MANAGING

MANAGING

Jon L. Pierce
University of Minnesota-Duluth

▲

Randall B. Dunham
University of Wisconsin-Madison

SCOTT, FORESMAN/LITTLE, BROWN HIGHER EDUCATION
A Division of Scott, Foresman and Company
Glenview, Illinois   London, England

To students of management:

May your educational experiences be enjoyable and rewarding. May you have a passion for learning about the science of management; may this passion drive your practice of management as well.

Jon
Randy

Credits begin on page 589, which is a legal extension of this copyright page.

Cover and part opener illustrations by Becky Cutler. Interior artwork by Candace Haught and PC&F Incorporated.

Library of Congress Cataloging-in-Publication Data

Pierce, Jon L. (Jon Lepley)
    Managing/Jon L. Pierce, Randall B. Dunham.
        p.   cm.
    Includes bibliographical references.
    ISBN 0-673-46011-8
    1. Management.   I. Dunham, Randall B.   II. Title.
    HD31.P49   1990
    658.4—dc20   89-38872
                                  CIP

1 2 3 4 5 6-VHJ-94 93 92 91 90 89

PREFACE

*T*he 1990s mark a turning point for American organizations and their managers. Many organizations are beginning to recognize the need for a new style of management and a new breed of manager. Managers have begun to question their purpose, their organization's structure and culture, and their leaders' visions and strategies. Increasing numbers are beginning to manage their organizations with high levels of employee involvement. Organizations smart enough to respond to these issues have initiated significant efforts aimed at professionalizing their management practices.

This book examines the aspects of the management process that you must learn to become an effective manager in a contemporary organization. Our discussion of management has two objectives. First, we believe students must learn that management requires both the skillful *and* the passionate application of scientific knowledge about organizations. Only by incorporating the science *and* art of management will you develop the knowledge and skills required of an effective manager, as well as the analytical and instinctive ability to determine when and how to use such knowledge and skills. Second, this book strives to fulfill a need for a concise presentation of the science of management. In short, the passion for managing must come from within you, and the art of management will stem from *your* skillful application of the science of management presented in *Managing.*

Organization of the Book

Learning about and practicing management can be stimulating, challenging, enjoyable, and fun. We have, therefore, incorporated a variety of features into this book and the supplements that accompany it to communicate information about management, to raise your interest in the subject matter and accompanying profession, and to encourage you to look forward to using this information in your own management career.

Manager Profiles

This book is divided into six parts, each of which begins with a profile of a manager who has found a unique way to achieve success.

- *Jack Welch,* General Electric, suggests that an organization that is tightly controlled stifles individuality; thus, his management style calls for opening up the organization. He encourages people to take initiative, pushes people hard, expects accomplishment and high performance, and shows little patience for those who do not measure up. (Part 1)

- *Lee Iacocca,* Chrysler, states that the ideal quality of a good manager is decisiveness. A manager needs to gather information, set priorities and timetables, and act decisively. Participative systems help bring information, ideas, and people into the management process so that managers can make effective organizational decisions. (Part 2)

- *Sara Westendorf,* Hewlett-Packard, claims that her management style is oriented toward several factors, including fun (make sure you enjoy what you do, since your enthusiasm will inspire others), leadership (be willing to do whatever it takes; lead through dedication and commitment; treat everyone equally), and humor (in high-pressure situations, a sense of humor can do an amazing job of diffusing tension and promoting teamwork). (Part 3)

- *A. Barry Rand,* Xerox, believes that achieving excellence, striving for continual improvement, and exceeding expectations are the key forces driving his motivation, hard work, and success. When Rand looks at himself in the mirror, the face looking back says that if you gave your maximum effort, everything is okay, but being number one without giving the maximum is unacceptable. (Part 4)

- *John Sculley,* Apple Computer, strongly believes that it is important for a manager to have a clear vision for the organization and views on how to position it within its external environment. It is also critically important that the manager communicate that vision to his or her subordinates. (Part 5)

- *Mary Kay Ash,* Mary Kay Cosmetics, has built her management style around seven basic principles: recognizing the value of people, praising them to success, tearing down the ivory tower, being a risk taker, creating a stress-free workplace, developing and promoting people from within, and keeping business in the proper place. (Part 6)

Part Divisions

Part 1 introduces you to the planning, organizing, directing, and controlling functions that define the management job. It discusses the management process and the managers who engage in it, the environments in which they operate, and the social and ethical responsibilities they bear. Part 1 also identifies various approaches to the practice of managing and the beliefs that guide these practices.

Part 2 explores the planning function, examining such critical aspects as decision making, managerial planning activities, effective planning tools and techniques, and ways in which managers develop the short-term and long-term strategic plans they need to guide their organization to success.

Part 3 addresses the organizing function and focuses on the ways in which managers structure and design organizations and assign authority.

Part 4 deals with the directing function. Here you will learn about organization members and the ways managers motivate, lead, and effectively use valuable human resources.

Part 5 examines the controlling function through which managers measure organizational effectiveness, and it explores strategies managers use to develop and change organizations in order to achieve or enhance effectiveness.

Part 6 offers a look at topics of growing importance to many organizations: the international arena, information systems, operating systems that produce goods and services, human resources, entre- and intrapreneurs, and the personal and organizational importance of career development.

Chapter Contents and Special Features

Each chapter begins with an outline of the major topics covered in the chapter and a list of learning objectives. Chapters end with a set of issues for review and discussion, a list of key terms, a list of suggested readings, and a case study that describes an organizational situation for you to analyze and resolve using information from the chapter. Between these openings and closings you will encounter a management text enhanced by special features to make these facts come alive. The following are a few samples from these features and some of the issues they present.

Student Learning Objectives

The objectives indicate areas of special importance to help you read the chapter effectively. By the time you have completed the chapter, you should be able to review and respond easily to the learning objectives. The following are a few of the approximately 150 objectives that appear in the book:

- Define management and what managers do. (Chapter 1)
- Discuss steps managers can take to encourage ethical behavior in organizations. (Chapter 3)
- Discuss the advantages and disadvantages of group decision making. (Chapter 6)
- Identify and differentiate the various approaches to departmentalizing jobs. (Chapter 9)
- Understand how people evaluate the fairness of the outcomes they receive from organizations. (Chapter 13)
- Describe how people use and abuse power. (Chapter 14)
- Discuss four major systematic approaches to assessing effectiveness and identify the major differences among these perspectives. (Chapter 16)
- Recognize the specific characteristics of good control systems and explain how each characteristic can improve the effectiveness of a control system. (Chapter 17)

A Closer Look

Chapters 1 through 18 each contain two special features, entitled "A Closer Look," that describe events in the real world that relate to material covered in the text. Each "Closer Look" allows you to see how a real organization has handled a managerial issue discussed in the chapter. Here are summarized excerpts from three of the thirty-six "Closer Looks" in the text:

- *Managerial Work: The Life of a Manager.* "[A] sixty-hour week is now standard among young 'workaholics,' and seventy-, eighty-, and ninety-hour weeks are not unheard of. . . . They spend over 95 percent of their time inside the walls of their own workplace. . . . First-level managers perform anywhere from 200 to 450 separate activities in a single eight-hour day. . . . The reality of life as a manager is not necessarily what it should be. The reality, from a manager's perspective, . . . " (Chapter 1)

- *Contingency Planning: Oh, for a Better Plan.* "It sounded good. Boston legal firm McCabe/Gordon was new and bold. It chose a small number of legal areas in which to concentrate its work. It sought and obtained big, leading-edge cases. In 1986, the firm moved into new headquarters above Boston's harbor. 'The offices were stunning, the lawyers among the brightest and best paid and the gleaming computer equipment seemed a beacon for the future.' In May of 1987, McCabe/Gordon fell apart. What went wrong was most probably . . . " (Chapter 5)

- *Conflict Management: Disagree with Your Boss? Let Your Peers Settle It.* " 'I don't agree with you, but you're the boss.' These words have been spoken millions of times to thousands of bosses. In recent years, however, a number of progressive companies have decided that simply being higher in the organizational hierarchy does not necessarily make a boss right. These companies have created a variety of 'speak up' and 'open door' policies, which typically allow a worker to skip over his or her boss and go directly to a higher-level manager to appeal an action the employee considers unfair or unwise. For many organizations, such as IBM, speak up and open door programs have worked well. For many others, however, . . . " (Chapter 14)

A Manager's Word

Each chapter in the first five parts contains "A Manager's Word," a feature that presents excerpts selected from the authors' interviews with people in unique positions that enable them to answer questions often asked by management students. Here are six samples from the more than fifty observations offered by these experts:

- *Walter Kiechel III,* writer/editor, *Fortune* magazine: [A] good manager has to . . . be able to listen to other people, hear what they're saying, and pay attention to what is heard. Dealing with people means taking into account their feelings and acknowledging your own. (Chapter 1)

- *Mary Ann Von Glinow,* University of Southern California: [T]here is an increased awareness in the marketplace of unethical kinds of activities. As a result, we're starting to see more corporate responses that try to deal with some of these kinds of issues . . . for example, widespread development of codes of ethics, or codes of conduct, and some statement of values in business organizations. (Chapter 3)

- *Phyllis A. Mason,* Baruch College: The crucial thing is that top management needs to communicate to the entire organization the objectives of the strategic planning unit, how the unit will work with the rest of the organization, the input that will be required from the rest of the organization, why the organization is doing strategic planning, how important it is to the organization's future, and so on. (Chapter 8)

- *Barbara M. Karmel*, president of the Reed Company: Managers often seem preoccupied with things that are too slow, inaccurate, or otherwise wrong rather than with looking for constructive, direct solutions to problems and for new windows of opportunity. (Chapter 13)
- *Michael J. Marx*, president of Selection Sciences, Inc.: [One of] the most serious communication problems [is] the exchange of information between senior management and the rest of the organization. Particularly in economically difficult times, management often fails to communicate what it sees as the problem, how it plans to deal with the problem, and the role employees play in the process. The resulting uncertainty felt by employees can have devastating effects on day-to-day and future operations of the organization. (Chapter 14)
- *Donald L. Hawk*, executive vice-president and manager, Texas Commerce Bancshares: Long ago, Peter Drucker said, "The purpose of an organization lies outside itself." Organizations that do not adapt to changing environments wither and die. (Chapter 18)

In Review

At the end of each chapter, a brief summary of the major issues discussed in that chapter helps you organize the information and place it in context. For example, part of the review section from Chapter 6 on decision making states:

Common decision-making problems include misunderstanding a situation and rushing decisions. Managers can counteract these problems by providing access to needed information, by training individuals and groups in systematic decision making, by providing adequate time for decision making, and by offering rewards that encourage effective decision making.

The review section in Chapter 6 also summarizes a four-step model that managers can use to make decisions more effectively and reiterates the issues managers should consider when determining whether to involve groups in the decision-making process.

Issues for Review and Discussion

After you have read each chapter and have studied its features, you should look at the end-of-chapter issues for review and discussion, which are designed to help you assess your mastery of the material. The following are a few samples of the approximately 150 discussion questions and exercises that appear in the book.

- What is the difference between organic and mechanistic management systems? between open and closed management systems? (Chapter 2)
- Why do you think contingency theories of management emerged? (Chapter 4)
- Describe the purposes of strategic planning and outline its advantages and disadvantages. (Chapter 8)
- Describe the stages in the evolution of conflict. (Chapter 14)
- How does the desire for personal control affect managers, and how can they balance it with organizational control systems? (Chapter 17)

- Explain what a management information system (MIS) is and discuss its purpose. (Chapter 20)
- Describe the steps that a large corporation, such as General Motors, could take to encourage intrapreneurial behavior. (Chapter 23)

Key Terms

At the end of each chapter is a list of important terms. After reading the chapter, you should be able to scan the list and quickly define each key term. If you are unsure of the meaning of any term, check its definition in the glossary of approximately 400 terms at the end of the book. The lists include such crucial management terms as *organizational culture* (Chapter 2), *Theory X* and *Theory Y* (Chapter 4), *nominal group technique* (Chapter 7), *self-managing work group approach* (Chapter 9), *cybernetic control* (Chapter 17), and *just-in-time (JIT)* (Chapter 21).

Suggested Readings

The end of each chapter also provides a list of suggested readings from a wide variety of sources, including books, academic journals, business publications, and articles from the popular press. Some of these are the original sources used for a particularly important part of the chapter; others expand on a critical issue in the chapter. Sometimes a suggested reading provides an organizational application of concepts examined in the chapter. We have chosen these readings to help you explore issues of interest and to give you an overview of the material currently being read by contemporary managers.

A Case Study

At the end of each chapter, you will find a case about one of a group of organizations as diverse as Environcare (Chapter 2), Xerox Corporation (Chapter 8), St. Amos Hospital (Chapter 16), and Maxim Insurance (Chapter 24). Each case informs you about an organization and asks you to apply the knowledge you have acquired from reading the chapter. The following is an excerpt from a case involving Bridgestone, a Japanese tire manufacturer:

> *Bridgestone is named after its founder, Ishibashi, whose name means "stone bridge." Shojiro Ishibashi founded Bridgestone in 1951 in Kurume, Japan, to produce tires using domestic capital and technology. In the years since, two principles have consistently guided the conduct of Bridgestone's business in both tires and chemical and industrial products. The first is an unswerving commitment to "enhancing the quality of life," a commitment served by the second principle: "serving society with products of superior quality." Bridgestone attributes its growth in large part to its emphasis on quality. The company exercises strict control over every aspect of tire production, from the manufacture of cords to the finishing process.*

This case then provides additional information on production and sales figures, strategic planning activities, and overseas investment considerations before concluding with a brief series of questions that draw on what you learned from the chapter.

Instructional Materials

A contemporary approach to teaching must incorporate rapidly developing modern technology. Our instructional package capitalizes on these new technologies to bring teachers and students the most stimulating and rewarding learning experience possible, offering a vast array of choices for testing, grading, and recordkeeping; for class design, planning, and teaching; for computerized learning; and for student-directed study.

Testing, Grading, and Recordkeeping

A printed test bank to accompany the text contains multiple-choice, true-false, completion, matching, and essay questions for each chapter. All of these questions are also available in computerized format, enabling teachers to select, edit, and create test items. These resources are designed to facilitate effective class management.

Instructor's Resource Manual (IRM)

Our *Instructor's Resource Manual* (IRM) is complete and detailed, providing an overview of each chapter contained in the book and answers to all learning objectives and issues for review and discussion. The IRM presents questions to stimulate discussion of the "Closer Looks" that appear in each chapter and offers suggested answers. The manual also furnishes answers to the questions found in the case studies, as well as additional questions and answers for each case. A second case, along with questions and suggested answers, is also presented for each chapter.

We are particularly proud of many of the manual's unique contributions. There are at least two original experiential exercises for each chapter to make the book's material come to life in a personal and interesting fashion. Essays on topics of special interest, such as Japanese management and organizational dysfunctions, are included for use as student handouts or as the basis of a class lecture.

Overhead Transparencies

A set of 125 full-color overhead transparencies is available to adopters of *Managing.* Some of these are reprints of important tables, figures, and artwork from the book; others have been created to further enrich classroom presentations.

Computerized Teaching Tools

We are offering two innovative computerized packages to enhance the management course.

You are likely to learn better when you have a personal interest in the material you are studying. You also learn better when you receive immediate feedback. Our *Self-assessment Exercises* provide both. After answering a series of questions about issues discussed in the text, such as job satisfaction, leadership style, stress, and receptivity to change, you are immediately given an on-screen image and a computer printout of your personal profile and its comparison to national and class norms.

An extremely easy-to-use database, the *Computerized Information Retrieval System* (CIRS) helps students and teachers pursue issues from the course in greater depth by allowing access to reference and abstract information from recent key management journals. Identifying an article on a topic and obtaining a summary of its content is as simple as typing the topic of interest. Retrieval on-screen or in printed form is quick and efficient.

New teaching technologies take a lot of time to develop and can be difficult to use. We have spent our time developing state-of-the-art technologies that will not intimidate you. Best of all, the instructional materials described to this point are provided to adopters free of charge, because we are committed to improving the quality of management education and want to make available every tool possible to those who are also committed to this end.

Compatible Resources

Three additional teaching resources are available from Scott, Foresman/ Little, Brown. One of these is a *Student's Resource Manual* designed specifically for this book. Others were developed by people with whom we have collaborated.

Student's Resource Manual. More than just a "study guide," the *Student's Resource Manual* provides pretests and posttests, along with an answer key, for each chapter. Chapter linking, chapter concepts, and key term sections also help you master the material.

Interactive Cases in Management. This software allows you to play the role of manager as you make day-to-day decisions in an organization. As you do so, the cases unfold quickly and realistically, illustrating the impact of various management strategies. These interactive cases concentrate on intra-organizational events. You will quickly learn that once a decision is made, its implications can be significant and long lasting.

Managerial Reality: Balancing Techniques, Practice, and Values. This book presents a realistic view of the balancing act required of contemporary managers, making clear that technique alone is not enough for organizational success. The strength of this book is that it stimulates serious, meaningful thought about the delicate issues faced by managers on an ongoing basis.

Acknowledgments

Substantial contributions to the design, development, and preparation of this book were made by a wide range of people. We have listened, and we have learned from each of them.

Four of these chapters were prepared by specialists, and we are grateful to them: Thomas Duff of the University of Minnesota-Duluth, management information systems (MIS); Peter J. Billington of Northeastern University-Boston, operations management; Heidi Vernon-Wortzel of Northeastern University-Boston, international management; and Ann Cope in consultation with Gene Dalton of Brigham Young University, careers.

To help you analyze the complexities of managing today's organizations from a variety of perspectives, we interviewed a group of important organizational experts, whose names and affiliations appear in the text, to provide the basis for each *A Manager's Word.* We thank them for their help in making these complexities come alive for our readers.

We recognize the importance of cases for a management text, and Philip C. Fisher of the University of South Dakota provided the expertise needed to locate and refine them for each chapter of the book and the *Instructor's Resource Manual.* We enjoyed working with Phil and greatly appreciate his dedication. We also are grateful to the Midwest Society for Case Research (MSCR), which gave Phil substantial assistance in supplying many of these cases, as well as many that appear in the IRM. We would also like to thank the many authors of the cases used in the book.

Each chapter in this book has gone through a number of versions. We especially appreciate the efforts of six reviewers who went beyond the call of duty, each reviewing chapters in several stages: Karen A. Brown, Seattle University; Lee G. Caldwell, University of Utah; David A. Cowan, Notre Dame University; David B. Greenberger, The Ohio State University; Robert F. Pethia, Western Kentucky University; and Roger Volkema, George Mason University. We also thank the following people, who reviewed the text or portions of it:

Mark G. Andersen	*Point Loma College*
Frank Aven	*California State Polytechnic University-Pomona*
Daniel Baugher	*Pace University*
William D. Biggs	*Beaver College*
Allen Bluedorn	*University of Missouri*
Kenneth J. Buck	*Oregon State University*
Jane Burman-Holtom	*University of Oklahoma*
Thomas M. Calero	*Illinois Institute of Technology*
David J. Cherrington	*Brigham Young University*
Raymond Cook	*University of Texas-Austin*
Richard DeLuca	*Bloomfield College*
Philip C. Fisher	*University of South Dakota*
Donald G. Gardner	*University of Colorado*

Roger Griffeth	*Louisiana State University*
Joyce Henson	*St. Peters College*
Russ Holloman	*Augusta College*
William Holstein	*SUNY at Albany*
Bruce H. Johnson	*Gustavus Adolphus College*
Ki Hee Kim	*William Peterson College*
Andrew Luzi	*University of Oklahoma*
Joseph W. McGuire	*University of California-Irvine*
Gus Manoochehri	*California State University-Fullerton*
Lyman W. Porter	*University of California-Irvine*
Samuel Rabinowitz	*Rutgers University-Camden*
Joseph C. Schabacker	*Arizona State University*
Richard Schallert	*Black Hawk College*
Paul L. Wilkens	*Florida State University*
Charles R. Williams	*Oklahoma State University*

We would like to thank the following organization and individuals for contributing to the teaching package, which, although not contained within the pages of this textbook, is linked closely to its use: AskSam Systems for providing the database program used in the computerized information and retrieval system; Cynthia Lengnick-Hall, University of Minnesota-Duluth, for the test bank and for her contributions to the *Instructor's Resource Manual;* and Loren Kuzuhara, University of Wisconsin, for his work on the IRM. We cannot overstate the importance of their contributions.

A number of individuals at Scott, Foresman and Company were instrumental in developing this project. We would like to acknowledge the help and support of Editorial Vice-President Jim Boyd, Acquisitions Editor Melissa Rosati, and Managing Developmental Editor Jane Steinmann. Developmental Editor Susan Moss provided the professional touch needed to refine our reader-friendly package. Project Editor Debra DeBord made sure we had the right words in the right places and guided our book through its final stages of production. Designer Julie Anderson created the book's design. Marketing Manager Brett Spalding ensured that we were attuned to the needs of the marketplace.

In closing, we would like to offer our special thanks to Randi K. Huntsman, who helped manage the preparation of this package from beginning to end. Once again, Randi has helped us turn an idea into a reality. Her assistance in writing, coordinating, and producing this book and its package is sincerely appreciated.

J.L.P.
R.B.D.

CONTENTS

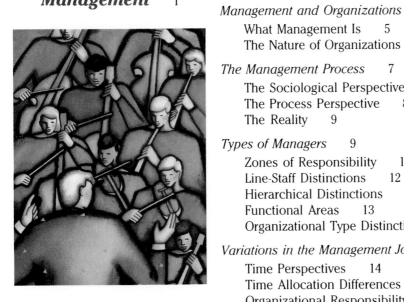

CHAPTER 4 *Schools of Management Thought: Approaches to Managing*   72

PART 4

Directing 271

MANAGER PROFILE
Addison Barry Rand 272

PART 5

Controlling   373

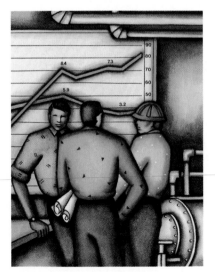

MANAGER PROFILE
John Sculley   374

PART 6

Special Topics   445

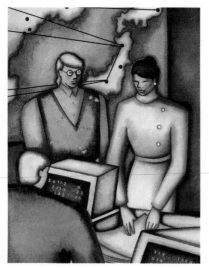

MANAGER PROFILE
Mary Kay Ash   446

PART 1 An Introduction to Management

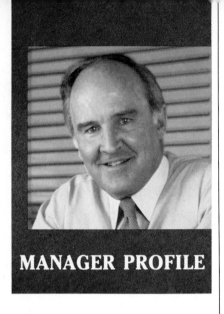

MANAGER PROFILE

Jack Welch

"Hero or villain? Corporate rejuvenator or destructive wheeler-dealer?"[1] Jack Welch, the top executive at General Electric, is described as a tyrant as well as a man who has established a strong espirit de corps among the top management group. He has been called "Mad Jack"; many current and former employees refer to him as "Neutron Jack," since he has eliminated nearly a quarter of all the jobs at GE.[2] Perceived as a tough guy, managing by fear and intimidation, Welch has lost the dedication of thousands of people, and yet he has been branded as a financial wizard and put into the same league as the J. P. Morgans of the American business world.[3]

Jack Welch rose to the top position at GE in 1981. Since that time he has taken a number of large and bold steps in an effort to change the organization. GE has trimmed its payroll by more than 100,000. Layers in GE's hierarchy have been removed, and middle managers who are not trained in tomorrow's technology continually fall by the wayside. Many of the corporation's less-profitable operations have been sold, there have been bold experiments with factory automation, and resources have been shifted from stodgy manufacturing to high technology and fast-growing services. GE has moved out of a number of long-standing business domains, such as television, and into investment banking, broadcasting, and high-tech manufacturing. Not only has Welch changed GE's corporate strategy, he has revamped the organization's structure, realigned GE's corporate culture, and watched corporate revenues grow by 48 percent.[4]

Accompanying the change in GE's business units, Welch has worked at making GE less bureaucratic. He has delegated authority, pushing it to lower levels; he has made the organization's structure wider and flatter by eliminating levels in the hierarchy; and he has adopted an informal and rigorous management style. In order to achieve integration among the organization's many business units, Welch has attempted to develop a team-oriented corporate culture. Camaraderie and communication are emphasized, almost to the extreme. Today GE's internal environment has been characterized as aggressive, argumentative, confrontational, tough, and iconoclastic. This is a far cry from GE's long-time history of being formal and gentlemanly. GE's internal environment used to be stable; today it is aggressively and boldly on the move. Whether or not it is moving in the right direction is open to debate. Some believe that instead of getting larger and larger, GE should become a "smaller, more focused, nimbler entity."[5]

[H]e has been branded as a financial wizard . . . .

During the 1950s, GE was one of the leaders in moving toward profit centers. Today Welch deals directly with the heads of GE's profit centers, limiting his involvement in the management of their operations to strategic and important personnel issues. It appears to be Welch's belief that the business unit directors should be left alone to run their divisions. He wants his managers to feel as though they own their operations, and therefore he encourages them to operate as entrepreneurs instead of seeing themselves as being on someone's payroll.[6] As long as they meet their financial targets, he does not intervene and heads do not roll. Since becoming CEO, he has installed eleven new managers at GE's fourteen business units.

A new breed of managers appears to stand at the core of Welch's GE management system. The development of a team system characterized by communication, candor, and trust seems to be critical. A measured amount of turmoil is seen as desirable, since turmoil is intended to challenge the organization and its management team, keeping them finely honed and on the winning edge. Strong performers are pushed to become stronger; the term *winaholics* is being used to characterize Welch's management team.[7]

Much of Welch's management philosophy appears to be built on the utilization of the organization's human resources. His vision suggests that an organization that is tightly controlled stifles individuality. Welch's management style calls for opening up the organization. He encourages people to take initiative and push themselves to develop better skills and to achieve. He pushes people hard, expects accomplishment and high performance, and shows little patience for those who do not measure up.

A measured amount of turmoil is seen as desirable . . . .

Welch has spent his entire career at GE. After receiving a Ph.D. in chemical engineering at the University of Illinois, he went to work in GE's plastics business. At age forty-five, he became GE's youngest CEO. His goal for GE is to make it number one or number two in every business in which it is engaged. He wants GE "to become the most competitive business enterprise in the world," and to be the most valuable corporation in terms of market capitalization.[8] Toward this end, Welch has

changed the emphasis of the company and is continually in the process of buying and selling businesses. GE is in such businesses as aircraft engines, major appliances, medical systems, plastics, investment banking, and broadcasting.

In Welch's estimation, a good manager is a person with a vision and the ability to articulate that vision to the entire business unit while listening through shared discussion. A good manager is someone who can "relentlessly drive implementation of that vision to a successful conclusion."[9] The successful manager who is going to survive as a part of Welch's team must be a self-starter, a visionary, and an orchestrator of others. The challenge for Welch is to be able to develop the organizational climate in which such independent managers can be melded into a strong top-management team.

Four times a year, the fourteen business leaders, the heads of corporate staff, and the CEO meet and discuss their business plans. It is a time for everyone to be an active participant. Challenging, criticizing, and offering constructive suggestions to further each business plan is the norm. It is through this type of confrontation, turmoil, tension, and conflict that Welch believes GE will find its advantage.[10]

While it has been claimed that Welch has built a strong team at the top, this strength may not have filtered down through the lower levels of the management hierarchy. In fact, disenchantment and dissatisfaction appear to be commonplace. Stress is leading to the burnout of many of GE's employees. According to Welch, he wants employees to see GE as a place where they will find a challenge, as a place where a worker who seeks an opportunity to develop his or her skills will find it. That is what

Welch's management philosophy has to offer. It is a work environment that is clearly not designed for everyone, "yet GE can be enormously exciting for those in the right place or attuned to the Welch mentality."[11]

1. Jack Welch: How good a manager? (14 December 1987), *Business Week*, 92.

2. What Welch has wrought at GE (7 July 1986), *Fortune*, 43.

3. *Business Week*, 93.

4. *Business Week*, 92.

5. *Business Week*, 94.

6. *Fortune*, 44.

7. *Business Week*, 92.

8. *Business Week*, 94.

9. *Business Week*, 96.

10. *Ibid.*

11. *Fortune*, 43.

1

The Nature of Management

Student Learning Objectives

After reading this chapter, you should be able to:

1. Define management and what managers do.

2. Understand the characteristics of organizations.

3. Distinguish between the sociological and process perspectives on management.

4. Discuss some of the categories of managers.

5. Identify variations in the ways managers execute the management process.

6. Specify the skills that managers need.

7. Give six reasons organizations need managers.

8. Distinguish between management as a process and management as a set of roles.

T hink for a moment about the types of management systems you have seen at your high school, at the places where you have held a job, at your college, and probably at many other places. Did you always understand why these organizations were managed as they were? Did you ever say to yourself, "There must be a better way to run an organization"? This book explores management and the philosophies and practices that guide managers so you can see *what* works and *why.* Knowledge, understanding, and a systematic approach are what you will need to become an effective manager.

Management and Organizations

Management in U.S. organizations has received a lot of criticism over the years in light of increasing productivity problems, deteriorating plants and machinery, lost ground in research and development, lack of competitive responsiveness at home and abroad, and increases in worker discontent. Some critics attribute the crises facing U.S. corporations to "bad management."[1]

What Management Is

The study of organizational management is relatively young; consequently, nearly every manager and writer about management has a favorite way to define the process. In general, **management** can be defined as the process of planning, organizing, directing, and controlling organizational resources (human, financial, physical, and informational) in the pursuit of organizational goals. **Managers** are organization members who are assigned the primary responsibility of carrying out the management process. As you will discover, there can be many levels of management and many activities that managers must plan, organize, direct, and control. Among these are the production (operations), marketing, human resource, finance, and accounting functions of an organization.

Managers are organization members whose primary responsibilities are to plan, organize, direct, and control organizational resources.

Chester Barnard defined management as a system of consciously coordinated activities of two or more persons.

The Nature of Organizations

Fifty years ago, Chester Barnard, the noted expert on management as a science, defined an **organization** as "a system of consciously coordinated activities of two or more persons."[2] This definition is still viable today. An organization is held together by the purposes and goals its members share. It may own buildings and equipment, but these do not define its nature. An organization is a social system, characterized by relatively enduring interaction patterns that link people to people and people to work as they pursue organizational goals.[3] Take away the interaction patterns in a hospital that link nurses with doctors, doctors with technicians, medical staff members with administrators, and all of these people with the patients they care for, and the essence of the hospital as a health care delivery system vanishes. The buildings and equipment remain, but the organization is gone.

Most people use the term *organization* to refer to a legal or registered entity. In this book, *organization* may bring to mind such corporations as Sears and CBS or such governmental bodies as the Environmental Protection Agency and Congress. You may also think of such organizations as the United Way and other charities, police and fire departments, or school systems. These are all organizations, but each often contains other, less readily identifiable organizations.

Sometimes it is easy to spot an organization within an organization. Tenneco, for example, is a conglomerate that is actually a collection of individual companies, such as Tenneco Oil Company, Tenneco Realty, Tennessee Eastman Company, and Tennessee Armature and Electric Company. The presence of organizations does not have to be so formal, however. The internal legal division and the accounting department of Tenneco Oil, for example, are organizations just as real as Tenneco itself. Each has distinct interaction patterns that link people to people and people to work, and each has members who share goals. Each is a work organization that transforms resources into goods and services (see Figure 1.1). Whether a manufacturing organization or

FIGURE 1.1 The Work Organization as an Import-Export System

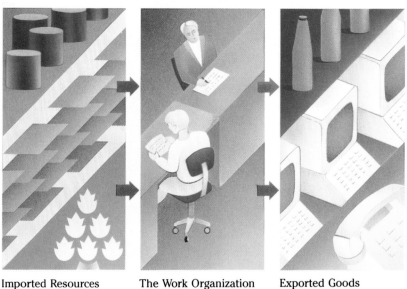

Imported Resources   The Work Organization   Exported Goods and Services

a governmental agency, a freestanding corporation or a tiny organization embedded in another, every organization must be managed through planning, organizing, directing, and controlling.

The Management Process

In the previous section, management was defined as a series of processes. The process (or activity) perspective focuses on the *actions* managers take. Another useful approach, known as the sociological perspective, defines management according to the *social positions* of organization members.

The Sociological Perspective

For many, the word *management* creates an image of a certain group of individuals in an organization. From this point of view, there are, for these individuals, two kinds of organization members: managers and everybody else. The **sociological perspective,** thus, defines management as the group of organization members that occupies the social position responsible for making sure that an organization achieves its mission (its "reason for being"). As you might expect, these people are called *managers.* The second group of organization members (the "everybody else") consists of workers, employees, laborers, troops, support staff, and technical analysts (the *nonmanagers*). An **organizational chart,** such as that shown in Figure 1.2, is a schematic drawing of the positions within an organization that can be used to distinguish

FIGURE 1.2   An Organizational Chart

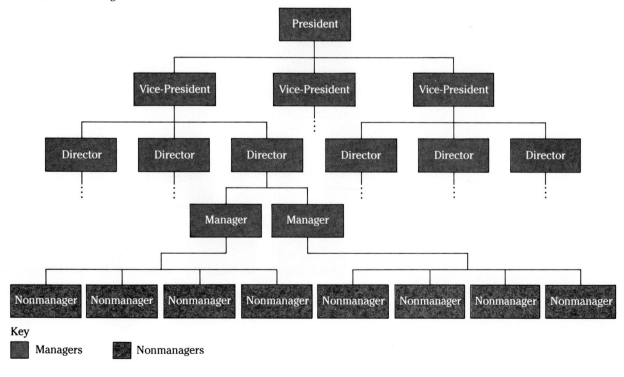

Key
■ Managers   ▨ Nonmanagers

Mary Parker Follett described management as the orchestration of people, work, and systems in the pursuit of organizational goals.

among these social positions. Notice that the management group in the chart spans several different levels and units (departments, sections, and divisions) in the organizational **hierarchy** (that is, its managerial levels of authority and responsibility).

The Process Perspective

One of the oldest and most widely adopted definitions of management is "the art of getting things done through people."[4] Mary Parker Follett, a pioneer in the study of management, described it as an activity concerned with the orchestration of people, work, and systems in the pursuit of organizational goals. The way in which managers accomplish this is the basis for the **process perspective.** This book adopts the process perspective to examine the roles, activities, and processes that managers engage in as they plan, organize, direct, and control their organization.

In 1916, French industrialist Henri Fayol described a "functional approach to management" and suggested that *all* managers perform similar activities. Whether they are top-level or low-level managers, whether their organization is as small as a hair stylist's shop or as large as the U.S. government, whether they manage a manufacturing organization or health care institution, whether they are in accounting or marketing, all managers must execute a universal set of management processes (see Figure 1.3).[5] Fayol's universal set has since been modified, and a useful process definition popular today includes four management functions: planning, organizing, directing, and controlling.

FIGURE 1.3   *The Universalism of Management*

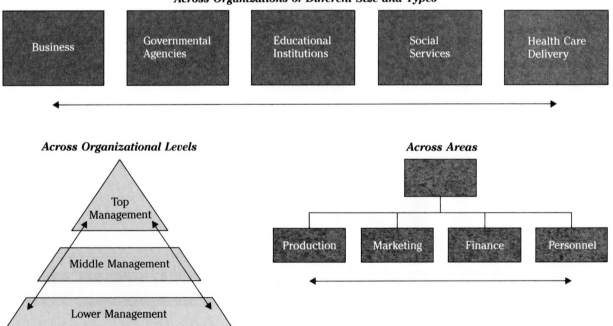

The **planning** function involves establishing organizational goals and defining the methods by which they are to be attained. The **organizing** function involves designing, structuring, and coordinating the components of an organization to meet organizational goals. The **directing** function involves managing interpersonal activities, leading and motivating employees to effectively and efficiently accomplish the tasks necessary to realize organizational goals. The **controlling** function involves monitoring both the behavior of organization members and the effectiveness of the organization itself, determining whether plans are achieving organizational goals, and taking corrective actions as needed. (Parts 2 through 5 of this text explore each of the four managerial functions in detail.) As shown in Figure 1.4, managers use all four functions when applying an organization's resources to achieve its goals.

The Reality

Do all managers actually perform all four sets of management functions? Evidence seems to indicate they do, although rarely in a controlled and systematic fashion.[6] Managers tend to navigate through their days by following a sequence of planning (identifying goals), organizing (designing the systems needed to meet goals), directing (energizing the systems through people), and controlling (measuring results against the plan).[7] This sequence does not mean, however, that managers plan on Monday, organize on Tuesday, direct on Wednesday, and control on Thursday. Rather, managers' days are seas of scheduled and unscheduled events, opportunities, and crises through which they navigate by using the four functions. Even for the highest-level managers, half of their activities last less than nine minutes each. Only 10 percent of their activities exceed one hour.[8] (See "A Closer Look: Managerial Work.")

Types of Managers

Now that you have an idea of what the management process is, consider the types of managers themselves. It is possible to classify managers by the nature of the position they hold. This section reviews some of the major categories of managers. The next section identifies how these differences affect a manager's job.

FIGURE 1.4   The Managerial Process

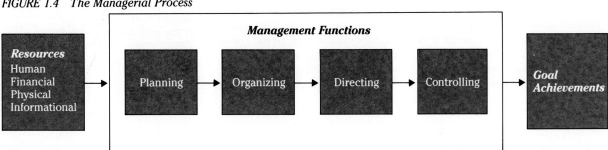

Source: Adapted from G. Terry (1972), *Principles of management,* Homewood, IL: Irwin, 4.

Managerial Work:
The Life of a Manager

Most of this book is organized around the four managerial functions of planning, organizing, directing, and controlling and the techniques that managers can use to carry out those functions. Real life, however, is seldom as organized and systematic. What is the life of a manager really like? People at the Center for Creative Leadership in Greensboro, North Carolina, have examined the daily routines of managers.[1] You might be interested in what the future holds if you become a manager.

For one thing, you can expect to work long hours. In a 1989 *Fortune* article, Walter Kiechel III argued that a sixty-hour week is now standard among young "workaholics," and seventy-, eighty-, and ninety-hour weeks are not unheard of.[2] If you are like most managers, you will spend most of this time working inside your own organization. Despite the importance of outside factors—such as customers, competitors, and suppliers—most managers spend little time interacting directly with these groups. They spend over 95 percent of their time inside the walls of their own workplace.

Expect not to be bored, especially if you become a first-level manager. There will be plenty to keep you busy. First-level managers perform anywhere from 200 to 450 separate activities in a single eight-hour day. The work is not repetitive; most managers find a tremendous amount of variety in their jobs. During a typical workday, a manager completes paperwork, makes and takes phone calls,

attends scheduled and unscheduled meetings, conducts inspection tours and visits at the workplace, has personal contact with many people, and addresses a wide range of work-related issues.

This level of activity will not allow you much time for contemplation. First-level managers encounter a new demand on their time almost every minute of the workday. Most of their activities, therefore, tend to be of very short duration. Trivial and important matters are often interspersed, and you will be expected to isolate and handle problems in rapid-fire order. Although this pace gives most managers little time to reflect or plan systematically, you should try to reserve some time for these activities. In fact, a 1989 study by the Northwestern Mutual Life Insurance Company revealed that one of the most critical, often missing resources for managing effectively is "quiet time."[3] As you will see later in this book, one of the factors that distinguishes effective from ineffective managers is how well they reflect on their work and systematically plan their actions.

Most managers do most of their work orally, not in writing. The managers studied by the Center for Creative Leadership conducted between 28 and 80 percent of their work orally. Managers need to be able to communicate well with their superiors, subordinates, and peers. You can expect to exchange a lot of information, the soul of the manager's job. You will spend much of your day get-

ting and giving information. If you do not get the information you need, you will not make good decisions or plans. If you do not give information to the people who need it, your activities will be in vain.

The reality of life as a manager is not necessarily what it should be. The reality, from a manager's perspective, also is not necessarily as others see it. If you were to ask the managers who were observed in the Center's study how many hours they spend at work, how often they are interrupted, how much time they spend working inside the organization, and other questions about how they spend their time, their answers would not match those of observers. Managers usually do not know how much time they devote to specific activities, and that is a problem. If managers do not know how they spend their day, how can they modify it to become more effective?

These *descriptions* of a typical managerial day are, therefore, not *prescriptions*. The reality is that a manager's day is hectic; thus, managers must attack the management process more systematically if they want to improve effectiveness.

1. M. W. McCall, Jr., A. M. Morrison, and R. L. Hannan (1978), *Studies of managerial work: Results and methods* (Technical Report No. 9), Greensboro, NC: Center for Creative Leadership.
2. The workaholic generation (10 April 1989), *Fortune*, 50ff.
3. Associated Press (13 April 1989).

FIGURE 1.5 The Management
Process Under Pressure

When you are up to your ears in alligators, it's hard to remember that your objective was to drain the swamp.

Zones of Responsibility

An organization can be viewed as a cake with three distinct layers, or *zones of responsibility:* the institutional zone, the managerial zone, and the technical core (see Figure 1.6 on page 12).[9] Managers can be classified according to the zones in which they operate.

The Institutional Zone. Managers in the **institutional zone** are primarily responsible for two aspects of an organization's external (outside) environment (see Chapter 2 for a detailed discussion of the components of an organization's external environment). First, they must establish their organization's importance to the external community by informing people outside of it and in other organizations. The institutional zone is where Lee Iacocca has been appearing for years in promoting Chrysler as an organization "Born in America."

Second, managers in the institutional zone are responsible for identifying the needs of the external environment and for finding ways in which their organization can satisfy those needs. Based on their perception of the marketplace, for example, managers in the institutional zone at Chrysler initiated the development of the minivan. In general, institutional zone managers fashion long-term strategies, plans, and objectives for the organization as a whole.

The Technical Core. Managers in the **technical core** have direct responsibility for producing and delivering an organization's goods and services. They manage the day-to-day activities of the organization. One set of technical core managers at a Chrysler plant, for example, oversees the people who operate the assembly of drive trains. Another set of technical core managers oversees the delivery of cars to distributors.

FIGURE 1.6   Zones of
Organizational Responsibility

Organization

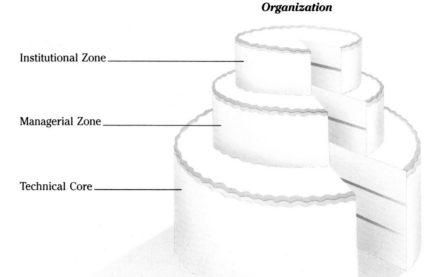

Institutional Zone

Managerial Zone

Technical Core

The Managerial Zone.   Sandwiched between the institutional zone and the technical core is the **managerial zone.** Here, managers create and manage systems to coordinate and integrate the various parts of the technical core. For example, at Chrysler such managers coordinate the work of those who produce cars with the work of those who deliver them. These managers also develop the specific operating strategies for implementing the overall plans and objectives set forth by upper-level managers. In general, managers in the managerial zone are responsible for translating the vision of the institutional zone managers into the realities of the technical core.

Line-Staff Distinctions

Another helpful way to classify managers is according to their direct involvement in producing an organization's goods or services (that is, whether they perform line or staff duties). **Line managers** have a *direct* responsibility for producing the service or product line of an organization. At Goodyear Rubber Company, for example, the department supervisor in charge of a tire molding department is a line manager. Every manager who links the tire molding department supervisor with the company president is a line manager.

It is the job of **staff managers** to *support* line managers, but staff managers are not directly involved in the production of goods or services. For example, staff managers in the legal department at Dairycraft, Inc., a manufacturer of stainless steel products for the dairy industry, do not manage the production or sale of stainless steel containers. Their job is to supervise lawyers, who advise line managers, who establish contractual relationships with suppliers, customers, and employees. Chapter 10 discusses line-staff authority in more detail.

Hierarchical Distinctions

Managers are also classified by their position in an organization's hierarchy. The lowest level consists of first-level managers who manage an organization's technical core. First-level managers direct nonmanagerial organization members and often have such titles as "unit manager" or "department manager." Those who manage first-level managers are referred to as second-level managers. Next come third-level managers, and so on, up to the top level. Although there is no rule about where the levels begin and end, people often describe managers' general positions in a hierarchy as lower-, middle-, and upper-level. Middle-level managers often have such titles as "division head" or "plant manager." Upper-level managers may be called "general manager," "director," "vice-president," or "president."

Functional managers oversee a specific set of organizational activities, such as human resource functions.

Functional Areas

Managers also are classified according to their area of specialized activity (also known as organizational function served). They are an organization's **functional managers.** "I'm in accounting," says one manager. "I've been transferred from marketing to production," says another. Functional areas should not be confused with the general management functions of planning, organizing, directing, and controlling. Instead, specialized functional areas describe the specific set of activities that a manager oversees. While these vary somewhat depending on the industry, it is common for organizations to have operations (production), marketing, finance, accounting, and human resource functions.

Organizational Type Distinctions

As you might expect, the sector of the economy (for example, government, education, or health care) in which an organization operates also influences the nature of a manager's job and, often, the titles used to designate the manager's position. A head nurse in a hospital, for example, can be the counterpart of a foreman or forewoman in a manufacturing shop. The dean of an engineering school may be doing work on a level comparable to that of a manufacturing organization's division head. These systems for categorizing managers' jobs are useful for describing where a manager operates in an industry. They are also important because the specific nature of managers' jobs varies substantially among categories.

FIGURE 1.7   The Distribution of Managers' Time Among Job Levels

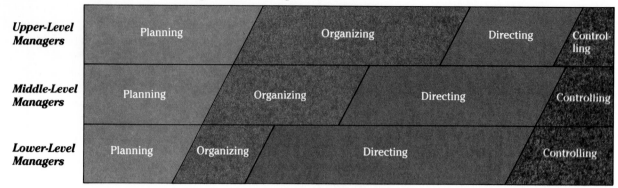

Proportion of Time

Variations in the Management Job

Although managing involves the same basic functions in any management setting, it flies in the face of common sense to say that all managers engage in exactly the same behaviors and activities as they conduct these functions.[10] Managers at Edina High School and managers at General Foods, for example, plan, organize, direct, and control their organization's operations. In one case, however, the focus is on the education of children. In the other, the focus is on the manufacture and distribution of food products. In addition to differences in content issues or problems faced, managers' jobs differ fundamentally in four ways: (1) the time frame they must consider, (2) the way managers allocate their time among the functions, (3) the organizational responsibility for which they are accountable, and (4) the skills needed to perform effectively.

Time Perspectives

As managers move from lower to higher levels in an organization, time frames often shift from the here-and-now to the distant future. Lower-level managers deliver current services and meet current production schedules. Upper-level managers, at least in some of the more progressive U.S. firms, regularly work with issues that will have impact five to fifteen years in the future. All managers should adopt appropriate time perspectives. Many organizations have lost their competitive edge by concentrating on quarterly profits at the expense of long-term needs.

Time Allocation Differences

One of the biggest variations among managers is in how much time they devote to each of the four functions. Level and functional area make the biggest difference. Upper-level managers, for example, typically spend more of their time planning and organizing than they do directing or controlling. Lower-level managers usually spend less time planning and organizing and more time directing and controlling.[11] Figure 1.7 illustrates how managers at different levels tend to distribute their time. Similar patterns exist across zones of responsibility.

FIGURE 1.8   *Required Skills for Successful Management*

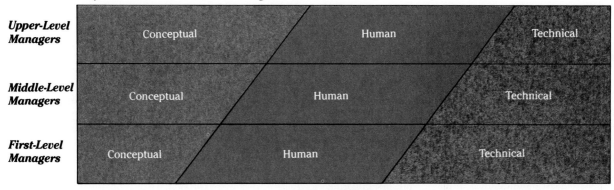

Amount of Skill Required

Source: Based on data from D. Katz (September-October 1974), Skills of an effective administrator, *Harvard Business Review,* 90-102.

Organizational Responsibility Differences

The way that managers plan, organize, direct, and control also varies according to their organizational responsibilities. For example, top-level managers devise strategic plans that encompass their entire organization. First-level managers, on the other hand, usually concentrate on an organizational subsystem, such as a department.

Skill Differences

Managers also vary in the skills they need and the degree to which they use each skill. For example, keeping the U.S. aerospace industry competitive requires managers whose mixture of skills differs from that of managers who train the astronauts or managers who assemble the rocket booster engines. All managers must be proficient in three categories of skill to be effective: technical, human, and conceptual.[12] The type and amount required, however, vary from level to level and from organization to organization (see Figure 1.8).

Technical skills enable managers to understand and use the tools, procedures, and techniques needed to perform a given task. Managers at lower levels, particularly in the technical core, usually need considerable technical skills to understand how the various components of their unit work. The relative importance of technical skills to managerial performance decreases for managers at higher levels in an organization.

Human (interpersonal) skills enable managers to work with and understand others, to lead, to motivate, to manage conflict, and to build group effort. Human skills are important to managers at all levels.

Conceptual skills enable managers to see, to diagnose, and to understand concepts at an abstract level of analysis. Although everyone needs conceptual skills, they are most important to managers in the institutional zone, who must devise plans based on probabilities, patterns, and connections. Conceptual skills provide upper-level managers with the ability to anticipate changes or to estimate the value of corporate strategies. (See "A Closer Look: Management in the 1990s.")

Management in the 1990s: The Times, They Are A'Changin'

Traditionally, the route to the top of corporate America has been through managing in blue chip industrial companies, but that route is likely to change. The Bureau of Labor Statistics (BLS), for example, estimates that by 1995 almost three quarters of all jobs in the United States will be in the service sector (including transportation, communication, trade, finance, real estate, and government), and some estimates raise that figure to 88 percent by the year 2000.[1] BLS projects that many of the new jobs will be in such areas as business services (for example, management consulting, public relations, and advertising), professional services (such as law, accounting, and engineering), maintenance and repair services for the highly technological equipment found in the workplace today, and financial services (particularly general financial management).

There is another change that will affect managers' futures, however. Middle-management positions are becoming an endangered species. For one thing, upper-level managers are being asked to do much of the analysis work previously done by their middle-level subordinates. For another thing, lower-level managers are becoming more active and making many of the day-to-day decisions formerly made by middle-level managers. Computers and new communications technology have taken over many information-handling

chores, and private contractors are being given legal, accounting, and other such tasks previously handled by an organization's middle-level managers. As a result, thousands of middle-level management positions are disappearing.

One other trend of note concerns the age of organization members. A 1989 *Fortune* article predicts that, by the year 2000, only 39 percent of the workforce will be under age thirty-five compared to 49 percent in 1989. Many organizations are dealing with this by recruiting older, even retired, managers but this strategy is not without problems. "Outfits with many senior employees worry about frustrating ambitious young hotshots, and managers sometimes feel awkward directing subordinates far older than themselves.[2]

Middle managers will be expected to use their technical skills much later in their career than once was the case. By drumming up new business, servicing clients, and continuing to add to profits rather than merely overseeing administration, many middle managers "will find their jobs riskier and more demanding, but also more purposeful and rewarding, than those of the old bureaucratic middle managers."[3]

In the 1990s, the fastest route to the top for managers may be through " . . . marketing, sales and then moving into general management. . . . [A]dmiration for the number

crunchers has diminished."[4] People on their way up should try to avoid mergers and reorganizations, organizations in slow rather than rapidly expanding industries, and bosses who feel threatened by their approach. They probably also should get a graduate degree as well as a B.S. or B.A. Perhaps most importantly, they must develop an "absolute, total dedication to being the boss."[5]

Those who succeed to top management can expect to be paid well for their work. As of the late 1980s, the average annual base salary for a top executive was $215,000 plus another 85 percent in bonuses. Increases in pay for top managers have outpaced inflation and are expected to continue to do so, but there is every indication that, more and more, managers will have to *earn* their pay. So, keep your technical skills sharp and prepare to add value to your organization.

1. Based on (2 February 1987), How managers will manage, *Fortune*, 47.
2. Making better use of older workers (30 January 1989), *Fortune*, 179.
3. *Fortune*, 1987, 48.
4. What makes top executives run? [An interview with Lester Korn, founder and chair of Korn/Ferry International, a large executive search firm] (14 April 1986), *U.S. News & World Report*, 52.
5. *Ibid.*

Managerial Roles

This section focuses on two questions: Why do organizations need managers? and How do managers spend their time? The work of Henry Mintzberg from McGill University provides a useful insight into both of these questions.

Why Organizations Need Managers

Organizations are tools created to achieve a set of objectives. Boswell Hospital in Phoenix, Arizona, was created to deliver high-quality health care. Hanover College in Hanover, Indiana, was created to provide a sound liberal arts education. The Miller Brewing Company was created to make a profit by manufacturing and selling beer. Every organization has a technical set of tasks that must be performed to convert its mission into reality. It is a manager's job to define an organization's goals, to determine how to achieve them, and to make them happen. There are six reasons organizations need managers:

1. Managers ensure that an organization serves its basic purpose—the efficient production of specific goods or services.
2. Managers design and maintain the stability of an organization's operations.
3. Managers choose the strategies needed to keep an organization adapting in a controlled way to its changing environment.
4. Managers ensure that an organization serves the ends of the people who control it.
5. Managers are the key informational link between an organization and its environment.
6. As formal authorities, managers are responsible for the operation of an organization's status system and serve as symbols of the organization in ceremonial activities.[13]

Every organization and organizational unit needs managers to plan, organize, direct, and control organizational resources in pursuit of organizational goals.

How Managers Spend Their Time

Managers must fill many roles as they carry out the four management functions (see Table 1.1). Henry Mintzberg grouped these roles into three categories: interpersonal, informational, and decisional.[14]

Interpersonal Roles. Managers fill several **interpersonal roles** because of their position in their organization. As a *figurehead,* a manager symbolizes the organization, signing legal documents and participating in such events as ground-breaking ceremonies or the opening of a new branch office. As a *leader,* a manager uses power, coordination techniques, and motivational tools to integrate the needs of individual subordinate organization members

TABLE 1.1 Major Managerial Roles

Interpersonal Roles	Informational Roles	Decisional Roles
Figurehead	Monitor	Entrepreneur
Leader	Disseminator	Disturbance handler
Liaison	Spokesperson	Resource allocator
		Negotiator

Source: Based on H. Mintzberg (1973), *The nature of managerial work,* Englewood Cliffs, NJ: Prentice-Hall.

with the needs of the organization as it pursues its objectives. As a *liaison,* a manager develops and cultivates relationships with individuals and groups outside of his or her area of direct responsibility to exchange information and coordinate the organization's many components. A supervisor, for example, may develop a network with other supervisors, and the chief executive officer (CEO) with other CEOs.

Informational Roles. Through **informational roles,** managers collect and disperse knowledge. As a *monitor,* a manager collects information about the organization and its environment from all available sources, including subordinates, peers, superiors, and liaison contacts. As a *disseminator,* a manager transmits information collected through the monitor role to subordinates in the organization. As a *spokesperson,* a manager transmits information about the organization (such as its policies or plans) to individuals and groups outside of the organization.

Decisional Roles. The third major role that managers must play are **decisional,** or **strategy-making, roles.** As an *entrepreneur,* a manager identifies opportunities for and threats to the organization and initiates changes to capitalize on these. As a *disturbance handler,* a manager reacts to and attempts to resolve day-to-day crises, such as conflicts between individuals or problems with other organizations. As a *resource allocator,* a manager schedules his or her own time; programs the work of subordinates; and controls decisions involving the allocation of other resources, such as money, supplies, and equipment. As a *negotiator,* a manager attempts to obtain beneficial solutions for the organization in nonroutine situations, such as arranging a contract with a supplier or negotiating a tax break from the state government in exchange for building a new plant in that state.

Although neither the functional (process) nor the role approach provides complete insight into many aspects of a manager's daily routine (such as how long each activity should last or the optimum frequency of interruptions), they do comprise a comprehensive and useful way of looking at the nature of management (see Figure 1.9). Managers can and should integrate the role-oriented approach with the traditional four-function process perspective, because it is, in part, through the interpersonal, informational, and decisional roles that managers execute the planning, organizing, directing, and controlling functions.

The Nature of Management in Review

There are at least two perspectives on and many definitions of management. This book uses a definition based on the process perspective. It views management as a combination of the processes of planning, organizing, directing, and controlling resources in pursuit of organizational goals. Managers put these four processes into effect. All managers plan, organize, direct, and control, so this set of functions can be considered universal, yet the specific ways in which managers apply the four functions vary with the type of management position they hold.

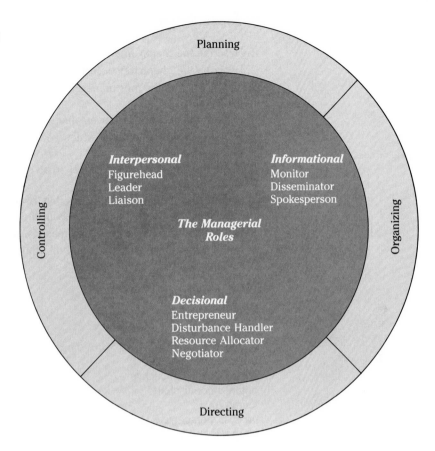

FIGURE 1.9 Managerial Roles and the Functions of Management

Through each of the major managerial roles, managers accomplish the four management functions of planning, organizing, directing, and controlling. The leadership role, for example, gives managers the authority they need to execute directing activities. The informational role provides leaders with the information they need to make decisions as resource allocators and negotiators.

Management positions vary according to zone, line or staff, hierarchical level, functional area, and organizational type. There are three zones of responsibility in an organization: the institutional zone (whose managers oversee the entire organization), the managerial zone (whose managers create the systems necessary to enact the plans developed in the institutional zone), and the technical core (whose managers supervise the people who produce the organization's goods and services). Line managers oversee the workers who produce an organization's goods and services. Staff managers counsel and advise line managers. Distinctions within an organization's hierarchy result in upper-level, middle-level, and lower-level managers. Functional managers oversee specific areas of a company, such as marketing, production, and finance. Managers can also be classified according to the industry in which their organization operates. Differences among types of managers produce differences in their time perspectives, in the way they allocate their time among the four functions, and in the profile of skills they need in order to manage effectively.

In carrying out the four major management functions, managers play three roles. To fill interpersonal roles, managers are required to be figureheads, leaders, and liaisons. To fill informational roles, managers become monitors, disseminators, and spokespeople. To fill decisional roles, managers act as entrepreneurs, disturbance handlers, resource allocators, and negotiators.

Issues for Review and Discussion

1. Describe the management process.
2. Describe the characteristics of an organization.
3. List and define the four managerial functions and explain how they are interrelated.
4. Explain the concept of universalism of management.
5. Explain several systems by which you could classify all of the managers from one large corporation.
6. Name the three managerial zones in an organization and describe what managers do in each.
7. Identify three types of skills needed by effective managers and relate their importance to the managers' levels in the hierarchy.
8. Identify and discuss at least two reasons organizations need managers.
9. Name three managerial roles and the duties managers perform in each.

Key Terms

management
managers
organization
sociological perspective
organizational chart
hierarchy
process perspective
planning
organizing
directing
controlling
institutional zone

technical core
managerial zone
line managers
staff managers
functional managers
technical skills
human (interpersonal) skills
conceptual skills
interpersonal roles
informational roles
decisional (strategy-making) roles

Suggested Readings

Flamholtz, E. G., (1987). *The inner game of management.* New York: AMACON.

Iacocca, L., with Novak, W. (1984). *Iacocca: An autobiography.* New York: Bantam; for a review of this book, see Heller, R. E. (1988). In Pierce, J. L., and Newstrom, J. W., eds. *The manager's bookshelf: A mosaic of contemporary views.* New York: Harper & Row, 145-49.

Kerr, S., Hill, K. D., and Broedling, L. (1986). The first-line supervisor: Phasing out or here to stay? *Academy of Management Review,* 11, 103-17.

Luthans, F. (1988). Successful vs. effective real managers. *Academy of Management Executive,* 2, 127-32.

Mintzberg, H. (1987). *Mintzberg on management.* New York: The Free Press.

Mintzberg, H. (July/August 1975). The manager's job: Folklore and fact. *Harvard Business Review,* 49-61.

Peters, T., and Austin, N. (1985). *A passion for excellence: The leadership difference.* New York: Random House.

Notes

1. C. Icahn (27 October 1986), What ails corporate America—and what should be done, *Business Week*, 101.
2. C. I. Barnard (1938), *The functions of the executive,* Cambridge, MA: Harvard University Press, 73.
3. A. K. Rice (1958), *Productivity and social organization: The Ahmedabad experiment.* London: Tavistock.
4. M. P. Follett (1949), *Freedom and coordination: Lectures in business organization,* London: Pitman.
5. H. Fayol (1949), *General and industrial management,* C. Storrs, trans., London: Sir Isaac Pitman and Sons, Ltd. (original work published in 1916); J. D. Breeze (1985), Harvest from the archives: The search for Fayol and Carlioz, *Journal of Management,* 11, 43-54.
6. M. W. McCall, Jr., A. M. Morrison, and R. L. Hannan (1978), *Studies of managerial work: Results and methods* (Technical Report No. 9), Greensboro, NC: Center for Creative Leadership.
7. R. A. Mackenzie (November-December 1969), The management process in 3-D, *Harvard Business Review,* 87.
8. H. Mintzberg (July-August 1975), The manager's job: Folklore and fact, *Harvard Business Review,* 49-61.
9. T. Parsons (1960), *Structure and process in modern society,* Chicago: Free Press; C. Perrow (1967), A framework for the comparative analyses of organizations, *American Sociological Review,* 32, 194-208.
10. W. W. Tornow and P. R. Pinto (1976), The development of a managerial job taxonomy: A system for describing, classifying, and evaluating executive positions, *Journal of Applied Psychology,* 61, 410-18; W. Whitely (1985), Managerial work behavior: An integration of results from two major approaches, *Academy of Management Journal,* 28, 358.
11. T. A. Mahoney, T. H. Jerdee, and S. J. Carroll, Jr. (1963), *Development of managerial performance: A research approach,* Cincinnati, OH: South-Western; T. A. Mahoney, T. H. Jerdee, and S. J. Carroll, Jr. (1965), The jobs of management, *Industrial Relations,* 4, 97-110.
12. D. Katz (September-October 1974), Skills of an effective administrator, *Harvard Business Review,* 90-102.
13. H. Mintzberg (1980), *The nature of managerial work,* Englewood Cliffs, NJ: Prentice-Hall, 94-96.
14. This discussion is based on Mintzberg, 1980.

A Conversation with Socrates

Seeing Nicomachides, one day, coming from the assembly for the election of magistrates, Socrates asked him, "Who have been chosen generals?"

"Are not the Athenians the same as ever, Socrates?" he replied; "for they have not chosen me, who am worn out with serving from the time I was first elected, both as captain and centurion, and with having received so many wounds from the enemy (he then drew aside his robe and showed the scars of the wounds) but have elected Antisthenes, who has never served in the heavy-armed infantry, nor done anything remarkable in the cavalry, and who indeed knows nothing, but how to get money."

"Is it not good, however, to know this," said Socrates, "since he will then be able to get necessaries for the troops?"

"But merchants," replied Nicomachides, "are able to collect money; and yet would not, on that account be capable of leading an army."

"Antisthenes, however," continued Socrates, "is given to emulation, a quality necessary in a general. Do you not know that whenever he has been chorus manager he has gained superiority in all his choruses?"

"But, by Jupiter," rejoined Nicomachides, "there is nothing similar in managing a chorus and an army."

"Yet Antisthenes," said Socrates, "though neither skilled in music nor teaching a chorus, was able to find out the best masters in these departments."

"In the Army, accordingly," exclaimed Nicomachides, "he will find others to range his troops for him, and others to fight for him!"

"Well then," rejoined Socrates, "if he finds out and selects the best men in military affairs, as he has done in the conduct of his choruses, he will probably attain superiority in this respect also."

"Do you say then, Socrates," he said, "that it is in the power of the same man to manage a chorus well, and to manage an army well?"

"I say," said Socrates, "that over whatever a man may preside, he will if he knows what he needs, and is able to provide it, be a good president, whether he have the direction of a chorus, a family, a city, or an army."

"By Jupiter, Socrates," cried Nicomachides, "I should never have expected to hear from you that good managers of a family would also be good generals."

"Come then," proceeded Socrates, "let us consider what are the duties of each of them, that we may understand whether they are the same, or are in any respect different."

"By all means," he said.

"Is it not, then, the duty of both," asked Socrates, "to render those under their command obedient and submissive to them?"

"Unquestionably."

"Is it not also the duty of both to appoint fitting persons to fulfill the various duties?"

"That is also unquestionable."

"To punish the bad, and to honor the good too, belongs, I think, to each of them."

"Undoubtedly."

"And is it not honorable in both to render those under them well disposed towards them?"

"That also is certain."

"And do you think it for the interest of both to gain for themselves allies and auxiliaries or not?"

"Certainly; but what, I ask, will skill managing a household avail if it be necessary to fight?"

"It will doubtless, in that case, be of the greatest avail," said Socrates; "for a good manager of a house, knowing that nothing is so advantageous or profitable and prejudicial as to get the better of your enemies when you contend with them, nothing so unprofitable and prejudicial as to

be defeated, will zealously seek and provide everything that may conduce to victory, will carefully watch and guard against whatever tends to defeat, will vigorously engage if he sees that his force is likely to conquer, and, what is not the least important point, will cautiously avoid engaging if he finds himself insufficiently prepared."

"Do not, therefore, Nicomachides," he added, "despise men skillful in managing a household; for the conduct of private affairs differs from that of public concerns only in magnitude; in other respects they are similar; but what is most to be observed, is, that neither of them are managed without men; and that private matters are not managed by one species of men, and public matters by another; for those who conduct public business make use of men not at all differing in nature from those whom the managers of private affairs employ; and those who know how to employ them, conduct either private or public affairs judiciously, while those who do not know, will err in the management of both."

Questions

1. What is Socrates' (470?–399 B.C.) main point?
2. Of what level of management is Socrates speaking?
3. What management roles and functions does he identify? How do these compare with the traditional process views? with Henry Mintzberg's views?
4. What else does this dialogue tell us about management in Greece in the fifth century B.C.?

From Xenophon (n.d.), *Memorabilia and Oeconomicus*, E. C. Marchant, trans., The Loeb Classical Library ed., Cambridge: Harvard University Press, 186–87.

2

Management and the Organizational Environment

Student Learning Objectives

After reading this chapter, you should be able to:

1. Identify and discuss key aspects of the general external environment.

2. Identify and discuss aspects of the task environment.

3. Identify the major problems that confront managers as a result of the relationship between an organization and its external environment.

4. Understand the importance of the boundary-spanning function.

5. Explain the difference between open and closed management systems.

6. Identify the major sources of structure that define the internal environment.

7. Discuss the managerial processes that play major roles in shaping the internal environment.

8. Define organizational culture and explain why it is important.

9. Specify and describe the five organizational functions and understand the importance of integrating them effectively.

M anagement does not exist in isolation. An organization and its managers must contend with two environments that encompass the structural, cultural, legal, economic, and social conditions within and surrounding the organization. This chapter explores these two environments and their components' demands on an organization's management system.

The External Environment

Every organization exists in an environment that extends beyond the organization's formal boundaries. This **external environment** represents a set of conditions, circumstances, and influences that surround and affect the functioning of an organization. CBS, for example, found Ted Turner to be part of its external environment several years ago when he attempted an unfriendly takeover. Several banks (particularly in Texas) faced serious economic problems when the price of oil went from $60 a barrel to under $20. In response to public pressure, Coca-Cola reintroduced its original-formula soft drink after a disappointing attempt to market "new" Coke. All of these are examples of how the external environment touches an organization.

The external environment is made up of many individuals (for example, customers, members of other organizations, local citizens), organizations (suppliers, civic groups, labor unions), and government bodies (regulatory agencies, legislators, local officials). It includes people who can influence an organization and its management system, as well as those who might be affected by the organization's actions. For most organizations, the external environment is large, diverse, and complex. As a result, organization scholars have partitioned it into two sections. The **general environment** is the overall environment within which an organization operates. The **task environment** is the more specific and immediate environment in which an organization conducts its business. Every organization must cope with both facets of its external environment.

The General Environment

As illustrated in Figure 2.1, the major components of an organization's general environment are its social and cultural context, the economic system surrounding the organization, the legal and political atmosphere, the technology from which knowledge and tools for reaching goals are derived, and the international climate. Managers in different general environments often adopt different management systems.[1] For example, the management group for a major manufacturer of computer systems in Minneapolis, Minnesota, is less likely to feel the need for lifetime commitment to employment than would its Japanese counterpart.

Just as an organization is affected by pressure from its general environment, the environment is influenced by organizational activity. One way in which an organization can affect the general environment is by influencing its local task environment. Consider, for example, the impact felt when IBM closed a distribution center in Greencastle, Indiana, leaving the city without its major employer.

*FIGURE 2.1 An Organization
and the General Environment*

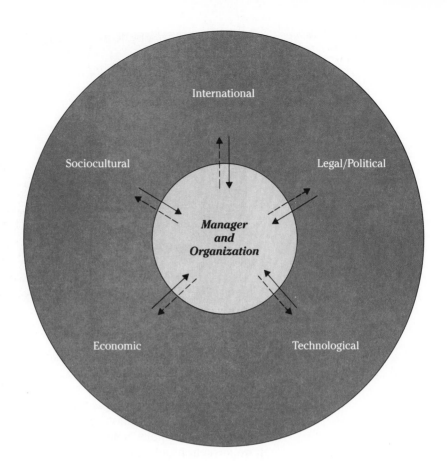

The Sociocultural Domain. The sociocultural domain consists of the
values, customs, mores, and demographic characteristics (age, education
level, mobility pattern, and the like) of the people within a society. Inasmuch as
most organizations are created to serve the needs of the members of a society,
it is easy to see how these organizations become manifestations of the social
and cultural forces that surround them.

The Economic Domain. Although organizations may be strongly influenced by the sociocultural domain, the fulfillment of these needs requires
resources (for example, land, labor, and capital). All societies develop rules to
govern the transfer of resources, and these rules define a society's economic
domain and govern such transactions. All organizations operate in at least one
type of economic system (for example, socialist, communist, or capitalist).
Each system has its own standards and institutions governing economic activity.

The health of the dominant economic system in which an organization
operates also affects its activities. Both for-profit and not-for-profit organizations are influenced by such economic conditions as inflation, recession,
depression, interest rates, and rates of international exchange. For example,
partly because of the growing national deficit, state universities throughout the
United States face declining budgets.

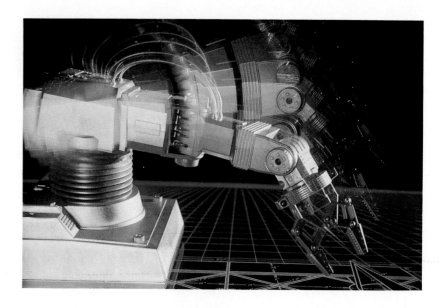

Technological advances in the use of robotics have revolutionized the manufacturing industry.

The Technological Domain.   *Technology* is the means by which an organization converts its inputs (such as raw materials, unfinished goods, and energy) into outputs (products or services). The technological domain includes the knowledge, processes, means, systems, hardware, and software available to an organization for this transformation process. In the past few decades, for example, optic fibers have facilitated communications, robots have revolutionized manufacturing, and lasers have assisted surgeons.

The Legal/Political Domain.   Many social values established by the sociocultural system are translated into laws that control and influence members of society. The laws are made by legislators and interpreted by the courts, which are expected to apply "the will of the people"; thus, the legal and political systems are inextricably linked. The will of the people changes over time (witness President Bush's "kinder and gentler America" presidential campaign theme), and political ideology affects organizations in many ways, including the extent to which selected laws are enforced, the levels of taxes and interest rates, and so on.

The International Domain.   Limited domestic resources, the availability of international currency, the search for new markets, and increasingly more vigorous competition are only a few of the forces that are bringing the international arena into the domain of increasing numbers of American organizations. The American automobile industry faces stiff competition from Japanese and German manufacturers. Even local liquor stores are influenced by international factors, such as the weather conditions in the Bordeaux region of France.

In sum, the sociocultural, economic, technological, legal/political, and international domains strongly affect organizational behavior and must, therefore, be a target of managerial attention. (See "A Closer Look: International Investment.")

International Investment: Europe Buys Back a Piece of the New World

In the eighteenth century, the United States of America claimed independence from its European master. Today Great Britain and such countries as France, West Germany, and Sweden are regaining some of their control over the former colonies. Today's weapons may seem less destructive, but they are much more powerful than those used over two centuries ago. The pounds, francs, marks, and kroners aimed at the United States have usually hit their targets.

In one recent year, over $10 billion worth of U.S. corporate assets were acquired through British takeovers alone. French interests assumed more than $1 billion of American holdings. According to *Business Week*, "A new, swashbuckling style of raider capitalism is in vogue across Europe. The economic recovery on the Continent has produced scores of cash-rich companies with too few investment opportunities. . . . "[1]

It is not surprising that U.S. corporations are attractive to European investors. Many of these excellent corporations have outstanding promise as established profit makers. Add to this the fact that the value of the U.S. dollar relative to its European

counterparts has been suppressed by at least 20 percent during recent years, and it is easy to understand what makes these companies appear as major bargains.

Should U.S. business go to war? Only if they want to bite the hand that feeds them. As noted by Jean-Jacques P. Netter of the French brokerage house Nivard Flornoy & Cie, "A few years ago the U.S. economy seemed so invulnerable, . . . Now it's the healthy Europeans saving ailing industrial America. It's bizarre."[2] Much of the money coming from Europe originated here as expenditures on European imports. Perhaps the returning monies will ease the huge trade imbalance.

Is it just the Europeans who are "buying American"? Clearly not. The Japanese have a penchant for American real estate. Tokyo's Shuwa Corporation now owns the Arco Plaza in Los Angeles and paid $625 million for it in cash. The luxury Hyatt Regency Waikiki Hotel belongs to Azabu Jidosha Corporation, a Japanese business that considered the $245 million price tag reasonable. Japanese investment in U.S. real estate is encouraged by the very low interest rates available to investors in Japan and the

limited real estate investment opportunities in their homeland. In one recent year alone, the Japanese spent $12.7 billion acquiring real estate in Phoenix, Seattle, San Diego, and other U.S. cities. Put quite simply, American real estate is too good a deal for the Japanese to resist.

What is the United States doing about this? Sometimes, turning the tables! According to a 1989 *Fortune* article, U.S. companies spent over $20 billion dollars in a recent year buying companies and plants in Europe. "In general, U.S. companies are superbly positioned to profit from the [European] market."[3] U.S. companies are also teaming up with foreign competitors. Texas Instruments and Japan's Hitachi, former adversaries in a lawsuit, are now collaborating to develop advanced memory chips.[4]

1. Europe goes on a shopping spree in the States (27 October 1986), *Business Week*, 54.

2. *Business Week*, 55.

3. The coming boom in Europe (10 April 1989), *Fortune*, 110.

4. Your rivals can be your allies (27 March 1989), *Fortune*, 66 ff.

The Task Environment

An organization's task environment is the means through which the general environment exercises its most immediate influences on the organization's management. The sociocultural domain describes the general values and mores of a society, but its people are the actual customers of an organization. They directly influence organizational operations and form part of the task environment. Managers should focus managerial strategies primarily on cur-

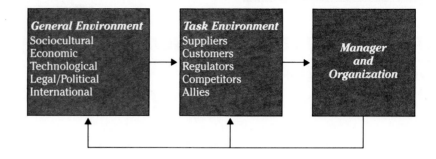

FIGURE 2.2 The Relationship Between Task and General Environments

General Environment	**Task Environment**	
Sociocultural	Suppliers	
Economic	Customers	*Manager and Organization*
Technological	Regulators	
Legal/Political	Competitors	
International	Allies	

A MANAGER'S WORD

The BATF (Bureau of Alcohol, Tobacco, and Firearms) regulates our industry with a firm hand. Wine labels and contents are rigorously monitored. Recent legislation on drunk driving has also had an enormous impact . . . . [T]he company in turn has spent millions in advertising to sensitize the public in developing responsible, moderate drinking patterns.

Claudia Conlon Appleby
Director, Public Relations
Sterling Vineyards

rent and potential customers rather than on the general beliefs, values, and mores of society as a whole. Figure 2.2 depicts the relationship between the two environments (general and task) and an organization.

The term *task environment* has been used to identify four components of an organization's external environment:

1. Suppliers—providers of materials, labor, capital, equipment, and work space
2. Customers/markets—including distributors and users
3. Regulatory and influence groups—for example, government agencies, unions, and professional associations (This group originally dealt only with regulatory groups. Here, unions, professional associations, and outside influence groups have been added to this category.)
4. Competitors—for both markets and resources[2]

A fifth component of the task environment includes *allies* (such as partners in joint ventures).[3] (See Figure 2.3.)

The relationship between an organization and its task environment is dynamic. Much as the task environment influences an organization, an organization attempts to control and influence the task environment. Most managers would agree that it is better to study and manage the external environment than to allow it to control an organization.

Uncertainty and Interdependence

As an organization and its external environment interact, managers confront two problems: uncertainty and interdependence. *Environmental uncertainty* arises because, under most circumstances, managers can neither control nor predict everything that will happen in their task environment. In 1989, for example, the FAA caused an unexpected disruption to Boeing's production schedule by requiring the company to reexamine the wiring of hundreds of its 737 planes after one crashed in Britain. *Interdependence* arises as organizations develop a variety of exchange relationships with other organizations.[4] For example, Northwest Outlet (a retailer) depends on the Hudson Bay Company, a manufacturer of wool blankets and clothing, to supply blankets for its customers.

Unless managed effectively, uncertainty and interdependence can interfere with the attainment of organizational goals. The discussion of strategic management in Chapter 8 explores techniques for achieving a fit between an organization and its environment.

FIGURE 2.3   The Task Environment

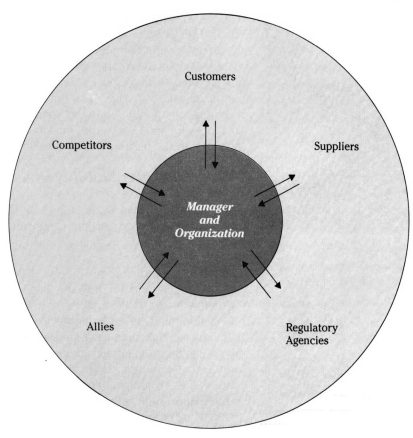

Linking Environments and Organizations

It is often difficult to determine where an organization ends and its environment begins. If someone asked you how large your college is, you would probably refer to the number of students who are enrolled, but are the students part of the organization or part of the external environment? If asked to describe the size of your hair stylist's shop, would you refer to the number of stylists who work there or to the number of customers? A major challenge facing managers is to link their organization with its external environment.

The Boundary-Spanning Process

The **boundary-spanning process** is one means through which organizations conduct transactions with their external environment. At General Mills, for example, when the market research department brings information into the organization about customer preferences, it performs a boundary-spanning activity. **Boundary roles** are the positions that link an organization to its external environment. Sales representatives, market researchers, and organizational lobbyists hold boundary roles.

Boundary spanners are the individuals who fill boundary roles. A boundary spanner operates both within and outside of an organization, as when a

James D. Thompson has contributed substantially to an understanding of the role of external environments and has developed strategies for managing them.

manager acts as a liaison between an organization and the external environment. The various managerial roles—figureheads, spokespeople—enable managers to span the boundaries between their organization and its environment.[5] Nonmanagers also can be boundary spanners. Purchasing agents, lawyers, and technological specialists often link an organization to its suppliers, regulatory bodies, and informational resources. Many organization members are informal boundary spanners, such as a waiter who learns about an especially good wine from customers and suggests that the wine steward include it in the restaurant's wine selection.

Environmental Stability and Segmentation

Organizational sociologist James D. Thompson has suggested that two characteristics of an organization's task environment significantly influence the behavior of effective managers: the degree of environmental change and the degree of environmental segmentation.[6]

Environmental change reflects the degree to which an organization's task environment is stable (undergoing few and slow changes) or shifting (undergoing frequent and rapid changes). During the late 1970s, domestic airlines operated within a fairly stable environment. During the 1980s, however, the U.S. government deregulated the airlines, causing numerous and frequent changes in flight schedules, airfares, and even airline ownership. Competition for new routes intensified, as did competition for new passengers. This previously stable environment changed rapidly.

Environmental segmentation describes the similarities and differences among components of the task environment and their demands on an organization. A **homogeneous task environment** is characterized by very little segmentation; the demands placed on an organization by the components of its task environment are quite similar. For example, most customers at The Badger Tap, a student bar near the University of Wisconsin, place essentially the same demands on the organization as do most of the bar's suppliers and competitors. Because of the similarity of their demands, these segments of The Badger Tap's task environment can be regarded as homogeneous. Conversely, a **heterogeneous task environment** is highly segmented or differentiated. For example, IBM developed its personal computer line to target part of a highly segmented market. Computer customers include groups with very different demands. Some want word processors, some graphics capabilities, some spreadsheets, and some scholarly capabilities. The computer needs of the Pentagon, a college student, and a business executive differ greatly.

The stability and segmentation of the task environment combine to define a variety of environmental conditions that managers encounter. The challenge is to design a management system that can meet the uncertainty, interdependence, and segmentation conditions presented by an organization's task environment.

Organic/Mechanistic Management Systems

Research provides evidence that an organization's external task environment strongly affects its organizational and management systems. British researchers Tom Burns and George Stalker examined the relationships among environmental conditions, management practice, and organizational design in twenty manufacturing firms in England and Scotland.[7] The study, which has had tremendous impact on the science of management, focused on the rate of environmental change in the firms' scientific technology and product markets. Burns and Stalker were able to identify two different systems of management practice: organic and mechanistic.

An **organic system** is characterized by:

- A flexible structure that can change when confronted with different kinds of task demands
- Loosely defined tasks to be performed by employees
- Consultative-type organizational communications (as opposed to a commanding type of relationship)
- Authority that flows more from knowledge centers (individuals, groups, or specialized departments) and the nature of relationships than from strict hierarchical positions

In contrast, a **mechanistic system** is characterized by:

- Clear definition and relative stability of tasks and responsibility
- Vesting of authority in position and its arrangement according to hierarchical level
- Communications in the form of a downward flow of instructions issued as commands

Burns and Stalker argued that organic and mechanistic management systems are appropriate for different kinds of environmental conditions. Dynamic environments, in which uncertainty is high and unique problems and events often arise, require an organic system. A mechanistic system is more compatible with stable environmental conditions.

Environmental studies conducted by Burns and Stalker and others give rise to a number of observations.[8] First, there appears to be a relationship between the characteristics of the task environment and the types of management systems an organization develops. To be effective, an organization must obtain the best possible fit between the environment and its management system(s). Second, organizations create different management systems to deal with the different amounts of uncertainty that managers face in performing their jobs. Organic management systems appear appropriate for high levels of environmental change and segmentation, mechanistic systems for more stable environments and lower levels of uncertainty.

Closed/Open Management Systems

Organic and mechanistic management systems are concerned with linking an organization's external environment to its internal design. *Open* and *closed* management systems look at the different approaches managers have regarding the organization-environment relationship.

Closed Systems. Years ago, classical management theorists proposed that organizations are rational systems that can be designed according to a specific set of laws. They asserted that organizations will be efficient if managers properly define the nature of the work, standardize work procedures, assign an appropriate division of labor, group tasks into departments, and specify appropriate authority and responsibility relationships. These primary forces, they said, are internal to the system and arise from the nature of the work itself. Thus, according to this perspective, an organization could be designed appropriately if managers paid attention to the relationships among these parts of the system. Much as an engineer designs a bridge according to the principles of physics, followers of classical management theorists believed managers design an organization by adhering to the principles of organization.

In contrast, behavioral management theorists believe that the forces defining an effective management system are to be found in the nature of individuals and groups. They reason that management systems must be designed to accommodate workers' social and self-fulfillment needs. Both the classical and behavioral management theories concentrate on the inner workings of organizations in an effort to achieve order, consistency, efficiency, and predictability. They consider that a manager working in such a system does not have to pay particular attention to the external environment. In fact, neither classical nor behavioral management theories explicitly include the environment in their models.

From both the classical and behavioral perspectives, managers look only within an organization to improve productivity and efficiency. The organization is considered a **closed system** that operates as though it were in a world by itself. As Figure 2.4 shows, the walls of a closed system are thick. They block out ideas, information, and external environmental forces. Any environmental uncertainty that penetrates the walls of an organization is absorbed at the institutional and managerial levels. Operations in the organization's technical core are not disrupted. The American automobile industry's refusal to believe in the shift to small and fuel-efficient cars is a classic example of a closed system at work. The goal of those within a closed system is to eliminate or control the uncertainty that originates in the external environment so that the management process is as easy and predictable as possible.

Open Systems.   A second perspective of an organization in relation to its external environment is the **open system** (review Figure 2.4). According to this perspective, an organization is a system that interacts with and depends on

FIGURE 2.4   *Open and Closed Systems Management*

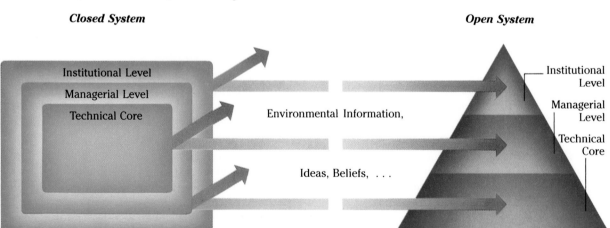

Closed System

Open System

Institutional Level

Managerial Level

Technical Core

Environmental Information,

Ideas, Beliefs, . . .

Institutional Level

Managerial Level

Technical Core

other systems. Consider the situation faced by banks in the United States. Banks cannot survive unless people and companies make deposits, take out loans, and purchase other banking services. Banks also depend on the federal government, which sets the cost of underlying money, as well as on state and federal regulations governing their bank charters.

Open systems advocates believe that an organization's survival depends on its ability to mesh with the larger environment. To cope with the external environment's inevitable intrusion and uncertainty, organizations must create management systems different from those found within a closed system. Rather than designing systems to ignore the external environment, managers must design systems sensitive and responsive to the environment. Managers who view their organization as an open system, therefore, face a major challenge. They must play an active role as organizational boundary spanners. They must carry information outward to influence the external environment and simultaneously serve as conduits through which external environmental factors can influence internal organizational operations. Such managers meet the public, talk to the press, and actively lobby regulatory and legislative bodies.

The open systems model suggests that an organization should create a number of open windows to let ideas, beliefs, information, and pressures from the environment influence the organization at each of its three levels (institutional, managerial, and technical core). Changes that confront organizations mean that the jobs of first-level managers increasingly will become externally oriented.[9] The institutional zone of management becomes more and more important as organizations become more dependent on coalitions with other organizations, as regulation of business expands, and as society increases its levels of expectations for social responsibility by organizations. Effective organizations will have to become more open to environmental information, allowing it to flow in at each hierarchical level and permitting organizations to influence the environment at each level as well.

Organic/mechanistic and closed/open systems are related, in that managers who adopt a closed systems perspective to the organization-environment relationship are likely to structure their organization following a mechanistic model. Conversely, managers who take an open systems approach are likely to fashion an organic internal design.

The Internal Environment

The **internal environment** of an organization consists of a wide range of factors within its formal boundaries. The internal environment includes the jobs that people perform; the work units, departments, divisions, and other structures in which they perform those jobs; the technologies people use to produce products and deliver services; the processes that managers use to guide workers; and, of course, the people who do the work—both managers and nonmanagers—together with their values and beliefs. These factors combine to form the climate of an organization. It is this climate that people "feel" when they perceive an organization as being, for example, cold and uncaring. Managers react to and must actively manage the components of their organization's internal environment.

Structures

Several structural features of an organization define its internal environment. Three salient sources of structure that researchers have identified are the design of jobs, the structural arrangement of an organization's work units (such as its departments), and the technology used within these units.[10]

Job Design. Part of a manager's responsibility is to divide the work that needs to be done into tasks and then to assemble these tasks into jobs. The way these tasks are assembled to form a job is known as **job design.** When designing jobs, managers generally have options. Consider, for example, the assembly of automobile engines. In the traditional American manufacturing process, employees stand along a conveyor belt. Their job is to add one or more parts to each engine as it passes by. The time elapsed between the beginning and the completion of the task is short. The nature of the task is simple, permitting a quick, efficient execution of the assigned work. This short-cycle task is repeated many times an hour as engine blocks move from employee to employee. Contrast this American design with the way engines are assembled at the Volvo plant in Kalmar, Sweden.[11] Swedish employees work together in teams to assemble an entire engine block. Each job consists of several tasks of varying complexity and duration. As a manager, you must design jobs appropriately for your subordinates.

Volvo's Kalmar plant uses a team approach for building cars rather than the traditional assembly line method. The results are better cars and happier workers.

Job design is a major influence on employees' work-related motivation, attitudes, and behaviors.[12] Managers must be attuned to this issue, because its consequences are so important. They must redesign jobs as necessary to incorporate new technologies or to improve performance. (Chapter 9 discusses job design in more depth.)

Work Unit and Organizational Structure. Just as job design specifies the manner in which tasks are assigned to individual jobs, **work unit design** groups jobs into structures usually consisting of a relatively small number of employees. In **organizational design,** top-level managers combine work units into larger collections, such as departments and divisions. Thus, work unit and organizational structure depict the "arena in which organizational action takes place."[13]

Organizational and work unit structure also concerns the interaction patterns that link people to people and people to work. An organization's interaction pattern reveals its authority structure. In organizations with *hierarchical* patterns, influence flows down from people in superior positions who command subordinates in much the same way as high-ranking military officers issue orders to the lower ranks. Interaction patterns can also be *reciprocal,* in which influence flows back and forth from one person to another. In organizations with reciprocal patterns, authority is shared in give-and-take relationships between superiors and subordinates. Reciprocal patterns are often found in professional companies, such as law offices, where general partners consult with junior partners regarding client case load and projected administrative expenses.

These two radically different approaches correspond to the mechanistic and organic structures described earlier. The bureaucratic structure of a mechanistic organization provides detailed rules and standard operating procedures to govern interactions between people and between people and their work. An organic structure lets authority flow between individuals based on their expertise and the nature of their task. Regardless of the general structure, the location of power bases within organizations can have a great impact.[14]

Technology. **Technology** refers to the processes that transform organizational resources into a product or service. For example, a carpenter's hammer, a surgeon's scalpel, a psychologist's counseling and therapeutic techniques, and a professor's teaching method are all forms of technology.

Technology strongly affects many facets of an organization, including job design; organizational and work unit (social system) structure; managerial control and coordination processes; and the behaviors, attitudes, and motivation of employees. Following World War II, for example, middle-management positions grew rapidly as organizations processed large amounts of information. Today, however, as computers process information, the number of middle-management positions in many organizations is being reduced.[15] Because of technology's importance in an organization's internal environment, managers must decide what types of technology to use and manage their relationship with other facets of the organization.

Processes

Organization and management scholars refer to certain organizational activities as *organizational processes.* Coordinating, decision making, and communicating are three of the most common organizational processes and are especially important parts of the internal environment.

Coordinating. The people, jobs, departments, levels, and other components of an organization must be coordinated. Part of a manager's task in dealing with the internal environment is to achieve this integration through the **coordinating process.** Managers generally use one of two approaches to coordinating. Those who use the **personal mode** deal directly with the people whose activities are to be coordinated. Managers adopting this approach have direct relationships with peers, subordinates, and superiors; hold group meetings; maintain informal contacts; and assign special integrators to coordinate two or more highly interdependent individuals or organizational units. Managers who use the **impersonal mode** assign rules, policies, and standard operating procedures to coordinate individuals and activities. Compared to the personal mode, this approach requires less person-to-person contact and lets managers coordinate the work of larger groups, because it frees them from having to tell each worker how a particular task should be performed. A routine of this nature appears in Figure 2.5 on page 36.

Decision Making. **Decision making** is the process through which a course of action is chosen. In some organizations, managerial and non-managerial personnel are encouraged or even required to participate in decision making. In other organizations, decisions are made only at high levels and often behind closed doors. The style of decision making within an organization, thus, may be open, as in the first instance, or closed, as in the second. Decision-making style has been tied to employee satisfaction, commitment to the organization, work motivation, goal acceptance, and performance.[16] Chapter 6 will discuss decision making in detail; however, as you read about the internal environment in this chapter, note that the way in which decision making is handled affects a number of dimensions of organizational effectiveness, as well as an organization's internal climate.

FIGURE 2.5   *An Impersonal Mode of Integration*

How to Wash Windows

Equipment

Stepladder   Pail of Warm Water   Paper Towels
Treated Dustcloth   Sponge   Ammonia or Cleaning Agent
Putty Knife   Squeegee (One-Bladed)

Frequency
As Needed

Procedure

1. Politely ask whoever is in the room to remove any nearby equipment that might be damaged. If it cannot be moved at this time, offer to come back later.
2. Put your ladder under the window to see if you can reach the top pane easily when standing on the third step from the top or lower.
3. Dust off frames and sills with your dustcloth.
4. Pour half a cup of ammonia into a pail of warm water.
5. Dip your sponge in the cleaning solution and squeeze it out enough so it doesn't drip; otherwise it will spot varnish on the sill or frame.

Source: *Custodial methods at the University of Minnesota* (1975), 47.

Communicating. **Communicating** is the process of transmitting information to organization members. Some organizations deliver formal communications through written messages. Some communicate verbally, either face-to-face or in group settings. In some organizations, communicating is a downward flow of information: bosses tell their subordinates, who tell their subordinates, and so on. In other organizations, communication is relatively unrestricted; it flows downward, upward, diagonally, and horizontally. The style of communication used by managers strongly influences their organization's internal environment. Employees who receive information almost exclusively in written form, for example, may perceive their work environment as being closed and impersonal.

In sum, managers use coordinating, decision-making, and communication processes to guide people within their organization's structure. The ways in which organization members respond to this guidance influence the organization's effectiveness.

People and Their Beliefs

Of course, the most carefully structured organization and smoothly applied managerial processes would be worthless without people in place to use them. A critical component of an organization's internal environment, thus, is its social system, which includes organization members and the values and beliefs they share. This section examines an organization's people and the culture that results from their combined values and beliefs.

Management and Formal Leaders.   In any organization, there are people who manage and people who are managed. Many organizations have a dominant key manager, whose decisions and control systems influence the character of their organization's internal environment. There are those who contend that "the 'CEO' factor—that elusive combination of charisma, personality and managerial style—remains one of the most important influences on a firm."[17] The environment created by a supervisor obsessed with task perform-

The most smoothly applied managerial processes would be worthless without people in place to use them.

ance, for example, differs dramatically from the environment created by a supervisor who is relaxed, sociable, warm, and supportive of subordinates' needs. H. Ross Perot, the founder of Electronic Data Systems Corporation, and Chrysler's Lee Iacocca have shaped the nature of their organization's internal environment. Sometimes the key manager's role is held instead by a dominant management group or powerful organizational coalition, such as the "Holy Trinity," the name given three powerful editors at *The New York Times.*[18]

The values, beliefs, and demographic characteristics (such as age, experience, education, and social class) of key upper-echelon managers affect an organization, the strategies it pursues, the demands on its employees, and its overall effectiveness.[19] For example, Donald Hambrick of Columbia University and Phyllis Mason of Baruch College have noted that "firms with young managers will be more inclined to pursue risky strategies than will firms with older managers." They also have hypothesized that significant organizational power brokers, such as the dominant coalitions, are more likely to emphasize growth and a search for new domains if they have a marketing background. Those from production tend to emphasize improving work methods and developing new technologies.[20]

Nonmanagerial Employees. Like managerial employees, nonmanagerial employees also differ from one another according to demographic characteristics; patterns of personality, attitude, motivation, and behavior; and group membership in, for example, committees and cliques. Both group and individual differences influence an organization's internal environment. A work environment containing employees with strong achievement motivation and a strong work ethic, for example, is likely to be more production oriented than a work environment in which employees have strong affiliation needs and a strong leisure ethic. As the profile of individuals and groups within an organization changes, so does the nature of the internal environment. Being sensitive and responsive to these environmental factors is a major challenge for managers.

Organizational culture is not a fad. It is driven by the need to equip the organization with the knowledge to operate in the real world . . . . We must nurture our culture to create an environment in which people can realize their full potential as individuals and, collectively, as an organization.

—Smith

Organizational Culture. Understanding an organization's culture is crucial for managers because, once an organizational culture has been established, it is relatively stable and highly resistant to change. New suggestions may be countered with such remarks as "Things aren't done that way around here." When asked why not, employees often have no logical explanation. Instead, they seem to rely on tradition or a mystical organizational embodiment of values.[21] This unseen presence, called **organizational culture,** can be considered " . . . a pattern of basic assumptions invented, discovered, or developed by a given group as it learns to cope with its problems of external adaptation and internal integration. . . . "[22]

This combination of shared beliefs, values, perceptions, language, and reactions to situations is a critical part of an organization's internal environment. In fact, an organization's survival may depend on its culture; researchers have observed that corporate culture influences the strategies that organizations choose to pursue and their effectiveness in doing so.[23] Comparing the effective EDS Corporation to struggling General Motors, for example, H. Ross Perot commented:

> *The first EDSer to see a snake kills it. At GM, first thing you do is organize a committee on snakes. Then you bring in a consultant who knows a lot about snakes. Third thing you do is talk about it for a year!*[24]

Organizational Culture: Recognizing and Imposing a Corporate Culture

Pericles, the father of Athens' Golden Age, made a speech in 431 B.C. outlining his picture of the ideal society. The focus of his speech was that the success of Athens was based on the values and beliefs Athenians shared.[1] Pericles' ages-old management tool, organizational culture, is now the latest corporate buzzword.

There have been many times when an appropriate culture has helped an organization prosper. A 1989 *Fortune* article, for example, profiled office furniture company Herman Miller, Inc., telling a story of a warm, caring culture that helped nurture the success of the company.[2] An inappropriate organizational culture, however, can be disastrous, as anthropologist Peter C. Reynolds discovered when he worked for a company he calls Falcon Computer.[3] An apparently successful company in the Silicon Valley, Falcon expanded rapidly from less than 50 to over 250 employees. Reynolds was on hand for this growth; he was still there when the company permanently closed its doors following a loss of over $32 million. Although there are many reasons for the company's failure, much of the blame rests with its attempts to create a new culture and impose it on the employees. In the process, its executives created a description of an "ideal" culture that differed so much from what employees knew to be true that it became a source of bitter amusement.

For example, according to the formal "values document" that purported to state the corporate culture at Falcon, management encouraged " . . . open, direct person-to-person communication as part of our daily routine,"[4] yet the document itself was created secretly by top managers, without input from middle managers, and distributed through the formal chain of command to employees only after it had been adopted. Another aspect of the corporate culture as set forth in the values document was " . . . to do it right the first time. We intend to deliver defect-free products and services to our customers on time. . . . "[5] Flaws were so common, however, that employees joked about Falcon's " . . . zero-defect program: Don't test the product and you'll find zero defects."[6]

Falcon Computer hired a management consulting firm to help the company define a corporate culture, conducted numerous meetings to discuss the concept, and spent a lot of money developing the values document to guide it. All of this was in vain, though; the company's actual practices belied its false image. According to Reynolds, an important lesson to be learned from Falcon is that, although it might seem desirable for an organization to try to promote a prevailing pervasive corporate culture,

. . . it makes more sense to accept cultural diversity as a fact of life and ask instead how it facilitates or impedes the larger goals of the organization. . . . Corporate culture is not an ideological gimmick to be imposed from above by management or management consulting firms but a stubborn fact of human social organization that can scuttle the best of corporate plans if not taken into account."[7]

1. A lesson from 431 B.C. (13 October 1986), *Fortune,* 161, 164.
2. Hot company, warm culture (27 February 1989), *Fortune,* 74ff.
3. Imposing a corporate culture (March 1987), *Psychology Today,* 33, 34, 36, 38.
4. *Psychology Today,* 34.
5. *Ibid.*
6. *Psychology Today,* 36.
7. *Psychology Today,* 38.

Climate

Much as the physical climate of an area is composed of such factors as temperature, humidity, and precipitation, an **organizational climate** is composed of such factors as structure, processes, and culture (see Figure 2.6). This climate is the prevailing organizational condition and reflects an organization's overall character or tone.[25] Prior to the court-ordered breakup of AT&T, comedienne Lily Tomlin played a telephone operator who answered customers'

FIGURE 2.6 The Internal
Environment and
Organizational Climate

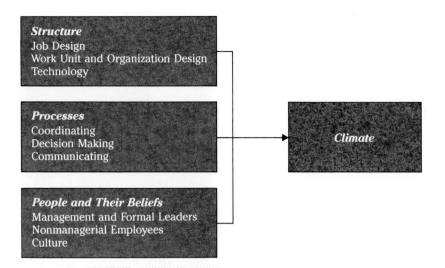

complaints with "We don't care. We don't have to. We're the telephone company"—a succinct characterization of a company's climate, or "personality."

The climate within an organization is a function of both its internal environment and its reactions to the external environment. You have seen that variations in job design, organizational and work unit structures, technologies, managerial processes, and employees create a wide range of environments. The organizational climate affects and is affected by employees' attitudes, motivation, and work-related behaviors. For example, the extent to which employees are willing to perform above and beyond the call of duty is likely to result from the type of climate within their organization.

The challenge for managers is to be aware of the climate that they produce with their managerial style. They cannot forget that an organization is a social system. An organization's level of innovation, the quality of its performance, and the way that its workers react to management are largely the result of its employees' attitudes. These attitudes are influenced to a certain degree by an organization's climate, and the climate is shaped largely by management.

Management and Organizational Functions

To address the components of their organization's internal environment, managers oversee the performance of many different types of activities. To coordinate such activities, managers frequently group them according to the organizational functions they serve, which include operations, marketing, accounting, finance, and human resource management.

Organizational Functions

This section concentrates on the internal environment represented by the organizational functions. As you read, you should realize that each of the three managerial roles (interpersonal, informational, and decisional) is carried out

FIGURE 2.7 *Managerial and Organizational Functions*

Integration of Organizational Functions

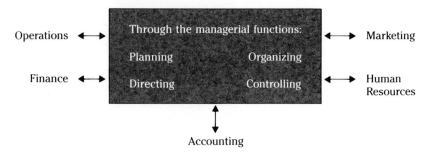

for each organizational function. Planning, organizing, directing, and controlling activities must be performed for each organizational function as well (see Figure 2.7).

Operations Management.   Every organization provides a product or service. **Operations management** applies planning, organizing, directing, and controlling activities to that part of an organization in charge of making the product. (When referring to operations management, the term *product* is used to include both goods and services.) Universities, for example, create and disseminate knowledge, so operations management in this case requires the building and operating of efficient systems—researchers, teachers, classes, classrooms, laboratories, and so forth—to develop and deliver information to student consumers. Oscar Mayer makes and sells meat products, so its operations management oversees systems for the acquisition of animals, slaughtering, packaging, and shipping the foods. Every organization (public or private, for-profit or not-for-profit, manufacturing or service) requires efficient, effective management of this production function. Operations managers try to accomplish this by using systems and activities to control production.

Marketing Management.   If operations managers do their job correctly, their organization can efficiently complete a product for consumers to buy. What makes an organization think that people would want to buy its product in the first place? How will people know about the product, and where will they go to find it? Marketing is the activity that identifies consumers' wants and needs so that an organization can develop appropriate products and services. Marketing also focuses on product distribution, promotion, and pricing.[26] **Marketing management,** therefore, applies the management process to satisfy customers' needs and wants through goods and services.

To achieve these goals, marketing managers gather and use the best information available to deploy their organization's physical, financial, and human resources in the most effective and efficient manner (see Figure 2.8).[27] They then develop plans in such areas as personal selling, advertising, pricing, sales, and distribution. When market researchers of Procter & Gamble, for example, found that two-income families with infants would be willing to pay for diapers that were thinner and kept babies drier longer, research and development staffs were instructed to come up with new absorbent materials and elastic designs. Finance departments directed money toward such development. Marketing managers targeted Wichita, Kansas, for a trial of the new product in October 1984 and bombarded consumers with commercials, advertisements, and discount coupons announcing its arrival. After a successful trial

FIGURE 2.8 The System of Marketing Management

Market knowledge and objectives balanced with corporate objectives help define an organization's marketing strategy.

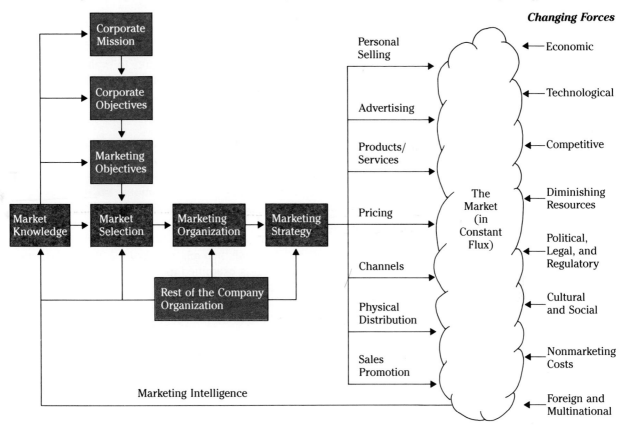

Source: R. W. Haas and T. R. Wotruba (1983), *Marketing management: Concepts, practice and cases,* Plano, TX: Business Publications, 6.

run, managers distributed the diapers nationwide in February of 1986. The results were immediately impressive.

Accounting Management. Accounting is the process of recording, classifying, summarizing, and reporting the financial transactions between an organization and its customers, creditors, suppliers, partners in joint ventures, employees, and government agencies. Nonmanagerial personnel, known as *accountants,* perform the accounting activity for organizations. **Accounting management** plans, organizes, directs, and controls the successful execution of these activities. In addition, it is the responsibility of accounting managers to organize financial information for use in other phases of organizational planning and control (for example, production planning and control, human resource planning and control).

Financial Management. **Financial management** is a staff function that applies the management process to an organization's financial assets. Although the importance of financial management activities varies from organization to organization, there are four primary financial functions:

1. *Planning*—preparing operating budgets and a master financial plan

2. *Acquiring* money—from sales, accounts receivable, notes, borrowing, long-term assets, stocks and bonds, and so on—and monitoring and planning for its use

3. *Distributing* money—regulating its flow to various stakeholders

4. *Evaluating*—assessing the use of an organization's assets

Financial managers use many quantitative measures to evaluate an organization's financial status across time. They interpret this financial information for the total management group so that it can be used for organizational planning and control.

Human Resource Management. **Human resource management** is the managerial function that tries to match an organization's needs and the skills and abilities of its employees. It attempts to motivate employees by offering rewards that meet their needs, wants, and expectations.[28] Human resource managers engage in such activities as staffing, training and development, compensation, and labor relations. If done well, the results are employees who are attracted to and stay with an organization, who attend work and perform acceptably, and who are satisfied with their job (see Figure 2.9). This extremely important organizational function is examined more fully in Chapter 22.

As social systems, organizations achieve their objectives through the people working in them. Organizational success, therefore, depends to a large extent on how well these human resources are managed.

Integration of Organizational Functions

For an organization to be effective, information from each of its subsystems must flow freely from one to another. Otherwise, the organization cannot operate as a unified whole and respond to changes from within and outside of its boundaries. The organization's production function, for example, cannot successfully be managed or make viable organizational contributions unless its managers receive information from marketing about the demand for the product and support from finance to make the product.

The internal environment, then, presents two challenges to managers. The first challenge is to manage each organizational function effectively. The second is to integrate these functions so they promote an organization's strategic position in its external environment.

FIGURE 2.9   *The Human Resource Management System*

Source: Modified from H. G. Heneman III, D. P. Schwab, J. A. Fossum, and L. D. Dyer (1983), *Personnel/human resource management,* Homewood, IL: Irwin, 8.

Management and the Organizational Environment in Review

Managers must contend with environments both within and outside of their organization. In the ordinary course of events, an organization interacts with its external environment in a dynamic relationship. Managers try to control forces within the external environment and, concurrently, the external environment exerts pressures on the organization. This external environment is large and complex, and it contains both general and task components. The general components include the culture in which the organization operates, the economic climate, the technological domain, the legal/political atmosphere, and the international domain. The task component includes an organization's suppliers, customers, competitors, a number of regulatory and influence groups, and allies.

Through interaction with the external environment, managers face varying degrees of uncertainty and change, as well as dependency on members of the task environment. Appropriate boundary-spanning activities help organization members exchange the information and knowledge necessary to deal effectively with the external environment.

Research has shown that management systems are and should be influenced by the external environment. Organic systems are better fitted to dynamic environments with high levels of uncertainty. Mechanistic systems, on the other hand, fit better when the external environment is quite stable. Classical management theorists suggested closed systems, to isolate organizations from their environments. Contemporary environments require open systems if an organization is to survive. The most effective organizations are sensitive and responsive to their external environment.

The internal environment consists of a number of different factors, including environmental structure, organizational processes, people and their beliefs, and organizational climate. These environmental factors affect the decisions made and actions taken by management groups and must be managed to achieve organizational efficiency and effectiveness. Managers attempt to do this by grouping organizational activities according to the function they serve: operations, marketing, accounting, finance, and human resource management. Each of these functions must be managed effectively, as must their interrelationships.

In sum, managers do not operate in isolation. They practice inside organizations, and organizations conduct business under pressure from both the external and internal environments.

Issues for Review and Discussion

1. Identify and briefly discuss each component of the general external environment.
2. What is an organization's task environment? Name the five components of the task environment.
3. What is the relationship between the general and task environments? What is their relationship with an organization?

4. Who acts as an organizational boundary spanner? Explain why it is important for organizations to have boundary spanners.

5. What is the difference between organic and mechanistic management systems? between open and closed management systems?

6. Identify and briefly discuss each component of the internal environment.

7. Name the three major sources of environmental structure and discuss the role played by each.

8. Discuss the concept of organizational culture and its importance to management.

9. Identify and briefly discuss the major organizational functions that take place in the internal environment.

Key Terms

external environment
general environment
task environment
boundary-spanning process
boundary roles
boundary spanners
environmental change
environmental segmentation
homogeneous task environment
heterogeneous task environment
organic system
mechanistic system
closed system
open system
internal environment
job design

work unit design
organizational design
technology
coordinating process
personal mode
impersonal mode
decision making
communicating
organizational culture
organizational climate
operations management
marketing management
accounting management
financial management
human resource management

Suggested Readings

Burns, T., and Stalker, G. M. (1961). Mechanistic and organic systems. In Burns, T., and Stalker, G. M. *The management of innovation.* London: Tavistock, 119-25.

Changing a corporate culture (14 May 1984). *Business Week,* 130-33, 137-38.

Deal, T. E., and Kennedy, A. A. (1982). *Corporate cultures: The rites and rituals of corporate life.* Reading, MA: Addison-Wesley; for a review of this book, see Marx, R. (1988). In Pierce, J. L., and Newstrom, J. W., eds. *The manager's bookshelf: A mosaic of contemporary views.* New York: Harper & Row, 46-56.

Hamel, G., Doz, Y. C., and Prahalad, C. K. (January-February 1989). Collaborate with your competitors and win. *Harvard Business Review,* 133-39.

Katz, D. R. (1987). *The big store.* New York: Viking Penguin.

Kilman, R. H., Saxton, M. J., and Serpa, R., and Associates (1986). *Gaining control of the corporate culture.* San Francisco: Jossey-Bass.

Naisbitt, J. (1982). *Megatrends: Ten new directions transforming our lives.* New York: Warner Books; for a review of this book, see Chamberlain, P. C. (1988). In Pierce, J. L., and Newstrom, J. W., eds. *The manager's bookshelf: A mosaic of contemporary views.* New York: Harper & Row, 207-11.

Peters, T., and Austin, N. (1985). *A passion for excellence: The leadership difference.* New York: Random House.

Schein, E. H. (1984). Coming to a new awareness of organizational culture. *Sloan Management Review,* 25, 3-16.

Sherwood, J. J. (1988). Creating work cultures with competitive advantage. *Organizational Dynamics,* 16, 4-27.

Wilson, I. H. (Winter 1978). Business management and the winds of change. *Journal of Contemporary Business,* 45-54.

Zald, M. N. (1981). Political economy: A framework for comparative analysis. In Zey-Farrell, M., and Aiken, M., eds. *Complex organizations: Critical perspectives.* Glenview, IL: Scott, Foresman.

Zuboff, S. (1988). *In the age of the smart machine: The future of work and power.* New York: Basic Books.

Notes

1. J. Child (1981), Culture, contingency and capitalism in the cross-national study of organizations, in L. L. Cummings and B. M. Staw, eds., *Research in organizational behavior,* Greenwich, CT: JAI Press, 303-56; M. Crozier (1973), Cultural determinants of organizational behavior, in A. R. Negandhi, ed., *Modern organizational theory,* Kent, OH: Kent State University Press, 219-28.

2. W. R. Dill (1958), Environment as an influence on managerial autonomy, *Administrative Science Quarterly,* 2, 409-43; J. D. Thompson (1967), *Organizations in action,* New York: McGraw-Hill.

3. P. E. Connor (1980), *Organizations: Theory and design,* Chicago: Science Research Associates.

4. M. Yasai-Ardekani (1989), Effects of environmental scarcity and munificence on the relationship of context to organizational structure, *Academy of Management Journal,* 32, 131-56; R. D. Luke, J. W. Begun, and D. D. Pointer (1989), Quasifirms: Strategic interorganizational forms in the health care industry, *Academy of Management Review,* 14, 9-19.

5. H. Mintzberg (1973), *The nature of managerial work,* Englewood Cliffs, NJ: Prentice-Hall.

6. Thompson.

7. T. Burns and G. M. Stalker (1961), *The management of innovation,* London: Tavistock.

8. P. R. Lawrence and J. W. Lorsch (1969), *Organization and environment,* Homewood, IL: Richard D. Irwin.

9. S. Kerr, K. D. Hill, and L. Broedling (1986), The first-line supervisor: Phasing out or here to stay? *Academy of Management Review,* 11, 103-17.

10. J. L. Pierce, R. B. Dunham, and L. L. Cummings (1984), Sources of environmental structuring and participant responses, *Organizational Behavior and Human Performance,* 33, 214-42.

11. P. G. Gyllenhammar (1977), *People at work,* Reading, MA: Addison-Wesley.

12. J. R. Hackman and G. R. Oldham (1980), *Work redesign,* Reading, MA: Addison-Wesley; R. W. Griffin (1982), *Task design: An integrative approach,* Glenview, IL: Scott, Foresman.

13. R. H. Hall (1987), *Organizations: Structure, processes, and outcomes,* Englewood Cliffs, NJ: Prentice-Hall, 56.

14. K. G. Provan (1989), Environment, department power, and strategic decision making in organizations: A proposed integration, *Journal of Management,* 15, 21-34.

15. A new era for management (25 April 1983), *Business Week,* 50-53.

16. J. L. Pierce and R. B. Dunham (1987), Organizational commitment: Pre-employment propensity and initial work experiences, *Journal of Management,* 13, 163-78; Pierce, Dunham, and Cummings, 214-42; J. Hage (1965), An axiomatic theory of organizations, *Administrative Science Quarterly,* 10, 289-320.

17. From an Executive Summary (p. 9) of E. F. Jackofsky, J. W. Slocum, and S. J. McQuaid (1988), Cultural values and the CEO: Alluring companions? *Academy of Management Executive,* 2, 1, 39-49.

18. The best of times at the New York Times (28 April 1986), *Business Week,* 46-48.

19. D. C. Hambrick and P. A. Mason (1984), Upper echelons: The organization as a reflection of its top managers, *Academy of Management Review,* 9, 193-206; R. J. House (1977), A 1976 theory of charismatic leadership, In J. G. Hunt and L. L. Larson, eds., *Leadership: The cutting edge,* Carbondale, IL: Southern Illinois University Press, 189-207.

20. Hambrick and Mason, 198-99.

21. P. Selznick (1957), *Leadership in administration,* Evanston, IL: Row, Peterson.

22. E. H. Schein (1985), *Organizational culture and leadership,* San Francisco: Jossey-Bass, 9.

23. D. R. Denison (1984), Bringing corporate culture to the bottom line, *Organizational Dynamics,* 13, 5-22; H. Schwartz and S. M. Davis (1981), Matching corporate culture and business strategy, *Organizational Dynamics,* 10, 30-48.

24. Ross Perot's crusade (6 October 1986), *Business Week,* 61.

25. W. H. Glick (1985), Conceptualizing and measuring organizational and psychological climate: Pitfalls in multilevel research, *Academy of Management Review,* 10, 601-16.

26. R. W. Haas and T. R. Wotruba (1983), *Marketing management: Concepts, practice and cases,* Plano, TX: Business Publications, 4-5.

27. Haas and Wotruba, 11.

28. H. G. Heneman III, D. P. Schwab, J. A. Fossum, and L. D. Dyer (1989), *Personnel/human resource management,* 4th ed., Homewood, IL: Irwin.

Environcare

By James Clinton, University of Northern Colorado

Environcare was incorporated in the state of Colorado in 1984 to provide pest-control services to homeowners and businesses with trees and ornamental shrubs. Located in Greeley, Colorado, the company was established by the owners of an indoor pest-control company who decided that tree and ornamental spraying would be a valuable complement to their existing line of business. Accordingly, they engaged Don Smith, who had been the general manager of Welco Spray, Inc. in Greeley, and established Environcare as a separate company.

The Lawn-Care Industry

In 1984 about 14,000 companies were in the lawn-care business, and total industry sales were expected to be about $2.75 million. Most lawn-care companies were local and privately owned, with annual revenues of less than $200,000. The giant of the industry was Chem-Lawn. Headquartered in Columbus, Ohio, it had 167 branches throughout the United States and served 1.3 million homes in 1983, with sales of $200 million. Other large companies included Lawn Doctor, Ever-Green Lawns, Orkin Lawn Care, and Nitro Green Inc. These companies either operated their own branches or had franchise units. Still, only 39 of the chemical lawn-care companies had revenues in excess of $1 million in 1983.

It was established that only 16 percent of the potential market of 50 million single-family residences used professional lawn-care service. The market had grown at a rate of 30 to 33 percent since 1975 and was forecasted to continue at the same rate of growth through the 1980s.

Other related firms in the lawn-care industry were landscaping companies and tree pruning and removal companies. Landscaping firms design lawns and gardens and provide sod, shrubs, trees, fences, and whatever is necessary to complete a landscape. They use creative talents to tailor landscapes to each customer's preferences and are almost exclusively local businesses. Tree companies prune, cut down, and remove trees either to improve the aesthetic appearance of a residence or to eliminate a blighted or diseased condition. They use expensive equipment, such as shredders and cherry-picker extension vehicles.

The growth of the industry was thought to be due to a combination of factors.

1. The public was becoming concerned about the possibly harmful health effects of handling chemicals. Homeowners, therefore, were more willing to allow commercial lawn-care companies to apply chemicals rather than doing it themselves.
2. Homeowners were placing a greater value on their leisure time and preferred to engage in activities other than yard work.
3. More families had two incomes and could afford lawn-care. In addition, because the professional lawn-care services bought fertilizer and chemicals in bulk, they could treat a lawn more cheaply than a homeowner could.
4. The professional lawn-care companies used specialized equipment that ensured the uniform application of chemicals. This produced more visually pleasing lawns than the homeowners achieved with home lawn spreaders.

Government Regulation

In accordance with the laws of the state of Colorado, pest-control employees had to be both bonded and licensed. Licensing was not required for the application of fertilizer but was required for the application of pesticides, which were usually toxic. A licensed individual was expected to know which chemical was appropriate to apply in various topographies, which problems were encountered in high winds, and how both liquids and powders could be combined to produce both a curative and a preventative effect. The bonding requirement ensured that a company could absorb the costs of accidents or damage to others due to chemical treatments.

If a chemical to be applied was highly toxic, employees had to be certified by the federal Environmental Protection Agency (EPA). Approximately fifteen categories of chemicals used in tree and ornamental shrubbery spray were categorized as dangerous.

Technology

The equipment used for lawn and tree spraying underwent many evolutionary changes from 1950 to 1980. Improvements increased the efficiency of pumps and produced smaller, more mobile pumps that permitted easier access to customers' lawns. Application times were reduced as a result. In fact, applications were accomplished so quickly that customers sometimes felt they were not getting their money's worth.

Developments in biological insect control raised the possibility that it might someday replace many pesticides. Parasitic wasps could be used to eat fly larvae, predatory snails could be used to control slugs, ladybugs could control aphids, and so on. In 1984, few companies had the expertise to conduct such operations, but biological control was growing in use, and "bug farms" or insectaries had begun commercial operations. The most well known of these was Rinocon-Vitova, which had three plants in California.

The Greeley Market

According to the U.S. Bureau of the Census, in 1980 there were 20,700 housing units in Greeley. In 1984, there were an estimated 21,300 units; slightly more than half of these were privately owned, single-family homes. The median value of single-family homes was $61,500. Greeley's physical area covered about 21 square miles, and its population was estimated to be 56,000. The median family income in 1980 had been $19,200. Families above the median income appeared to be twice as likely to use spray treatments as lower-income families.

In 1984, Don Smith estimated that about one third of Greeley's residents were having their lawns chemically treated by commercial firms. For $125, a homeowner could receive treatments to fertilize the lawns, kill weeds, and destroy harmful insects. He estimated that only about 2000 residents used spray services for trees and ornamental shrubs. Typically, this would involve two treatments per

year at $35 per application. Smith further estimated that tree-spraying services to local government facilities, schools, business properties, and apartments or condominiums in Greeley amounted to $40,000.

Greeley is located along Colorado's northern Front Range. This is an area approximately twenty miles wide and about seventy-five miles long, which includes the cities of Fort Collins, Longmont, Loveland, Boulder, and Denver. Fort Collins, Longmont, and Loveland are all within thirty-five miles of Greeley. Boulder and Denver are slightly more than fifty miles away. Don Smith estimates that the Fort Collins market potential is about the same as Greeley's, that Longmont and Loveland together have about half the market potential of Greeley, and that Boulder's potential is about five times that of Greeley's.

Don Smith's former employer, Welco Spray, Inc., and Greeley Spray Service had divided most of the Greeley market for chemical lawn treatments and tree shrub spray service evenly for several years. In 1983, two franchise operations, Ever-Green Lawns and Nitro-Green, entered the chemical lawn-treatment business in Greeley. In addition, there were about fifteen smaller companies that provided spray service or lawn care in Greeley.

Don Smith planned to rely primarily on radio advertising on two Greeley radio stations to obtain public recognition. He believed that his prospective customers would listen to the radio for community programs and announcements. Ads would be broadcast just prior to the spraying seasons. He also planned to advertise in three newspapers, with readers in Boulder, Loveland, and Fort Collins. The firm planned to have an exhibit booth at local home and garden shows held each spring in Greeley, Boulder, and Fort Collins.

Don Smith planned to use telephone canvassing to reach commercial customers. Finally, he

decided to send out direct mailings to the customers of the parent company and selected residential and commercial customers in Greeley and Boulder.

Don Smith had a long-term goal of $500,000 in sales. While he was devoting all of his time to the start-up of Environcare's tree- and shrub-spraying business, he recognized that there were many avenues for expansion. Geographical expansion and chemical lawn service were obvious directions. Although ruling out the landscaping business, he was very interested in the possibilities of biological pest control, but for the time being he said, "Before we can even consider expanding our line of services, we have to learn how to walk before we can run."

Questions

1. What key components of Don Smith's general environment are described in this case?
2. What are the key components of his task environment?
3. What problems and opportunities are represented by each?
4. What type of internal environment would be most appropriate, given Environcare's external environment?

3

Social Responsibility and Managerial Ethics

Student Learning Objectives

After reading this chapter, you should be able to:

1. Define social responsibility and trace its historical development, including the two principles on which contemporary attitudes toward corporate social responsibility are based.

2. Name and discuss three levels of commitment to social responsibility.

3. Compare and contrast two divergent views on corporate social responsibility.

4. Discuss the relationship between social responsibility and the law.

5. Define ethics and distinguish them from social responsibility.

6. Understand individuals' and organizations' responsibility for ethical behavior and list some sources of unethical behavior.

7. Identify utilitarian and formalistic ethics and discuss how they affect decision making.

8. Discuss steps managers can take to encourage ethical behavior in organizations.

A manager's primary responsibility is to achieve organizational effectiveness. Most of this book, in fact, is devoted to describing how managers can meet this responsibility. Managers have an equally pressing duty to behave ethically, however, and to honor social values when pursuing effectiveness goals.

Some managers and their organizations do a good job of meeting both responsibilities. Control Data Corporation, for example, has built plants in Minneapolis, St. Paul, and Washington, DC, to provide jobs and develop an economic base for inner-city residents of poor urban areas. Other organizations and their members do not do as well. Financial wizard Ivan Boesky was sentenced to prison and paid the U.S. government $100 million because he profited unfairly from information that others did not have. Metropolitan Edison, the operator of Pennsylvania's Three Mile Island nuclear plant, withheld information and lied to the public immediately following the nuclear disaster at that plant.[1] Exxon was slow to respond to its 1989 Alaskan oil spill.

These examples show something about the ethics and socially responsible—or irresponsible—behavior of managers and organizations. This chapter looks at the external and internal environments discussed in Chapter 2 from the perspective of how managers respond to matters posed by these environments. A manager today must ask, "What is socially responsible behavior?" "What is ethical behavior?" and "What is management's responsibility in dealing with each of these issues?"

The Nature of Social Responsibility

Many members of society argue strongly that managers must consider the impact of their decisions and actions on society as a whole and must assume responsibility for their activities. They assert that managers should take steps to protect and improve the welfare of society.[2]

All managers must obey the law, but social responsibility goes beyond the requirements of law. **Social responsibility** is an organization's obligation to engage in activities that protect and contribute to the welfare of society.[3] An organization's social responsibilities are shaped by its culture and the historical period in which the organization operates.[4] Just as a society's values, norms, and mores change over time, so does the definition of socially responsible behavior.

A Historical Perspective

At the start of the twentieth century, there were few corporate acts of charity. Instead, wealthy businesspeople gave as individuals from their personal wealth to charitable causes. This *principle of charity,* which suggests that those who have plenty should give to those who do not, increasingly influenced individuals in the business community to use some of their corporate power and wealth for the social good. For example, steel magnate Andrew Carnegie put much of his great wealth to work for education. Over time, other business leaders adopted and spread the idea that business has a responsibility to society beyond simply providing necessary goods and services.[5]

The *principle of stewardship* also shaped contemporary views on social responsibility. This principle asserts that organizations have an obligation to the public. Because corporations control vast resources, they are obliged to serve society's needs. In this way, managers and the corporations become the stewards, or trustees, for society.[6]

Attitudes toward social responsibility have changed throughout business history. These changes can be grouped into three phases: profit-maximizing, trusteeship, and quality-of-life (see Figure 3.1).

Phase One: Profit-Maximizing Management. During the period of economic scarcity in the nineteenth and early twentieth century, most American business managers felt they had one primary responsibility to society: to underwrite the country's economic growth and oversee the accumulation of wealth. Business managers could pursue, almost single-mindedly, the objective of maximizing profits. Essentially, managers felt that what was good for business was good for the country.

Phase Two: Trusteeship Management. After the Great Depression, the number of privately held American corporations declined. So, too, did the strong and probusiness ethos. Organizations found themselves having to respond to the demands of both internal and external groups, such as stockholders, customers, suppliers, and creditors. With this new emphasis on social responsibility, trusteeship management emerged. The job of corporate managers was to maintain an equitable balance among the competing interests of all groups with a stake in the organization. Pressure from these groups led to the use of some of the corporate economic wealth to meet social needs.

Phase Three: Quality-of-Life Management. In the 1960s, a new set of national priorities began to develop, and the pressure on managers to behave in socially responsible ways intensified. Such issues as poverty, pollution, and deteriorating inner cities raised widespread concern about the quality of life in the United States. The consensus was that managers had to do more than achieve narrow economic goals. They should manage the quality of life by helping develop solutions for society's ills. The principles of charity and stewardship were firmly in place.

FIGURE 3.1 A Historical Perspective on Social Responsibility

Proportion of Firms Adopting Each Perspective

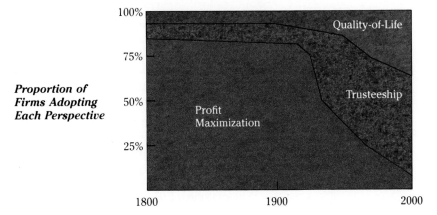

FIGURE 3.2 *Organizational Stakeholders*

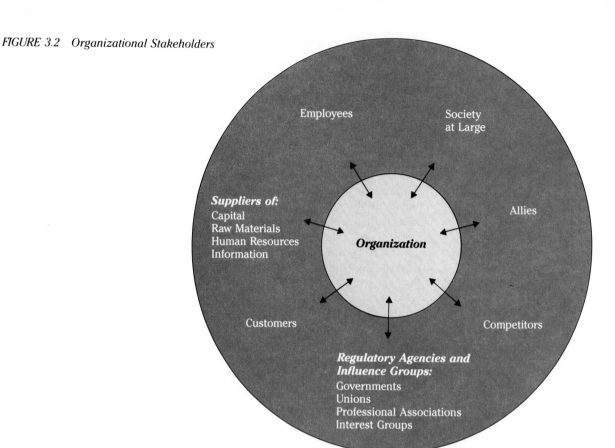

Social Responsibility and Organizational Stakeholders

The internal and external groups that emerged during the trusteeship management period have grown in strength and size. Today, every manager must be aware of the needs of stockholders, customers, suppliers, creditors, and all the men and women—managers and nonmanagers—who work full- or part-time for an organization. Figure 3.2 shows the variety of individuals and groups who are organizational stakeholders.

The large number of stakeholder groups complicates management's social responsibility. An organization should be responsive to everyone, but there are many groups, each with its own needs, and these needs may conflict. How, for example, can an organization meet its investors' interests *and* community needs for money to build a new library?

One way in which organizations can identify and communicate issues of public interest to both internal and external stakeholders is through a social audit. A **social audit** is a detailed examination and evaluation of an organization's social performance.[7] Figure 3.3 illustrates the audit process followed by some organizations. A thorough social audit involves sophisticated strategic planning and evaluation. In the United States, social audits are voluntary, and few organizations go to such lengths. Many aspects of the process are pursued more aggressively by organizations in other countries, including Germany, France, and Norway, where social audits are mandated by law.

The majority of the top 500 corporations in the United States include infor-

FIGURE 3.3   The Social Audit

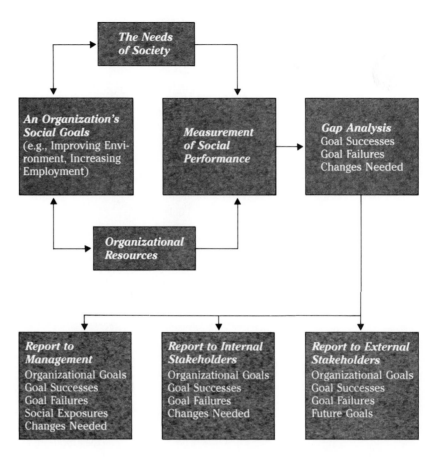

mation about their social performance in their annual reports. Some also prepare a special report that details their activities that are of interest to the general public. General Motors, for example, regularly prepares a public interest report that outlines the areas included in its social audit. Inspection of its table of contents (see Table 3.1 on page 54) shows GM's involvement in such issues as automotive safety, the depletion of ozone, alternative fuels, and programs for minorities and women.[8]

Levels and Types of Social Commitment

What makes managers in some organizations respond so vigorously to social issues, while others seem to do only what they are forced to do by law? The intensity with which managers involve their organization in social issues varies according to the principles that motivate them (see Table 3.2 on page 54).[9] At the lowest level of social commitment are the organizations whose managers adhere to the principle of *social obligation.* These managers confine their responses to social issues within the guidelines mandated by prevailing laws and the operation of the economic system. Social contributions are viewed as the responsibility of individuals, not of the organization. A manager adhering to this principle, for example, might obey the letter of environmental protection laws yet allow pollution when no legal punishment is likely.

At a middle level of commitment are organizations whose managers go beyond fulfilling mere social obligations. These managers adhere to the princi-

TABLE 3.1 Table of Contents: GM Public Interest Report

Contents	
An Overview	Page

Source: *1988 General Motors public interest report* (16 May 1988).

TABLE 3.2 Levels of Social Commitment

Social Obligation (Lowest Level)	Social Responsibility (Middle Level)	Social Responsiveness (Highest Level)
Reactive	Prescriptive	Proactive
Proscriptive	Does more than required by law	Anticipates and prevents problems
Adheres to legal requirements	Does more than required by economic considerations	Searches for socially responsible acts
Adheres to economic considerations	Avoids public stands on issues	Takes public stands on issues

ple of *social responsibility* and try to make their actions keep pace with—rather than lag behind—social norms, values, and expectations of performance.[10] Frequently seen as "good corporate citizens," socially responsible organizations are willing to assume a broader responsibility than that prescribed only by law and economic requirements. Managers adhering to this principle, for example, are likely to try to reduce pollution if they consider certain levels to be dangerous, even if the levels are legally acceptable.

At the highest level of social commitment are organizations whose managers are *socially responsive*. Managers in socially responsive organizations communicate and interact with external groups to anticipate social issues and to prevent problems, as well as to correct problems after the fact. When managers at IBM planned massive automation at the Lexington typewriter plant, they evaluated the possible effects on the local labor market and the economy. Demonstrating socially responsive behavior, IBM managers then implemented corrective action *before* the problems could occur.

How do organizations in the United States perform when they are rated according to these three principles? Although many organizations still are driven by the principle of social obligation, an increasing number demonstrate

TABLE 3.3   *Degree to Which U.S. Business Community Supports Socially Responsible Activities Over Time:*
CEOs and Business School Deans

Corporate Support For:	Was Five Years Ago		Is Now		Will Be in Five Years	
	CEO	Dean	CEO	Dean	CEO	Dean
Higher education	49.1%	20.5%	65.6%	29.9%	72.2%	50.8%
Ethical practice codes	48.7	12.8	70.8	35.0	74.8	47.4
Minority hiring and training	34.5	21.6	52.6	33.3	63.2	27.8
Charitable and philanthropic	28.4	23.7	56.0	27.1	71.1	33.7
Pollution control	24.6	6.0	31.6	14.4	39.3	18.8
Quality of work life program	22.6	11.2	47.8	28.4	75.7	61.6
Building and ground beautification	22.3	13.7	33.0	18.5	36.7	25.6
Environmental protection laws	20.2	3.5	26.1	8.1	31.5	18.2
Community renewal and revitalization	18.9	9.3	30.4	16.1	43.1	22.0
Arts and cultural	17.2	20.9	32.8	28.9	51.3	36.9
Handicap hiring and training	13.9	4.6	28.1	14.2	42.3	16.1
Minority business	11.7	7.2	17.0	8.6	22.9	8.9
Political action committee	11.3	18.4	40.0	41.8	60.7	54.6
Consumer protection laws	10.4	6.5	15.7	9.5	20.5	13.0
Executive loan to governments	9.3	10.0	14.8	11.6	22.9	19.1

All numbers represent the percentage of respondents indicating considerable or extensive support for an activity.

Source: R. Ford and F. McLaughlin (1984), Perceptions of socially responsible activities and attitudes: A comparison of business school deans and corporate chief executives, *Academy of Management Journal,* 27, 672.

a growing social consciousness. Others are adopting attitudes of social responsibility and social responsiveness.[11] Table 3.3, for example, shows how the relative importance of fifteen specific social issues have changed over time.

Diverging Views on Social Responsibility

Not everyone agrees that contemporary organizations should be driven by the principles of charity and stewardship. Proponents of corporate social responsibility have suggested that firms that take a major role in tackling social issues are good investment risks and will eventually be more profitable than less socially responsive firms. Current research, however, does not show a simple relationship between social responsibility and profitability.[12] As a consequence, the profitability claim cannot legitimately be used to argue either for or against corporate social responsibility, but other arguments can be made on both sides.

Arguments for and Against Social Responsibility

Those who argue in favor of organizations' acting in socially responsible ways have offered several reasons, among them:

- The assumption of social responsibility balances corporate power with corporate responsibilities.

The Exxon Corporation's social responsibility came into question in March 1989, when its tanker Exxon Valdez crashed and spilled over 10 million gallons of oil into Prince William Sound. Exxon was criticized for the tanker pilot's negligence, for a lack of preparation for such a disaster, and for belated cleanup efforts.

- Social initiatives taken by organizations tend to promote goodwill, public favor, and corporate trust, and these may contribute to the long-run success of the organizations.
- Organizations' acts of social responsibility help correct the social problems (such as air and water pollution) the organizations create.[13]

Sociologists have suggested that, because society has many needs, an organization can be categorized according to: (1) the needs it fulfills and (2) the benefits that society derives from the organization's existence.[14] Critics of corporate social responsibility have, in essence, used the sociologists' analysis to propose that organizations specialize. According to this way of thinking, a corporation is a particular type of organization that exists to provide goods and services and to earn profits. Curing society's social ills is the responsibility of other organizations, including governmental and charitable organizations. Among some of the major arguments against corporate social responsibility are the following:

- The costs of socially responsible behavior lower a corporation's operating efficiency and, therefore, weaken its ability to offer goods and services at the lowest possible competitive cost.
- The costs of socially responsible behavior are often passed along in the form of lower dividends to stockholders, lower wages for employees, or higher prices for consumers.
- Individuals in the business community are trained in such areas as marketing, finance, and manufacturing, not in dealing with social problems.[15]

These and other arguments for and against corporate social responsibility have resulted in the emergence of two distinct sides to the social responsibility debate.

Side One: An Argument Against. Economist Milton Friedman of the University of Chicago has argued that managers should not be required to earn profits for business owners while simultaneously trying to enhance societal welfare.[16] According to Friedman, these two goals are basically incompatible and will lead to the demise of business as we now know it. Friedman also has suggested that forcing organizations to engage in socially responsible behavior may actually be unethical, because it requires managers to spend money that really belongs to other individuals, which otherwise would be given back to stakeholders in the form of higher dividends, wages, and the like.

Side Two: An Argument in Favor. Keith Davis, professor emeritus at Arizona State University, provides another perspective.[17] To Davis, organizations are members of society. Because they take resources from society for their own use, they have a responsibility to return to society a value for those resources. Society should be able to determine the nature of the value to be returned and to expect organizations to assist in solving social problems.

Where Corporate America Stands Today

Given the many arguments for and against corporate involvement in addressing society's needs, it seems appropriate to ask, "Where does corporate America stand today?" (see Figure 3.4). In the 1950s and 1960s, people in the United States became increasingly conscious of the wide-scale importance of large organizations to society. During this gestation and innovation phase, managers became aware of the need to be socially responsive. During the development and expansion phase of the 1970s, organizations began formally to act on this awareness. Corporate social reports started to appear, and social audits became more common. Finally, today's maturity and institutionalization phase is one in which "many of the changes that were anticipated in the Sixties and Seventies have in fact taken place . . . . "[18] Using data collected by *Fortune,* a recent study demonstrated that the financial performance of an organization is an important indicator of its subsequent level of corporate

FIGURE 3.4 The Growth of Attention to Social Issues

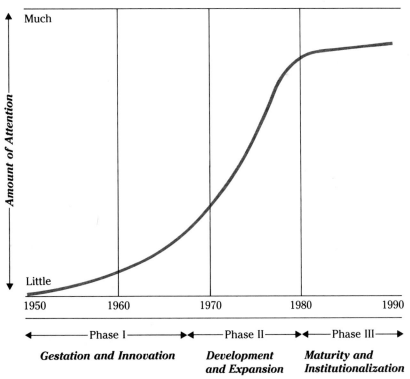

Source: L. E. Preston (1986), Social issues in management: An evolutionary perspective, in D. A. Wren and J. A. Pearce II, eds., *Papers dedicated to the development of modern management,* Chicago: Academy of Management, 52.

TABLE 3.4   *Agreement with Statements for Corporate Acceptance of Social Responsibility*

Statements	Total % of Agree Strongly and Mildly Agree	
	CEOs	Deans
Responsible corporate behavior can be in the best economic interest of the stockholders.	92.2%	90.1%
Efficient production of goods and services is no longer the only thing society expects from business.	88.8	92.1
Long-run success of business depends on its ability to understand that it is part of a larger society and to behave accordingly.	87.0	86.1
Involvement by business in improving its community's quality of life will also improve long run profitability.	78.4	75.7
A business that wishes to capture a favorable public image will have to show that it is socially responsible.	77.6	76.2
Social problems, such as pollution control, sometimes can be solved in ways that produce profits from the problem solution.	71.9	75.6
If business is more socially responsible, it will discourage additional regulation of the economic system by government.	70.7	68.3
If business delays dealing with social problems now, it may find itself increasingly occupied with bigger social issues later such that it will be unable to perform its primary business tasks.	55.2	57.4
The idea of social responsibility is needed to balance corporate power and discourage irresponsible behavior.	36.5	55.0
Other social institutions have failed in solving social problems so business should try.	27.8	32.3
Since businesses have such a substantial amount of society's managerial and financial resources, they should be expected to solve social problems.	16.6	31.8

Source: R. Ford and F. McLaughlin (1984), Perceptions of socially responsible activities and attitudes: A comparison of business school deans and corporate chief executives, *Academy of Management Journal*, 27, 670.

social responsibility. Although there was little evidence that socially responsible behavior can improve performance, good financial performance does appear to be followed by subsequent socially responsible behavior.[19]

A survey of 116 chief executive officers and 203 college business school deans reports that many consider it important for today's corporations to take an active role in solving social problems (see Tables 3.4 and 3.5).[20] The study also shows that both groups believe that business support of corporate involvement in addressing social problems has increased.

Legality and Social Responsibility

Organizations can adopt any of a number of strategies to deal with issues of social responsibility. One way to define these strategies is along the dimensions of legality and responsibility.

TABLE 3.5   Disagreement with Statements Against Corporate Acceptance
of Social Responsibility

Statements	Total % of Mildly Disagree and Disagree Strongly	
	CEOs	Deans
Business already has too much social power and should not engage in social activities that might give it more.	77.0%	73.1%
If business does become socially involved, it will create so much friction among dissident parties that it will be unable to perform its economic mission.	69.3	77.2
A firm that ignores social responsibility can obtain a competitive advantage over a firm that does not.	69.3	44.1
Involvement in socially responsible activities threatens business by diverting time and money away from its primary business purpose.	68.1	60.9
It is unwise to allow business to participate in social activities where there is no direct way to hold it accountable for its actions.	67.6	67.0
Business is most socially responsive when it attends strictly to its economic interests and leaves social activities to social institutions.	64.7	57.4
Business leaders are trained to manage economic institutions and not to work effectively on social issues.	60.5	49.5
Business will become uncompetitive if it commits many economic resources to social responsibility.	49.1	47.3
If social programs add to business costs it will make business uncompetitive in international trade.	44.7	33.8
Business will participate more actively in social responsibility in prosperous economic times than in recession.	24.6	9.0
Consumers and the general public will bear the costs of business social involvement because businesses will pass these costs along through their pricing structure.	15.8	5.0

Source: R. Ford and F. McLaughlin (1984), Perceptions of socially responsible activities and attitudes. A comparison of business school deans and corporate chief executives, *Academy of Management Journal*, 27, 671.

The Four Faces of Social Responsibility

Four approaches to social responsibility have been identified: illegal and irresponsible, illegal and responsible, legal and irresponsible, and legal and responsible.[21]

Illegal and Irresponsible. Some organizations behave illegally and irresponsibly. For example, an investigation was launched in early 1988 to examine claims that some companies were taking advantage of the catastrophic Pennsylvania Ashland Petroleum tank collapse by dumping their own toxic wastes into the already polluted Monongahela River. Dumping this type of material into the river is prohibited by law, and it is clearly irresponsible to contaminate the water. Today, an illegal and irresponsible strategy is highly risky and may be fatal to an organization, because a broad spectrum of society no longer tolerates such behavior.

Social Responsibility: The Wine Industry

Side by side in an issue of *The Wine Spectator* were two stories. The first bore the headline "Cancer Study Recommended" and described a proposed study to investigate whether urethane in wine and other alcoholic beverages causes cancer in humans. The U.S. Food and Drug Administration believes that urethane, a natural by-product of fermentation, exists in "minute amounts in some wines, brandies, beers, distilled spirits and liqueurs."[1] The study would cost more than $1 million and would include laboratory tests to determine whether the small doses of urethane in some wines can lead to cancer.

The second article bore the headline "Mondavi Strikes Back at Critics." It said that Napa Valley vintner Robert Mondavi was embarking on a "personal mission to 'educate ourselves and the world' about wine's beneficial qualities" and to show that wine is a healthy product.[2] Mondavi has undertaken this campaign because he feels the wine industry is not doing enough to counter accusations such as those expressed by health and consumer activists in California. These critics are urging wine pro-

ducers to put warning labels on their bottles stating, for example, the health risks to pregnant women if they drink wine.

To Mondavi, wine is a food and an "essential part of the gracious way of living," a message he believes should be taken to the public.[3] The San Francisco-based Wine Institute, however, does not want to make sweeping claims that wine is healthful, apparently fearing that such claims might legitimize lawsuits from individuals who claim they were misled and subsequently became injured or ill as a result of drinking wine. Given the Wine Institute's unwillingness to combat these claims more aggressively, Mondavi has launched his own educational campaign. He plans to involve "priests, rabbis, philosophers, physicians, artists and poets and others to expound on the contributions wine has made to civilization."[4]

These two stories from *The Wine Spectator* emphasize the type of dilemma organizations often face. It can be argued that, if urethane is present in wine and can cause cancer, a socially responsible organization would want to know this and take

steps to eliminate the hazard. A fiscally responsible organization, however, does not want to decrease its earnings. A vote to support the study is probably a vote to reduce profitability, because consumers are likely to reduce wine consumption if they think there is a chance the claim is true. People tend to believe that "if it is serious enough to study, it must be a problem."

What about Mondavi's plans? Is there anything wrong with educating the public? Although many argue that wine does have beneficial qualities, is it socially responsible behavior to present only positive information about a product without mentioning the hazards? Is it possible to promote wine as a product in a socially responsible manner? The wine industry is not the first business, nor will it be the last, to experience the frustrations of balancing profitability and social responsibility.

1. Cancer study recommended (31 January 1988), *The Wine Spectator*, 8.
2. Mondavi strikes back at critics (31 January 1988), *The Wine Spectator*, 8.
3. *Ibid.*
4. *Ibid.*

Legal and Irresponsible. Some organizations can operate without violating a single law but still not act in a socially responsible manner. For example, beer companies produce commercials that appeal to underage drinkers, and casinos sometimes make special offers that encourage people to trade their Social Security checks for gambling chips. Prior to the explosive tragedy of Pan Am's flight 103 over Lockerbie, Scotland, the airline chose not to notify passengers of a terrorist threat to bomb a New York–bound flight. All such organizations are acting within the limits of the law, but it can be argued that they endanger the well-being of society.

Illegal and Responsible. Some organizations follow strategies that are socially conscious and responsible but that violate the letter of the law. When American Telephone and Telegraph Company was found guilty of discriminating against women, for example, the company undertook an affirmative action program to improve working conditions for women, only to have a group of male workers sue for discrimination.

Legal and Responsible. Finally, some organizations obey the law and, at the same time, engage in socially responsible behavior. For example, the Minneapolis-based Dayton organization gives a percentage of its profits to charity, an act that is both legal and highly socially responsible. Many organizations believe that it is possible to play by the rules, turn a profit, and still be a good corporate citizen.

The Role of a Corporate Board

What role should a board of directors play in seeing that an organization meets its legal and social responsibilities? It has been argued that most corporate boards " . . . include numerous first-rate people doing what amounts to a second-rate job."[22] Some say that the design of a board restricts the independence of its members and basically renders them ineffective in their monitoring role.[23]

Perhaps boards of directors could do a better job of monitoring if people outside organizations were invited to become board members.[24] Outsiders give a board a broader base of power and knowledge and enable it to be more independent and, therefore, better able to monitor objectively management decisions and actions.[25] These are strong arguments, but the existing (although limited) evidence shows no significant relationship between the number of insiders on boards and corporate involvement in illegal acts.[26] In fact, a 1989 study showed that corporate boards are more likely to adopt golden parachutes (sizable payments to top managers if a corporate takeover occurs) when they have more external directors on their boards.[27] Perhaps insiders are simply more effective at concealing illegal activities. At any rate, it appears likely that responsible behavior is encouraged by outside members who feel free to ask hard questions without worrying that it will affect their jobs or working relationships.

In sum, to act in a socially responsible way requires managers to consider the effect of their decisions on the well-being of society; thus, managers must ask themselves what their actions do *to* and *for* society. When similar considerations are made at a personal level, managers must rely on their ethics to help them choose an appropriate course of action.

The Nature of Managerial Ethics

Ethics are the standards and codes of conduct that define what is right, wrong, and just in human actions. Managers' decisions and actions affect the health, safety, morale, and behavior of all organization members. For example, at General Motors, massive plant closings followed large pay increases for high-level executives. In another example, flawed decision making led to the death of the entire crew of the space shuttle *Challenger*.

Unfortunately, ethical issues often do not fall neatly into categories of right and wrong. Attempts to do what is ethical can be complex, revealing that there

Through socialization, new members of a society adopt at least some of the values, norms, and mores of that society and develop a definition of ethical conduct.

are varying degrees of rightness and wrongness. Suppose, for example, that two students each missed passing their management course by only five points. The first student wants the professor to adjust his grade in exchange for sexual favors. The second student wants the professor to adjust the grade because her spouse died during the semester, and she received passing grades on all exams except the one she took the day after the funeral. Most people would agree that the professor who agrees to adjust the first student's grade is acting unethically. The second student's case is not so clear-cut.

Of course, behaving ethically involves more than just helping others and behaving honestly. Ethics arise in all issues associated with human relationships. For managers, ethical issues surface in numerous interactions with an organization's external and internal stakeholders.

Ethical considerations, like considerations of social responsibility, are influenced by existing social values, norms, and mores. The two are also similar in that both revolve around concerns for the well-being of others. Ethical considerations, however, also differ from those of social responsibility. Ethical judgments are based on personal values that have been learned over a number of years. They usually arise in situations that do not influence society as a whole. Frequently, in fact, ethical judgments affect only one person, the people in a manager's organization, or an organization's stakeholders, rather than society as a whole. Ethics usually involve one person's judgment and behavior, whereas social responsibility usually involves those of entire organizations. In short, ethics are primarily a personal issue; social responsibility is an organizational issue.

Sources of Ethics

People in all societies create standards and codes of conduct to govern their dealings with one another, but not all societies have the same definitions of right, wrong, and just. In the United States, for example, kickbacks to purchasing agents are generally considered unethical. In some countries, however, kickbacks are an accepted business custom. Religious, educational, and cultural organizations, as well as the family unit, pass on culture from one generation to the next.[28] Through this socialization process, people develop beliefs about what is right, wrong, and just to arrive at a definition of ethical conduct.

Managerial Ethics

Managerial ethics are not fundamentally different from other ethics. Usually, they are only a matter of applying personal ethics in an organizational context. What are a manager's ethical responsibilities? Managers are responsible for the decisions and actions they take on their own initiative. They also are ethically responsible for actions they take under another's direction. In other words, managers are not relieved of ethical responsibility just because their boss "ordered" them to behave unethically. Managers who must choose whether to behave unethically or to lose their job face a painful decision, but the ethical choice is to lose their job. Similarly, students who must either cheat on an exam or fail a course behave unethically if they cheat, regardless of the consequences.

Managers also are ethically responsible for the behavior of subordinates who follow their instructions. If managers tell subordinates to behave in a

Ethics: How Much Are Those Ethics in the Window?

You have probably figured out by now that money cannot buy love. The question today in business schools around the country seems to be, "Can money buy ethics?" At least one influential businessperson seems to think so. John Shad, the former chair of the Securities and Exchange Commission, recently turned over $20 million of his own funds to Harvard and spearheaded the raising of an additional $10 million from other Harvard alumni. The purpose of the gift, according to Shad, was to teach students that ethics pay.

Shad is very interested in improving the ethical behavior of students who represent future businesspeople. After all, $20 million is greater than the annual operating budget of almost every graduate school of business in the United States. With it and the other $10 million, Harvard intends to develop better business ethics through faculty research, teaching improvement grants, and increased opportunities for students to explore the impact of ethical issues.

Will this be enough? The school requires M.B.A. students to take only a "short course" on ethics—a mere seven classes and ten and one-half hours.[1] Furthermore, the school previously denied tenure to its two M.B.A. ethics teachers. Shad's gift may not achieve its purpose if Harvard merely "goes through the motions."

What are other schools doing that do not have $30 million to spend on teaching ethics? Whatever they want to do, apparently. In a recent survey, 89 percent of all accredited business schools reported that they teach ethics. About one fifth have created separate, free-standing courses. The rest attempt to integrate the teaching of ethics into existing classes. Most that do have separate ethics courses offer them as electives. Unfortunately, elective ethics classes traditionally have not been very popular among students unless they are considered an easy A. It may be that the only students who choose the elective are the students who least need ethical development. Lastly, there is tremen-

dous variation in the intensity and quality of the training. Often, a case approach is used that may make students *aware* of ethical considerations as they discuss and debate the issues posed but may not *change* ethical values, and many schools seem to concentrate on teaching students what is "right." As *Newsweek* concluded, "Even in today's complex world, knowing what's right is comparatively easy. It's doing what's right that's hard."[2]

The question is whether business school courses—elective or mandatory, free-standing or intermixed— can change students' ethics. Unfortunately, there is little conclusive evidence of such an effect, but the search for ways to monitor ethics must continue if tomorrow's businesspeople are to consider ethics as more than just an option.

1. Ethics experience at Harvard Business School (March 1989), *The Academy of Management news*, 19, 3.
2. The business ethics debate (25 May 1987), *Newsweek*, 36.

---

manner that the managers consider unethical, the managers are responsible for the subordinates' unethical behavior. Managers are equally responsible if they instruct subordinates to behave in a manner that the subordinates consider unethical. Managers are even ethically responsible when they fail to act if their inaction allows unethical behavior to occur. They are also responsible if the organizational policies, practices, and structures they create lead to unethical behavior.[29]

An Organization's Responsibility

The foregoing discussion makes it sound as if managers are ethically responsible for everything that happens inside organizations. In fact, some people argue that the "real role of the chief executive is to manage the values of the organization."[30] Top managers, with their key organizational roles and formal authority, can and should infuse a sense of moral reasoning and ethically guided decisions and behavior into their organization's culture. By being good role models, by reinforcing ethical behavior and punishing un-

When the individual at the top of an organization demonstrates that ethical behavior is important, it gets translated into formal programs designed not only to teach ethics but to sensitize employees with respect to values and concerns within the company.

—Von Glinow

"You are either going to be part of the corruption or part of the forces working against it," declared Kathy Laubach, whose husband Vincent blew the whistle on his employer— the U.S. Department of the Interior.

ethical behavior, and by making explicit what ethical conduct is, top managers help ensure that the expectation of ethical behavior, as well as the ethical behavior itself, permeates organizational culture.[31] In fact, research has shown that unethical behavior can be reduced through steps as simple as issuing statements that support ethical behavior.

Top management, of course, is not exclusively responsible for instilling and enacting ethical behavior. Every organization member carries the values, norms, and mores of society into the organization. With this goes responsibility for his or her personal conduct. The responsibility for moral reasoning and ethical conduct, therefore, falls on each member. With this in mind, some organizations encourage their members to report unethical behavior. **Whistleblowing** refers to a member's disclosure that someone within the organization has engaged in an illegal, immoral, unethical, or illegitimate act.[32] Traditionally, whistleblowing has been discouraged both by group norms and by company practice, but more organizations are actively encouraging such action today because it is the ethical thing to do.

To persuade employees to blow the whistle inside an organization (rather than to the press or to regulatory agencies), many organizations have set up internal systems to handle complaints. When surveyed about corporate ethics, in fact, over 70 percent of U.S. corporations responding said they had written codes of conduct, and over 35 percent had formal training programs encouraging ethical behavior.[33] Some companies, such as General Dynamics, have an ombudsperson, whose job includes soliciting whistleblowing and dealing with it in-house.

Ethical and Unethical Managerial Behavior

Managers should behave ethically, but do they? Consider the following:

- A study reported in *Fortune* magazine showed that 117 (11 percent) of 1043 major corporations have been involved in blatant illegalities.[34]
- A *Wall Street Journal* survey reported that four out of ten executives said they were asked to behave in unethical ways on the job.[35]
- Although the vast majority of managers believe that managers should apply ethics to business practices, many report that they simply do not live up to these standards. Nearly two thirds indicate that generally accepted unethical practices were being conducted within their industries, an increase over the degree of unethical practices in the early 1960s.[36]

Such observations of widespread illegality and unethical behavior underscore the importance of keeping a "continual vigilance . . . focusing attention on values and ethical behavior."[37]

Influences on Unethical Behavior

Why do managers choose to behave unethically? Sometimes they simply do not take time to think about the implications of their behavior. Managers are commonly overworked and highly stressed. Under these conditions, people sometimes do things they later regret. It also has been shown that people placed in competitive situations are more likely than others to behave un-

FIGURE 3.5   The Impact of Rewards and Punishment on Unethical Behavior

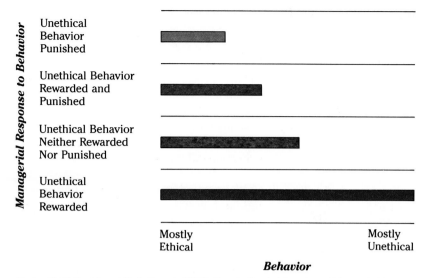

Source: W. H. Hegarty and H. P. Sims, Jr. (1979), Organizational philosophy, policies, and objectives related to unethical decision behavior: A laboratory experiment, *Journal of Applied Psychology*, 64, 331-38.

 ethically. The behavior of one's superiors also strongly influences a manager to make ethical or unethical decisions.

Another reason managers sometimes behave unethically involves their personality characteristics.[38] Persons most likely to behave unethically are those who believe that the ends justify the means, that events are due to luck or chance (not to their actions), and that economic and political values are of great importance.

As shown in Figure 3.5, rewards and punishment are among the most powerful determinants of ethical or unethical behavior. People who receive rewards for unethical behavior (such as receiving a pay increase for providing kickbacks to customers) are much more likely to behave unethically than those who are not rewarded for such behavior. The use of punishment for unethical behavior, however, can lead to higher levels of ethical behavior, even when rewards for unethical behavior are also present. Rewards and punishment probably influence the ethics of behavior because rewards increase the likelihood that such behavior will be repeated, and punishment decreases the likelihood of repetition (more on this idea appears in Chapter 13). Reward and punishment also call attention to potentially unethical behavior.

Ethical Standards and a Manager's Dilemma

No independent set of standards exists for ethical behavior in organizations. Ethics for organizations are based on the ethics of the society within which the organizations exist. The societal standards that guide ethical behavior should be used to guide the decisions and actions of managers who operate within society. When managers confront an ethically difficult decision, they should consider how these standards apply to their situation and should try to incorporate the most relevant ones within their moral reasoning.[39]

There are several standards that managers can use to guide ethical decision making.[40] *Utilitarian theories* concentrate on the social consequences that an anticipated action is likely to produce. Manager Lynn Butler, for example,

FIGURE 3.6 A Janus-Headed
Model of the Ethical Process

*Managerial decision making must
look both forward and backward to
address utilitarian and formalistic
needs.*

Past   Future

*Generally speaking . . .
[ethical codes of conduct] are
not enough and must be
accompanied by an ongoing
process of implementation. A
process of implementation
differs somewhat from a formal
code of ethics in that it tends to
be more specific, concentrating
on two main objectives:
ensuring compliance with
company standards of conduct
and linking a corporate culture
that values ethics with survival
and profitability in a highly
competitive world.*

—Von Glinow

might create a training program for minority employees so that the Equal
Employment Opportunity offices will leave her organization alone. Another
ethical standard deals with *rights*. Decision makers who apply this standard are
concerned with respecting the rights to which people are entitled. For example,
Dave Freer would respect his subordinates' right to free speech and not ask
them to refrain from speaking out at a prolife rally. A third ethical standard is
based on the *theory of justice*, which emphasizes fair and impartial acts.
Manager Ben Jordan, for example, might create an affirmative action program,
not because he is required to, but because it is a fair response to past
discrimination.

It sounds reasonable that managers should consider the social consequences, the rights of others, and other ethical standards when making decisions; however, doing so does not prevent managers from encountering ethical
dilemmas from time to time. Consider, for example, the dilemma posed by new
scientific developments. In one such case, the Environmental Protection
Agency permitted BioTechnica International, Inc., to test genetically altered
organisms on a Wisconsin farm.[41] The dilemma is whether the potential
benefit to the human race is greater than the cost and risks associated with
releasing genetically altered organisms into the environment.

Many managers' ethical dilemmas arise when balancing utilitarian and
formalistic needs (see Figure 3.6). Managerial decision making in the utilitarian ethic is future oriented. It seeks innovations, improves techniques, and
promotes change as ways to meet organizational goals and the evolving needs
of the external environment. Decision making in the formalistic ethic is concerned with preserving current definitions of right and just, maintaining tradition, and perpetuating organizational and societal heritage. In the BioTechnica
case mentioned earlier, a utilitarian ethic would favor the new technology and
release of the organisms. A formalistic ethic, however, would favor minimizing
potential risks to people and the environment. Managers must continually
reconcile new practices with accumulated wisdom that has shaped current
behavior and thought.[42]

Encouraging Ethical Behavior

How can organizations guide managers as they cope with ethical decisions
and the dilemmas they may pose? Organizations can encourage ethical behavior by considering both long- and short-term factors.[43] For the long term,
managers should develop their organization's culture so that it supports the
learning—and, if necessary, the relearning—of personal values that promote
ethical behavior. For example, when decisions are made, managers should
explicitly and publicly explain the ethical factors that accompany each alternative. Managers also should nurture an organizational culture that supports
and values ethical behavior—for example, by encouraging organization members to display signs of ethical values through whistleblowing.

To encourage ethical standards in the short term, managers should:

- Consider the personality characteristics of people applying to join the
  organization. Either avoid personalities that are prone to unethical behav-
  ior or make sure that policies block unethical tendencies.
- Make public statements that ethical behavior is important and expected.
- Develop organizational policies that specify ethical objectives.
- Reward ethical behavior and avoid rewarding unethical behavior.

- Punish unethical behavior and avoid punishing ethical behavior.
- Be sensitive to the potential for unethical behavior when placing members into competitive situations and take appropriate steps to avoid it.[44]
- Take into account that, when decisions require moral judgment, group decision making generally results in higher levels of moral reasoning than does individual decision making.[45]

Implications for Managers

The guidelines for promoting ethical behavior discussed in this chapter are just that—suggestions. No one can tell you which one or how many of these guidelines you should adopt. Any decision you make that involves ethics is likely to be based on values you have already learned and experiences you have already had. Rest assured, as a manager you *will* be asked to make decisions that involve ethics. Some of these decisions will affect only you. Others will affect subordinates, superiors, or even the organization. What will you do, for example, when you encounter organizational policies and practices that you consider inappropriate? Are you willing to blow the whistle and perhaps put your own career at risk?

Although there are many behaviors that are clearly ethical or unethical, the vast majority of decisions managers must make fall into "gray" areas. When others cannot agree on whether a particular behavior is ethical, your personal values and the cultural values of your organization come into play. Think about the nature of ethics and the various guidelines discussed in this chapter. Then let your behavior reflect your values.

Organizations are becoming increasingly active in addressing such social concerns as the need for reforestation.

Social Responsibility and Managerial Ethics in Review

Organizations at the start of the twentieth century were concerned mostly with making profits and leaving the well-being of others up to individual acts of charity. After the Great Depression, however, people began to demand that organizations share some of their profits to improve society. Today, all managers must be aware of what society expects from their organizations and whether their actions will meet expectations.

This is not an easy task. There are many external and internal stakeholders, and one group's needs may conflict with another's. Many organizations try to specify current social issues and their response to them through a social audit. The level of commitment found in an organization's response is determined largely by the principles it follows and ranges from performing only those socially responsible acts that are imposed by laws and regulations to initiating policies and programs that try to anticipate social issues before they become problems.

There are many arguments for and against corporate social responsibility. These arguments have been encapsulated into two points of view. Those who believe that organizations should not be concerned about social responsibility base many of their arguments on the costs involved and on whether organizations should shoulder those costs on behalf of society. Those in favor of corporate social responsibility feel that organizations benefit from society and, therefore, have an obligation to improve it.

An organization's response to social issues can be classified according to its relationship with the law. Organizations who behave illegally and irresponsibly flout the law and public opinion. Some organizations obey the letter of the law but not the spirit. Other organizations break the law in the midst of their attempts to act responsibly. A fourth category of organizations manages to adhere to laws and regulations and still respond to society's needs. One way to promote an organization's adherence to the law and attention to social issues is to put its board of directors in charge of monitoring decisions and behaviors. This charge may be best met if the board includes members from outside as well as inside the organization.

The societal values, norms, and mores that shape an organization's social responsibility considerations also influence the ethics of individuals. Every society has a set of standards to guide the behavior of its citizens, although acceptable codes of conduct for one society may be judged more harshly by another. Like social responsibility considerations, ethical considerations address the well-being of others, but on a smaller scale. These personal values are learned through one's family and through religious, educational, and cultural experiences.

A manager's personal ethics become managerial ethics when applied to situations in organizations. Managers bear a tremendous ethical responsibility for the actions they take, for the actions others take at their behest, and even for the results of their failure to act. They also bear responsibility for encouraging others to act ethically. Although many people might behave unethically under certain conditions, there are steps managers can take to promote ethical behavior, including developing an organizational culture and organizational policies and practices that reflect a high ethical standard for both managers and nonmanagers.

Issues for Review and Discussion

1. Define both ethics and social responsibility. How are they alike? How do they differ?
2. Identify and discuss the two principles guiding contemporary acts of social responsibility.
3. What are the major points of disagreement between Milton Friedman and Keith Davis on corporate social responsibility?
4. Discuss the distinction among social obligation, social responsibility, and social responsiveness.
5. List several sources of unethical managerial behaviors.
6. Discuss the steps that managers can take to encourage ethical behavior by all organization members.

Key Terms

social responsibility   ethics
social audit   whistleblowing

Suggested Readings

Blanchard, K., and Peale, N. V. (1988). *The power of ethical management.* New York: William Morrow.

Carroll, A. B. (1984). *Social responsibility of management.* Chicago: Science Research Associates, Inc.

Dierkes, M., and Antal, A. B. (1986). Whither corporate social reporting: Is it time to legislate? *California Management Review,* 28, 106-21.

Klein, J. I. (1989). Science and subterfuge. *Academy of Management Executive,* 3, 59-62.

Preston, L. E. (1986). Social issues in management: An evolutionary perspective. In Wren, D. A., and Pearce, J. A. II, eds. *Papers dedicated to the development of modern management.* Chicago: Academy of Management, 52-57.

Toffler, B. L. (1986). *Tough choices: Managers talk ethics.* New York: John Wiley.

Notes

1. L. Wolfson (3 January 1988), Helping business handle crises, interview with Steven B. Fink, President of Lexicon Communications Corp., *Wisconsin State Journal,* 2, 8.
2. K. Davis and R. L. Blomstrom (1971), *Business society and environment: Social power and social response,* New York: McGraw-Hill.
3. K. Davis and W. C. Frederick (1984), *Business and society: Management, public policy, and ethics,* 5th ed., New York: McGraw-Hill.
4. D. Votaw and S. P. Sethi (1973), *The corporate dilemma: Traditional values versus contemporary problems,* Englewood Cliffs, NJ: Prentice-Hall; S. P Sethi (1975), Dimensions of corporate social performance: An analytical framework, *California Management Review,* 17(3), 58-64.
5. M. Heald (1970), *The social responsibilities of business: Company and community, 1900-1960,* Cleveland, OH: Case Western Reserve Press.
6. W. C. Frederick, K. Davis, and J. E. Post (1988), *Business and society: Corporate strategy, public policy, ethics,* New York: McGraw-Hill.
7. A discussion of the social audit can be found in R. A. Bauer and D. H. Fenn, Jr. (1972), *The corporate social audit,* New York: Russell Sage.
8. General Motors Corporation (1988), *1988 General Motors Public Interest Report,* Detroit, MI: Author, 1.
9. Sethi, 63.
10. Sethi, 62.
11. Frederick, Davis, and Post, 32.
12. K. E. Aupperle, A. B. Carroll, and J. D. Hatfield (1985), An empirical examination of the relationship between corporate social responsibility and profitability, *Academy of Management Journal,* 28, 446-63.
13. Frederick, Davis, and Post, 36-39.
14. T. Parsons (1960), *Structure and process in modern society,* Glencoe, IL: Free Press; P. M. Blau and W. R. Scott (1962), *Formal organizations: A comparative approach,* San Francisco: Chandler Publishing Company.
15. Frederick, Davis, and Post, 39-43.
16. M. Friedman (September 1970), The social responsibility of business is to increase profits, *The New York Times Magazine,* 33, 122-26; M. Friedman (April 1971), Does business have social responsibility? *Bank Administration,* 13-14.
17. K. Davis (1973), The case for and against business assumption of social responsibility, *Academy of Management Journal,* 16, 312-22.
18. L. E. Preston (1986), Social issues in management: An evolutionary perspective, in D. A. Wren and J. A. Pearce II, eds., *Papers dedicated to the development of modern management,* Chicago: Academy of Management, 56.
19. J. B. McGuire, A. Sundgren, and T. Schneeweiss (1988), Corporate social responsibility and firm financial performance, *Academy of Management Journal,* 31, 854-72.

20. R. Ford and F. McLaughlin (1984), Perceptions of socially responsible activities and attitudes: A comparison of business school deans and corporate chief executives, *Academy of Management Journal,* 27, 666-74.

21. The four faces of social responsibility (May-June 1982), *Business Horizons,* 19-27.

22. H. Geneen (1984), *Managing,* New York: Doubleday, 258.

23. P. F. Drucker (1973), *Management: Tasks, responsibilities, practices,* New York: Harper & Row; H. Mintzberg (1983), *Power in and around organizations,* Englewood Cliffs, NJ: Prentice-Hall.

24. Directors aren't doing their jobs (16 March 1987), *Fortune,* 117-19.

25. I. F. Kesner, B. Victor, and B. T. Lamont (1986), Board composition and the commission of illegal acts: An investigation of Fortune 500 Companies, *Academy of Management Journal,* 29, 789-99.

26. Kesner, Victor, and Lamont.

27. H. Singh and F. Harianto (1989), Management-board relationships, takeover risk, and the adoption of golden parachutes, *Academy of Management Journal,* 32, 7-24.

28. Parsons.

29. T. J. Peters and R. H. Waterman, Jr. (1982), *In search of excellence: Lessons from America's best run corporations,* New York: Harper & Row, 26.

30. J. I. Klein (1989), Science and subterfuge, *Academy of Management Executive,* 3, 59-62.

31. J. G. Longenecker (1985), Management priorities and management ethics, *Journal of Business Ethics,* 4, 65-70.

32. M. P. Miceli and J. P. Near (1984), The relationship among beliefs, organizational position, and whistle-blowing status: A discriminant analysis, *Academy of Management Journal,* 27, 687-705.

33. Ethics on the job: Companies alert employees to potential dilemmas (14 July 1986), *The Wall Street Journal,* 17.

34. I. Ross (December 1980), How lawless are big companies? *Fortune,* 57-63.

35. Ethics in America (31 October-3 November 1983), *The Wall Street Journal,* 33.

36. S. N. Brenner and E. A. Mollander (January/February 1977), Is the ethics of business changing? *Harvard Business Review,* 57-71.

37. B. Z. Posner and W. H. Schmidt (1984), Values and the American manager: An update, *California Management Review,* 26(3), 202.

38. W. H. Hegarty and H. P. Sims (1978), Some determinants of unethical decision behavior: An experiment, *Journal of Applied Psychology,* 63, 451-57; W. H. Hegarty and H. P. Sims, Jr. (1979), Organizational philosophy, policies, and objectives related to unethical decision behavior: A laboratory experiment, *Journal of Applied Psychology,* 64, 331-38.

39. L. Hosmer (1987), *The ethics of management,* Homewood, IL: Irwin, 107-9.

40. D. J. Fritzsche and H. Becker (1984), Linking management behavior to ethical philosophy: An empirical investigation, *Academy of Management Journal,* 27, 166-75.

41. J. Wilke (7 May 1987), BioTechnica to get OK to test genetically-altered bacteria, *Boston Globe,* 61.

42. F. N. Brady (1985), A Janus-headed model of ethical theory: Looking two ways at business/society issues, *Academy of Management Review,* 10, 570.

43. R. B. Dunham (1984), *Organizational behavior: People and processes in management,* Homewood, IL: Irwin.

44. Dunham, 495.

45. M. L. Nichols and V. E. Day (1982), A comparison of moral reasoning of groups and individuals on the "defining issues test." *Academy of Management Journal,* 25, 201-8.

Frank Pearson and the Allied Research Corporation

By David B. Thompson and Michael J. DiNoto, University of Idaho

Dr. Frank Pearson was an associate director of medical research for the Allied Research Corporation, where he supervised a research team assigned to develop therapeutic drugs. The team's duties included establishing procedures to test drugs for effectiveness, safety, and marketability. Dr. Pearson was the only physician on the research team and had been employed by Allied since 1980.

In the spring of 1985, the team was engaged in the development of loperamide, a liquid drug for treatment of diarrhea in infants, children, and the elderly. The proposed formula contained forty-four times the concentration of saccharin permitted by the Federal Drug Administration (FDA) in twelve ounces of a soft drink. Accordingly, the team agreed that the formula was unsuitable for use and suspended work on the project.

In March of 1986, Allied's marketing division issued a directive to resume the research and development of loperamide. The company intended to file an investigational new drug application with the FDA, to continue laboratory studies on loperamide, and to complete the formula. In Dr. Pearson's professional judgment, however, there was no justification for seeking permission from the FDA to continue to develop the drug because of the heated controversy over the safety of saccharin. He made his position clear to the other team members. The team, however, decided to continue the research despite Dr. Pearson's objections.

Dr. Pearson met with his supervisor, Dr. Antonucci. During the meeting, Dr. Pearson stated that, in his professional opinion, the decision to pursue the development of loperamide was medically unsound. He also told Dr. Antonucci that he believed continuing his work on the loperamide research would violate his Hippocratic oath, a generally accepted standard of medical ethics. The risk, he said, that saccharin might be harmful should prevent testing the formula on children or the elderly, especially when an alternative formula might soon be available

Dr. Antonucci responded that the company had no intention of testing the formula on any human subjects unless and until the FDA gave its approval. He assured Dr. Pearson that all proper procedures would be scrupulously observed in the development and testing of the drug. He also emphasized the differences between the development and testing phases of research projects in general and suggested that continuing to do research would, in his opinion, violate no law or professional code of ethics. He also stressed the need to work constructively with the marketing division.

At the end of the meeting, Dr. Pearson remained unpersuaded, and Dr. Antonucci asked him to choose another research project. He assured Dr. Pearson that the request would be honored and that no salary adjustment would be made. Dr. Pearson responded that, even so, he interpreted this offer as a demotion.

Later in the day, Dr. Pearson submitted his letter of resignation to Dr. Antonucci. It said, in part, "Upon learning that you believe that I have not 'acted as a Director' and have displayed inadequacies as to my inability to relate to the marketing division and that I am now—or soon will be—demoted, I find it impossible to continue my employment at Allied." Dr. Antonucci accepted the resignation without comment.

Questions

1. What are the ethical issues in this case?

2. If the FDA had given permission to test the drug, would that permission make the testing ethical? Explain.

3. What alternatives were open to Dr. Antonucci? Which should he have taken?

4. Was Dr. Antonucci correct in dealing with Dr. Pearson as he did?

4

Schools of Management Thought: Approaches to Managing

Student Learning Objectives

After reading this chapter, you should be able to:

1. Identify the early management pioneers, their views of organizations, and their contributions to the classical theory of management.

2. Understand the major elements of Taylor's approach to scientific management.

3. Explain the significance of the Hawthorne studies.

4. Discuss the emergence of the human relations movement and describe how it views workers in organizations.

5. Identify the major contributors to the behavioral theory of management, their views of organizations, and their contributions to the management literature.

6. Explain the systems theory perspective of managing organizations.

7. Identify and describe three contemporary perspectives of management.

8. Understand the difference between the *science* and the *art* of management.

*M*anagers and management scientists develop theories of managing. These theories offer different approaches to planning, organizing, directing, and controlling. As you will recall from the discussion of the internal environment in Chapter 2, the style managers use when coordinating, making decisions, and communicating greatly influences the climate of their organization. This chapter explores the major approaches to managing and the beliefs, or schools, of management thought that guide managers. It also explains why one manager's approach may be different from another's.

The Classical School

Managers have needed efficient planning, organizing, staffing, decision-making, and control systems since ancient times. Now there are books, journals, professional societies, and schools to which managers can turn. Our ancestors, however, had to learn to manage primarily through trial and error. Although history provides some insight into managerial practice, it was the consequences of the Industrial Revolution that stimulated sustained and systematic efforts to understand organizations and their management. These efforts resulted in the emergence of well-defined schools of thought on how to approach the practice of management. Management literature, professional associations, and schools of management also arose to create and disseminate knowledge about managers and their organizations.

The **classical school** of management thought and practice emerged during the late 1800s and early 1900s as managers struggled with organizational complexities brought on by the Industrial Revolution. Organizations were growing larger and more complex, their technologies more sophisticated. These new organizations demanded that managers control inventory and production, schedule and coordinate work, integrate diverse work systems, and manage human resources. There was little information, however, to guide managers on how to perform these activities. It was not until the 1800s and early 1900s that a new breed of industrial managers, most of whom had an engineering background, consciously set out to develop "principles" of organizational management and, thus, to find practical solutions to the problems facing managers.

Classical management theorists proposed that there was "one best way" to manage a complex industrial organization. Their theories assumed that people make logical, rational decisions while trying to maximize personal returns from their work experiences. This reliance on the maxims of economic and mechanical rationality for the ideal management of organizations is the cornerstone of the classical school, an approach based on: the scientific management movement in the United States; Henri Fayol's work in France on classical administrative theory; and the work of German sociologist Max Weber, who developed a model of the bureaucratic organization.

The Scientific Management Movement

Scientific management refers to "that kind of management which conducts a business or affairs by standards established by facts or truths gained through systematic observation, experiment, or reasoning."[1] Promoters of the

Charles Babbage advocated division of labor as a way of lowering costs and boosting productivity.

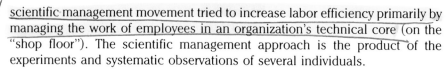

scientific management movement tried to increase labor efficiency primarily by managing the work of employees in an organization's technical core (on the "shop floor"). The scientific management approach is the product of the experiments and systematic observations of several individuals.

Charles Babbage.   Charles Babbage (1792-1871) was one early contributor to the scientific management movement. He argued that organizations could realize greater profit if employees specialized in performing job activities. Along with classical economist Adam Smith, Babbage advocated a division of labor and the design of jobs so that each employee performed only a small set of simple tasks. Babbage also believed that managers should conduct time studies to determine how long it should take to perform each task. He noted that "if the observer stands with his watch in his hand before a person heading a pin, the workman will almost certainly increase his speed."[2] Managers could then use such time study information to establish standards for expected performance levels and to reward employees with bonuses based on the degree to which they exceeded those standards.

Frederick W. Taylor has been called the "father of scientific management."

Frederick W. Taylor.   The best known of the scientific management theorists was Frederick W. Taylor (1856-1915). An engineer and consultant, Taylor observed what he considered to be inexcusable work methods in the steel industry.[3] Workers often brought their own, poorly designed tools to the workplace. Job training typically was haphazard, and workers themselves often determined machine speed and workpace. Hiring frequently occurred on a "first-come, first-hired" basis rather than on individuals' skills and abilities. Managers worked side by side with laborers, often ignoring such management responsibilities as planning and organizing work.

Taylor severely criticized managers for failing to manage effectively and for allowing workers to determine their own methods and pace. He believed that managers should develop and implement the "science" of work and that laborers would function effectively by following its principles.

Throughout the technical core, Taylor set out to establish the science of work. Focusing on the task of handling pig iron, he was convinced that, using scientific principles, he could identify the "one best way" to pick up a 92-pound piece of pig iron, hold it, walk with it, and lay it down. Through time-and-motion and fatigue studies, Taylor identified a "science" of pig iron handling that enabled an average laborer to increase the amount of pig iron handled from 12-1/2 tons to 48 tons a day.

By using the same approach, Taylor created sciences of shoveling coal, iron ore, and ash.

Press the forearm hard against the upper part of the right leg just below the thigh, . . . take the end of the shovel in your right hand, . . . and when you push the shovel into the pile, instead of using the muscular effort of your arms which is tiresome . . . throw the weight of your body on the shovel . . . .[4]

Taylor's approach to scientific management called for:

1. *Developing the science of work* using time, motion, and fatigue studies to identify the "one best way" to perform a job and the level at which it can be performed

2. *Adhering absolutely to work standards,* not allowing the daily production rate identified through the science of work to be changed by the arbitrary whim of either manager or employee

3. *Selecting, placing, and training workers scientifically,* assigning workers to the most interesting and profitable tasks for which they are suited

4. *Applying a financial incentive system* that encourages workers to perform efficiently and effectively by tying pay to output: low production leads to low pay, high production to high pay

5. *Using specialized functional supervision* by a number of expert managers to oversee workers on the different aspects of their work rather than by one general manager who supervises an entire department (Taylor referred to this as "functional foremanship." This text refers to it as *functional supervision.* [See Figure 4.1.])

6. *Keeping labor-management relations friendly,* because a cooperative alliance between employee and employer helps ensure the willing application of the scientific principles of work.[5]

One of the furthest-reaching aspects of Taylor's work was a new philosophical approach to managing work and people. To be successful, Taylor stated, the scientific management approach would require a mental revolution on the part of both labor and management. Employees and managers would have to understand the scientific management principles and work together in harmony, accepting new work roles and new methods. Only through this mental revolution would labor and management achieve both increased output and higher wages.

Frank and Lillian Gilbreth were pioneers in the scientific management movement.

The Gilbreths.   Frank and Lillian Gilbreth, a husband and wife team, also pioneered the scientific management movement. Frank Bunker Gilbreth (1868-1924) focused on improving work methods to enhance productivity and efficiency. With her background in psychology and management, Lillian Moller Gilbreth (1878-1972) viewed scientific management as a technique to help workers reach their full potential.

The Gilbreths developed a scheme to classify the motions used in performing a job. They referred to motion as a *therblig,* Gilbreth spelled backwards. Their classifications included such motions as grasping, holding, and moving. Their motion scheme documented the relationship between types and frequencies of motion and worker fatigue, demonstrating that unnecessary motions waste energy. By separating appropriate from inappropriate motions, the

FIGURE 4.1
Functional Supervision

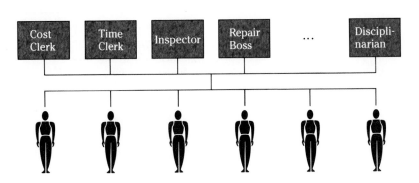

Henry Gantt created the Gantt Chart to aid production and control.

Gilbreths helped make more of a worker's energy available for job performance.

Like Taylor, Frank Gilbreth concentrated on developing the science of work. Through his famous study of bricklaying, he devised ways to increase the average output of individual bricklayers from 120 to 250 bricks an hour. Lillian Gilbreth pioneered modern human resource management, especially the scientific selection, placement, and training of employees. Together, the Gilbreths were interested in developing individual workers through training programs, improved work environments, and a healthy psychological outlook. They were so convinced of the benefits of such efforts that they even applied their management principles to raising their twelve children, as described in the book and movie *Cheaper by the Dozen*.

Henry Gantt.   Henry Gantt (1861-1919), an associate of Taylor's at Midvale, Simonds, and Bethlehem Steel, added two techniques to scientific management. The Gantt chart is used by managers to summarize work activities and identify those that should be performed simultaneously or sequentially (see Figure 4.2). Gantt's other contribution was the minimum-wage-based system, in which employees receive a minimum daily wage whether or not they achieve their specified daily work objectives.

Gantt also recommended that employees receive monetary incentives in the form of bonuses for work beyond the expected standard. Furthermore, he proposed bonuses for supervisors whose subordinates reached their daily standard and additional bonuses if all workers reached their goals, because he felt that this would encourage supervisors to manage subordinates more effectively.

Classical Organization Theory

Whereas scientific management focuses on the management of an organization's technical core, **classical organization theory** concentrates on the management of an entire organization. Contributors to classical organization

FIGURE 4.2   Gantt Chart for Lil'America Builders

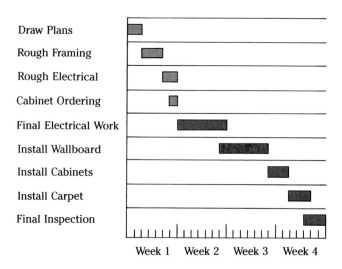

theory were concerned with the structure of an organization and with designing processes that would make its operations rational, ordered, predictable, efficient, and effective. Classical organization theorists viewed organizations as giant machines created to achieve goals. They believed that a basic set of universal laws or principles govern the design and operation of effective organizations. Two primary contributors to classical organization theory were Henri Fayol and Max Weber.

Henri Fayol. Henri Fayol (1841-1925) worked for fifty-eight years with Commentry-Fourchambault, a French coal and iron processing organization. His perspectives on management grew out of this experience and his formal training as a mining engineer. Fayol attributed his success as a manager to the methods he used rather than to personal talent. He felt that other managers could be just as successful if they had appropriate guidelines for managing complex organizations.

Fayol paid particular attention to managerial activities. He believed that all managers perform all five of the managerial functions he identified (planning, organizing, directing, coordinating, and controlling), but he recognized that the nature of managerial work differs from manager to manager. Fayol identified fourteen principles that he believed should guide managers in the management of an organization's functions (operations, marketing, finance, accounting, and security). The following are some of the most distinguishing principles:

1. *Division of labor*—improved levels of efficiency through specialization result in reduced learning time, fewer activity changes, and increased skill development
2. *Authority*—the right to give orders should always carry responsibility fitting to its privilege
3. *Unity of command*—each employee reports to only one superior, thus avoiding confusion and conflict
4. *Subordination of individual interest to the common good*—the needs of individuals and groups within an organization should not take precedence over the needs of the organization as a whole
5. *Centralization*—levels at which decisions are made should depend on the specific situation; no level of centralization or decentralization is ideal for all situations
6. *Scalar chain*—the relationship among all levels in the organizational hierarchy and exact lines of authority should be unmistakably clear and followed at all times
7. *Order*—there should be a place for everything (and everyone), and everything (and everyone) should be in its place

Fayol felt the application of the principles he identified should be flexible, noting that:

> . . . there is nothing rigid or absolute in management affairs, it is all a question of proportion. . . . [A]llowance must be made for different changing circumstances . . . . [6]

Max Weber saw the bureaucratic organization as that organizational form most capable of attaining the highest degree of efficiency and superior precision, stability, and reliability.

Despite Fayol's call for flexibility, many managers who adopted his fourteen principles applied them rigidly. In fact, it is the strict application of these principles that characterizes the classical approach.

Max Weber. Max Weber (1864–1920), a German lawyer and sociologist, was convinced that there was an appropriate design for an efficient, effective organization.[7] In Weber's model of this "rational organization," labor should be divided according to specialization. Each employee's authority and responsibility should be clearly defined as the official duties of the position, not as the duties of the particular individual who holds that position. Weber also proposed that a well-defined hierarchy be set up to eliminate ambiguity and to specify the nature of relationships among jobs within an organization.

Weber's vision of an ideal organization included an elaborate set of rules specifying the rights and duties of employees and a set of procedures involved in each work situation, which were to be applied uniformly throughout the organization. As a result, Weber's bureaucratic organization would be impersonal, rigid, and routine in meeting its goals of speed, precision, order, unambiguity, continuity, and predictability.

Closing Thoughts

Although the classical school of management did not provide a totally unified approach, there were many similarities among its contributors. Classical management was, to a very large extent, prescriptive: it described how people should manage organizations. Just as engineers specify the appropriate way to build bridges, managers were to follow a rational approach and a set of principles to build and operate organizations. Through the classicists' work to identify "one best way," systems were developed that led to greater organizational productivity.

The contributors to the classical school of management agreed on many issues, such as the importance of a division of labor, order, standard operating procedures, and centralization of authority. There were, however, a few areas of disagreement. For example, there were radical differences in thinking about supervision in the technical core; compare Fayol's unity of command principle to Taylor's call for functional supervision. Disparity also arose between the prescriptions and reality. For example, Fayol instructed managers to apply his fourteen principles flexibly, but classical managers tended to apply them rigidly. Similarly, Taylor called for friendly labor-management relations, but the typical classical approach was often cool, impersonal, and adversarial.

The classical school of management thought has a number of critics. Many argue that its description of organization members as rational and economically motivated is incomplete. Critics claim that when managers ignore the social needs of workers, organizations do not provide adequate motivation and reinforcement programs. Managers following the classical model frequently find themselves in destructive confrontations rather than eliciting productive cooperation.

A final area of criticism revolves around the classicists' attempts to identify universal principles for efficient management. Although many of the classical principles may be appropriate for organizations operating in simple, nonturbulent environments, they are less well suited to conducting business in shifting and heterogeneous environments.

Robert Owen was an early industrialist who saw the need for effective human resource management.

The Behavioral School

The classicists' preoccupation with the technical (machine) side of organizations left a void. This space was filled by behavioral management theorists, who viewed organizations from social and psychological perspectives. The contributors to the **behavioral school** were concerned about the welfare of employees and wanted to treat them as more than mere cogs in the industrial wheel.

Early Contributors

Instead of viewing organizations as machines with perfectly designed mechanical systems, behavioral thinkers envisioned a social system. In this social system was a people-to-people and people-to-work network so smoothly linked and efficient that it would accomplish organizational goals. Effective management of this social system would require managers to understand the nature of individuals and groups, as well as their patterns of interaction.

Hugo Munsterberg, the "father of industrial psychology," taught managers to use psychological principles to enhance organizational effectiveness.

Robert Owen.   British industrialist Robert Owen (1771-1858) was one of the first managers to recognize the need for good overall management of an organization's human resources. Owen called for managers that treat workers with respect and dignity, for better working conditions, for reduced hours of work, for meals for the workforce, and for restrictions on the use of children as a labor source.

Hugo Munsterberg.   After establishing a psychological laboratory at Harvard in 1892, Hugo Munsterberg (1863-1916) concentrated on applying psychological concepts to organizational settings. He, too, was concerned with the human side of organizations. Considered the father of industrial psychology, Munsterberg documented the psychological conditions associated with different levels of productivity. He taught managers to match workers with jobs and to motivate workers after placing them in jobs.[8]

Walter Dill Scott.   While on the faculty at Northwestern University, Walter Dill Scott (1869-1955) argued that managers were not effectively using the human factor in organizations. Although Scott agreed with the classicists' argument that employees are economically motivated, he also emphasized that people are social creatures with needs for recognition and social membership. Scott believed that if managers did not consider employees' social needs, organizational effectiveness would be hindered. He asserted, therefore, that management should work at improving employees' attitudes and motivation as a means to increase worker productivity.

Walter Dill Scott suggested that employees are not only motivated by economic rewards, but also by a set of social needs.

Mary Parker Follett.   Management philosopher, consultant, and educator Mary Parker Follett (1868-1933) called management "the art of getting things done through others."[9] She believed that a natural order between management and employees could be achieved through leadership. This leadership was not, however, to be accomplished through the traditional use of formal authority by superiors over subordinates. Rather, a manager's influence and power should flow naturally from his or her knowledge, skill, and personal contact with employees.

Chester Barnard. Chester Barnard's (1886–1961) major contribution to management is his discussion of formal and informal organizations. Managers consciously create formal organizations to achieve goals. Informal organizations arise spontaneously as employees interact and form bonds. Whereas classical management thinking asked managers to focus on the design and management of the formal organization, Barnard's work sensitized managers to the informal organization and its ability to aid communication, provide leadership, maintain cohesiveness, strengthen individual feelings of integrity and self-respect, and influence the effectiveness of management practices.[10]

A Transition: The Hawthorne Studies

Between 1924 and 1933, a series of worker productivity studies was conducted at the Hawthorne Plant of the Western Electric Company in Chicago. These studies, widely known as the Hawthorne studies, have strongly influenced the course of behavioral management theory (see "A Closer Look: The Hawthorne Studies").* Prior to the Hawthorne studies, managers had increased productivity primarily through developing better tools and improving machines and work methods. The Hawthorne studies initially focused on the relationship between worker productivity and such factors as the illumination of the workplace, the length of coffee breaks, the length of the workday, and the nature of pay plans. The researchers expected that improvements in these work environment factors would yield improvements in productivity.

Surprisingly, the results of these studies were often inconsistent with expectations. In fact, at times, productivity actually increased when decreases were expected (such as when illumination levels were decreased). In an attempt to understand the confusing pattern of results, a large number of workers were interviewed. The interviews suggested that a human/social element operated in the workplace and that productivity increases were as much an outgrowth of group dynamics as of managerial demands and physical factors.

Classical management theorists expected each employee in a group to maximize pay by producing as many units as possible. Instead, Harvard professor Elton Mayo observed that informal work groups emerged with their own leaders, influence systems, norms for appropriate behavior, and pressures for conformity. An individual who produced above the maximum level was considered a "rate-buster" and was pressured by co-workers to slow down. Anyone who produced under the minimum level was a "chiseler" and was urged to speed up. The social pressures within the group powerfully affected workers' productivity.

The Hawthorne studies failed to uncover a simple relationship between improvements in physical working conditions and increases in worker productivity. They did, however, emphasize the importance of human considerations for worker effectiveness and documented, for the first time, the tremendous power of an informal work group and the influence of the social environment on workers' attitudes and behaviors. The studies provided a transition between

* The Hawthorne studies have been much discussed and often misrepresented. The discussion here is consistent with the review of the Hawthorne studies published by the Academy of Management as part of its celebration of 100 years of modern management: R. G. Greenwood and C. D. Wrege (1986), The Hawthorne studies, in D. A. Wren and J. A. Pearce II, eds., *Papers dedicated to the development of modern management,* Chicago: Academy of Management, 24-35.

The Hawthorne Studies: Shedding Light on Worker Productivity

A series of studies conducted at the Hawthorne Works of the Western Electric Company near Chicago, usually referred to as the Hawthorne studies, has had a significant impact on the management of work.[1] Studies involving illumination levels were conducted between November 1924 and April 1927 by D. C. Jackson and G. A. Pennock. These studies were intended to identify lighting levels that would produce optimal productivity. In the first experiment, however, productivity increased both when illumination was increased and when it was decreased. Overall, productivity bounced up and down without an apparent direct relationship to illumination level.

A second study had an experimental group that experienced illumination changes and a control group for which illumination was held constant. Production increased in both groups to an almost equal extent. In yet a third experiment, lighting levels were decreased over time. As a result, productivity increased for both the experimental and the control group (at least until an extremely low level of illumination was reached).

The first major study of the Hawthorne studies themselves was conducted over a twenty-four-experimental session between April 25, 1927, and February 8, 1933. These relay-assembly-test-room (RATR) experiments explored the degree to which variations in length of rest periods, of the working day, and of the working week influenced productivity. As was the case for the illumination study, productivity fluctuated during the stages of the RATR experiments.

Again, these variations could not be explained by the expected factors.

Many reports of the Hawthorne studies suggest that any change conducted during the Hawthorne studies increased productivity. This is not exactly true, and it is not the primary reason these studies are so important. The importance of the Hawthorne experiments is a function of how researchers and scholars explained the unexpected findings. As early as September 1928, an extensive interviewing program elicited comments from workers that helped identify the causes of fluctuations in productivity. Conclusions as to why the Hawthorne effects occurred vary. According to Elton Mayo, for example,

What actually happened was that six individuals became a team and the team gave itself wholeheartedly and spontaneously to cooperation in the experiment. The consequence was that they felt themselves to be participating freely and without afterthought, and were happy in the knowledge that they were working without coercion from above or limitation from below.[2]

Mayo seemed to feel that the experiments satisfied workers' needs and shifted their attention from preoccupation with personal problems to concentration on productivity.

George Pennock, who conducted the RATR experiments, has stated:

Emotional status was reflected in performance; and the major component of this emotional conditon was at-titude toward supervisor. The influence from these studies was inescapable that the dominant factor in the performance of these employees was their mental attitude.[3]

Another perspective on the Hawthorne effects comes from the independent writings of Whitehead and Chase, who both suggested that a major reason the "Hawthorne effect" produced increases in productivity was that being a part of the experiments made the workers feel important.[4] Even members of the control groups felt important; thus, their productivity was said to increase as a result.

1. R. G. Greenwood and C. D. Wrege (1986), The Hawthorne studies, in D. A. Wren and J. A. Pearce II, eds., *Papers dedicated to the development of modern management*, Chicago: Academy of Management, 24-35.

2. E. Mayo (1945), *The social problems of an industrial civilization*, Boston: Division of Research, Graduate School of Business Administration, Harvard University, 72-73.

3. G. A. Pennock (1930), Industrial research at Hawthorne: An experimental investigation of rest periods, working conditions and other influences, *Personnel Journal*, 8, 297.

4. T. N. Whitehead (1938), *The industrial worker* (2 vols.), Cambridge: Harvard University Press; S. Chase (1941), What makes workers like to work, *Reader's Digest*, 38, 15-20.

the task-oriented classicists, who thought managers should enhance productivity through technical systems, and the emerging human relations advocates, whose behavioral approach focused on individual needs for recognition and peer interaction.

The Human Relations Movement

Rising negative reactions to the impersonality of scientific management and bureaucratic theory, combined with evidence from the Hawthorne studies, helped ignite the **human relations movement.** Turning from task-oriented styles of management, advocates focused on employees in the belief that satisfied workers are productive workers. A manager following the human relations guidelines would be supportive and paternalistic, creating and nurturing cohesive work groups and a psychologically healthy environment for workers. This social model, thus, proposed that increased productivity depended on the degree to which an organization could meet workers' needs for recognition, acceptance, and group membership.

The Behavioral Science Movement

Advocates of the **behavioral science movement** stressed the need to conduct systematic and controlled studies of the human side of organizations. They also believed that the classicists' rational/economic model and the social model espoused by human relations advocates were incomplete representations of workers. The model proposed by Abraham Maslow, Douglas McGregor, and other behavioral scientists suggested that employees have a strong need to grow, to develop, to maintain a high level of self-regard, and consequently to be actively involved.

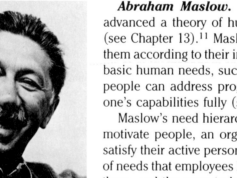

Abraham Maslow was the architect of the hierarchy of human needs.

Abraham Maslow. In 1943, psychologist Abraham Maslow (1908-70) advanced a theory of human motivation that many managers later adopted. (see Chapter 13).[11] Maslow identified five sets of human needs and arranged them according to their importance. At the bottom of the hierarchy are the most basic human needs, such as for food and water. As these needs are satisfied, people can address progressively higher ones, such as the need to develop one's capabilities fully (see Figure 4.3).

Maslow's need hierarchy theory had specific implications for managers. To motivate people, an organization must offer its members the opportunity to satisfy their active personal needs. Maslow helped managers identify the types of needs that employees have, the order in which employees are likely to satisfy them, and the ways to help them do so. For example, organizations can help employees meet their physiological needs by providing a base salary sufficient to pay for food and shelter. Organizations can offer benefit programs, such as retirement plans, to help employees meet their safety and security needs. Maslow, thus, provided a rational model of human behavior based on workers' needs.

While Maslow recognized the importance of lower-level needs, he emphasized the significance of the insatiable growth needs of self-esteem and self-actualization at the top of the hierarchy. These growth needs can be strong motivators of human behavior, but designing growth experiences into the work context so that organization members can satisfy these needs is a challenge for managers.

FIGURE 4.3 Maslow's
Hierarchy of Needs

Douglas McGregor.   Douglas McGregor (1906–64) and his ideas on Theory X and Theory Y management represent another major contribution to the behavioral science movement.[12] McGregor called the traditional approach to management "Theory X." **Theory X** describes workers as inherently disliking work, lacking ambition, resistant to change, gullible, dull, and indifferent to organizational needs.

In contrast, the **Theory Y** view of management suggests that people like work, are motivated to achieve objectives to which they are committed, and are capable of self-direction and self-control. People are not considered naturally passive or resistant to organizational needs, although they have become so as a result of their experiences in organizations. According to the Theory Y approach:

> *The essential task of management is to arrange organizational conditions and methods of operation so that people can achieve their own goals best by directing their own efforts toward organizational objectives.[13]*

Managers can do this by creating structures and processes that encourage employees to become actively involved in executing their organizational roles. Techniques discussed later in this text, such as the decentralization and delegation of authority, job enlargement, and the use of goal setting, are some of the management practices a Theory Y manager can use to encourage employees to exercise self-direction and self-control.

McGregor's Theory Y, like Maslow's work, focuses managers' attention on an employee model that is more complex than either the classicists' rational/economic model or the human relationists' social model. Theory Y depicts employees as having complex motivational patterns, with behavior strongly influenced by their need to fulfill their human potential.

Other Contributors.   Rensis Likert from the University of Michigan and Harvard's Chris Argyris concentrated on how organizational and management systems affect employees' attitudes and behaviors. Both advocated the development of open and flexible organizations. Argyris, for example, argued that

Raymond Miles, from the University of California at Berkeley, called for expanded employee involvement in organizational affairs.

classically designed organizations (bureaucracies) make demands on employees that are incompatible with the needs of growing, self-actualizing individuals.[14] He suggested, as Likert did, that management should create organizational systems that create a greater opportunity for employees to exercise self-direction and self-control.

During the early 1960s, Raymond Miles, from the University of California at Berkeley, called for expanded employee involvement in organizational affairs. Believing that the employee group is a major untapped resource, he suggested that managers should involve workers in decision making to increase organizational performance. His human resource perspective suggests that these performance increases lead to greater employee satisfaction and heighten employees' willingness to become even more involved in organizational activities.[15]

Closing Thoughts

The behavioral school introduced the importance of personal and social considerations to the management task. It stimulated managers' thinking about employees and the need to design organizations that were more open and flexible than Weber's bureaucratic model. Like the classicists, however, proponents of the behavioral school tended to believe there was "one best way" to manage all organizations.

Contemporary Management Thought

The past few decades have been marked by the refinement, extension, and synthesis of both classical and behavioral management thinking. **Sociotechnical systems theory,** for example, tries to counteract the one-sided approach taken by the classical and behavioral schools by balancing the technical and social-psychological sides of an organization.[16] The perspectives of both classical and behavioral management have been combined and incorporated into a number of new management models.

The Systems Perspective

THEORY Z

A MANAGER'S WORD

What used to be termed "management" is now examined as organization behavior/organization management, production/ operations management, and strategic management. Each functional specialization within management has developed independently of the others.

Thomas A. Mahoney
Frances Hampton Currey Professor
of Organization Studies
Vanderbilt University

One of the contemporary approaches to management views an organization as a complete system. A **system** can be defined as a set of interrelated elements that functions as a unit for a specific purpose. **Systems theory** is presented in this discussion not as a separate theory of management, but as a way of viewing organizations. Systems theorists see organizations as complex networks of interrelated parts that exist in an interdependent relationship with the external environment.[17]

This interrelationship affects all components of an organization's internal environment. Managers from different departments need to communicate with one another; they also need to understand the degree to which the activities of their own department affect and are affected by the activities of other departments. When an automaker's accounting department reports increased revenues from the sale of luxury sedans, for example, its marketing department may expand the advertising campaign for that model, and production departments might produce more cars. The boundaries between an organization's internal divisions must be open for such give-and-take of information.

The relationships among internal organizational systems also call for an open relationship between an organization and its external environment.[18] Managers are expected to be sensitive to the needs of the environment as they take resources from and interact with it while pursuing organizational goals. For example, logging companies reseed areas they deforest, and restaurants heed customers' demands for nonsmoking areas. Two of the three contemporary theories on organizational management (contingency theories and the McKinsey 7-S framework) were derived from a systems-theory perspective.

Contingency Perspectives

Contemporary theorists see the "one best way" approach desired by both classsical and behavioral theorists as too simplistic. They believe that, although a particular managerial strategy may succeed in some situations, it may fail in others. According to various **contingency perspectives,** the techniques a manager should use depend (*are contingent*) on the situation.

A contingency theory of decision making, for example, might suggest that the centralized authority and highly directive leadership style found in the classical approach is effective when a manager has a well-developed body of knowledge that defines the most effective way to proceed. If workers and managers know an effective way to convert iron ore into pig iron, for example, there is very little need for them to collaborate in deciding which techniques should be used to perform this task. Contrast this with situations in which there are high levels of environmental uncertainty and little or no developed knowledge to guide work methods. Such situations require managers to use more consultative and participative decision strategies. For example, the decision in 1989 by B. Dalton and Waldenbooks to remove *The Satanic Verses* from their shelves following Iran's threats to kill the book's author could have required meetings with the publisher, staff attorneys, board of directors, and even the State Department. The public outcry that caused the book stores to reinstate the novel indicates how difficult it is to make the correct decisions under such conditions.

In today's complex organizations, effective managers must go beyond the simplistic strategies of the past. Contingency perspectives help managers diagnose a situation and be flexible about adopting an approach. Throughout the remainder of this book, contingency perspectives guide discussion of the management process, from planning through controlling.

The McKinsey 7-S Framework

A second contemporary perspective on organizational management to come from a systems-theory perspective is the **McKinsey 7-S framework.**[19] The research conducted through McKinsey and Company, a large management consulting organization, revealed that there are seven interdependent organizational factors that must be managed harmoniously. The critical components in the McKinsey 7-S framework—*S* factors—include the following:

1. *Strategy*—the plans or courses of action that allocate an organization's scarce resources and commit it to a specified action

Japanese Management Methods: Japanese Management Arrives Just in Time

Most U.S. corporations have dealt with the demand for increased productivity, concerns over quality, and the need to enhance profitability by throwing millions of dollars at potential high-technology solutions. How have the Japanese dealt with the same problems? Although they have not been shy in applying new technology, the Japanese have emphasized the importance of management and the key role of employees in the successful development of business.

In 1982, for example, General Motors finally gave up and closed its plant in Fremont, California, because of apparently unresolvable problems with gross absenteeism, employee grievances, and wildcat strikes. The company eventually joined forces with Toyota Motor Corporation under a joint venture known as New United Motor Manufacturing, Inc. (NUMMI), and Japanese managers reopened the Fremont plant. They introduced some new technology, but the primary changes involved management, delivery systems, assembly lines, and work teams run by the workers—many of whom were former employees of the GM-operated plant. More recently, Chrysler and Mitsubishi initiated a joint effort in Illinois. In fact, "Japan's Auto Valley, which cuts through six heartland states, already provides more than 15,000 assembly jobs."[1]

How well have the new management approaches worked? The 2500 NUMMI employees are producing roughly the same number of cars that previously took twice as many GM employees to assemble, grievances have virtually disappeared, and absenteeism has dropped to around 2 percent. According to Joel D. Smith, a UAW representative at the NUMMI plant, "We have the same members, the same building, the same technology—just different management and a different production system."[2]

The importance of strong employee loyalty appears to be paramount. To develop this loyalty, Japanese managers have created a situation of mutual trust by treating employees as equals. Gone are the executive parking lots, elite dining rooms, and fancy offices. Sometimes even the titles go, as at a U.S.-based Honda plant where employees are called associates rather than employees. Another important factor in the Japanese development of loyalty among American employees is minimizing layoffs. In fact, when business conditions were bad at a Japanese-managed tire plant in Danville, Kentucky, managers permitted a buildup of inventory, assigned some workers to house-cleaning tasks, and shifted some of the production from one of their Japanese factories to the Danville plant to retain workers. According to D. William Childs, general manager of human resources at the NUMMI plant, "The Japanese philosophy is to make people an important item, as opposed to the typical U.S. philosophy that workers are just an extension of machines."[3]

Other modifications at the Fremont plant included a production change known as a "just-in-time" delivery system that typically keeps no more than a few hours of excess parts in inventory. Remaining supplies arrive just in time to be used. Job design changes are not only permitted but encouraged, as Japanese managers urge employees to find faster ways to perform their work with greater quality. Similar actions expand the nature of jobs for employees. Each employee does several jobs under the team system. They become more highly skilled. Work is spread out, making for a more flexible organization.

Will the success of these Japanese management techniques endure? Only time can tell, but many U.S. organizations evidently think so as more begin to experiment with just-in-time deliveries, team approaches, and so on. Some American managers have noted that many of these techniques actually originated in the United States in the 1930s and, therefore, are not Japanese but simply good management practices. Regardless of their origin, most are clearly attributed to the Japanese today, and it is the Japanese who have stimulated their expanded use in the United States.

1. Japan's gung-ho U.S. car plant (30 January 1989), *Fortune*, 98.
2. The difference Japanese management makes (14 July 1986), *Business Week*, 47.
3. *Business Week*, 49.

2. *Structure*—an organization's design, such as the number of its hierarchical levels and the location of authority within them
3. *Systems*—proceduralized reports and routines
4. *Staff*—important personnel groups within an organization, described demographically (for example, the ages of engineers, the functional background of M.B.A.'s)
5. *Style*—the way key managers behave when pursuing an organization's goals; also refers to an organization's cultural style (for example, consultative or dictatorial)
6. *Skills*—the distinctive abilities of an organization's key personnel
7. *Superordinate goals* (*shared values*)—the significant meanings or guiding concepts an organization instills in its members, such as when members are encouraged to experiment with new methods even if they risk failure[20]

Because of their interdependent relationship, a change in one *S* factor may require adjustment of the others. A change in an organization's strategy, for example, may call for a change in its structure. According to the McKinsey model, managers of effective American organizations have achieved a good fit among these seven variables.

The Theory Z Perspective

During the 1970s and 1980s, American business organizations were seriously affected by Japanese competitors. American scholars identified a number of management practices common to Japanese organizations that appeared to account for much of their effectiveness. (See "A Closer Look: Japanese Management Methods.") Whether these practices could be transplanted successfully to American organizations was an issue for debate. Some argued that unique cultural differences would prevent American organizations from adapting Japanese management practices. Others felt that Japanese practices could be successful in American organizations, often noting that they were basically American in origin anyway.

In 1981, management professor William Ouchi offered **Theory Z** to integrate the merits of the Japanese (Theory J) and American (Theory A) management styles.[21] Theory Z is less a major theory of management than it is a set of organizational and management style characteristics. As summarized in Figure 4.4 on page 88, Theory Z emphasizes terms of employment, decision making, responsibility, evaluation and promotion, control, career paths, and concern for employees. Some successful American organizations that practice Theory Z management include Eastman Kodak, Hewlett-Packard, IBM, and Procter & Gamble.

Ouchi espouses Theory Z as a universally superior approach to managing over the traditional American approach. As such, Theory Z appears to reflect a return to the outdated "one best way" thinking of behavioral management theory. Despite this, Ouchi's work has heightened American industry's awareness of an alternative to the still popular classical approach.

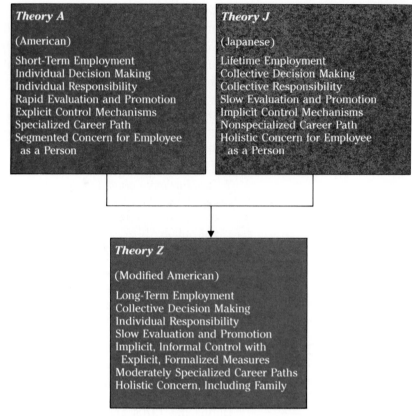

Theory A

(American)

Short-Term Employment
Individual Decision Making
Individual Responsibility
Rapid Evaluation and Promotion
Explicit Control Mechanisms
Specialized Career Path
Segmented Concern for Employee
 as a Person

Theory J

(Japanese)

Lifetime Employment
Collective Decision Making
Collective Responsibility
Slow Evaluation and Promotion
Implicit Control Mechanisms
Nonspecialized Career Path
Holistic Concern for Employee
 as a Person

Theory Z

(Modified American)

Long-Term Employment
Collective Decision Making
Individual Responsibility
Slow Evaluation and Promotion
Implicit, Informal Control with
 Explicit, Formalized Measures
Moderately Specialized Career Paths
Holistic Concern, Including Family

Source: Adapted from W. Ouchi (1981), *Theory Z*, Reading, MA: Addison-Wesley, 58.

Closing Thoughts

The contemporary schools of management thought have had a unifying effect, combining the classicists' technical focus with the behavioralists' social elements. This combination has alerted managers to the interdependence of organizational subsystems and to the importance of integrating them to achieve efficiency and effectiveness. The contemporary era also has sensitized managers to the fact that no one set of principles is appropriate in all situations. Under some circumstances, the classical approach is effective. Under other circumstances, the behavioral model works best. Under still others, managers should integrate and apply ideas from both the classical and behavioral models.

*Management science has
provided a sound framework
for optimizing decisions in
well-structured situations . . . .
Much of managing is an art
of coalition formulation, the
exercise of political influence,
and guiding behavior in
unstructured situations. Management science currently
provides little guidance in
these issues.*

—Mahoney

Management: Art or Science?

The question of whether management is an art or a science has often been asked. The answers are diverse, and debate over the issue periodically surfaces in academic circles. In practice, a manager's job involves both science and art. A *science* is a body of knowledge that has evolved through controlled, system-

In practice, a manager's job involves both science and art. Effective managers expand their knowledge and develop the personal skills and passion necessary to apply their knowledge artfully.

atic investigation. It provides descriptions, explanations, and predictions about the phenomena under investigation. There is a large body of scientific management literature based on such analyses. The *art* in management appears in the application of the knowledge derived by scientific investigation. Science discusses and documents; art creates.

> *Just as artists need to master their crafts, business managers need to perfect their skills in dealing with people and in expressing themselves verbally; just as artists need visions and passion to realize them, managers need imagination and audacity to redesign their organizations; and just as great masters communicate their visions, great leaders inspire those who work for them.*[22]

A body of management knowledge has been developed through systematic and controlled inquiry, but managers who rely only on this knowledge deny the importance of feelings, hunches, intuition, and common sense. Effective managers expand their knowledge and develop the personal skills and passion necessary to apply that knowledge artfully.

Schools of Management Thought in Review

Management theories help managers understand and anticipate organizational events and, thus, allow them to manage more effectively and efficiently. There are several schools of management thought and, therefore, various approaches to the practice of management. Although no one grand theory has emerged, each school offers a distinctly useful perspective.

The classical school included the scientific-management movement and classical organization theory. It emphasized the economic rationality of decisions and the role of economic incentives as primary motivators. Classical theorists, although occasionally paying lip service to the importance of a friendly labor-management climate, tended to focus on the mechanical side of an organization. Workers were treated as nonthinking, nonfeeling robots and were reduced to the role of cogs in the organizational wheel. The classicists felt that their prescriptions for designing and running the organizational machine defined the "one best way" to manage.

The Hawthorne studies provided a transition from classical to behavioral management theories, which emphasized the human side of organizations and the importance of personal and social factors as motivators. The human relations movement saw organizations as social systems and proposed that the way to increase productivity was to satisfy workers. The behavioral scientists saw employee involvement as the key to greater organizational efficiency and effectiveness. Like the classicists, behavioralists believed that their theories provided the "one best way" to manage organizations.

The contemporary school draws from the best of earlier theories. Although some contemporary theories, such as Theory Z, provide "new" ideas, the most important recent advances develop contingency perspectives. Recognizing that organizations are neither mere machines nor pure social systems, contingency theories arising from this system-theory perspective deal with both the technical and the human side of organizations. Managers must recognize the interdependence of these two systems.

Contemporary theories propose that there is no "one best way" to practice management. Instead, managers must develop diagnostic skills to assess each situation, identify the appropriate managerial style for that situation, and be flexible enough to match their behavior to that demanded by the situation. The information they draw on to perform this balancing act is considered the fruits of the science of management. The manner with which they apply this knowledge can be considered an art.

Issues for Review and Discussion

1. Who were the major contributors to the scientific management movement, and what were their respective contributions?
2. Name and discuss Taylor's six prescriptions for effective scientific management.
3. Explain the basic differences between the work of Taylor and his European counterparts, Henri Fayol and Max Weber.
4. What were the Hawthorne studies? What effect did they have on the practice of management?
5. Why do you think contingency theories of management emerged? How do these theories differ from the classical and behavioral schools of management thought?
6. Give an example of a situation involving a human resource department and a marketing department that illustrates the importance of a systems-theory perspective.
7. Identify and discuss four attributes of Theory Z.

Key Terms

classical school
scientific management
classical organization theory
behavioral school
human relations movement
behavioral science movement
Theory X

Theory Y
sociotechnical systems theory
system
systems theory
contingency perspectives
McKinsey 7-S framework
Theory Z

Suggested Readings

Bisesi, M. (1988). A review of *Theory Z: How American business can meet the Japanese challenge.* In Pierce, J. L., and Newstrom, J. W., eds. *The manager's bookshelf: A mosaic of contemporary views.* New York: Harper & Row, 263-67.

Maidique, M. A. (1983). The new management thinkers. *California Management Review,* 26, 151-61.

Miles, R. E. (1975). Managers' theories of management. In Miles, R. E., *Theories of management: Implications for organizational behavior and development.* New York: McGraw-Hill, 31-50.

Robbins, S. P. (February 1977). Reconciling management theory with management practice. *Business Horizons,* 38-47.

Van Auken, P. M., and Ireland, R. D. (1979). An historical review of management philosophy. *Academy of Management Proceedings,* 39, 7-11.

Notes

1. G. D. Babcock (1927), *The Taylor system in Franklin management,* 2nd ed., New York: Engineering Magazine Company, 31.

2. C. Babbage (1832), *On the economy of machinery and manufactures,* London: Charles Knight, 132.

3. F. W. Taylor (1947), *Scientific management,* New York: Harper and Brothers.

4. F. W. Taylor (1912), *The art and science of shoveling,* testimony before a Special Committee of the U.S. House of Representatives.

5. Taylor, 1947.

6. H. Fayol (1949), *General and industrial management,* C. Storrs, trans., London: Sir Isaac Pitman and Sons, Ltd., 19.

7. M. Weber (1922), *The theory of social and economic organization,* A. M. Henderson and T. Parsons, eds. and trans. (1947), New York: Oxford University Press.

8. H. Munsterberg (1913), *Psychology and industrial efficiency,* New York: Arno Press.

9. M. P. Follett (1918), *The new state,* Gloucester, MA: Peter Smith.

10. C. I. Barnard (1938), *The functions of the executive,* Cambridge, MA: Harvard University Press.

11. A. H. Maslow (1957), *Motivation and personality,* New York: Harper & Row.

12. D. M. McGregor (November 1957), The human side of enterprise, *Management Review*, 22-28, 88-92; D. M. McGregor (1960), *The human side of enterprise*, New York: McGraw-Hill.

13. D. M. McGregor (9 April 1957), The human side of enterprise, *Proceedings of the 5th Anniversary Convocation of the School of Industrial Management*, Cambridge, MA: Massachusetts Institute of Technology, 15.

14. C. Argyris (1957), *Personality and organization*, New York: Harper and Brothers.

15. R. Miles (1964), Conflicting elements in managerial ideologies, *Industrial Relations*, 4, 77-91; R. Miles (1975), *Theories of management: Implications for organizational behavior and development*, New York: McGraw-Hill, 42.

16. E. L. Trist (1981), The sociotechnical perspective: The evolution of sociotechnical systems as a conceptual framework and as an action research program, in A. H. Van de Ven and W. F. Joyce, eds., *Perspectives on organization design and behavior*, New York: John Wiley & Sons, 19-75.

17. R. A. Johnson, F. E. Kast, and J. E. Rosenzweig (1963), *The theory and management of systems*, New York: McGraw-Hill.

18. *Ibid.*

19. R. T. Pascale and A. G. Athos (1981), *The theory and management of systems*, New York: McGraw-Hill.

20. Pascale and Athos, 81.

21. W. Ouchi (1981), *Theory Z: How American business can meet the Japanese challenge*, Reading, MA: Addison-Wesley.

22. H. Boettinger (January-February 1975), Is management really an art? *Harvard Business Review*, 54.

A Job Interview with Sterling Manufacturing

By Phil Fisher, University of South Dakota

Clayton Odland sat in disbelief as the personnel manager explained to him, "You see, our experience with young men such as yourself is that you will stay with us only long enough to gain some experience and then leave to go to work for a smaller company."

"How can he say that?" Clayton thought. "I want to work for Sterling. Where did I go wrong?" Shaken by the realization that he was not going to get a job offer, Clayton thought back over the events of the day to try to understand what he had said or done to make the personnel manager decide not to offer him a job.

Clayton's first interview with Sterling Manufacturing had been on the campus of State University, where Clayton was nearing the end of his senior year. Majoring in personnel management and scheduled to graduate with honors, Clayton had been sure that he would have many job opportunities, but the offer to visit a Sterling plant was especially exciting for him. Sterling was one of the largest manufacturers in the world, with plants locating throughout the United States, Canada and Europe. Former Sterling executives served on the Cabinet of the President of the United States. A career with Sterling seemed to offer unlimited possibilities.

Despite Sterling's size and enormous prestige, at the on-campus interview Clayton had felt relaxed and confident. Donald Vodicka, the Sterling manager conducting the interview, was a State University graduate himself and had advanced to a position of considerable responsibility in the twelve years he had been with Sterling. An accounting graduate whose position was in the financial area at Sterling headquarters, he assured Clayton that he could arrange for him to visit one of Sterling's divisions to interview for a position in personnel management.

About two weeks after the interview, Clayton received a letter inviting him to visit a Sterling facility in Michigan. Now, as he sat in a red leather chair in the personnel manager's impressive paneled office, Clayton's mind raced back over the events of the day.

He had arrived at the Sterling building on schedule, traveling by cab from the hotel at which the company had made a reservation for him. The first person he met was Jim Pflanz, who was not much older than Clayton and had been working for Sterling for only a year. He talked about his work for Sterling, which mainly consisted of interviewing applicants for jobs and occasionally traveling to a college campus to interview seniors for management trainee positions. He also outlined Clayton's schedule for the day, which was to consist of a series of interviews with managers within the personnel department; lunch in the executive dining room; and a final interview with Mr. Merrigan, the head of the division's personnel department.

The second person Clayton saw that day was Luis Portillo. Mr. Portillo described the manner in which Sterling prepared its young management trainees for positions of responsibility. Clayton could expect to spend his first four to six years with Sterling in a series of appointments of six months' to two years' duration. He would probably spend some months interviewing job applicants, as had Jim Pflanz. He would probably have an assignment working in industrial relations as the first level of appeal in grievances filed by the union. He would no doubt spend some time learning the details of administering Sterling's pension and health benefits. The details of the company's training program varied somewhat for different people, but it was the company's policy to assure that its managers were well prepared through both experience and training before investing them with substantial authority.

Clayton asked Mr. Portillo about his responsibilities at Sterling. Mr. Portillo replied that he was responsible for reviewing the way departments were organized in the division. Clayton had enjoyed his college course in organization theory and asked about the possibility of a training assignment with Mr. Portillo. Mr. Portillo replied that he often did have a management trainee assigned to him, but as the work was rather complex and required some knowledge of the way in which the company worked, trainees were assigned there only after three or four years of experience.

At the close of Clayton's interview with Mr. Portillo, Jim Pflanz appeared and escorted Clayton to his next stop, which was with Stuart Davis. Mr.

Davis worked in the industrial relations section, which was responsible for administering the labor contract that covered the employees of this division of Sterling. Mr. Davis described the functions of his department and the types of assignments typically filled by management trainees. Although apparently less intellectually challenging than the work of Mr. Portillo's department, the thought of having the opportunity to resolve real conflict gave the industrial relations department a lot of appeal to Clayton.

After Mr. Davis finished describing the industrial relations function, he asked Clayton if he had any questions. Clayton then asked what Sterling did to motivate its employees. At this, Mr. Davis seemed a little annoyed. As if he were explaining something to a child, he leaned forward and said, "Listen, it's very simple. Every job has a standard. If people meet that standard, we leave them alone. When they don't meet the standard, we take disciplinary action." This was not the approach favored by Clayton's professors at State University, but he did not comment.

At the close of their session, Mr. Davis escorted Clayton to the executive dining room, which was on the top floor of the building. He ushered Clayton into a richly appointed small restaurant, where they were joined by Mr. Portillo and three other men, including Richard Merrigan, the head of the personnel function for the division. Mr. Merrigan led the way to a table for six, where he took a seat at

one end and invited Clayton to sit at his right hand. Clayton noted that Jim Pflanz had not joined them but supposed that he had other obligations.

The lunch was a heady experience for Clayton. The surroundings were sumptuous, befitting a corporation of Sterling's reputation, and the lunch was delicious. Two waiters hovered at their table, filling water glasses and coffee cups and attending to every word or gesture from Mr. Merrigan and the others. The conversation centered on labor problems in the division's plant in Great Britain and on Sterling's difficulty in dealing with British labor unions. The Sterling executives included Clayton in the discussion, explaining the differences in labor law between Great Britain and the United States. Clayton commented that it was too bad that relations between the company and its workers were so rigid.

At the close of the meal, Mr. Davis asked Clayton what he thought of the dining room. Clayton expressed his delight at so magnificent a place and Mr. Davis laughed. "Well, if you come to work here, it will be many years before you see the inside of it again." Clayton then understood why Jim Pflanz had not joined them.

After lunch, Clayton had one more interview before meeting with Mr. Merrigan. It was with one of the men who had joined them for lunch, and who, as it turned out, was responsible for administering the division's benefits. The work he described seemed terribly dull, more clerical than managerial, but Clayton could

recognize the necessity to become familiar with it.

The final stop before checking out with Jim Pflanz was his interview with Mr. Merrigan. Despite the prospect of a long and probably often boring training period, Clayton was enthusiastic about the opportunity to someday be a member of the inner circle at this large, powerful company. He expressed that enthusiasm to Mr. Merrigan but immediately saw that the decision had already been made, and there would be no job at Sterling Manufacturing for Clayton Odland.

Questions

1. What school of management thought appears to underlie the management practices at Sterling Manufacturing?
2. How are these assumptions reflected in Sterling practices?
3. What school of management thought does Clayton Odland appear to ascribe to?
4. How did he express these assumptions?
5. What do you think would have happened if Clayton had gone to work for Sterling?

PART 2 *Planning and Decision Making*

Lee Iacocca

Lee Iacocca has been fired as president of the Ford Motor Corporation, but he has also been credited with the turnaround of Chrysler. He has been called a skillful manager and mentioned as a possible presidential candidate. Others have characterized him as lucky and fortuitous. Iacocca has been described as "fast-talking," "straight-shooting," "blunt," "boastful," and "hard-hitting." Who is Lee Iacocca? What kind of manager is he?

Iacocca began working as a mechanical engineer at Ford. After entering sales, he quickly climbed the ladder to become general manager of a Ford division. As "Father of the Mustang," he was promoted to vice-president of the corporate car and truck group. Following accomplishments in the Lincoln-Mercury division and work with the Mark III, he was promoted to the presidency of Ford. Eight tumultuous years later, Iacocca was fired. Shortly thereafter he was brought into the battle-ridden, struggling Chrysler Corporation.

> *The starting point for good management is with the effective use of one's own time.*

Iacocca's management style and philosophy revolve around a number of concepts. The ability to identify, recruit, and surround himself with good people has been a key to Iacocca's success at Chrysler. According to Iacocca, a manager who surrounds him or herself with weak managers will not only have his or her own work to do, but will have to continually check up on the work of others. Hiring good people and delegating authority is critical to effective organizational management. Iacocca

has also seen that teamwork is crucial. As a manager, he sees his role as one of developing teamwork through the use of his own interpersonal skills.

During his years as a serious student active in extracurricular pursuits at Lehigh and Princeton, Iacocca established the foundation of his management philosophy: the effective use of time and communication. Iacocca's philosophy suggests that the starting point for good management is with the effective use of one's own time. Those who are good at managing their time effectively are self-motivated and, therefore, more productive. Through personal time management, people can be accountable to themselves. Self-motivation and personal accountability are important factors of success, especially for those in highly responsible and independent positions of management. Time management can facilitate a results orientation, promote a focus of the achievement of goals, and stimulate organized and creative thinking. Finally, managers serve as leaders and role models for those below them. A manager who uses self-direction and self-control effectively, through example, motivates others to do the same.

Managing others is not accomplished solely through delegation and role modeling. Iacocca is also a charismatic leader. He has brought a vision to Chrysler, and, through his interpersonal style, this vision has found its way to others. He has inspired people and built their confidence in themselves, in their organization, and in the product they produce. His strong sense of patriotism, in an industry embattled by foreign competition, has inspired others. He has been willing to take risks and make personal sacrifices at

Chrysler, all in an effort to make the organization successful.

To manage time well, a manager must be disciplined enough to take time to organize. In Iacocca's life, this consists of taking time each week (Sunday evenings) to write out goals, priorities, and a timetable for the upcoming week. This weekly planning effort is always carried out with a vision toward long-range goals.

Iacocca is convinced that the ability to communicate is everything.

Building on his strong beliefs in time management, goal setting, and evaluation of priorities, Iacocca has implemented a quarterly planning and review process. Each quarter, managers are asked to write down their goals and priorities and their plans for accomplishing them. These documents are shared with superiors to assure that their plans are realistic and consistent with the larger scheme of organizational activities. Iacocca believes that, through the interactive process between superior and subordinate, a team-oriented relationship will develop. Planning documents form the basis for quarterly reviews. According to Iacocca, the theory behind this procedure is that employees who set their own goals are more motivated and consequently more productive. The process makes the employee's activities more purposeful and organized.

Iacocca is convinced that the ability to communicate is everything. Obviously, this includes the ability to speak and to write precisely and clearly. In addition, managers must develop the ability to listen. Listening is especially important when

attempting to solve problems. Good communication shows that management cares and is open to the ideas of others. To a large extent, Iacocca sees communication as a tool through which managers motivate others to act, react, and work as a team pursuing the goals of the organization. Through open communication, people feel part of the team, which in turn prompts people to act more positively.

Iacocca's style includes elements of participative management. He believes in the use of a committee system. He wants every employee to know exactly where he or she fits into the organizational scheme of things. It is important, for example, that the production manager knows what the marketing manager is doing and vice versa. When Iacocca arrived at Chrysler, nobody understood the interaction and dependency among the different functions in the company. He suggested that the people in manufacturing, marketing,

and engineering maintain constant communication with one another. At Chrysler, they barely knew each other existed. Today the importance of dialogue permeates Iacocca's entire organizational system. Quality circles, for example, are used as a way of producing dialogue and involvement among production employees.

The ideal quality of a good manager, according to Iacocca, is decisiveness. A manager needs to gather information, set priorities and timetables, and act decisively. Participative systems help bring information, ideas, and people into the management process so they can act as managers and make effective organizational decisions.

Source: L. Iacocca with W. Novak (1984), *Iacocca: An autobiography*, Toronto: Bantam Books; R. E. Heller (1988), A review of *Iacocca: An autobiography*, in J. L. Pierce and J. W. Newstrom, eds., *The manager's bookshelf: A mosaic of contemporary views*, New York: Harper & Row, 145-49.

5 Planning

Student Learning Objectives

After reading this chapter, you should be able to:

1. Understand the steps of the planning process and a manager's role as a planner.

2. Distinguish among various types of plans.

3. Explain the concept of goals and understand how goals contribute to organizational efficiency and effectiveness.

4. Explain what is meant by multiple plans.

5. Explain a goal hierarchy.

6. Discuss MBO and associate it with one of the major schools of thought about management.

7. Understand why organization members often resist planning and discuss actions that can be taken to overcome this resistance.

8. Discuss the role of a planning specialist.

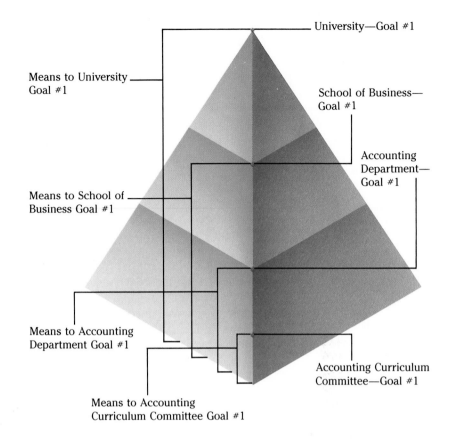

FIGURE 5.2 Network of Organizational Plans

When departmental goals in an organization's technical core are realized, they become the means by which the organization's divisions accomplish their goals. Accomplishing the division's goals, in turn, enables the organization to achieve its overall goals.

University—Goal #1

Means to University Goal #1

School of Business— Goal #1

Accounting Department— Goal #1

Means to School of Business Goal #1

Means to Accounting Department Goal #1

Accounting Curriculum Committee—Goal #1

Means to Accounting Curriculum Committee Goal #1

Another approach to planning is **domain/directional planning,** in which managers develop a course of action that moves an organization toward one identified domain (and, therefore, away from other domains).[11] Within the chosen domain may lie a number of acceptable specific goals. For example, high-school senior John Mathews has decided that he wants to major in a business-related discipline in college. During the next four years he will select a variety of courses from the School of Business curriculum but never specify a major. After conveniently earning credits within this chosen domain, John will accumulate enough credits to graduate with a major in marketing. John has never engaged in goal planning, but in the end he will realize one of many acceptable goals within an accepted domain. Unlike goal planning, which moves an organization toward a specific goal, domain planning simply moves an organization in a particular direction. Situations in which managers are likely to engage in domain planning include:

1. When there is a recognized need for flexibility (for example, when the payoff associated with a set of goals cannot yet be determined, but managers must begin to act)
2. When people cannot agree on goals
3. When an organization's external environment is unstable and highly uncertain
4. When an organization is starting up or is in a transitional period

Occasionally, coupling of domain and goal planning occurs, creating a third approach, called **hybrid planning.** In this approach, managers begin with the more general domain planning and establish their commitment to move in a

FIGURE 5.3 The Dynamics of Hybrid Planning

As the stages progress, the number of goals within the chosen domain decreases. By Stage III, the planners have decided on a single goal and create an action statement that will move them toward that goal.

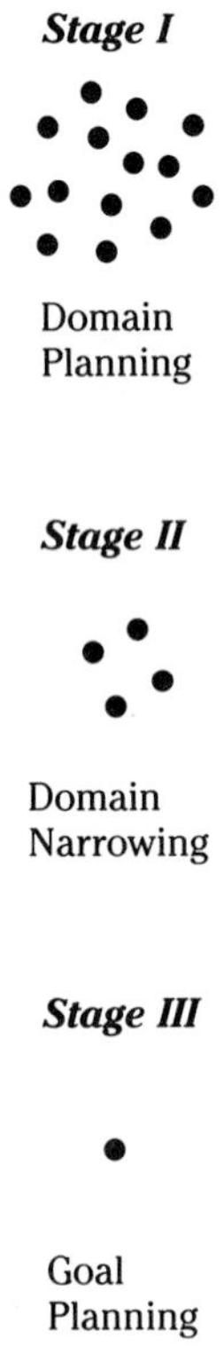

Stage I

Domain
Planning

Stage II

Domain
Narrowing

Stage III

Goal
Planning

particular direction. As time passes, their preferences sharpen, and managers are able to make the transition to goal planning as they identify increasingly specific targets within the selected domain.

Figure 5.3 illustrates the dynamics of hybrid planning. In Stage I, planners pursue domain planning. Their movement from Stage I to Stage II represents an accumulation of knowledge, which narrows the domain. As they learn even more, the planners reduce the domain even further and enter Stage III. At this point, they can select a particular goal and create appropriate action plans.

Some managers achieve success without moving from Stage I. In the mid-1980s, for example, a number of organizations succeeded by being in the right place (the computer domain) at the right time, even though they never developed specific goals. Many of these lucky companies later failed, however, when their environments changed and they did not have specific goals and accompanying action plans to guide their reactions. For example, one of the "hottest" computers on the market for a short while was the Osborne. Osborne just happened to have the right computer at the right time; it fit the market demand. As the market changed, however, Osborne failed to plan appropriately and was not prepared to respond with a new generation of computers. Osborne found itself incapable of meeting market demands and eventually lost its market. Generally, long-term success (organizational performance) is likely to be greater if an organization reaches Stage III and establishes specific goals.

Consequences of Goal, Domain, and Hybrid Planning. Setting goals not only affects performance directly but also encourages managers to plan more extensively. That is, once goals are set, people are likely to think more systematically about how they should proceed to realize these goals.[12] When people have vague goals, as in domain planning, they find it difficult to draw up detailed, systematic action plans and, therefore, are likely to perform less effectively. Research evidence clearly suggests that performance is higher when goal planning has taken place.[13] (See "A Closer Look: Planning" for an example of successful goal planning.)

Although goal planning is generally preferable, there are conditions that call for domain planning. Under such conditions, managers should try to combine goal planning with domain planning. This process may take place at various hierarchical levels. For example, domain planning is likely to prevail at upper levels in an organization, where managers are responsible for dealing with the external environment and task uncertainty is high. Goal planning (that is, formulating goals compatible with the chosen domain) is likely to prevail in the technical core, where there is less uncertainty.

Step Three: Premising

During the third step of the planning process, managers establish the premises, or assumptions, on which their action statements are built. The quality and success of any plan depends on the quality of the assumptions on which it is based. Even one inappropriate assumption can produce a poor or unrealistic decision. Throughout the planning process, assumptions must be brought to the surface, monitored, and updated.[14]

Managers derive information by scanning their organization's internal and external environments (see the discussion in Chapter 8 on organizational and informational scans). They use this information to make assumptions about

Planning: Rubbermaid Bounces Higher Every Year

If you had bought $1000 in Rubbermaid stock early in 1980, your investment would have been worth over $10,000 within seven years. During that period you would have watched your company's sales double and its earnings triple, not bad for a company that makes boring rubber and plastic "stuff" for homes.

How has Rubbermaid achieved such strong performance and why has it been recognized by *Fortune* as one of the country's most admired corporations year after year? Rubbermaid sets specific objectives, listens closely to consumers and retailers, and plans carefully.

"Rubbermaid has a sustained growth record it credits to a strong strategic plan for good times and bad."[1] The company has set and realized annual objectives of 15 percent growth in both sales and earnings per share; however, these objectives have not been realized without planning. Rubbermaid expects new products (those less than five years old) to account for at least 30 percent of sales.

To support its expectations for new product sales, Rubbermaid attempts to develop and release as many as 200 new products each year. Over 90 percent of these are successful. How is such a high hit rate obtained? According to *Fortune*, the company "maintains that enviable record by making a fetish of keeping in touch with customers. For instance, it tests color preferences year round through consumer focus groups in five cities, then confirms the results by quizzing people in shopping malls."[2]

Not all of Rubbermaid's market research is done by market researchers. Executives read customers' letters and woo buyers who visit the company's corporate offices. The executives willingly spend their time at these activities because customers and buyers generate product ideas and provide feedback about existing products. Their ideas are regularly converted into profit-making products, and profits are shared with executives in the form of bonuses.

Why aren't all companies as successful? Many give much of the credit for Rubbermaid's achievements to Stanley Gault, who took over as chairman and chief executive in 1980. Gault's formula for success is to watch the market and work at it twenty-four hours a day.

1. America's most admired corporations (30 January 1989), *Fortune*, 70.
2. Why the bounce at Rubbermaid? (13 April 1987), *Fortune*, 77-78.

the likelihood of future events. In the next phase of the planning process, they will develop action statements based on these assumptions. For example, a manufacturing firm that plans to expand its scale of operations might forecast changes in the prime lending rate. Basing its expansion plan on an assumption that the prime is going to rise in six weeks, the firm might borrow its needed capital within the next two weeks. While the company does not know for sure that the prime is going to rise, its forecast suggests an 80 percent chance that it will. This assumption is built into the organization's expansion plans.

Through forecasting, organizations try to answer such questions as: "What technological advances are on the horizon?" "How will consumers react to a proposed change in our product?" Forecasting may be based either on personal experience and expectation or on systematic, empirical research. In both cases, managers base their forecasts on assumptions. **Premising,** therefore, involves forecasting what is likely to happen inside and outside an organization. When managers make forecasts about environmental events that might affect an organization's movement toward its goals and use these forecasts to generate information for their action statements, they are engaged in the premising activity.

In sum, premising helps managers develop assumptions—premises—about future events. Managers use these premises to develop alternative courses of action.

Step Four: Determining a Course of Action

In the fourth stage of the planning process, managers decide how to move from their current position toward their goal (or into their identified domain). They develop an action statement that details what needs to be done, when, how, and by whom. The way in which an organization gets from its current position to its desired future position is determined by the course of action that managers choose. Choosing a course of action involves: *determining alternatives* by drawing on research, experimentation, and experience; *evaluating alternatives* in light of how well each would help the organization reach its goals or approach its desired domain; and *selecting a course of action* after identifying and carefully considering the merits of each alternative.

Step Five: Formulating Supportive Plans

The planning process seldom stops with the adoption of a general plan. Managers often still need to develop one or more supportive, or derivative, plans to bolster and explain their basic plan. For example, suppose that an organization decides to switch from a five-day, forty-hour workweek to a four-day, forty-hour workweek in an attempt to reduce employee turnover. This major plan would require the creation of a number of supportive plans. Managers might find it necessary, for example, to develop a new plan for personnel policies dealing with the payment of daily overtime. New administrative plans would be needed for scheduling meetings, handling phone calls, and dealing with customers and suppliers. Even a new maintenance arrangement for cleaning the facilities would be required.

Planning and Controlling

After managers have moved through the five steps of the planning process and have drawn up specific plans, they must monitor and maintain their plans. Through the controlling function, managers observe ongoing organizational activity, compare it to the goals formulated during the planning process, and take corrective action if they observe unexpected and unwanted deviations. The planning and controlling activities are closely interrelated. Planning feeds controlling by establishing the standards against which behavior will be compared during the controlling process. Monitoring (controlling) behavior provides managers with input that can help them prepare for upcoming planning periods. (Managerial controlling will be discussed in more detail in Chapter 17.)

Types of Plans

Managers create many different types of plans to guide operations and to monitor and control organizational activities. In this section, several commonly used plans are discussed: hierarchical, frequency-of-use (repetitiveness), time-frame, organizational scope, and contingency plans.

Hierarchical Plans

Each of the three major hierarchical levels in an organization—institutional, managerial, and technical core—is generally associated with a particular type of plan. Plans based on a hierarchical perspective are interdependent.

Strategic plans are generally associated with the institutional level. They define an organization's long-term vision, specify what business the organization is in and hopes to be in, and stipulate how the organization intends to make its vision a reality. To a large extent, strategic plans define how an organization will integrate itself into its task environment. For example, following the Surgeon General's report on the health hazard of cigarette smoking in the 1960s, managers at Philip Morris, R. J. Reynolds, and other tobacco organizations acquired firms in the food, beverage, and petroleum industries as part of a diversification strategy to maintain the survival of their organizations.

Managers use **administrative plans** to allocate organizational resources and to coordinate their organization's internal subdivisions. These plans, therefore, are associated with the organizational responsibility of middle management. For example, the R. J. Reynolds executive group's plans to pioneer the development of smokeless cigarettes required the allocation of massive amounts of money over several years to sponsor that product's development and marketing. The executive group canceled production of the new cigarette after a trial marketing period.

Operating plans cover the day-to-day operations of an organization and, thus, govern the workings of the organization's technical core. The network of organizational plans discussed earlier suggests that an organization's operating plans are nested within and support its subdivisions' administrative plans, which are nested within and support its strategic plans.

Frequency-of-Use Plans

Another category of plans is frequency-of-use, or repetitiveness, plans. Some plans are used repeatedly, and others are used for a single purpose. **Standing plans** are designed to cover issues that managers face repeatedly. For example, managers may be concerned about employees' tardiness, a problem that may occur often in the entire workforce. These managers might decide to

Planning can influence the effectiveness of an entire organization. Managers use administrative plans to allocate organizational resources and to coordinate their organization's internal subdivisions.

develop a standing policy to be implemented automatically each time an employee is late for work. The procedure invoked under such a standing plan is called a **standard operating procedure (SOP).** Some of the most common standing plans are policies, rules, and procedures.

As broad-based statements of understanding or general statements of intent, **policies** establish limits within which decisions are to be made but allow decision makers some discretion in making these decisions. For example, a policy statement pertaining to employees' acceptance of gifts and/or entertainment might be "No employee shall accept favors and/or entertainment from an outside organization that are substantial enough in value to cause undue influence over one's decisions on behalf of the organization." Such a statement provides employees the opportunity to decide what types of gifts and/or entertainment are acceptable. This type of policy may be set forth formally in writing and placed in company manuals and other customary printed guidelines. Other policies may be implied from the spoken statements or actual practices of managers. The top management group from the Radisson Corporation may make a practice of promoting from within merely for convenience, yet this practice may be interpreted as policy and rigorously followed by the managers of its various hotels. Managers, therefore, must exercise caution so that their spoken statements and customary practices are not interpreted as policy if they are not intended as such.

Rules, like policies, are standing plans that guide actions. Rules specify what employees are supposed to do or not do. For example, many organizations have launched no-smoking campaigns and have developed organizational rules to support them. Unlike policies, rules do not permit organization members to exercise individual discretion. Instead, rules specify what actions will be taken (or not taken) and what behavior is allowed or prohibited.

Like rules, **procedures** are standing plans that guide action rather than thinking. Procedures establish customary ways for handling certain activities: hiring an assistant, participating in a pension plan, ordering from a supplier, and the like. The major distinguishing feature of a procedure is that it specifies a chronological series of steps that must be taken to accomplish a particular task. For example, Melissa Gulley, a student seeking admission into a specific degree program at the School of Business and Economics at the University of Minnesota-Duluth, must follow this procedure: (1) she secures candidacy papers from the school's adviser for student affairs, (2) she obtains a current transcript from the registrar, (3) she completes the application-for-candidacy forms, (4) her adviser reviews the application form and indicates approval, (5) the application form is filed with and reviewed by the school's student affairs adviser, and (6) Melissa is informed of her acceptance.

Single-use plans are developed for unique situations or problems and are usually replaced after one use. Managers generally use three types of single-use plans: programs, projects, and budgets. **Programs** are single-use plans that consist of a complex set of policies, rules, procedures, and other elements necessary to carry out a course of action. Many organizations, for example, have programs that train employees to use computers. **Projects** have the same characteristics as programs but are generally narrower in scope, are less complex, and frequently support or complement programs. For example, Employers Insurance of Wausau provides traditional home, auto, and life insurance policies, but its managers have created project teams to investigate nontraditional insurance for such activities as the construction of the San Francisco Bay Area Rapid Transit tunnel or the construction of a nuclear power plant on the San Andreas fault. **Budgets** are single-use plans, expressed in numerical terms, that deal with the allocation and use of organizational activities for a specified accounting period. For example, a budget plan allows the State of Maine's Department of Transportation to spend only a certain amount on office supplies and equipment during the 1990 fiscal year. Sometimes called *numerized programs,* budgets are most commonly expressed in dollar terms but may be expressed as hours worked, as units sold, or in any other measurable unit.

Time-Frame Plans

Some activities that require planning are completed quickly, while others do not see completion for years. **Short-range plans** cover activities that unfold relatively quickly. In most organizations, the short range varies from the next several hours to the next several months. A newspaper may run a three-month campaign to boost circulation; a city government may plan street repairs over a two-week period; a computer software company may run a crash, six-month program to develop a new data base. **Medium-range,** or **intermediate, plans** usually encompass a one-to-five-year period. **Long-range plans** generally are for a period of more than five years (see Figure 5.4)

Short-, medium-, and long-range plans differ in more ways than the amount of time they cover. Typically, the further a plan is projected into the future, the more uncertainty planners encounter. As a consequence, long-range organizational plans are usually less specific than shorter-range plans. Also, long-range plans are usually less formal, less detailed, and more flexible than short-range plans in order to accommodate such uncertainty. Long-range plans also tend to be directional. For example, ten years ago a small manufacturer of tools developed a plan for the eventual use of robotics in manufacturing. Short-range

FIGURE 5.4   *How Long Is a Long-Range Plan?*

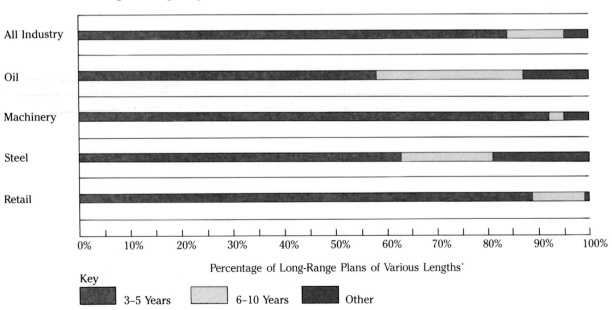

Percentage of Long-Range Plans of Various Lengths*

Key

■ 3–5 Years   □ 6–10 Years   ■ Other

* Long-range is less than three years or more than ten years.

Source: L. W. Rue (December 1973), The how and who of long-range planning, *Business Horizons,* 29.

plans, in contrast, tend to be goal plans. Two years ago, this same manufacturer developed a plan to implement a fully automated and computer-integrated system for manufacturing pliers.

Organizational Scope Plans

Plans vary in scope. Some plans focus on an entire organization. For example, the president of the University of Minnesota advanced a plan to make the university one of the top five in the United States. The strategic plan for realizing this goal focuses on the entire institution (as opposed to a similar plan that might be focused on the health science unit).

Other plans are narrower in scope and concentrate on a subset of organizational activities. For organizations that operate multiple divisions or a number of different businesses, there are **business/divisional-level plans.** Divisional-level plans focus on a division's competitive position in its market and on the ways in which it can complement other divisions. During the late 1980s, for example, Philip Morris used revenues generated by 7Up to promote the growth of Miller High Life beer.

At a still narrower focus are **unit/functional-level plans.** Plans at this level are focused on the day-to-day operation of lower-level organizational units. For example, a marketing manager might create a plan for pricing decisions, and the personnel manager might create a plan for handling the compensation of the organization's top performers.

Divisional-level and unit-level plans are also referred to as **tactical plans.** Tactical plans focus on subsets of an organization's overall programs, activities, and systems. They are designed to help an organization accomplish its strategic plans. Tactical plans developed to improve the functioning of organizations typically include policies, rules, procedures, programs, and budgets.

Contingency Plans

You will recall that the planning process is based on certain premises about what is likely to happen in an organization's environment. **Contingency plans** are created to deal with what might happen if these assumptions turn out to be wrong. Contingency planning, thus, is the development of alternative courses of action to be implemented if events disrupt a planned course of action. A contingency plan allows management to act immediately if an unplanned occurrence, such as a strike, boycott, natural disaster, or major economic shift, render existing plans inoperable or inappropriate. Airlines frequently develop contingency plans, for example, to deal with terrorism and air tragedies. Most contingency plans are never implemented, but when needed, they are of crucial importance. (See "A Closer Look: Contingency Planning.")

Goals

Goals are an inherent part of effective managerial planning. Setting specific and challenging goals contributes more to planning effectiveness and organizational performance than working under "no-goal" or "do-your-best-goal" conditions. There are two types of organizational goals.[15] **Official goals** are

Contingency Planning: Oh, for a Better Plan

It sounded good. Boston legal firm McCabe/Gordon was new and bold. It chose a small number of legal areas in which to concentrate its work. It sought and obtained big, leading-edge cases. In 1986, the firm moved into new headquarters above Boston's harbor. "The offices were stunning, the lawyers among the brightest and best paid and the gleaming computer equipment seemed a beacon for the future."[1]

In May of 1987, McCabe/Gordon fell apart. Gone were the flashy offices. Gone were many leading attorneys who formed splinter groups and left the firm to practice on their own. The rising star had fallen. What went wrong? The firm's failure cannot be tied to a lack of legal competence; these were good attorneys. The business plan crafted for the firm appears at fault. "Their failing was not their specialties of bankruptcy and litigation or their marketing. It was most probably a combination of poor planning and bad luck."[2]

It seems McCabe/Gordon planned to concentrate on the cases of only one or two immense clients at a time. Most of these clients were located far from Boston. Rather than spend time developing a Boston-based group of regular clients, the firm went for flashier, highly publicized cases, wherever they might be found.

A problem with the McCabe/Gordon plan was that the loss of even one of its large clients would deal a destructive blow. This is exactly what happened, when the firm's extreme legal aggressiveness in a case for the billionaire Hunt brothers in Dallas was followed by their dismissal from the case. The firm was left with an insufficient caseload to support its large staff. Without a broad client base, another huge account was needed. Unfortunately for McCabe/Gordon, this time there weren't enough billionaires with legal problems to go around.

According to observers, the McCabe/Gordon plan was bold but too risky. The company was done in by the lack of an adequate contingency plan should a client, such as the Hunts, be lost.

1. Boston's fallen legal star (12 May 1987), *Boston Globe*, 45.
2. *Boston Globe*, 54.

an organization's general aims as expressed in public statements, in its annual report, and in its organizational charter. One official goal of a hospital, for example, might be to "heal the sick." Official goals are usually ambiguous and oriented toward achieving the acceptance of an organization's constituent groups. **Operational goals** reflect managers' specific intentions. These are the concrete goals that organization members are to pursue.[16] For example, an operational goal for a hospital might be to increase the number of patients by 5 percent.

Functions and Dysfunctions

The importance of goals is apparent from the purposes they serve. Successful goals do the following:

1. Guide and direct the efforts of individuals and groups
2. Motivate individuals and groups, thereby affecting their efficiency and effectiveness
3. Influence the nature and content of the planning process
4. Provide a standard by which to judge and control organizational activity

In short, goals help define organizational purpose, motivate accomplishment, and provide a yardstick against which progress can be measured.

A number of dysfunctional consequences are associated with goals:

1. The methods and means created to accomplish organizational goals may themselves become the goal (means-ends inversion).
2. The goals of an organization may be in conflict with the personal goals of employees or society.
3. Ambiguous goals may fail to provide adequate direction.
4. Goals that are too specific may inhibit creativity and innovation.
5. Goals and reward systems are often incompatible. Goals frequently lead people to do things for which rewards are unavailable, whereas rewards encourage people to do other things. For example, a university encourages faculty members to be better teachers but rewards them primarily for good research.[17]

Multiple Goals and the Goal Hierarchy

Peter Drucker, management scholar, consultant, and writer, believes that to achieve organizational success, managers must try to achieve several goals simultaneously.[18] In most organizations, perhaps the most basic goal is to earn profits, followed by organizational growth, and so on (see Figure 5.5). Hewlett-Packard Corporation, for example, has established the seven corporate goals listed in Table 5.1. Sometimes, though, units within organizations may pursue goals that actually conflict with the goals of other internal units. The innovation goals of a research and development department, for example, might conflict

FIGURE 5.5   Stated Corporate Goals

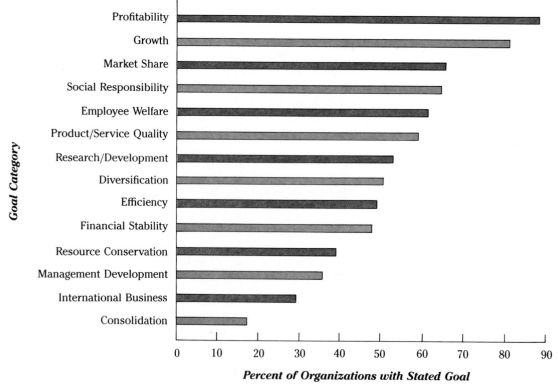

Percent of Organizations with Stated Goal

Source: Data from Y. K. Shetty (1979), New look at corporate goals, *California Management Review*, 22, 72.

with the production department's goal of efficiency.[19] Managers must be able to integrate the network of goals and resolve internal conflicts.

Broad organizational goals (productivity, innovation, profitability, and so forth) are likely to be broken down into subgoals at various levels within an organization. The complexities posed by many interrelated systems of goals and major plans can be illustrated by a **goal hierarchy.**[20] As Figure 5.6 on page 112 shows, an organization sets organizational-level, divisional-level, departmental-level, and job-related goals. Managers must take care that lower-level goals combine to achieve higher-level goals.

Goal Formulation

There are two different views that depict the process by which organizational goals are formulated. The first view focuses on an organization and its external task environment. You will recall from Chapter 2 that an organization's task environment is made up of a wide range of individuals and groups—owners investors, customers, and so on—who have a stake in the organization. Organizational goals emerge as managers try to maintain the delicate balance between their organization's needs and those of its external environment.[21]

The second view concentrates on a set of dynamics within an organization's internal environment. Internally, an organization is made up of many individuals, coalitions, and groups who continually interact to meet their own interests and needs.[22] They bargain, trade, and negotiate and, through these political processes, organizational goals eventually emerge.

Neither the formulation of goals by satisfying the external environment nor by balancing the needs of the members of the internal environment provides long-term organizational success. Goals must fit an organization into its external environment, while satisfying the needs of external constituent groups. In addition, goals must enable an organization's internal components to work in harmony. For example, the goals of its marketing department need to mesh with those of its production and finance departments. The challenge for managers is to balance these forces and preserve the organization.

TABLE 5.1 Hewlett-Packard's Corporate Goals

Profit. To achieve sufficient profit to finance our company growth and to provide the resources we need to achieve our other corporate objectives.

Customers. To provide products and services of the greatest possible value to our customers, thereby gaining and holding their respect and loyalty.

Field of interest. To enter new fields only when the ideas we have, together with our technical, manufacturing, and marketing skills, assure that we can make a needed and profitable contribution to the field.

Growth. To let our growth be limited only by our profits and our ability to develop and produce technical products that satisfy real customer needs.

People. To help our own people share in the company's success, which they make possible: to provide job security based on their performance, to recognize their individual achievements, and to help them gain a sense of satisfaction and accomplishment from their work.

Management. To foster initiative and creativity by allowing the individual great freedom of action in attaining well-defined objectives.

Citizenship. To honor our obligations to society by being an economic, intellectual, and social asset to each nation and each community in which we operate.

"New Look at Corporate Goals" by Y. K. Shetty. © 1979 by the Regents of the University of California. Reprinted from the *California Management Review*, Vol. 22, No. 2 by permission of The Regents.

FIGURE 5.6   Goal Hierarchy

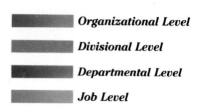

Organizational Level

Divisional Level

Departmental Level

Job Level

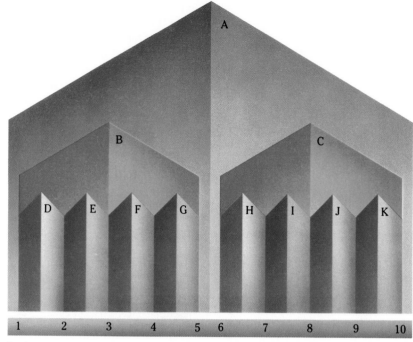

Source: M. D. Richards (1978), *Organizational goal structures*, St. Paul, MN: West, 27.

What Makes Goals Work?

Much is known about the characteristics of effective individual goals (see Chapter 13). Although group and organizational goals have been studied less, it is probably safe to assume that most of the knowledge about individual goals also applies to group and organizational goals; therefore, effective organizational goals should:

1. Be difficult but reachable with effort
2. Be specific and clearly identify what is desired
3. Be accepted by and have the commitment of those who will help achieve the goals
4. Be developed by employees if such participation will improve the quality of the goals and their acceptance
5. Be monitored for progress regularly

MBO: A Special Case

QUALITY CIRCLE MANAGEMENT

Management by Objectives (MBO) is both a philosophy of management and a planning and controlling technique.[23] As a philosophy of management, MBO assumes that people are capable of self-direction and self-control (recall the discussion of Theory Y in Chapter 4). Through employee involvement, organizational performance increases, and workers become more satisfied and committed to further involvement.

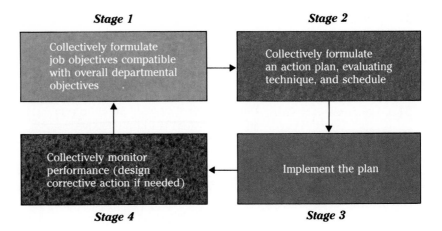

FIGURE 5.7 *The Management by Objectives (MBO) Process*

Stage 1

Collectively formulate job objectives compatible with overall departmental objectives

Stage 2

Collectively formulate an action plan, evaluating technique, and schedule

Stage 3

Implement the plan

Stage 4

Collectively monitor performance (design corrective action if needed)

As a technique, MBO increases employee involvement in planning and controlling activities. Although there are many variations in the practice of MBO, it can be seen as a process through which managers and their subordinates collaborate to identify common goals, to define the results expected from each individual, and to use these measurements to guide the operation of their unit and assess individual contributions.[24] Rather than managers' telling subordinates "These are your goals"—the classical approach—managers and subordinates together decide what subordinates' goals should be. After a set of goals has been established and accepted, employees help develop an action plan for achieving their goals. In the final stage in the MBO process, employees develop control processes, monitor their own performance, and recommend corrections if unplanned deviations occur. At this stage, the entire process begins again. Figure 5.7 depicts the major stages of the MBO process.

Research has clearly documented many instances in which MBO programs have increased organizational effectiveness. Because some managers have failed to design or manage their MBO programs adequately, however, there have been failures. After reviewing 185 studies of MBO programs, one researcher concluded that they are effective under some circumstances, but not all.[25] For example, MBOs tend to be more effective in the short term (less than two years), in the private sector, and in organizations removed from direct contact with customers. For MBO programs to be effective, managers must be philosophically committed to the MBO concept, they must identify the conditions under which they propose to use such programs, and they must evaluate the likelihood of success. Among the factors that affect the success of an MBO program are the following:

- The intensity of upper-level managers' commitment to an MBO system. Half-hearted commitment is associated with a higher failure rate.
- The time element. Is there enough time for employees to learn how to participate in an MBO process—that is, to learn how to set meaningful goals, to develop good action statements, and to develop effective monitoring systems? Is there enough time for employees to learn how to assume responsibility in a new organizational context? Is there enough time for employees and managers to collaborate in a joint planning and controlling process?

- The legitimacy of the system. Is it integrated into an overall philosophy of management, or does it seem to be a gimmick to seduce employees into being more productive?
- The integration of employees' goals. Are goals for each employee integrated well enough into the goals of the larger organizational unit?

Managers must provide an appropriate context for design and maintenance if an MBO system is to be effective.

Formal Organizational Planning in Practice

Studies indicate that, in the 1950s, approximately 8.3 percent of all major American firms (one out of every twelve) employed a full-time long-range planner. By the late 1960s, 83 percent of major American firms used long-range planning. Today it is estimated that nearly all American corporations with sales over $100 million prepare formal long-range plans.[26] Most have formal plans that extend five years into the future, and about 20 percent extend at least ten years.

Encouraging Planning

In a survey of Fortune 500 CEOs . . . , 89 percent agreed that a crisis in business is as inevitable as death and taxes, but fully 50 percent admitted that they or their companies did not have a written crisis-management plan in place.

—Fink

In spite of the advantages to be gained by planning, there is evidence that many managers resist it. Some feel that there is not enough time to plan, or that it is too complicated and costs too much. Others worry about the possible consequences of failing to reach the goals they set. In spite of these and other reasons, resistance to planning can be overcome. Some techniques for encouraging planning include:

- Developing an organizational climate that encourages planning. Top managers should support lower-level managers' planning activities—for example, by providing such resources as personnel, computers, and funds—and should serve as role models through their own planning activities.
- Training people in planning
- Creating a reward system that encourages and supports planning activity and carefully avoids punishment for failure to achieve newly set goals
- Using plans once they are created

Managers can involve subordinate managers in the planning process in an attempt to overcome resistance to planning.

Does Planning Really Pay Off?

Managers of organizations in complex and unstable environments may find it too difficult to develop meaningful plans, yet it is precisely conditions of environmental complexity and instability that produce the greatest need for a good set of organizational plans. In order for managers to invest the time and energy needed to overcome resistance to planning, they must be convinced that planning does, in fact, pay off.

Studies suggest that firms that engage in planning are more financially successful than those that do not.[27] For example, the median return on investment for a five-year period was 17.1 percent for organizations engaged in strategic planning, vs. 5.9 percent for those that did not.[28] Similarly, of seventy large commercial banks, those that had strategic planning systems outperformed those that did not.[29]

Although planning clearly has observable benefits, it can be expensive. The financial commitment can be large for organizations with a formal planning staff. Even so, research suggests that planning is warranted. It is imperative, therefore, that managers develop formal plans.

The Location of the Planning Activity

Classical management thinking advocates a separation of "planning" and "doing." According to this school of thought, managers plan for technical core employees and formulate most of their organization's plans for the upper levels of the organization with little participation from lower-level managers and workers. In contrast, behavioral management theorists suggest involving organization members in drawing up plans that would affect them. Implementation of an MBO program, for example, is one means through which this participative planning can be realized. Researchers at the Tavistock Institute in England have promoted the idea of *self-managed work groups* as a means of expanding the level of employee involvement. According to this plan, work groups assume a major role in planning (as well as in organizing, directing, and controlling) the work assigned to them. Many organizations—for example, Volvo and Motorola—have had successful experiences with employee involvement in the planning and controlling activities.

Many organizations have successfully involved employees in planning and controlling activities.

Planning Specialists

To keep pace with recent increases in organizational complexity, technological sophistication, and environmental uncertainty, many organizations use **planning specialists.** Professional planners work singly or in groups to develop organizational plans and to help managers plan. Boeing, General Electric, and Ford are among the many organizations with professional planning staffs. These specialists may serve as planning advisers to top management or may assist lower-level managers (for example, functional managers) with planning. Planning specialists helped develop United Airlines' crisis management plan.

A planning staff's goals are varied.[30] Its primary responsibility is to assist line managers in developing strategies for achieving organizational objectives. It also should coordinate the complex array of plans created for the various levels within an organization. Finally, a planning staff should provide encouragement, support, and skill for developing formal organizational plans.

Some of the forces that have led organizations to create formal planning departments include the recognition that:

- Planning takes time, and the presence of a planning staff can reduce a manager's workload.
- Highly competitive and rapidly changing environments frequently require an organization to make coordinated and systematic moves quickly. Professional planners develop contingency plans that can be implemented quickly to meet environmental changes.
- In highly centralized organizations, operating units are interdependent, and their planning must be integrated. A planning department can span organizations both horizontally and vertically to create highly integrated planning systems.
- Effective planning often requires more objectivity than employees with a vested interest in a particular set of activities can provide.
- Planning has become so sophisticated that specialists are needed.

Planning in Review

Planning is the process through which managers establish goals and detail the methods by which these goals will be attained. There are five major stages in the planning process. First, an organization establishes its preplanning foundation, which reviews past events and describes the current situation. In the second step, the organization sets forth goals based on the preplanning foundation. In the third step, managers forecast what is likely to happen in the organization's internal and external environments in order to develop alternative courses of action. In the fourth step, managers identify possible courses of action for meeting their objectives, evaluate each alternative, and select a course of action. In the fifth step, planners develop the supportive plans necessary to accomplish the organization's major plan of action. Once implemented, that plan must be monitored and controlled so that it meets the goals established in the second step.

Managers create many types of plans based on hierarchical, frequency-of-use, time-frame, and organizational scope perspectives. Contingency plans to be used in case of unexpected events or wrong assumptions are critical for effective management in highly turbulent environments.

Goal development is an important part of the planning process. Goals developed for employees, for departments, and for an entire organization can greatly enhance organizational effectiveness. Evidence reveals that performance is higher when organizations, as well as individuals, operate under difficult (but attainable), specific goals.

Plans reduce uncertainty and risk, focus attention on goals, and enhance understanding of the external environment. Although most major organizations engage in formal organizational planning, many managers fail to plan appropriately. Lack of time, uncertainty about the future, and fear of failure are among the reasons managers give for their failure to plan. A number of tactics have been developed to encourage managers to plan, and formal planning staff positions have been developed. Although an organization's success is sometimes a question of being in the right place at the right time, sustained success requires careful, systematic planning.

Issues for Review and Discussion

1. Define managerial planning.
2. What is the relationship between planning and decision making?
3. Identify and briefly describe each stage in the planning process.
4. Compare and contrast three different types of planning.
5. What are multiple goals? What is a goal hierarchy? How are these concepts related to one another?
6. Briefly describe the two different views of the goal formulation process and explain how they differ.
7. Describe the MBO process and the philosophy behind it.

Key Terms

planning
goals
action statements
goal planning
domain/directional planning
hybrid planning
premising
strategic plans
administrative plans
operating plans
standing plans
standard operating procedure (SOP)
policies
rules
procedures
single-use plans

programs
projects
budgets
short-range plans
medium-range (intermediate) plans
long-range plans
business/divisional-level plans
unit/functional-level plans
tactical plans
contingency plans
official goals
operational goals
goal hierarchy
Management by Objectives (MBO)
planning specialists

Suggested Readings

Drucker, P. F. (1959). Long-range planning: Challenge to management science. *Management Science*, 5, 238-49.

Fink, S. (1986). *Crisis management: Planning for the inevitable.* New York: American Management Association. For a review, see Markham, S. (1988). In Pierce, J. L., and Newstrom, J. W., eds. *The manager's bookshelf: A mosaic of contemporary views.* New York: Harper & Row, 285-90.

Schnaars, S. P. (1988). *Megamistakes: Forecasting and the myth of rapid technological change.* New York: Free Press.

Notes

1. R. M. Fulmer and T. T. Herbert (1978), Decline and fall of Santa, *Exploring the new management,* 2nd ed., New York: Macmillan, 65-66.
2. G. A. Steiner (1969), *Top management planning,* London: MacMillan, 6, 7.
3. United once more (22 June 1987), *Time,* 46-47.
4. H. Koontz and C. O'Donnell (1972), *Principles of management: An analysis of managerial functions,* New York: McGraw-Hill, 113-14.
5. B. E. Goetz (1949), *Management planning and control,* New York: McGraw-Hill.
6. P. Lorange and R. V. Vancil (1977), *Strategic planning systems,* Englewood Cliffs, NJ: Prentice-Hall; Steiner.
7. K. G. Smith, E. A. Locke, and D. Barry (1986), *Goal setting, planning effectiveness and organizational performance: An experimental simulation,* unpublished manuscript, University of Maryland, College of Business and Management, College Park, Maryland.
8. Koontz and O'Donnell, 124-28.
9. J. F. Clemens and D. F. Mayer (1987), *The classic touch: Lessons in leadership from Homer to Hemingway,* Homewood, IL: Dow Jones-Irwin, 147.
10. Steiner, 7; M. B. McCaskey (1974), A contingency approach to planning: Planning with goals and planning without goals, *Academy of Management Journal,* 17, 281-91.
11. McCaskey.
12. P. C. Earley, P. Wojnarocki, and W. Prest (1987), Task planning and energy expended: An exploration of how goals influence performance, *Journal of Applied Psychology,* 47, 107-14; P. C. Earley and B. Perry (1987), Work plan availability and performance: An assessment of task strategy priming on subsequent task completion, *Organizational Behavior and Human Decision Processes,* 39, 279-302.
13. Smith, et al.
14. R. H. Kilman (1984), *Beyond the quick fix,* San Francisco: Jossey-Bass, 50-51.
15. C. Perrow (1961), The analysis of goals in complex organizations, *American Sociological Review,* 26, 854.
16. P. E. Connor (1980), *Organizations: Theory and design,* Palo Alto, CA: Science Research Associates, 92-96.
17. R. M. Steers (1977), *Organizational effectiveness: A behavioral view,* Santa Monica, CA: Goodyear, 20-23.
18. P. F. Drucker (1954), *The practice of management,* New York: Harper and Brothers.
19. J. Hage (1965), An axiomatic theory of organizations, *Administrative Science Quarterly,* 10, 289-320.
20. M. R. Richards (1978), *Organizational goal structures,* St. Paul, MN: West, 27.
21. J. D. Thompson and W. J. McEwen (1958), Organizational goals and environment, *American Sociological Review,* 23, 23-30.

22. R. M. Cyert and J. G. March (1963), *A behavioral theory of the firm,* Englewood Cliffs, NJ: Prentice-Hall.

23. Drucker; A. P. Raia (1974), *Managing by objectives,* Glenview, IL: Scott, Foresman.

24. G. S. Odiorne (1979), *M. B. O. II,* Belmont, CA: Fearon.

25. J. N. Kondrasuk (1981), Studies in MBO effectiveness, *Academy of Management Review,* 6, 419-30.

26. J. J. Reitz and L. N. Jewell (1985), *Managing,* Glenview, IL: Scott, Foresman, 66.

27. W. Lindsay and L. Rue (1980), Impact of the organization environment on the long-range planning process: A contingency view, *Academy of Management Journal,* 23, 385-404; D. Herold (1972), Long-range planning and organizational performance: A cross-valuation study, *Academy of Management Journal,* 15, 91-102; C. Saunders and F. D. Tuggle (1977), Toward a contingency theory of planning, presented at the 37th Annual Meeting of the Academy of Management, Orlando, FL; S. S. Thune and R. House (1970), Where long-range planning pays off, *Business Horizons,* 13, 81-87.

28. E. H. Bowman (1976), Strategy and the weather, *Sloan Management Review,* 17, 53.

29. D. R. Wood and R. L. LaForge (1979), The impact of comprehensive planning on financial performance, *Academy of Management Journal,* 22, 516-26.

30. Steiner, 117.

Product Development Planning at Display Electronics

By Phil Fisher, University of South Dakota

The Display Electronics Corporation manufactures computer-driven electronic displays. These include such products as athletic scoreboards for college football stadiums; voting displays used by state legislatures; time-and-temperature signs used by banks; and larger displays sold as electronic billboards to coliseums, truck stops, and gambling casinos. In the early 1980s, opportunities for new products using this technology seemed endless.

Display Electronics grew as fast as company managers could develop marketing channels and raise funds to support the manufacture and sales of their new products. Despite this growth, company profits were irregular, and average return on sales was lower than company goals. Dr. Arthur Keene, the company president, became concerned that new product development was being driven more by technological than by economic considerations. Dr. Keene, who has a Ph.D. in electrical engineering, decided to put more emphasis on the profit potential of products at the earliest stage of development.

His first step was to create a marketing committee composed of himself, the vice-president for engineering, the vice-president for sales and two members of his staff, and a representative of the company's advertising agency. The function of this committee was to review all new product development projects twice a month. The project managers, usually

---

September 19, 1986

Product Design Procedure

1. All new product or product enhancement ideas are submitted to the marketing committee for consideration using Display Electronics Form No. 44.

2. Upon preliminary approval by the marketing committee, the idea is submitted to engineering for design feasibility, estimated time and cost to complete the design, and estimated cost of the product. These data are presented to the marketing committee for final approval.

3. Upon final approval by the marketing committee, the development project is funded and scheduled for completion.

4. A project manager is assigned by the Engineering Vice-President to manage each design project. It is his or her responsibility to successfully complete the project on schedule and within budget.

---

electrical engineers, who actually managed the development of new products, met with the committee as their projects were being reviewed. The procedures to be followed by the committee and project managers were outlined in the memorandum by Dr. Keene titled *Product Design Procedure.*

Dr. Keene further outlined the information to be required by the marketing committee for evaluating new product proposals. He did this by setting the requirements for product development requests in the memorandum titled *Product Development Request,* which became Display Electronics Form No. 44.

September 19, 1986

Product Development Request

1. New Product _____   Product Enhancement _____

2. Purpose: (check all appropriate items)
   _____ Reduce manufacturing cost
   _____ Take advantage of new market
   _____ Another product in an existing product line
   _____ Uses existing parts and subassemblies
   _____ Uses existing distribution system
   _____ Improves product reliability
   _____ Other _____

3. Describe the new product idea. Carefully specify all key features.

4. Describe the market for the new product and the proposed method of distribution. Project total market size for the next five years.

5. Estimate the number of units that will be ordered and Display Electronics market share during the first year, the second year, and the third year. State product price at which these order quantities are feasible. State sensitivity of the market to product price. Carefully outline all assumptions made in arriving at your order projections.

6. List and describe all current and potential competitive products. Include company name, product description (brochures and manuals if available), market share, pricing, etc.

7. Describe the proposed marketing strategy for the new product (e.g. top of line, minimum first cost, complete system, etc.).

8. Describe the general manufacturing method and reference to currently used manufacturing methods.

9. Describe any unusual requirements and how these requirements are related to product success (e.g. critical product introduction date, special finish, size or weight, low power, etc.).

10. Additional comments as appropriate.

Questions

1. What type of plans are being outlined in this case?
2. How does the planning process developed at the Display Electronics Corporation relate to the planning process stages outlined in this chapter?
3. Which organization members are most likely to resist this process?
4. Do you see any other problems that might arise from the use of this planning process?

6 Decision Making

Student Learning Objectives

After reading this chapter, you should be able to:

1. Describe the nature of decision making.

2. Explain the types of organizational decisions.

3. Distinguish among choice making, decision making, and problem solving.

4. Understand how individual attributes, such as cognitive style, personality, and motivation, affect decision making.

5. Compare and contrast the rational/economic (classical) and administrative (behavioral) models of decision making.

6. Describe the conditions under which managers should use groups for decision making.

7. Discuss the advantages and disadvantages of group decision making.

8. Identify and discuss the most common problems that managers face when making decisions.

9. Discuss the tactics that managers can use to make their decision making more effective.

The decision makers who launched the space shuttle Challenger *claimed they were unaware of information that might have prevented the explosion that killed seven crew members.*

D uring the late 1980s, the nation's air traffic controllers were on the verge of unionizing. One of their major grievances was that the Federal Aviation Administration (FAA) was making policy decisions about air safety without consulting those who were watching over the nation's airlines. Many claimed, for example, that the number of near collisions was rising dramatically and could be traced directly to these policy decisions.

In 1986, the spacecraft *Challenger* exploded, killing the seven people aboard and significantly setting back the United States space program. Those in control of the final decision to launch the *Challenger* claimed they were not fully aware of lower-level engineers' long-expressed concerns over the booster's "O-rings" and concerns that the temperature on the morning of the launch was too low for safety.

In both of these incidents, the decision makers had insulated themselves from critical information sources. These examples highlight a significant challenge for management: developing effective organizational decision-making and problem-solving systems.

The Nature of Decision Making

Decision making is the lifeblood of any organization and the essence of management.[1] It is not unusual for a manager to face decisions about hiring and firing, product specifications, and return on investment all in the same business day.

Choice Making, Decision Making, and Problem Solving

Although many managers use the terms *choice making, decision making,* and *problem solving* interchangeably, these three activities are different.[2] **Choice making** refers to the narrow set of activities associated with choosing one option from a set of already identified alternatives. Choice making is involved when manager Denise Siefkas selects one of five applicants to hire for a quality-control job opening. **Decision making** is an intermediate-sized set of activities. It begins with problem identification and ends with choice making. Decision making is involved when Denise, faced with a large number of returned products due to defective manufacturing: 1) identifies three possible causes for the defective products, 2) concludes that the best way to deal with this problem is to have a quality-control inspector examine each product, and 3) selects an applicant to be hired for the new quality-control job. **Problem solving** refers to the broad set of activities that involves finding and implementing a course of action to correct an unsatisfactory situation or to capitalize on an opportunity. It includes not only decision making but also implementing, monitoring, and maintaining the decision. Problem solving would be involved if all of the choice-making and decision-making steps were followed and if Denise implemented the chosen course of action and followed up to make certain that the addition of the quality-control person solved the problem of defective products' being delivered to customers.

Many occasions give rise to the need for decisions.[3] First, a current state of affairs may fall short of a goal or an ideal.[4] A publisher, for example, may find that its book sales are not reaching target projections for the current fiscal year. Second, a problem or crisis may arise like that confronting managers of Procter & Gamble when their Rely tampon was accused of causing toxic shock syndrome among users. A third decision occasion may occur when managers want to take advantage of an opportunity. Du Pont, for example, is trying to develop a sucrose polyester, which its researchers discovered accidentally while researching weight gain in premature babies, into a fat substitute similar to the sugar substitute aspartame (NutraSweet). A fourth occasion for making decisions is, of course, to maintain the status quo—to preserve a high sales volume, to maintain suppliers' contentment, and so on. The fifth reason that managers make decisions is proactive. Carrying out their entrepreneurial role, managers seek new opportunities and ventures for their organization. McGraw-Hill's decision to purchase Data Resources was a search for new ventures that would contribute to McGraw-Hill's objective of serving the worldwide need for knowledge. Decision situations need not be limited to one purpose. A hijacking, for example, can present a nation's government with a crisis but, simultaneously, offer the opportunity to forge a closer alliance with another government or to strengthen certain areas of its foreign policy (see Figure 6.1).

Types of Decisions

Every day managers must make many different types of decisions. When should an organization construct a new building? How should a company react to a competitor's price cut? Is it time to develop and market a new product? This section discusses some of the many types of decisions that confront managers.

FIGURE 6.1   Decision Making, Choice Making, and Problem Solving

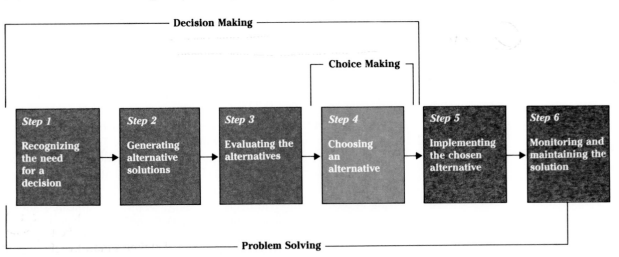

Source: Adapted from G. P. Huber (1980), *Managerial decision making*, Glenview, IL: Scott, Foresman, 8.

Reprinted by permission of UFS, Inc.

Means vs. Ends Decisions. Decisions may be oriented toward the way to achieve goals or toward the goals themselves. **Means decisions** concern procedures or actions undertaken to achieve particular goals—in other words, *how* a goal is to be reached. **Ends decisions** are oriented more specifically toward achieving a goal. For example, in the mid-1980s, IBM's goal (the result of an ends decision) was to reduce the size of its workforce. To achieve this goal, the company decided to offer an early retirement program to encourage employees to leave the IBM workforce voluntarily. The means to reaching the ends goal of a reduced workforce was to encourage early retirement. In practice, means and ends decisions often are linked. Ends decisions are more likely to be successful when they are combined with means decisions. (See Chapters 16 and 17 for more information about means and ends goals.)

Decision Levels. Managers make decisions that affect various levels of organizational responsibility. At the broadest level, **strategic decisions** reflect management's strategies for positioning an organization in its external environment. For example, Brad Rogers, a manufacturer of peat-based briquettes, made a strategic decision to begin marketing his company's products in a new state. At an intermediate level, **managerial,** or **tactical, decisions** specify how an organization intends to integrate its institutional level with its technical core and how it will coordinate work systems within the technical core. Because Brad decided to market the briquettes in other states, for example, he had to decide how to allocate resources for the expanded organizational operations. At a narrower level, **operating decisions** deal with the day-to-day operations of an organization. Brad must coordinate daily activities, such as customer contacts, sales reports, and delivery problems, to handle the expanded operations. Because organizations are dynamic, integrated entities, the effects of decisions at one level are likely to be felt at many other levels. Operating decisions ultimately affect strategic decisions, just as strategic decisions affect decisions made at lower levels.

Programmed vs. Nonprogrammed Decisions. Some decisions cover routine circumstances and can turn into formal company policy. **Programmed decisions** are routines that deal with frequently occurring situations, such as employees' requests for vacations. In programmed decisions, managers make a real decision only once, when the program is created. Subsequently, the program specifies procedures to follow when similar circumstances arise. The creation of these routines results in the formulation of rules, procedures, and policies. Programmed decisions are not necessarily confined to simple issues, such as vacation policies. They also are used to deal with very complex issues, such as the types of tests a doctor needs to conduct before performing major surgery on a patient with diabetes.

Nonprogrammed decisions generally are made in unique or novel situations. Nonprogrammed decisions are necessary when no prior routine or practice exists to guide the decision-making process. For example, when the first Sears employee with acquired immune deficiency syndrome (AIDS) was identified, a decision had to be made about whether the employee could continue to work as long as he was able. The decision required special consideration and could not have been made at that time simply by referring to a policy manual.

FIGURE 6.2   Degree of Certainty and Decision Making

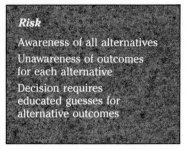

Uncertainty	**Risk**	**Certainty**
Unawareness of all alternatives	Awareness of all alternatives	Awareness of all alternatives
Unawareness of outcomes even for known alternatives	Unawareness of outcomes for each alternative	Awareness of all outcomes related to each alternative
Decision requires creativity and willingness to take risk in the face of uncertainty	Decision requires educated guesses for alternative outcomes	Decision can identify the best solution

Circumstances
Completely
Unknown ◄——————— Level of Certainty ———————► Circumstances
Completely
Known

Conditions of Certainty, Risk, and Uncertainty.   Managerial decisions also can be characterized by the conditions of certainty, risk, and uncertainty under which they are made (see Figure 6.2). When a decision maker is aware of all available alternatives and the factors (outcomes) associated with each, a state of **certainty** exists. Under these conditions, decision making requires the collection and use of accurate, measurable, and reliable information. Under conditions of **risk,** managers are aware of all available alternatives but do not know what will happen if they choose a particular alternative. When decisions are made under risk, managers must collect information that helps them estimate as accurately as possible the probable outcome of each alternative. Under conditions of **uncertainty,** a decision maker is not aware of all possible courses of action. Managers making decisions under high levels of uncertainty should conduct comprehensive and systematic research about their alternatives to help them look at best and worst alternatives.

Decision Making: The Process and Managerial Practices

Ask several managers how they make decisions and solve problems and many will probably say, "I don't know," "There are no rules; you just do it," and "I just do what feels right." In reality, good decision makers, acting either consciously or unconsciously, follow a fairly consistent pattern.

The Process

Earlier in this chapter, a distinction was made among choice making, decision making, and problem solving. This section examines in greater detail the first four steps involved in the decision-making process (review Figure 6.1). Steps 5 and 6, implementing the chosen alternative and monitoring and maintaining the solution, are discussed at some length in Chapters 16, 17, and 18.

Step One: Recognizing the Need for a Decision.   The first step in the decision-making process consists of recognizing that a decision is needed. (Much of the following discussion assumes the existence of a problem, but

②
✗
Correctly identify problem(s)
We often find the correct
solution to the wrong problem

The first step in the decision-making process is to identify the problem and define the situation in detail.

opportunities can also give rise to the need for decision making.) Problem recognition begins when a signal alerts the decision maker that a decision is needed. A tardy employee, slipping sales, or an angry supervisor are signs that something is wrong. Sometimes people identify problems automatically. For example, suppose Tanya discovers that her old stereo is not working. This sends her an obvious signal that she has a problem and that she needs to decide whether to have her stereo fixed or to buy the expensive new system she wants.

After the decision maker has been alerted to the need for a decision, he or she must analyze the situation along the following guidelines:

1. *Differentiate between events and the language used to describe them.* Managers should make sure they are looking at an event and not at how it might be interpreted—perhaps incorrectly—by others. Suppose Eric, a union leader, says that a labor-management conflict stems directly from management's continued exploitation of the workforce. His statement may be more a description of his perception of events than an objective analysis of true causes and effects.

2. *Specify the degree of precision of available information.* Managers must evaluate the degree of certainty that surrounds a problem. If, for example, manager Sarah Morgan complains that subordinates are lazy and sales have dropped, her boss must know whether Sarah's statement is based on actual performance data.

3. *Determine underlying causes* rather than placing blame or giving credit. If sales are low, is it because salespeople are lazy, or has consumer demand for the product decreased?

4. *Look for several causes.* When people identify only a single cause of a problem, they are probably overlooking information that might help them formulate a solution.

5. *Be specific.* Managers should diagnose a problem as explicitly as they can and communicate as clearly as possible what the problem is and why it has arisen.[5]

Identifying, analyzing, and coming to understand a problem can be extremely difficult. Furthermore, problems and crises frequently introduce uncertainty and discomfort. For these reasons, people sometimes avoid or take problem definition for granted. They tend to gloss over the first step in the decision-making process and rush to Step Two.

Step Two: Generating Alternative Solutions. After a problem has been identified, diagnosed, and understood, a manager is ready to move into the second stage of the decision-making process—generating a set of alternative solutions. (Chapter 7, "Tools for Planning and Decision Making," describes a number of useful techniques for identifying decision alternatives.) In developing these solutions, decision makers first must specify the goals they hope to achieve through their decision. Are they trying to reduce costs, improve product quality, or increase sales? Once they have determined their goals, they can search for alternative means of reaching them.

Alternative solutions generally fall into two categories: existing solutions and custom solutions. **Existing solutions** are alternatives that have been used (or at least considered) by other decision makers in similar situations. For example, many organizations purchase programs—compensation systems, for

instance—that have worked well in other organizations. Existing solutions are frequently applied, with or without modification, to new situations. Existing solutions sometimes prove an easy way out—perhaps *too* easy a way out. In failing to consider fresh information, managers might define problems poorly and identify solutions inadequately.

Custom solutions are developed specifically for a current situation. It is at this stage that creativity can be introduced into the decision-making process through modifying existing alternatives, combining alternatives, or developing new alternatives.

Step Three: Evaluating Alternatives. Once managers have derived a list of alternative solutions, they must evaluate how well they expect each alternative to meet the specified goals and objectives. For example, how well would each alternative reduce costs, improve quality, or increase sales? Research, experimentation, and previous experience are common tools for this stage of decision making. Next, managers need to focus on each alternative's strengths and weaknesses, pros and cons, and probable consequences. In addition, it is important to evaluate the feasibility of each alternative.

Step Three of the decision-making process usually eliminates many of the alternatives on the managers' list. Some are too expensive. Others offer too much risk or uncertainty. Modifying the O-rings on a space shuttle's engine just before lift-off, for example, would be too risky an alternative if the procedure had never been tested. Still other alternatives simply are not feasible, such as those that are illegal or unethical.

Step Four: Choosing an Alternative. If several alternatives remain under consideration after the evaluation process, managers make judgments and choices. Some quantitative and qualitative tools to help managers select an alternative are presented in Chapter 7, but it is the managers themselves who ultimately must decide. There are three decision criteria: optimizing, maximizing, and satisficing. If managers **optimize,** they try to find the best possible decision. When managers **maximize,** they make a decision that meets the maximum number of criteria. To **satisfice,** managers try only to find the first satisfactory solution. The decision-making process can change substantially, depending on which approach a manager chooses. It usually takes more time, for example, to maximize than to satisfice, and still more time to optimize (if this is even possible).

Alternative Approaches: The Need for Flexibility. The variety of situations confronting managers calls for various approaches to decision making.[6] The *computational* approach is a rational, mechanical process applicable when parties agree on the desired outcomes and when a well-developed body of knowledge exists to instruct an organization on how to proceed. Relevant information, including facts regarding the problem and desired outcomes, is turned over to an expert. This expert, who may be a manager, staff manager, or subordinate, interprets the existing knowledge, makes the decision, and directs others on how to respond. When Ford Motor Company detects a safety problem with one of its cars, for example, engineers are the experts who develop a solution.

The *judgmental* decision-making approach is used when managers agree on their goals but do not know how to achieve them. In this situation, experts share their knowledge, ideas, and opinions with the managers, and both groups use creativity to develop solutions. The judgment resulting from such interaction is used to arrive at a decision. For example, when Chrysler's managers noted a drop in station wagon sales in the late 1970s, they sought a wide range of input and generated many alternative solutions. The judgmental solution was to develop a minivan.

In the *compromise* decision-making approach, there is no agreement on goals. Individuals or groups who disagree about preferred outcomes bargain but limit the number of negotiators to one representative for each interest group. The ultimate aim is to reach a compromise for which each group member feels ownership, such as when departments agree on a release date for a new product.

The *inspirational* decision-making approach is characterized by extremely high levels of uncertainty, because there is no agreement on either goals or methods. This type of decision situation calls for a commitment to resolving the impasse, for continued dialogue, and for the open and complete sharing of information. It also calls for creativity and intuition. The structured techniques discussed in Chapter 7 can aid inspirational decision making.

Managers need to be flexible in their approaches to decision making. Under some conditions, they need to be able to make decisions and direct others. At other times, they need to allow other experts to make decisions and provide necessary direction. Still other conditions call for any one of a number of group decision processes.

Managerial Practices

Although the decision-making models described to this point show how decisions should be made, many managers do not actually follow these models. Many behaviors are unconscious acts driven by habit. Many people have not learned when it pays to be systematic in decision making. There are times when a habitual or intuitive response is not necessarily bad; a manager who has internalized the goals of an organization and has developed a good sense of the management process may be able to handle uncomplicated problems quite easily from instinct. In this approach lies part of the art of management. It is important for managers to be able to diagnose the situations that they face, to judge the importance of a decision, and to determine whether to decide systematically or instinctively. (See "A Closer Look: Intuition in Management.")

Intuition in Management: If It Feels Good, Do It

Decisions should be based on the best information available coupled with a decision maker's best judgment and intuition. "What frightens me about business schools is that they train their students to sound wonderful. But it's necessary to find out if there's judgment behind their language."[1] This concern, expressed by Robert Bernstein, chairperson of Random House publishers, preceded his argument that the best managers must be more than "business-school-glib, number-crunching, fast-trackers."[2]

What is the all-too-often missing element? *Intuition:* the ability to identify good decisions through gut feelings. Although management is a science and sophisticated databases can provide the information people need to make decisions, these scientific techniques cannot replace a manager's intuition in making final decisions. Managers should take advantage of the scientific techniques available, but, as Roger Straus, president of Farrar, Straus & Giroux, says, it is a shame if the availability of scientific methods leads to "shunting intuition aside and going by the numbers."[3]

So important is the role of intuition in management that Roy Rowan, writer and editor at *Fortune* magazine, has written a book entitled *The Intuitive Manager.*[4] In his book, Rowan argues that, even though logic and analysis are important for effective management, "[T]he last step to success frequently requires a daring intuitive leap."[5] In today's business world, decisions rarely can be made with certainty. There is seldom one correct answer to a problem. The best managers recognize this and are willing to use intuition as an important decision-making tool. Eden Collinsworth, publisher of Arbor House, enthusiastically agrees with Rowan that the most effective managers are not afraid to combine the intuitive art of management with science: "People may think of me as decisive and businesslike. I think of myself as artistic."[6]

1. The intuition factor (25 April 1986), *Publishers Weekly,* 29.
2. *Ibid.*
3. *Publishers Weekly,* 30.
4. R. Rowan (1986), *The intuitive manager,* Boston: Little, Brown.
5. *Publishers Weekly,* 30.
6. *Ibid.*

Despite the fact that a systematic approach to decision making has been proven effective, studies show that managers seldom progress smoothly through the stages.[7] The process is marked by frequent interruptions, delays, and periods of acceleration. Failures due to undesired results and poor planning frequently force a return to earlier stages of the process.

Individual Decision Making

Four general models of the individual as a decision maker have been identified (see Table 6.1).[8] The first of these, the *irrational person model,* suggests that many decisions stem from a variety of fears, anxieties, and drives.[9] The second model, the *creative/self-actualizing model,* assumes that individuals pursue total development of their inner selves rather than look for an external goal, such as profit seeking.[10] Contemporary managers, however, deal mostly with the last two models: the *classical* model and the *behavioral* model.

TABLE 6.1   Four Decision-Making Models

The Irrational Person	The Creative/Self-actualizing Person
Has a variety of fears, anxieties, and drives	Pursues total development of the inner self
Decisions are driven by the unconscious motives underlying these fears and anxieties.	Decisions are driven by desire to develop the self even at the expense of external factors.

The Rational/Economic Person	The Administrative Person
Is rational and deals with objective facts	Is aware of only certain alternatives
Is economically motivated	Is limited by restricted cognitive capacity
Decisions are driven by objective rationality and a search for the best possible alternative.	Decisions are driven by a desire to identify and select the first acceptable alternative.

A Classical (Rational/Economic) Decision-Making Model

Classical, or rational/economic, decision-making models were most popular during the early part of this century. They portray decision makers as rational in behavior, as dealing with objective and verifiable facts, and as economically motivated. Decision makers are supposed to be completely informed, infinitely sensitive, and, therefore, able to make decisions under conditions of **objective rationality.** By knowing all possible alternatives and their probable consequences, decision makers rationally select the "one best" alternative. This classical decision-making model discounts as unnecessary the effects of the attitudes, emotions, or personal preferences of the decision maker.

A Behavioral (Administrative) Decision-Making Model

Whereas the classical model argues that decision makers are aware of all possible alternatives, the behavioral, or administrative, decision-making theory proposes that this is seldom the case and that it is unrealistic to think otherwise. According to this model, decision makers cannot possibly be aware of all the consequences for each alternative or their probability of occurring. Behavioral theory suggests that most decision makers actually choose the first satisfactory solution they identify. That is, they satisfice.

According to Nobel-Prize winner Herbert Simon's administrative model of decision making, people operate in the realm of **bounded rationality.**[11] They try to behave rationally within the limits of their information-processing capabilities and within the context of their attitudes and emotions. They engage in restricted searches for information; have limited information-processing capabilities; rely on familiar sources of information; and, as a result, construct simplified models of reality on which to base their decisions. At best, they satisfice in their decision-making behaviors.

Individual Differences in Decision Making

Some people make decisions quickly, others slowly. Some people consider a large amount of information before reaching a decision, others a small amount. Although it is not fully understood why people behave differently when making decisions, cognitive and personality attributes appear to account for a number of these individual differences.

Cognitive Attributes.   An individual's cognitive attributes affect the *judgmental* aspects of decision making. Relevant cognitive processes include intelligence, learning, remembering, and thinking. They affect problem recognition, comprehension, and diagnosis; the storage, retrieval, and assimilation of information for the development of alternative solutions; and the ability to store, retrieve, and process information for the evaluation of alternatives. Differences in intelligence, for example, mean that some people can process only relatively small amounts of information before becoming overloaded and, thus, tend to base their decisions on relatively small amounts of specific information.

Personality Attributes.   Personality and motivational attributes tend to affect decision-making *style*. Those with a high propensity toward risk tend to make rapid decisions because they process less information and spend less time evaluating it before making a decision. People with dogmatic personalities have fixed, narrow perspectives on life and, thus, often consider only the small set of alternatives that fits their existing view of the world. Individuals with calm, reflective personalities lean toward long-term planning and decision making. Those who are uncomfortable accepting uncertainty (a personality characteristic called *tolerance for ambiguity*) tend to be problem avoiders. People with intermediate levels of tolerance for ambiguity tend to be problem solvers; they anticipate difficulties and deal with them as they arise. People possessing a high tolerance for ambiguity tend to be problem seekers; they go out of their way to find potential opportunities and develop decisions to capitalize on them.

Group Decision Making

Spotted on an old Volkswagen minibus in New Orleans was a bumper sticker that read: *GROUPS DO IT BETTER!!!* Many believe that two heads are better than one, that people involved in decision making feel a sense of ownership in the decision, and that group decision making is safer because everyone shares in the risk. Organizational committees and task forces often do make excellent decisions, but they can make unwise and ill-fated decisions as well. Why the mixed results?

Group decision making has both assets and liabilities.[12] A thorough understanding of them can help you, as a manager, determine when to encourage or to discourage group decision making and how to improve the quality of group decisions (see Table 6.2). Perhaps that bumper sticker in New Orleans should have read: *GROUPS DO IT BETTER: SOMETIMES!*

TABLE 6.2 *Assets and Liabilities of Group Decision Making*

Assets	Liabilities
Greater knowledge and information	Negative social pressure
More perspectives on issues	Premature decisions
More alternatives identified	Individual domination
Great acceptance of decisions	Interference of personal goals
Better problem comprehension	

Assets or Liabilities
Disagreements can generate ideas or cause hard feelings.
Diverse interests can broaden perspectives or cause conflict.
Increased risk taking can be beneficial or costly.
Increased time spent can improve decisions or waste time.

Source: N. R. F. Maier (1970), Assets and liabilities in group problem solving: The need for an integrative function, in N. R. F. Maier, ed., *Problem solving and creativity: In individuals and groups*, Belmont, CA: Brooks/Cole, 431-44.

Assets and Liabilities of Group Decision Making

Sheer size has its advantages. Large groups possess increased knowledge and information, multiple outlooks and opinions, and a greater number of potential solutions. On the other hand, "too many cooks can spoil the soup." Social pressure may cause a group to focus more on reaching agreement than on making a good decision, resulting in a premature or inappropriate decision. In addition, although a group's primary goal should be to make a quality decision, members may "take sides" and devote too much energy to winning and too little to making a good decision. Sometimes, one individual can overwhelm other group members, limiting the group's usefulness and causing resentment.

Several group factors can serve either as assets or liabilities, depending on the situation. Disagreement among members can provide the spark needed to generate new ideas, but it can also lead to hard feelings and threaten the group's existence. Members' diverse, conflicting interests can provide a variety of perspectives on the situation under discussion, but they can also produce conflict that threatens the group and, therefore, the quality of its decisions. Groups also are prone to making decisions that are riskier than the decisions made by individuals, which may be either desirable (as in many entrepreneurial decisions) or disastrous. Finally, groups often require more time than do individuals to come to a final decision, which uses more resources and slows the decision process. This tendency can benefit an organization, however, if it means that the group thoroughly understands the decision situation and follows a good decision-making model.

The arguments for and against group decision making suggest that choosing this approach requires careful thought. Managers must evaluate whether, for a particular situation, the assets outweigh the liabilities.

Group Properties

Several group characteristics that can influence the decision-making process are discussed in this section.

Group Size.   The size of a group can substantially influence its activity and effectiveness.[13] For example, a group of five to seven members is usually viewed as the optimal size. When a group is larger, members' satisfaction declines, as do both their ability to achieve a consensus and the participation level of individual members.

Spatial Arrangements.   People sitting at a table tend to talk to those next to them and to those directly across from them, but people who sit at the opposite corners of a long, narrow table have difficulty speaking to one another. This restriction in the flow of information frequently splinters the group into cliques, and groups with cliques operate differently from those without them. Cliques may have conflicts with one another, possibly becoming competitive and unable to achieve consensus or arrive at a decision.

Group Homogeneity/Heterogeneity.   Group members can be similar or different in such characteristics as education, work experience, aptitudes, and attitudes. A homogeneous group encourages the building of good interpersonal relationships, which facilitates communication, coordination, and greater chances for reaching consensus. Heterogeneous groups have one major advantage, however, in that members possess a greater variety of information and ideas. Decision quality can increase as a result of such diversity.[14]

Group Cohesiveness.   Cohesiveness is the psychological glue that holds a group together (see Chapter 12). In a cohesive group, members are loyal to the group, tend to identify with each other, and want to work for group goals.[15] Noncohesive groups struggle more with communication, power relationships, and getting to know and understand one another; however, the presence of conflict and low levels of pressure toward conformity may improve the quality of a noncohesive group's decisions.

Group Phenomena

Managers should be aware of several interesting phenomena that affect group decision making.

Social Presence.   You have probably noticed that you often feel and behave differently when there are other people around than you do when you are alone. This difference is due to the psychological and physical arousal caused by the presence of others. Have you ever been in a play or given a talk in front of a large audience? Did your heart race? Did your palms sweat? Did you feel extremely alert? These are all reactions to the presence of others.

Under some conditions, decision making is enhanced by the presence of others (**social facilitation**). Under other conditions, it is impaired (**social impairment**). The difference depends largely on the nature of the task, on the level of arousal produced by the presence of others, and on an individual's tolerance for high levels of arousal. For easy tasks, when people are dealing with familiar things, their performance improves, even with very high levels of

Group size and spatial arrangements influence employee interaction and, thus, overall group effectiveness.

Groupthink was at work in the 1970s when U.S. President Richard Nixon and his advisers decided to launch a cover-up of the Watergate break-in. As a result, Nixon's presidency faltered and failed.

arousal. For difficult or new tasks, however, performance begins to suffer at moderate or higher levels of arousal.

If decision making involves simple, routine, or familiar situations, managers should permit individuals to work in the presence of others; the resulting arousal will help increase their performance levels. If decision making deals with complex, difficult, and unfamiliar situations, managers should urge workers to perform the activity privately, because the presence of others probably will impair effective decision making due to overarousal.

Group Shift. Social psychologists have documented that group decisions often are riskier than those made by individual members.[16] Although **cautious shifts** occur, it is far more common to find **risky shifts** in group decision making. Several factors explain why group shifts occur.

First, through group discussion and the sharing of ideas and information, *familiarization* with the decision situation increases. As a result, group members pursue alternatives that they previously considered too risky. Second, *diffusion of responsibility* often occurs in groups. When individuals feel less personal responsibility for their group's decision, they are more willing to accept decisions that are riskier than they would have made individually. Third, most groups have at least one member willing to make riskier decisions than are other group members. These high risk takers also tend to be *risk persuaders,* who convince others to take greater risk. Finally, both risky and cautious shifts can be caused by *cultural values.* As group members strive for approval and status in the eyes of others, they try to behave in a socially approved fashion. When the cultural values of the group (or organization) favor risk, individuals perceive this and take greater risks. Similarly, when group values favor caution, members become more cautious.

Groupthink. **Groupthink** is a phenomenon that can cause highly capable groups to make terrible decisions.[17] According to Irving Janis of Yale University, groupthink is based on a group's desire to obtain consensus at almost any cost. The urge for unanimity can be so strong that dissent is almost eliminated. In the 1970s, for example, President Richard Nixon and his advisers decided to launch a cover-up of the Watergate break-in. Despite clear evidence to the contrary, they refused to accept that the cover-up would fail. Group members rallied behind Nixon's claims that what they had done was for the good of the country, and they chose not to raise individual concerns in group meetings. Any objections were quickly quashed. As a result, Nixon's presidency faltered and failed. In short, groupthink leads to bad—sometimes catastrophic—decisions. (Chapter 12 discusses groupthink more thoroughly and explores a variety of remedies.)

When Should Groups Make Decisions?

 Individuals and groups respond in terms of the context they experience; the major task of top management is to shape that context so it will get the decisions it wants.

—Perrow

In deciding whether to assign decision responsibilities to individuals or to groups, managers should carefully consider the following:

1. If a problem is moderately difficult, groups have a clear advantage over an individual.
2. Problems that can be divided lend themselves to group problem solving.
3. Groups with five to seven members are the most desirable, and a range of four to ten members is acceptable.

Failure Through Isolation: The Challenger Disaster

Before January 28, 1986, twenty-four space shuttle flights had been successfully completed. There hadn't been so much as a single injury to any crew member. On that cold day at Cape Canaveral, final preparations were made for the twenty-fifth lift-off. On board were seven men and women who placed their lives in the hands of NASA decision makers. At 11:38 A.M. eastern standard time, *Challenger* was launched into the bright Florida sky. Seventy-four seconds later, the shuttle exploded, and all seven aboard were killed.

What caused the fatal accident of the spaceship *Challenger?* Did the mechanical failure of an O-ring on one of the solid fuel booster rockets cost the lives of seven people? Yes and no. It is true that the explosion occurred when the O-ring failed, but most agree that the *reason* the accident occurred was that NASA made a faulty decision to launch under adverse conditions:

[I]t has become clear that the disaster represents a managerial failure. . . . [T]he tragically flawed decision to launch was no fluke. It was the almost predictable result of a pat-tern of mismanagement that has spread throughout the agency. . . . The people at the top ended up isolated, a grimly instructive example of a problem that can overtake any organization, governmental or corporate.[1]

Before the launch of *Challenger*, engineers at Morton Thiokol, the company that made the solid fuel booster, analyzed the weather conditions and unanimously concluded that a launch would not be safe: the O-rings might fail. Repeatedly challenged by Lawrence Mulloy, chief of the solid rocket booster program at the Marshall Space Flight Center, Thiokol engineers repeated their concerns and stood their ground. Finally, Mulloy went over their heads and convinced Joe Kilminster, Thiokol's vice-president for space booster programs to sign a launch go-ahead. The rest is history.

How could such a poor decision have been made? NASA was aware that the failure of a primary O-ring probably would cause disaster. Engineers with presumably the greatest technical knowledge believed that the rings might fail under the prevailing weather conditions. Apparently, Mulloy changed his decision strategy. He required "proof of probable failure" to abort a launch rather than "evidence of probable success" to initiate it. In addition, the top decision makers who ultimately decided to launch were isolated from the lower-level engineers and their concerns. The NASA decision makers had been lulled into complacency by their twenty-four successes.

NASA's decision-making process was flawed: "This was an absolutely preventable thing. This accident never should have happened. Never."[2] "NASA's highest decision makers had either not heard about the contractors' fears or ignored them. So *Challenger* blasted into the Florida sky on its brief, one-way flight to oblivion."[3]

1. NASA's challenge: Ending isolation at the top (12 May 1986), *Fortune*, 26.
2. A serious deficiency (10 March 1986), *Time*, 38.
3. *Time*, 42.

---

4. Groups made up of individuals who differ in experience, interest, and personal characteristics tend to be more productive than groups of similar individuals.
5. Partly structured interaction improves group functioning.
6. Extreme status differences between group members—for example, president and secretary together—can inhibit group processes.
7. Groups that are too cohesive can bog down in groupthink and become overly concerned with presenting a united front to outsiders. Moderately cohesive groups with a good communication system and an appropriate set of norms can function effectively.[18]

In sum, managers should decide whether to use groups or individuals in the decision-making process based on the characteristics of the situation.

Problems in the Decision-Making Process

Two of the most common problems facing decision makers are the tendencies to misunderstand the situation and to rush the decision-making process.

Misunderstanding a Situation

To understand a decision occasion, a manager must coordinate and organize a great deal of relevant information. If this information is incomplete or organized poorly, the manager may easily misconstrue the situation. Consider the case of Bill Bass, a manager inspecting information about product return levels. If Bill sees information on returns organized by day of shipment and by quality-control inspector, he might conclude that the problem is linked to two particular quality-control inspectors who seem to have a heavy work load on Mondays. If the information is organized by customer, Bill will see that most of the returns are from one large customer whose regular standing order is always filled from the Monday morning production run.

Although it can be relatively straightforward to organize *concrete* information about costs, schedules, and units produced, the sheer quantity of such information can make it extremely difficult to make sense of it all. Giving meaning to *abstract* information is even more difficult. As a consequence, a manager's perceptions of and reactions to situations are not always accurate.

Managers also may misinterpret a decision situation if they mistake the symptoms of a problem for the problem itself. If Diane Gray, a manager experiencing high absenteeism from her subordinates, tries to control absenteeism—for example, by docking wages for unapproved absences—she may be able to force people to appear for work. If, however, high absenteeism is only a symptom of an underlying problem, such as job dissatisfaction, Diane's solution does not address the true problem. It may, therefore, reappear in another fashion, such as a work slowdown.

Rushing the Decision-Making Process

For many reasons, perhaps to save money or to avoid the uncertainty associated with problems, both individual and group decision makers often tend to rush the decision-making process. The results are inadequately defined problems, limited searches for and development of possible solutions, and inadequately evaluated courses of action.

For example, a company may discover that sales in the previous quarter were lower than desired. In a rush to attack the problem, the company defines the situation as a problem of too few sales representatives. If managers had cast the problem in a different light, such as "sales volume is $500,000, but we targeted it at $750,000," the problem would be defined as $250,000 of unmet targeted sales. Using that definition, managers can generate more possible solutions—hiring additional sales representatives, increasing or changing advertising, or marketing the product in different outlets. With more possible solutions, the managers are closer to solving their real problem.

Because many decision makers dislike uncertainty, they tend to overlook unusual alternatives in favor of readily available and previously used solutions. In their haste, decision makers often overgeneralize and assume that solutions from vaguely similar situations are appropriate for new situations. Decision makers also develop a similar familiarity with certain sources of information and alternatives. Although this approach is handy and fast, these comfortable alternatives limit the range of choices.

Improving Decision Making

Managers can take a number of steps to improve the decision-making process. They can use heterogeneous groups, for example, to expand the information base, to define problems thoroughly, to encourage searches for alternatives, and to evaluate alternatives. Managers can also appoint a devil's advocate, a person whose role is to examine and possibly challenge alternatives and tentative decisions. A devil's advocate helps a group focus on the possibly undesirable consequences of some alternatives or the possibly desirable consequences of others.

Another step managers can take to improve the decision-making process is to develop an internal organizational environment that makes it safe for members to pursue new ideas. Giving employees the freedom to try new things, as well as to fail or to be wrong occasionally, stimulates the search for solutions and for new ways of doing things. One organization that systematically encourages many of its employees to devote a portion of their workday to search for opportunities is 3M (Minnesota Mining and Manufacturing). One result of this policy was the development by a 3M employee of "Post-it" notes, a phenomenally successful product that fulfilled a previously unmet need.

Training organization members in systematic decision making, providing them with the tools to collect the necessary information, and allowing them adequate time to make decisions can go a long way toward improving organizational decision making. Supporting these actions with reward systems that emphasize careful, effective decision making will reinforce their importance.

Decision Making in Review

 Decision making is the process through which a course of action is chosen. In a systematic decision-making model, managers proceed through four steps: 1) recognizing that a decision is needed and defining its nature, 2) generating a list of possible solutions, 3) evaluating these alternatives, and 4) choosing one or more solutions. Problem solving involves these steps, plus a fifth and a sixth step that implement the chosen decision and monitor and maintain its effectiveness. Unfortunately, many managers do not follow a systematic decision model. Furthermore, there are many differences from person to person in how decisions are made. Knowledge of these differences can help managers select decision makers wisely and improve their effectiveness.

Organizations tend to rely on groups when faced with decision occasions, but there are both assets and liabilities to group decision making, as well as factors that can go either way. Managers who are aware of these can determine whether to use a group and how to improve its effectiveness.

Common decision-making problems include misunderstanding a situation and rushing decisions. Managers can counteract these problems by providing access to needed information, by training individuals and groups in systematic decision making, by providing adequate time for decision making, and by offering rewards that encourage effective decision making.

Issues for Review and Discussion

1. Briefly define decision making.
2. Identify and explain three types of decisions.
3. Identify and discuss the differences among the three types of conditions under which decision making takes place.
4. How are decision making and problem solving related?
5. Discuss the influence of personality and cognitive factors on individual decision making.
6. Identify the assets and liabilities associated with group decision making.
7. Identify three group properties that influence decision making. Briefly discuss the role of each.
8. Define and explain groupthink.
9. Identify one major problem associated with decision making. How can this problem be managed so that decision making is more effective?

Key Terms

choice making
decision making
problem solving
means decisions
ends decisions
strategic decisions
managerial (tactical) decisions
operating decisions
programmed decisions
nonprogrammed decisions
certainty
risk
uncertainty

existing solutions
custom solutions
optimize
maximize
satisfice
objective rationality
bounded rationality
social facilitation
social impairment
cautious shifts
risky shifts
groupthink

Suggested Readings

Cotton, J. L., Vollrath, D. A., Froggatt, K. L., Lengnick-Hall, M. L., and Jennings, K. R. (1988). Employee participation: Diverse forms and different outcomes. *Academy of Management Review,* 13, 8-22.

Ford, C. H. (1977). The "elite" decision makers: What makes them tick. *Human Resource Management,* 16, 14-20.

Janis, I. L. (1988). *Crucial decisions: Leadership in policy making and crisis management.* New York: Free Press.

Janis, I. L. (1983). Groupthink. In Blumberg, H. H., Hare, A., Kent, V., and Davies, M., eds. *Small groups and social interaction,* vol. 2. New York: John Wiley & Sons, 39-46.

Lindblom, C. E. (1959). The science of muddling through. *Public Administration Review,* 19, 79-88.

Mintzberg, H., Raisinghani, D., and Theoret, A. (1976). The structure of "unstructured" decision processes. *Administrative Science Quarterly,* 21, 246-75.

Quinn, R. E. (1988). *Beyond rational management.* San Francisco: Jossey-Bass.

Schweiger, D. M., Sandberg, W. R., and Ragan, J. W. (1986). Group approaches for improving strategic decision making: A comparative analysis of dialectical inquiry, devil's advocacy, and consensus. *Academy of Management Journal,* 29, 51-71.

Simon, H. (March 1965). Administrative decision making. *Public Administrative Review,* 31-37.

Notes

1. B. M. Bass (1983), *Organizational decision making,* Homewood, IL: R. D. Irwin, 2; H. A. Simon (1960), *The new science of management decision,* Englewood Cliffs, NJ: Prentice-Hall.

2. G. P. Huber (1980), *Managerial decision making,* Glenview, IL: Scott, Foresman, 8-9.

3. Simon.

4. P. L. Koopman, J. W. Broekhuysen, and M. Meijn (1984), Complex decision making at the organizational level, in P. J. Drenth, H. Thierry, P. J. Wilems, and C. J. DeWolff, eds., *Handbook of work and organizational psychology,* New York: John Wiley & Sons, 831-54.

5. A. Elbing (1978), *Behavioral decisions in organizations,* Glenview, IL: Scott, Foresman, 74-83.

6. J. D. Thompson and A. Tudin (1959), Strategies, structures and processes of organizational decisions, in J. D. Thompson, P. B. Hammond, R. W. Hawkes, B. H. Junker, and A. Tudin, eds., *Comparative studies in administration,* Pittsburgh, PA: University of Pittsburgh Press, 195-216.

7. H. Mintzberg, D. Raisinghani, and A. Theoret (1976), The structure of "unstructured" decision processes, *Administrative Science Quarterly,* 21, 246-75.

8. M. J. Driver (1979), Individual decision making and creativity, in S. Kerr, ed., *Organizational behavior,* Columbus, OH: Grid Publishing, 59-91.

9. S. Freud (1920), *A general introduction to psychoanalysis,* New York: Pocket Books.

10. C. Argyris (1957), *Personality and organization,* New York: Harper & Row; C. G. Jung (1957), *The undiscovered self,* Boston: Little, Brown; A. H. Maslow (1962), *Toward a psychology of being,* Princeton: Van Nostrand; D. McGregor (1960), *The human side of enterprise,* New York: McGraw-Hill.

11. H. A. Simon (1976), *Administrative behavior,* New York: Free Press.

12. N. R. F. Maier (1970), Assets and liabilities in group problem solving: The need for an integrative function, in N. R. F. Maier, ed., *Problem solving and creativity: In individuals and groups,* Belmont, CA: Brooks/Cole, 431-44.

13. L. L. Cummings, G. P. Huber, and E. Arendt (1974), Effects of size and spatial arrangements on group decision making, *Academy of Management Journal,* 17, 460-75.

14. J. P. Wanous and M. A. Youtz (1986), Solutions diversity and the quality of group decisions, *Academy of Management Journal,* 29, 149-59.

15. L. N. Jewell and H. J. Reitz (1981), *Group effectiveness in organizations,* Glenview, IL: Scott, Foresman, 5-6.

16. R. D. Clark III, W. H. Crockett, and R. L. Archer (1971), Risk-as-value hypothesis: The relationship between perception of self-others, and the risky shift, *Journal of Personality and Social Psychology,* 20, 425-29; J. H. Davis, P. R. Laughlin, and S. S. Komorita (1976), The social psychology of small groups: Cooperative and mixed-motive interaction, *Annual Review of Psychology,* 27, 501-41; L. B. Rosenfeld (1973), *Human interaction in the small group setting,* Columbus, OH: Charles E. Merrill.

17. I. L. Janis (1971), Groupthink, *Psychology Today,* 5, 43ff; I. L. Janis (1982), *Groupthink: Psychological studies of policy decisions,* 2nd ed., Boston: Houghton Mifflin.

18. H. J. Reitz and L. N. Jewell (1985), *Managing,* Glenview, IL: Scott, Foresman.

AgBanCorporation

By Lowell Bourne, Eastern
Illinois University

Ken Ormiston, a successful businessman in Heartland, Iowa, had been a Director of AgBanCorporation since 1980. As he studied his briefing book for the directors' April 1986 meeting, he realized that the normally perfunctory vote to declare the 28-cents-per-share quarterly dividend would not be routine. In fact, Mr. Ormiston saw this as one of the most crucial votes he had cast during his tenure on the Board of Directors.

AgBanCorporation, headquartered in Heartland, Iowa, was a multibank holding company with twelve affiliate banks. Total consolidated assets amounted to just slightly more than $900 million. Ten of the affiliates with combined assets of $600 million were located in small farming communities along Iowa's southern border. The others were located in Heartland— a city of over 150,000 people with a diverse industrial base—and its suburbs.

Throughout the 1970s, AgBanCorporation's earnings and assets grew at 12 percent per year. Although many observers considered AgBanCorporation's management team to be one of the best in the Midwest, the firm's success during this period was largely due to the prosperity of its customers, especially farmers and those closely allied with agriculture. This period was characterized by strong grain prices, good growing conditions in AgBanCorporation's service area, and a general feeling of prosperity as agricultural land prices rose about 14 percent per year.

Unlike several agricultural lenders, AgBanCorporation maintained stringent lending standards during the 1970s and carefully secured its agricultural loans with ample collateral, usually land and/or major pieces of farm equipment. For example, a farmer needing $50,000 to plant crops in the spring was required to provide collateral valued at $75,000 to secure the loan. Furthermore, the bank required land buyers to have a 40 percent down payment.

Although these lending standards appeared tight at the time, they were insufficient to insulate the bank from the disaster which befell its borrowers during the early 1980s. The early 1980s were not good years for agriculture in the United States. Other countries were becoming increasingly aggressive competitors, limiting the export opportunities available to U.S. farmers, and the strong dollar caused U.S. grain to be priced out of many foreign markets. Consequently, grain prices were low throughout the period. Low grain prices coupled with extraordinarily high interest rates forced the price of agricultural land to reverse its upward trend and to begin a seemingly endless downward slide.

The farmers in AgBanCorporation's service area would have had difficulty enough coping with these problems, but their situation was exacerbated by five consecutive years of well-below-average rainfall. Their crop production was far below normal in three of those years and almost nonexistent in two others. As a consequence, many of AgBanCorporation's loans to farmers, agricultural suppliers, and even area merchants became problems for both the borrower and the lender. AgBanCorporation's income statements, shown in Figure 6A, indicate the impact of these loans on the firm's profitability.

The first quarter of 1986 was a particularly bad one from the standpoint of earnings. Many banks, including AgBanCorporation, undertook reviews of their agricultural loan portfolios and concluded that many loans were uncollectible and several others were

FIGURE 6A AgBanCorporation Comparative Income Statements (in 000's)

	1985	1984	1983	1982	1981
Interest Income	$93,899	$81,115	$72,372	$66,061	$52,929
Interest Expense	64,405	55,732	50,535	46,509	37,328
Net Interest Income	29,494	25,732	21,837	19,552	15,601
Provision for Loan Losses	7,391	4,910	2,168	2,116	1,242
Income After Provision for Losses	22,103	20,473	19,669	17,436	14,359
Other Income	8,174	5,947	4,045	3,629	2,931
Other Expense	27,033	23,845	17,954	15,859	11,839
Pretax Net Income	3,244	2,575	5,760	5,206	5,451
Tax Expense (Benefit)	(1,000)	(2,377)	48	20	1,028
After-Tax Net Income	$4,244	$4,952	$5,712	$5,186	$4,423

highly questionable. In most instances, the borrowers no longer had the capacity to repay their loans, and the value of the collateral had fallen to the point where it was insufficient to cover the loan. AgBanCorporation's review resulted in a 6.3-million-dollar provision for loan losses in the quarter to offset the large scale write-offs of agricultural loans and to strengthen the loan loss reserve. AgBanCorporation's first quarter 1986 financial statements were contained in Mr. Ormiston's briefing book and are shown in Figure 6B. After review by the Board of Directors, they were to be released to the public.

AgBanCorporation's Board of Directors meets quarterly. Standing items of business for each meeting are review of the financial statements for the quarter just concluded, review of the financial forecast for the next four quarters, dividend action, and approval of the press release containing the quarterly financial statements and the dividend action.

Two days prior to the meeting, each director receives a briefing book containing fairly detailed information concerning the meeting's agenda. In addition to including several routine items for the Board's consideration, the briefing book for the April meeting contained the material shown in Figures 6B through 6E concerning the standing agenda items.

Questions

1. Since Chairman Mayvis has no reservations about declaring a dividend, why do you suppose Mr. Ormiston sees this as such a crucial vote?

2. Do you believe Mr. Ormiston should vote "for" or "against" declaring the regular quarterly dividend? Explain your reasoning.

3. Why is it likely that some members of the board will vote for a different decision than they would choose if they were to make a decision alone?

4. What changes, if any, should be made in the press release prior to its being made public?

FIGURE 6B AgBanCorporation
Income Statement for the First
Quarter, 1986 (in 000's)

Interest Income	$22,365
Interest Expense	15,214
Net Interest Income	7,151
Provision for Loan Losses	6,318
Income After Provision for Losses	833
Other Income	5,046
Other Expense	7,641
Pretax Net Loss	(1,762)
Tax Expense	309
After-Tax Net Loss	$(2,071)

FIGURE 6C Memorandum for Your Eyes Only

To: The Directors of AgBanCorporation
From: Bill Golladay, Controller
Subject: Earnings Forecast
Date: April 1986

My staff has prepared the following forecast of AgBanCorporation's after-tax net income during each of the next four quarters.

Period	Amount (in 000's)
2Q86	$100
3Q86	200
4Q86	200
1Q87	350

As usual, this forecast is the output of our own econometric model. Input data consists of national, regional, and local data as well as the firm's internal plans. We are 95 percent confident that 2Q86's actual net income will be within 7 percent of the forecast. The margin of error is 16 percent in the other forecasts.

After-tax net income will be depressed in each of these quarters due to anticipated loan losses of approximately $1 million per quarter. These write-offs will have a direct impact on earnings because of the desire to maintain the allowance for losses at its present level. We have very few unrealized gains in the securities portfolio, so earnings will not benefit to the previous extent from taking these gains.

FIGURE 6D   *Memorandum for Your Eyes Only*

To: The Directors of AgBanCorporation
From: Bob Mayvis, Chairman and CEO
Subject: Recommended Dividend Action
Date: April 1986

Despite the $2 million loss suffered by AgBanCorporation during the first quarter, I strongly recommend the declaration of a regular dividend in the amount of $.28 per share payable May 15, 1986, to common stockholders of record May 1, 1986. A dividend of $.28 per share has been declared and paid during each of the past sixteen quarters. A cash disbursement of $504,000 would result.

Maintenance of the dividend is important, in my opinion, for three reasons. First, the declaration of the regular dividend in the face of the loss is tangible evidence of your confidence in AgBanCorporation's financial health. Secondly, many of our stockholders count on our dividend for at least a portion of their living expenses. Inasmuch as many of these people have suffered a financial hardship from the area's agricultural problems, I see no reason to compound their plight by reducing or eliminating the dividend as long as the firm has the ability to declare it. Finally, maintenance of the dividend will provide some measure of protection against what I fear may be a precipitous drop in the price of our stock once the loss is announced. A substantial decline in the stock price would make it much less expensive for a "corporate raider" to acquire an influential position in our stock and, ultimately, rob us of our independence. Our stock is currently trading at $21 per share, or 69 percent of book value, whereas the stocks of our peers sell for slight premiums to book value. I fear this discrepancy may draw unwanted attention to us. We are somewhat vulnerable to a takeover because some of our stockholders, particularly those who joined us as a result of our merger with the suburban banks, feel uncomfortable with our exposure to the agricultural sector. They may be motivated sellers if the dividend is not maintained.

As you may remember, our 13 percent note held by the P_____ Insurance Company contains a covenant prohibiting the declaration of dividends whenever our cumulative net income for the prior four quarters falls below $1 million. AgBanCorporation's net income for the four quarters ending with 1Q86 exceeds this amount; however, if the 2Q86 forecast by Bill's staff is anywhere near correct, and I fear it is, our net income for the four quarters then ending will not reach that minimum required by the covenant. I have no reason to believe that P_____ will, even temporarily, waive the covenant.

FIGURE 6E   *Proposed Press Release*

FOR IMMEDIATE RELEASE

Heartland, IA—Today, AgBanCorporation reported a net loss of $2,071,000 for the first quarter of 1986. Chairman Bob Mayvis reported that the loss was caused by a substantial increase in the provision for loan losses resulting from an extensive review of the firm's ag-related loans. Net income is expected to be depressed until the agricultural sector improves. The Board of Directors declared a $.28 per share dividend payable May 15, 1986, to common stockholders of record May 1, 1986.

7

Tools for Planning and Decision Making

Quantitative Tools

Qualitative Tools

Tools for Planning and Decision Making in Review

Student Learning Objectives

After reading this chapter, you should be able to:

1. Understand why managers need quantitative planning and decision-making tools.

2. Describe the types of quantitative planning and decision-making tools managers need.

3. Identify and explain some quantitative planning and decision-making tools available to managers.

4. Understand why managers need qualitative planning and decision-making tools.

5. Identify and explain some of the qualitative planning and decision-making tools available.

6. Determine when it is appropriate to use each qualitative planning and decision-making tool.

7. Explain the difference between quantitative and qualitative planning and decision-making tools and understand why it is important for managers to balance the use of each type.

You are probably convinced by now that you must be able to plan and make decisions effectively to be a good manager. Simply knowing this, however, is not enough to make you a good manager, any more than it is enough to know you must be able to work with wood and nails to be a good carpenter. You must have access to and know how to use a good set of tools to be a carpenter or a manager.

Consider this chapter your planning and decision-making "toolbox," in which you will find substantial help for planning and decision making. Some of these tools are **quantitative tools** that provide a way to examine, measure, and express information in numbers. Typically, these tools rely on mathematical and statistical models, and many require sophisticated computer analyses.

Your toolbox also contains a number of **qualitative tools** designed for collecting and processing ideas, opinions, and judgments. Think of these as thought-processing procedures. They identify whether planning and decision making should be conducted by individuals or by groups and then offer structure to guide these activities.

Quantitative Tools

Quantitative decision-making tools are a significant aspect of the *science* of management. These models typically use *objective measures* to quantify management information in numeric terms. By manipulating numbers, a manager can ask a sophisticated "what-if" question and look at a mathematical or statistical model for the answer rather than putting the organization through an actual trial-and-error situation. Many of these procedures have been particularly useful to managers of production and operations (see Chapter 21). A break-even model, for example, can estimate what would happen to an organization's profits if it closed one of its four plants, dropped one of its three product lines, and added a third shift of workers at the remaining plant. The same model could also predict the effects on profits if production were to be increased by 15 percent or 25 percent.

As you read, the precision of the models may seem like the perfect answer to all planning and decision-making problems. It is true that, using quantitative tools, managers can anticipate the probable outcomes for various alternatives and plan accordingly. It is important to note, however, that the effectiveness of the models depends on the quality of the assumptions on which they are based. In other words, a poor mathematical model of reality gives very precise—but very inaccurate—estimates. Managers have to capitalize on their intuition and personal skills—the *art* of managing—as well as on the precision of mathematical models.

Quantitative tools can save time and reduce errors that may occur as a result of purely subjective decisions.

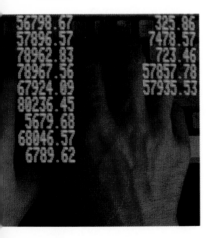

Inventory Plans and Decisions

Cindy Mertes is the owner of Progressive Video Images (PVI). Her company offers consumers a number of services related to home videotape systems. One such service is converting home movies into videotapes. PVI also copies photographs and slides onto videotape and adds music and titles to produce a high-quality product.

Cindy Mertes has to decide how many blank VHS tapes to request in her next tape order. She expects to use a total of 10,000 VHS tapes during the next twelve months, and each tape costs her $4. Her standard weekly order is for slightly fewer than 200 tapes. Because she occasionally has a very busy week and runs short on tapes, Cindy has considered placing a larger order. To buy more tapes, however, she might have to borrow money to pay for them, to insure the larger inventory against loss, and to rent additional storage space.

With all of these considerations, Cindy is having a difficult time deciding how many tapes to order. To help her make the decision, she investigated the various costs associated with ordering and maintaining inventory. The following are some of the facts that she turned up:

1. PVI uses 10,000 VHS tapes per year.
2. Each tape costs $4 to purchase.
3. The administrative costs of placing and receiving an order (including payment for the merchandise and clerical, accounting, and stocking costs) average about $100 per order.
4. The cost of keeping tapes in inventory is about 12.5 percent of the value of the tape inventory per year, including the cost of insurance, rent, and interest on loans to purchase extra (stored) tapes.

Cindy can answer her inventory problem by using a quantitative tool such as **economic order quantity (EOQ),** a mathematical model for identifying the amount of inventory to order. To use EOQ, managers must know their inventory use (*IU*), product cost (*PC*), cost of procuring inventory (*PI*), and annual inventory carrying costs (*CC*) to solve the following equation:

$$EOQ = \sqrt{\frac{2 \times IU \times PI}{PC \times CC}}$$

To determine the best inventory order for PVI, Cindy uses the information that she has uncovered:

Inventory annual use (*IU*) = 10,000 units
Procuring inventory cost (*PI*) = $100
Product cost (*PC*)   = $4
Carrying costs (*CC*)   = 12.5 percent

and plugs it into the EOQ formula:

$$EOQ = \sqrt{\frac{2 \times 10,000 \times \$100}{\$4.00 \times .125}} = 2000$$

As the equation shows, the best number of tapes for PVI to order is 2000. The EOQ is a simple model, and its advantages are obvious. Cindy should remember, however, not to become too dependent on the EOQ model (or any other model, for that matter). If reality differs from Cindy's assumptions, she may find herself with a bad solution. For example, Cindy could lose considerable money and competitiveness if the price of tapes drops right after she orders 2000 tapes.

Resource Allocation: Linear Programming

With **linear programming (LP),** another quantitative model, managers not only can control inventory but can also identify the appropriate quantity of product to manufacture. They can decide how many employees to hire, allocate advertising dollars, and plan any other task that involves minimizing an objective (for example, material waste or labor cost) or maximizing an objective (profit). LP helps managers calculate the best combination of resources and activities, and Cindy Mertes hopes it will help her solve a problem at PVI.

During the past six months, most of PVI's business has come from two of the company's services: converting movies to videotapes and custom editing customers' tapes. Unfortunately, the employees who perform these two services are competing for equipment and other resources.

Figure 7.1 illustrates the processes and resources involved in producing PVI's two competing services. Table 7.1 lists some of the facts that Cindy identified by researching this problem. The movie department staff is currently converting forty-four hours of movies a day. In doing so, they are using the facilities of the movie department forty-four hours a day and need forty-four hours of audio department time. The video department staff is producing six hours of custom editing a day. To do so, they are using video department facilities eighteen hours a day and need six hours of audio department time. The present total demand for audio department facilities (44 + 6 = 50) has exceeded the total capacity of the audio department and has led to the need to contract for audio work at another studio at $150 an hour.

FIGURE 7.1   Resource Usage at PVI

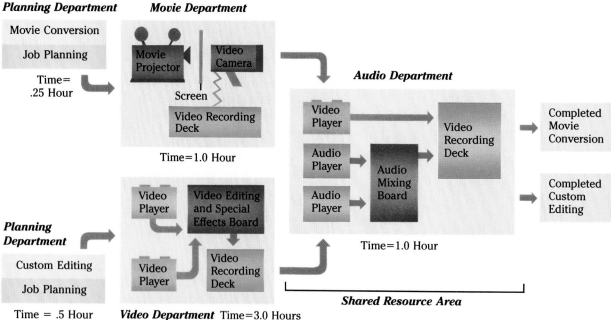

Note: All times shown are those required to prepare a one-hour-long completed product.

TABLE 7.1 *Production and Revenue Data for Conversions and Editing*

| Department | Number of Hours Required per Hour of Completed Product | | Capacity per Day (in Hours)* |
	Movie Conversions (c)	Custom Editing (e)	
Planning (P)	.25	.50	16
Movie (M)	1.0	0.0	48
Video (V)	0.0	3.0	24
Audio (A)	1.0	1.0	48
Profit margin	$40	$150	

*Planning capacity based on hours worked by the two people who do planning. Video department capacity based on around-the-clock use of one available video room. Movie and audio department capacities based on around-the-clock use of two available rooms each.

The following is a list of current daily profits and contracting costs for PVI:

1. Movie conversion profits (44 units/day @ $40) = $1760
2. Custom editing (6 units/day @ $150)   =   900
3. Audio contracting costs (2 hours/day @ −$150) = − 300
    Total Current Daily Profits $2360

Linear programming will help Cindy determine if she can maximize total profits and reduce conflict through the best combination of movie conversion and custom editing. Cindy will solve the following equation by using LP:

$$\text{PROFIT}_{max} = \$40X_c + \$150X_e$$

where
X_c = Units of movie conversions to be produced
X_e = Units of custom editing to be produced

Cindy is aware of several constraints as she tries to maximize profits. One is the capacity of her audio department, which has sixteen hours of planning time available per day. The movie department has two staffs, each of which is available for twenty-four hours a day (three people each working eight-hour days). The video department has one staff available for twenty-four hours a day. The audio department has two staffs, each of which is available for twenty-four hours a day. In LP, these constraints define "constraint equations" and can be obtained by using the information in Table 7.1:

$$.25c + .50e \leq 16.0 \text{ (available planning department time)}$$
$$1.0c + 0.0e \leq 48.0 \text{ (available movie department time)}$$
$$0.0c + 3.0e \leq 24.0 \text{ (available video department time)}$$
$$1.0c + 1.0e \leq 48.0 \text{ (available audio department time)}$$

By solving simultaneous linear equations with a computer program, Cindy determined that PVI should produce forty units a day of movie conversions and eight units a day of custom editing. (It is beyond the scope of this book to fully discuss simultaneous linear equations. In fact, computers can help you solve equations far more complex than those contained in this example.) This solution not only maximizes profits, it also eliminates the need for PVI to contract out audio work. Furthermore, it will significantly reduce the conflict between the video and movie staffs. When Cindy places these numbers into the first equation, she finds that her daily profits will be $2800:

$$\text{PROFIT}_{max} = (\$40 \times 40) + (\$150 \times 8) = \$2800/\text{day}$$

This figure represents an additional $440 a day of profits, a 19 percent increase that will amount to additional profits of more than $100,000 a year.

Under this solution, both the video and audio departments will be operating at full capacity. The planning department will have two hours of excess capacity. Finally, the movie department will have a full eight hours a day of excess capacity. To Cindy, it sounds almost too good to be true. Many managers have a tendency to look at the precise mathematical results of these solutions and to assume that they provide a totally accurate reflection of reality. As you know, however, a mathematical solution is only as good as the assumptions on which it is based. If Cindy's estimates (shown in Table 7.1) are wrong, her solution is wrong. She also has to make sure not to let a computer program inhibit her creativity.

Scheduling and Sequencing

How many lines do you wait in during a typical week? Meg Malde-Arnosti of St. Paul, Minnesota, listed some of her waiting times during one week:

Line	Waiting Time (Minutes)
Parking lot checkout	7
Fast food counter	4
Airport ticket counter	29
Taxi stand	12
Hotel check-in	15
Gas station	6
Grocery store checkout	19
Football stadium entrance	14
Football stadium rest room	13
Bank teller	6
Physician's office	27

If this week is typical for Meg, she is spending over 130 hours a year waiting in line—the equivalent of over 16 workdays. At some point, she may give up on the gas station line and go to a less busy gas station. Perhaps next time she will avoid the grocery store that kept her waiting 19 minutes for her to give *them* her money. Are the businesses involved so shortsighted that they cannot staff adequately to reduce people's waiting times?

Queuing Models. Most organizations would agree that, ideally, customers should not have to stand in long lines, but adding staff to avoid these lines costs money. **Queuing models** (a *queue* is a line) can help managers identify the best number of waiting lines. These models balance an organization's costs of having lines against what it costs to lose customers or their goodwill.

Greg's Wash and Buff uses a state-of-the-art brushless car wash system. Greg's washes a large number of cars and usually has reasonable waiting

When managers use PERT or CPM, they construct a network that shows the flow of work that must be accomplished to complete a project.

times. Greg's also offers a hand-applied hard wax for $39.95. Although demand has been strong for the waxing service, Greg's has only one employee who waxes cars, and most customers have been forced to wait in long lines for their wax jobs to be completed.

Recently, fewer customers have been asking for wax jobs, so Greg's asked consultant Donald Cole to determine whether the company should hire an additional waxer. Donald conducted an analysis for both a one- and two-person waxing staff, estimating such factors as the amount of time it takes to wax a car, how often customers request wax jobs, and the cost of wages for waxers. He also estimated the cost of customer dissatisfaction, lost goodwill, and lost business to be about $10 for each hour that a customer spends waiting in line for a wax job. Using his estimates and a computer queuing program, Donald found that, even though a second waxer would spend a lot of time doing nothing, a two-person waxing operation would substantially reduce waiting times for wax jobs and enhance Greg's profitability by $43 a day.

PERT and CPM. While queuing models deal specifically with waiting time, *program evaluation and review technique (PERT)* and the closely related *critical path method (CPM)* can be used to schedule and coordinate any project that can be broken down into a series of interdependent tasks or activities.

PERT and CPM provide estimates of expected completion time for an entire project. They can also provide detailed information for each activity, including the earliest or latest start time and the earliest or latest finish time. To use these quantitative tools, managers construct a network that depicts the flow of work that must be accomplished to complete a project. The network is made up of paths connecting the project's events and activities. All but one of the paths contain activities that can experience some delays before they jeopardize the overall completion of the project. The one path containing no slack time, the *critical path,* takes the greatest amount of time to complete. The time necessary to complete the overall project, thus, is the amount of time required to complete the critical path. (See "A Closer Look: PERT.")

Predicting/Forecasting

PVI must buy tapes without knowing whether their price will drop; a building contractor must schedule an electrical inspection in the hope that the electricians will have finished on time. Decision making requires making assumptions about the future, so managers must often rely on their subjective feelings and best guesses as they plan. The more accurate their feelings, the better prepared they are. Experience tends to improve managers' judgment and ability to forecast events, and there are quantitative methods available to help. The best managers combine intuition and the conscientious use of quantitative tools.

Break-Even Analysis. **Break-even analysis** is the identification of the point at which sales revenues will equal the total cost of producing a product or service. Managers use break-even analyses primarily for financial planning. Sales that fall below the break-even point create financial losses; sales above the point produce profits.

To conduct a break-even analysis, managers must first estimate fixed costs, variable costs, and a sales price per unit. Fixed costs are those incurred

PERT: Scheduling for Lil'America Builders

Recently, Butch Ledworowski of Lil'America Builders contracted to remodel the basement of a single-family home. So that he could identify a probable completion date and so that he could manage the project effectively, Butch conducted a PERT analysis. First he drew Figure 7A, called a PERT network, which showed the flow of work for the project. In this diagram, each arrow identifies a specific activity required by the project. The numbered circles indicate the beginning and end points of activities. Arrows indicate which activities must be completed before another activity begins.

For each activity, Butch provided optimistic, most probable, and pessi-mistic estimates of the time that would be required for completion. Some of these estimates are shown in Table 7A.

Once Butch had a diagram of the workflow and estimates for each activity, he could use a PERT analysis to identify the following:

1. The critical path that would take the longest time to complete
2. The earliest possible starting and finishing day for an activity
3. The latest possible starting and finishing day for an activity without the project's being delayed
4. The amount of slack time for each activity (that is, acceptable delay time that would not slow the entire project)

The results of a computerized PERT analysis for this project determined that 22.4 working days could be expected for completing the critical path (and, thus, the entire project). Some of the estimates for individual activities appear in Table 7B.

Butch used the results of the PERT analysis to tell the owners when they could expect their project to be completed, to schedule the various components of the job, and to monitor and control progress of the project.

FIGURE 7A   PERT Network Used by Lil'America Builders

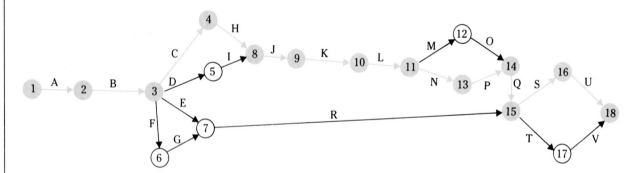

A-V represent activities.
1-18 represent beginning and ending points of activities.

regardless of how many units are produced. These usually include building costs, equipment and tool costs, insurance, and so on. Variable costs change, depending on how many units are produced, and include such factors as raw materials, labor, and supplies. Variable costs are usually expressed in terms of how much it costs to produce one additional unit of a product. Sales price per unit is simply the amount of revenue generated by each unit of sales. When

TABLE 7A Time Completion Estimates

Activity	Description	Start, End Point	Time Estimates (Days) Opti-mistic	Prob-able	Pessi-mistic
A	Draw plans	1,2	1.0	2.0	3.0
B	Rough framing	2,3	2.0	3.0	4.0
C	Rough electrical	3,4	1.0	2.0	3.0
G	Cabinet ordering	6,7	0.2	0.5	1.0
H	Electrical inspection	4,8	0.4	0.5	1.0
I	Heating inspection	5,8	0.5	0.7	1.0
T	Install cabinets	15,17	0.8	1.0	1.2
U	Install carpet	16,18	0.8	1.0	1.5
V	Final inspection	17,18	0.4	0.5	1.0

A-V represent activities.
1-18 represent beginning and ending points of activities.

TABLE 7B Individual Activity Estimates

Activity	Starting Day Earliest	Latest	Finishing Day Earliest	Latest	Slack Time
A	0.0	2.0	0.0	2.0	0.0
B	2.0	2.0	5.0	5.0	0.0
C	5.0	5.0	7.0	7.0	0.0
G	6.0	9.7	6.5	10.2	3.7
H	7.0	7.0	7.6	7.6	0.0
I	6.0	6.9	6.7	7.6	0.9
T	20.3	20.8	21.3	21.8	0.5
U	21.3	21.3	22.4	22.4	0.0
V	21.3	21.8	21.9	22.4	0.5

A-V represent activities.
1-18 represent beginning and ending points of activities.

these three pieces of information are known, the break-even point can be identified using either a graphic or an algebraic solution.

Figure 7.2 shows a break-even analysis PVI conducted to investigate the feasibility of a potential new service—restoring old movie films. According to the figure, the break-even point—where the total costs (fixed plus variable) and total revenues lines cross—is 800 restorations (units). In other words,

FIGURE 7.2 *Break-Even Analysis at PVI*

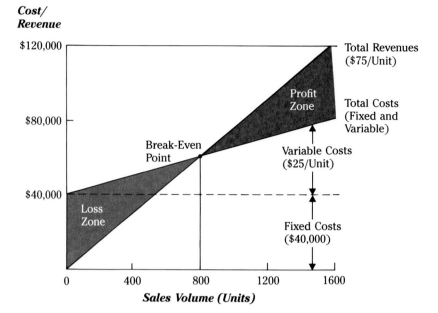

annual sales below 800 units will generate losses, and sales of more than 800 will generate profits at the rate of $50 per unit (sale price of $75 less $25 variable cost). With a capacity for 1600 movie restorations a year, Cindy's potential profit for the operation is 800 × $50, or $40,000.

Although Cindy solved her break-even analysis on a graph, she could have used the following equation:

$$\text{Break-even point} = \frac{FC}{P - VC}$$

where
FC = Fixed costs
P = Price per unit
VC = Variable cost per unit

$$\text{PVI's break-even point} = \frac{\$40,000}{\$75 - \$25} = 800 \text{ Units}$$

Notice how easy it would be for Cindy to repeat a variety of break-even analyses for different assumptions. She might ask what would happen to the break-even point if fixed costs were increased or decreased, or what would happen if the market would bear only a charge of $60 per unit.

Time Series Analysis. Managers often must predict future trends. **Time series analysis** examines past data for trends and forecasts what would happen in the future if a given trend were to continue. If PVI were to consider opening a second facility, for example, Cindy might use a time series analysis. The home video market seems to be expanding rapidly, and PVI's current facility is being used at nearly its full capacity. Because she must order equipment capable of handling the appropriate mix and volume of video formats, Cindy would like to know how much the home video market is likely to expand and in which formats (VHS, Beta, and 8mm).

Figure 7.3 illustrates the use of a relatively simple and popular time series analysis known as *trend analysis*. Trend analysis develops a statistical equa-

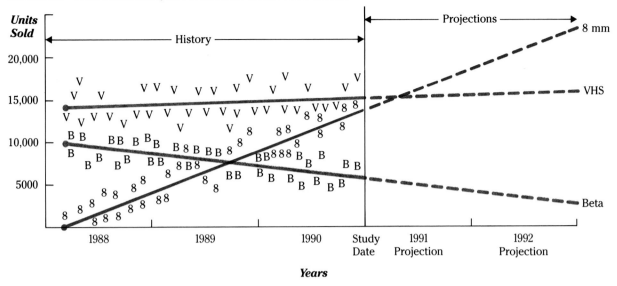

FIGURE 7.3   Time Series Analysis Forecasts for Home Video Market

Years

tion from past performance and projects into the future. In Figure 7.3, the thirty-six-month history of PVI's market area is plotted for each of the three video formats. The solid line shown for each format represents the statistical solution that best describes its past trend. The dashed extension of each line shows the forecast for the next twenty-four months.

The analysis also shows when—sometime near 1991—8mm sales are expected to exceed VHS sales. Figure 7.3 also suggests overall increases in the home video market. Because 8mm sales are increasing more rapidly than Beta sales are decreasing, Cindy can use this information to plan her second facility. Her first location has more than enough Beta capacity, so the second facility can ignore Beta and concentrate on the 8mm format to meet the expected demand.

Managers must use this model cautiously, however. Because it is based on the assumption that past trends will continue in the future, this model is most useful in stable environments. In using trend analysis, for example, Cindy must consider the volatility of the home video market. If 8mm prices drop substantially, 8mm sales might climb even more rapidly, and VHS sales might fall. The relatively new Super VHS format might change the 8mm trend. It is also possible that the market could become saturated (how many video recorders will a family want in one home?). Because time series analysis assumes that past trends will continue, such effects cannot be forecast.

Causal Modeling.   Like time series analysis, **causal modeling** attempts to forecast events in statistical terms. Causal models, however, document the causes of past events and try to predict and explain future events using cause-and-effect relationships. Suppose the trends shown in Figure 7.3 were caused by a combination of the price of tapes in each format, the availability of prerecorded movies, and advertising. As long as these factors remain constant, future projections based on time series analyses should be reasonably accurate. As soon as one or more of these factors change, however, time series projections become imprecise. Causal models take into account the probable effects of such changes.

The causal models used most often in business are based on a statistical procedure known as **regression analysis.** Regression analysis develops a mathematical model (equation) that describes the relationship of one or more causal variables to a variable that is dependent on the causal variables.

Greg's Wash and Buff can provide an example of the use of regression analysis. Greg's wanted to predict how many wax jobs it would sell in a given month. Its managers also wanted to obtain information about other factors in the sale of wax jobs, such as the degree to which sales are determined by price and the time needed to get the job done. Greg's convinced members of the Metropolitan Car Wash Association to participate in a study, the data from which were used to identify the appropriate values for a, b, c, d, and k in the following equation:

$$Y = aX_1 + bX_2 + cX_3 + dX_4 + k$$

where
Y = Number of wax jobs sold
X_1 = Price of wax job
X_2 = Average time in system
X_3 = Advertising budget
X_4 = Washes per month
k = A constant

When Greg's conducted regression analysis on this information, the resulting equation captured the apparent cause-effect relationship among the four factors and actual wax job sales:

$$Y = (-4)X_1 + (-3)X_2 + (.1)X_3 + (.06)X_4 + 110$$

This equation represents the experience of the car wash companies that participated in the study. Greg's tested the equation to see how well it applied to Greg's Wash and Buff. Greg's charges $39.95 per wash, has an average time in the system of 60 minutes, has an advertising budget of $175, and does 10,500 washes per month. As the following equation shows, Greg's should be selling 417.7 wax jobs per month:

$$Y = -4(39.95) + -3(60) + .1(175) + .06(10,500) + 110 = 417.7$$

Inasmuch as Greg's actually sells about 450 wax jobs per month, its managers concluded that the prediction was quite good.

The information from the regression analysis allows Greg's to identify what it can do to change the number of wax jobs that it sells. For example, it is likely to sell six additional car waxes for every 100 additional cars washed. Reducing the price of a wax job by $10 probably would only increase demand by 40 wax jobs a month (-4×-10). Perhaps most important, the equation suggests that reducing time in the system from 60 minutes to 22.5 minutes (as the earlier queuing example showed that adding a second waxer would do) would increase sales of wax jobs by 112.5 per month (-3×-37.5). The $4494.38 in additional revenue generated by these additional wax jobs (39.95×112.5) would more than make up for the $1680 in wages paid each month to the second waxer ($56/day \times 30$ days).

In sum, quantitative tools can help managers divide complex, difficult problems into smaller, more easily manageable parts. Managers can use these tools to learn things that they otherwise could learn only through risky trial-and-error experiments. The models encourage managers to pay closer attention to the factors that influence the effectiveness of their business decisions. What is needed now is broader recognition that the art of management improves when it is integrated with quantitative tools from the science of management.

Qualitative Tools

Whereas quantitative tools generate mathematical or statistical solutions to managers' problems, qualitative tools help generate the information, ideas, and judgments that managers need for planning and decision making. Whereas quantitative (and some qualitative) techniques are focused on selecting the most desirable from among a set of options, qualitative tools focus most heavily on identifying options.

Decision Trees

One qualitative tool often used as both a leadership and a decision model is the **decision tree** developed by Victor Vroom of Yale University and Philip Yetton of the University of New South Wales in Australia (see Figure 7.4). A decision tree helps managers select the best planning and decision-making

FIGURE 7.4 Vroom-Yetton Decision Tree

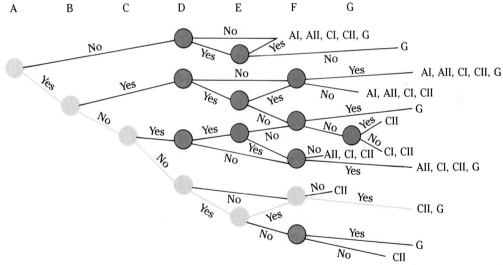

Questions

A. Is one solution better than another?
B. Is there sufficient information to make a high-quality decision without help from subordinates?
C. Is it clear exactly what problem needs to be solved?
D. Is acceptance by subordinates important for effective implementation?

E. If the decision is made independently of subordinates, will it be accepted by them?
F. Do subordinates share the organizational goals to be attained in solving this problem?
G. Is it likely that subordinates will disagree about the best solution?

Note: The highlighted path refers to the Wisconsin Tissue Mills example discussed in the text.

Source: Adapted from V. H. Vroom and P. H. Yetton (1973), *Leadership and decision making*, Pittsburgh, PA: University of Pittsburgh Press.

approach for a particular situation according to the amount of subordinate involvement appropriate for those conditions. Vroom and Yetton described five approaches:

1. *Autocratic I (AI).* A manager makes plans and decisions alone, without any input from subordinates.
2. *Autocratic II (AII).* A manager asks for information from subordinates, who may or may not be informed as to why they are being asked. The manager then makes the plans and decisions alone.
3. *Consultative I (CI).* A manager shares the situation with subordinates and asks each individually for information and an evaluation of the problem. No group meetings are held. The manager makes the plans and decisions alone.
4. *Consultative II (CII).* A manager shares the situation with subordinates as a group and asks the group for information and evaluation of the problem. The manager makes the plans and decisions alone.
5. *Group (G).* A manager shares the situation with subordinates as a group and asks the group for information and evaluation of the problem. The manager accepts and implements the plan or decision agreed on by the group.

Suppose that Melanie Castleberry is a manager who wants to use the decision tree shown in Figure 7.4. She begins on the left and answers question *A.* Melanie then either follows the branch *up* (if her answer to question *A* was no) or *down* (if her answer to question *A* was yes) to the next question. She repeats this process until she arrives at the right-hand end of a branch. Next to each branch is a list of all the appropriate strategies for a particular situation. If more than one alternative appears at the end of a branch, Melanie can use either the one with the lowest costs or the one she prefers if cost is not an issue.

Consider an example of the model in actual use. Wisconsin Tissue Mills is a moderately large paper and paper products manufacturing company located in the Fox River Valley of Wisconsin. A few years ago, Vice-President of Manufacturing Bill New and other executives recognized that the company could make substantially more profits by improving quality and cutting costs at its plants. The question was how to do it. Should Bill and his co-executives identify the changes to be made, or should lower-level managers and professionals be involved in the planning process? The highlighted path in Figure 7.4 identifies the branch of the decision tree appropriate for this situation.

A: Is one solution better than another? **YES**

B: Is there sufficient information to make a high-quality decision without help from subordinates? **NO**

C: Is it clear exactly what problem needs to be solved? **NO**

D: Is acceptance by subordinates important for effective implementation? **YES**

E: If the decision is made independently of subordinates, will it be accepted by them? **YES**

F: Do subordinates share the organizational goals to be attained in solving this problem? **YES**

Bill New and his executive colleagues identified two acceptable strategies that Vroom and Yetton would have called Consultative II (CII) and Group (G). The approach Wisconsin Tissue Mills finally selected resembles the CII approach, and it incorporates aspects of the G approach. A number of quality groups were formed and given responsibility for identifying and evaluating possible actions for improving quality and reducing costs. The groups presented the executives with plans, cost estimates, and projected results. The top executives then made a final decision on whether to implement each plan.

Under circumstances such as those at Wisconsin Tissue Mills, the Vroom-Yetton model can prove very successful.[1] Both management and employees at the company were enthusiastic about the way the decision was handled. The results were better product quality, increased profits, and improved morale.

Brainstorming

Brainstorming is a qualitative tool designed to stimulate people to develop alternatives during the planning and decision-making process.[2] Brainstorming encourages the sharing of ideas in a setting free of the interruptions and risks of immediate evaluation and discussion. A set of basic ground rules governs a brainstorming session: no one may evaluate or criticize the ideas of others, and people are encouraged to be freewheeling in creating ideas. The more ideas produced, the better, and individuals are urged to "take off" on others' ideas ("hitchhiking").

To conduct a brainstorming session, the group is informed about the problem and asked to generate as many solutions as possible within a specified period of time. Participants are encouraged to suggest whatever comes to mind, no matter how unusual. It is emphasized that all ideas generated belong to the group, not to individuals, and criticism is forbidden.

All ideas from a brainstorming session are recorded for later evaluation by either the group or the manager, depending on which planning and decision-making strategy is being followed. Because the purpose of the technique is to generate many creative ideas, it is expected that many of the ideas eventually will prove to be of little use. The hope is that, among the many ideas offered, one or more will prove useful.

Some of the purported advantages of the brainstorming technique include a reduced dependence on a single authority figure, maximized output for a short period of time, and its enjoyable and stimulating qualities.[3] In fact, compared to more traditional group processes, brainstorming does work well.[4] The number and quality of ideas are better, and costs per idea generated tend to be more favorable. Through the brainstorming process, group members tend to focus on the task at hand, and, as a result, interpersonal conflict and pressures toward conformity decline. In addition, ideas generated by group members are likely to be accepted by the group.

Unfortunately, the aspects of brainstorming that help make it successful also create some problems. Because ideas are not evaluated, the only product of a brainstorming session is a list of ideas. There is no plan, there is no solution, and the initial problem still exists. This lack of closure can create dissatisfaction among participants, especially when someone else (a manager or another group) evaluates the ideas that the brainstorming group has generated.

Synectics

The Greek word *synectic* means "the joining together of different and apparently irrelevant elements."[5] The **synectic technique,** designed to develop creative ideas, attempts to integrate "diverse individuals into a problem-stating problem-solving group."[6] This technique gets people to focus on developing a single, insightful solution and includes developing, evaluating, and critiquing ideas.

As shown in "A Closer Look: Synectics," the outcome of the synectic process is a single unique plan or decision that has undergone considerable evaluation. The process tends to produce innovative ideas. It also generates a list of the advantages and disadvantages of the chosen plan or decision and suggestions for dealing with the disadvantages.

Although the synectic approach can be quite useful for creative planning and decision making, its cost is high. Furthermore, it produces only one potential solution to a problem. If that solution turns out to be unusable, the problem remains, and the process has failed.

The Delphi Technique

Solutions to problems that come from groups in which participants interact face-to-face often are of lower quality than solutions that come from individuals who work alone on the same problem. To address this concern, Norman C. Dalkey and his associates at the Rand Corporation developed the Delphi process.[7] The **Delphi technique** is a qualitative tool that facilitates planning and decision making by gathering information and opinions from a group without physically assembling its members. Instead, information is exchanged through questionnaires. The Delphi technique is particularly useful when a problem would benefit from group participation but it is not feasible to assemble individuals for a meeting because of time constraints, geographical dispersion, or desires to remain anonymous.

Suppose Chemical Bank, a huge conglomerate, were to encounter a significant decline in the amount of money being deposited at its banks. Suppose further that its executives conclude that the way to increase deposits is through nontraditional investment instruments—not mere copies of its competitor's investments, but *new* investment instruments. Top executives would like to hear ideas from some of Chemical's many bankers throughout the country, but bringing them together to address this issue would be extremely difficult and expensive. The Delphi technique could help.

The Delphi technique generally consists of several stages:

1. *Development of the Delphi question and the first inquiry.* The coordinator prepares a written statement of the problem and sends it to each group member, along with a questionnaire requesting suggestions and potential solutions to the problem. At Chemical Bank, for instance, coordinator Matthew Harr selects twenty-five banks and appoints one banker from each to participate. Matt sends all twenty-five bankers a statement that reads, in part, "Chemical needs to identify potential new investment instruments to increase deposits at the banks." The questionnaire asks each banker in the Delphi group to present his or her ideas for potential new instruments and emphasizes that, at this stage, ideas need not be fully developed or completely evaluated.

Synectics: A Phone That Can't Be Beaten (or Stolen)

Get several of your friends together and spend one half hour brainstorming on the following issue: ways to vandalize a pay telephone. Feel free to come up with ideas that are as wild and unusual as possible. No matter how creative your solutions, they have probably all been used on phones owned by the New York Telephone Company. In fact, repairing and replacing damaged and stolen pay phones has become a major expense for the company.

New York Telephone decided to use the synectic approach to solve this vandalism problem. They enlisted the help of George Prince, developer of the synectic approach, and followed the five steps of the process.[1]

At the *problem-statement stage,* the scope of the problem was described, and it was agreed that an ideal solution to the problem would involve the total elimination of all pay phone vandalism and theft.

At the *goal-wishing stage,* a wide range of "wishes" was generated. One participant, for example, wished for an indestructible phone booth door that would open only after the insertion of money. Another participant wished that pay phones could be designed like punching bags, capable of withstanding repeated blows. Another wished the phones could be disguised as fire hydrants. This idea was hitchhiked on by someone who wished the phone could be as indestructible as a fire hydrant. Continued discussion led to a wide range of creative ideas.

During the *excursion stage,* the leader suggested that the group follow up its ideas about indestructibility from the perspective of the

Wild West. Discussion followed on the indestructibility of the bank safe, the indestructible relationship between a cowboy and his horse, and other equally "destruction-proof" ideas.

The *forced-fit stage* required participants to apply their Wild West ideas from the excursion stage to the problem of pay phone vandalism and theft in modern-day New York. When someone followed up on the idea of the impenetrable safe, for example, the suggestion was to build phones right into the walls of buildings. The idea of the indestructible pillars of rock found in western canyons gave rise to a suggestion for designing phones with no external appendages.

At the *itemized-response stage,* a single solution to the problem of van-

dalism and theft of pay phones was specified. The group documented its advantages, its possible drawbacks, and ways to reduce these limitations.

The solution was to design a pay phone that resembles a bank's automated teller and to build it into the wall of a building so it fits flush with the wall. The phone should have no appendages, not even buttons. Instead of a handset, it would have a speakerphone. Instead of a dial or buttons, the wall would have touch-sensitive areas. If a caller wanted privacy, he or she could attach a Walkman-type headset.

1. G. Prince (1980), *Problem solving strategies: The synectic approach,* Del Mar, CA: CRM McGraw-Hill Films.

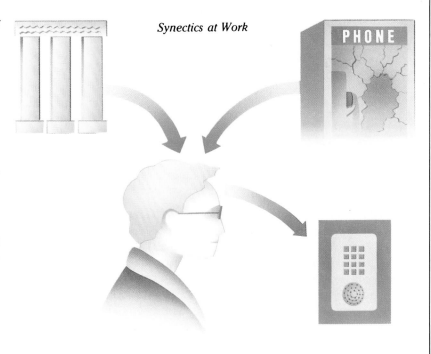

Synectics at Work

2. *The first response.* Each participant, independently and anonymously, records his or her comments, suggestions, and potential solutions and returns them directly to the Delphi coordinator.

3. *Analysis of the first response, feedback, and the second inquiry.* The coordinator prepares a written summary of all comments and sends it to each participant, along with another questionnaire. At Chemical, Matt reviews the returned questionnaires and develops a list that includes all suggestions from the twenty-five Delphi members. He prepares and sends a second questionnaire to the participants that begins with the statement "Attached is a list showing all of the ideas the group has generated on potential investment instruments. Please review them, list suggestions on how you would refine each, and briefly evaluate the degree to which you believe the idea would be likely to generate increased deposits."

4. *The second response.* Each participant, again independently and anonymously, records his or her responses to the questionnaire and sends them directly to the coordinator. Matt reviews this input, summarizes it, and makes yet another mailing.

5. *Continuation of the process.* The Delphi coordinator continues to follow this procedure until a clear solution emerges, a point of diminishing returns is reached, or a vote is taken. When finished, Chemical Bank's Delphi group has produced a list of ideas for potential new instruments, has refined descriptions of each, and has evaluated each instrument's strengths and weaknesses.

Like the other qualitative decision tools, the Delphi technique has both strengths and limitations. As you have learned, the technique can involve many participants, even if they are physically separated from one another. The technique tends to produce a large amount of information and many high-quality ideas. Many of the dysfunctions of face-to-face groups (such as pressure to conform and interpersonal conflict) can be greatly reduced. The technique is slow, although computer networks and electronic mail systems can greatly reduce this problem.[8] The delays and the impersonality of the process do little to build group cohesiveness or commitment to the solution. In addition, group members need good written-communication skills to participate effectively in a Delphi exercise. Participants also have to be motivated to produce timely, constructive responses. Finally, the success of the technique requires a coordinator who is adept at interpreting, translating, and summarizing input from members at each stage of the process.

))) **A MANAGER'S WORD**
Nominal group technique has become incorporated as a standard operating group process for planning, problem solving, and decision making in contemporary organizations throughout the world.

Andrew H. Van de Ven
3M Professor of Human Systems Management and Director Minnesota Innovation Research Program

Nominal Group Technique (NGT)

The **nominal group technique (NGT)** is a highly structured, interactive group decision-making process designed to generate a large number of creative potential solutions to a problem, to evaluate these solutions, and to rank them from best to worst.[9] The NGT can also be used to identify problems, evaluate their magnitude, and rank them from most to least critical. The NGT process consists of four major steps. It begins with a silent, individual generation of ideas, followed by a round-robin recording of these ideas. Next, the ideas are discussed and evaluated sequentially by the group. Finally, there is a confidential vote on the relative importance of the ideas.

At the beginning of an NGT session, a "leader" presents a description of the problem to be addressed by the group. When, in response to the recommendations generated by the Vroom-Yetton decision tree, managers at Wisconsin Tissue Mills decided to form twelve NGT groups to develop ideas for product quality and profitability improvements, the following statement was made:

Wisconsin Tissue recognizes the opportunity for employee groups to contribute further to cost reduction, production improvement, and product quality. Specifically, what suggestions could your group make for actions or organizational changes at Wisconsin Tissue to facilitate cost reduction, improve production, and enhance product quality?

Immediately, Step One—a silent generation of ideas—begins. Each group member works independently for five to ten minutes, generating and recording ideas. This phase of the process is identical to and has all the advantages of a short individual brainstorming session.

During Step Two, ideas are combined into a master list. First, the leader asks one member of the group to state an idea and records it on a list without discussing it. A second member of the group is then asked for one idea, and it is recorded. This process is continued round-robin, each member giving one idea at a time, until all ideas have been listed. Lists of ideas generated by employee groups at Wisconsin Tissue Mills typically contained more than thirty suggestions for quality and cost improvements.

In Step Three, the leader reads the first idea from the list and asks if any member would like to ask for or provide clarification of its meaning. Members then can briefly express their opinions about the strengths and weaknesses of the idea. Each item on the list is discussed sequentially in this way.

Step Four consists of a confidential vote on the merits of the various ideas. Each member of the group is asked to work alone and select a small number of ideas from the list (usually five to seven) that he or she feels are most important. Each member then ranks the ideas and votes on them by assigning points based on his or her ordering. Individual votes are recorded anonymously on index cards and submitted to the leader, who tallies them. After the

In a nominal group session, members attempt to identify solutions to an important problem. They do so by working alone to generate ideas, together to discuss the ideas, and then alone to vote on them. The result is a rank-ordered list of potential solutions.

voting, the ideas are ranked. The aggregation of individual votes determines the relative importance of ideas. At Wisconsin Tissue Mills, the voting process typically identified three or four ideas that were rated highly by most members of the group, another four or five ideas considered moderately promising, and about twenty ideas that group members agreed were less promising.

The NGT can be an extremely effective tool. It generates a large number of ideas, many of which are of high quality. It also produces a lot of low-quality ideas, but these "wash out" based on the vote. People have strong feelings of accomplishment and commitment to the solutions arrived at by the group. Members also feel committed to their group, enjoy the process, and feel a strong sense of having done a satisfying job because they can clearly see the results of their work.

[P]ractitioners too often rely only on the NGT, to the exclusion of other group and organizational development processes. . . . NGT [is] but one step in a larger process of program planning and organizational problem solving.
—Van de Ven

The NGT process also has costs, however. It takes a couple of hours to implement, and it requires advanced planning. The high level of structure reduces feelings of involvement for some members. This structure also reduces the direct interaction among participants and, therefore, does not work well when situations require negotiation between two or more parties. Furthermore, the process can succeed only if all members agree to abide by the rules. As noted by its creators, André L. Delbecq of Santa Clara University and Andrew H. Van de Ven of the University of Minnesota, the technique is best suited for complex situations that require the judgment of a number of experts and for which no single person has the only "right" solution.

In sum, qualitative tools can help managers perform a number of managerial tasks. Many techniques structure group interaction in ways that reduce the liabilities often associated with group decision making, while simultaneously capitalizing on the assets associated with group processes (see Chapter 6). Because each technique is designed for specific purposes, managers need to use them carefully in the appropriate settings.

Tools for Planning and Decision Making in Review

Managers use a variety of tools as they plan and make decisions. Some of these tools are quantitative; they use mathematical and statistical models of planning and decision making. Inventory models help managers balance inventory needs with the costs of procuring and maintaining supplies and products. Managers with resource-allocation problems can use linear programming to identify the best ways to use scarce resources. Managers with waiting-line problems can use queuing models to identify the best number of lines to maintain. Complex projects can be organized, scheduled, and monitored using program evaluation and review techniques (PERT). Break-even analysis, time series analysis, and causal models are quantitative tools that deal with forecasting events.

Qualitative tools concentrate on the generation and processing of ideas, opinions, and judgments. Decision trees help managers determine the appropriate degree of worker participation in planning and decision making. When the decision tree indicates that worker participation in planning or decision making is appropriate, managers can use other qualitative tools to get workers' contributions. During brainstorming, a group of individuals generates as many innovative ideas as possible. During synectics, a group develops and evaluates a single, highly creative solution. The Delphi technique provides a way to capitalize on group processes without physically assembling the group's members. Finally, nominal group technique integrates aspects of all these approaches into an effective face-to-face approach for addressing single-issue problems.

Decision-making tools can provide a systematic, effective approach to planning and the science of management. Used badly, both qualitative and quantitative models may erode intuition, passion, and the art of management.

Issues for Review and Discussion

1. Describe the purpose of an inventory planning and decision model, such as EOQ (economic order quantity).
2. Discuss the information that a manager must have before using linear programming to solve a resource allocation problem.
3. Use PERT (program evaluation and review technique) to outline a plan for writing a term paper.
4. Select a technique that could be used by your college bookstore to project the demand for 5-1/4-inch floppy disks for the upcoming academic year, and explain your selection.
5. How could the student-body president at your college use the Vroom-Yetton model to determine the degree to which others should be involved in planning the annual budget? Explain your answer step-by-step.
6. Describe a situation in which brainstorming would be an appropriate qualitative tool for a manager to use.
7. Identify the two biggest potential drawbacks of the synectic approach to planning and decision making.
8. Under what conditions should a manager use the Delphi technique rather than the nominal group technique?

Key Terms

quantitative tools
qualitative tools
economic order quantity (EOQ)
linear programming (LP)
queuing models
break-even analysis
time series analysis

causal modeling
regression analysis
decision tree
brainstorming
synectic technique
Delphi technique
nominal group technique (NGT)

Suggested Readings

Fox, W. M. (1987). *Effective group problem solving.* San Francisco: Jossey-Bass.

Moore, C. M. (1987). *Group techniques for idea building.* Newbury Park, CA: Sage.

Murnighan, J. K. (1981). Group decision making: What strategies should you use? *Management Review, 70,* 55-62.

Render, B., and Stair, R. M., Jr. (1986). *Microcomputer software for management science and operations management.* Boston: Allyn and Bacon.

Notes

1. A. G. Jago (1982), Leadership: Perspectives in theory and research, *Management Science,* 28, 315-36; R. J. House and M. L. Baetz (1979), Leadership: Some empirical generalizations and new research directions, in B. M. Staw, ed., *Research in organizational behavior,* vol. 1, Greenwich, CT: JAI Press, 341-423.

2. A. F. Osborn (1957), *Applied imagination,* New York: Scribner's.

3. R. W. Napier and M. K. Gershenfeld (1985), *Groups: Theory and experience,* 3rd ed., Boston: Houghton Mifflin, 334.

4. D. W. Taylor, P. C. Berry, and C. H. Block (1958), Does group participation when using brainstorming techniques facilitate or inhibit creative thinking? *Administrative Science Quarterly,* 3, 23-47; J. K. Murnighan (1981), Group decision making: What strategies should you use? *Management Review,* 70, 55-62.

5. W. J. Gordon (1961), *Synectics: The development of creative capacity,* New York: Harper & Row, 3.

6. *Ibid.*

7. N. C. Dalkey and O. Helmer (1963), An experimental application of the Delphi method to the use of experts, *Management Science,* 9, 458-67; A. L. Delbecq, A. H. Van de Ven, and D. H. Gustafson (1975), *Group techniques for program planning: A guide to nominal group and delphi processes,* Glenview, IL: Scott, Foresman.

8. Delbecq, et al.

9. A. L. Delbecq and A. H. Van de Ven (1971), A group process model for problem identification and program planning, *Journal of Applied Behavioral Science,* 7, 466-92; A. L. Delbecq and A. H. Van de Ven (1971), Nominal versus interactive group processes for committee decision-making effectiveness, *Academy of Management Journal,* 14, 203-11.

Harvey Industries

By Donald F. Condit, Lawrence Institute of Technology

Harvey Industries, a Wisconsin Company, was incorporated in 1950 and specializes in the assembly of high-pressure washer systems and in the sale of repair parts for these systems. The products range from small, portable high-pressure washers to large, industrial installations for snow removal from vehicles stored outdoors during the winter months. Typical uses for high-pressure water cleaning occur for automobiles, airplanes, buildings, engines, ice cream plants, packing plants, swimming pools, and machinery. Harvey's industrial customers include General Motors, Ford, Chrysler, Delta Airlines, United Parcel Service, and the Shell Oil Company.

Although the industrial applications are a significant part of its sales, Harvey Industries is primarily an assembler of equipment for coin-operated self-service car wash systems. The typical car wash is of concrete block construction with an equipment room in the center flanked on either side by a number of bays. Cars are driven into the bays, where the driver can wash and wax the car, utilizing high-pressure hot water and liquid wax. A bill changer is available to provide change for the equipment and the purchase of various products from a coin-operated dispenser. These products include paper towels, a white-wall cleaner, and an upholstery cleaner. Harvey supplies its customers with all of the equipment, supplies, and products necessary for operation.

In recent years, Harvey Industries has been in financial difficulty, losing money in three of the previous four years. The most recent year's results are a loss of $17,174 on sales of $1,238,674.

The company employs twenty-three people with the management team consisting of the following key employees:

President
Sales manager
Manufacturing manager
Controller
Purchasing manager

The abbreviated organization chart in Figure 7B reflects the reporting relationship of the key employees and the three individuals who report directly to the manufacturing manager.

The Current Inventory Control System

The current inventory control "system" consists of orders for stock replenishment being made by the stockroom foreperson, the purchasing manager, or the manufacturing manager when one of them notices that inventory is low. An order for re-

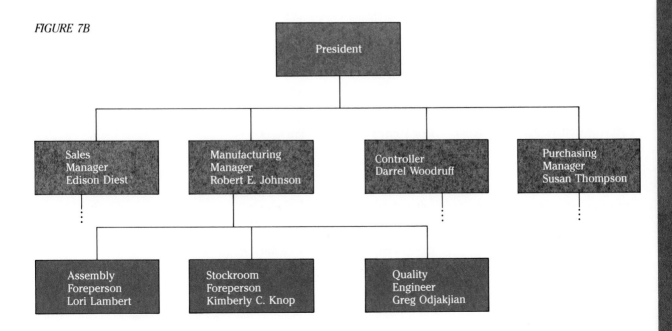

FIGURE 7B

plenishment of the inventory is also placed whenever someone (either a customer or an employee in the assembly area) wants an item that is out of stock.

Some inventory is needed for the assembly of the high-pressure equipment for the car wash and industrial applications. There are current and accurate lists of materials for these, which are generally known well in advance of the scheduled time of production.

The majority of orders is for repair parts and supplies used by the car washes, such as paper towels, detergent, and wax concentrate. Because of the constant and rugged use of the car wash equipment, there is a steady demand for various repair parts.

The stockroom is well organized, with items stored in locations according to each vendor. The number of vendors is limited, and each vendor generally supplies many different stock items. For example, the repair parts from Allen Bradley, a manufacturer of electric motors, are stocked in one location. These parts are used to provide service for the many electrical motors used for car wash high-pressure pump and motor assemblies.

Because of the large number of repair parts, there are generally two employees working in the stockroom, the stockroom foreperson and an assistant, both of whom handle customer orders. Many customers come to Harvey's plant to get the parts or supplies they need. Other orders come by telephone and are shipped by United Parcel Service the same day.

Some inventory is stored on the shop assembly floor. This consists of low-value items, which are used every day, such as nuts, bolts, screws, and washers. These items do not amount to a large percentage of Harvey's purchases; unfortunately, the assembly area is often out of one of these basic items, and this causes a significant amount of downtime for the assembly lines.

Paperwork is kept to a minimum. A sales slip listing the part numbers and quantities sold to a customer are generally filled out for each sale. If the assembly department needs items that are not stocked on the assembly floor, someone from that department enters the stockroom and withdraws the necessary material. No paperwork is done for items removed for use on the assembly floor.

The company carries 973 different items in stock. Purchases amounted to $314,673 last year. Although the company does not use a computer, it does have accurate records on how much money was spent on each part last year. An analysis of that data showed that $220,684 was spent on just 179 of the parts.

Harvey Industries purchases items from both manufacturers and wholesalers. Fortunately these suppliers carry most of the items Harvey purchases in stock so that Harvey can usually replenish its inventory in two or three days after submitting an order.

Harvey Industries' recent losses have caused its auditing firm to become concerned about the company's ability to continue in business. Recently the company has been selling excess land adjoining its manufacturing facility to generate the cash to meet its financial obligations. Also of concern is the rising level of money tied up in inventory. At the last audit, inventory was valued at $124,324.

The New President

Because of the recent death of the owner, the trust department of a Milwaukee bank, as trustee for the estate, has taken over the company's affairs and appointed a new president, Cindy Herring. Cindy quickly identified many problem areas, among them inventory control. To solve the problem, she retained a consultant to make specific recommendations concerning a revised inventory control system.

Questions

1. Pick a quantitative planning and decision-making tool you feel would be useful to Cindy. Briefly explain how and why this tool would be used.

2. Pick a qualitative planning and decision-making tool you feel would be useful to Cindy. Briefly explain how and why this tool would be useful.

3. What recommendations would you make to Harvey Industries' new president?

8 Strategic Management: Planning for Environmental Fit

Student Learning Objectives

After reading this chapter, you should be able to:

1. Understand the concept of strategic management and its importance.

2. Discuss the advantages and disadvantages of strategic planning.

3. Name and discuss the three levels of strategic planning.

4. Describe the nine steps involved in the strategic planning and implementation process.

5. Understand the three major problems addressed by a strategic plan.

6. Describe the ways in which organizations can resolve strategic planning problems.

7. Explain the concept of strategic business units, the way in which they are classified according to market factors, and the strategies appropriate for use with each classification.

8. Describe the three generic approaches to organizational strategy.

9. Discuss the reasons for strategic planning in both small and not-for-profit organizations.

*T*he previous three chapters explored the importance of systematic planning and decision making in guiding an organization toward the successful accomplishment of its goals and objectives. What goals and objectives should an organization pursue? Is it the mission of Humana Hospital in Louisville, Kentucky, to provide state-of-the-art treatment of heart problems or to develop new procedures for a variety of medical problems? Does Compaq Computer Corporation want to focus on small business computers or on personal computers? Does the Cadillac Division of General Motors wish to compete against Mercedes in the ultra-luxury market or against the Lincoln-Mercury Division in the lower luxury market? These are all questions of organizational strategy and strategic management, and answers to such questions help guide an organization into its environmental niche.

The Concept of Strategic Management

Strategic management is that part of the management process concerned with achieving an overall integration of an organization's internal divisions, while simultaneously integrating the organization with its external environment. Strategic management does this in two basic ways. First, it considers formulation—the planning that leads to the development of organizational goals and specific statements of action. Second, it involves implementation—the design and use of organizational subsystems and resources to operate strategic plans. Strategic management, then, formulates and implements tactics that try to match an organization as closely as possible to its task environment for the purpose of meeting its objectives.

Strategic Planning

Strategy is the art and science of combining the many resources available to achieve the best match between an organization and its environment. Top managers' active, conscious attempts to design a scheme to position an organization within its external environment are known as **strategic planning.** An organization's **strategic plan** outlines its long-term vision and specifies its reason for existing, its strategic objectives, and its operational strategies. An organization's strategic plan, thus, answers a set of fundamental questions: *What* business is it in or does it want to be in? *What* kind of organization is it or does it want to be? *How* is it going to operate to achieve this strategic position?

An **organizational mission,** a statement that specifies an organization's reason for being, answers the question "What business[es] should be undertaken?" This mission is set forth in a **mission statement.** It encapsulates managers' vision for their organization based on its internal and external environments, its capabilities, and the nature of its customers or clients. The mission statement for Lil'America Builders, the small construction company mentioned in Chapter 7, simply states that the company is and will remain in the business of home remodeling.

Note that two different organizations can have almost identical mission statements but very different operational strategies. Table 8.1 provides an abstract of two hypothetical alternative strategic plans for Lil'America Builders. The mission statement and strategic objectives in the two plans are identical, but the operational strategies are different.

A MANAGER'S WORD

Strategic planning, like anything else, can be done well or done badly. . . . Organizations that are only interested in paying lip service to strategic planning probably get very little benefit from it.

Phyllis A. Mason
Professor
Baruch College

TABLE 8.1 *Strategic Plans for Lil'America Builders*

Plan #1	Plan #2
A. Mission Statement	A. Mission Statement
We are in and will remain in the business of home remodeling.	We are in and will remain in the business of home remodeling.
B. Strategic Objectives	B. Strategic Objectives
1. For profits to constitute 15-20 percent of the charge to the homeowner for individual remodeling projects	1. For profits to constitute 15-20 percent of the charge to the homeowner for individual remodeling projects
2. To increase the dollar value of business conducted by 10-15 percent per year	2. To increase the dollar value of business conducted by 10-15 percent per year
3. To make project cost estimates accurate enough so that overruns average less than 3 percent of the project bid and underruns average less than 5 percent of the bid	3. To make project cost estimates accurate enough so that overruns average less than 3 percent of the project bid, and underruns average less than 5 percent of the bid
4. To make project completion time estimates accurate enough so that all projects are completed within five days of the initial scheduled completion date	4. To make project completion time estimates accurate enough so that all projects are completed within five days of the initial scheduled completion date
5. To be recognized as one of the top three remodeling contractors in the city based on the quality of work completed	5. To be recognized as one of the top three remodeling contractors in the city based on the quality of work completed
6. To obtain at least 50 percent of our business through word-of-mouth based on prior clients	6. To obtain at least 50 percent of our business through word-of-mouth based on prior clients
C. Operational Strategies	C. Operational Strategies
1. To hire highly skilled carpenters and pay them well enough to encourage long-term commitment to the company	1. To hire young, inexperienced carpenters, pay them moderately low wages, and teach them carpentry skills
2. To control costs by using subcontractors for all non-carpentry work (heating, electrical, wallboard, painting, carpeting)	2. To control costs by using subcontractors for heating and electrical work
3. To control quality by inspecting work quality and progress on all jobs at least once a day	3. To control quality by inspecting work on each job on completion of each major segment of the project
4. To schedule and control all jobs using PERT analyses*	4. To have the owner of the company schedule and control all jobs because of his experience in scheduling projects
5. To obtain a microcomputer to support the business and to use quantitative planning tools	5. To hire an accounting firm to meet financial responsibilities
6. To plan and monitor all project schedules according to a computerized PERT analysis	
7. To create and use a computer program to develop project bids based on input, such as number of square feet, type of existing construction, and quality of materials	

Note: These plans have been simulated.

*PERT analysis is described in Chapter 7.

Strategic objectives state definable, measurable accomplishments that, when realized, fulfill an organization's mission statement. Each of Lil'America's strategic plans, for example, shows six strategic objectives ranging from the amount of profit the company would like to earn per job to the percentage of business it wants to gain through the recommendations of satisfied customers (review Table 8.1). Finally, **operational strategies** specify the actions that managers are to take to accomplish these objectives. Lil'America has two different operational strategies, depending on which strategic plan it decides to use (review Table 8.1).

Strategy Components. Strategic plans set forth an organization's long-term goals; its intermediate objectives; and its purpose, or basic role, in society. As managers construct a strategic plan, they must consider several factors:

- **Scope**—an organization's present and planned interactions with its environment. Scope also identifies the organization's domain, such as the markets in which it expects to compete, and the nature and character of these interactions, such as methods of competition. Butch Ledworowski, Lil'America's owner, for example, considered whether to restrict the business solely to home remodeling and how to obtain customers.

- **Resource deployment**—an organization's distribution of its resources in pursuit of its goals. Butch decided to allot money for skilled carpenters' salaries, for a microcomputer, and for the development of a computer program.

- **Competitive advantages**—an organization's unique position compared to other organizations in its task environment, such as exceptional skill in direct mail marketing

- **Synergy**—the positive results that emerge from the combination of scope, resource deployment, and competitive advantages (see Figure 8.1). The major business of Humana Hospital, for example, is routine hospital care, yet research activities conducted by Dr. William C. DeVries enabled Humana to perform artificial heart transplants. The synergistic effects may have allowed Humana to attract business and profitability through the publicity that ensued.

The Importance of Operational Strategies. Whereas strategic objectives specify what an organization hopes to accomplish, operational strategies describe how this is to be done. Operational strategies, therefore, should be specified only after strategic objectives have been chosen. Lil'America established its third strategic objective regarding accurate cost estimates, for example, before developing its operational strategies for controlling costs—using

FIGURE 8.1 Strategy Components

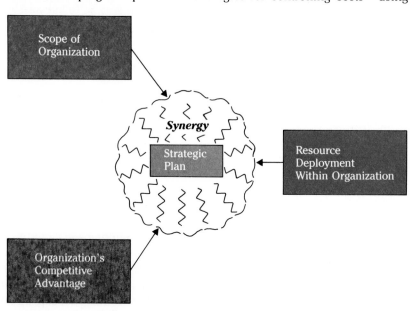

subcontractors, microcomputers, and PERT analyses. If managers permit organizations to be driven by operational strategies rather than by the more important strategic objectives, they undermine the sense of direction that people need to guide and coordinate organizational activities.

The Levels of Strategic Planning

In most organizations, strategic planning takes place for at least three levels: corporate, business unit, and functional (although in smaller, single organizations such as Lil'America, there are only two—corporate and functional).[1]

Corporate Strategy.   At the corporate level, strategic planning establishes the mission for an entire organization. Usually plotted by top management, **corporate strategy** addresses two major questions: "What business[es] will the organization engage in?" and "How will resources be distributed?" Corporate-level strategy enacted in 1989, for example, determined that Sears, Roebuck and Company should lower prices and offer national name brands to compete with discount stores such as Kmart.

Business Unit Strategy.   A business unit, often referred to as a strategic business unit (SBU), is a segment of an organization with a distinct mission, external market, and strategy for dealing with that market. Allstate Insurance Group, for example, is a business unit within Sears. **Business unit strategy,** therefore, concerns the functioning of SBUs and primarily focuses on synergy and competitive advantage. Synergy at this level involves the means by which business units can be integrated within the larger organization. Competitive advantage recognizes and takes advantage of an SBU's unique position relative to its competitors.

Functional Strategy.   A **functional strategy** is a comprehensive plan showing how management intends to guide a particular functional area, such as marketing, finance, or production, within a business unit. Functional strategy should support and conform to the strategy of the business unit. If, for example, the strategic plan for Allstate specifies that insurance sales should constitute 20 percent of Sears' business, Allstate's marketing department would identify potential customers while its underwriting department would devise the auto, home, and health policies to be sold.

It is important that managers integrate the strategy developed at each level to support and reinforce one another. At Sears, managers in the service division should integrate their strategies with those developed by the major appliance sales division, which, in turn, complement strategies created by the advertising group, thereby contributing to the corporate-level strategy adopted for the entire national chain.

Strategic Management Styles

The personalities and preferences of an organization's managers strongly influence the strategies they develop. Managers have three distinct styles of strategic planning: entrepreneurial, adaptive, and planning.[2]

In the *entrepreneurial style,* one person—typically the founder of the organization—develops plans based on personal beliefs, experiences, and intuition,

The Allstate Insurance Group is a business unit within Sears, Roebuck and Company. Allstate's Direct Marketing Center provides direct mail and telemarketing services for the Sears family of companies and for other major corporations.

The crucial thing is that top management needs to communicate to the entire organization the objectives of the strategic planning unit, how the unit will work with the rest of the organization, the input that will be required from the rest of the organization, why the organization is doing strategic planning, how important it is to the organization's future, and so on.

—Mason

which often involve substantial uncertainty and risk. Sam Jacobson, founder of PDQ and Pick Kwik food stores, is an entrepreneur who based his retailing approach on the belief that customers would be willing to pay a higher price to obtain a needed product quickly and conveniently.

In the *adaptive style*—sometimes called the "science of muddling through"—managers move an organization forward timidly, defensively, and through a series of small (often disjointed) steps.[3] Rather than trying to shape the environment, adaptive managers monitor activities in the environment and react to them. After watching Beta sales decline, for example, SONY defensively issued a series of minor improvements and additional features to its machines before finally abandoning the format and switching to VHS production.

Managers who use a *planning style* develop a comprehensive organizational plan. They analyze the environment, identify opportunities and threats, and formulate rational methods of coping with both according to the capabilities of the organization. For example, Sears' decision to sell its Tower in Chicago was a result of the comprehensive, systematic approach that characterizes the planning style of strategic management.

No one strategy works best for all organizations. The entrepreneurial approach may be appropriate for a small, new organization with a strong leader striving to find its niche in the marketplace. The adaptive model may be the only choice available to an organization, such as an individual chapter of the Girl Scouts, whose mission is specified and cannot be changed. Managers of most established organizations can use the systematic approach of the planning style to fit their organization into its task environment. Even within an organization, styles are likely to differ over time or across business units. The entrepreneurial style that may work for an organization's research and development department may be inappropriate for the marketing department, which requires an adaptive style to meet the needs, values, and wants of potential consumers.[4]

The Advantages and Disadvantages of Strategic Planning

Strategic plans sometimes succeed—and sometimes create problems. The primary advantage of strategic planning is that it makes an organization more systematic. A systematic organization directs a greater percentage of its efforts toward specific objectives, which makes it more efficient than a less systematic organization. A strategic plan also reduces guesswork on the part of managers, because it tells them specifically what the organization hopes to accomplish and how it plans to do so.

Probably the single biggest problem with strategic planning occurs when planners become so enthralled with their own importance that they fall out of touch with the organization's realities and its environment and, subsequently, develop inappropriate plans. Most observers have concluded that this is what happened when R. J. Ferris, then CEO of United Airlines, developed a new strategy to create Allegis, a "total travel partner" consisting of an airline (United), a car rental company (Hertz), and a hotel chain (Hilton). This strategy failed for a variety of reasons, among them the loss of United's identity as a premier airline. Other potential problems associated with strategic planning include managers who are slow to react when a carefully developed plan

Former Allegis CEO Richard Ferris envisioned that passengers who traveled on United would also stay at a Westin or Hilton Hotel and rent a car from Hertz. This "fly-sleep-drive" strategy failed for a variety of reasons. Ferris' abrupt dismissal exemplifies the quick and drastic action of boards of directors under certain circumstances.

is failing because they were so certain it would succeed and plans that stifle rather than facilitate the effects that were intended, as when a meticulously constructed plan drives all future decisions—even though managers' instincts detect the need for a change.

The Strategic Planning and Implementation Process

Strategic planning is a process that covers several steps, from the initial examination of the current state of affairs, through the creation of a plan, to the final checks on how the plan is affecting daily performance (see Figure 8.2).[5]

Step One: Planning Awareness

The first step in developing a strategic plan is to take stock of the status quo: an organization's current mission; its goals, structure, strategy, and performance; the values and aspirations of its major stakeholders and power brokers; and the nature of its environment. This assessment documents the point of departure for the future strategic plan. For Lil'America Builders, Step One revealed that: the organization was exclusively in the home remodeling business; it experienced slow but steady growth in profits; it employed skilled workers who seemed committed to the organization; and it maintained a strong, but not fully used, base of satisfied customers.

FIGURE 8.2   The Strategic Planning Process

The complete strategic planning process requires nine steps. As you can see, Steps Three and Four can be conducted concurrently. Note that Steps Three and Four must both be completed before Step Five can be completed.

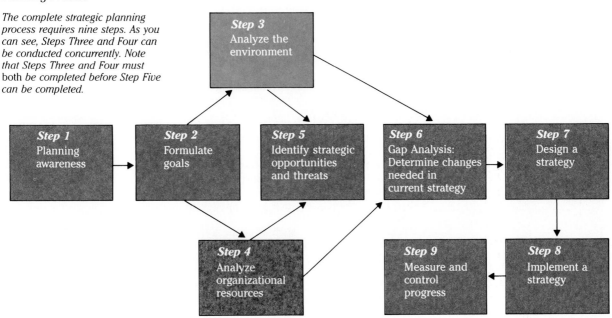

Source: C. W. Hofer (1986), *Strategy formulation: Issues and concepts,* 2nd ed., St. Paul, MN: West. While this particular model was developed primarily for the business unit level, it is useful for strategic planning at any of the three levels.

Step Two: Formulating Goals

During the second step of the strategic planning process, managers describe exactly what their organization wishes to accomplish in the future. Formulating goals requires managers to verify and affirm their organization's reasons for existence, define its mission, and establish strategic objectives. When conducting this step, Butch Ledworowski concluded that he was basically happy with the nature of Lil'America's business and the company's degree of success. He felt, however, that the company's goals should be modified and specified, among them: 1) to increase profits to a 15-20 percent margin per job; 2) to increase the dollar volume of business by 10-15 percent per year; and 3) to capitalize more on word-of-mouth advertising.

Step Three: Analyzing the Environment

Once managers have formulated their organization's goals, they must look at the factors in its external environment that might affect their ability to achieve those goals (see Table 8.2). An **informational (environmental) scan** is a process by which managers can collect information from their organization's general and task environments to identify indicators of opportunities and threats so that a strategy can be designed to address them. It is particularly important that an informational scan detect trends and changes in the environment, especially as the rate of change in the external environment escalates, because managers need an accurate set of assumptions on which to base their strategy.

Managers get environmental information in several ways. The historical evaluation conducted in Step One often reveals important information. Sometimes the experiences of other organizations that have encountered similar situations provide valuable information. Managerial intuition can identify relevant factors, too. Some data are available from government sources, and business and trade publications offer analyses. Lil'America's environmental scan revealed that: 1) new housing starts are expected to level off soon due to

TABLE 8.2   The Focus of Environmental Scanning

General Environment
1. *International information,* such as activities of foreign competition, resource availability, governments and interest groups, and international monetary events
2. *Political information* from local, regional, and national political developments
3. *Cultural information,* such as social movements and changes in values and societal needs
4. *Technical information,* such as technological innovations and licensing and patent information
5. *Economic information,* such as changes in rates of inflation, employment levels, and fluctuations in consumer prices

The Task Environment
1. *Supplier information,* such as resource availability and supplier behavior
2. *Regulatory agencies information,* such as current and pending regulatory activity
3. *Competitor information,* such as pricing strategies, advertising trends, and product/service characteristics
4. *Customers/market information,* such as distribution channels, market potential, pricing, and changes in customers' wants

an anticipated overbuilding of residential homes, 2) inflation is causing interest rates to rise, and 3) people are spending more leisure time at home. The environmental scan also indicated some potential problems, including an anticipated shortage of highly skilled labor.

Step Four: Analyzing Organizational Resources

The promise of future possibilities is very exciting, but what is an organization capable of right now? That is the question addressed by the fourth step of the strategic planning process. An organizational analysis, also referred to as an **organizational scan,** identifies an organization's present strengths and weaknesses by examining its internal resources. By analyzing such items as its technological capabilities, human resource capacities, and structural design, managers hope to discover what their organization possesses that makes it better able (or less able) than its competitors to meet the goals formulated in Step Two. For Lil'America, the organizational scan revealed technological capabilities, human resources, and financial strength to move toward the growth specified in its new goals. It was clear, however, that the desired level of growth would require resources not currently in place, including advertising and other business acquisition methods, additional skilled human resources, and greater training.

Step Five: Identifying Strategic Opportunities and Threats

In Step Five, managers use the information provided by environmental and organizational scans to identify opportunities to meet their goals and the threats that could thwart them. For example, Lil'America's environmental and organizational scans identified an opportunity for the company to meet its goal of increasing the dollar volume of business by specializing in sunroom additions and entertainment centers that would capitalize on the at-home leisure ("couch potato") phenomenon. The major threat to be considered was the predicted shortage of highly skilled workers.

Step Six: Performing Gap Analysis

Gap analysis identifies the expected difference between where managers want the organization to go and where it will go if they maintain current strategy. A performance gap is said to exist when managers must change goals and strategies to meet threats or to take advantage of opportunities. For example, Lil'America's gap analysis revealed that current strategy requires hiring highly skilled carpenters, but the information produced by Butch's scans shows that they probably will not be available. This gap between his wishes and reality requires a change in strategy if he intends to meet his goal of increased business.

Step Seven: Designing Strategy

At the seventh step of the strategic planning process, managers determine whether a new strategy is needed, and if so, what it should be. If gap analysis identified no expected gaps, managers continue with the existing plan. More often, though, gap analysis reveals that some changes in strategy are needed. Sometimes, managers need to make only minor modifications, as when an image problem can be rectified by a simple change in advertising. At other times, major changes in organizational strategy are required, such as entering a new market or even merging with another organization.

Making changes in strategy involves three steps: identifying the specific actions necessary, evaluating alternatives, and selecting one or more for implementation. Having reviewed the results of his gap analysis, for example, Butch questioned whether Lil'America should merge with SF Construction, a local competitor, to acquire the workers needed. He therefore met with owner Maggie Henry, and both parties explored the possibility. After the meeting, Butch evaluated the alternative by submitting it to four tests that can be used to judge the acceptability of a proposed strategy: (1) *goal consistency test* (are goals, objectives, and policies consistent with one another?), (2) *frame test* (are managerial efforts and organizational resources focused on the crucial issues or problems?), (3) *competence test* (can existing organizational resources and competencies be used?), and (4) *workability test* (is it likely to achieve the desired objectives?).[6] These tests convinced Butch that the merger alternative was not an acceptable strategy, in large part because Maggie's goals included expansion into new home construction, which was inconsistent with Butch's goal of remaining solely in home remodeling. After evaluating the remaining alternatives, Butch ultimately decided on trying to hire workers from competitors in outlying areas.

Step Eight: Implementing Strategy

At the eighth step of the strategic planning process, managers find ways to put the ideas from the strategic plan designed in Step Seven into action at each level of their organization. A corporate-level strategy must spawn compatible

"I'd like to take this opportunity to analyze our conceptual arsenal, discuss our competitive strategies, and formulate a posture statement."

James Stevenson from the *Harvard Business Review*

strategic plans for each business unit. Within each business unit, supportive functional strategies must be developed. For a large organization, this can be a time-consuming undertaking because, as the overall strategy filters downward, managers at each level must follow the full strategic planning process to develop strategies for the major organizational subdivisions and for each major functional area. Fortunately, for a small organization, such as Lil'America, implementing strategy is somewhat easier. Butch placed a hiring notice in the classified ads and phoned a few of his contacts in the construction industry. He was interviewing prospective skilled workers within a few days.

Step Nine: Measuring and Controlling Progress

At this final step of the strategic process, managers evaluate the effectiveness of the strategy in action. They check to see if it conforms to the strategy that they laid out in Step Seven and is accomplishing the goals that they set forth in Step Two. Managers also must control the progress of the implemented plan by making sure that appropriate work systems, such as those necessary for communication, are in place. The results of the evaluation and control measures conducted during this final step of the process tell managers if actions need to be taken to enforce a strategy that is not being followed or to modify a strategy that is not working. At Lil'America, Butch was able to hire enough skilled workers from his competition to offer remodeling services for sunrooms and entertainment centers. He will continue to evaluate and monitor the workers to see if they "mesh" with members of his existing workforce, and to determine whether the new business does indeed increase dollar volume by 10-15 percent per year.

In sum, the strategic planning process is a systematic, nine-step procedure that may seem long and complicated—and it is (review Figure 8.2). Strategic management is too important, however, to just "wing it." It is the primary tool that managers have for mapping the path their organization should take, for guiding it along that path, and for making sure it arrives at the intended destination.

Perspectives on Strategic Management

Various scholars and managers have offered their perspectives on the process of strategic management. These perspectives are useful to planners who want to think through and develop a comprehensive, effective strategic plan.

Problems Faced: The Adaptation Approach

As you have seen, strategic plans must fashion a careful match between an organization and its environment. Professors Raymond E. Miles of Emory University and Charles C. Snow of Pennsylvania State University discuss this match in their *adaptation approach* to strategic planning. They argue that the development of a match between an organization and its environment requires the solution of three basic kinds of problems: entrepreneurial, engineering, and administrative (see Figure 8.3).[7]

The *entrepreneurial problem* is to define an organization's mission. In new organizations, this problem is basically one of turning insight and vision into a

FIGURE 8.3   The Adaptive Cycle

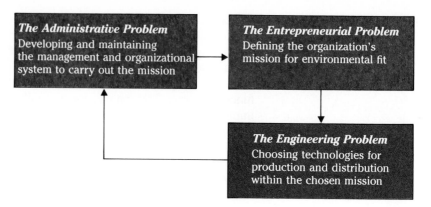

product or service and delivering it effectively. This is what engineer Kenneth Harry Olsen did in the late 1950s when he decided that the world needed a small, rugged, inexpensive minicomputer to compete with the giant mainframes. In providing such a product through his Digital Equipment Corporation, Olsen laid the groundwork for the personal computer revolution.

The *engineering problem* describes the creation of a way to implement the solution chosen at the entrepreneurial stage. Specifically, managers have to select technologies capable of producing and distributing their organization's products or services to the environment. If Sears, for example, adopted a strategy to let consumers charge purchases to their Discover credit card accounts using home computers, an engineering solution to this entrepreneurial plan might require that all Discover cardholders be given a phone number that their computers could dial to connect to the Sears system, a personal password to initiate the transaction, and software to help them order.

The *administrative problem* is one of developing, refining, and maintaining the management and organizational systems that let organization members carry out the strategic plan (see Chapters 9-11). In the Sears example, the administrative solution would have to include creating software to make the new system work, arranging phone service, letting Discover cardholders know about the service, and fashioning a campaign that tells the general public about this new advantage to owning a Discover card.

Ways to Face the Problems: Strategic Approaches

Miles and Snow identified four ways managers can approach the entrepreneurial, engineering, and administrative problems. Three of these ways—as a defender, a prospector, and an analyzer—are often associated with success (see Table 8.3). A fourth, the reactor approach, is usually considered a strategic failure.

Defenders.   Managers in **defender organizations** develop strategies that they hope will create and maintain a stable niche in the market for their organization's products or services. A defender strategy is best suited to organizations operating in relatively stable environments. If there is a major shift in its environment, a highly structured defender organization has difficulty being flexible enough to respond appropriately. Its tight structure and control also mean that new information is slow to reach managers. Perhaps the best known and most successful defender organization is McDonald's. The market chosen

TABLE 8.3   *Strategic Approaches*

Type of Organizational Strategy	Problem		
	Entrepreneurial	*Engineering*	*Administrative*
Defender	How to "seal off" a portion of the total market to create a stable set of products and customers	How to produce and distribute goods or services as efficiently as possible	How to maintain strict control of the organization to ensure efficiency
Prospector	How to locate and exploit new product and market opportunities	How to avoid long-term commitments to a single technological process	How to facilitate and coordinate numerous and diverse operations
Analyzer	How to locate and exploit new product and market opportunities while simultaneously maintaining a firm base of traditional products and customers	How to be efficient in stable portions of the domain and flexible in changing portions	How to differentiate the organization's structure and processes to accommodate both stable and dynamic areas of operation

Source: Based on R. E. Miles and C. C. Snow (1978), *Organizational strategy, structure, and process,* New York: McGraw-Hill.

by McDonald's is narrow, confined to the fast-food consumer; the company is a model of efficiency in dealing with the engineering problem; and its strict control in dealing with the administrative problem is legendary.

Prospectors.   **Prospector organizations** are innovative. Their managers move rapidly from one domain to another in search of new possibilities and attempt to create change within their own industry as a way of gaining an edge over the competition. Prospector organizations invest heavily in individuals and groups who scan the external environment for opportunities. 3M, for example, encourages many of its people to use 15 percent of their time away from day-to-day operations for discovery. Not surprisingly, a prospector strategy works best in an environment characterized by a high level of change.

Analyzers.   **Analyzer organizations** are a true blend of both defender and prospector styles. They attempt to balance the risk and aggression of a prospector with the conservative, protective nature of a defender. In many ways, an analyzer organization reduces risk—or "hedges its bets"—by conducting both stable and changeable businesses. One of the most successful analyzers has been Procter & Gamble, a company that operated as a defender organization for years by firmly establishing itself in the relatively narrow hand soap market. After decades of success, the firm began to incorporate prospector activities as it sought products to complement its soap business. Many of the products initially developed via the prospector mode, such as Crest toothpaste and Duncan Hines cake mixes, are now managed successfully with a defender approach.

Reactors.   **Reactor organizations** are so called because they tend to react to environmental events before they analyze the meaning and possible consequences of such events. Reactor organizations often fail because they develop strategy poorly, create an inadequate structure, and do not respond appropriately to changes in environmental conditions. In short, reactor organizations do not succeed because they do not systematically and effectively

As a defender organization, Procter & Gamble operated for years within a narrow market for hand soap. Today the company uses the prospector approach to identify and establish itself in new market areas.

Defender Organizations: Can MCI Analyze Its Way to Renewed Success?

A defender organization is one that creates a product or service in a fairly narrow area. By being fiercely competitive, the defender tries to seal off its portion of the total market and guard it against competitors, thus protecting a stable market niche. MCI is a good example of a company that has used the defender strategy to its advantage.

Almost twenty years ago, MCI selected a narrow service: cut-rate long-distance phone calls. At that time, American Telephone and Telegraph Company held a monopoly on long-distance services in the United States. MCI brashly attacked, challenged the monopoly in court, won the legal battle, established a 10 percent market share, and adopted a defender strategy to protect its share of the market. By virtually all standards, MCI's selection of a defender stance succeeded immensely.

A defender organization generally does not fare well, however, if its external environment changes substantially—which is what has happened in the long-distance calling marketplace. Largely because of

MCI's successful challenges, the Federal Communications Commission issued a series of rulings that decreased long-distance phone call rates by over 30 percent between 1984 and 1987. In 1986, MCI showed a $448 million loss. The question became: could MCI continue with a defender strategy and regain profitability? The answer: apparently not.

In its fight to recapture its previously successful position, MCI is trying an analyzer strategy, a combination of defender and prospector strategies. As a defender, MCI is trying to retain its solid base of existing residential customers. As a prospector, it is pursuing new markets, among them corporate long-distance customers, toll-free users (with 800 numbers), and international callers. MCI is supporting its prospector side by using new technologies. For example, the company has introduced computerized network phone services and added digital transmission lines that are ideal for computer communications.

Another aspect of the MCI analyzer strategy is to change its image. MCI

has long prided itself on its image as a maverick, both in marketing and delivering services. Now, it is shifting that image to a service-oriented company that customers feel they can influence, rather than the other way around. Recognizing that changes of this magnitude are difficult to accomplish alone, MCI struck an interesting deal that made IBM owner of 17 percent of MCI and gave IBM a position on the MCI board of directors. Among other advantages, this move let MCI capitalize on IBM's solid reputation as a service-oriented corporation.

A defender strategy served MCI well for almost two decades; however, the organization has moved on. Overall, MCI's new analyzer strategy cut internal operating costs by $100 million in 1986 alone and, in 1987 and 1988, reduced interest payments on loans by $15 million. Will the change from a defender to an analyzer organization achieve the desired results? Only time will tell, but observers seem to feel that this change gives MCI its best chance of success for the future.

attack strategic planning and implementation. Although a reactor organization may limp along for a while, the only way it is likely to experience long-term success is by converting to one of the other three approaches and becoming a different kind of organization.

This is what happened at Chrysler Corporation in the 1970s. The once-profitable organization began to flounder and to turn from a defender into a reactor. When Lee Iacocca took over Chrysler in 1978, he converted the corporation into an analyzer. In 1984, for example, Chrysler took prospective action in its risky introduction of minivans. By the late 1980s, Chrysler held most of the minivan market and was in the process of converting it into a defender operation. It was, at the same time, prospecting in joint ventures with Japanese organizations.

Ways to Configure an Organization: Business Portfolios

The nine-step strategic planning process does not automatically provide solutions to the strategic problem. Rather, it helps managers seek solutions systematically. Supplementing—not replacing—these nine steps is a technique that provides a framework for strategic solutions. When organizations that engage in many different businesses want a comprehensive approach to strategic planning, they sometimes adopt a *business portfolio* approach.[8] The portfolio approach to strategic planning proceeds through three phases: (1) developing strategic business units, (2) classifying them using a portfolio matrix, and (3) selecting an approach to manage each unit.

Strategic Business Units.   In the first phase, an organization identifies its strategic business units. You will recall from the earlier discussion of business unit strategy that a **strategic business unit (SBU)** is a segment of an organization with a distinct mission, external market, and strategy (or potential strategy) for dealing with that market. In some organizations, SBUs are formally designated as divisions, departments, or subsidiaries. Regardless of its formal designation, an SBU is essentially a portion of an overall organization that could constitute a freestanding business.

The Portfolio Matrix.   In the second phase, the organization places each SBU into a portfolio matrix. A **portfolio matrix** categorizes an SBU according to its relative market growth and market share into one of four distinct categories (see Figure 8.4 on page 184):

1. **Stars** are SBUs with a relatively large portion of a high-growth market. The compact disk SBU of SONY is a star, because it possesses the industry's largest share of the CD market, which is itself increasing at an extremely rapid rate.
2. **Cash cows** are SBUs with a large share of a low-growth market. The refrigerator SBU for General Electric is a cash cow because, although the overall market for refrigerators is not growing substantially, GE maintains a large share of that market.
3. **Question marks** (sometimes called *wildcats*) possess a relatively small share of a rapidly growing market. Western Union's computerized information service is a question mark for that corporation. There is no doubt that the market for on-line information services is growing rapidly, but Western Union presently possesses only a relatively small share of it.
4. **Dogs** are SBUs with a small portion of a low-growth market. Dogs are clearly not the glamorous part of a portfolio. In fact, they often cannot support themselves and drain cash from other parts of an organization. Over 40 percent of SBUs can best be classified as dogs.[9]

Selecting a Business Approach.   Once an SBU is identified and classified, the final phase of the portfolio approach involves selecting an approach to manage it. Managers often use one of four grand strategies to achieve long-term objectives:

FIGURE 8.4 *The Business Portfolio Matrix*

Source: A. Gerald (June 1976), A note on The Boston Consulting Group concept of competitive analysis and corporate strategy, *Intercollegiate Case Clearing House,* ICCH 9-175-175.

1. **Growth strategy**—used for stars and for question marks that an organization hopes to transform into stars, this strategy requires the organization to invest substantial amounts of capital in the SBU to increase its market share.

2. **Stable growth,** or **hold, strategy**—appropriate for most cash cows and some dogs, this strategy allocates only the resources necessary to avoid loss of market share.

3. **Retrenchment,** or **turnaround, strategy**—implemented when an SBU fails to perform as expected, as when a question mark fails to become a star, this strategy tries to stimulate markets by finding new uses for existing products, by changing the image of a product, or by modifying a product in a search for a market niche. Sales of Retin-A, for example, rose significantly after the acne treatment was discovered to have the potential to reduce wrinkles and reverse precancerous skin conditions.

4. **Divestiture strategy**—this strategy is used when managers want to eliminate an SBU, either by selling it or by closing it. Divestiture gets rid of dogs that no longer generate a profit and would be difficult to improve, cash cows expected to stop producing, and stars whose sale can generate cash needed to support other parts of an organization's portfolio.[10]

Generic Strategies

A slightly different way of looking at strategies was developed by Michael Porter of the Harvard Business School.[11] Porter describes three strategies—cost leadership, differentiation, and focus—that managers pursue to establish a competitive niche in the market. These three business-level strategies are

A Turnaround Strategy:
M–I–C–K–E–Y M–O–N–E–Y

The years between 1966 and 1984 were grim ones for the Disney corporation, despite the fact that its theme parks were still profitable. Its movie studios churned out mostly failures, and Disney images had pretty much disappeared from the TV screen. "Mickey Mouse" profits were all the company could create. In 1984, Disney was considered ripe for a corporate takeover.

In 1984, things changed at Disney. New owners bought a 25 percent share of the corporation. In return, they demanded a total management overhaul and a new, aggressive, strategic plan. The results have been impressive. Michael D. Eisner, the new chairman and chief executive, and Frank G. Wells, the new president and chief operating officer, decided it was time to attack today's entertainment marketplace with new vigor and a new perspective. How have they done it? Through a two-part strategy designed to show growth and develop strength.

Emphasizing the importance of strategic planning, Disney recently named Lawrence P. Murphy as its new senior vice-president for strategic planning and development. This move met with widespread admiration, as noted by *Fortune* when it named Murphy one of 1989's "Fortune People on the Rise."[1]

The first part of Disney's turnaround strategy focuses on its existing assets, including its theme parks, hotels, and cartoon characters. They have been marketed aggressively and have incorporated modern technologies, such as computer outlets for the Disney comics. In 1988 Disney opened the first of its very successful "Disney Stores," which sell clothing and souvenirs bearing the likeness of Disney characters. Strategic plans call for the opening of 100 stores by 1992.

The second part of the Disney strategy focuses on creating new properties. Disney has entered the modern world of movie entertainment with extremely profitable Touchstone Pictures, including *Outrageous Fortune, Who Framed Roger Rabbit, Ruthless People*, and *Tin Men*. Disney's strategy also has been aimed at the small screen once again. Under Murphy's direction, the company recently acquired an independent TV station in Los Angeles. Nationally, the Disney Channel's subscriber base on cable TV has grown immensely, and Disney has had successes with such network shows as *The Golden Girls.*

A creative hybrid of existing and new business opportunities is epitomized by the May 1989 opening of a combined movie studio/tour attraction on the grounds of the Disney complex in Florida. The opening of new high-end and moderate hotel accommodations preceded the opening of the new attraction.

The new strategy is far from fully implemented. Recently, Disney divested itself of its real-estate unit for about $400 million, a $200 million profit in less than three years. To raise cash, Disney is trying to sell its Epcot Center property in Orlando, Florida, for over $1 billion. It plans to invest the money from these sales into what Eisner and Wells hope will be Disney's future star SBUs: more new hotels, a new European Disneyland theme park, and other major entertainment investments. One likely acquisition for Disney would be a distribution channel for its movies—in other words, movie theaters.

The current strategic plan for Disney is quite different from its 1984 plan. After scanning Disney's external environment and internal capabilities, its new managers targeted products and services they believed would give Disney a solid base for its turnaround. They created a strategy, followed it, monitored its progress, and revised it when necessary. Due to their sound strategy—if not to magic—the kingdom is healthy once again.

1. Fortune people—on the rise (24 April 1989), *Fortune*, 320.

known as **generic strategies** because they are applicable to a wide range of organizations. Recently it has been shown that appropriate matches of these strategies with the environment and an organization's structure can lead to enhanced success.[12]

Cost leadership strategy requires managers to sell their organization's products or services more cheaply than its competitor does. This strategy can work well if the product is much like the higher-priced competitor's. The Tandy Corporation, for example, introduced a line of IBM-compatible personal computers in the 1980s and marketed them primarily as cheaper—not better—versions of the IBM computer. A **differentiation strategy** tries to convince potential customers that the organization is different from its competition in a meaningful way. Instead of competing with IBM through low cost, for example, Compaq captured substantial portions of the personal computer market by offering the first mass-marketed personal computer to use the fast 80386 chip. Managers who use a **focus strategy** concentrate their resources on competing within a specific segment in a total market in an attempt to become more efficient. The segment might be a geographic location (American Family Insurance concentrates on the Midwest), a particular customer group (BMW concentrates on higher-income professionals), or any other identifiable segment of the market.

Special Cases: Small and Not-for-Profit Organizations

Research has shown that relatively few of the tens of thousands of small and not-for-profit organizations throughout the country engage systematically in strategic planning, even though strategy is just as important to their success as it is to that of larger corporations. Many of the strategic planning techniques discussed in this chapter can be used by small and not-for-profit organizations. In addition, small organizations need to contemplate certain special considerations.

Small Organizations

To people in many small organizations, the strategic planning process appears complex, expensive, formal, and time consuming. For these reasons, managers of many small organizations avoid strategic planning. As Lil'America's experiences show, however, planning is valuable to organizations of all sizes.

In some ways, strategic planning is easier in small organizations because they and their external task environments are generally less complex. In addition, because of the more manageable size of a small organization, strategic planning can often be conducted by one, or a few, managers. For these reasons, the strategic planning process can be considerably less formal, less complex, less costly, and less time consuming for a manager of a small and structurally simple organization than it is for a larger organization. On the other hand, because small organizations often struggle from day to day merely to survive, their managers find it difficult to take the time required to conduct strategic planning. As more and more managers of small organizations recognize that strategic planning saves time in the long run and enhances effectiveness, strategic planning will become more popular.

Not-for-Profit Organizations

Not-for-profit organizations, whether they are private or public, exist for many different reasons.[13] Some are large national organizations with far-

reaching missions; others affect only those people in the immediate community. Most provide protection, social services, health care, entertainment/recreation, and education. Although they may not operate for profits, these organizations still must be managed, and strategic management is an important part of this process.

Managers of not-for-profit organizations are less likely than their counterparts in for-profit organizations to engage in systematic strategic planning. Even when they do, their plans tend to be shorter term.[14] Managers in many of these organizations infrequently reexamine their organization's mission, and because only a few individuals hold control, strategic planning is often ignored.

Recently, however, some not-for-profit organizations have begun to use strategic planning. One reason they are forced to do so is because they will fail if they do not, as when a local theater group cannot project revenues accurately enough to assure creditors that invoices will be paid. Economic factors can also encourage not-for-profit organizations to use strategic planning, as is the case when federal funds are cut for low-income housing projects. Competition for services also can force even large not-for-profit organizations to use strategic plans. The U.S. Postal Service, for example, has operated at a loss for years—despite several rate increases—and has gained a reputation for slow service from uncaring employees. Increased sales services from such for-profit competitors as Federal Express and United Parcel Service are causing postal administrators to explore alternative strategies—for example, postal service available through Sears stores and pickup of overnight mail envelopes by carriers on their normal route.

Although there are not yet any good strategic planning models specifically tailored to not-for-profit organizations, their managers can follow the guidelines presented in this chapter. Given their financial objectives, not-for-profit organizations should focus on efficiency rather than on profitability. In addition, measures of effectiveness are likely to concentrate on the degree to which an organization serves the external environment rather than on the degree to which the organization benefits from the environment. With the need for "volunteerism" stressed by the last two American presidents, not-for-profit organizations grow in importance. So, too, does their need for strategic management.

Strategic Management in Review

Strategic management is systematic, long-term planning that positions an organization within its external environment. A strategic plan specifies the organization's mission (which businesses it will undertake), strategic objectives (the definable and measurable accomplishments associated with the mission), and operational strategies (the actions to be used to accomplish the objectives).

Strategic planning typically is performed for three levels in an organization—corporate, business unit, and functional—and reflects the personalities and preferences of an organization's managers. The entrepreneurial style of strategic planning is characterized by bold initiatives. The adaptive style is defensive and allows the environment to shape an organization. The planning style reflects systematic development of a comprehensive plan to position an organization within its task environment.

Implementing a strategic plan involves a nine-step process, which managers begin with a planning awareness stage. They proceed to formulate their organization's goals, analyze its external environment and internal resources, and identify existing and potential opportunities and threats. At this point, managers perform a gap analysis to see where the current strategy may fall short of meeting expectations, and they design a new strategy to address those shortcomings. After implementing the new strategy, managers must then measure and control its progress to see that it is being carried out as intended and produces the desired results.

Various perspectives exist regarding strategic management. The adaptation approach maintains that strategic plans must address entrepreneurial, engineering, and administrative problems. The business portfolio approach to strategic planning classifies strategic business units according to market share and market growth. A third strategic approach is based on a scheme of generic strategies designed to establish a market niche for an organization's products or services.

Although the managers of many small and not-for-profit organizations ignore strategic planning, they must fit these organizations into their environments. In doing so, they can benefit by following the models of strategic management presented in this chapter.

Issues for Review and Discussion

1. Describe the purposes of strategic planning and outline its advantages and disadvantages.
2. Identify the three levels of strategic planning and discuss why it is important to integrate planning across these three levels.
3. Discuss how analyses of the external environment and of organizational resources can identify strategic opportunities and threats.

4. What is gap analysis, and why is it a critical step in the strategic planning process?
5. Describe the relationship among the entrepreneurial, engineering, and administrative problems and explain how they are addressed by strategic planning.
6. Compare and contrast defender, prospector, and analyzer organizations. Explain why reactor organizations seldom succeed.
7. Why might an organization want to include stars, cash cows, *and* dogs in its business portfolio?
8. Discuss the special problems that face a manager of a small organization during strategic planning.
9. Suppose you are the director of United Way, a not-for-profit organization that receives public donations and distributes the money to other service organizations, such as the Boy Scouts of America. How would you incorporate what you know of strategic planning to fit the goals of your organization?

Key Terms

strategic management	defender organizations
strategy	prospector organizations
strategic planning	analyzer organizations
strategic plan	reactor organizations
organizational mission	strategic business unit (SBU)
mission statement	portfolio matrix
strategic objectives	stars
operational strategies	cash cows
scope	question marks
resource deployment	dogs
competitive advantages	growth strategy
synergy	stable growth/hold strategy
corporate strategy	retrenchment/turnaround strategy
business unit strategy	divestiture strategy
functional strategy	generic strategies
informational (environmental) scan	cost leadership strategy
organizational scan	differentiation strategy
gap analysis	focus strategy

Suggested Readings

Below, P. J., Morrisey, G. L., and Acomb, B. L. (1987). *The executive guide to strategic planning.* San Francisco: Jossey-Bass.

Huff, A. S., Reger, R. K. (1987). A review of strategic process research. *Journal of Management,* 13, 211-36.

Notes

1. A. A. Thompson and A. J. Strickland III (1983), *Strategy formulation and implementation: Tasks of the general manager,* Plano, TX: Business Publications.
2. H. Mintzberg (1973), Strategy-making in three modes, *California Management Review* 16, 44-53; H. Mintzberg (1973), *The nature of managerial work,* Englewood Cliffs, NJ: Prentice-Hall.
3. C. E. Lindblom (1958), The science of "muddling through," *Public Administration Review,* 19, 79-88.

4. V. Govindarajan (1988), A contingency approach to strategy implementation at the business-unit level: Integrating administrative mechanisms with strategy, *Academy of Management Journal,* 31, 828-53.

5. D. Schendel and C. W. Hofer (1979), Introduction to strategic management, in D. E. Schendel and C. W. Hofer, eds., *Strategic management: A new view of business policy and planning,* Boston: Little, Brown, 1-29; A. D. Szilagyi, Jr. (1984), *Management and performance,* Glenview, IL: Scott, Foresman.

6. *Ibid.*

7. R. E. Miles and C. C. Snow (1978), *Organizational strategy, structure, and process,* New York: McGraw-Hill; R. E. Miles, C. C. Snow, A. Meyer, and H. Coleman (1978), Organizational strategy, structure, and process, *Academy of Management Review,* 3, 546-62.

8. B. Hedley (1977), Strategy and the business portfolio, *Long Range Planning* 10, 9-15; Schendel and Hofer; I. Macmillan, D. C. Hambrick, and D. L. Day (1982), The product portfolio and profitability—a PIMS-based analysis of industrial product businesses, *Academy of Management Journal* 25, 510-31; A. Gerald (June 1976), A note on The Boston Consulting Group concept of competitive analysis and corporate strategy, *Intercollegiate Case Clearing House,* ICCH 9-175-175.

9. Hambrick and Day.

10. J. A. Pearce II (1982), Selecting among alternative grand strategies, *California Management Review* 24, 23-31.

11. M. E. Porter (1985), *Competitive advantage: Creating and sustaining superior performance,* New York: The Free Press.

12. D. Miller (1988), Relating Porter's business strategies to environment and structure: Analysis and performance implications, *Academy of Management Journal,* 31, 280-308.

13. R. Lachman (1985), Public and private sector differences: CEO's perceptions of their role environments, *Academy of Management Journal* 28, 671-80; B. P. Keating and M. O. Keating (1980), *Not-for-profit,* Glen Ridge, NJ: Thomas Horton and Daughters.

14. M. S. Wortman, Jr. (1979), Strategic management: Not-for-profit organizations, in D. E. Schendel and C. W. Hofer, eds., *Strategic management: A new view of business policy and planning,* Boston: Little, Brown, 353-81; Schendel and Hofer.

Xerox Corporation

By J. David Hunger, Thomas Conquest, and William Miller, Iowa State University

Xerox introduced the world's first convenient office copier in 1959, and its sales exploded, rising from $33 million a year to $3.6 billion by 1974. Its profits mushroomed from $2 million to $331 million, and the price of its stock soared from $2 a share to $172. The company grew to 100 times its former size. In that short period, photocopying machines dramatically transformed the nature of office work. Xerography made carbon paper and mimeograph machines obsolete and drastically reduced typing time. By the end of 1970, Xerox held the dominant position in the worldwide office copier market, with 95 percent of the market.

This monopolistic market share was seriously eroded in the 1970s, due to increased competition from many sources. Xerox had built its business by creating the plain paper copying market and then by protecting it with a solid wall of patents; however, in 1975, the company signed a consent decree with the Federal Trade Commission, in which Xerox agreed to license other companies wanting to use its process. Their seventeen-year patent protection was also expiring, and Xerox' technology could increasingly be used by anyone.

Recognizing that the copying industry was not going to continue to grow at its previous rate, Xerox positioned itself to become a major competitor in the "Office of the Future" market by creating an office products division. In 1981, Xerox executives reported to their stockholders that the overriding corporate objective over the next decade was to be one of the leading companies in enhancing office productivity. "In order to accomplish this," the report said, "Xerox must maintain and strengthen its position of leadership in reprographics—as we refer to our total copying and duplicating business—and emerge from the 1980s as a leading systems company that is a major factor in automating the office."

Problems

By the autumn of 1982, the chief executive officer of the Xerox Corporation, David Kearns, was facing some difficult problems. His company had just suffered a 39 percent drop in third-quarter earnings. This was Xerox' fourth consecutive quarterly decline and the picture did not appear brighter for the current quarter. Much of the profit decline had been attributed to narrower profit margins brought on by steep price cutting on many copier models in response to increasing competition, especially from the Japanese. In addition, Xerox' profits had been reduced by severance costs of trimming its workforce; by the strength of the dollar, which eroded the values of its sales made abroad; and particularly by the sluggish U.S. economy. Xerox had reduced its workforce by 2174 employees in 1981, the first such reduction in the company's history. Further reductions occurred in 1982,

with more predicted for the coming year. Kearns had watched Xerox' share of the plain paper copier market slip from 95 percent to about 45 percent in 1982. In addition, Xerox stock had slipped to less than $40 in 1982.

Xerox' attempts to lessen its dependence on the competitive copier market by moving into the broader office automation area had been less than spectacular. The office products division had only one profitable quarter in its seven-year history and had losses of approximately $90 million in 1981. Kearns had admitted recently to market analysts that he did not expect the unit to be profitable until 1984. The division had recently been reorganized in an attempt to deal more effectively with some of the problems. Shortly after the reorganization, however, two of the key executives from the office products division resigned to form their own company.

The Office of the Future

The high cost of management, professional, and clerical workers in combination with the increasing capabilities of electronic office equipment established office automation as a major growth market for the 80s. White-collar salaries had become a huge and seemingly intractable cost of doing business. In 1980, 60 percent of the $1.3 trillion paid in wages, salaries, and benefits in the United States went to office workers. At the same time, the cost of electronic office equipment fell. Computer memory became cheaper at an annual rate of 42 percent over the five years prior to 1982 and the price of the logic chips that give computers their intelligence dropped about 28 percent a year.

Although office automation made sense in theory, the market did not develop as quickly as Xerox and others hoped. According to a competitor, Wang Laboratories, only 60 or so of the largest industrial corporations had acquired as many as 100 electronic office work stations; a much smaller number had linked them into networks.

Many reasons were given for the slow growth of this market. First of all, the recession caused many organizations to cut back on capital spending programs. Second, there was a lack of convincing studies on the savings associated with office automation. Third, in developing automation for managers and professionals, there was a problem in specifying exactly what steps or processes these individuals went through in doing their jobs. Fourth, top management did not feel comfortable with computer terminals on their desks. Fifth, there was uncertainty over the type of networking system that would prevail, and this made customers postpone purchasing networks. Finally, despite managers' universal desire to find better ways of doing work, office automation remained poorly understood.

Still, Dataquest, Inc., a California-based market research firm, estimated that U.S. shipments of equipment that could be linked to form electronic offices would grow 34 percent a year through 1986. Total revenues were predicted to grow between $12 and $15 billion.

This anticipation of a booming market for office automation brought dozens of companies into the competition. AT&T, IBM, and Xerox all declared the market to be a key to their future. In 1981, the top three minicomputer companies, Digital Equipment, Hewlett-Packard, and Data General, launched office automation systems within thirty days of one another. Analysts saw IBM, Wang, Digital Equipment, and Xerox as being in the best position to capture large pieces of this growing market, yet there appeared to be enough profitable niches to reward any company that could fill customers' needs.

Xerox Marketing

Xerox had traditionally been a single product line company, selling copiers to large businesses through its own sales and service force. This changed as it diversified its product line and redefined its customer base. The company revamped its copiers, offering a wider range of products to smaller businesses as well as larger companies. With their move into electronic office systems, a systems approach to marketing became necessary.

To meet the marketing problems associated with the company's new concepts, Xerox experimented with new distribution techniques. Independent distributors and dealers were contracted to sell products not only to end users, but also to original equipment manufacturers (OEMs), who resold the products as part of larger systems. These distribution systems reduced the company's expenses, thereby increasing margins while unburdening the company's own salesforce.

Xerox also planned to use retail chains, as well as its own retail stores, to reach small businesses. By 1982, it had already opened approximately thirty retail stores throughout the U.S. and had plans to open more. These outlets were named *The Xerox Store* and were designed to make small business operators comfortable in a store with a familiar name and reputation. In addition to selling Xerox' equipment, these outlets also carried brand-name equipment of other manufacturers, including competitors for home and office use. Most of this equipment complemented Xerox' own products and included Apple Computers, Hewlett-Packard calculators, Matsushita dictating machines, and a host of other products.

According to industry analysts, Xerox had three major marketing strengths. Its sales and service staff was the largest in the industry. The company had many financial resources to fund challenging, new product developments. Finally, the Xerox name was a household word, which gave customers a feeling of confidence about getting products serviced.

Analysts agreed that if the company had any weaknesses, it was a lack of expertise in marketing complex office products and systems. There were apparently great differences between marketing stand-alone copying machines and marketing more complex information-handling and processing systems. By 1981, Xerox had captured 13 percent of the word processor market but only about 1 percent of the small business office systems market.

September 1982

In September 1982, Xerox took the industry by surprise when it announced an agreement to acquire Crum & Forster, an insurance holding company, for about $1.65 billion in cash and securities. Crum & Forster was the nation's fifteenth largest property-casualty insurer, with $1.6 billion in premiums and $171 million in profits in 1981. The Xerox offer was twice the previous market price of the Crum & Forster stock.

Kearns gave several reasons for the acquisition: (1) Xerox believed that property-casualty insurance offered the best growth opportunities in the insurance industry. (2) The company perceived the acquisition as an expansion of Xerox' financial services, to complement the Xerox Credit Corporation. Formed in 1979 to help Xerox customers finance their purchases of Xerox equipment, this subsidiary had profits of about $35 million in 1981. (3) The acquisition would provide investment income, which Xerox needed to support its research in copiers, duplicators, and other office equipment.

Xerox watchers wondered whether the company had lost confidence in its office automation business. One analyst said, "My hunch is that office products may never be profitable for them. They've lost momentum." Kearns, however, disagreed. "This is a very aggressive strategy to grow this business with two market segments very different from each other. We concluded we could leverage the balance sheet at this time to branch out to other areas for a better return to our shareholders."

Questions

1. What are the major strategic planning issues that Xerox had dealt with in the late 1970s and early 1980s, following its consent decree with the Federal Trade Commission?

2. What evidence do you see here of corporate level strategic planning? business unit level planning? functional level planning?

3. What is your analysis of the Crum & Forster acquisition from a business portfolio standpoint?

4. From a strategy perspective, how would you have evaluated Xerox' quest in 1982 to be a dominant company in the "Office of the Future"?

5. Had Xerox CEO David Kearns asked you in 1982 to develop a strategic plan to take the company into the 1990s, what questions would you have asked him?

PART 3 *Organizing*

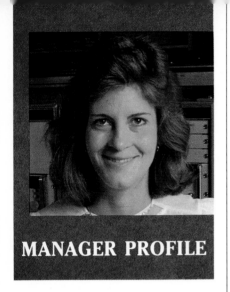

MANAGER PROFILE

Sara Westendorf

From earning a B.A. in German and linguistics to receiving a B.S. in computer engineering, from having a career in social work to being a manager of design engineers, from Massachusetts to California—such has been the path of Sara Westendorf. Today while she heads a division at Hewlett-Packard, she is primarily concerned with doing things that are interesting and enjoyable, making sure that she is always in a position where she is learning something new. "My goal has always been to make the people and projects that I am responsible for successful. Doing a top-notch job will make the promotions come my way." In six years and after three promotions, thirty-five-year-old Westendorf is research and development manager for Advanced Manufacturing Systems (AMSO) at Hewlett-Packard.

Sex-role stereotyping (maybe), a caring for people (obviously), a drive to excel, perfectionism, and a problem-solving orientation have played major roles in Westendorf's career choices. Following graduation from high school in Amherst, Massachusetts, Westendorf worked as a nurses' aide in West Germany and then went on to earn a B.A. in German and linguistics from the University of Rochester. During this time, she did social work and eventually pursued an M.S.W. at Rutgers University. After two and one half years of developing caring relationships with the children and families who were a part of her case load, Westendorf began to experience frustration and, possibly, occupational burnout. She found herself dealing with problems for which her formal training had not equipped her, emotionally or technically.

She talks about working with a family with fifteen children aged fourteen and under. One of the babies belonged to the fourteen-year-old daughter, another to the twelve-year-

old daughter. "Just as I was starting to feel good that the third grader with a truancy problem had achieved a perfect school attendance record for two weeks, two of the other children dropped out of school. Just as I was starting to feel good about the seventh grader staying away from liquor and dope for a week, the sixth grader overdosed on 'reds' and the mother spent the grocery money to get high herself." Experiences of this nature were taking their toll. As Westendorf tells it, "I would have done anything to help those kids, but frankly, the futility of my best efforts was so overwhelming that it seemed like the only way to preserve my sanity was to stop caring, in the same way many of the experienced social workers seemed to have done." Instead, Westendorf fantasized about becoming an engineer, and shortly thereafter she turned that dream into a reality.

She is always in a position where she is learning something new.

At Princeton University and then at the University of Illinois, Westendorf turned her attention to designing functional computers. In 1976 she received a B.S. in computer engineering, and today she manages an engineering unit. Recognizing her need for formal training in business economics, and management, she is planning on pursuing an M.B.A. degree.

Westendorf now manages R&D for Hewlett-Packard's Advanced Manufacturing Systems Operation. Formed in 1984, AMSO's mission is to apply HP's measurement and computation expertise in providing custom-integrated testing systems that improve customers' product and process quality. AMSO produces integrated test systems with an aerospace/military market focus and in-process/service-bay vehicle analyses for the automotive industry.

AMSO is organized into four functional areas—manufacturing, marketing, finance, and research and development. The R&D unit is responsible for designing and implementing computer systems. Within the R&D unit, Westendorf's managerial responsibilities include providing the leadership the organization needs to meet its goals of profitability and customer satisfaction. She sees her success as largely dependent on the caliber and expertise of the people in her organization. As a consequence, she places a premium on human resource recruitment and development, and on providing an excellent working environment. She says, "If an engineering team has the right expertise for the job and the individuals are enthused about the project they're working on, then productivity, profitability, and customer satisfaction will follow." Westendorf sees her job as providing the right environment and developing a sense of enthusiasm and project commitment among her subordinates.

Westendorf's management style has significant roots in her educational experiences. Her social-work education and work experiences helped her develop several interpersonal skills that are necessary in the highly political and sensitive organizational environment. She also credits her experiences with giving her a sense of resourcefulness. "Working in agencies operating on shoestring budgets instilled the attitude of doing whatever it takes to get the job done." Finally, her frustration with social work left Westendorf with an appreciation for the importance of job satisfaction. "Enhancing your job satisfaction is important, because the more you enjoy your job, the better you'll do at it."

Westendorf's engineering educa-tion and work experiences provided her with another set of important ingredients of her management philosophy. Her technical background equipped her to understand the organization's product line. "No matter what business you're in, whether it's perfume or rifles, understanding your product line is essential to being successful in a management position." Understanding the customer is equally important. Westendorf feels that her engineering background helps her understand the product, and that this background provides her with the opportunity to better understand the customer and the needs the organization is attempting to fulfill.

"The more you enjoy your job, the better you'll do at it."

Several other factors—making it fun, making effective use of mentoring, keeping up a sense of humor, and managing by walking around—highlight Westendorf's management style and play an important role in her success:

Regarding fun—make sure you enjoy what you are doing. As a manager your enthusiasm about a project will inspire the workers and make them productive.

Regarding leadership—be willing to do whatever it takes. Leading through dedication and commitment to getting the job done will inspire others to do the same. Being boss does not mean you are any more important than everyone else; treating everyone equally is important in promoting a spirit of teamwork.

Regarding humor—especially in high-pressure situations, a sense of humor can do an amazing job of diffusing tension and promoting teamwork.

Managing by walking around

(MBWA) is a management process that has become part of the Hewlett-Packard way. Westendorf notes that some decisions must be made in the privacy of one's own office, yet most decisions are best made with the involvement of employees. She says, "I find myself coming up to people and saying, 'I've been thinking about whether we ought to keep bidding minicomputer products into our system, or whether we ought to go to a lower-cost, PC-based controller, and I'd be interested in hearing your thoughts on the matter.'" This process accomplishes a number of things:

You soon have a good feel for who knows what.

Workers feel good that you cared enough to ask for their opinion.

You will probably get some good information that will help you make the right decision.

You will have more grassroots support for your decision from the people who felt involved in making the decision.

If the decision is later questioned, you will know who to go to for back-up information.

You will have effectively communicated to the trenches some of the issues you are wrestling with, and the "troops" seem to appreciate knowing these things.

Finally, Westendorf notes that MBWA is a good way to validate a decision once it has been made, or to see if there are any better ideas floating around before the decision is finalized.

What outstanding perspective makes Sara Westendorf a successful manager? According to her, it is "a results-oriented, can-do, get-the-job-done-no-matter-what-it-takes attitude."

9 Organizing and Coordinating Work

Student Learning Objectives

After reading this chapter, you should be able to:

1. Understand what managers do when they engage in the organizing activity.

2. Understand the difference between the formal and informal organization.

3. Distinguish among the classical, behavioral management, and work group approaches to the organizing of jobs.

4. Identify and differentiate the various approaches to departmentalizing jobs.

5. Identify the ways managers coordinate the levels of an organization's hierarchy.

6. Identify the ways managers coordinate units at the same level in an organization's hierarchy.

7. Identify and discuss the problems managers face when integrating individuals, jobs, and organizational units.

*T*hink about all of the activities employees perform at your university: scheduling courses, cleaning windows, ordering supplies, maintaining student records, teaching classes, preparing food, and so on. If you were to make a comprehensive list, you would probably identify several thousand different tasks. The managerial activity of organizing attempts to bring order and direction to the work of an organization. This chapter and the two that follow discuss the ways in which managers organize.

The Nature of Organizing

Organizations are systems created to achieve a set of goals through people-to-people and people-to-work relationships. Each system has its own external and internal environments that define the nature of those relationships according to its specific needs. A hospital, for example, has organizational needs that are different from those of a university, which are different from those of a museum or of the federal government. **Organizing** is what managers do when they design, structure, and arrange the components of an organization's internal environment to facilitate the attainment of organizational goals. For example, to meet its goal of delivering high-quality health care, a hospital may organize both in- and outpatient facilities, locate its emergency room on the first floor of the building to prevent delays in treating critical cases, prepare meals, provide room cleaning services, and so forth. The people-to-people and people-to-work relationships—that is, the organization—created for a hospital's housekeeping department differ from those for its surgical unit because each department has a different set of goals.

Managers organize by defining and coordinating work at a number of different levels: tasks are grouped to form jobs, jobs are combined into departments, and departments are organized into divisions (see Figure 9.1 on page 201). Organizational activities are supported by a variety of systems. The authority and communication systems, for example, that link a large hospital with its satellites provide computerized information exchanges on such matters as budgets and medical information. Personnel move back and forth between the organizations, providing human skill and expertise. Managers must organize the systems needed to fulfill all of the organization's coordination needs.

Within any organization, there are both formal and informal components. The **formal organization** exists as a result of the official structures and systems managers design through the organizing activity.[1] The formal organization usually contains a structured decision-making, communication, and command system that helps people pool their time, energy, and talents to reach common objectives. (See "A Closer Look: Formal Organization.")

The **informal organization,** in contrast, exists when two or more people interact for a purpose or in a manner beyond that specified by managers. Informal organizations evolve in a natural, unplanned manner, but they may also form intentionally. A group of nurses at a nursing station between shifts may contain some members who want to socialize, others who want a snack, and some who want a place to wait for a ride home. Because members of the informal organization exchange information, satisfy individual needs, and influence one another, the informal organization may have direct and significant implications for managers of the formal organization.

Formal Organization: Runner's World *Goes the Distance Through Organization*

Runner's World magazine has a monthly circulation of 350,000 copies and requires the services of a number of full-time employees. To help these employees operate efficiently and effectively, *Runner's World* has a formal organization that specifies their responsibilities and clarifies the links among jobs and departments.

In 1966, *Runner's World* had no organization and no employees. In that year, seventeen-year-old Bob Anderson, tired of the lack of good information about running, produced a twenty-eight-page first issue of a magazine he called *Distance Running News*. Bob was writer, editor, publisher, and marketing manager—totally alone in the venture. He used $100 of savings to print and sell 1000 copies of his new magazine at $.75 a copy.

In 1967, Bob was still running the company by himself, but he recognized that one person alone could not guarantee the continued growth and success of the magazine. By 1970, he had moved the company from Kansas to California, changed the name of the magazine to *Runner's World*, developed an international network of part-time correspondents, and hired a full-time assistant.

Eventually, Bob created a formal organization designed to coordinate work efficiently and effectively. He still carried the titles of editor and publisher, but the organization also had an executive editor, a managing editor, a photo editor, a features editor, a columns editor, and a copy editor. There were directors of production, creative arts, advertising, sales, circulation, and human resources. Each director had a staff.

Job descriptions specified the responsibilities of each employee. People with similar jobs supported a particular function (for example, advertising) and were grouped into departments. Each department had a director, who was responsible for supervising the department's employees and managing its activities successfully. Directors reported to executives, who coordinated related departments.

Bob and his managers created a variety of formal rules and regulations to encourage fair and consistent treatment of individual employees. At the same time, these rules and regulations set guidelines for the operation and coordination of jobs and departments. They specified who would make decisions and how they would be implemented.

Running requires one step at a time. Competitive running, however, requires coordination, stamina, and long-term planning. The same is true for the running of an organization. In 1966, Bob Anderson founded his magazine and developed it one step at a time. With its rapid success, however, one step at a time proved insufficient to reach the goal, and Bob passed the baton to Rodale Press in 1985.

The new owners streamlined the structure. Today, with the help of computers, twenty-five full-time staff members publish the widely popular magazine. The current lean structure—the creative arts, advertising, sales, and circulation directors all make do with one secretary, for example—enables it to compete in the competitive publishing race.

Source: S. P. Robbins (1983), *Organization theory: The structure and design of organizations*, Englewood Cliffs, NJ: Prentice-Hall, 3-5; current data from industry statistics and direct communication with *Runner's World*.

In the formal organization, managers prescribe expected behaviors through job descriptions, rules, policies, and operating procedures. In contrast, informal behaviors arise from the needs, norms, values, and standards of organization members. The formal organization in a company that assembles bathroom exhaust fans, for example, might specify the time to show up for work and the method to be used to assemble the fans. The informal organization, however, may define a social norm stating that employees should not produce more than a certain number of fans per hour.

Managers need to recognize that both formal and informal organizations exist and that both influence the overall efficiency and effectiveness of their organization.

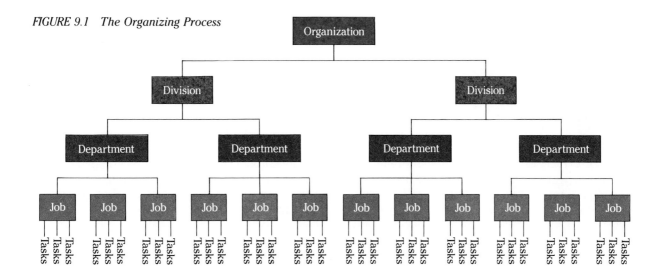

FIGURE 9.1 The Organizing Process

Organizing Jobs

An organization achieves its goals through the work done by its members. To facilitate this, managers organize various tasks into jobs. Before the Industrial Revolution, the dominant approach to job design was the **craft approach,** in which a single skilled worker designed and built products one at a time from beginning to end. For example, a craftsperson raised and sheared sheep, washed and carded the wool, dyed it with berries or blossoms that he or she had gathered, dried and spun it into yarn, and wove it into clothing.

Following the Industrial Revolution, however, the craft approach nearly disappeared. Today wool clothing is usually the result of the combined efforts of sheep ranchers, textile mills, weavers, and dyers—all separate enterprises, separate organizations, and separate workforces. Although some potters, artists, weavers, and furniture makers still craft products individually, the craft approach has been replaced almost entirely by four other approaches to job design: classical, behavioral, contingency, and work group.

In the craft approach, a skilled potter designs and builds one product at a time from beginning to end.

The Classical Approach

In the **classical approach,** labor is divided into jobs made up of a few simple, repetitive, standardized tasks. Adam Smith first illuminated the economic advantages said to accompany the specialization, standardization, and simplification of work in his classic book *Wealth of Nations* (published in 1776).[2] Succeeding generations of managers built on the idea of the division of labor, and Frederick W. Taylor and other advocates of scientific management brought Smith's concepts into twentieth-century organizations.[3] Even today, managers routinely divide labor and design jobs along the lines of work specialization, standardization, and simplification.[4] Commonly used techniques that harken back to Taylor include **vertical specialization,** which removes planning and controlling activities from production employees, and horizontal specialization, which creates many low-skill-level, repetitive jobs.

The classical approach to job design was seen as a way to achieve greater productivity, efficiency, control, and standardization of work. For decades, its supporters touted that it increased labor effectiveness, lowered production costs, and made system performance more predictable.[5] Its critics have argued, however, that jobs designed solely according to the classical approach may lead to problems for both organizations and their members. They have suggested that employees occupying simplified, low-skill-level, repetitive jobs eventually perceive them as monotonous and, thus, become bored and dissatisfied. Boredom and job dissatisfaction, they claim, eventually translate into absenteeism, turnover, and various other forms of output restriction.[6] Saab recognized the problems caused by the classical approach more than fifteen years ago. Nevertheless, many organizations still use it today.

The Behavioral Approach

The classical approach to job design tried to make organizations efficient and effective by making work simple, but, in the late 1940s and early 1950s, behavioral management advocates suggested that perhaps the same objective could be attained by making work interesting. The **behavioral approach** rejects the idea of treating people like automated machines, continuously performing simple and repetitive activities. Behavioral theorists noted that, although machines have no emotions, people do. When people's feelings are negative, their needs are not met, and their motives are frustrated, workers and their organizations suffer.

Job Enlargement and Job Enrichment. To interest and motivate workers, behavioral management advocates first introduced two alternative job design strategies.[7] **Job enlargement** adds breadth to a job by increasing the number and variety of activities performed by an employee. For example, an insurance clerk's job, which consists primarily of repeatedly completing one type of insurance application, can be horizontally enlarged by adding other forms to be typed, filing duties, and communication with clients and agents to maintain insurance histories. **Job enrichment** adds depth to a job by adding "managerial" activities (planning, organizing, directing, and controlling) to an employee's responsibilities. The insurance clerk's job could be vertically loaded by allowing the worker to make decisions about accepting new policy applications, rejecting claims, and so on.

The Job Characteristics Model. An expansion on the ideas of job enlargement and job enrichment is found in the **Job Characteristics Model (JCM)** developed by J. Richard Hackman of Harvard University and Greg Oldham of the University of Illinois. This model (see Figure 9.2) specifies the critical job components that lead to positive results for both an organization and its workers. According to the JCM, if a job has high levels of the five "core" components, a worker will perceive the job as meaningful, will develop a sense of responsibility for the outcome of the work, and will understand the results of his or her efforts. These three psychological states are expected to lead to job satisfaction; motivation; high-quality work performance; and a reduction in

Bored people build bad cars. That's why we're doing away with the assembly line.

Working on an assembly line is monotonous. And boring. And after a while, some people begin not to care about their jobs anymore. So the quality of the product often suffers.

That's why, at Saab, we're replacing the assembly line with assembly teams. Groups

of just three or four people who are responsible for a particular assembly process from start to finish.

Each team makes its own decisions about who does what and when. And each team member can even do the entire assembly singlehandedly. The result: people are more involved. They care more. So there's less absenteeism, less turnover. And we have more experienced people on the job.

We're building our new 2-liter engines this way. And the doors to our Saab 99. And we're planning to use this same system to build other parts of our car as well.

It's a slower, more costly system, but we realize that the best machines and materials in the world don't mean a thing, if the person building the car doesn't care.

Saab. It's what a car should be.

Saab claims that, because employees are no longer bored by the monotony of the assembly line, they care about the products they make and will build a better-quality car.

[T]he characteristics of jobs really do make a difference, and it appears to be a very substantial difference in the reactions people have to their work and to their behavior on the job.

—Hackman

FIGURE 9.2   The Job Characteristics Model

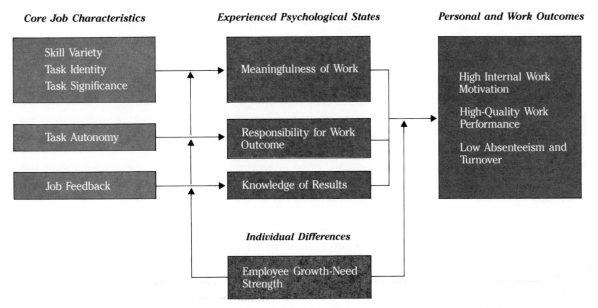

Source: J. R. Hackman and G. R. Oldham (1976), Motivation through the design of work: Test of a theory, *Organizational Behavior and Human Performance*, 16, 250-79.

absenteeism, tardiness, and turnover behaviors. The five core components (items 1-5), plus two supplemental socially oriented components specified by the JCM, include:

1. *Skill variety*—the extent to which a job requires an employee to use a broad set of skills and abilities
2. *Autonomy*—the amount of independent thought, freedom, and discretion an employee is permitted to exercise in performing a job
3. *Task significance*—the degree to which a job affects the lives, well-being, and/or work of other people
4. *Task identity*—the extent to which a job produces a complete, identifiable piece of work (that is, the job is done from beginning to end and has a visible outcome)
5. *Job feedback*—the degree to which an employee receives information about the effectiveness of his or her task performance directly from the job as it is being performed
6. *Agent feedback*—the degree to which a worker receives clear information about the effectiveness of his or her work from supervisors, co-workers, and/or clients
7. *Dealing with others*—the amount of human interaction an employee experiences while performing a job[8]

The Contingency Approach

A number of management scholars have argued that neither the classical nor the behavioral approach to job design is universally most appropriate. According to the **contingency approach** to job design, managers should organize work and design jobs to fit the characteristics of the worker who will perform that job, the organization's technology, and other design characteristics of the organization.[9]

Initially, proponents of the contingency approach focused their attention on the fit between individual characteristics (such as an employee's work ethic level) and job design characteristics. It was suggested that people have different needs and personality characteristics and, therefore, respond differently to job designs.[10] Some employees, for example, prefer routine jobs, while others respond more favorably to complex jobs. Individuals with strong esteem, growth, and achievement needs (that is, higher-order needs) should be most compatible with complex jobs.

In addition to initial suggestions that managers consider the fit between individual differences and job design characteristics, several other contingency models have emerged. For example, a dynamic, organic organization using rapidly changing technologies is not likely to function well if jobs are overly specialized and routine. The incumbents of such jobs would be unlikely to keep up with the changing demands of such an environment. It also means that a mechanistic organization with simple, routine, unchanging technologies has little need for complex jobs.[11]

Because there is no one best way to design jobs, it appears that managers must use a contingency approach and consider the fit between job design, worker make-up, technology, and an organization's internal and external environments.

The Self-managing Work Group Approach

So far this chapter has focused on the design of work for individuals. Some types of work, however, are not well suited to being performed by a single individual. In the **self-managing work group approach,** managers assign work to an entire group rather than to individuals.[12] The group is given the authority to create the processes needed to accomplish their assigned work and to handle internal problems. For example, at Butler Manufacturing in Sioux City, Iowa, self-managing teams have replaced the traditional assembly line for the construction of grain driers.[13] Each construction team, operating autonomously, performs a wide variety of tasks, and team members change job assignments frequently so that they eventually learn the entire range of assembly activities. Quality inspection; employee training, development, and discipline; performance appraisals; work scheduling; and other managerial activities are conducted by the group through a combination of planned and spontaneous meetings.

Work in a self-managing group is designed to offer variety, autonomy, significance, task identity, feedback, and opportunities for human interaction. Group members participate in their own management and, as a result, are more likely to accept, support, and actively pursue the procedures and goals set by the group. Participating in what traditionally have been management decisions tends to fulfill various growth needs and leads to satisfaction for many employees. This approach, however, also moves organizational control from the hands of traditional managers to those of workers. Managers and workers must be able to accept this transformation, or the approach will fail. (See "A Closer Look: Work Teams.")

Work Teams: Only People Can Give Wisdom to the Machines

The mechanization of muscle-power in the first Industrial Revolution led to simpler and simpler tasks that demanded little of workers except the use of their hands. Management neither expected nor wanted broader worker involvement. In the new Industrial Revolution now under way, capital consists of information technologies that require workers' mental commitment and responsibility for entire systems rather than for narrow tasks.[1]

Until recently, the majority of work performed in the United States was directed by the hands of people. Today, the bulk of work is guided by machines. When people were the instrument of production, managers were taught to control employees. Now that machines do the work, emphasis is shifting to teaching managers to loosen their control and encourage workers to use their creativity and initiative in controlling machines.

Modern plants in the United States rely heavily on robotics and other computer-driven systems for manufacturing. The Ex-Cell-O Corporation in Americus, Georgia, is typical. Ex-Cell-O manufactures a variety of plastic car parts, such as the shiny colored covers used for bumpers. In the past, each bumper cover was spray-painted by a worker. Now, the job is done by robots—and quality and productivity are much higher. Employees at Ex-Cell-O's plant are responsible for operating and maintaining the robotics systems rather than directly producing the products.

The nature of work changes substantially when robotics take over production. Even though robotics and computerization have reduced the likelihood of a worker making a simple production error, human errors in operating the technology can be magnified to dreadful levels: witness the nuclear accidents at Three Mile Island and Chernobyl. It is a fact of life in business today that "[w]e're moving increasingly into dangerous, unforgiving technologies that can't be operated safely with uncommitted people."[2]

More and more organizations are turning to teamwork to nurture commitment to the organization and to manage the new technologies effectively. When Shenandoah Life Insurance Company placed employees into semiautonomous work teams of five to seven members, the time required to handle a policy conversion decreased from twenty-seven to two days. Overall, 50 percent more policies were handled with a smaller number of employees. Procter & Gamble, a leader in the use of teams, claims that its team-based plants are 30 to 40 percent more productive than their traditional plants. Volvo's team-oriented plants in Sweden are reported to have production costs 25 percent lower than the company's conventional plants.

Loosened controls, better use of employees' ideas, greater commitment, and stronger motivation go hand in hand in developing a more effective and more satisfied workforce. Enlightened managers are discovering that one of the best decisions they can make is to allow workers to help make decisions. The solutions are not easy but the direction is clear: this is the decade of the worker!

1. Based on a statement by Japanese labor expert Haruo Shimada, Getting man and machine to live happily ever after (20 April 1987), *Business Week*, 61.
2. Lyman D. Ketchum in Management discovers the human side of automation (29 September 1986), *Business Week*, 71.

Departmentalization: Grouping Organizational Activities

Just as individual tasks need to be organized into jobs, jobs must be organized into larger units (such as work groups and departments), and work units into divisions. Otherwise, the control of jobs and the coordination and integration of work is extremely difficult. The process of grouping jobs into organizational units and those units into larger units is referred to as **departmentalization.**

Organizations use departmentalization to answer the question "What activities do we want to coordinate at one place in the organizational hierarchy?" For example, does Zimbrick, a large automobile dealer in the Midwest, want to locate (and therefore coordinate) all salespeople in one department, or does it want to coordinate new-car sales in one organizational unit and used-car sales in another? As shown in Figure 9.3, managers group activities at all levels of an organization. Groupings at the very top of an organization refer to the superstructure of the entire organization, and many of the strategies discussed here are also used when developing superstructures (see Chapter 11).

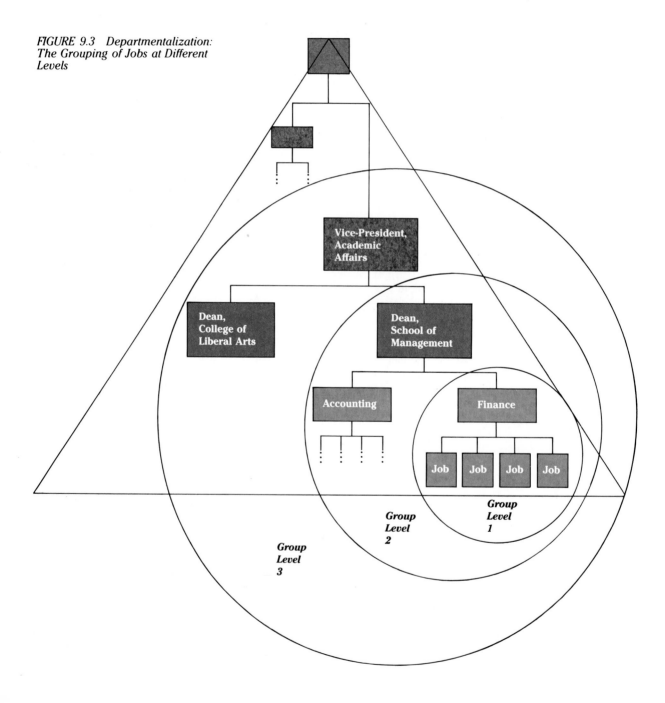

FIGURE 9.3 Departmentalization: The Grouping of Jobs at Different Levels

Through the years, managers have tried various ways to group (departmentalize) organizational activities. One method organizes activities around the type of *customer* or customer needs served by an organization, as when department stores separate men's, women's and children's clothing. Another method groups activities around the *equipment* used, such as the separation of sanding and painting when making furniture. The following sections discuss four other common approaches.

Departmentalization by Function

Managers create **functional departments** by grouping activities according to the nature of the work performed. Activities that support an organization's operations system, for example, are placed in an operations department (see Figure 9.4). Similar activities are coordinated from a common place in the organizational hierarchy. A marketing department, for example, controls only marketing activities. Each functional unit may be broken down further for coordination and control purposes. Although the names given to functional departments may vary from one organization to another, common terms in for-profit organizations are operations, marketing, finance, accounting, human resources, engineering, and research and development.

Functional departments offer a number of advantages. Because people who perform similar functions work together, they can specialize and benefit from one another's expertise. Decision making and coordination are easier, because managers need to be familiar with only a relatively narrow set of activities. Functional departments at high levels of the hierarchy use an organization's resources more efficiently because a department's activity does not have to be repeated across several organizational divisions. On the negative side, strong functional grouping may prevent people from seeing the totality of an organization. Communication and coordination across departments can be prob-

is necessary

FIGURE 9.4   Functional Departmentalization

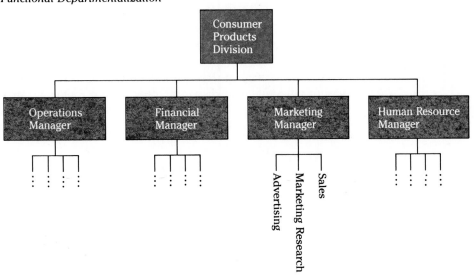

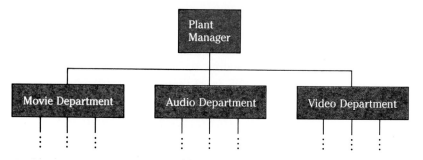

lematic, and conflicts often emerge when each functional department attempts to protect its own turf.

Departmentalization by Product/Service

Ex. Phillip morris
Procter + Gamble
In **product/service departmentalization,** activities related to the development and delivery of a single product (or closely related group of products) are grouped together. Progressive Video Images, for example, has movie, audio, and video units (see Figure 9.5).

The product/service departmentalization approach can be logical and efficient. Procter & Gamble, for example, produces and markets both soap and food. Each of these product lines has unique technical and business properties and problems, so the company separates the activities that produce Ivory Soap from those that result in Crisco. This approach also is useful when an organization wishes to treat product/service lines as independent business units, because managers can more readily assess the profitability of each product line. On the negative side, this approach has the potential disadvantage of creating destructive competition between departments for organizational resources, as people are encouraged to be responsible for *their* product line. Another potential disadvantage is that, if managers do not use standardized practices to run their departments, it can create coordination problems.

Departmentalization by Territory

Territorial (geographical) departmentalization is often used when organizations have widely dispersed operations or offices. American Family Insurance, for example, has three separate territories, and the regional office in each handles the insurance issues that arise in its particular region (see Figure 9.6).

The territorial approach has many logistical and practical advantages. It moves operations closer to raw materials, to distribution systems, and to customers. Sometimes geographic variations in laws, regulations, and customs change the nature of doing business enough so that territorial arrangements are necessary. For example, regulations on the sale and servicing of insurance differ from state to state, and each American Family Insurance Company regional office is responsible for complying with the regulations within its own territory. On the negative side, territorial offices may undermine each other by

FIGURE 9.6 Territorial
Departmentalization

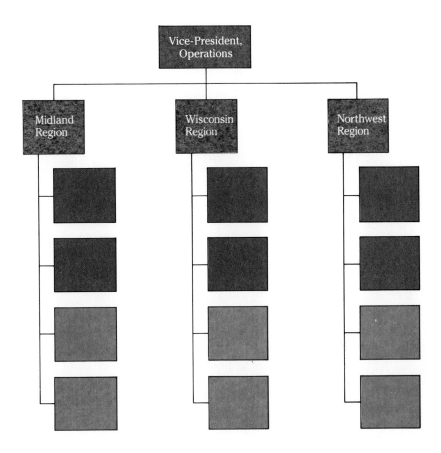

competing for organizational resources, and geographical dispersion can make it difficult for an organization to enforce uniform standards. The physical separation of organizational divisions can also create communication and coordination problems.

Departmentalization by Project

Project departments are generally created to address specific, often unique, organizational goals and cease to exist once that goal has been achieved—that is, when the project has been completed. A medical equipment manufacturer, for example, might want to design an artificial heart. Project departments typically have an organic management system. Authority and positions of leadership shift as members bring their particular expertise to various phases of the project. Communication, coordination, and control systems are continually adjusted, and the people-to-people and people-to-work relationships change frequently to accommodate the uncertain nature of the project.

Managers can create a project department in a number of ways. One approach is to hire or transfer a group of employees to *form a new department* solely to work on the project at hand (see Figure 9.7). A second method managers use to create a project department involves the *matrix* approach, an organizational arrangement in which two overlapping structures are used (see

FIGURE 9.7   New Department Approach to Project Departmentalization

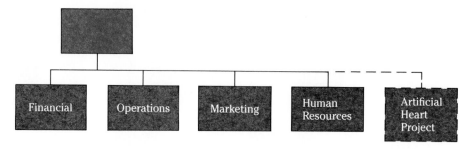

Chapter 11). This type of project department is staffed with workers from various parts of the organization who may be released from their regular responsibilities, either on a part-time or full-time basis. When they are required to perform their regular duties in addition to those of the project department, these individuals are accountable to their home department as well as to the project department. The department developing an artificial heart, for example, may want the organization's marketing department to lend them Susan Hessney to conduct hospital surveys, operations employee Sandra Nossiter to conduct feasibility studies, and employees Lucinda Turley and Steve Sidwell from clerical services for typing and filing tasks.

A primary advantage of creating a new department for a project is that it produces a group of people who are concentrating on a single organizational role and chosen for their ability to do so. The drawback is that, once the project is finished, they have no remaining organizational role to fulfill. The matrix approach makes it easy to choose qualified members from almost anywhere in an organization who are familiar with a wide range of organizational issues, but this can be disruptive, because members must divide their time, attention, and energy between their regular and special assignments.

FIGURE 9.8   Hybrid Approach to Departmentalization: The Comfort-Living Corporation

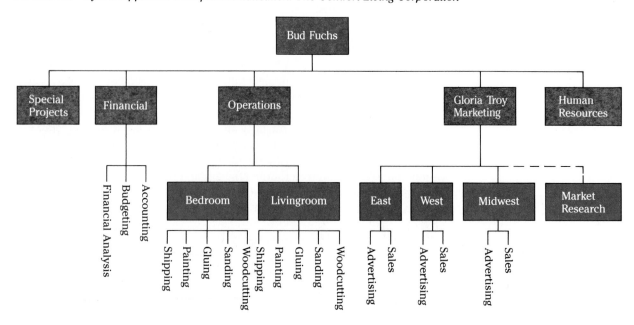

The Hybrid Approach to Departmentalization

Rather than limiting themselves to just one departmentalization strategy, managers in most organizations use a number of approaches. The **hybrid approach** calls for the simultaneous use of two or more departmentalization strategies. Figure 9.8 illustrates the hybrid approach to departmentalization that managers have taken at Comfort-Living Corporation, a home furnishings manufacturer and distributor. Bud Fuchs, owner of Comfort-Living, has organized top-level management according to organizational function and special projects. The operations department is subdivided by product into bedroom and livingroom departments. Gloria Troy, supervising the marketing department's territories, also is currently heading up a special project department on market research.

Span of Control

How large a salesforce can one sales manager supervise? How many executive vice-presidents should report to the president of an organization? **Span of control,** also referred to as *span of management* and *span of supervision*, refers to the number of subordinates and activities that a manager oversees.

Why It Is Important

Managers must consider span of control when departmentalizing so they do not create a span that is too large to handle. What is the limit to the number of people and activities that any one manager can effectively manage? During the classical management period, many people tried to determine an ideal span of

There is a limit to the number of people and activities that one manager can handle.

control. Most argued in favor of greatly limiting a manager's span of control. Some proposed that limitations on a manager's attention, energy, and knowledge should restrict the span of control to five or six employees. Others argued that the nature of work and the limitations of the human brain should produce an increasingly narrower span of control as one moves up an organization's hierarchy. At the top, a manager would be responsible for no more than six people but, at lower levels, a much wider span would be acceptable.

In practice, there is no universally ideal span of control. If a span is too limited, a manager's talents may be underutilized. If the span is too large, a manager may have too much work to perform any of it effectively. It would be virtually impossible, for example, to have one manager directly supervise the work of fifty staff accountants and all of their projects at the same time. From the subordinates' perspective, a span that is too large may prevent them from getting needed supervisory support. None of the fifty accountants would be likely to get the training and support needed to perform effectively and to grow if one manager supervised them all. On the other hand, too small a span might result in too much supervision. In such cases, managers often baby-sit subordinates, not allowing them enough freedom to be effective.

The size of a manager's span has other organizational implications as well. An organization with a wide span of control—that is, many subordinates reporting to one manager—is relatively flat. Narrower spans make a taller organizational structure with multiple levels of management. The additional costs associated with this shape can be substantial. DANA Corporation, an auto parts manufacturer, changed the shape and reduced the costs of its organizational structure by decreasing the size of its management and administrative group from 475 to 84 people, and by paring the number of hierarchical levels from 15 to 5.

Determining the Appropriate Span

Because of the importance of span of control, managers should consider at least three factors when determining the span appropriate for their organization: the individual supervisor, the employee group, and the situation.[14]

The Individual Supervisor. A number of manager/supervisor characteristics should influence the span of control decision. Some managers, for example, believe that their subordinates are capable of self-direction and self-control; others do not. Those in the former group may be able to handle a broad span because their burden is lessened by allowing subordinates to exercise some self-management. Managers who believe in delegating authority and can do so effectively may be able to handle a larger span than managers who need to be intimately involved in each subordinate's work.

The Employee Group. Employee competence is also a factor in the span of a manager's control. A highly professional group, a seasoned group, or a group of individuals with high levels of independence all permit managers a wider span of control than groups with less experience, competence, or independence. Thus, for an accounting firm at which all accountants are CPAs with at least five years of field experience, span of control can be much larger than that at a firm where most accountants are fresh out of college and lack work experience.

The Situation.   The nature of the situation also affects span of control. The more uncertain a task, for example, the smaller the span must be. The same holds true for highly interdependent tasks. In both cases, a narrow span of control provides managers and subordinates with the frequent and unrestricted communication they need for coordination and control. Managers of research labs, for example, can supervise only a small number of assistants because of the daily need to evaluate and direct experiments. Contrast this with a regional sales supervisor whose primary contacts with twenty sales representatives are phone calls to check on weekly sales results and six "motivational" meetings a year.

Coordinating Organizational Activities and Units

When work is divided and various jobs and departments are created, someone must integrate and coordinate these organizational subsystems. To many, the coordinating activity *is* the essence of organizing. After all, the purpose of organizing is to achieve an integration among the diverse organizational parts and systems. **Coordinating** links two or more organizational units so that they work harmoniously. Coordinating, for example, links the production of textbooks with the sale of textbooks; it connects the admission of students to a university with the supply of services needed to provide a high-quality education. Organizations have two basic kinds of coordination needs: vertical and horizontal.

Vertical Coordination

To meet organizational goals, managers must coordinate the hierarchical levels. The institutional level, for example, must be coordinated with the technical core. **Vertical coordination** links people and units that are separated by hierarchical level. For example, if Bo Dandison, owner of the Sit'n'Sip chain of coffee shops, decided to boost sales through increased advertising, he would tell Rob Clouse, his marketing manager, to come up with a new ad campaign. Rob, in turn, would ask territorial managers to contribute ideas and provide Bo with final recommendations. It would then be the marketing department's duty to launch the chosen campaign.

Managers can achieve vertical coordination in a number of ways. For example, in small, uncomplicated organizations or within individual organizational units, superiors and subordinates can meet face-to-face. This *direct supervision* enables people to communicate, provides direction and assistance, and integrates activities across organizational levels.

Another way managers coordinate work across levels in the hierarchy is through *standardization* of activities. Large spans of control, high communication needs, a desire for uniformity in operations, and physical dispersion all create pressure to standardize activities. Suppose, for example, that Julie Pearson Davis is a manager at a collection agency whose span of control has gone from the supervision of five subordinates to that of twenty. This increase has made it more difficult for her to deal face-to-face with each subordinate on all issues. If activities are standardized, Julie can handle this increase by developing rules and procedures to govern such routine activities as what to do if someone claims he or she has already made the payment being requested. Of course, there will always be exceptions and unique events for which rules and procedures have not been and, in fact, should not be created. At this point, the *exception principle* takes over, and managers concentrate their efforts on matters that deviate from routine, such as a customer who threatens the physical safety of a collection agency employee.

A third way to achieve vertical coordination is through *goal statements.* When the nature of work makes it difficult to designate the specific behaviors that are needed, managers can create a hierarchy of goals. The general manager of the Scott, Foresman higher education division, for example, might specify a goal of increasing sales by 15 percent in the next year. The vice-president of sales and marketing then assigns a sales goal to each of the division's regional managers. They, in turn, assign sales goals to their subordinates. This set of interrelated goals guides the actions of lower-level employees, and their accomplishments become the means through which the next higher level achieves its goals, and so on to the top of the hierarchy.

Horizontal Coordination

Horizontal coordination occurs within a single hierarchical level and, thus, make it possible for managers to coordinate organization members and units that do not have a hierarchical relationship. Through horizontal coordination, for example, the efforts of manufacturing and sales departments are integrated, and resources are shared. By allowing managers at the same hierarchical level to work together, horizontal coordination also relieves bottlenecks in the hierarchy. For example, if Gregory Christofferson, a director of purchasing, can ask Meg Weant, the director of finance, for permission to

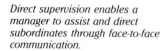

Direct supervision enables a manager to assist and direct subordinates through face-to-face communication.

deviate from his allotted budget, he does not need to work through higher-level managers.

Horizontal coordination can be achieved in several ways.[15] In many instances, managers can use the same direct supervision, standardization, and goal statement techniques that bring about vertical coordination. Additional techniques are also available. Perhaps the simplest way to achieve horizontal coordination is through *direct contact*—that is, having two managers with a common problem communicate directly with one another, as Gregory and Meg did in the example just mentioned.

When the volume of contact between two organizational units becomes extremely heavy, management may assign an employee to act as a *liaison* to facilitate communication between the units. An organization designing a new jet airplane, for example, might create a liaison to help coordinate the efforts of those designing the jet's engine with the team responsible for designing the airframe. Under other circumstances, an *integrator* might be appointed. The role of an integrator is more complex than that of a liaison. Liaisons primarily encourage and facilitate an exchange of information so that coordination can be achieved between interdependent units. Integrators, on the other hand, are expected to provide leadership and directly influence the direction taken through their expertise.

When conditions are highly uncertain, an integrator alone may not be able to coordinate highly heterogeneous, interdependent organizational units. To deal with this type of situation, a linking manager must be given the formal authority to command action. Shifting from a reliance on the influence that stems from someone's expertise to actual, formal authority is a shift from an integrator to a *managerial linking role.* The integrator may say, "Here is a way to solve the problem, and this is why I think you should choose this solution." A linking manager, however, has the authority to say, "*Do* it this way."

Direct contact and liaison/integrator roles work well in coordinating a limited number of organizational units, but when problems arise involving a number of organizational units, managers may have to form a *task force.* A task force is a temporary group, generally comprising representatives from the several units experiencing the difficulty, that comes into existence to tackle a particular problem and then dissolves when the problem is resolved. If the problem needs continual attention, not a one-time solution, the task force becomes permanent and is referred to as a *task team.*

Although it violates Fayol's principle of unity of command, there are times when it is necessary to give two or more independent units command authority over an activity to bring about appropriate integration. Consider the case of Universe Products Limited, a manufacturer of electrical, chemical, mechanical, and aerospace products. Historically, the company coordinated all of its engineering and research activities out of its aerospace division; however, this functional grouping ultimately was unable to attend adequately to special engineering projects. To resolve this problem, management created a second command system for its space projects. Members of the engineering and research group are now accountable to both their functional (aerospace) boss and to a Venus, Mars, or Space-Lab project manager (see Figure 9.9). These two overlapping structures represent the matrix approach discussed earlier.

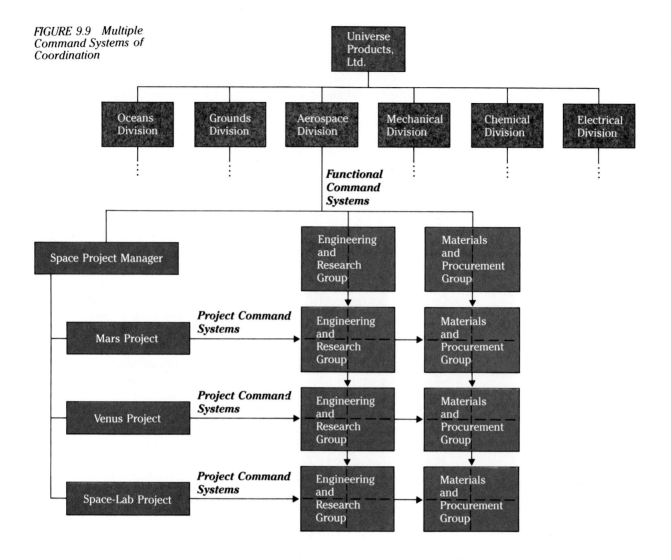

FIGURE 9.9 Multiple Command Systems of Coordination

Organizing and Coordinating Work in Review

Organizing is the management function of designing an organization and its internal systems with people-to-people and people-to-work interaction patterns. This design must take into account the formal organization created by managers and the informal organization that arises spontaneously as organization members interact. The primary purpose of organizing is to integrate various organizational units so that an entire system is efficient and effective.

The first step in organizing is to group tasks into jobs. Before the Industrial Revolution, one worker crafted an entire product from start to finish, but the craft approach has been replaced by four other approaches. The classical approach is based on a strict division of labor that tries to increase productivity by concentrating on work specialization, standardization, and simplification. The behavioral approach focuses on employees and tries to make jobs more interesting through job enlargement and enrichment. The contingency approach tries to match a job to workers and the organization. The self-managing work group approach attempts to increase productivity by allowing workers to participate in the managerial processes that accompany production.

The next step in organizing is to group jobs into larger units and then place those units into larger organizational divisions. This is called departmentalization, and one method of achieving it is to group jobs according to the activities performed. Traditional groupings include departmentalization by the customer/client group served, the process or equipment used, organizational function, territory, product/service, and projects. In practice, most organizations use a hybrid approach to combine methods of departmentalization.

A third part of the organizing process requires managers to decide how many people one manager can supervise effectively. This is known as span of control, and it affects the size of various organizational units and the shape of an organization's overall hierarchy. There is no ideal size; instead, the appropriate span for a given organizational situation should be determined in large part by the nature of the task, the managers involved, and the characteristics of subordinates.

Coordinating is another, perhaps the most important, major organizing activity. There are two ways in which coordinating must be done in organizations. Vertical coordination links people and activities from different levels of the hierarchy. Horizontal coordination links people and activities from the same organizational level. There are numerous techniques managers can use to achieve both vertical and horizontal coordination. Choosing a technique or combination of techniques depends on the specific coordination needs of an organization.

Issues for Review and Discussion

1. Define organizing and discuss its purpose.
2. Specify the differences between formal and informal organizations.
3. Identify and differentiate among the four contemporary approaches managers use to design jobs.
4. Identify and briefly describe four different forms of departmentalization.
5. What is the hybrid approach to departmentalization?
6. Define span of control and explain how it affects an organization.
7. Identify the two basic coordination needs that organizations have and discuss three different mechanisms that managers use to meet them.

Key Terms

organizing
formal organization
informal organization
craft approach
classical approach
vertical specialization
horizontal specialization
behavioral approach
job enlargement
job enrichment
Job Characteristics Model (JCM)
contingency approach

self-managing work group approach
departmentalization
functional departments
product/service departmentalization
territorial/geographical departmentalization
project departments
hybrid approach
span of control
coordinating
vertical coordination
horizontal coordination

Suggested Readings

Dow, G. K. (1988). Configurational and coactivational views of organizational structure. *Academy of Management Review,* 13, 53-64.

Fisher, K. K. (1989). Managing in the high-commitment workplace. *Organizational Dynamics,* 17(3), 31-50.

Griffin, R. W. (1982). *Task design: An integrative approach.* Glenview, IL: Scott, Foresman.

Hackman, J. R. (1977). Work design. In Hackman, J. R., and Suttle, J. R., eds. *Improving life at work,* Santa Monica, CA: Goodyear, 96-162.

Manz, C. C., and Sims, H. P., Jr. (1987). Leading workers to lead themselves. *Administrative Science Quarterly,* 32, 106-28.

Pierce, J. L. (1980). Job design in perspective. *The Personnel Administrator,* 25, 67-74.

Reynolds, E. V., and Johnson, J. D. (1982). Liaison emergence: Relating theoretical perspectives. *Academy of Management Review,* 4, 551-59.

Scott, W. G. (1961). Organization theory: An overview and an appraisal. *Academy of Management Journal,* 4, 7-26.

Wall, T. D., Kemp, N. J., Jackson, P. R., and Clegg, C. W. (1986). Outcomes of autonomous work groups: A long-term field experiment. *Academy of Management Journal,* 29, 280-304.

Notes

1. C. Barnard (1938), *The functions of the executive,* Cambridge, MA: Harvard University Press.
2. A. Smith (1776), *The wealth of nations,* New York: Modern Library, Inc.
3. F. W. Taylor (1947), *Scientific management,* New York: Harper & Brothers; F. B. Gilbreth and L. M. Gilbreth (1910), *Applied motion study,* New York: Sturgis and Walton Co.; H. L. Gantt (1910), *Work wages and profits,* New York: The Engineering Magazine Co.
4. J. L. Pierce and R. B. Dunham (1976), Task design: A literature review, *Academy of Management Review,* 1, 83-97.
5. J. L. Pierce (1980), Job design in perspective, *The Personnel Administrator,* 25, 67-74.
6. M. R. Blood and C. L. Hulin (1967), Alienation, environmental characteristics and worker responses, *Journal of Applied Psychology,* 51, 284-90; Pierce.
7. F. Herzberg, B. Mausner, and B. Snyderman (1959), *The motivation to work,* New York: Wiley; F. Herzberg (January/February 1968), One more time: How do you motivate employees? *Harvard Business Review,* 54-62.
8. J. R. Hackman and G. R. Oldham (1975), Development of the job diagnostic survey, *Journal of Applied Psychology,* 60, 159-70; J. R. Hackman and G. R. Oldham (1976), Motivation through the design of work: Test of a theory, *Organizational Behavior and Human Performance,* 16, 250-79; J. R. Hackman and G. R. Oldham (1980), *Work redesign,* Reading, MA: Addison-Wesley.
9. Hackman and Oldham, 1975; Pierce and Dunham; C. Hulin and M. R. Blood (1968), Job enlargement, individual differences and worker responses, *Psychological Bulletin,* 69, 41-55; C. Argyris (1957), *Integrating the individual and the organization,* New York: Wiley; F. Herzberg (1966), *Work and the nature of man,* Cleveland, OH: World; F. R. David, J. A. Pearce III, and W. A. Randolph (1989), Linking technology and structures to enhance performance, *Journal of Applied Psychology,* 74, 233-41.

10. R. W. Griffin (1982), *Task design: An integrative approach,* Glenview, IL: Scott, Foresman; Pierce and Dunham; Hulin and Blood.

11. L. W. Porter, E. E. Lawler III, and J. R. Hackman (1975), *Behavior in organizations,* New York: McGraw-Hill; J. L. Pierce, R. B. Dunham, and R. S. Blackburn (1977), Social systems structure, job design, and growth need strength: A test of a congruency model, *Academy of Management Journal,* 22, 223-40; J. L. Pierce (1984), Job design and technology: A sociotechnical systems perspective, *Journal of Occupational Behavior,* 5, 147-54; J. W. Slocum, Jr., and H. P. Sims, Jr. (1980), A typology for integrating technology, organizations, and job design, *Human Relations,* 33, 143-212.

12. M. Bucklow (1972), A new role for the work group, in L. E. Davis and J. C. Taylor, eds., *Design of jobs,* Middlesex, England: Penguin; Hackman and Oldham, 1980.

13. Hackman and Oldham, 1980, 165-68.

14. J. C. Worthy (January 1950), Factors influencing employee morale, *Harvard Business Review,* 61-73; D. D. Van Fleet and A. G. Bedeian (1977), A history of the span of management, *Academy of Management Review,* 2, 356-72; J. G. Udell (1967), An empirical test of hypotheses relating to span of control, *Administrative Science Quarterly,* 12, 420-39.

15. J. R. Galbraith (1974), Organization design: An information processing view, *Interfaces,* 4, 28-36.

Oscar Metz Tool Company

By James C. Hodgetts, Memphis State University

The Oscar Metz Tool Company was a closely held manufacturer of bottling and canning equipment located in a large midwestern city. It was organized in the early 1920s and in recent years had experienced rapid growth. The company hopes to double in size in the next ten years. At present, Metz employs approximately 300 people. It manufactures bottling and canning equipment to order. The entire management group takes great pride in the quality of the company's products and in the company in general.

Arnold Parker, executive vice-president, sought an investigation of the organizational structure of the company's manufacturing division. A preliminary investigation revealed several problems:

1. A tendency on the part of lower-echelon managers to try to shift decisions to their supervisors
2. Confusion on the part of most front-line supervisors regarding the functions and authority of the management levels above them
3. A tendency to bypass intermediate levels and to take problems and complaints to the vice-president of manufacturing, and even to the president

Further investigation resulted in the discovery of the following organizational problems.

The Organizational Problem in the Shop

The line management group in manufacturing consists of: vice-president of manufacturing Karen Bednarski, shop superintendent James Marshall, night general supervisor Doug Gilbert, nine day supervisors, and four night supervisors. Manufacturing staff includes: production control manager Bill Young and chief engineer Bill Ewing. Although the manufacturing functions of the supervisors are clearly defined, there are few clear-cut lines of authority. James Marshall believes he reports to the president, but Karen Bednarski believes that Marshall reports to her. Marshall believes that the nine day supervisors report to him, but this opinion is not shared by many of the supervisors. They made the following comments:

1. The supervisor of the miscellaneous machining department says he reports to Karen Bednarski.
2. The supervisor of the lathe department also says he reports to Bednarski.
3. The supervisor of the grinder department says he reports to Bednarski *and* to the miscellaneous machining supervisor.
4. The supervisor of the milling machine department says he reports to Bill Young *and* to Karen Bednarski.
5. The supervisor of maintenance says he reports to James Marshall *and* to Karen Bednarski.
6. The supervisor of the drilling department says he reports to Marshall and to Bednarski.
7. The supervisor of the tool and die room says he reports to Karen Bednarski and, to a minor degree, Bill Ewing.
8. The supervisor of assembly says he reports to the president, to Arnold Parker, and to James Marshall.
9. The supervisor of the heat treatment department says he reports to Marshall.

In summary, it appears that only one of the nine day supervisors reports entirely to James Marshall. Only three acknowledged a partial responsibility to him, and five did not even mention his name when asked to name their immediate boss. The only undisputed authority Marshall appears to have is in connection with the heat treatment department; however, he believes he is in charge of the entire shop.

The Organizational Problem in Production Control

Bill Young says he supervises the work of the shipping supervisor, the final inspection supervisor, and six clerks. Both the final inspection supervisor and the shipping supervisor say they report to both Bill Young and Karen Bednarski. The milling department supervisor says he reports to Young as well as to Bednarski. Other comments from the production supervisors also indicate that Young has some authority over them.

The Organizational Problem on the Night Shift

Discussions with the four night supervisors indicate differences of opinion about lines of authority on the night shift. Bednarski believes that the night general supervisor reports to her. So does Marshall. Marshall also believes that Gilbert reports to the president, but Gilbert says this is definitely not correct and that he reports to Bednarski. Bednarski believes that the night lathe supervisor reports to the day lathe supervisor; still, Gilbert does not believe a night lathe supervisor has been appointed but believes that this should happen and that this person should report to him. The person who believes he is the night lathe supervisor says he reports to Gilbert. Bednarski believes that the night supervisor of assembly reports to the day supervisors of both assembly and milling; however, the night supervisor of assembly says he reports to the day supervisor of assembly and to Doug Gilbert. Gilbert says this person reports to him. Both the night shipping supervisor and the night milling supervisor say they report to Bednarski, but Gilbert says he is their immediate supervisor.

Questions

1. How do you account for the discrepancies in perceived reporting relationships?

2. What problems are likely to occur from these inconsistencies?

3. Draw an organizational chart of the Oscar Metz Tool Company.

4. Which reporting relationships make the most sense to you?

10 Authority, Delegation, and Decentralization

Student Learning Objectives

After reading this chapter, you should be able to:

1. Distinguish among influence, power, and authority.

2. Understand the major views on the meaning of authority.

3. Identify and understand the various types of authority relationships.

4. Understand the processes through which influence is exercised inside organizations.

5. Discuss how, when, and why organizations use delegation.

6. Distinguish between centralized and decentralized authority.

7. Identify factors that managers should consider to determine the appropriate degree of centralization for their organization.

W ho makes commitments on behalf of an organization? How? These are questions of influence, power, and authority. The answers depend, in part, on the type of authority system that managers create to distribute and use their organization's power, influence, and authority. Deciding what type of authority system to create is part of the managerial activity of organizing and a major challenge facing managers. Compare, for example, two midwestern utility companies. In one, the president of the organization accepts or rejects all appointments of new employees. In the other, the authority for making these decisions is given to employees in the human resources department, several levels below the president. This chapter examines the nature of organizational power and authority, looks at several types of authority systems, and reviews the processes managers use to transfer authority from one organization member to another.

Managerial Influence: Power and Authority

Inexperienced managers often assume their organization's work *will* be successfully accomplished because formally defined jobs and departments specify how the work *should* be done. Things work this way for some people, in some jobs, at some times, but usually this is not the case. In most situations, formal job definitions and coordinating strategies are not enough to get the work done. Organizations must somehow galvanize their workers into action; to do so, they must use influence. **Influence** is a person's ability to produce results and to bring about a change in his or her environment. People derive influence from interpersonal power and authority.

Interpersonal Power and Its Sources

The people inside organizations influence one another and shape organizational events. Managers, for example, can tell subordinates what to do and, in many cases, how to do it. Nonmanagers can share ideas for cost-cutting measures with supervisors or encourage co-workers to form a union. **Interper-**

People derive influence from interpersonal power and authority.

sonal power enables individual organization members to exert influence over others and over their organization.[1] There are several types and sources of interpersonal power (see Chapter 14), three of which are

- *Reward power*—the power a person has because people believe that he or she can bestow rewards or outcomes, such as money or recognition, that others desire
- *Coercive power*—the power a person has because people believe that he or she can punish them by inflicting pain or by withholding or taking away something they value
- *Legitimate power*—the power a person has because others believe that he or she has a right to influence them and that they ought to obey[2]

In practice, many organization members have—and need—more than one form of power. For example, when a manager makes a decision and directs others, employees usually follow this directive because of the legitimate power the organization gives the manager. What if, however, the new manager is Fred Kooperstein, the company president's son, and employees resent "this young hotshot who got the job only because of his dad"? What if the new manager is Patricia Quinlin, a newly graduated M.B.A. from Northwestern University, whose blue-collar subordinates do not think a "college kid" can possibly know how they should do their jobs?

In these and other cases, legitimate power alone might not be enough. In reality, workers seldom give automatic and unconditional compliance to any manager. (After all, did you always do exactly as your parents told you? Do you always do exactly what your professor asks?) To reinforce their legitimate power, then, managers also must use other forms of power. If workers think Fred has the ability to fire them, their perceptions may give him coercive power. If Patricia tells her subordinates she will pay a year-end bonus to any employee whose use of new tools leads to an increase in production output, she is using reward power if the employees believe her and follow through. Many public and private organizations have formal reward and punishment programs that managers can use to enhance their legitimate power.

Authority

Many equate authority with legitimate power. Max Weber saw **authority** as the legitimate right of a person to exercise influence.[3] According to Weber, this perception that someone has the legitimate right to exercise influence can stem from such sources as legal systems, situational demands, relationships between people, tradition, and charismatic personalities. In the U.S. Army, for example, anyone wearing a lieutenant's uniform possesses the right to command privates, and privates have the obligation to comply. Contrast this with a project department, where influence is based on the expertise each participant brings to a task. The next sections explore the types of authority found in organizations and their sources.

Classical View of Authority. One view of authority arises from the classical approach to management. According to **classical authority theory,** authority is the *institutional right* of organizations to act, to decide, and to exercise influence. What this means for organizations in the United States, for

The acceptance view of authority is oriented toward people's views of their working relationships.

example, is that a group of stockholders can transfer rights to a board of directors, which, in turn, can transfer a large portion of its rights to the chief executive officer. As authority flows from the institutional level down to the technical core, all managers eventually possess some formal authority to act, to decide, and to exercise influence.

Acceptance View of Authority. A second perspective on authority is anchored in the nature of interpersonal relationships rather than in a formal hierarchy of authority. In the **acceptance view of authority** proposed by Chester Barnard and other behavioral management advocates, authority flows upward from subordinates to superiors, based on the nature of the relationship between people and their perception of this relationship.[4] According to the acceptance view, the relationships between employees and their superiors become authoritative when the subordinates view those relationships as legitimate. Subordinates consider relationships legitimate—and, therefore, authoritative—and will comply when four conditions are met:

1. Subordinates understand the nature of the request.
2. Subordinates perceive that the request is consistent with the goals and values of the organization.
3. The request is compatible with the subordinates' personal interests.
4. Subordinates are mentally and physically capable of complying with the request.

These four conditions define what is acceptable to an employee and, thus, identify his or her *zone of acceptance.*[5] Managers should make sure their requests fall within their subordinates' zone of acceptance. Otherwise, their requests are likely to be met with resistance or at least with something less than full support.

Situational View of Authority. A third perspective is the **situational view of authority** proposed by Mary Parker Follett. She argued that, rather than one person's giving orders to another, both should agree to take orders from the situation. Under these conditions, ultimate authority would reside in the will and consent of the people who perform a particular task. Like Barnard, Follett treated acceptance as the key to establishing authority relationships. Unlike Barnard, however, Follett strongly emphasized the importance of considering each situation according to its particular demands. It is the knowledge and skills of people in relation to the task being executed that determines who will exercise authority, not those people's positions in the organizational hierarchy. Authority in a project department, for example, may change hands more than once, depending on whether a project is in the developmental stage, in the experimental phase, or in the process of generating a final report.

Exercising Authority

In all three views of authority, it is how subordinates perceive a manager's legitimacy that is important. When people perceive an attempt at influence as legitimate—whether because of hierarchical right, the nature of the relationships between people, or the situation itself—they concede its authority and willingly comply. When formal superior-subordinate relationships exist, managers may often rely on the power of formal authority to encourage workers to comply, keeping in mind that directives must fall within the zone of acceptance.

In many situations, however, formal superior-subordinate relationships do not exist. For example, the interaction patterns of employees assigned to committees and task forces often are not prescribed in advance. Much influence, in fact, is informal. Consider, for example, the great power wielded by many corporate secretaries, who decide how many and which pieces of mail the boss will see and who screen the boss' telephone calls.[6]

The sources of power in any organization, thus, are varied. Some are subtle, others obvious. Some are planned, formal parts of the organizational structure. Some are spontaneous and informal outgrowths of particular personalities in particular situations. In many cases, power flows to those individuals and groups who are most capable of coping with an organization's critical problems and uncertainties.[7] For example, when an organization is embroiled in a number of lawsuits that threaten its existence, its legal department will gain considerable power and legitimate influence over organizational decisions. Managers should be aware of the complexities of power and cultivate a climate that will use it to further the goals of their organization.

Even though management theories differ somewhat in the details as they address the role of managerial influence, one important universal message comes through. The ability to influence organization members is an important resource that must be used if a manager is to succeed. Saying "I am the boss" may help, but this alone is seldom powerful enough to achieve adequate influence. Organizations must provide managers with the influence tools they need, and managers must use them effectively. (See "A Closer Look: The Redistribution of Authority.")

Authority Relationships

As part of the organizing activity, managers must design an organization's authority system. This design creates **authority relationships** between people and between people and their work. There are three different types of authority found in these relationships: line, staff, and functional authority.

Line Authority

Line authority is a *command* authority. Line authority gives a manager the organizational right to make decisions and to commit the organization to action. Line authority is represented by the chain of command: an individual positioned above another in the organizational hierarchy has the institutional right to make decisions, to issue directives, and to expect compliance from the lower-level employees in his or her span of control. Figure 10.1 on page 228 traces the line authority for claims adjusting in an insurance company. In this figure, the regional operations director has direct responsibility for providing claims service to the insured. Authority for this service flows directly from this director to a regional claims manager, to branch managers, to claims managers, and then to the claims representatives who provide the actual claims service.

The Redistribution of Authority: Can It Help Saturn Run Rings Around Toyota and Intel Chip Away at the Competition?

There is no question about who holds supreme authority in a traditional U.S. auto plant. The plant manager has virtually total authority, and he or she alone decides whether to share this authority with anyone else. If General Motors' plans for its new Saturn facility are fully executed, however, a new day will dawn in corporate America. With its new Saturn plant, GM intends to cut labor hours in half and bring the costs of its cars closer to those of its Japanese competitors. Although robotics are expected to increase effectiveness, GM also plans a radical redistribution of power through the widespread use of participative management. According to GM Chairperson Roger B. Smith, this $4 billion project will be "the key to GM's long-term competitiveness."[1] According to Richard G. LeFauve, president of the Saturn subsidiary of GM, the success of this venture will depend heavily on such practices as the team approach to work.[2]

Work groups at the new Saturn plant will consist of a handful of employees who will elect their own boss and will decide who does which jobs. Each work unit will use a personal computer to coordinate the maintenance of equipment, the ordering of supplies, and the administration of

work and vacation schedules. Workers will be paid a salary instead of an hourly wage and can earn substantial bonuses for good performance. If a work group needs another member, candidates will be interviewed by work group members themselves.

In short, power at the Saturn plant will lie in the hands of the workers. If cutbacks are needed, employee committees will decide whether to issue layoffs or to curtail work hours. Such questions are unlikely to arise, however, because almost 5000 of Saturn's 6000 workers will be protected from layoffs unless a "catastrophic event" should occur. Why does GM expect this bold experiment to work? Because, along with authority and power, workers will be responsible for controlling costs, managing quality, and making the plant profitable. The company is convinced that employees are able to do so if given the opportunity and sufficient support.

Although not at as daring a level as at the Saturn plant, semiconductor giant Intel is also redistributing power in hopes of enhancing organizational effectiveness. The company has simply "grown too big and its markets too turbulent for one manager to control it so closely."[3] The once-profitable Intel, with its highly centralized structure, posted operating

losses of $255 million in 1985–86 alone. Intel's chief executive, Andy Grove, stated publicly that corporate giants must become agile or die. Although Grove admits that it is hard to follow his own advice, he has decentralized Intel along product lines and placed power in the hands of managers in each of the company's three major operating units. Grove's hopes? To restore confidence to the company, return it to money-making status, and position it to respond quickly to market opportunities. Did the actions work for Intel? The 1989 Fortune 500 list profiles a newly profitable Intel, now ranked 150 (up from 200). Sales have risen 50 percent and profits have been up over 80 percent.[4] General Motors and Intel, previously profit-making leaders in the United States, have seen hard times in recent years. How do they "spell relief"? DECENTRALIZATION

1. Will Saturn ever leave the launchpad? (16 March 1987), *Business Week*, 107.
2. Back to the future at Saturn (1 August 1988), *Fortune*, 63ff.
3. Can Andy Grove practice what he preaches? (16 March 1987), *Business Week*, 68.
4. The Fortune 500 largest U.S. industrial corporations (24 April 1988), *Fortune*, 358–59.

Staff Authority

Staff authority is *advisory* authority.[8] It is authority in the form of counsel, advice, and recommendation. Unlike line managers with formal command authority, people with staff authority—for example, staff managers—derive their power primarily from their expert knowledge and from the legitimacy they can establish in their relationships with line managers. For example, lawyer

FIGURE 10.1 Line Authority

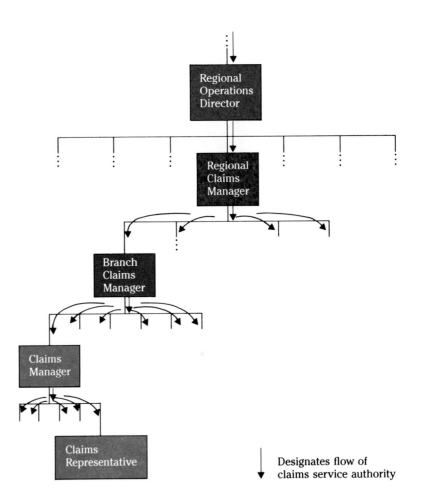

Designates flow of
claims service authority

Don Reynolds cannot dictate a contract negotiated between his organization's personnel department and its unionized employees. Instead, Don, in a staff capacity, advises contract negotiators about the advisability of the language in the contract.

Organizations often have trouble getting their line managers to listen to and accept advice from staff personnel. Line managers often feel that staff people are isolated from the realities of their department and that, therefore, their advice is of limited value. In addition, because line managers are responsible for the action taken, many want to make their own decisions about what needs to be done, how it needs to be done, and why. To solve this problem, many organizations have formally modified the role of staff personnel and the type of authority they are permitted to exercise. These variations in staff authority include compulsory staff consultation, concurring authority, and functional authority for staff personnel. These tactics are intended to move staff personnel from a purely advisory role toward broader authority (see Figure 10.2).

Compulsory staff consultation forces line personnel to discuss issues with staff personnel before taking action. Under this system, for example, purchasing agent Ann Stypuloski is required to contact Don Reynolds' legal department before signing an agreement to buy raw materials. Through this arrangement, organizations hope to create better-informed line managers who take advantage of the resources of staff managers.

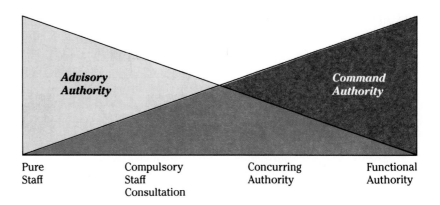

FIGURE 10.2 Variations in Staff Authority

Advisory Authority			Command Authority
Pure Staff	Compulsory Staff Consultation	Concurring Authority	Functional Authority

Some organizations have tried a slightly different approach to make sure their line managers listen to staff departments. They assign a staff member **concurring authority.** That is, a designated staff member can formally approve or disapprove an action to be taken. For example, if the quality inspection department has concurring authority, the production manager will have to obtain the approval of the quality inspection department before making changes in production methods. Concurring authority, in effect, gives staff members the right to veto actions proposed by line managers.

Functional Authority

The third way of expanding staff authority is to vest staff members with functional authority. **Functional authority** is the right to direct or control specific activities that are under other managers' span of control. Functional authority allows a manager (line or staff) to command specific processes, practices, and policies related to the activities undertaken by personnel in other departments. Whereas line authority runs vertically in a traditional organization, functional authority cuts across the vertical chain of command and flows horizontally and diagonally across the hierarchy. The human resources department, for example, may create policies guiding an organization's compliance with equal employment regulations. As managers in such departments as marketing and operations promote and hire employees, the human resources department makes all final decisions to assure compliance with the organization's equal employment opportunity policies (see Figure 10.3 on page 230).

Delegating Authority

Although managers may exercise line, staff, or functional authority, they must transfer some of their formal authority to others for their organization to function effectively. **Delegation** is the process managers use to transfer formal authority from one position to another within an organization and, thus, to put the authority system they have designed into place. Architects delegate authority to draftspeople, senior law partners delegate authority to junior lawyers, high-school principals delegate authority to vice-principals, and so on. It is important to note that delegating authority does not reduce the authority of the architects, senior partners, or principals, nor does it relieve them of their

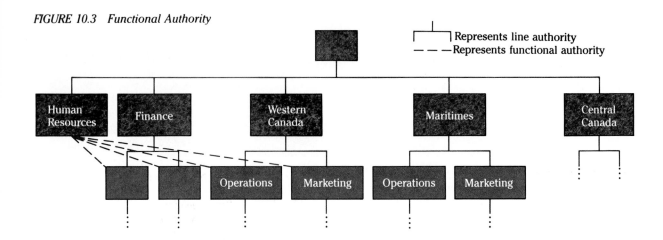

FIGURE 10.3 *Functional Authority*

Represents line authority
— — — Represents functional authority

responsibility. To delegate means to grant or to confer; it does not mean to surrender. A manager who delegates authority in no way abdicates the institutional right to act on behalf of the organization. The manager who delegates effectively retains authority but does not exercise it unless the delegatee fails to act appropriately.

How much authority can a manager delegate? Theoretically, managers can delegate the right to do anything they have authority over, unless their source of authority prohibits doing so. For example, Kelly Bell, president of a national shoe distributor, may delegate authority over all hiring, firing, marketing, and production, but she may retain the authority to make long-term strategic plans and to keep the company in compliance with the law. Realistically, most managers usually retain and manage critical tasks, delegating as many others as possible. (See "A Closer Look: Delegation.")

The Delegation Process

There are four stages in the delegation process, although it rarely unfolds in an orderly fashion from one step to the next. Figure 10.4 on page 232 depicts those stages. In the first stage, the delegator identifies a block of work to be transferred from one area in the organization to another and assigns this activity to an employee or group of employees. For example, Charlie Dawkins, founder of a medium-sized accounting firm on the East Coast, has been the coordinator of his community's annual holiday parade for eight years. He has elected to remove himself from direct involvement in this activity but wants his firm to continue to sponsor the event. Charlie decides to turn the activity over to the firm's vice-president, Laurie O'Donnell.

In the second stage of the delegation process, the delegator transfers authority—the organizational right to command—to the delegatee. Until this point, the delegator is the active participant, assigning activities and transferring authority. The subordinate is passive, listening to the delegator's requests and receiving authority. As often happens in organizations, Charlie combined the first and second stages by sending Laurie a memo telling her of his decision and stating that, should she accept the assignment, she would have full authority to manage the parade.

A CLOSER LOOK

Delegation: Dance to the Music or Pay the Piper

Delegating is one of the areas in which new managers are the weakest. It requires a clear understanding of the task at hand, the ability to communicate your expectations, and the skill to follow up on the task once it has been delegated.[1]

Busy managers must learn to delegate if they are to capitalize on the skills and knowledge of their subordinates, or else they will become immersed in details and unable to cope. According to Jack Smith, the director of support operations in the customer service division of Trans World Airline's information systems group, "People are motivated when they feel as if they are a part of the business and understand where they fit in. . . . We've found that sharing information and treating employees as business partners, not just workers, is highly motivating."[2]

In spite of its advantages, though, many managers find it extremely difficult to delegate. One reason is that "a lot of people in . . . corporate life feel that delegating is an admission that there's something they can't do."[3] Delegation should be added to the list of important tasks that a manager does well. According to Peter Drucker, "The greatest delegator was Franklin D. Roosevelt who 'did' an absolute minimum."[4]

Delegation must be done well or the consequences can be devastating. Poor delegation can lead to legal, moral, political, and professional shambles, as people learned from the Iran-Contra affair that almost derailed Ronald Reagan's presidency, has continued to haunt George Bush, and changed the lives of many other people. Reagan conducted his administration according to his belief that "there's no limit to what you can do if you don't mind who gets the credit."[5] He recommended to managers: "Surround yourself with the best people you can find, delegate authority, and don't interfere as long as the policy you've decided upon is being carried out."[6] Even before the scandal emerged, however, *Fortune* noted, "Critics fault Reagan for not wading deeply into the substance of decision-making. . . . Management experts caution corporate leaders against disdaining detail to the extent Reagan does."[7]

Things obviously went wrong for Reagan. According to Drucker, this outcome could have been anticipated because Reagan made "one of the most common but also most unforgiving management mistakes—[he] confused delegation of authority with abdication of responsibility."[8] For delegation to be effective, the delegatee must keep the delegator completely informed. One of the things that made Roosevelt such an effective delegator is that he required regular reports and upward responsibility. Reagan, however, allowed—and, in some cases, possibly required—his delegatees to keep him in the dark. The results for Reagan, his administration, and the country were catastrophic.

1. How to manage a staff (November 1986), *Business Week Careers*, 107.
2. *Ibid.*
3. John Sears, Ronald Reagan's former campaign manager, as quoted in What managers can learn from manager Reagan (15 September 1986), *Fortune*, 35.
4. Management lessons of Irangate (24 March 1987), *Wall Street Journal*, 32.
5. Ronald Reagan as quoted in *Fortune* (15 September 1986), 36.
6. *Fortune*, 33.
7. *Fortune*, 35, 38.
8. *The Wall Street Journal*, 32.

Charlie and Laurie are now at the conditional third stage in the delegation process. At this stage, the delegatee either accepts or rejects the task assignment and the accompanying authority. If Laurie were to refuse the task, the delegation attempt would be blocked, and Charlie would have to start again by assigning the activity to someone else. If Laurie were to accept the assignment and authority, the delegation process would continue.

The fourth, and final, stage in the process is the creation of the delegatee's obligation to perform the assigned tasks and to use the delegated authority properly. By accepting the assignment and its accompanying authority, Laurie becomes accountable to Charlie and is responsible for completing the assigned work. At this stage, both Charlie and Laurie have authority to complete the task, and both are responsible for how it is performed. Ultimately, however,

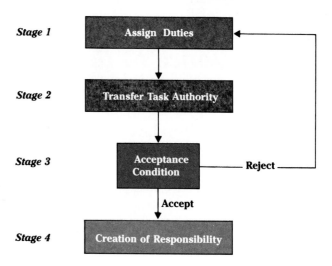

FIGURE 10.4 The Delegation Process

Stage 1 Assign Duties

Stage 2 Transfer Task Authority

Stage 3 Acceptance Condition — Reject

Accept

Stage 4 Creation of Responsibility

Laurie will produce the parade. If things go well, she will accept credit; if not, she will have to answer to Charlie—who will have to respond to community criticism.

Delegation is not confined to a downward process in which authority is transferred from one level to those below it in the organizational hierarchy. Managers can delegate upward to transfer control to a higher level. Kevin Carlson, for example, may have the authority to negotiate the sale of 10,000 tires to WalMart, but when WalMart asks for a guaranteed ten-day delivery schedule, Kevin may ask Karen LaBonte, his boss, to decide if the company should make such a commitment. Even though Kevin has the authority to make the decision, he delegates it upward to Karen. Lateral delegation is also possible. If WalMart asks Kevin to sign a sales contract that guarantees his organization will not sell tires to any other company in the same city, Kevin can decide whether to sign, or he can delegate laterally by asking his organization's lawyer to decide if the contract would be legal. Authority delegation is lateral when line managers transfer authority to staff advisers or to people in other line departments.

Barriers to Effective Delegation

Managers are often unwilling to run the risk of things going wrong if others are given authority for decisions, and, moreover, share the natural inclination of all of us to think that we know best what should be done.
25 —Pfeffer

In the best of all possible worlds, managers would delegate efficiently, and others would accept their new responsibilities enthusiastically and carry them out to perfection. In the real world, however, the delegation process does not always go so smoothly. Some of the barriers to effective delegation reside in the abilities and beliefs of the delegator. Managers, for example, can be so poorly organized that they are incapable of planning delegated activities. Even managers who are fully capable of delegating may not want to do so because they lack confidence in others' abilities to do a job well, and they fear being held personally accountable for the work of others. Conversely, some managers may be afraid that others will do the delegated task so well that their success will be a personal threat. Some managers want so strongly to dominate and influence others that they resist delegating authority.

Another reason some managers do not delegate is that they fear losing control should conditions become turbulent. In fact, when an uncertain en-

232   Chapter 10   Authority, Delegation, and Decentralization

"All I need is a chair. I delegate everything."

Drawing by Joseph Farris; © 1983 The New Yorker Magazine, Inc.

vironment poses problems, threats, and crises that cry out for delegation and for opening up the system, many managers react in just the opposite fashion. They pull back the reins, reduce delegation of authority, rechannel information to themselves, and attempt to take personal charge. This phenomenon has been referred to as *threat rigidity.*[9]

Managers are not the only organization members who can have difficulty with the delegation process. Some of the barriers to effective delegation reside with those who would assume the new responsibilities. Some employees, for example, feel they cannot handle additional responsibility. Others are reluctant to accept delegation because they fear their managers will criticize them if they fail to execute the task well. Still others simply do not want any extra work. If workers perceive no benefit to themselves (whether from an organizational or a personal reward system), managers may have difficulty inducing them to assume additional responsibility.

Delegation must be done well or the results can be devastating, as illustrated by the Iran-Contra affair during the presidency of Ronald Reagan.

Overcoming Barriers to Delegation

No matter where they reside, the barriers to delegation are not easily overcome. Organization members at the top must create a climate in which delegation can be effective by encouraging managers to release some of their personal hold on authority and to inspire subordinates to pick it up. Managers must be persuaded to give others a chance to expand their organizational roles. In addition to providing the opportunity, delegators also must deliver the tools that delegatees need to be successful. Managers must become resource providers, part of a support system, and trainers to prepare employees for expanded organizational roles. Equally important, managers must set aside the tendency to insist that delegated tasks be done their way. When assigning tasks and transferring authority, managers should permit employees to experiment, to make mistakes, and to learn from those mistakes.

The largest danger faced when real authority is delegated is that people at lower levels in the organization will not see the big picture— how their activities fit in with the overall objective. . . . Information about the firm, its operations, its performance, and particularly about the interrelationship among activities is invaluable in addressing this problem.

—Pfeffer

All of a manager's good intentions will come to naught, however, unless employees also want to expand their roles, to assume additional responsibilities, and to learn new skills. It is not enough for managers to give employees the opportunity to expand their horizons. Employees must allow themselves to try new things, to make mistakes, and to seek the guidance and resources they need to succeed in their new roles. For instance, when Charlie asked Laurie to coordinate the holiday parade, she thought, "I've never done anything like this before. What if I fail? Wow, will I need help." When she decided to accept, she said to herself, "I'll give it a shot. I'll have to rely on Charlie a lot, but I'll try." Finally, employees may need to recognize that some organizations do not immediately reward workers who have taken on new responsibilities. People in those organizations sometimes have to reward themselves by taking pride and pleasure in their own personal development, at least for a while, but effective delegators should monitor their delegatees' actions and reward success. Otherwise, delegatees may conclude that their boss does not care whether they can do the job well or not.

Classical Principles for Effective Delegation

People's attitudes toward authority and responsibility have a long history of causing organizational problems. Many people like to accumulate and exercise influence over the individuals and events around them, but they often do not want the responsibility when things go wrong. Oliver North and John Poindexter, for example, accumulated and wielded a great deal of influence during Ronald Reagan's presidency but tried mightily to avoid accountability for their actions during the hearings held after the surfacing of the Iran-Contra affair.[10] Such conflict between the desire to influence and the desire to escape the consequences creates a delicate situation. Early writers on management tried to address this predicament by creating a set of principles that managers could use to guide the delegation process:

- *Parity of authority and responsibility*—employees should not exercise more influence than they can be held accountable for, but they must have enough authority to do the work for which they are held accountable.
- *Responsibility is absolute*—"to delegate" does not mean "to give away" authority or to be relieved of responsibilities.
- *Scalar principle*—lines of authority must be clear as they run from the very top of the organization to its lowest levels.
- *Unity of command*—each subordinate should be accountable to only one superior.[11]

Although these classical principles can serve as useful guides, they are not universally applicable to delegation. They neglect an organization's occasional need to operate as a self-managing system. They tend to ignore that people-to-people and people-to-work interactions must evolve out of the demands of the current situation.[12] They also ignore situations that require dual authority designs, such as a matrix structure; thus, there are cases in which management should violate these classical principles.

Decentralization of Authority

Some managers delegate authority extensively, others hardly at all. The extent to which formal authority is concentrated within the hierarchy of an organization determines its degree of *centralization* or *decentralization*.[13] At the extreme, absolute **centralization** exists when authority is concentrated at a single, central point in the organization. **Decentralization** exists when authority is diffused throughout an organization.[14] In the utility companies described at the beginning of this chapter, for example, hiring authority was centralized at the company in which the president approved the hiring of all new employees. In the second company, however, those decisions were made by members of the human resources department. The second company, thus, has a more decentralized structure. In practice, all organizations are somewhere between the two extremes of absolute centralization and absolute decentralization.

Decentralization: Its Nature and Importance

A highly centralized organization is typically designed so that all important organizational decisions are made at a high level in the organization (see Figure 10.5). Upper-level managers or advisers to the institutional level make the decisions considered important and provide directives for lower-level organization members to follow; thus, a decision to adopt a merit pay system would be made at the top, with lower-level managers ordered to implement the plan.

With decentralization, authority is pushed down to the lowest possible hierarchical level (see Figure 10.6). In a highly decentralized organization, authority is spread throughout the organization both horizontally and vertically.

FIGURE 10.5   A Highly Centralized Organization

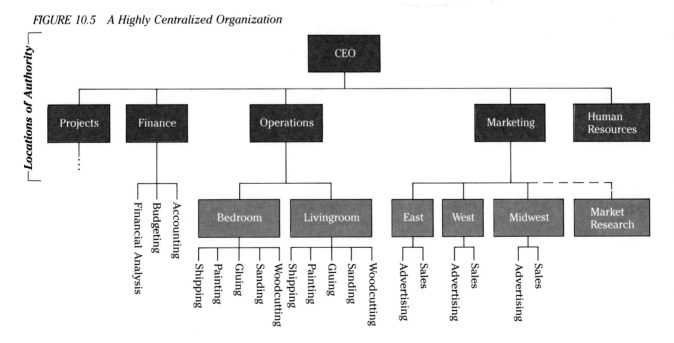

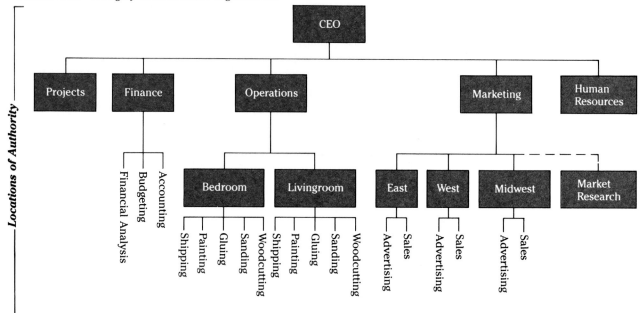

FIGURE 10.6 *A Highly Decentralized Organization*

Very-low-level managers and nonmanagers are expected to make important decisions that pertain to their organizational units. In a decentralized organization, the decision to implement a merit pay system could be made within a single unit or department.

People often confuse decentralization of authority with delegation of authority or participation. *Decentralization* refers to the extent to which, by design, authority is spread throughout an organization and, thus, characterizes the organization's structure. *Delegation* is the process through which authority is transferred, thus enabling an organization to become increasingly decentralized. *Participation* also involves a distribution of authority; however, through delegation and decentralization, superiors transfer authority to subordinates so that they can make decisions independently, whereas in participation, superiors and subordinates make decisions together.[15]

Organizations vary in the degree to which their work units, departments, and divisions are decentralized.[16] In fact, organizational units need varying degrees of centralization and decentralization to accommodate differences in the work they perform, the environments with which they have to deal, and so on. Reporting of on-the-job accident rates to the Occupational Safety and Health Administration (OSHA) usually needs to be centralized to facilitate effective, efficient reporting of inquiry statistics. Responsibility for the prevention of accidents, however, is often best decentralized to allow better control over hazardous situations. Before determining whether an organization or organizational unit should be made more decentralized, managers must first ascertain its current level of centralization. The questionnaire in Figure 10.7 shows some of the criteria for determining various degrees of centralization. The higher the score, the greater the centralization of authority.

Every organization needs an appropriate degree of decentralization to cope with the demands of its external environment, to coordinate activities within its formal structure, to do its particular kind of work, and to manage the attitudes and capabilities of its members. The appropriate degree of decentralization

FIGURE 10.7   *The Measurement of Centralization*

Circle your response to each of the following items as they apply to the organization in question.

1. How much direct involvement does top management have in gathering the information input that they will use in making decisions?
   - a. none
   - b. little
   - c. some
   - d. a great deal
   - e. a very great deal

2. To what degree does top management participate in the interpretation of the information input?
   - a. 0–20%
   - b. 21–40%
   - c. 41–60%
   - d. 61–80%
   - e. 81–100%

3. To what degree does top management directly control the execution of the decision?
   - a. 0–20%
   - b. 21–40%
   - c. 41–60%
   - d. 61–80%
   - e. 81–100%

For Questions 4 through 10, use the following responses:
   - a. very great
   - b. great
   - c. some
   - d. little
   - e. none

4-10. How much discretion does the typical first-line supervisor have over
   4. establishing his or her unit's budget?
   5. determining how his or her unit's performance will be evaluated?
   6. hiring and firing personnel?
   7. personnel rewards (i.e., salary increases, promotions)?
   8. purchasing of equipment and supplies?
   9. establishing a new project or program?
   10. how work exceptions are to be handled?

Scoring: For all items, a = 1, b = 2, c = 3, d = 4, e = 5. Add up the score for all ten items. The sum of the item scores is the degree of centralization (out of a possible 50). Scores of 40 or above indicate high centralization; of 20 or below very low centralization (i.e., decentralization).

Source: S. P. Robbins (1983), *Organization theory: The structure and design of organizations*, Englewood Cliffs, NJ: Prentice-Hall, 88.

enables an organization to: (1) react in a timely fashion to changes in the external environment, (2) deal with complex combinations of business activities, (3) cope with organizational growth and change, (4) place those most familiar with the work in positions to manage it, (5) relieve managers of information and decision overload, and (6) motivate and improve the organization's human resources.

Environmental uncertainty, turbulence, and organizational growth bring with them an increasing need for an organization to collect and process information. A decentralized structure allows a greater number of workers to monitor and react to these environmental conditions—more individuals have the authority to interpret environmental demands and the organization's capacity to respond and to make decisions on behalf of the organization. Decentralization is not a universally preferable way to design an organization's authority system, however. There are a great many reasons centralization of authority may be a preferable arrangement in some cases. For example, under stable environmental conditions, centralization can let managers exercise needed control over organizational activities. The concentration of authority in the hands of a few organization members—as envisioned in Fayol's centralization, unity of command, and unity of direction principles—can help bring about consistency of operations, because only a limited number of people are providing direction to the organization. Military organizations operate this way out of necessity.

Managers must find the best match between the degree of decentralization and their organization's external and internal environments. The challenge facing managers is to balance the advantages of decentralization without losing the coordination, integration, and control advantages provided by centralization.

Determinants of Appropriate Decentralization

As you probably know by now, there is no one best way to accomplish a particular goal in management. There is no ideal degree of decentralization for every organization, its units, and various situations. There are, however, several factors that managers should consider when designing their organization's authority. Table 10.1 summarizes some of the conditions under which centralization and decentralization of authority are likely to be observed.

The External Environment. Decentralization is well suited to uncertain and rapidly changing external environments. The unpredictability of such environments demands that organizations acquire and process considerable amounts of information rapidly. Furthermore, they must respond quickly and appropriately to that information. Decentralization allows an organization to avoid the delays and information and decision overloads that would occur if all information had to be collected, analyzed, and responded to at a central source of authority.

The Organization. Various features of an organization affect decisions about decentralization. For instance, the strategy it pursues should influence the type of authority system it creates. A strategy of product diversification, for

TABLE 10.1 *The Decentralization Decision*

Conditions	Appropriate Matches	
	Centralized	*Decentralized*
1. The external environment		
Stability	Stable	Unstable
Uncertainty	Certain	Uncertain
2. The organization		
Strategy	Narrow	Diverse
History/culture	Closed	Open
Growth rate	Slow	Rapid
Change rate	Slow	Rapid
Size	Small-med.	Large
Complexity	Simple	Complex
3. The work		
Decision costs/risks	High	Low
Technology	Routine	Nonroutine
Task interdependence	Low	High
4. The people		
Upper managers—willing to "let go"	No	Yes
—confidence in lower managers	Low	High
Lower managers—managerial abilities	Low	High
—training needs	Low	High
—control desires	Low	High
—motivation needed	Low	High

example, dictates a need for decentralization, because the complexity of doing business in many markets would overwhelm a single manager.

Size and complexity also affect decentralization decisions. The larger an organization, the more it needs decentralization. Size eventually overwhelms an individual manager's span of control, and lower-level managers must take over some of the organizational decisions. Likewise, the more complex an organization, the more it needs decentralization. Regardless of its size, a complex organization needs decentralization to deal with its wide variety of organizational groups and types of decisions. Large *and* complex organizations, such as Procter & Gamble or IBM, need especially high levels of decentralization.

The Work. The nature of the task is also relevant to decentralization. Tasks that involve considerable interdependence, such as delivering a baby with a caesarean operation, are better suited to decentralization because it allows more careful monitoring of the work at a "local" level. The same is true for tasks that involve considerable uncertainty and nonroutine technologies and, thus, require frequent consultation, advice, or direction. For these reasons, research and development disciplines are usually decentralized. In contrast, routine and nonambiguous tasks, such as converting taconite pellets to ingots or rolled steel, are well suited to centralization, in which decision making is handled higher in the organization.

The People. The appropriate degree of decentralization for a particular organization is influenced by its managers' characteristics. Upper-level managers are fully in charge under centralization; lower-level managers take over under decentralization. Decentralization is unlikely to occur, therefore, unless upper-level managers are willing to release some of their authority to, and have confidence in the abilities of, lower-level managers.

The potential psychological effects of decentralization on lower-level managers should not be overlooked. To the extent that these managers like to exercise control over their work, they find decentralization satisfying. Decentralization can also pose disadvantages for lower-level managers. It places major responsibilities and the worries and burdens associated with this work directly on their shoulders. The result may be longer hours and more intense work, often increasing the amount of stress that workers experience.

Managers should take all these considerations into account when making decentralization decisions. Often these factors point to the same conclusion, making the manager's task easier, but when signals are mixed, the decentralization issue becomes difficult. At that point, managers have to weigh the importance of each factor, as shown in Table 10.1, to arrive at a balanced decision.

Authority, Delegation, and Decentralization in Review

Organization members are able to influence others in the organization to the extent that they have the power and authority to do so. Authority provides individuals (and groups) the right to influence others. Merely having the authority given to them by their organization may not be enough, however, for managers to influence subordinates. The ability to exert authority usually requires managers to develop an adequate interpersonal power base that adds to their legitimate power. This is done by incorporating other sources of power, such as reward and coercion.

An organization tries to control the influence patterns of its members by creating formal authority systems. There are three views of the types and sources of authority: classical, acceptance, and situational. The one belief shared by all three views is that managers must see to it that employees perceive managerial directives to be legitimate. If they do, they tend to comply, in part because they have learned to do so.

The authority system that managers design defines their organization's authority relationships. There are three types of authority found in these relationships: line, staff, and functional. Managers receive some of their line, staff, or functional authority because someone has delegated it to them. Although delegators may transfer authority and responsibility for certain tasks to others, the delegators remain ultimately responsible for such tasks. Delegating is a way to cope with large and complex workloads, but there are both managers and subordinates who resist delegation. Organizations must overcome this resistance by encouraging managers to develop, by training employees, and by providing the resources employees need to meet new challenges.

The amount of delegation that occurs in an organization determines its degree of decentralization. A highly decentralized authority system delegates authority to the points in an organization's hierarchy where decisions are implemented. Decentralization is appropriate for the high levels of environmental and task-induced uncertainty that accompany nonroutine technologies. An organization should determine the level of decentralization appropriate for its specific needs by examining its external environment, the size and complexity of the organization, the work performed in the organization, and the people who do the work.

Issues for Review and Discussion

1. Define influence, authority, and power and explain why organizations must manage each.
2. Compare and contrast the classical, acceptance, and situational views of authority.
3. Discuss various means by which organization members gain influence over organizational behavior.
4. Define delegation and discuss the process.
5. List some of the barriers to effective delegation and actions that managers and nonmanagers can take to overcome these barriers.
6. Identify the principles that early writers on management believed should guide the delegation process and explain why managers must sometimes violate these classical principles.
7. What forces do (and should) influence the degree of decentralization within an organization's authority system?

Key Terms

influence
interpersonal power
authority
classical authority theory
acceptance view of authority
situational view of authority
authority relationships
line authority

staff authority
compulsory staff consultation
concurring authority
functional authority
delegation
centralization
decentralization

Suggested Readings

Barnard, C. I. (1986). The theory of authority. In Matteson, M. T., and Ivancevich, J. M., eds. *Management classics*, 3rd ed., Plano, TX: Business Publications, 211-19. (Reprinted from *The functions of the executive*, 1938.)

Kanter, R. M. (1979). Power failure in management circuits. *Harvard Business Review*, 57, 65-75.

Kotter, J. P. (1985). *Power and influence.* New York: Free Press. For a review, see McGee, G. (1988). In Pierce, J. L., and Newstrom, J. W., eds. *The manager's bookshelf: A mosaic of contemporary views.* New York: Harper & Row, 158-67.

Notes

1. The problems associated with defining power and the major approaches are discussed in A. T. Cobb (1984), An episodic model of power: Toward an integration of theory and research, *Academy of Management Review*, 9, 482-93.

2. W. G. Astley and P. S. Sachdeva (1984), Structural sources of intraorganizational power: A theoretical synthesis, *Academy of Management Review*, 9, 104-13; J. R. P. French, Jr., and B. Raven (1959), The bases of social power, in D. Cartwright, ed., *Studies of social power,* Ann Arbor, MI: Institute for Social Research; D. J. Hickson, C. R. Hinings, C. A. Lee, R. E. Schneck, and J. M. Pennings (1971), A strategic contingencies' theory of intraorganizational power, *Administrative Science Quarterly,* 16, 216-29; G. R. Salancik and J. Pfeffer (1977), Who gets power—and how they hold on to it: A strategic-contingency model of power, *Organizational Dynamics,* 5, 3-21.

3. M. Weber (1947), *The theory of social and economic organization,* Glencoe, IL: Free Press.

4. C. Barnard (1938), *The functions of the executive,* Cambridge, MA: Harvard University Press.

5. Barnard; H. A. Simon (1976), *Administrative behavior,* 3rd ed., New York: Macmillan.

6. Executive secretary: A new rung on the corporate ladder (21 April 1986), *Business Week,* 74-75.

7. Hickson, et al.; Salancik and Pfeffer.

8. H. Stieglitz (1974), On concepts of corporate structure, *The Conference Board Record,* 11, 7-13.

9. B. M. Staw and J. Ross (1987), Behavior and escalation situations: Antecedents, prototypes and solutions, in L. L. Cummings and B. M. Staw, eds., *Research in organizational behavior,* vol. 9, Greenwich, CT: JAI Press, 39-78;

B. M. Staw, L. E. Sandelands, and J. E. Dutton (1981), Threat-rigidity effects in organizational behavior: A multilevel analysis, *Administrative Science Quarterly,* 26, 501-24.

10. Passing the buck: How the President's men attempted to evade accountability (27 July 1987), *Time,* 8-9.

11. H. Fayol (1949), *General and industrial management,* London: Pitman (English translation, 1916).

12. M. P. Follett (1930), Some discrepancies in leadership theory and practice, in H. C. Metcalf, ed., *Business leadership,* London: Pitman; Salancik and Pfeffer.

13. R. H. Hall (1982), *Organizations,* Englewood Cliffs, NJ: Prentice-Hall; J. Hage and M. Aiken (1967), Program change and organizational properties: A comparative analysis, *American Journal of Sociology,* 72, 503-19.

14. C. R. Leana (1987), Power relinquishment versus power sharing: Theoretical clarification and empirical comparison of delegation and participation, *Journal of Applied Psychology,* 72, 228-33; D. M. Schweiger and C. R. Leana (1986), Participation in decision making, in E. Locke, ed., *Generalizing from laboratory to field settings: Research findings from industrial-organizational psychology, organization behavior, and human resource management,* Boston: D.C. Heath; E. A. Locke and D. M. Schweiger (1979), Participation in decision-making: One more look, in B. M. Staw, ed., *Research in organizational behavior,* vol. 1, Greenwich, CT: JAI Press, 265-340.

15. Leana.

16. R. H. Hall (1962), Intraorganizational structural variation: Applications of the bureaucratic model, *Administrative Science Quarterly,* 7, 295-308; E. Litwak (1961), Models of organizations which permit conflict, *American Journal of Sociology,* 76, 177-84; P. R. Lawrence and J. W. Lorsch (1969), *Organization and environment,* Homewood, IL: R. D. Irwin.

Bank Second Marriages: Conflict in Family Integration

By Dean A. Dudley, Eastern Illinois University

Jamestown National Bank was a very successful and profitable bank located in Jamestown, a city in South Central Arkansas. Jamestown's economy is equally divided between agriculture and the economic activity generated by a branch of the state university. With an enrollment of 20,000, in addition to Jamestown's 35,000 population, the university creates a service economy that tends to even out the ups and downs of farm income.

With total assets of $200 million, Jamestown National had experienced rapid, but balanced, growth through acquisition of three smaller banks in surrounding farming communities. These acquisitions through the bank's parent holding company, Jamestown Bancshares, were now operated successfully as branches of Jamestown National. The acquired banks' loan portfolios and personnel were merged easily with Jamestown National's, and they contributed to the growth of the parent bank. This stable growth contributed also to the reputation of Jamestown National's president and chief executive officer, Richard Hodgdon.

Richard Hodgdon was an anomaly in the local banking community. The son of migrant workers who had settled in Jamestown, he had to work especially hard to establish his business career. He was employed as a teller by Jamestown National immediately on his graduation from Jamestown High School. Through hard work and dedication to the bank, he progressed from the teller line to the loan office to the executive vice-presidency over a period of fifteen years. Then, on the sudden death of the bank's president, Hodgdon was asked to accept the presidency. He agreed and, over the next six years, guided Jamestown National successfully through the acquisition negotiations.

Although the bank had grown, Hodgdon was still able to manage with a personal touch. He relied on verbal rather than written communications whenever possible and could frequently be found on the main banking floor or at one of the branches, talking with customers and employees. He often initiated loan applications from the bank's more valued customers himself. The bank's board of directors, its employees, and its customers accepted Hodgdon at face value: his lack of a college degree receded into the background. He enjoyed the respect of his customers and the confidence of his board.

Enter Inland Marine

Then Hodgdon's world was jarred. Inland Marine Bankcorp, a large out-of-state bank holding company, made an offer to Jamestown National's shareholders to acquire their stock. Inland Marine was a large corporate bank headquartered in a major city in an adjoining state. It had grown and diversified by acquiring banks in its neighboring states through its holding company. These acquired banks were all operated as branches of Inland Marine.

Inland Marine's acquisition of Jamestown was not exactly an unfriendly takeover, but it was not friendly either. Even though the offer was generous, Inland made no real effort to keep Jamestown National's officers and employees informed of future plans for them should the merger be approved. The merger was tied up for over a year by regulatory authorities. For this period, Hodgdon and his staff remained uncertain about their future. Inland Marine's silence was explained as being based on competitive reasons and on the possibility of regulatory disapproval. Accordingly, Hodgdon did not discuss contingency plans with the members of his staff. Shortly after the merger was approved, Inland Marine announced that Hodgdon would continue as chief executive officer.

The First Monday

Hodgdon was standing at the teller line on the first Monday morning after the acquisition thinking about how he had spent the weekend. Chris Besse, the Inland Marine regional vice-president to whom Hodgdon now reported, had ordered that all Jamestown National signs be covered with temporary Inland Marine signs. Hodgdon and other key employees had spent the weekend tying canvas Inland Marine signs over all the Jamestown National signs in the county. He was at that moment checking the pockets in the work table in front of the teller line to make sure that Inland Marine deposit tickets had replaced the old ones.

"What the hell are you doing to my bank, Richard?" It was a voice that Hodgdon recognized. He turned to face Joseph Seniw, a retired professor of zoology at the university. "I woke up this morning to find that the bank I have been dealing with for thirty years doesn't exist anymore. You mean to tell me, Richard, that my savings are being controlled by some big city? Richard, haven't you been doing your job?"

"Excuse me, Mr. Hodgdon," Jane Gunton, Hodgdon's secretary, interrupted, "Mr. Besse wants to talk to you. He says it's important."

"Tell him I'll call right back. I'm talking to a customer."

"But he says it's really . . . "

"That's enough, Jane." Hodgdon spoke deliberately, and with force.

Jane Gunton was worried as she returned to her desk. She had never heard that tone in Hodgdon's voice before.

"See, Richard, now you are some kind of 'yes man' for a big city outfit. What's happening to the world when my bank isn't my bank, and my banker is some kind of messenger for some out-of-state slicker?" continued Joseph Seniw.

I don't need this today, thought Hodgdon. Today of all days, I don't need this. "Oh, come on Joseph. You exaggerate . . . " Hodgdon broke off in midsentence when he saw Jane Gunton approaching out of the corner of his eye. There was an urgency in her stride. He turned to meet her.

"It's Mr. Besse again. He is furious, Mr. Hodgdon," she whispered.

"It's OK, Jane. I'll handle it."

Hodgdon welcomed the cool darkness of his office, even though the light on his phone was blinking ominously. He jabbed the blinking button and picked up the handset.

"Hello, Chris, what can I do for you this morning?"

"Well, you can begin by answering the damn phone when I call you." There was acid in Besse's voice.

"But I was talking to a customer. I . . . "

"Look, Richard, we pay you a hell of a lot of money to run that bank and report to us. Other people get paid to talk to customers. You can't do both. If you want to be a loan officer trainee, we might be able to arrange it."

"Chris, our customers are our blood. I've been talking to these people for twenty years."

"In the meantime, who is running that operation? Jane?" The acid had disappeared from Besse's voice. It was now a cool monotone.

This thing is getting out of hand, Richard thought to himself. "Chris, let me call you back. OK? I'll call you back within an hour."

"Make sure that you do," Besse said. "I have some really important things to discuss with you. That's why I have been trying to get you on the phone for twenty minutes. Call back within an hour, and let's get this straightened out." His tone had softened ever so slightly.

The line was silent before the dial tone buzzed its message in finality.

Questions

1. What questions should Richard Hodgdon ask himself in the following hour?
2. Does Hodgdon have any power in this situation? What is the source of Chris Besse's power?
3. What should Hodgdon say when he calls Besse?
4. What could Hodgdon have done to prevent this unpleasant situation?
5. Is Besse right? Can Hodgdon run the bank and talk to customers too?

11 *Organizational Design*

Student Learning Objectives

After reading this chapter, you should be able to:

1. Understand the importance of structural, process, and contextual dimensions to organizational design.

2. Describe the differences among functional, divisional, hybrid, and matrix forms of organizational design.

3. Identify the three key managerial roles found in a matrix organization and discuss their purpose.

4. Relate the importance of the classical (bureaucratic) model to organizational design.

5. Name and discuss two behavioral models of organizational design.

6. Identify the major features of organic organizations.

7. Describe the relationship between each of the major contextual features and organizational design.

*P*icture two houses. In the first, there are very few windows and doors, many corners, and small rooms; furniture is everywhere, and the hallways are crowded. The second house, by contrast, is open and spacious. The walls and furniture do not restrict movement. It has been said that organizations are like houses; just as an architect designs the features of a house, managers design the features of an organization. **Organizational design**—the creation of an organization's structure and the systems that help the organization operate—is a major purpose of the organizing function of management.

Organizational Dimensions

Much like the design of a house and the anatomy of the human body, organizations have many different features. Some concern the *structure* of an organization, some define its *processes,* and still others concern the *context* in which it operates. Together, the structure and process features of an organization (or organizational unit) define its overall design. The contextual features are the primary determinants of that design.

Structure

Just as an architect designs the features of a house, a manager designs the features of an organization.

Like the physical structure of a house, **organizational structure** identifies and distinguishes the individual parts of an organization and ties them together to define an integrated whole.[1] Organizational structure differs from the physical structure of a house, however, in that it encompasses more than inanimate characteristics of walls, doors, and windows. Organizational structure includes the interaction patterns that link people to people and people to work, and, unlike a house, structural dimensions of organizations frequently evolve.

Some important components of an organization's structure include the following:

- *Decentralization of authority*—the degree to which decision-making authority is spread throughout the organization as opposed to being concentrated (centralized) at the top
- *Formalization*—the extent to which the norms of the organization are set forth in written records, documents, and procedure manuals
- *Standardization*—the extent to which work activities are described in detail and performed uniformly throughout the organization
- *Complexity*—the number of specialized job types or subsystems within the organization, the number of levels in the organizational hierarchy, and the number of geographical locations from which the organization operates

Consider these components as they relate to the organizational structure of Progressive Video Images. Because Cindy Mertes makes most of the decisions from the top of the organization, the company has a centralized structure. There is a high degree of formalization attained through the organization's employee handbook, which outlines the policies on hiring, firing, paying, retiring, and the like. A manual specifies the procedures PVI staff should follow in performing such tasks as converting movies to videotapes and custom editing videotapes. The organization is not very complex; there are only three hierarchical levels and the number of specialized job types is small.

Because there is no one best structure for all situations, a wide variety of structures exists. Managers choose and combine structural features to create departments and divisions to meet their organization's needs.

Process

Another feature of an organization's design concerns the systems created to deal with such organizational processes as decision making, coordinating, and communicating. For example, a decision-making system can either permit employees to participate in the decision-making process or enable managers to hand down edicts already "carved in stone." A coordination system can be personal (based on direct contact between managers and subordinates, task forces, and so on) or impersonal (relying on written rules, policies, and standard operating procedures). Information exchanged during the communication process (see Chapter 14) can flow directly from workers to the company president or can be channeled through several layers of management.

There is no one best way to design decision-making, coordination, communication, or other organizational processes to meet an organization's goals. Managers must examine their organization's needs and design these processes to be consistent with and to support the structure of the organization and the context in which it operates.

Context

When architect Cynthia Allen designs a house, she creates a structure and the systems that take into account the characteristics of its inhabitants. The needs of a family with children, for example, differ from those of a retired couple, one of whom uses a wheelchair. Cynthia also considers the environment in the proposed location. A house in Marquette, Michigan, needs a structure capable of supporting tons of standing snow on its roof and an excellent heating system, whereas prospective home buyers in southern Texas are more concerned about effective air conditioning. Similarly, the structure and process features that define an organization's design should be appropriate for the **organizational context,** or circumstances and conditions in which it operates. Contextual design influences are discussed in more detail later in this chapter. For now, you should note that some important contextual considerations include an organization's goals, size, technology, external environment, and people.

Organizational Superstructures

When Cynthia Allen plans a house, she begins by thinking about its overall design—a one-story ranch? a two-story colonial? a split-level?—and then focuses on the pieces that combine to form rooms. Managers are the architects of an organization's design. They, too, frequently begin with an overall design and create their organization's **superstructure,** which defines the division of activities at the top of the organizational hierarchy, thus providing the organization's primary structural form.[2] The superstructure used at the institutional level is the dominant approach for the grouping of organizational activities. It reflects managers' attempts to balance the efficient, effective operation of their organization's internal environment and its strategic response to the external environment. An organization's superstructure also specifies who has the power and legitimacy to guide its operations.

There are several traditional superstructure designs available to managers, as well as a more complex approach known as the matrix superstructure.

Traditional Superstructures

The three most common traditional superstructures are the functional, divisional, and hybrid. Each is an appropriate design for particular combinations of goal, technological, and environmental conditions.

Functional Superstructure. In a **functional superstructure,** upper-level managers are organized around the basic organizational functions—operations, marketing, finance, and so on—in a manner similar to the departmentalization-by-function approach adopted at lower levels (see Chapter 9). The organization shown in Figure 11.1, for example, uses a functional superstructure to group together all marketing activities, such as market research, advertising, and sales. The coordination of any of these activities with those of other functional areas must be done at a higher level in the organization than if the functions were not separated by the structure. The advantages and disadvantages of a functional approach to departmentalization (noted in Chapter 9) also apply to a functional superstructure design.

Divisional Superstructure. When managers design an organization's superstructure according to *non*functional factors—products, territories, projects, and so on—they create a **divisional superstructure.** The divisions most often created are product and territorial divisions, similar to the departmentalization approach for those groupings discussed in Chapter 9. Figure 11.2 on page 250 shows the superstructure of a retailing organization with operations in a number of different states. Figure 11.3 on page 251 shows a product-based superstructure.

One of the biggest advantages of a divisional superstructure design is that it can overcome both the inefficiencies caused by information overload and the bottlenecks that may affect upper-level managers in functional superstructures. For example, bank president Byron Hopkins uses input provided by the bank's personal, small business, and commercial divisions to focus on overall strategic issues. The three division heads take responsibility for strategic and operating issues within their own divisions. This customer-based divisional superstructure improves Byron's control over internal operations because day-to-day operating responsibilities are delegated to the various divisions. The resulting reduction in the demands placed on Byron allows him more time to manage strategic activities.[3]

One of the disadvantages of the divisional superstructure is that an organization can lose the economies of scale associated with the functional grouping of

FIGURE 11.1   A Functional Superstructure

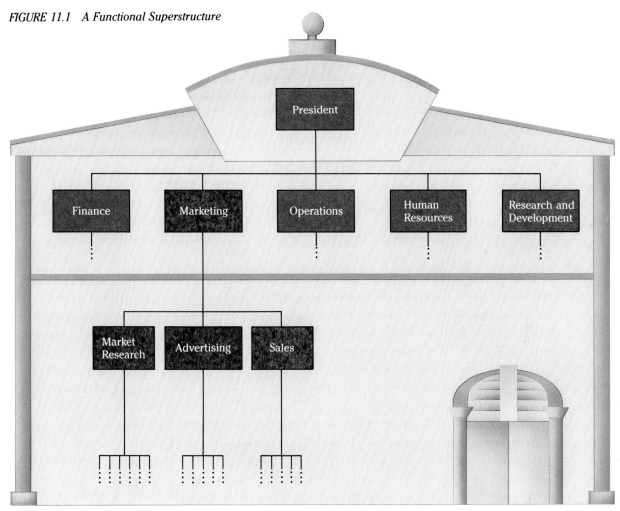

Note: The green portions identify the marketing functional group in the organizational superstructure.

activities. For example, each division might have its own marketing unit. Sharing such resources as equipment and personnel among divisions also can be more difficult than under a functional arrangement.

Hybrid Superstructure.   Few managers adopt a purely functional super-structure or a divisional superstructure consisting of only one divisional basis (for example, product or territory). Instead, most combine the characteristics of two or more structural approaches to create a **hybrid superstructure.** The superstructure of Levi Strauss, for example, has such a hybrid form (see Figure 11.4 on page 252). Near the top of this superstructure are eight product divisions (each containing its own marketing and manufacturing facilities) and four functional groups (consisting of research and development, corporate legal, market research, and traffic and transportation). The functional units serve each of the product divisions. For example, all research and development work for the eight divisions is done by the single R&D unit.

A hybrid superstructure may be adopted by managers of organizations that cannot support the costs of duplicating functional or other resources across

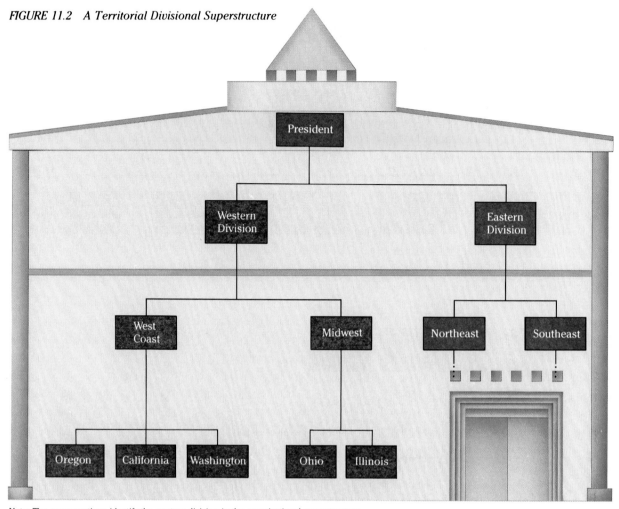

FIGURE 11.2   A Territorial Divisional Superstructure

Note: The green portions identify the western division in the organizational superstructure.

divisional lines. A hybrid superstructure can also give organizations high levels of efficiency by grouping particular units functionally and yet separating groups where necessary. It makes sense, for example, for Levi Strauss to be efficient by having just one legal group. It also makes sense to place manufacturing and marketing in each product division so that those functions can capitalize on the advantages of product divisions. Overall, a hybrid superstructure makes it easier for the Levi organization to manage its wide range of products and markets.

The Matrix Superstructure

Developed in the early 1960s to help solve the management problems emerging in the aerospace industry, a **matrix superstructure** uses two or more integrated, coexisting structures simultaneously. What distinguishes a matrix superstructure from a hybrid superstructure is its gridlike intersection of multiple lines of authority and responsibility. As is true at the departmental level, managers can create a matrix in many different ways. They can, for example, blend function with territory, territory with product, or function with

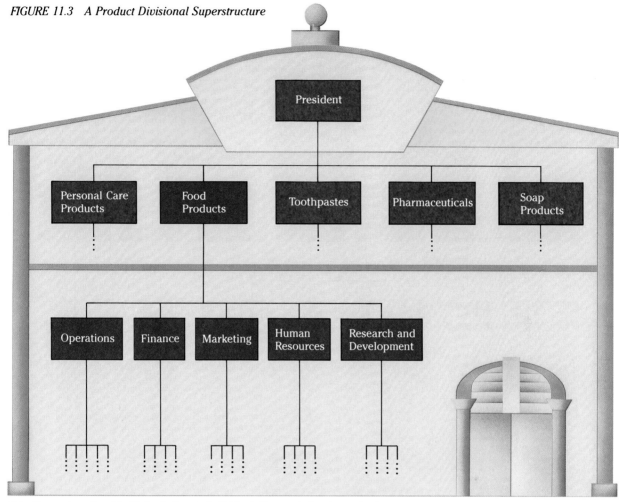

FIGURE 11.3   A Product Divisional Superstructure

Note: The purple portions identify the food products division in the organizational superstructure.

territory with product. The company shown in Figure 11.5 on page 252, for example, superimposes a product division over a functional group to create its matrix superstructure. The functional finance, marketing, operations, and human resources units give the matrix a vertical structure, while the product division gives it a horizontal structure.

A major advantage to a matrix structure is its *dual authority system,* which allows all units to benefit from dual authorities and requires some employees (usually managers in the upper hierarchical levels) to be accountable to two bosses at the same time. In Figure 11.5, for example, Manager A is responsible to the vice-president of operations as well as to the manager for Product A.

The advantage presented by the dual authority system can turn to disadvantage, however.[4] For instance, if a publisher's production manager needs more time to create a high-quality book but the company's marketing manager says that delay will result in fewer sales, how does the book's project director reconcile this with the director of marketing? Conflict, ambiguity, responsibility gaps, and the structural complexity of the matrix have caused many managers to try and then abandon it. The design remains popular, however, among many of the giant firms, such as Honeywell, IBM, and General Electric.

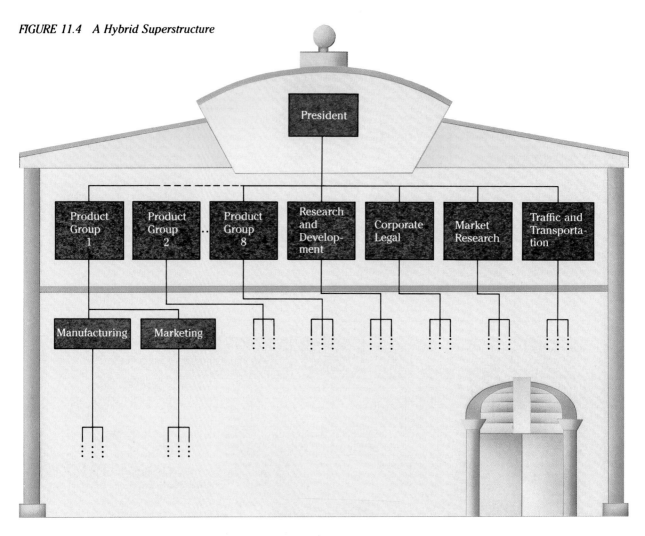

FIGURE 11.4   A Hybrid Superstructure

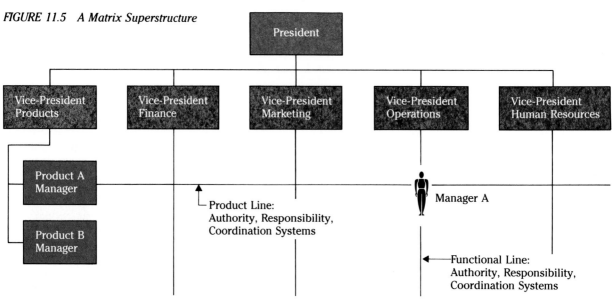

FIGURE 11.5   A Matrix Superstructure

Organizational Forms: The Coming of the Network Organizations

A new corporate look is emerging. Recently, a company called Ocean Pacific Sunwear generated $15 million in sales with only 67 employees; Electronic Arts, a software firm, $20 million in revenues with 75 employees; and Lewis Galoob Toys Inc., over $58 million in sales with just 115 employees. None of these organizations had even a single employee involved in the manufacturing of products. How could these companies perform that way? They use the newest corporate structure, the "network organization." A network organization maintains a very small central organizational structure. It then relies on other companies and suppliers to perform its manufacturing, marketing, distribution, or any number of the other crucial business functions typically done in-house.

When Galoob selects a toy for its product line, it contracts with an outside firm—often in Hong Kong or China—to manufacture and package the product. The toys are then shipped to the United States, where they are distributed by commissioned manufacturers' representatives. Even accounts receivable are handled by an outside credit firm, so what do David Galoob, president of the company, and his brother Robert, executive vice-president, spend their time doing? They make the critical decisions and coordinate the various organizations on which they depend. You might say that Galoob is an idea

and coordination business. The Galoobs make money by selling toys that never touch the hands of a Galoob employee. The Galoobs have discovered that network organizations can sometimes be even more fickle than a traditional organization. After a bad year, however, Galoob bounced back and generated $6.6 million in profits and $140 million in sales between April 1988 and March 1989.[1]

Many network organizations in the United States arose out of their founders' desire to capitalize on lower labor costs found in other countries; however, many have extended this idea to capitalize on other potential advantages of the network structure. For example, network organizations need less capital and maintain lower overhead costs, because they do not build their own facilities and they employ a minimum number of employees per dollar of sales. They can move more quickly on a product or service idea or can adapt other advanced technologies more easily than can their traditional counterparts. Network organizations also tend to support an entrepreneurial spirit. The focus is on creativity, and profitable ideas that might not emerge in a traditionally structured organization are encouraged.

There are, however, some potential disadvantages to the network structure. Many firms, such as Tektronix, which uses Seiko to manufacture its monitors, have discovered

that their suppliers often compete in the same marketplace. A network organization usually has less control over production facilities than does a traditional organization. If a supplier decides to sell its manufacturing capacity to a competitor, the network organization must look elsewhere. This decreased control can also affect product quality. If a supplier does not conform to the network organization's standards, the network organization may not be able to remedy the situation quickly. Many people argue that networking causes a loss of the design and manufacturing expertise usually maintained by in-house production and that creativity and future product ideas are hampered.

No one knows for sure whether the network structure is here to stay. It is known, however, that

With less bureaucracy, they are well suited to an era in which managers and workers are demanding a bigger say in their jobs. . . . All in all, the network structure allows companies to zero in on what they do best and leave the rest to other experts.[2]

1. Media general report (28 April 1989).
2. And now, the post-industrial corporation (3 March 1986), *Business Week*, 64, 66.

There are three key management roles in a matrix superstructure (see Figure 11.6).[5] A **top leader** heads the multiple command system of a matrix organization. It is his or her responsibility to ensure a true balance of authority among the managers in the next layer—the matrix bosses. A **matrix boss** manages one of the organization's overlapping systems, working with other matrix bosses on such matters as scheduling work, coordinating resources, and

FIGURE 11.6   Key Matrix Superstructure Roles

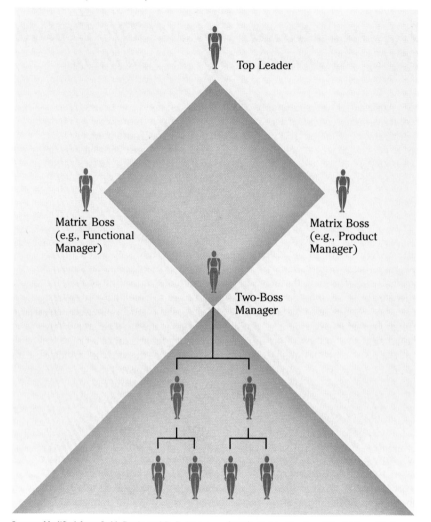

Source: Modified from S. M. Davis and P. R. Lawrence (1977), *Matrix,* Reading, MA: Addison-Wesley, 24, 27.

appraising employee performance. Matrix bosses do not have complete control over the people they supervise or over their immediate subordinates—two-boss managers. A **two-boss manager** is at the point of intersection of two or more multiple structures and, therefore, is directly responsible to more than one matrix boss. To manage their own organizational unit successfully, two-boss managers must be able to confront and influence senior managers when demands conflict, while remaining loyal to the matrix bosses.

In sum, the dual-authority system of a matrix design can be a two-edged sword. It requires matrix bosses and two-boss managers to form a consultative relationship, rather than the traditional superior and subordinate relationship—which can create both a beneficial professional atmosphere and high levels of conflict. If effectively managed, however, conflict can contribute to the skills and knowledge base of an organization's managers. Even so, it is time consuming and often requires frequent meetings and conflict-resolution sessions. These drawbacks are simply the price managers must pay if they are to benefit from the advantages of a matrix superstructure—a price well worth it for organizations requiring its special features but a waste of money for organizations that can use a simpler superstructure effectively.

Design Approaches

All superstructure designs have their roots in three basic models: classical, behavioral, and organic. As you read, remember that managers must create a design for each formal organizational arrangement—work unit, department, division, and entire organization—that matches the unit's or organization's purpose, technology, environment, and members.

Classical Design and the Bureaucratic Model

As you will recall from Chapter 4, classical management scholars, such as Henri Fayol, Frederick Taylor, and Max Weber, believed that a universal set of laws governed the efficient and effective functioning of organizations. They tried to identify these laws and to establish a set of principles to guide the organizing process. Although the classicists did not agree on all issues, one major organizational design—the **bureaucratic model** most often associated with Max Weber's work—emerged from the classical period.[6] The term *bureaucracy* has become emotionally charged and synonymous with red tape and inefficiency.[7] This is unfortunate, because the bureaucratic model can create a high level of speed, order, predictability, and consistency of operations.

Few organizations have a purely bureaucratic design, but most possess at least some bureaucratic characteristics.[8] Chief among these is the emphasis on obeying one leader rather than many. This characteristic arises from Weber's well-defined hierarchy of authority, which specifies the lines of communication, command relationships, and the channels through which individual accountability should flow. A bureaucratic design, thus, centralizes its authority system and bases its legitimacy on inherent rationality. In the U.S. Marine Corps, for example, it is rational for a commander to order troops into action. After all, there would hardly be time for a battalion to take a break during a firefight to see if members could agree on a course of action. Other distinguishing features of the bureaucratic organization include: its reliance on a set of rules that specify employee rights and duties and on standard operating procedures to control work-related activities; its selection of people based on their technical competence; its advancement of organization members based on their tenure and technical competence; its insistence on impersonal interpersonal relations; and its reliance on a division of labor, individual specialization and routine tasks.

When a bureaucracy runs well, it can be a model of order, stability, consistency, and predictability. Even when running well, however, a bureaucratic design has drawbacks. For one thing, it is less than ideal as environmental uncertainty increases and as tasks become increasingly nonroutine.[9] At Hewlett-Packard, for example, the development and design of information systems requires a much more open and flexible working environment than that which would be created by a highly programmed and controlled bureaucracy. A bureaucratic design also does not work well when an organization depends on its members' creativity and interdependencies.[10] For example, the collaboration needed to identify and develop movie ideas at Disney's Touchstone Studios would be inhibited by the rigid structure of a bureaucracy. Other problems frequently associated with bureaucracies include:

- Human problems, such as alienation, frustration, low morale, and lack of motivation that frequently stem from a high level of division of labor and imposed control
- The tendency to ignore the social and psychological sides of the organization, such as the informal organization
- Rules and procedures that become ends in and of themselves, replacing original goals
- Tedious and time-consuming delays in the flow of information because internal communication must follow the chain of command
- The tendency to become inflexible and incapable of responding quickly to environmental complexity and turbulence or to complex tasks and non-routine technologies

Throughout the classical period, managers popularized the use of the bureaucratic organization. During the past few decades, however, managers have experienced increasing inefficiencies associated with this design. As a result, alternative designs have been adopted.

Behavioral Models

As you will recall from Chapter 4, such people as Hugo Munsterberg, Walter Dill Scott, Mary Parker Follett, and Chester Barnard argued that the classical approach to management fails to consider the human side of organizations. Their work led to the development of **behavioral models,** which focused less on the rational and mechanical aspects of organizational design and more on its social and psychological sides. Two behavioral model design approaches are sociotechnical systems theory and Rensis Likert's System 4 organization.

Sociotechnical Systems Theory. Eric Trist and K. W. Bamforth's classic studies on alternative methods of coal mining, and the research of others at England's Tavistock Institute, led to the development of **sociotechnical systems theory,** a design perspective that proposes balancing an organization's human side with its technical and mechanical side (see Figure 11.7).[11] According to the sociotechnical model, managers should design organizations from two premises. First, they should recognize that two systems operate inside every organization: a technical system that focuses on the tasks that produce the organization's product or service and a social system that contains the people-to-people interactions that sustain both the formal and informal organizations. The technical systems involved in the manufacture of paper, for example, include machines and such activities as debarking, grinding, washing, bleaching, and cooking wood. The social system that runs the machines and performs these activities includes individuals and groups whose motivation, interest, ideas, insights, creativity, and needs also must be maintained. Unless managers pay attention to the social and psychological needs of this side of their organization, the technical side will not operate efficiently and effectively.

FIGURE 11.7 *The Sociotechnical Systems Perspective*

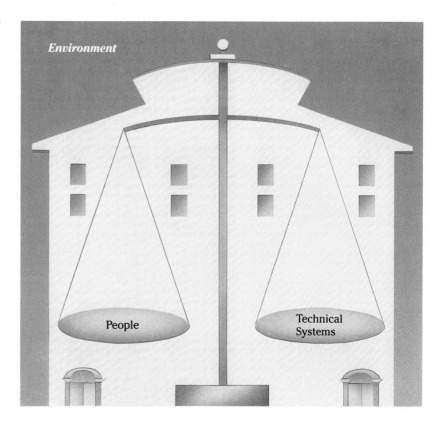

Likert's System 4 Organization. As a social scientist at the University of Michigan's Institute for Social Research, Rensis Likert found a significant relationship between organizational design and effectiveness. He was most concerned with eight features of organizations: leadership, motivation, communication, interaction, decision making, goal setting, control, and performance goal setting. Through his research, Likert observed four design approaches that incorporate these features, which he referred to as Systems 1 through 4. Systems 2 and 3 have received little attention; the System 1 organization is similar to a bureaucratic model. Likert classified the most effective design approach as a **System 4 organization.** Table 11.1 on page 258 summarizes the characteristics of a System 4 organization and contrasts them with a System 1 organization.

Structurally, a System 4 organization has a traditional hierarchy laced with a hierarchy of groups (see Figure 11.8 on page 259), similar to the increasingly popular circular organization.[12] Each manager is a member of several groups. For example, Renée Barnhart is the vice-president of the marketing division shown in Figure 11.8. She is a member of the firm's executive group, which is made up of the heads of the legal, operations, finance, and human resources departments. Renée also is a member of the marketing group, which includes the directors of promotion and sales. She also belongs to a community relations group that has members both from other parts of the organization and from outside of the organization.

Their participation in and connecting function with so many groups imbues managers with **linking pin roles,** so that they become a major conduit through which information and influence flow. Renée represents the promo-

TABLE 11.1 System 1 and System 4 Organizations

System 1 Organization	System 4 Organization
1. **Leadership** shows little confidence or trust in subordinates, seldom soliciting their ideas and opinions. Subordinates are not free to discuss job problems with superiors.	1. **Leadership** shows confidence and trust in subordinates in most matters, soliciting their ideas and opinions. Subordinates are free to discuss job problems with superiors.
2. **Motivation** focuses on physical, security, and economic issues using fear and sanctions. Negative attitudes toward the organization are dominant among employees.	2. **Motivation** draws on a full range of motives through participatory methods. Positive attitudes toward the organization are dominant among employees.
3. **Communication** flows mostly downward. Information is often distorted, inaccurate, and viewed with suspicion by subordinates.	3. **Communication** flows throughout the organization in all directions. Information exchanged tends to be accurate and trusted by subordinates.
4. **Interaction** is closed and restricted. Subordinates have little influence on departmental goals, methods, and activities.	4. **Interaction** is open and extensive. All organizational members, managers and nonmanagers, can influence departmental goals, methods, and activities.
5. **Decisions** take place mostly at the top of the highly centralized organization.	5. **Decisions** take place at all levels of decentralized organization, often using group processes.
6. **Goal setting** is performed at the top of the organization. Group participation is discouraged.	6. **Goal setting** is based on group participation and emphasizes high but realistic goals.
7. **Control** is centralized and great importance is placed on apportioning blame for mistakes.	7. **Control** is decentralized and great importance is placed on self-control and problem solving.
8. **Performance goals** are usually low. Managers make little commitment to developing the human resources of the organization.	8. **Performance goals** are usually high. Managers are committed to developing the human resources of the organization through training.

Source: Adapted from R. Likert (1967), *The human organization*, New York: McGraw-Hill, 197-211.

tions and sales departments when decisions are made at the executive level. In addition, she can bring information about decisions made in operations or human resources back into the marketing group. As a linking pin, then, a manager connects the executive and marketing groups, facilitating vertical, horizontal, and diagonal organizational relationships. This promotes problem-solving, planning, and controlling activities, because it brings together a wide range of people and knowledge when needed. It discourages one-on-one, superior-subordinate relationships because many individuals are included in critical activities. The design also encourages managers from various departments in the executive group to help each other with functional decisions.

Organic Models

For highly uncertain environments and technologies, some people believe that even the behavioral models are too rigid a design. These people have drawn on the work of British researchers Tom Burns and George Stalker to create an organic design (see the discussion in Chapter 2 on organic and mechanistic management systems).[13] In stark contrast to the classical bureau-

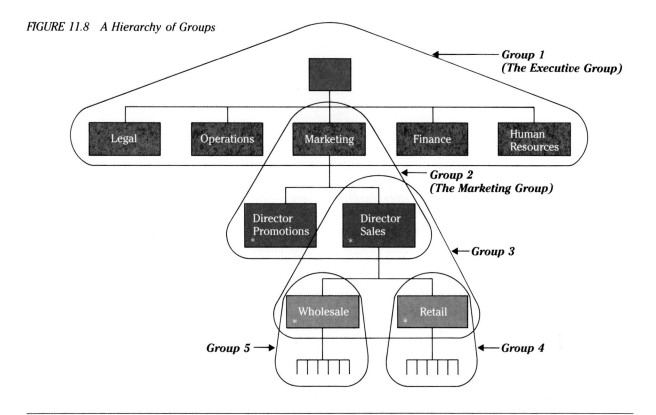

FIGURE 11.8 A Hierarchy of Groups

Group 1
(The Executive Group)

Legal   Operations   Marketing   Finance   Human Resources

Group 2
(The Marketing Group)

Director Promotions *   Director Sales *

Group 3

Wholesale *   Retail *

Group 5 →   ← Group 4

*Linking pin role

cratic design, an **organic organization** is fluid and dynamic and is capable of evolution, redesign, and adaptation to both internal and external environmental forces (see Figure 11.9 on page 260).[14]

Consider the organization design of W. L. Gore and Associates, the company that produces and markets Goretex fabric. Each of the company's 28 plants employs no more than 200 people, all of whom are encouraged to work with every other employee in a kind of corporate free-for-all. There are few chains of command, few hierarchies, few titles, and few formalized rules and policy statements. There is little fixed or assigned authority and responsibility. When people are hired, they are told to look around for something that they would like to do that will help the organization be successful. It sounds like anarchy, but Gore claims that its sales and earnings have been increasing at a 40 percent annual rate.[15]

Although W. L. Gore and Associates is an extreme example, an organic design does allow goals, rather than highly formalized rules or standard operating procedures, to direct employees. Authority is vested in individuals and groups as a function of the task they are working on and the expertise they bring to that task. The loosely coupled, decentralized hierarchical system changes as necessary to respond to environmental pressures, task needs, and participant expertise. Informal and spontaneous interactions facilitate the sharing of information and ideas. Participative decision making is common. Communication networks emerge and evolve to meet the needs of organization members and the changing nature of the tasks. Control systems are personal and rely heavily on feedback about process and outcomes.

FIGURE 11.9 Structures of
Organic and Mechanistic
Organizations

Organic ———————————————————————— Mechanistic

High Complexity Low Centralization Low Formalization Low Standardization High Person Specialization High Task Specialization	Low Complexity High Centralization High Formalization High Standardization Low Person Specialization Low Task Specialization

Design Influences

Because no single design is universally effective, managers must examine the circumstances inside and outside of their organization to determine the most appropriate and effective design. In some cases, for example, highly mechanistic characteristics will be effective; in other cases, such a design could lead to the organization's demise. As noted early in this chapter, managers must consider several *contextual* factors, or contingencies, that influence design decisions: external environment, technology, goals, size, and characteristics of organization members.

The External Environment

Particularly since the early 1960s, people who study organizations have stressed the importance of designing them so they can respond to their external environments. For example, organizations operating in the fiercely competitive airline industry must contend with threats of organizational buyouts, price wars, changing schedules, and competition for lucrative routes. The uncertainty that accompanies such unstable and unpredictable environmental conditions requires a flexible organizational design, such as that found in the organic models. In stable environments, however, organizations have little need for flexibility. The continuity and lack of environmental change, thus, enable managers to use standard operating procedures, centralized authority systems, and other efficient characteristics of mechanistically designed organizations, such as are found in the bureaucratic model.

In addition to considering the design influence that the external environment exerts on an organization as a whole, managers must judge the effects of the individual external environments that surround each organizational unit.[16] For example, Colgate-Palmolive's production department, operating under relatively stable environmental conditions, might do well with a mechanistic structure, while its marketing group, operating in a more turbulent environment, might need an organic structure. In fact, the greater the differentiation among units, the greater the need for the use of special integrators, task forces, and matrix superstructures.

Culture

The culture that permeates an organization and the attitudes toward authority within that culture often strongly influence organizational design. This effect is readily apparent in comparing organizations from around the world. For example, researchers have attributed many of the structural differences between British and American organizations to the fact that authority in British society often stems from tradition, whereas authority in the United States is based more on law and reason.[17] French organizational sociologist Michael Crozier attributes the strength of the bureaucracy in France to the value that society places on protecting individuals from those with power.[18] When compared to their German counterparts, American organizations emphasize individualism and the need for achievement, which is reflected in the design of many contemporary U.S. organizations.[19] Finally, Japanese organizations and their group management systems may reflect the dominant role of society over that of individuals in Japanese culture.[20]

Technology

People often define technology as the machinery that an organization uses, but, as you discovered in Chapter 2, an organization's technology includes any process or technique that converts inputs to outputs, whether it is turning high-school students into college graduates or transforming bolts of material into business suits.[21] Most organizations use one overall technology, but each unit within an organization also uses its own technology to accomplish its assigned task. For example, within a university, the routine technology used by the food service department to produce lunch in the cafeteria exists side by side with the nonroutine technology used in the biomedical research laboratory to pursue cancer research. The primary technology of the entire university is based on the development of new knowledge and its exchange through direct, interpersonal interaction; thus, this technology focuses on the creation, transformation, and exchange of ideas.

Pioneering work on the relationship between technology and organization design was done by British organization scholar Joan Woodward. In the early 1960s, she studied the relationship between technology and a number of organizational design features (span of control, hierarchical levels, decentralization of authority, and so on) in 100 British manufacturing firms.[22] Woodward noted that, as the technology became more complex, the number of hierarchical levels in an organization's structure increased. So, too, did top management's span of control and the size of the organization's staff. Based on these and other observations, it appears that managers must consider the technology that will be used when structuring their organization. If it will be routine, a mechanistic (bureaucratic) design probably will be appropriate.[23] Organic designs, however, are better suited for organizations whose tasks and accompanying technology are nonroutine.[24]

Alfred Chandler observed a close relationship between the types of goals pursued by an organization and its structure.

Goals

Alfred Chandler, while on the management faculty of the Massachusetts Institute of Technology, observed a close relationship between the types of goals pursued by an organization (its strategy) and its structure.[25] He analyzed the history of such firms as General Motors, Standard Oil, Du Pont, and Sears and noted that each had used simple and centralized structures when dealing with limited product lines; however, as the firms took on more complex goals, adopted new products, entered new markets, and increased output, they decentralized their organizational structures.

Recent research has shown that the strategies chosen by an organization's managers determine the tasks it undertakes, the technology it uses, and the environments in which it operates. Subsequently, these organizational attributes (tasks, technology, and environment) have a strong impact on the design the organization adopts.[26] The design, in turn, places constraints on the goals managers are likely to adopt in the future. A mechanistic organization, for example, is likely to pursue goals that emphasize higher levels of productivity and operating efficiency. On the other hand, organizations that want to pursue innovation must be designed more openly and flexibly and must permit exchanges among individuals and highly heterogeneous groups.[27]

Size

The size of an organization influences its design in many ways. As a department expands, a manager's span of control increases and coordination and control pressures mount. In response to these increased pressures, organizations frequently make structural changes, which often result in more organizational units, more hierarchical levels, and an even more complex structure.

As organizations become larger, managers often increase the number of specialized departments (especially staff departments) and increase job specialization. Individuals often become responsible for the performance of a narrow range of activities. In the early days at Progressive Video Images, for example, employee Carri Kessler was involved in virtually all of the company's business activities. On a given day, she often would work on 35mm stills, 8mm movies, VHS and Beta tapes, and transfers from film to video. As the company grew, however, it developed specialized departments. Now Carri works exclusively at transferring 8mm movies to VHS videotape.

Often accompanying increased specialization is greater standardization and formalization, more delegation of authority, and increased decentralization of structure. Lower-level employees are permitted to make decisions to relieve upward pressure and bottlenecks in the hierarchy, but these decisions are guided by elaborate sets of policies, rules, and standard operating procedures. Upper-level management can then operate under the exception principle, handling only those issues that fall outside of the formal guidelines and delegating specific assignments to lower-level employees.

Organizational size also affects coordination and control activities. Managers tend to rely increasingly on impersonal modes of coordination and control as size increases. As a result, large organizations tend to be mechanistic in design.[28]

People

The attitudes, values, beliefs, commitments, and behaviors of an organization's members influence its design and, ultimately, its effectiveness. If employees are not good at self-direction and self-control, for example, the organization must rely on a mechanistic design.[29] If, on the other hand, an organization's employees are highly professional, organizationally committed, self-directed, and self-controlled, they work better with a less mechanistic design. Workers motivated by safety, security, and social needs tend to be comfortable in and work well with a bureaucratic design. Employees with

Organizational Redesign: The Post Office Looks for New Zip, Kodak for More Snap

The Peter Principle holds that people rise to their personal level of incompetence. Robert J. Samuelson believes that "the same dynamic affects large companies; they tend to expand to their level of incompetence and inefficiency."[1] Many companies have been living proof of the organizational Peter Principle. They have diversified into areas where they are inept; have focused too heavily on a small number of products, like Eastern Kodak Company; or have concentrated on operations at the expense of marketing, like the U.S. Postal Service.

For years, Kodak focused on what has now become a mature photo industry. After a ten-year low in profits and stiff competition from such companies as Fuji Photo Film Company, Kodak has been trying to improve business by diversifying its narrow product line to include printers, optical memory systems, and disposable cameras. Perhaps more important, however, are changes in its corporate structure. According to Kodak's chairman, Colby H. Chandler, the company is being broken into a number of autonomous units that will market new products better and will encourage additional new products to keep Kodak competitive.

Another familiar giant with problems is the U.S. Postal Service, which is finding that such organizations as United Parcel Service, Federal Express, and Purolator continue to grow at its expense. Former Postmaster General Preston Robert Tisch intended to turn the overgrown, 700,000-person bureaucracy into a more aggressive, businesslike provider of mail delivery services. According to Tisch, restructuring the organization was necessary to " . . . change it from an operating mentality to a marketing mentality."[2] Tisch initially agreed to local postmasters' suggestions for making Sunday deliveries in Manhattan's West Side to get rid of a backlog of mail, developed account teams to deal with major corporate customers, and took a more flexible approach to using automation. He seemed willing to admit error and bail out when mistakes were made, as the nine-digit zip code idea may prove to be. These and similar moves led *Business Week* to note that, "If Tisch leaves his mark on the Postal Service, it is most likely to be by making the organization more responsive to the public."[3]

Unfortunately, beginning early in 1988, Congress forced Tisch to take steps that will make the Postal Service less responsive. To save money,

Sunday mail pick-up was terminated, lobby hours were shortened, and modernization was delayed. Congress won the short-term battle, and Tisch resigned. It remains to be seen whether actions taken since Tisch's resignation, such as trial installation of Postal Service outlets in Sears stores, will be enough to prevent the demise of the Postal Service's new marketing orientation.

The steps that both Kodak and the U.S. Postal Service (under Tisch's guidance) took were designed to remedy their problems through restructuring. They tried to capitalize on their organizational strengths and to eliminate their weaknesses. In effect, they tried to become exceptions to the Peter Principle by rising to their true level of *competence.* Kodak may succeed, but the meddling of Congress seems only to have shoved the Postal Service farther down the road to failure: calls for its privatization have begun.

1. How companies grow stale (8 September 1986), *Newsweek,* 45.
2. Bob Tisch is putting more zip in the post office (24 November 1986), *Business Week,* 72.
3. *Ibid.*

strong growth needs, however, find more challenge and greater satisfaction in an organically designed organization.[30]

The values, beliefs, attitudes, and commitments of powerholders likewise play a major role in shaping organizational design.[31] Managers who subscribe to Theory X, for example, are likely to design tightly controlled, bureaucratic organizations to keep a watchful eye over workers' actions. Theory Y managers, on the other hand, believe in an individual's capacity to exercise self-direction and self-control and, thus, are more likely to adopt an organic design. Personality factors also influence managers' design preferences. Such factors as authoritarianism (discussed in Chapter 12) can be particularly important. A manager with a highly authoritarian personality, for example, feels that power and status should be clearly defined and specified within organizations. This type of person, thus, is likely to create a centralized, formalized structure with a distinct hierarchy of authority.

In sum, managers should review an organization's internal and external environments, technology, goals, and other contextual factors when considering a structural design. They then should compare the compatibility of design alternatives with existing and anticipated conditions. Through this systematic approach, managers can select and implement an overall design with supporting superstructures and processes to meet their organization's requirements.

Organizational Design in Review

As a part of the organizing process, managers must decide how to design the overall organization. Managers should consider structural, process, and contextual dimensions to arrive at an appropriate superstructure and accompanying systems. There are at least two types of traditional superstructures. A functional superstructure approach groups activities around the major types of tasks performed by an organization, such as operations, marketing, finance, and human resources. A divisional superstructure is based on arrangements similar to those used for departmentalization at lower levels: products, territories, customers, and so forth. A hybrid superstructure combines two or more of these approaches so that managers can benefit from the advantages of each.

Many managers of organizations that operate in complex, turbulent environments have come to rely on a newer design called a matrix superstructure. This approach allows managers to overlap several organizational arrangements simultaneously. The intersections of authority in this complex arrangement require three managerial roles: top leader, matrix boss, and two-boss manager. This structure has advantages, but it also creates many challenges for those who have to deal with its complexities.

All organizational designs are based on essentially three models. The first is the bureaucratic (mechanistic) structure advocated by the classicists. Behavioral models, such as sociotechnical systems theory and Likert's System 4 design, counter the classicists' concentration on organizations' technical side by stressing their human elements. The third model, based on organic design, permits an organization's structure to evolve quickly in response to changes in the internal and external environments.

Managers contemplating various models and structures when designing organizations must take certain contextual factors into account. Environmental considerations, their organization's culture, the type and complexity of the technology to be used, their organization's goals, its size, and the attributes of organization members give rise to variations in organizational design. To be most effective, a chosen design must be compatible with these factors.

Issues for Review and Discussion

1. Explain the roles of structure, process, and context in defining organizational design.
2. What are the differences between the functional and divisional forms of organizational superstructure?
3. What are some advantages of a hybrid superstructure? What are the disadvantages?
4. Identify three major managerial roles that are found in a matrix organization and discuss each.
5. What are some problems commonly associated with a bureaucracy?
6. Compare and contrast the bureaucratic and System 4 approaches to organizational design.
7. Under what conditions is an organic design appropriate?
8. Explain how environmental conditions influence the design of an effective organization.

Key Terms

organizational design
organizational structure
organizational context
superstructure
functional superstructure
divisional superstructure
hybrid superstructure
matrix superstructure
top leader

matrix boss
two-boss manager
bureaucratic model
behavioral models
sociotechnical systems theory
System 4 organization
linking pin roles
organic organization

Suggested Readings

Crosby, P. (1988). The eternally successful organization. New York: McGraw-Hill.

Gribbins, R. E. (1988). A review of *The adaptive corporation*. In Pierce, J. L., and Newstrom, J. W., eds. *The manager's bookshelf: A mosaic of contemporary views*. New York: Harper & Row, 268-74.

Hellriegel, D., and Slocum, J. W., Jr. (1973). Organizational design: A contingency approach. *Business Horizons*, 16(2), 59-68.

Kets de Vries, F. R., and Miller, D. (1984). *The neurotic organization*. San Francisco: Jossey-Bass.

Lawler, E. E. (Summer 1988). Substitutes for hierarchy. *Organizational Dynamics*, 17(1), 4-15.

Mintzberg, H. (January/February 1981). Organization design: Fashion or fit? *Harvard Business Review*, 59, 103-16.

Toffler, A. (1985). *The adaptive corporation*. Toronto: Bantam Books.

Notes

1. R. H. Miles (1980), *Macro organizational behavior,* Santa Monica, CA: Goodyear, 18; R. H. Hall (1987), *Organizations: Structures, processes, and outcomes,* Englewood Cliffs, NJ: Prentice-Hall.

2. R. Robey (1982), *Designing organizations: A macro perspective,* Homewood, IL: Irwin.

3. R. E. Hoskisson (1987), Multidivisional structure and performance: The contingency of diversification strategy, *Academy of Management Journal,* 30, 625-44.

4. W. F. Joyce (1986), Matrix organization: A social experiment, *Academy of Management Journal,* 29, 536-61.

5. S. M. Davis and P. R. Lawrence (1977), *Matrix,* Reading, MA: Addison-Wesley, 11-24.

6. M. Weber (1922), *The theory of social and economic organization,* A. M. Henderson and T. Parsons, ed. and trans. (1947), New York: Oxford University Press.

7. P. M. Blau, and M. W. Meyer (1987), *Bureaucracy in modern society,* New York: Random House.

8. E. Litwak (1961), Models of bureaucracy which permit conflict, *American Journal of Sociology,* 67, 177-84; R. H. Hall (1962), Intraorganizational structural variation: Application of the bureaucratic model, *Administrative Science Quarterly,* 7, 295-308.

9. Litwak; C. Perrow (1967), A framework for the comparative analysis of organizations, *American Sociological Review,* 32, 194-208; A. H. Van de Ven and A. L. Delbecq (1974), A task contingent model of work unit structure, *Administrative Science Quarterly,* 19, 183-97; W. A. Randolph and G. G. Dess (1984), The congruence perspective of organization design: A conceptual model and multivariate research approach, *Academy of Management Review,* 9, 114-27.

10. C. Argyris (1973), Personality and organization theory revisited, *Administrative Science Quarterly,* 18, 141-67; C. Argyris (1957), *Personality and organization,* New York: Harper & Row; W. Bennis (1965), Beyond bureaucracy, *Trans-action,* 2, 31-35; R. Blauner (1964), *Alienation and freedom,* Chicago: The University of Chicago Press.

11. E. Trist and K. W. Bamforth (1951), Some social and psychological consequences of the long-wall method of coal getting, *Human Relations,* 4, 3-38.

12. R. Likert (1967), *The human organization,* New York: McGraw-Hill; R. Likert (1961), *New patterns in management,* New York: McGraw-Hill; R. L. Ackoff (1989), The circular organization: An update, *Academy of Management Executive,* 3, 1, 11-16.

13. T. Burns and G. M. Stalker (1961), *The management of innovation,* London: Tavistock.

14. Litwak; Hall, 1962; G. Hage (1965), An axiomatic theory of organizations, *Administrative Science Quarterly,* 10, 289-320.

15. Classless capitalists (9 May 1983), *Forbes,* 122, 124.

16. P. R. Lawrence and J. W. Lorsch (1967), *Organization and environment,* Homewood, IL: R. D. Irwin.

17. S. Richardson (1956), Organizational contrasts on British and American ships, *Administrative Science Quarterly,* 1, 189-207.

18. M. Crozier (1964), Bureaucracy, integration, and alienation, *The bureaucratic phenomenon,* Chicago: The University of Chicago Press.

19. A. Reudi and P. R. Lawrence (1970), Organizations in two cultures, in J. W. Lorsch and P. R. Lawrence, eds., *Studies in organization design*, Homewood, IL: R. D. Irwin.

20. W. G. Ouchi (1981), *Theory Z: How American business can meet the Japanese challenge*, Reading, MA: Addison-Wesley.

21. Randolph and Dess.

22. J. Woodward (1965), *Industrial organization: Theory and practice*, London: Oxford University Press.

23. Perrow; Van de Ven and Delbecq.

24. J. W. Alexander and W. A. Randolph (1985), The fit between technology and structure as a predictor of performance in nursing subunits, *Academy of Management Journal*, 28, 840-59; J. V. Singh (1986), Technology, size, and organizational structure: A reexamination of the Okayama study data, *Academy of Management Journal*, 29, 800-12.

25. A. D. Chandler, Jr. (1962), *Strategy and structure: Chapters in the history of the American industrial enterprise*, Cambridge, MA: MIT Press.

26. H. Mintzberg (1979), *The structuring of organizations*, Englewood Cliffs, NJ: Prentice-Hall.

27. J. L. Pierce and A. L. Delbecq (1977), Organization structure, individual attitudes, and innovation, *Academy of Management Review*, 2(1), 27-37; M. Aiken and J. Hage (1971), The organic organization and innovation, *Sociology*, 5, 63-82; Burns and Stalker.

28. Singh.

29. D. McGregor (1960), *The human side of enterprise*, New York: McGraw-Hill.

30. L. W. Porter, E. E. Lawler III, and J. R. Hackman (1975), *Behavior in organizations*, New York: McGraw-Hill.

31. J. Child (1972), Organization structure, environment, and performance: The role of strategic choice, *Sociology*, 6, 369-93; J. R. Montanari (August 1977), *Operationalizing strategic choice*, a paper presented at the 37th National Meeting of the Academy of Management, Orlando, FL; D. C. Hambrick and P. A. Mason (1984), Upper echelons: The organization as a reflection of its top managers, *Academy of Management Review*, 9, 193-206.

Arnco Products Company

By Kenneth L. Jensen,
Drury College

The Arnco Products Company was founded in 1952 as a glass container supplier for the beer and soft drink segment of the beverage industry. Over the years, it branched into supplying other industries with glass containers. The first area was the dairy industry, which used returnable glass bottles for their delivery sales. Arnco then developed other forms of glass containers to allow it to expand into supplying food packers with jam and jelly glasses, which were reused by consumers. Eventually the company became known as a specialist supplier of reusable glass containers. In all of the industries to which it sold, Arnco maintained high quality levels and sold at prices higher than their competitors.

When Cindy Yates became president of Arnco, she replaced her aunt, Karin Wasner. Wasner was an engineer and designer who concentrated her efforts on operation, particularly quality control. It was her belief that high-quality products would sell themselves. Yates, on the other hand, had left a major manufacturer of consumer goods, where she had been the national sales manager. Her strong suit was in the development of accounts and channels of distribution. She believed that sales representatives (reps) should cultivate major accounts by providing the types of services that such accounts demanded.

At the time Cindy Yates became the president of Arnco, company sales had been flat for several years. This came about because of the increased use of cans, plastic containers, and nonreturnable bottles in the beverage industry. The one favorable factor was the increased use of returnable glass bottles in states requiring deposits on all beverage containers for environmental reasons. Yates believed that there was a new opportunity for Arnco if the company could take advantage of it. She came to believe that the company should investigate the characteristics and requirements of its customers, as well as the ability of Arnco's sales organization to meet their needs. To do this, she asked her staff to do an analysis of Arnco's existing sales network and a study of customer buying patterns.

Arnco's Sales Organization

Arnco's sales force consisted of twenty sales reps organized on a geographical (territorial) basis. There were two regional managers supervising the sales reps. Each rep was expected to call on and service all accounts in his or her territory—an average of 100 accounts per rep. Two thirds of the accounts were in the beverage industry, with an increasing number of food packers and a decreasing number of dairy accounts.

Because of the broad diversity of customer requirements, Arnco's product line was quite extensive. Each rep sold all items in the line. This required a great deal of knowledge on the part of the sales force, for beer and soft drink customers had different product requirements than food packers. Beverage accounts were concerned more with the serviceability of the container. Food packers tended to be more concerned with print requirements for container labels.

Once an order was placed, Arnco shipped directly to customers from either of two warehouses. One was located at company headquarters in Lancaster, Pennsylvania. It served all accounts east of the Mississippi River. The other warehouse was in Denver, Colorado, and handled the remainder of the country. Orders were mailed in each day by the sales reps, processed at the warehouse, and then filled and shipped by truck to the customer. The order-processing time varied from one to four days, depending on the mail service and the volume of orders received on any one day. Truck delivery times varied from one to four days also; thus, total delivery time could vary from two to eight days once a customer placed an order.

Promotional efforts were totally concentrated in direct selling. No advertising had ever been used in the trade press, nor had direct mail ever been used. When calling on an account, Arnco's representatives tended to stress their product quality and the

FIGURE 11A   Arnco's Sales Organization

company's reputation to get the order.

Arnco's customers purchased glass containers either through negotiating the purchase or through letting the purchase out for bids. Customers who used the bidding process typically wanted products made to their specifications and required more time on the part of Arnco's sales representatives. Arnco's survey showed that nearly 25 percent of their accounts used the bidding process exclusively and that about three fourths used bids for 60 percent or more of their purchases. The survey also showed a strong relationship between the size of the customer and the use of competitive bidding, with the larger accounts using bidding more often than the smaller accounts.

The survey identified the importance of factors customers used to select their supplies. The top five factors, in order of importance, were the following:

1. Quality
2. Speed of delivery
3. Service
4. Reputation
5. Price

The survey also showed that the larger customers who relied more on the bidding process placed more importance on speed of delivery than did smaller customers.

Another aspect of the survey examined competition from the customers themselves, who made some of their own containers. The survey showed that slightly fewer than 50 percent of their customers produced some of their own containers and that fewer than 10 percent made more than 40 percent of their required containers. None of their accounts produced more than 80 percent of their own containers.

After considering the results of the work done by her staff, Cindy Yates came to believe that the sales force would be more effective with a different organizational structure. She wondered what kind of structure was needed.

Questions

1. What do you think leads Cindy Yates to believe that the current structure needs improvement? What other changes might be made?
2. What are the most important aspects of the sales force's task environment?
3. What should be the basis for the sales force structure?
4. Prepare a new organizational chart for Arnco's sales force.

PART 4 Directing

MANAGER PROFILE

Addison Barry Rand

After holding several sales jobs in suburban department stores, A. Barry Rand joined the Xerox Corporation as a sales trainee in 1968. After two years of hard work and self-denial, Rand's persuasive talents and passion for selling paid off. In 1970, Rand was recognized as the top salesperson in his district and ranked third among Xerox' national salesforce. Rand's twenty years with Xerox have been characterized by commitment, the setting of difficult goals, successful performance, and upward mobility. His performance record has positioned him as a possible candidate for the corporate presidency of Xerox.

Wanting to win—
and winning—is a way of life
for this manager.

After graduation from high school, Rand headed to Rutgers University to study medicine, yet his sights were really set on a career in sales. He transferred to American University and graduated in 1968 with a degree in marketing. After being recruited by IBM and Exxon, Rand chose to accept an offer as a trainee with Xerox. He saw Xerox as an organization that prompted individuality. It was an organization in which a young person who wants to win would have ample opportunity to do so. Wanting to win—and winning—is a way of life for this manager. As he says it, "I thought I was always supposed to win and that's the way life was supposed to be."[1]

Rand's strong sales performance helped put him in the spotlight at Xerox. Not only was he seen as a good salesperson, he understood marketing. Emerging opportunities gave him the chance to demonstrate managerial talents as well as a passion for excellence. These factors, and a little luck, enabled him to move rapidly through a number of marketing management positions. From 1980 to 1984, he was promoted from corporate director of major account marketing, into and out of vice-presidencies in account marketing and field operations, and into the vice-presidency of Xerox' Eastern operations. In January of 1986, Rand was named vice-president and general manager of Xerox' National Marketing Distribution Organization. He was elected a corporate officer in May 1986 and, in December of 1986, he was appointed to his present position of vice-president of Xerox Corporation and president of the company's U.S. marketing group. His corporate vice-presidency places him on a team of twenty top-level executives in the $13 billion multinational corporation.

As president of the U.S. marketing group, Rand is responsible for an operation that generates nearly $5 billion in sales and employs a salesforce of 33,000 people. For all practical purposes, his operation is responsible for the "bread and butter" of Xerox.[2] The division is responsible for marketing, direct sales, and service of Xerox products and services to major accounts and commercial customers throughout the United States. Rand is also playing a central role in Xerox' challenge to its Japanese competitors. In recent years, the Japanese have made major inroads into a market that once belonged to Xerox. Today Xerox is positioning itself to take this market back, and Xerox chairman and CEO David T. Kearns has identified Rand as the man who will lead the "multinational giant's initiative against the Japanese."[3]

In response to this challenge, Rand has embarked on a major change in Xerox' strategy. This strategic change will necessitate a major change in the organization's internal culture. The essence of his strategy will be to place greater emphasis on customer satisfaction. Rand says, "We have got to develop an obsession with satisfying customers, . . . We've got to do everything we can to make sure that we get the affirmative vote of our customers."[4] According to Rand, Xerox historically has been an internally oriented organization. This internal orientation is reflected in the organization's drive for efficiency. The customer, says Rand, "doesn't necessarily care how lean we are. He cares about us meeting his needs."[5] Rand is steering Xerox toward building a customer responsive product and service-oriented organization. If he is successful, many speculate that he will become Xerox' next corporate president.

Being number one without giving the maximum is unacceptable.

Rand also finds himself responsible for meeting a number of the company's cost-cutting goals while increasing efficiency and productivity. Herein lies another part of his managerial philosophy. Instead of cutting costs by laying off a portion of the organization's workforce, Rand's approach is driven by the simultaneous achievement of cost cuts and the maintenance of employee morale and security.

Achieving excellence, driving for continual improvement, and exceeding expectations may be key forces behind Rand's motivation, hard work, and successful track record. He credits his middle-class parents with instilling in him high expectations and the drives for achievement and continued self-betterment. In 1970, when he became Xerox' number-three national salesperson, his father might have asked why he was third and not second or first. When Rand looks at himself in the mirror, the face looking back says that if you gave your maximum effort, everything is okay, but being number one without giving the maximum is unacceptable.

Rand claims that his teamwork experiences with athletes of all ethnic backgrounds played a major role in preparing him for success in the corporate world. High expectations, ambition, preparation, and performance have enabled him to break into corporate management by the age of forty-three. These same factors are likely to carry him even higher and to more success in the decades to come.

At Xerox, Chairman and CEO Kearns sees Rand as a talented executive. "Barry has a tremendous amount of experience and he is an aggressive executive with a great background in marketing," says Kearns.[6] He believes Rand's drive, standards of excellence, aggressiveness, and experience with marketing will play a key role in Xerox' effort to combat the Japanese marketing challenge.

1. Barry Rand—Xerox's $5 billion man (January 1988), *Ebony,* 118.

2. A black's climb to executive suite (22 May 1987), *Business Day: The New York Times,* D1, D4.

3. Can this man keep team Xerox no. 1? (August 1987), *Black Enterprise,* 58.

4. *Business Day,* D1.

5. *Ibid.*

6. *Black Enterprise,* 60.

12 Organization Members: The Nature of Individuals and Groups

Student Learning Objectives

After reading this chapter, you should be able to:

1. Understand the nature and purpose of the directing activity.

2. Discuss how people learn and how managers can use this knowledge to benefit an organization.

3. Explain why personality differences are important to an organization.

4. Understand the nature of attitudes and how they can influence organizational effectiveness.

5. Discuss the four stages of the perceptual process and what is needed to manage each stage effectively.

6. Identify the factors that encourage group formation and cohesion.

7. Understand the six major stages of group development.

*D*irecting, the third major management function, is the process through which employees are led and motivated to make effective, efficient contributions to the realization of organizational goals. To execute the directing function successfully, managers must understand the nature of individuals *and* groups, much as they need to understand capital in order to execute financial activities. After all, an organization is a social system; its work is accomplished through its individual members and through such groups as work teams, project groups, committees, and quality circles.

The Nature of Individuals

Susan Siegrist and Karlene McBride were classmates in high school and college. They both majored in business and graduated at the same time, but there the similarities end. Today, ten years after graduation, Susan is performing well as the associate dean of a fine midwestern university. She works closely with the treasurer and comptroller, oversees the preparation of the annual budget, and has close contact with the office of alumni. Karlene, in contrast, has held more than a dozen different jobs since graduating from college. She has never received a promotion at any of them. She is presently working as a publicist for the consumer products division of a large manufacturing firm. Her previous job was as assistant to the administrator of a small hospital. Before that, she worked in the real estate department of an insurance company. In each job, Karlene has felt increasingly less motivated and more dissatisfied with her responsibilities and her colleagues.

Everyone enters an organization with a variety of needs, abilities, attitudes, personality factors, and perceptual and learning styles. Together, these individual differences exert a tremendous influence on people's reactions to their work, on their ability to work effectively, and on the degree to which they serve the interests of their organization. People may be an organizational resource, but they are not standardized, automated machines. They are human and must be directed by managers who understand various human characteristics. The way in which managers work with (or against) employees' motivation, attitudes, skills, and abilities is crucial to an organization's success.

Motives

All individuals have needs, wants, desires, and expectations—**motives**—that push them to perform various types of behavior. When people's motives are met, they feel happy or satisfied. When they are not, people feel unhappy or dissatisfied. Consequently, individuals are continuously motivated to do things that satisfy their wants, needs, desires, and expectations and to avoid doing things that frustrate this satisfaction.

Motivation is an internal force that makes an organization member put forth a certain amount of effort to accomplish a task. People are motivated, for example, to come to work, to remain on the job, to do things for the organization "above and beyond the call of duty"—or they are motivated to skip work (and interview for another job or sleep late), to quit their job altogether, or to do as little for the organization as they can get away with.

Employee performance appears to be determined by accurate role perceptions, the skills and abilities needed to perform a task, and the motivation to accomplish it.

Although motivation is not the only determinant of the way employees behave, it certainly plays a central role. Employee performance level appears to be determined largely by three factors: (1) accurate role perceptions (an employee knows what is to be done and how), (2) the skills and abilities needed to perform a task, and (3) the motivation to put forth the necessary effort to accomplish the task. A manager cannot elicit behavior from employees—selling products, serving customers, meeting budgets, and so on—unless they are motivated to engage in that behavior. In turn, employees' motivation is unlikely to be intense and appropriately channeled unless some of their needs, wants, desires, and expectations can be satisfied in the process. In short, organization members are motivated to meet their organizational responsibilities when they feel that doing so also meets their personal motives. Chapter 13 examines several need and motivation theories.

Abilities

Performance, as you have seen, is a function of both motivation and ability. Motivation accounts for the *desire* to perform; ability accounts for the *capability*. Two people with identical levels of motivation perform differently if their levels of ability differ. For example, Sandra Rainer and Glen Wilson, trainees in the accounting department of a textile mill, may both be highly motivated to achieve and succeed, but Sandra, who has a stronger mathematical ability, may work more effectively.

Of course, the performance of any job requires a combination of abilities. Sandra and Glen not only need mathematical ability but must be able to read and write, to follow directions, and to get along with others. The levels of various abilities differ substantially from person to person and can differ significantly across time for one individual. Sandra may have stronger mathematical skills than Glen, but Glen may have more persistence and a better ability to work with others. For large groups of people, statistics reveal a *bell curve distribution* for most abilities. The bell curve shows that, in the general population, most people have about average ability levels (see Figure 12.1). Few people have abilities that approach very low or very high levels. This holds true for both physical abilities (strength, flexibility, and coordination) and intellectual abilities (thinking, memory, and reasoning).

Different jobs, of course, require different types of abilities. Some jobs require conceptual abilities, some require interpersonal abilities, and some require technical abilities (see Chapter 1). Accounting trainees, for example, require a different mixture of these abilities than do investigative reporters or associate deans. The abilities that are relevant to the successful performance of a particular job depend on the nature of the job, the design of the job, and the types of technology available. The necessary mix varies not only from one job to another and across jobs at the same level in an organizational hierarchy, but from one level to another. It stands to reason that the higher up in the organizational hierarchy a manager rises, the stronger his or her conceptual and interpersonal abilities must be.

As a manager, you will need to exercise your ability to tell people what to do, how to do it, and when to have it done. You will have to motivate them to do as you ask and to meet the organization's goals. To do so, you must be capable of matching the demands of specific jobs to the abilities of your employees. If motivation is constant, one theory suggests that an employee's performance is

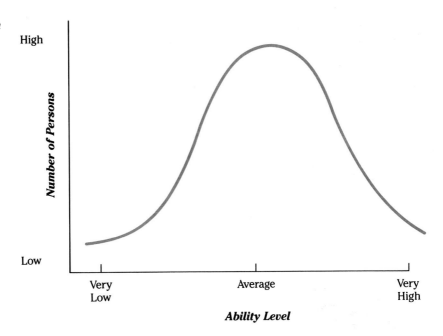

FIGURE 12.1 Ability Distribution

High

Number of Persons

Low

Very
Low   Average   Very
High

Ability Level

primarily determined by the degree of correspondence between his or her abilities and the ability demands of the job.[1] If the match between employee and job is not a good one, problems lie ahead. Chapter 22 discusses techniques managers use to try to achieve a good fit.

Learning

Except on very simple tasks, a person's performance improves with time and training until he or she reaches a final level of competence. Like performance, the rate of learning (that is, the acquisition of skills) is influenced by a person's motivation and ability.

Learning seldom occurs at a steady rate. When learning a new task, for example, people seem to learn fairly quickly at the beginning, but then their learning speed tapers off. Sometimes they reach a plateau at which they seem to learn little, if anything. Although plateaus are common, they are not a necessary part of the learning process. Plateaus usually follow a temporary lack of motivation, inefficient performance methods, or poor training techniques. Although a plateau can provide a brief respite from rapid learning, it delays the point of reaching full proficiency. Appropriate training techniques and incentives can usually shorten or eliminate plateaus. After breaking away from a plateau, people learn fairly rapidly again until they reach their final level of mastery.

Figure 12.2 illustrates the learning curves for people learning to enter computer data and shows how ability and motivation can affect both the level and rate of learning (note the trends discussed in the prior paragraph). Donna has the lowest ability, the slowest rate of learning, and the lowest final proficiency level, and she takes the longest to reach that final level. Mark has a higher ability than Donna, a more rapid rate of learning, and a higher final proficiency level, and he takes less time to reach it. Randi's ability level is also high and about on par with Mark's, but she has received an incentive from the organiza-

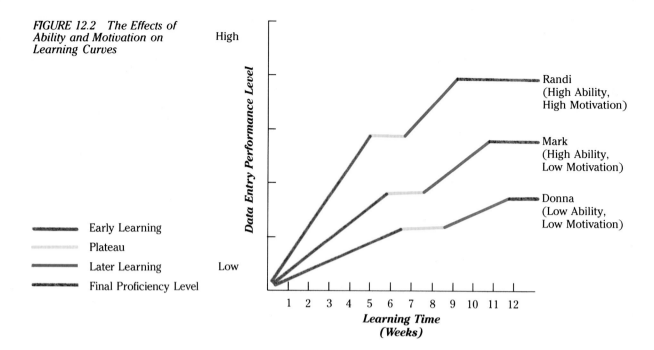

FIGURE 12.2 The Effects of Ability and Motivation on Learning Curves

Early Learning
Plateau
Later Learning
Final Proficiency Level

tion to learn data entry quickly. Her high ability level, coupled with her high motivation level (due to the incentive), have resulted in a rate and level of learning that are higher than those for either Donna or Mark. The next chapter will explore the most effective ways for managers to enhance motivation.

Personality

Although learning is determined by abilities and motivation, a person's general nature is largely determined by his or her personality. **Personality** is a combination of the psychological characteristics and traits that make up a unique style of behavior. Psychologists think that personality characteristics tend to be quite stable over time and that any significant changes usually occur only gradually. An employee who is impulsive and restless is not likely to become cautious and sedentary. An employee who is orderly and obedient is not likely to become disorderly and rebellious. Psychologists have identified many personality factors, some of which are of particular importance in an organizational context.

Locus of Control.   All people experience positive and negative consequences of their behavior. They receive praise, raises, and promotions. They also get criticism, demotions, and warnings. Some people believe that their success and failure are determined by their own actions and abilities. They have what psychologists call an **internal locus of control.** Conversely, individuals who believe that other people, circumstances, or just plain luck account for their success and failure have an **external locus of control.**

Individuals with an internal locus of control may be easier to motivate than people with an external locus of control, because they are more likely to understand that success must be *obtained,* not just received. Some employees with an external locus of control believe there is little point in working hard because they feel perpetually unlucky, think that "what will happen will happen," or believe that the cards have been stacked against them from the beginning. People with an external locus of control, however, can be motivated to work effectively if given specific, appropriate direction. They also are not as likely to take failure personally, as are people with an internal locus of control.

Authoritarianism. Another aspect of personality that affects job performance is a person's beliefs about authority. An **authoritarian** person believes that power and status should be clearly defined, that organizations must concentrate authority in the hands of a few leaders, and that this authority should be obeyed. Authoritarian leaders tend to be effective if they have authoritarian subordinates. Authoritarian subordinates expect to receive orders and are likely to feel frustrated if given only suggestions or general instructions from an unauthoritarian leader. Subordinates who are not authoritarian, however, tend to examine the appropriateness of the orders they receive, which frustrates an authoritarian leader. It is important that an organization's leaders recognize the levels of authoritarianism that subordinates respond to best and manage them appropriately.

Dogmatism. A person with a high level of **dogmatism** has a rigid belief system and sees the world from a narrow perspective. Highly dogmatic individuals feel uncomfortable when presented with ideas that are not consistent with their own views of the world. Within an organizational context, they like to know the rules and to follow them closely. When faced with new ideas, they tend to resist. When faced with problems, they try to apply solutions that worked in a similar situation in their experience.

Dogmatic personalities fit well into an organizational setting that presents few uncertainties and that specifies courses of action. They are unlikely to waste time, for example, thinking about alternative ways to view an already highly structured task. In contrast, people with low levels of dogmatism spend significant amounts of time and energy thinking about all sorts of alternatives and are better suited to jobs that require creativity.

Although they seem to work well under pressure, people with a Type A personality may be likely to suffer from stress-related illnesses.

Type A and Type B Personalities. One classification of personality types has important implications not only for the ways in which people work but also for their physical health and well-being. Some people, for example, are never late for an appointment. They are always rushed and very competitive. They walk, eat, and talk quickly and try to do several things at once. They have what is referred to as a Type A personality. A person with a **Type A personality** works intensely, impatiently, and under great pressure. An individual with a **Type B personality,** in contrast, has a less-pressured style and tends to be more easygoing and relaxed.

Type A people tend to work better under time pressure than do their Type B counterparts. Type A people tend to focus on here-and-now issues but may fail to consider long-term concerns. Type B people, in contrast, are often more willing to take the time necessary to explore options; to evaluate alternatives carefully; and to develop well-thought-out, complete solutions. As is true for the other personality factors, it is important to an organization that managers understand the relative strengths and weaknesses of each type so that they can match individuals to organizational demands. (See "A Closer Look: Personality.")

Personality: Lots and Lots of Personality

Picture four adults sitting in a room answering over 100 questions on the order of "In a group, do you often introduce others or wait to be introduced?" and "Would you rather work under someone who is always kind or always fair?" The people then score the test, discover the label that corresponds to their personality type, and eagerly begin comparing notes. What is happening here? Is this the latest board game craze? the newest survey put out by *Good Housekeeping?* Possibly, but the chances are far greater that you are seeing employees taking a personality test.

Known as the Myers-Briggs Type Indicator (MBTI), this increasingly popular personality test was completed by approximately 1.5 million people in 1986, with nearly half of those at such companies as Apple, AT&T, Citicorp, Exxon, GE, Honeywell, 3M, and the U.S. armed forces. MBTI is based on a theory initially proposed by Swiss psychologist Carl Jung in the 1920s and further developed by Katherine Briggs and her daughter, Isabel Briggs Myers. A person's answers to the test are divided and classified into 16 different personality types (see Table 12A).

Why is this test so popular? Certainly one reason is that it is interesting to discover your personality classification and how it compares to that of others. MBTI proponents argue that there is more to it than that, however. Knowledge of personality types can help managers understand why subordinates and coworkers behave the way they do and anticipate how they are likely to behave in certain circumstances. For that reason, most businesses use the MBTI for developmental purposes, such as getting groups to work together more effectively. Understanding the personality types of group members helps managers assign roles best filled by particular personality types. For example, managers can match the personality type often found in accountants and other "numbers people" (ISTJ traditionalists) to that of "idea people" (ENTP conceptualizers); during idea sessions, the "numbers people" can help translate ideas into figures, which might keep the company from making a disastrous move.

In some ways, the broad use of this test may be a fad, yet " . . . the theory may well be less significant than the communications it seems to foster. Talking about what type you are and what type I am and the differences between the two often proves to be an unthreatening way for people to raise and resolve problems."[1] If it does turn out to be a fad, the MBTI is at least based on a solid instrument, and it's fun, too.

1. Ideas and information for this "Closer Look" were obtained from Personality tests are back (30 March 1987), *Fortune*, 74-76, 80, 82.

Attitudes

In addition to differences in organization members' motives, abilities, and personalities, people also differ in their attitudes. An **attitude** consists of the beliefs, feelings, and intentions about behavior that people have toward a person, an event, a task, or an organization. An attitude consists of three components. The **cognitive component** includes *what people think they know* about a person, task, or the like and is generally descriptive. For exam-

TABLE 12A   The Sixteen Different Personality Types

		Sensing Types (S)		Intuitive Types (N)	
		Thinking (T)	Feeling (F)	Feeling (F)	Thinking (T)
Introverts (I)	Judging (J)	**ISTJ** Serious, quiet, earn success by concentration and thoroughness. Practical, orderly, matter-of-fact, logical, realistic, and dependable. Take responsibility.	**ISFJ** Quiet, friendly, responsible, and conscientious. Work devotedly to meet their obligations. Thorough, painstaking, accurate. Loyal, considerate.	**INFJ** Succeed by perseverance, originality, and desire to do whatever is needed or wanted. Quietly forceful, conscientious, concerned for others. Respected for their firm principles.	**INTJ** Usually have original minds and great drive for their own ideas and purposes. Skeptical, critical, independent, determined, often stubborn.
	Perceiving (P)	**ISTP** Cool onlookers—quiet, reserved, and analytical. Usually interested in impersonal principles, and how and why mechanical things work. Flashes of original humor.	**ISFP** Retiring, quietly friendly, sensitive, kind, modest about their abilities. Shun disagreements. Loyal followers. Often relaxed about getting things done.	**INFP** Care about learning ideas, language, and independent projects of their own. Tend to undertake too much, then somehow get it done. Friendly, but often too absorbed.	**INTP** Quiet, reserved, impersonal. Enjoy theoretical or scientific subjects. Usually interested mainly in ideas, little liking for parties or small talk. Sharply defined interests.
Extroverts (E)	Perceiving (P)	**ESTP** Matter-of-fact, do not worry or hurry, enjoy whatever comes along. May be a bit blunt or insensitive. Best with real things that can be taken apart or put together.	**ESFP** Outgoing, easygoing, accepting, friendly, make things more fun for others by their enjoyment. Like sports and making things. Find remembering facts easier than mastering theories.	**ENFP** Warmly enthusiastic, high-spirited, ingenious, imaginative. Able to do almost anything that interests them. Quick with a solution and to help with a problem.	**ENTP** Quick, ingenious, good at many things. May argue either side of a question for fun. Resourceful in solving challenging problems, but may neglect routine assignments.
	Judging (J)	**ESTJ** Practical, realistic, matter-of-fact, with a natural head for business or mechanics. Not interested in subjects they see no use for. Like to organize and run activities.	**ESFJ** Warm-hearted, talkative, popular, conscientious, born cooperators. Need harmony. Work best with encouragement. Little interest in abstract thinking or technical subjects.	**ENFJ** Responsive and responsible. Generally feel real concern for what others think or want. Sociable, popular. Sensitive to praise and criticism.	**ENTJ** Hearty, frank, decisive, leaders. Usually good in anything that requires reasoning and intelligent talk. May sometimes be more positive than their experience in an area warrants.

ple, Jill Peters is an investigative reporter who knows that her newspaper employs editors, reporters, and photographers. The **affective component** of an attitude is *how people feel* about a person, task, or the like and arises from their reactions to the cognitive component of the attitude. Jill is unhappy that her newspaper has too few photographers and too many editors. Finally, the **behavioral tendency component** of an attitude identifies *how people intend to behave* toward a person, task, or the like. Jill intends to quit unless the situation changes.

People are not born with attitudes. They acquire them gradually through personal experience; through learning based on information provided by others; and by associating one person, task, organization, or the like with another about which they already have formed an attitude. Although firmly held attitudes are resistant to change, they can and do evolve through this same learning process. Managers who wish to change a worker's attitude must first recognize the relationship among the three attitude components and then choose an appropriate method for influencing attitude change—exposing employees to new organizational experiences, for example, or giving them information that will change their cognitions, feelings, or behavioral intentions.

Employees' attitudes can strongly influence behaviors within an organization. Some of the attitudes that researchers have found to be important to organizational functioning are job satisfaction, job involvement, and organizational commitment. These attitudes influence rates of employee turnover, absenteeism, tardiness, unionizing activity, and job performance. An attitude survey administered to Sears employees in Chicago, for example, showed that employee satisfaction with supervision, amount of work, kind of work, financial rewards, career future, and company identification was a powerful predictor of which employees came to work the day after a snowstorm paralyzed transportation systems.[2]

Job Satisfaction. As you have seen, all attitudes have cognitive, affective, and behavioral tendency components. **Job satisfaction** is the affective component of people's attitudes toward their work; it reflects how people feel about their job. Job satisfaction can affect various behaviors (such as absenteeism and turnover); thus, job satisfaction levels strongly influence an organization's effectiveness.

People's overall job satisfaction is composed of their feelings on many dimensions of the work and work environment. Eight dimensions that are important in almost any work setting are people's feelings about: the work itself, the amount of work, physical conditions, co-workers, supervision, compensation, promotions, and company policies and practices. Workers display all possible permutations of these components of overall job satisfaction. A worker may be highly satisfied with pay and promotional opportunities, for example, but dissatisfied with co-workers and supervisors.

Job and Work Involvement. Attitudes of particular importance to organizations are their employees' involvement with work in general and with their own job in particular.[3] **Job involvement** concerns an employee's psychological attachment to a particular job. Employees who have a high level of job involvement are strongly psychologically attached to their jobs. Jill Peters, for example, often dogs a story for her newspaper for days on end, reluctantly taking breaks or diverting her attention. **Work involvement** refers to an employee's devotion to or alienation from work in general. Jill works harder at her reporting job than she has at anything else in her life. Her job involvement is stronger than her work involvement.

Organizational Commitment. The organizational commitment attitude goes beyond that of job and work involvement. **Organizational commitment** is an active association between individuals and organizations such that com-

FIGURE 12.3   *Organizational Commitment: Its Determinants and Consequences*

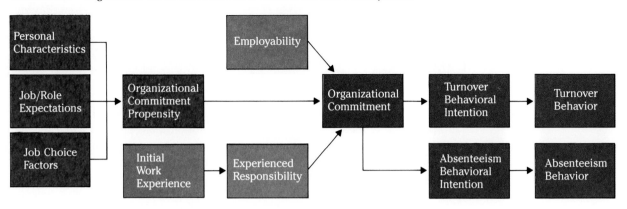

mitted employees are "willing to give something of themselves in order to contribute to the organization's well-being."[4] A strong organizational commitment includes: (1) a belief in and an acceptance of an organization's values and goals, (2) a willingness to put forth considerable effort on the organization's behalf, and (3) a strong desire to remain a member of that organization.[5] Much of the importance of organizational commitment lies in its effects on absenteeism and turnover behaviors.[6] A 1989 study, however, suggested that commitment, when based on a personal attachment to the organization, can enhance performance. Unfortunately, when based mostly on the cost of leaving, commitment can hurt performance.[7]

People who commit themselves to organizations do so for a number of reasons. They may have a propensity to commit themselves to organizations, they may possess certain personal characteristics, or they may have worked in jobs that promoted a sense of responsibility.[8] By knowing about these factors, managers can choose employees who are likely to become committed. Managers can also use this knowledge to identify the types of work experiences that foster employees' commitment. The potential importance of organizational commitment is illustrated in Figure 12.3, which specifies a number of the determinants and consequences of organizational commitment. This figure also makes clear that both the antecedents and consequences of organizational commitment are involved in a complex process.

Good managers understand the nature and psychological makeup of individuals. They use this knowledge to identify desired qualities in subordinates, to nurture their development, and to direct them to facilitate organizational effectiveness. The next section explores the ways in which employees perceive their organizational experiences and the actions that managers can take to direct this perceptual process.

The Perceptual Process

Perception is the process by which a person gains information from the environment, organizes it, and derives its meaning. Managers, therefore, try to direct this perceptual process so that subordinates view managerial directives and other information as intended.

FIGURE 12.4
The Perceptual Model

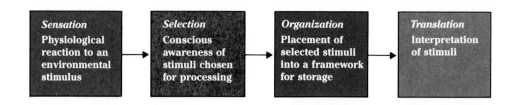

People react to their perceptions of an organization, whether or not those perceptions match objective reality. If a subordinate perceives that the next sales forecast is due on Thursday, even though the manager said it was due on Tuesday, there has been a problem in perception. No matter how carefully a manager plans and guides subordinates, things are sure to go awry unless workers perceive these plans as the manager intends. For this reason, effective managers must manage perceptions as well as reality.

Before any environmental stimulus, such as a memo or a performance appraisal, is understood by an individual, it must pass through four steps: *sensation, selection, organization,* and *translation* (see Figure 12.4).

Sensation

Sensation is the body's physiological reaction to an environmental stimulus, such as a ringing telephone. In effect, at the sensation stage of perception, the body acknowledges the presence of the stimulus.

Selection

People use *selection* to reduce the number of stimuli they perceive to a manageable subset. Sometimes a *perceiver's characteristics* influence the weeding-out process. Suppose, for example, that Clare Lynch and Cecilia Lause, co-workers at an insurance company, walk into the company cafeteria together. Clare is hungry. She is very likely to pay attention to the food on display and does not even check to see whether there are any empty chairs available. Cecilia brought her lunch to work and has already eaten at her desk. She has come to the cafeteria to chat and unwind. Cecilia does not notice any of the appealing food but sees immediately that there are three or four chairs empty at tables where people from her department are sitting.

In addition to a perceiver's characteristics, two other factors can influence the selection decision substantially. A *stimulus' characteristics* are important. For example, intensity (a bright light, loud noise, and so on) attracts attention. Novelty makes people notice a stimulus that is different from the others with which they are familiar. The *context* in which a stimulus is presented also plays an important part in the selection process, which is why a manager might deliver an important message in person rather than through a memo that arrives with the rest of an employee's mail.

Organization

Once a person has selected certain stimuli for further processing, he or she *organizes* and stores them until they can be translated. The process is somewhat like storing papers in a file cabinet until they are needed. The methods workers use to store information influence both the ease with which they can retrieve it later and the meaning they ultimately derive from it. A secretary, for example, who throws every meeting's notes in a random heap in a storage closet definitely influences his or her ability to prepare a quarterly report. Just as most secretaries select file folders, individual data files, or another organizational scheme for storing notes, perceptual organization places selected stimuli into a mental framework for storage and eventual use.

Because a message that is effectively organized when it is sent is more likely to be effectively organized when it is received, managers should try to influence subordinates' organization. For example, people are more likely to associate two stimuli if they are physically similar, so many offices encourage the use of color-coded files and other such materials. Second, because people tend to associate stimuli that are physically close to one another, it makes sense for managers to group place-related messages and materials physically together, such as filing press reports about an escaped convict with the investigation report. Third, managers can present related pieces of information at the same time so that workers connect the stimuli. Managers also can prevent the association of dissimilar stimuli by letting some time elapse between their presentation. ("This is what I have for you on the Northwest sales territory. I'll give you the Midwest sales material tomorrow.")

Translation

People use the *translation* stage of perception to give meaning to the various stimuli they have sensed, selected, and organized. Unfortunately, a number of perceptual phenomena can distort the translation of stored stimuli. For example, a *stereotype* effect can cause a perceiver to feel that a person, an object, or an event possesses the same properties as the group to which it belongs, when in fact it may not. A *primacy effect* occurs if a perceiver gives disproportionate weight to the *first* pieces of information received about a person, an event, or an object; for example, the first few minutes of an interview with a job candidate may prove critical. If, however, a perceiver feels that it is the most recent information that counts, a *recency effect* can distort reality. *Perceptual readiness* occurs when a person perceives the characteristics of an event according to the way he or she anticipated them, rather than according to what actually takes place. If an employee expects management to be unfair and insensitive, for example, the worker might perceive his or her boss' lateness to a meeting as a snub rather than as the result of an unexpected phone call. This phenomenon often leads to self-fulfilling prophecy (the process through which a person changes to match expected characteristics).[9] *Perceptual defense* is the tendency to defend existing perceptions against contradictory information, as when a subordinate who believes the boss to be highly ethical refuses to believe a co-worker's claims to the contrary.

At each of the four steps of the perceptual process, perception of reality may be either distorted or processed as the message sender intended. By understanding that your own and other people's perceptions often are distorted, you improve your perceptual effectiveness. Although people seldom obtain completely accurate perceptions, understanding the source and the likelihood of perceptual errors can go a long way toward improving perceptual capabilities.

The Nature of Groups

Organizations are social systems. They cannot be treated like mere collections of individuals acting independently. Virtually all organizational goals are achieved by individuals interacting. To be effective as a manager, therefore, you must understand the nature of groups.

A **group** is a set of two or more people who interact, who perceive themselves to be a group, and who have a common purpose or work toward the accomplishment of a common purpose or goal. Organizations create **formal groups** to serve an organizational objective; departments and committees are formal groups. Typically, managers identify one or more objectives for a group and specify who will be its members. Jill Peters, for example, is part of the metropolitan news department of her newspaper. Formal groups may also form, however, as the result of employee initiative in highly open and organic organizational settings. **Informal groups** arise spontaneously, such as when a few marketing managers regularly take their coffee breaks together; such group activity may or may not be helpful in reaching organizational objectives.

Group Formation and Cohesion

People join some groups because they offer safety and security. Just as, thousands of years ago, membership in a cohesive group protected people from predators in the environment, membership in a cohesive group within an organization, such as a union, can protect members from harassment by those who oppose the group. People also join groups and become committed to them if they like the other members of the group. Nothing holds a group together as tightly as mutual affection and admiration between members. People also join and stay in groups whose activities interest them. Many groups can have high levels of cohesion even when members do not especially like each other if they enjoy the group's activities, and if belonging to the group is a requirement for participating in the activities.

People also join and stay with groups if belonging helps them achieve their goals. These goals can be personal, as when a worker joins the company's bowling team to learn how to bowl and to enhance his or her reputation as an involved employee. The goals can be social, as when a person joins an organization to promote humanitarian treatment of political prisoners. Group membership can also provide participants with esteem and status. A new member can share in an established, respected group's esteem and status and build his or her own esteem in the eyes of group members. People take pride in serving on and being known to serve on prestigious committees and boards.

People also are attracted to groups because of the power they offer. A person may find opportunities to influence other group members and, thus, may acquire power. Paula Reid, for example, is an expert on microcomputer data bases. Her regional sales manager has just formed a task force to computerize the tracking of sales records. Paula quickly volunteered to join this group because she will have a chance to influence her boss with her expertise and her co-workers with her willingness to help. There is also power in numbers. A group of individuals is likely to exert more influence than is any one person

A group is a set of two or more people who interact, who perceive themselves to be a group, and who work toward the accomplishment of a common purpose or goal.

working alone. A lone telephone operator's request that the company change to a flex-time schedule would probably not carry as much clout as would a petition from the company's entire workforce.

One effect of a high level of group cohesion is that members tend to be quite satisfied with their group experiences. After all, cohesion is, in large part, a function of the degree to which a group meets the needs of individual members. High levels of cohesion do not necessarily increase performance, however.[10] If the goals of a group match those of its organization, members are likely to perform effectively. If group goals are inconsistent with organizational goals, though, organizational goals will not be met even if the group's goals are. Furthermore, highly cohesive groups can be very effective at executing dysfunctional activities, such as work slowdowns or stoppages. Managers need both to foster strong cohesion within a group (by identifying members' needs and by designing groups that satisfy those needs) and to direct it toward organizationally desirable goals.

Group Norms

In one of two groups of reporters with whom Jill Peters works, daily meetings start promptly, members contribute relevant material, and joking and complaining take a back seat to finishing a story. In the other group, meetings usually start late, are often interrupted by irrelevant reports and complaints, and break down into bickering between members who want to investigate certain aspects of a story and those who think the investigation should not "go looking for trouble." In each of these groups, different norms are operating.

Group norms stipulate the limits of expected and acceptable behavior for group members. For example, group norms specify acceptable levels of performance, the ways in which members are to interact, and the things members must not do. Sometimes norms are formalized into writing; more often they are passed from member to member verbally or through example. Groups may have different norms, depending on their members' values and their organization's norms. For example, in some organizations it is acceptable for production workers to interact informally with executives. In others, it is not (in fact, some organizations separate these two groups to the extent of having "executive" and "nonexecutive" restrooms and cafeterias). Group norms, then, are the means by which groups guide and control the behavior of their members.

Managers should be aware of the significance that group norms can have for an organization and of members' conformity to these norms. Norms can signal sources of support for or resistance to organizational activities. When "service with a smile" is a group norm and not just an organizational slogan, customers can expect to be greeted courteously. When Jill Peters' group works as hard as possible to produce a thorough, balanced story, the group's norms support the newspaper's goal of presenting thorough, balanced news to its readers. Groups whose norms are inconsistent with organizational goals can pose problems, however, as when a group sets an informal production ceiling below that desired by the organization. Managers can work to develop groups, to shape group norms, and to satisfy group needs, thereby making these groups work as organizational allies.

Group norms guide employees' behavior, specifying how they should interact and perform their duties.

Groupthink: Pearl Harbor— Why the Fortress Slept

The early months of 1941: *"MAGIC (the code name used for the intelligence branch which had cracked the Japanese secret codes) supplied plenty of warning signals showing that Japan was getting ready for massive military operations."[1]*

March 1941: *"A dawn patrol attack launched against Pearl Harbor from one or more Japanese aircraft carriers could achieve complete surprise."*

November 27, 1941: *"This dispatch is to be considered a war warning. . . . [A]n aggressive move by Japan is expected within the next few days. . . . Execute appropriate defensive deployment."*

December 6, 1941: *"I am certain the Japanese are going to attack Pearl Harbor."*

In spite of these and other warnings, Admiral H. E. Kimmel, Commander-in-Chief of the Pacific Fleet, and his high-level group of naval commanders concluded that "there was no chance of a surprise air attack on Hawaii at that particular time." The result of their conclusions was felt at 8:00 A.M. (Hawaii Time):

Sunday, December 7, 1941: *"While most navy personnel were on weekend leave or just awakening in their bunks, the first wave of attack planes began to sweep over the island of Oahu. Bombs were dropped at will on the 96 unprepared American ships sitting at anchor in Pearl Harbor. Over 2000 men were killed. Thousands more were injured or missing. The U.S. Pacific fleet was devastated."*

How could Kimmel and his group have ignored such clear warnings and left their fleet unprepared for attack? Because, according to Irving L. Janis, they allowed *groupthink* to convince them that Pearl Harbor was safe despite all evidence to the contrary.

This military group exhibited some of the classic symptoms of groupthink. Kimmel had surrounded himself with extremely loyal advisers. A highly cohesive group, these people interacted socially as well as for business purposes. Their feelings of personal security appeared to reinforce their perceptions of military security. The groundwork for illusions of invulnerability was firmly in place.

The group norm was "Pearl Harbor is safe." When warnings from outside the group suggested otherwise, members focused on reasons to reject the warnings rather than on reasons to accept and react to them.

If an individual member expressed doubts (as Kimmel himself did on December 6, 1941), other members quickly closed ranks to assure the doubter that all was well. Their desire for uniformity and agreement with the group stance, combined with stereotypes they had formed of the enemy, allowed members to rationalize that there was no danger.

This naval group was not the only one so complacent. In fact, the views of Kimmel and his commanders were reinforced by apparently similar beliefs held by army commanders on Oahu and by President Roosevelt's War Council in Washington. Each group suffered from the groupthink phenomenon. In addition, the groups supported the development and maintenance of groupthink in each other by hesitating to share information that might upset the status quo of the other groups. Collective groupthink at work among the three main groups responsible for the defense of Pearl Harbor turned out to be a potent ally of the Japanese bombardiers.

1. Information for this "Closer Look" was obtained in an interview the authors conducted with Irving L. Janis and from his book (1982), *Groupthink: Psychological studies of policy decisions and fiascoes,* 2nd ed., Boston: Houghton Mifflin, 72-96.

Groupthink: A Special Problem

Irving Janis of Yale University has documented a special phenomenon known as **groupthink** (see "A Closer Look: Groupthink").[11] Groupthink happens when group members have illusions of invulnerability that lead them to accept excessive risks. Even when warned, members rationalize their way out of believing in impending problems. They also believe that the group's purpose is so righteous that they do not question the morality of its assumptions or tactics. They use negative stereotyping to degrade outsiders who question the group and put intense pressure on other members to conform to group norms. If information from outside the group conflicts with its position, members protect it by developing what Janis has called "mind guards" to filter out the objectionable information. Groupthink produces such a strong desire for consensus and cohesiveness that it overwhelms a group's desire and ability to make realistic decisions. There are several actions a manager can take to prevent or reduce the effects of groupthink, among them encouraging each group member to evaluate ideas openly and critically, discussing plans with outsiders to obtain their reactions, and assigning a devil's advocate role to one or more members to challenge ideas.

The Impact of Group Membership on Individuals

A MANAGER'S WORD

Conflict over group leadership and member uncertainties about leader-member relationships are obstacles that must be overcome if a group is to reach maturity. Changing leadership at each stage of development would require the group to keep dealing with these same issues, making it difficult or impossible to move on to the later stages of group development.

Linda N. Jewell
Management Consultant
and Author

Group membership carries certain responsibilities. A member of any group or organization occupies one or more roles. Each role defines a set of expectations for the member's behavior. In reality, organization members often experience contradictions and/or uncertainty about their roles. **Role ambiguity** is uncertainty about the requirements of a role. "Am I supposed to be a reporter or a writer?" Jill Peters may wonder. Individuals differ substantially in their *tolerance for ambiguity.* For some people, a moderate amount of ambiguity provides an enjoyable challenge. For others, even minor ambiguity creates major problems. **Role conflict** occurs when people occupy several roles whose expectations contradict one another or when the demands of their roles conflict with their personal preferences. Role conflict can cause even more stress, dissatisfaction, and performance problems than does role ambiguity. Sometimes there is simply too much to do, because roles either carry too many expectations or pose overwhelming demands. In such cases, people feel *role overload,* a form of role conflict. Regardless of its cause, role overload prevents people from meeting all of the expectations their roles create and can cause psychological and even physical discomfort.

The job of managing role expectations and keeping contradictions to a minimum falls jointly on the individual who holds the roles and the manager(s) who assign them. Managers should periodically evaluate and review role assignments, checking for evidence of role ambiguity, role conflict, and role overload. Employees should look for these signs when accepting new roles and, occasionally, while executing old ones.

Group Development and Facilitation

Like people, groups go through various stages as they mature, and their capacity for performance is not the same at each stage. Research has identified six stages in group development (see Figure 12.5).[12] At each stage, there are steps that managers can take to facilitate a group's development (see Table 12.1 on page 291).

Orientation (Stage 1). As a group first forms, members do not know each other within the group context (even if they know each other outside of the group). They are often uncertain about the group's purpose, its rules, its

FIGURE 12.5   The Stages of Group Development

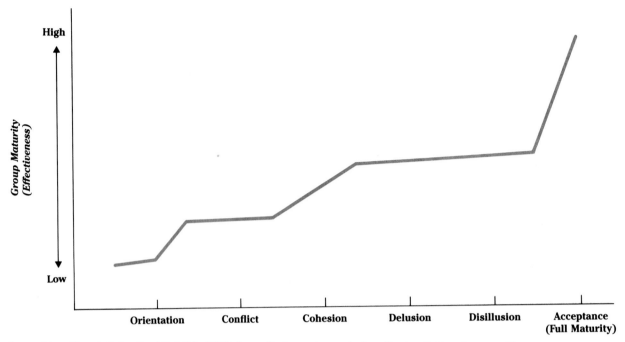

Source: Adapted from L. N. Jewell and H. J. Reitz (1981), *Group effectiveness in organizations*, Glenview, IL: Scott, Foresman, 20.

leadership, and their own roles as group members. During this first stage, they exchange information, ask questions about other group members, and attempt to define the nature of the group.

Conflict (Stage 2).   Following the orientation stage, individual differences among group members surface. Often members compete for leadership and disagree about procedures and even the merits of the group itself. Tension and hard feelings may arise. The group may divide into subgroups that set off in different directions. Because the conflict stage is unpleasant and often ineffective, many groups try to deny its onset or deal with its issues superficially; however, forcing a group to bypass the conflict stage greatly increases the chances of regression to it at a later date. It is far better to accept the stage as a necessary part of group development and to concentrate on effective ways to shorten its duration and minimize its impact.

Cohesion (Stage 3).   During the cohesion stage, group members work through personal differences, develop a set of norms, agree on their roles, and establish operating procedures to guide future activities. It is in this stage that a true sense of group identity emerges for the first time. For many groups, the cohesion stage is so effective and gratifying that further development seems unnecessary. For groups that are to be relatively short-lived (such as a task force), this is not always a bad idea. Further significant improvement is likely only if a group manages to reach the full maturity stage of acceptance.

Delusion (Stage 4).   If a group develops beyond cohesion, it is likely to evolve into a stage of delusion, in which members believe that significant problems no longer exist. After all, they overcame the problems of conflict and

TABLE 12.1 *Guidelines for Group Development*

Orientation Stage
- Provide a strong leader who is willing and able to structure and guide the group.
- Offer group members the opportunity to share, discuss, and exchange ideas and information.
- Assign or have the group develop specific group goals.
- Assign or have the group define group roles for each member.
- Provide answers to members' questions about the group.

Conflict Stage
- Accept conflict as necessary for further group development and allow it to emerge.
- Allow testing of group norms by members.
- Allow subgroups to form but maintain at least some total group interactions.

Cohesion Stage
- Provide a fair, nonpower-seeking leader who will work for the good of the group.
- Develop a system for addressing and resolving disagreements (conflict).
- Encourage a sense of group identity.
- Encourage written and/or public statements from the group as a whole.
- Develop and formalize a permanent operating structure to guide group actions.

Delusion Stage
- Accept delusion as a normal stage necessary for further group development.
- Avoid the onset of groupthink by watching for symptoms and taking corrective steps as needed.
- Avoid prolonged continuation of delusion by challenging its unrealistic bases.

Disillusion Stage
- Accept disillusionment as necessary for further development and allow it to occur openly.
- Force the development of disillusionment by identifying and presenting group problems.
- Allow subgroups to form but maintain at least some total group interactions.
- If the existing leader is unwilling or unable to manage conflicts, replace the existing leader with a directive leader who can do so.
- Emphasize how and why the group can mature effectively.

Acceptance Stage
- Provide a leader with good interpersonal skills who will work for the good of the group, either by replacing the existing leader or by changing the leader's behavior.
- Encourage open, honest discussion of issues and discourage differences that focus on personalities.
- Dissolve subgroups through rewards for commitment to the total group.
- Identify to the group the unique qualities and contributions of each member.
- Develop communication channels to exchange information accurately and realistically.
- Use issue-oriented decision-making techniques.

achieved effectiveness during the cohesion stage. It is at the delusion stage that a group may fall prey to groupthink and commit disastrous errors due to its false sense of perfection.

Disillusion (Stage 5).   For a group to advance to maturity, it must pass through the painful stage of disillusionment, in which the bubble of delusion bursts. Members are shocked that problems still confront the group, and they

A few specific suggestions for an individual who wants to help his or her group achieve maturity include: (1) be fully active and participate in the group, so that other members know what you have to offer in the way of information, skills, and other resources; (2) encourage the active participation of other group members, especially any who appear to have opinions, information, and skills that are different from your own; (3) make an effort to interact with group members you do not know; and (4) avoid initiating or encouraging conflict over a personal agenda that is irrelevant to the group's purpose.

—Jewell

make few significant improvements in effectiveness. Cohesiveness decreases, and members may be tempted to leave the group. Absenteeism and tardiness are common. Subgroups may emerge again, and interpersonal conflict is frequent. Members blame each other for allowing the group to be deceived by the delusion stage. Pessimism about the group's future grows. Although unpleasant, this "group puberty" seems to be necessary if a group is to reach full maturity. If a group skips it, there is always pressure to return to this painful stage. It is better to live through it and to manage its impact rather than trying to avoid it completely.

Acceptance (Stage 6).   With appropriate care and direction, a manager can move a group out of disillusionment and into acceptance, which characterizes a fully mature group. At the acceptance stage, members discuss their differences rather than fighting over them. They aggressively attack issues and deemphasize personal interests. Any divisive subgroups that may have formed tend to dissolve, and a stronger sense of group identity emerges. Each member's distinctive qualities are recognized and appreciated. Communication flows freely. Time and resources are used effectively and efficiently. Group effectiveness increases more rapidly than ever before, as does members' satisfaction.

In sum, a fully mature group can be a great asset to an organization, but shortcuts to maturity seldom work. The successful path to maturity begins when a group first forms, and the group requires careful management throughout its entire course of development.

Organization Members in Review

People react differently to and have varying levels of involvement with the work experience, depending on their motives, abilities, learning rates, personalities, and attitudes. Managers must consider the differences from person to person, as well as within each person, in order to use an organization's human resources most effectively.

People's reactions to their organizational environment are based on their perceptions, whether or not these perceptions match objective reality. The perceptual process has four steps: sensing environmental stimuli, selecting certain stimuli for further processing, organizing the selected stimuli, and translating the organized stimuli to derive meaning from them.

Much of the work accomplished in organizations is performed by groups. Many different factors attract individuals to groups and contribute to the development of cohesion. Cohesion can either benefit or injure an organization, depending, in part, on the nature of group norms and on their level of consistency with organizational goals. Sometimes extremely high levels of cohesion can lead to groupthink, a phenomenon in which groups act disastrously in the face of conflicting information.

Being part of a group means assuming roles that carry particular expectations. It is important that managers carefully define and manage roles to minimize the psychological and physiological discomfort that can result when contradictions in role expectations cause ambiguity or conflict.

Groups differ dramatically in their nature and effectiveness. The most effective groups become competent only after passing through a number of stages of development. In the beginning (orientation stage), a group searches for its identity. Then the group usually encounters a conflict stage. Successful further development leads to cohesion and then to a period of delusion, when members falsely believe that all is well. When this bubble bursts, disillusionment sets in. Through careful management, however, the disillusion stage can be turned into an acceptance stage. At this final point, full group maturity and effectiveness can be realized.

Issues for Review and Discussion

1. Discuss how differences in personality affect organization members' reactions to their experiences.
2. Why is it important for managers to care about the attitudes of organization members?
3. Identify and briefly describe each of the four major stages in the perception process.
4. As the leader of a group, what steps could you take to develop cohesion within your group?
5. As a group member, what can you do to reduce the likelihood that groupthink will develop?
6. Briefly describe the actions you could take as the leader of a group to facilitate movement through each of the six stages of group development.

Key Terms

motives	job satisfaction
personality	job involvement
internal locus of control	work involvement
external locus of control	organizational commitment
authoritarian	perception
dogmatism	group
Type A personality	formal groups
Type B personality	informal groups
attitude	group norms
cognitive component	groupthink
affective component	role ambiguity
behavioral tendency component	role conflict

Suggested Readings

Blau, G., and Boal, K. (1989). Using job involvement and organizational commitment interactively to predict turnover. *Journal of Management,* 15(1), 115-27.

Janis, I. I. (1982). *Groupthink: Psychological studies of policy decisions and fiascoes,* 2nd ed. Boston: Houghton Mifflin.

Jewell, L. N., and Reitz, H. J. (1981). *Group effectiveness in organizations.* Glenview, IL: Scott, Foresman.

McCormack, M. H. (1984). *What they don't teach you at Harvard Business School.* New York: Bantam Books. For a review of this book, see Barber, A. E. (1988). In Pierce, J. L., and Newstrom, J. W., eds. *The manager's bookshelf: A mosaic of contemporary views.* New York: Harper & Row, 89-96.

Mowday, R. T., Porter, L. W., and Steers, R. M. (1982). *Employee organization linkages: The psychology of commitment, absenteeism, and turnover.* New York: Academic Press.

Organ, D. W. (1988). *Organizational citizenship behavior.* Lexington, MA: Lexington Books.

Notes

1. R. V. Dawis, G. W. England, and L. H. Lofquist (1967), *A theory of work adjustment: A revision,* Minnesota Studies in Vocational Rehabilitation, Bulletin 47, Minneapolis.

2. F. J. Smith (1977), Work attitudes as predictors of attendance on a specific day, *Journal of Applied Psychology,* 62, 16-19.

3. S. Rabinowitz (1981), Towards a developmental model of job involvement, *International Review of Applied Psychology,* 30, 31-50; S. D. Saleh and J. Hosek (1976), Job involvement: Concepts and measurements, *Academy of Management Journal,* 19, 213-24.

4. R. T. Mowday, L. W. Porter, and R. M. Steers (1982), *Employee organization linkages: The psychology of commitment, absenteeism, and turnover,* New York: Academic Press.

5. L. W. Porter, R. M. Steers, R. T. Mowday, and R. V. Boulain (1974), Organizational commitment, job satisfaction, and turnover among psychiatric technicians, *Journal of Applied Psychology,* 59, 603-9.

6. G. Blau and K. Boal (1989), Using job involvement and organizational commitment interactively to predict turnover, *Journal of Management,* 15(1), 115-27.

7. J. P. Meyer, S. V. Paunonen, I. R. Gellatly, R. D. Goffin, and D. N. Jackson (1989), Organizational commitment and job performance: It's the nature of the commitment that counts, *Journal of Applied Psychology,* 74(1), 152-56.

8. J. L. Pierce and R. B. Dunham (1987), Organizational commitment: Pre-employment propensity and initial work experiences, *Journal of Management,* 13, 163-78.

9. R. Rosenthal and L. Jacobsen (1968), *Pygmalion in the classroom,* New York: Holt, Rinehart & Winston; R. L. Dipboye (1982), Self-fulfilling prophecies in the selection-recruitment interview, *Academy of Management Review,* 7, 579-86.

10. R. M. Stogdill (1972), Group productivity, drive, and cohesiveness, *Organizational Behavior and Human Performance,* 8, 26-43.

11. I. L. Janis (1971), Groupthink, *Psychology Today,* 5, 43ff; I. L. Janis (1982), *Groupthink,* 2nd ed., Boston: Houghton Mifflin.

12. L. N. Jewell and H. J. Reitz (1981), *Group effectiveness in organizations,* Glenview, IL: Scott, Foresman.

The Patterson Operation

By James M. Todd and
Thomas R. Miller,
Memphis State University

Carrington, Inc., is an international company engaged in the production and distribution of pharmaceuticals, proprietary drugs, and cosmetics and toiletries. In its worldwide operations, Carrington employs over 15,000 people and has sales of over $500 million annually.

At the Mid-South plant of Carrington, Inc., management was faced with problems of low productivity, low employee morale, and high unit costs in the section responsible for the assembly of various kinds of packages containing assorted products made by the company. These "prepaks" or "deals," as they were referred to within the organization, were prepared to customer specifications. Each package might contain from 24 to 480 items, and the total number of packages for a customer ranged from 10 to 1500 units. Most of these packages were prepared so that the retailer could set them up as free-standing, point-of-sale promotional displays. Assembling the deals was essentially a job shop process, and prior to the events described here, the "assembly room," was located in a part of the main plant known as Section 10.

The employees in Carrington's manufacturing and assembly operations were unionized, and the firm used a Halsey 50-50 Incentive Plan, a time-saved bonus plan. Under the Halsey Plan, if a worker could produce the standard output in less than the standard time, that worker received a bonus of 50 percent of the hourly wage rate multiplied by the time saved. For example, an employee who completed ten standard hours of work in eight hours would be paid for eight hours plus one of the two hours saved; thus, if the hourly pay rate were $8, the worker would earn $72 for the day.

Problems with Section 10

The assembly of prepaks in Section 10 utilized roller type conveyor belts, which supplied each worker with the products to be included in a particular package. The working conditions were outstanding in that the work area was very clean, well-lighted, and air conditioned. An attractive cafeteria for employees was available in the same large building.

In spite of good working conditions and the chance to earn extra pay through the company's incentive system, the operation in Section 10 had encountered a marked trend of increases in unit costs and decreases in output per labor hours. In fact, over the most recent two-year period, cost figures revealed that the section was below the break-even point. Contributing to this deteriorating situation was low productivity and a failure of employees to meet the work standard. This latter problem was made particularly evident by the fact that no employees were able to earn a bonus under the incentive plan.

Discipline in Section 10 was poor, and supervisors constantly had problems. A number of grievances had been generated. Morale was not helped by the fact that employees quite often found themsleves being moved from one assembly line to another. This tended to increase production costs because the employees had little chance of learning one operation before being moved to another. Workers in Section 10 lacked a spirit of mutual cooperation; an attitude of "that's not my job" was prevalent.

Working in Section 10 was unpopular. The manual labor there was perceived as harder than the automated work in other areas. Also, word had spread that no one could "make bonus" working there. Eventually, through the bidding system used by the organization, the workforce in Section 10 came to consist, in large part, of young, inexperienced employees; problem workers; and malcontents. As manager Colleen McHugh described the situation, "Section 10 had the pits of the workforce."

A New Operation

Management at Carrington was also confronted with a severe space problem for its expanding operations. Several alternatives were considered, but none seemed to offer an economically feasible solution. In near desperation, a brainstorming session of managers led to a decision to move a large part of the assembly of the deals to a facility already leased by the company and presently used as a warehouse. This facility was located on Patterson Street, and for this reason the new deal room became known in the company as the "Patterson operation."

The new facility fell far short of providing work space and conditions comparable to those in Section 10. The building was located in an entirely separate area approximately three miles from the main plant in a neighborhood of run-down, low-income housing and other warehouse operations.

The building housing the Patterson operation had been thought to be acceptable only for warehouse use. It was an older brick structure with a number of large open bays for shipping and receiving. The building was dark, poorly ventilated, not air condioned, and inadequately heated. It was poorly suited for use by workers involved in assembly operations. Temperatures averaged approximately 50 degrees during the winter months and well over 90 degrees in the summer. There was no cafeteria or food service, and employees either brought their own lunch or went to a small neighborhood grocery in the vicinity and bought food. Other worker facilities, such as rest rooms and break areas, were poor. In summary, conditions contrasted sharply with Section 10 and its clean, air-conditioned, well-heated facilities in a good neighborhood and with a first-class cafeteria available.

Despite these obstacles and seemingly against their best judgment, management, pressed for manufacturing space, decided on the move to the Patterson warehouse. Little money was spent on modifications.

Results of the Move

Moving to Patterson involved the transfer of approximately forty low-seniority employees from the main plant. All of these workers were managed by Ed Donnelly, Jr., a new first-line supervisor.

As foreman, Donnelly made some drastic changes in the assembly operation. He set up the assembly line so that individual workers could work on the same job until that particular order was completed. The situation was entirely different from Section 10, where an employee could work on as many as three different assemblies during the day. The repetition of working on the same line enabled workers to develop speed, which facilitated their earning bonuses.

The new foreman introduced some other innovations. He allowed employees the opportunity to influence decisions concerning their work hours and the times of their rest breaks. While at the main plant the playing of radios in a production area was not permitted, at Patterson it gradually became acceptable to have radios playing, usually at a high volume. Other "nonstandard" conditions existed at Patterson. Unlike Section 10, employees did not have to observe dress codes, wear bonnets, or refrain from wearing jewelry on the

job. Because of the rather remote location of Patterson from the main plant, managers or supervisors visited the new facility rather infrequently. Where violations of company policies existed, management took a somewhat liberal attitude.

In order to have a place to eat or take a break, the employees got together and furnished a small room with enough tables and chairs to modestly equip a rather austere dining and rest break area. Eventually this room was air conditioned. The employees asked to get the company to furnish some paint so they could repaint the room.

With these and other changes, a shift in worker attitudes began to evolve. Employees came to view Patterson as their own company. There was a willingness to assist others when possible. Productivity increased to such an extent that employees received bonuses. The jobs at Patterson became more popular, and the composition of the workforce changed from one of inexperienced workers to one in which older and more qualified people began to actively bid for the jobs. Over the first four years of operation, only one grievance was filed at the Patterson operation and, during the first year of operation, productivity was 32.8 percent higher than it had been in Section 10.

Ed Donnelly, Jr., was promoted and replaced by Susan Wilcox-Garner, who continued to run the operation in the same manner as Donnelly. She continued to get the employees to participate in decision making. For example, the employees decided to change work hours at Patterson during the summer months. Work hours had been from 7:30 A.M. to 4:00 P.M.; the employees changed them to two hours earlier because of the nearly unbearable heat of the late afternoon in the warehouse. This change in work schedule was not in accordance with company policy but was tolerated by management. The workers at Patterson really preferred an even earlier workday, but this was not feasible due to coordination problems in receiving goods from the main plant.

Another interesting development at Patterson was the formation of an employee softball team called the Patterson Warriors. Normally, the company fields a team composed of players from all units instead of from one particular section. Again, Patterson employees did this independently without reference to overall company policy.

Currently, work records at the Patterson operation concerning absenteeism, tardiness, and turnover are not better than in the main plant. In a few cases, they are slightly worse, although management does not consider this difference to be significant; however, the very low grievance rate, the high level of worker morale, and the better productivity are pleasant surprises to management.

The activities of the Patterson operation are fairly well known among the managers at the Mid-South plant of Carrington. Management reactions range from positive to negative, with other managers ambivalent about Patterson. All however, seem to agree that it is, at least, interesting.

Questions

1. To what do you attribute the improvement in productivity at the Patterson operation as compared to Section 10?
2. What principles do you see at work here?
3. Why do you think that some managers at the main plant are negative or ambivalent about the Patterson operation?

13 *Motivating Organization Members*

Student Learning Objectives

After reading this chapter, you should be able to:

1. Name and describe the three traditional managerial approaches to motivation.

2. Explain why managers must know the needs of their employees in order to motivate them.

3. Describe ways to encourage desired behaviors and to discourage undesired behaviors from a reinforcement theory perspective.

4. Understand how people evaluate the fairness of the outcomes they receive from organizations.

5. Identify the characteristics of goals that most effectively motivate performance.

6. Understand why people choose and actively pursue particular alternatives.

7. Name the steps an organization must take to help employees translate effort into performance.

*R*ecently, Blue Cross/Blue Shield of Illinois wanted to use selection tests to identify well-qualified applicants for its job openings. After investigating many abilities that were expected to be important determinants of performance, the organization identified several for each job group and tested for these when it selected employees. This strategy for hiring employees gave Blue Cross/Blue Shield a significantly improved workforce. Even after these steps were taken, however, management could still see major performance differences from person to person that could not be explained simply on the basis of differences in ability. When Blue Cross/Blue Shield investigated, it found that the major factor distinguishing the best of the employees from those performing at lower levels was *motivation*—the amount and direction of energy that employees exerted when performing their jobs.

Traditional Motivational Approaches

As previously noted, people's abilities and skills make performance possible, but motivation makes them choose to use those abilities and skills to accomplish things. Without adequate motivation, even the most capable person performs poorly. **Motivation** energizes, directs, and sustains human behavior. Students must be motivated to do well in school; organization members must be motivated to do well at work. In fact, a survey of *Fortune* 500 chief executives identified employee motivation as one of the top three issues of concern to their organizations.[1]

Traditionally, managers have used three approaches to motivate employees' performance. The first is based on economic factors, the second on social considerations, and the third on the nature of the work itself. Like Hagar's wife in the cartoon below, some managers use only one approach. The best contemporary managers, however, incorporate aspects of all three.

- *The economic approach.* The economic model assumes that people are rational and economically motivated. The economic approach to motivating employees was popularized through the classical school. As part of his approach to scientific management, Frederick Taylor developed a financial incentive system called the *differential wage rate system*. A worker who produces nothing during the day earns no wage; the more the worker

Reprinted with special permission of King Features Syndicate, Inc.

produces, the more he or she earns. Money can, in fact, motivate people to accept even unpleasant jobs, and it can motivate them to perform at a relatively high level.[2] This is one reason that many contemporary organizations use the economic approach for certain jobs, such as sales. Unfortunately, when managers rely too heavily on the power of the dollar, they fail to use other, possibly more effective, motivators.

- *The social approach.* The social model of motivation proposes to make the work experience socially pleasant. If this can be done, proponents argue, workers will be both satisfied and motivated to perform their jobs effectively, because people are social and need acceptance and recognition. Managers who use this approach provide work opportunities that are socially rewarding: they offer opportunities for co-workers to interact, develop cohesive work groups, provide employees with recognition, and treat workers humanely. Social factors can motivate and satisfy organization members, but, just as the economic model overemphasizes money as a motivator, some managers overemphasize social factors and neglect other potential motivators.

- *The nature-of-work approach.* Neither the economic model nor the social model of motivation addresses the nature of work itself. A more contemporary perspective on motivation deals specifically with this issue. A manager who uses this perspective believes that work can be interesting for organization members and that it is a manager's job to motivate employees by making the work interesting. The manager focuses on employees' needs for esteem, growth, and personal development. The nature-of-work model of motivation has been responsible for much job enlargement and job enrichment activity during the past few decades (see Chapter 9). Again, it is unfortunate that many of the managers who have used the nature of work as an approach to employee motivation have done so at the exclusion of other motivation factors.

A MANAGER'S WORD

I see a stick-to-carrot [approach to motivation] ratio of 10:1. Managers often seem preoccupied with things that are too slow, inaccurate, or otherwise wrong rather than with looking for constructive, direct solutions to problems and for new windows of opportunity.

Barbara M. Karmel
President
Reed Company

In sum, the economic, social, and nature-of-work models of employee motivation focus on only a subset of an employee's total need structure. As a consequence, each has failed to achieve high and sustained levels of employee motivation. For example, managers who motivate using only money fail to satisfy employees' social and growth needs and risk having less than fully satisfied and motivated employees. An effective motivational strategy should recognize that employees have a complex set of needs and that an effective long-term motivational strategy must address each set of needs to be fully effective. The content theories address workers' complex need structures and, thus, provide a more comprehensive approach.

Content Theories

Content theories (also known as need theories) of motivation are based on the simple premise that all people have needs. Some needs are inborn, such as the need for food and water, and are called **innate needs.** Others, such as the need for self-esteem, are **acquired needs** learned through experience. Regardless of their source, if a person's needs are not met, he or she is dissatisfied. If these needs are met, people feel satisfied. Part of a manager's job is to determine which needs have not been met (and, thus, are active) among subordinates and to find ways for employees to meet their needs while contributing to the achievement of their organization's goals.

Maslow's Need Hierarchy Theory

The most widely known theory of human needs was set forth by Abraham Maslow in his **need hierarchy theory.**[3] According to Maslow, people have a set of five innate needs that they try to satisfy in a particular order (see Figure 13.1). The most basic human physiological needs have the greatest urgency and appear at the base of Maslow's hierarchy. As these needs are met, satisfaction results, permitting an individual to focus increasing amounts of attention on meeting higher-level needs. Most people move upward in the hierarchy as they attempt to satisfy unmet needs.

Physiological and survival needs include the most basic chemical needs for food, water, sex, sleep, and other physiological requirements. *Safety and security needs* involve the desire for protection from threats (including assault, robbery, disease, and extremes of temperature). *Social needs* include the need for affiliation and a sense of belonging, such as emotional needs for love, friendship, and affection. *Ego and esteem needs* involve the desire for self-respect, self-esteem, and the esteem of others. *Self-actualization,* the desire for self-fulfillment, involves the need "to become more and more what one is, to become everything that one is capable of becoming."[4] According to Maslow, most needs can be fully met, except for the need for self-actualization. No matter what you become or what you achieve, the self-actualizing need can always cause you to strive to become better and to achieve even more.

FIGURE 13.1 Maslow's Hierarchy of Needs

The lower-level needs are referred to as "deficiency" needs in Maslow's two-level version of the theory. He referred to the upper-level needs as "growth" needs.

Alderfer's ERG Theory

Clayton Alderfer from Yale University refined the ideas of Maslow and others into a perspective known as the **Existence, Relatedness, and Growth (ERG) Theory.**[5] As Figure 13.2 shows, Alderfer presents a three-level hierarchy containing the same needs as those Maslow described but partitioned differently. His *existence needs* include the physiological and material safety needs identified by Maslow. *Relatedness needs* include all of Maslow's social needs, plus social safety and social esteem needs. *Growth needs* include self-esteem and self-actualization needs.

Four components—satisfaction progression, frustration, frustration regression, and aspiration—are the key to understanding Alderfer's ERG theory. The first of these, *satisfaction progression,* is in agreement with Maslow's theory and refers to the process through which higher-level needs become increasingly important as lower-level needs are satisfied. The second component, *frustration,* occurs when a person attempts but fails to satisfy a particular need. The resulting frustration may make satisfying the unmet need even more important to the individual—unless he or she repeatedly fails to satisfy that need. In this case, Alderfer's third component, *frustration regression,* can cause a person who experiences repeated frustration to shift attention to a lower-level, more concrete and verifiable need. Lastly, the *aspiration* component of the ERG model notes that, by its very nature, growth is intrinsically satisfying. The more one grows, the more one wants to grow; therefore, the

FIGURE 13.2   Alderfer's ERG Theory

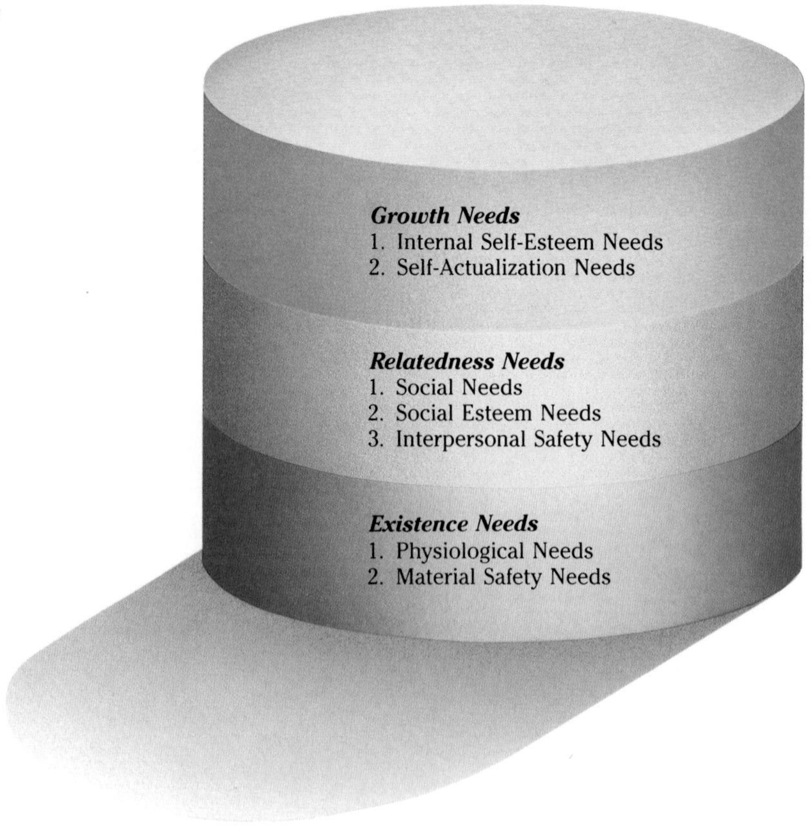

Growth Needs
1. Internal Self-Esteem Needs
2. Self-Actualization Needs

Relatedness Needs
1. Social Needs
2. Social Esteem Needs
3. Interpersonal Safety Needs

Existence Needs
1. Physiological Needs
2. Material Safety Needs

more a person satisfies the growth need, the more important it becomes, and the more strongly he or she is motivated to satisfy it.

Consider Elizabeth, a recent college graduate initially motivated by her salary and benefits to repay her college loans. Thus, as Elizabeth's existence needs were satisfied, she concentrated more on (and was motivated by) relatedness needs, especially the opportunities to develop friendships at work and to work effectively as a team player. After these needs were met to a reasonable degree, she shifted her attention to growth needs, focusing on the importance of significant job accomplishments. Repeatedly frustrated by a boss who denied her challenging assignments, Elizabeth ultimately stopped trying to meet her growth needs and concentrated once again on relatedness needs The message to managers is that workers who are unable to satisfy a given level of needs are likely to redirect their attention elsewhere, perhaps to an area in which the results of their efforts are less valuable to the organization.

Needs for Achievement, Affiliation, and Power

Not all human needs are present at birth. People also acquire needs through a learning process based on personal and organizational experiences. Because each person has different experiences, the type and strength of individual needs vary from person to person. Three acquired needs—the needs for achievement, affiliation, and power—play key roles within an organizational setting.[6]

The need for affiliation is the desire for warm and friendly relationships with others. People with a strong affiliation need want to please people and to win their respect and affection.

The Need for Achievement. The **need for achievement,** which involves a desire to accomplish difficult and challenging objectives, is learned during childhood. High-need-for-achievement individuals find achievement satisfying whether or not anyone else even notices. They prefer relatively difficult challenges to simple ones, but only if they perceive a reasonable likelihood of success. They value immediate feedback about goal progress and tend to become quite absorbed in a task until they succeed. For example, basketball player Jim Camp is likely to take practice shots with a 40-60 percent chance of success because of his strong need for achievement. Similarly, an employee choosing between a competitor's job offer and an in-house promotion is likely to turn down the one that is too easy or that has a limited chance of success in favor of the offer where success is possible but not assured.

Managers can take systematic steps to capitalize on the need for achievement. A good place to start is in the employee selection process. If a job opening provides challenge, feedback, and opportunity for personal success, applicants high in the need for achievement are likely to perform better (because they need to achieve under challenging circumstances). A job that provides little challenge or, conversely, that is virtually unachievable is best filled by a person low in the need for achievement.

The Need for Affiliation. The **need for affiliation** is the desire for warm and friendly relationships with others.[7] People with a strong affiliation need want to please people and to win their respect and affection. They seek approval and reassurance from others and are genuinely concerned about others' interests and feelings. Because of this, they are easily influenced by the norms and expectations of other individuals and groups. For instance, supervisor Jeffrey Stephens goes out of his way to help his subordinates whenever he can. He does so because he genuinely wants to help and because it makes him feel good. Jeffrey has a high need for affiliation.

People with a high need for affiliation are satisfied by organizational experiences that provide social opportunities; thus, they like to work closely with co-workers or customers. If forced to work alone, they become unhappy. A manager whose workers have strong affiliation needs must recognize that they will take steps to satisfy this need. If the manager does not offer opportunities for satisfaction in a way that benefits the organization, such as by placing these workers in work groups, they will try to satisfy their affiliation needs in another manner—perhaps by wasting time gossiping with co-workers. Managers should, therefore, match people with high affiliation needs to jobs that provide affiliation opportunities. High-affiliation-need individuals often make excellent salespeople, for example, and work well in teams. People with a low affiliation need—for example, many systems analysts, computer programmers, and research specialists—work best alone.

The Need for Power. The **need for power** involves a desire to control others and to influence their behavior.[8] Depending on how it is used, this need can have a significant positive or negative effect on managerial success.

There are two types of power, either of which (or a combination of which) can satisfy the need for power. *Personalized power seeking* involves dominating others for the sake of domination. Personalized power seekers often overlook their organizational responsibilities in favor of personal concerns because having power makes them feel good about being powerful. A manager who tries to build an "empire" by developing a strong power base simply because he or she enjoys power is a personalized power seeker. *Socialized power seeking,* on the other hand, involves acquiring power in order to benefit a group. Socialized power seekers use power to motivate and positively influence others and to help meet group goals. This is what officer manager Mark Schmeling does when he uses his influence to convince the MIS manager to assign Mark's subordinates the microcomputers they need to manage their customer accounts effectively.

Except under unusual circumstances, organizations should avoid hiring personalized power seekers. If managers discover people who act this way, they should place them in positions in which they have very little contact with others—a nonmanagerial job, for example, that is closely controlled and offers little leeway for the use of power—so they cannot manipulate people for the sake of manipulation. Socialized power seekers, however, should be sought for important leadership roles that will allow them to exercise power for the benefit of the organization, such as helping a work group succeed.

Herzberg's Motivation/Hygiene Theory

Frederick Herzberg developed a unique perspective on employee needs.[9] He argued that different sets of needs play different roles in the overall scheme of motivation and satisfaction in organizations. This perspective has strongly influenced motivational practices during the last three decades.

In the 1950s, Herzberg asked 200 accountants and engineers to reflect on their work experiences and to identify those associated with: (1) extreme dissatisfaction and lack of motivation and (2) extreme satisfaction and motivation.[10] After analyzing these "critical incidents," Herzberg observed that certain issues were at the heart of dissatisfying experiences, and other issues were at the heart of satisfying experiences. He then concluded that people's needs could be grouped into two categories, which correspond to negative and positive experiences: hygiene and motivator needs.

Hygiene Needs. **Hygiene needs** are not directly related to the work itself. Instead, they relate to the context of a job and consist of such factors as pay, working conditions, co-workers, supervision, and security (like the factors that satisfy the existence and relatedness needs included in Alderfer's ERG theory). Hygiene needs focus on the need to avoid pain and must be met to avoid dissatisfaction. Meeting these needs, however, does not necessarily provide satisfaction or motivation. Supplying employees with clean working conditions, for example, will satisfy them initially. After a short while, though, such conditions will be taken for granted. They are no longer capable of producing strong, long-term satisfaction or motivation. Dirty working conditions, on the other hand, will cause employee dissatisfaction and eventually will reduce work motivation.

Herzberg often refers to hygiene needs as "dissatisfiers" because they are so often associated with dissatisfaction. In fact, Herzberg's research indicated that hygiene needs accounted for 69 percent of all reported dissatisfying experiences but only for 19 percent of the satisfying experiences (see Figure 13.3).

Motivator Needs. **Motivator needs,** such as achievement, recognition, responsibility, and advancement (like Alderfer's growth needs), center on a long-term need to pursue psychological growth. When motivators are present, employees are motivated to be high performers. For example, workers who achieve production goals, meet a sales target, or are assigned extra responsibility for a job well done are likely to have their motivator needs met. Herzberg states that meeting motivator needs will produce satisfaction; thus, he calls them "satisfiers." In fact, Figure 13.3 shows that, in Herzberg's research, motivators were involved in 81 percent of satisfying incidents but in only 31 percent of dissatisfying events. Herzberg's biggest lasting contribution to management probably has been his creation of an awareness of the potential power of these needs for motivating and satisfying organization members.

FIGURE 13.3   Needs Associated with Satisfaction and Dissatisfaction

Source: Data derived from F. Herzberg (1968), One more time, how do you motivate employees? *Harvard Business Review,* 46, 54-62.

Dissatisfaction

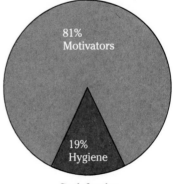

Satisfaction

FIGURE 13.4 *The Motivation/Hygiene Motivational Strategy*

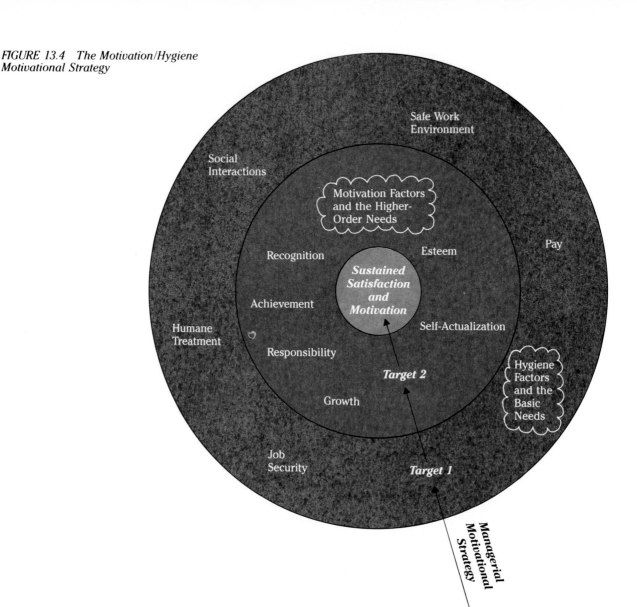

Implications. Herzberg's work suggests a two-stage process for managing employee satisfaction and motivation (see Figure 13.4). First, managers should address hygiene factors so that basic needs are met and employees do not become dissatisfied. They must make sure that workers are adequately paid, that working conditions are safe and clean, that workers have opportunities for social interaction, and that treatment by supervisors is humane. When these conditions are met, employees should not be job dissatisfied and should not be motivated to avoid work or perform poorly. After these conditions are met, managers should proceed to the second stage and address the much more powerful motivators. They must make sure that workers experience recognition, responsibility, achievement, and growth. If motivator needs are ignored, neither long-term satisfaction nor high motivation is likely. When motivator needs are met, however, employees feel satisfied and are motivated to perform well.

Motivating Employees: Workers Bag More Money, but A&P Reduces Labor Costs

In the late 1970s, rivals called Great Atlantic & Pacific Tea Co. the worst-run supermarket chain in the business. Shoppers were deserting A&P in droves. Managers doubled as baggers, and worker morale reached an all-time low. By 1982, after four straight years of losses, A&P had shrunk to 1,016 stores from 3,468 in 1974. But then A&P found an important resource: its employees.[1]

In a four-year period, A&P's operating profits increased 81 percent. The value of the stock doubled. Store sales jumped almost 25 percent. Employee satisfaction improved substantially. In fact, average overall earnings for employees also increased. What accounts for the turnaround at A&P? A large portion of this newfound success can be traced to a novel incentive plan that offers workers financial bonuses if they can help trim labor costs or increase sales volume.

In 1981, all eighty-one A&P stores in the Philadelphia area were closed for lack of profitability. A&P Chairman James Wood believed that one of the reasons A&P had encountered such serious problems was the lack of " . . . motivation you find at a family business . . . . The idea of people getting a piece of what they are trying to achieve has always appealed to me enormously."[2] Accordingly, Wood worked with Thomas R. McNutt, president of the local United Food & Commercial Workers (UFCW) labor union, to develop the unique plan that they hope will be the salvation of A&P. Six of the stores were bought

and reopened by employees, and another sixty stores were opened based, in part, on the viability of the new incentive plan.

How does this unique plan work? It starts with workers accepting a 25 percent cut in pay in exchange for the store's promise of a bonus if labor costs can be cut to 11 percent of sales or less. In fact, if labor costs can be cut to as little as $9\frac{1}{2}$ percent of sales, the company presents workers with a bonus equal to $1\frac{1}{2}$ percent of all of the store's sales.

What do employees do to earn their bonus? They work harder and increase their productivity and efficiency. They also attend twice-weekly meetings with the store's manager. They meet on a regional basis as well, during which time they are encouraged to make suggestions that reduce labor costs directly or increase sales volume. Employees in Richmond, Virginia, for example, noticed that customers who came to the store during peak times and found checkout lines stretching into aisles would leave rather than deal with the congestion. The employees' suggestion was to widen the aisles at the checkout counters. The results were more customers and greater sales. After heeding the suggestion of employees at a store in Philadelphia, managers noted sales soaring after ethnic foods were added to the inventory.

The company has clearly benefited from the incentive plan, but so have employees. Thousands who would otherwise have become unemployed through store closings have retained

their jobs. Philadelphia workers now earn almost a dollar per hour more in base wages and bonuses than the average food store employee earns elsewhere in the city.

A&P's experience emphasizes that incentive plans can benefit both organizations and employees. To quote Thomas McNutt, "You'd be amazed at the willingness of people to participate when they can say anything without fear of reprisal."[3] A&P is now exploring the use of such incentive plans at more of its stores. They are now in place at hundreds of the company's 1170 stores in the United States and Canada. It is likely the plan will work elsewhere if employees accept it and believe that, through their efforts, they can benefit themselves as well as the organization.

How has A&P done lately? Earnings for 1988 were $103.4 million on sales of over $9.5 billion. As of May 1989, projections were for $127.5 in profits on over $10 billion of sales. In addition, by February 1989, A&P had acquired over 97 percent of the stock of Borman's supermarket chain following a $76 million cash tender for the chain. The great A&P is growing again.[4]

1. How A&P fattens profits by sharing them (22 December 1986), *Business Week,* 44.
2. *Ibid.*
3. *Ibid.*
4. Standard & Poors report for *Dow Jones News Service* (2 May 1989).

Criticism. Although Herzberg's work contains important ideas for managers, his theory has been the subject of considerable controversy.[11] It has been argued, for example, that even if Herzberg is correct in noting that hygiene factors seldom produce satisfaction or motivation, this does not mean they *never* can do so.[12] Perhaps managers simply have failed to make hygiene factors work well as motivators. (Herzberg's research showed that hygiene factors were associated with satisfying experiences 19 percent of the time.) For instance, appropriately administered monetary bonuses have been successful in motivating work attendance, performance, and satisfaction.[13] "A Closer Look: Motivating Employees" examines how A&P grocery stores used a financial incentive system to improve employee productivity.

In sum, content theories deal with the importance of human needs and the dissatisfaction that occurs when they are unmet. Each theory shows that people are motivated to meet their needs and that, when they do so, they feel satisfied. The content theories, thus, identify what motivates people. They do not, however, specify how managers can motivate workers, nor do they offer much guidance for understanding how people choose a course of action when faced with two or more alternatives, any of which could satisfy their needs. The reinforcement and process theories help complete this picture.

Reinforcement Theories

Managers often note that people repeat some behaviors more often than others. Diana Brown, for example, is frequently late for work. Her co-worker, Brett Spalding, is continually offering production improvement suggestions. What encourages people to behave in a particular way? According to **reinforcement theories,** people repeat behaviors that result in desirable consequences and avoid behaviors that produce undesirable consequences. This idea is known as the *law of effect.*

Important Factors

According to reinforcement theorists, one way a manager can encourage an employee to repeat a behavior is to provide a desirable consequence, or reward, after the behavior is performed. A desirable consequence is anything that satisfies an active need or that removes a barrier to need satisfaction. It can be as simple as a kind word or as major as a promotion, both of which are examples of **positive reinforcement**.

Another technique for making a desired response more likely to be repeated is known as **negative reinforcement.** Managers use negative reinforcement when they remove something unpleasant from an employee's work environment in the hope that this will encourage the desired behavior. Grocery clerk Garry Fielding, for example, is responsible for affixing product/price labels to the store's shelves and sorting redeemed customer coupons. Garry does a good pricing job, but he detests sorting coupons. His boss, Philip Howrigan, would like Garry to finish pricing in time to check inventory before the store closes each night, but Garry seldom is done in time. Philip tells Garry that he will reassign the coupon sorting task to someone else on those days that Garry can finish pricing by 6 P.M. If removing his most hated task prompts Garry to work faster at pricing, Philip's use of negative reinforcement will have reinforced that desired behavior.

When it is necessary to discourage a subordinate from repeating an undesirable behavior, a manager must do something that frustrates the employee's need satisfaction or that removes a currently satisfying circumstance. **Punishment** makes it less likely that a person will repeat an undesired behavior because it is followed by an undesirable consequence. If Philip were to dock Garry's pay $25 every time he failed to finish pricing by 6 P.M., he would be punishing Garry's "foot-dragging."

It should be noted that managers have another alternative, known as **nonreinforcement,** in which they provide no consequence at all following an employee's response. Nonreinforcement eventually reduces the likelihood of that response reoccurring, which means that managers who fail to reinforce an employee's desirable behavior are likely to see that desirable behavior less often. If Philip never rewards Garry when he finishes pricing on time, for instance, Garry probably will stop trying to beat the clock. Nonreinforcement can also reduce the likelihood that employees will repeat undesirable behaviors, although it does not produce results as quickly as punishment does. Furthermore, if there are other reinforcing consequences present, nonreinforcement is not likely to be effective. For example, if Garry is reinforced by pleasant social interactions with co-workers during unofficial breaks, Philip must do more than just ignore Garry's behavior if he wants to convince him to quit taking unofficial breaks.

How often does a manager need to provide reinforcement or punishment? **Continuous schedules of reinforcement,** which reinforce or punish every time a behavior is performed, are the most effective for shaping behavior. Employees who are rewarded for every production increase and students who are penalized for every late paper learn appropriate behavior much more quickly than do those who receive feedback less consistently. Of course, it is not realistic to expect that a manager with many other responsibilities can be available continuously for this purpose. **Intermittent schedules of reinforcement** provide a consequence following some (but not all) responses. A company that rewards salespeople with a day off for every thousand units sold reinforces according to an intermittent schedule.

Reinforcement theories build on the knowledge provided by content theories. Managers can use the content theories to help identify those things subordinates positively or negatively value and can follow up using the knowledge from reinforcement theories to shape desired behavior by providing these positively or negatively valued outcomes. For example, if her manager discovers that Suzanne values relatedness opportunities, the manager can offer her social recognition for success.

Organizational Behavior Modification (OBM)

The term **organizational behavior modification (OBM)** is used to describe the systematic management of behavior within organizations. For example, a manager using OBM can tell subordinates what he or she wants them to do and which consequences will follow if they do or do not choose to comply. OBM also takes advantage of *social learning,* in which people watch others and see the consequences that follow their behavior. An employee who sees a co-worker rewarded for behaving in a certain way learns to behave similarly in an attempt to be rewarded.

One way to begin the OBM process is to identify the specific behaviors that management expects from workers.

A Step-by-Step Procedure. To begin the OBM process, managers must specify which behaviors are expected. For example, do they wish to motivate employees to generate money-saving ideas, to reduce absenteeism, or to increase their productivity? After identifying the desired behaviors, managers should determine the reinforcers that employees will positively value. They must find out, through formal surveys or simple interaction, subordinates' needs and interests and the value they place on particular outcomes. Otherwise, something that they thought would be a reward may backfire and punish behavior instead.

Managers must consider two types of motivators when they try to determine outcomes: extrinsic and intrinsic.[14] **Extrinsic motivators** are rewards provided by someone other than the person being motivated. **Intrinsic motivators** arise from within the individual. If Cynthia Biron, data entry supervisor, offers Earl Karn, key operator, a bonus in exchange for the timely completion of a special project, she is using an extrinsic motivator to coax improved performance. If Earl works hard to complete the project because he enjoys a difficult task or because it is a matter of pride, the motivation is intrinsic. This is also the point in the OBM process at which managers must decide whether to use punishment. If so, they must identify and prepare to use consequences that are considered negative by employees.

Next, managers of the OBM process must choose appropriate learning techniques for their programs: positive reinforcement, negative reinforcement, punishment, or a combination of these. Once they have selected a learning device, such as positive reinforcement, they must decide whether to use a continuous reinforcement or an intermittent reinforcement schedule.

The next important step is to specify for employees the behavior-reinforcement links that have been chosen. Managers should tell workers, "If you behave this way, you will receive the following reinforcers" and "If you behave this other way, you will receive the following punishment." It is at this stage that employees are told the focus of the OBM program. It makes very clear what behavior is desired and what consequences the organization is prepared to provide for this behavior.

The last steps in an OBM program involve measuring how employees are actually behaving and providing the promised consequences in a timely fashion. If a person behaves as desired, reinforcement should follow quickly. If a worker behaves in an undesired manner so that punishment is necessary, it also should be administered quickly. The effective use of OBM requires managers to behave systematically, following the many steps required in an orderly fashion. While OBM programs are never easy to design or administer, they can be strong motivators with excellent results (see "A Closer Look: OBM").[15]

Ethics and OBM. OBM can shape the behavior of organization members, but is it ethical? After all, it specifies a systematic approach for controlling people so they will behave as an organization wants them to. Does this take away individuality and invade privacy? Is it humane? Does it open the door to wide-scale abuse of organization members? The answer to all these questions is both yes and no. OBM can be used to manipulate people, but it can also be used for the good purpose of helping them. Many weight-reduction and quit-smoking programs apply OBM principles. Industrial safety programs use OBM to teach workers how to operate equipment. OBM programs teach salespeople effective techniques and provide rewards for successful sales.

OBM: Flying High at Scandinavian Airlines

Sales performance for reservations agents at Scandinavian Airlines was at an all-time low. A consultant hired to investigate and improve the situation found that agents were making firm booking offers during only 34 percent of potential sales opportunities. They were making round-trip bookings during only 17.5 percent of the opportunities. The only behavior that managers were measuring was the number of calls every agent took each day, and even this behavior was not being reinforced systematically.

An OBM program was designed to change the agents' behavior. The consultant helped the airline identify a desired response for agents: to provide specific booking offers to customers and to give them supporting information to encourage them to book flights. The consultant developed a system the airline could use to measure the frequency of each desired response. Appropriate responses were reinforced through feedback, social recognition, awards, gifts, and special assignments. Inappropriate responses received mild punishment or no response at all. Most reinforcement was provided using intermittent schedules.

The OBM program at Scandinavian Airlines seemed to be a tremendous success. Reservations agents offered customers specific bookings and gave them the necessary supporting information 80 percent of the time. The frequency of successful round-trip bookings increased from 17.5 percent to over 30 percent. The financial impact for the airline was substantial, even considering the costs of the training required. OBM was working well at Scandinavian Airlines.[1]

1. For additional information, see E. J. Feeney, J. R. Staelin, R. M. O'Brien, and A. M. Dickinson (1982), Increasing sales performance among airline reservation personnel, in K. M. O'Brien, A. M. Dickinson, and M. P. Rosow, eds., *Industrial behavior modification: A management handbook*, Maxwell House, NY: Pergamon Press, 141-58.

OBM simply describes the processes through which people learn. The individuals who apply these processes can put them to ethical or unethical, harmful or beneficial, use. When used appropriately and explained fully, OBM can show employees that managers care. It lets workers know what their managers expect of them. Managers who use OBM appear willing to help workers meet their organization's expectations and to reward desired behavior. In fact, it can be argued that managers behave unethically if they do *not* systematically use their knowledge: every time managers react or fail to react to subordinates' actions, they influence subsequent behavior. If managers do not use OBM, they may waste employees' time and energy and inadvertently encourage undesired behavior by failing to reward those who follow the rules and perform effectively.

Process Theories

Process theories go beyond content and reinforcement theories to provide a more complete understanding of human feelings, beliefs, and expectations. **Process theories** focus on the reasons people choose to behave in certain ways and on the reasons they react as they do to organizational events.

Distributive Justice and Equity Theory

Distributive justice is a question of fairness between workers and their organization.

Lillie Chalmers has just been given a pay raise, and she is furious. Why was Lillie happier yesterday than she is today earning 6 percent more? When asked this question, she replied:

My starting salary a year ago was $30,000, which I thought was reasonable pay for a new customer relations representative with a fresh M.B.A. During the last year, I have worked extremely hard and, if you ask me, have clearly shown that I am the most effective rep in the entire office. The value of what I give the company is much more than a lousy $30,000. I looked forward to today because I knew annual raises would be announced. I felt my effectiveness easily merited a 10 percent increase. When I found out I only got 6 percent, I checked with two of my friends who became reps about the same time I did. Keith Kastle, who isn't nearly as good as I am, also got a 6 percent raise. Mae Hedding, who is probably second best in the office, got a 9 percent raise and she doesn't even have an M.B.A. It just isn't fair!

Distributive Justice.   One of the reasons Lillie reacted negatively to her pay raise involves what George Homans has called the principle of **distributive justice.**[16] Simply put, distributive justice is a question of fairness: does Lillie believe that a fair exchange has occurred between herself and the organization? Because Lillie feels that she has given more to the organization than she has received, she is dissatisfied, and her future motivation is threatened.

Equity Theory.   In addition to being upset because of a lack of distributive justice, Lillie was angry about the unfairness she perceived when she compared her situation to that of her co-workers. **Equity theory,** as proposed by J. Stacy Adams, suggests that people compare their own situation—that is, what they contribute vs. what they receive—to the situation they perceive for other people (an individual, a group, one's self in another situation, or one's idealized self).[17] When people perceive their contributions and results to be equal to the contributions and results of others, they see the situation as equitable (fair). When people feel that the situation is fair, they feel satisfied. When they feel satisfied, they are motivated to maintain the state of equity.

People may perceive a situation to be inequitable (unfair) under two conditions. People who feel overrewarded perceive that they are getting more than they should, considering their contributions. Whereas overreward does not usually cause a manager many difficulties (how likely is Mae to complain that her pay increase is too high?), *considerable* overreward can make people feel guilty. Guilt can produce dissatisfaction and motivation to seek a state of equity, perhaps by workers' increasing their inputs.

The second condition of inequity, underreward, does pose a problem for managers. In this situation, workers feel that those to whom they compare themselves are getting "a better deal." When people perceive underreward, as Lillie did, they feel angry, tense, and dissatisfied and will be motivated to do something to reestablish a state of perceived equity. For instance, Lillie is considering reducing her contributions by lowering her performance. Another solution would be to increase her results, perhaps by demanding a bigger raise. She also might try to change the situation of the people to whom she is comparing herself, by persuading Mae to work harder or by telling her boss about the times Keith has cheated on his weekly status reports. Another alternative for Lillie in dealing with this perceived underreward is to change her perceptions and to decide that she is simply not as valuable to the organization as she had previously believed. She also might conclude that it is inappropriate to compare herself with Mae and Keith and identify another person with whom to compare herself. If all else fails, of course, Lillie can escape this unfair situation by leaving her job.

Together, the principles of distributive justice and equity theory can help managers recognize that organization members evaluate what they receive from the organization in a very personal manner.

Motivating Through Goals

Goal theory specifies that particular kinds of goals motivate organization members most effectively. Although somewhat narrow in scope, this theory is straightforward, easily understood, and the theory most completely supported by research evidence.[18]

Important Goal Characteristics. Four characteristics enhance the motivating power of goals: *goal specificity, goal difficulty, goal acceptance,* and *goal commitment.*[19] As Figure 13.5 shows, workers who have a goal, even if it is quite general, usually perform better than those who work without any goals at all (goal specificity). Furthermore, certain types of goals are more effective than others (goal difficulty). Goal acceptance is the degree to which workers accept a goal as their own ("I agree that this report must be finished by 5 P.M."). Goal commitment is more inclusive, referring to one's level of attachment to or determination to reach a goal ("I *want* to get that report done on time").

People with difficult goals perform better than those with easy goals (note the two bottom bars in Figure 13.5), but goals that are perceived as impossible are not very effective.[20] Difficult goals must be considered reachable to be effective. A difficult goal also should be specific to be maximally effective.

FIGURE 13.5   *The Effects of Goals on Performance*

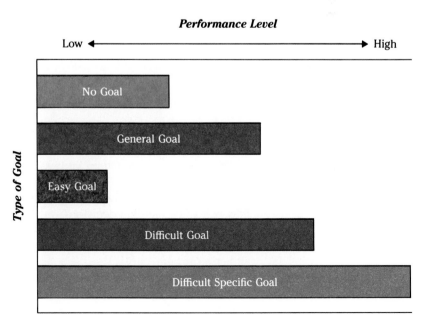

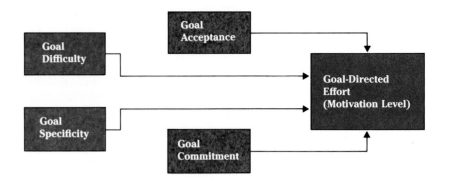

FIGURE 13.6 A Model
of Goal Setting

Thus, the most commonly expressed goal "I'm going to do my best" is not very effective because it is too general. Goals can fail to motivate people if managers assign goals without making sure that subordinates have accepted or committed themselves to them. Figure 13.6 summarizes the conditions necessary to maximize goal-directed effort (motivation), a major contributor to subsequent performance.

A Manager's Role.   What can you do as a manager to encourage goal acceptance and commitment? Set difficult, specific, and reasonable goals and make certain that subordinates perceive them as reasonable. Make goals public, rather than private.[21] If necessary, provide employees with the training and support needed to make goals reachable. Offer feedback that lets people know when they are approaching the goal; feedback reinforces employees for being on target or provides information that suggests a rechanneling of efforts. Avoid using threats; a positive, success-oriented approach is usually more effective.

Whereas goal acceptance occurs before people begin working on a task and can be encouraged through *promises* of reward, goal commitment can be nurtured throughout the performance period as workers *receive* rewards for progress. Encourage the development of work group norms that contribute to goal commitment. Use legitimate authority to encourage the setting of specific and difficult goals. Stimulate workers to develop a sense of ownership in goals, thus producing goal acceptance and commitment.

Watch intently for examples of what [the employee] does right and reward him [or her] for it by glance, bonus, smile, promotion, newsletter item, and so on.
—Karmel

Expectancy Theory

It is 8:30 on a Saturday morning. Kit Pratt is trying to decide how to spend her day. Her husband has asked her to go with him and another couple to a football game. Unfortunately, Kit has a final exam scheduled for Monday. Kit has until 9 A.M. to decide whether she will study until noon and then go to the game or skip the game and study all day. Which alternative will Kit choose, and how will she make this decision?

Expectancy theory states that Kit will make her decision by thinking through the implications of each alternative and choosing the one that is most attractive to her.[22] In fact, expectancy theory is a general model that can be useful in a wide variety of situations. Which job offer should you accept? Which classes should you sign up for? Should you go to work today or stay home?

In addition to stating that a person will select the most attractive alternative, expectancy theory specifies that the more attractive the selected alternative, the more highly motivated the individual will be to pursue it. If Kit concludes that staying home to study is only slightly more attractive than going to the football game, she will choose to stay home but will not be highly motivated to do so. In fact, it might be possible for her husband to change her mind without too much difficulty. If, however, staying home to study is much more attractive, Kit will choose to stay home and be highly motivated to do so. It will be very difficult for her husband or anyone else to convince her to go to the game.

In expectancy theory, the overall attractiveness of an alternative is referred to as the **Force** driving a person to choose that alternative (motivation strength). People consider three basic issues when they evaluate the attractiveness of alternatives: expectancy perceptions, instrumentality perceptions, and valence perceptions.

Expectancy Perceptions. For a given alternative, the **expectancy perception** is the perceived likelihood that effort will lead to a particular performance level. Consider Kit's expectancy perceptions as she evaluates the two alternatives:

1. If I study all day (effort), I am reasonably certain that I will get a high score (performance) on the exam. Maybe there is a 20 percent chance that I will get only a moderately good score, but I see no chance of anything lower.
2. If I study only a few hours this morning and then go to the game, I see a very slim chance of getting a high exam score. I might have a 50-50 chance of getting a moderate score that way, but it is also quite possible that I could get a low exam score.

Instrumentality Perceptions. Kit has identified three possible performance levels: high, medium, and low exam scores. What outcomes might follow each of these performance levels? The **instrumentality perception** is the perceived likelihood that a given performance level will lead to one or more outcomes. Here are Kit's instrumentality perceptions:

1. If I get a high score on the exam (performance), I am almost certain that I will be given an *A* for the course (outcome).
2. If I get a moderate exam score, I have equal chances of being given an *A* or a *B* for the course.
3. A low exam score gives me no chance of an *A* for the course. In fact, a low exam score makes it pretty sure I will get a *C* (although I suppose there is a chance I could still get a *B*).

Kit is now close to making her decision. Only one final consideration remains: valence.

Valence Perceptions. **Valence** is the value attached to an outcome. How does Kit feel about her grades?

My current grade point average is 3.05. I know I have to maintain at least a 3.00 to be admitted to the M.B.A. program I just applied to. Although I value an A somewhat more than a B, I would be pleased with either an A or a B, since either helps me get into graduate school. A grade of C, however, would be a serious problem because it would drop my GPA below 3.0.

Making the Decision. As noted earlier, Force represents a person's drive to engage in a particular behavior. The strength of this Force derives from the combination of expectancy, instrumentality, and valence perceptions. In essence, expectancy theory says that people will be motivated to perform at a high level to the degree to which they believe (1) that they can accomplish the expected performance level, (2) that the performance will lead to outcomes, and (3) that the outcomes have value. Although Force scores can be calculated using a mathematical equation, most people mentally evaluate a decision, as Kit has done. Because Kit values admittance to the M.B.A. program so highly, she cannot risk receiving a *C,* which is possible if she goes to the game. Kit, therefore, will be highly motivated to stay home and study.

Expanded Expectancy Theory

Expectancy theory deals with the processes involved in choosing among alternatives. It also indicates that the enthusiasm with which a person pursues an alternative depends on how attractive the alternative is (Force). The expanded expectancy model, originally developed by Lyman Porter from the University of California-Irvine and Edward Lawler III from the University of Southern California, provides an understanding of employee motivation, performance, and satisfaction. As shown in Figure 13.7, the model illustrates what happens after a choice is made by incorporating ideas from each of the theories discussed earlier in this chapter. This complete model, although somewhat complex, provides a realistic picture of how people react to their organizational experiences. (Notice that the three boxes on the model's left-hand side are the factors that determine the attractiveness of an alternative. Assuming that this is the chosen alternative, the rest of the model illustrates what happens next.)

The greater the Force, the more highly motivated a person will be to expend energy pursuing that alternative. A strong Force, therefore, encourages strong commitment to a goal once it has been selected. A strong Force is also associated with a high level of effort, as shown in Figure 13.7. If an individual has the necessary personal capabilities, he or she can translate this effort into performance.

FIGURE 13.7   Expanded Expectancy Theory

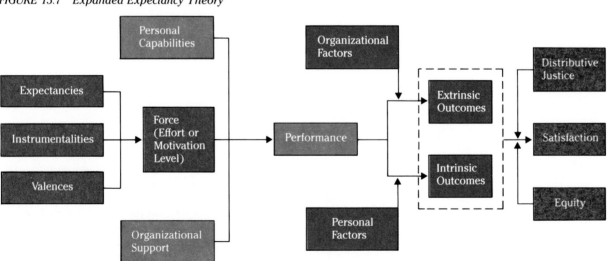

Managers can use this to their advantage if, after persuading workers to choose an alternative, they follow through by seeing to it that the workers have the capabilities necessary to succeed and by providing the promised rewards. For example, Pamela Fullerton, a sales manager who has just convinced sales representative Mari Hall to choose a high sales goal and to devote considerable energy toward achieving that goal, cannot yet rest easy. The expanded expectancy model clarifies that Pamela must ensure that Mari has the capabilities to meet the goal. Does Mari, for example, have the interpersonal skills and product knowledge required to make the sales? Is there adequate organizational support—product samples, documentation of the products' merits, appropriate supply and delivery mechanisms, and so on?

Pamela also must help sustain Mari's high effort and performance once they have been achieved. To do so, Pamela must identify outcomes—such as increased travel allotments, bonuses, and special recognition—that Mari values and must give them out in such in a way that Mari considers them a fair reward for her efforts. The rewards also must seem fair in comparison to those given to other salespeople.

If Pamela can meet all these conditions, she is likely to have a highly effective, satisfied salesperson. If Pamela can convince Mari that hard work in the future—effort that translates into performance—will also lead to valued, fair, and satisfying outcomes, then Mari will again choose to work hard and, in all likelihood, will succeed again.

Motivating Organization Members in Review

Being capable of doing something does not mean that a person will choose to do so and will follow through to the point of effectiveness. It is motivation that energizes, directs, and sustains the human behavior necessary to turn a capable employee into an effective one. Traditional managerial approaches to motivation tried to energize workers by satisfying various sets of human needs. The economic model of motivation popularized by the classicists assumed that work is inherently unpleasant and that organizations should provide enough money to compensate employees for this unpleasantness. The social model of motivation assumed that the satisfaction of social needs would lead to effective performance. The nature-of-work approach argued that jobs that offer interesting, challenging work would motivate and satisfy workers.

Contemporary theoretical models offer more specific details. The content theories, such as Maslow's and Alderfer's need-hierarchy theories (and, to some extent, Herzberg's motivation-hygiene theory), explain why individuals value outcomes as they do. The reinforcement theories show that providing or withholding valued outcomes following a behavior can encourage or discourage future repetition of that behavior. The process theories, such as distributive justice, equity theory, and goal theory, help managers understand some of the processes that organization members follow as they react to their work experiences.

Each of the theories presented in this chapter provides something useful for a manager who wants to motivate people. The expanded expectancy theory attempts to integrate the major points from each of the content, reinforcement, and process theories into a model that helps managers develop and maintain employees' motivation, performance, and satisfaction.

Issues for Review and Discussion

1. Describe the economic, social, and nature-of-work approaches to motivation.
2. Describe the type of worker who would *not* be motivated by the nature-of-work approach to motivation; by the social approach.
3. Outline an organizational behavior modification program to reduce absenteeism among workers at your favorite restaurant.
4. Use equity theory to describe a situation in which you might be unhappy even though you received an *A* in a course.
5. Explain why the goal "I'm going to do my best" is not effective for motivating high performance.
6. According to expectancy theory, how does a worker determine the attractiveness of an alternative?
7. From an expectancy theory perspective, identify five reasons that high effort can lead to low performance.

Key Terms

motivation
content theories
innate needs
acquired needs
need hierarchy theory
Existence, Relatedness, and Growth
   (ERG) Theory
need for achievement
need for affiliation
need for power
hygiene needs
motivator needs
reinforcement theories
positive reinforcement
negative reinforcement
punishment

nonreinforcement
continuous schedules of reinforcement
intermittent schedules of reinforcement
organizational behavior modification
   (OBM)
extrinsic motivators
intrinsic motivators
process theories
distributive justice
equity theory
goal theory
expectancy theory
Force
expectancy perception
instrumentality perception
valence

Suggested Readings

Herzberg, F. (1968). One more time: How do you motivate employees? *Harvard Business Review, 46,* 54-62.

Kerr, S. (1975). On the folly of rewarding A, while hoping for B. *Academy of Management Journal, 18,* 769-83.

LeBoeuf, M. (1987). *The greatest management principle in the world.* New York: Berkley.

Locke, E. A., and Latham, G. P. (1984). *Goal setting: A motivational technique that works!* Englewood Cliffs, NJ: Prentice-Hall.

McClelland, D. C. (November-December 1966). That urge to achieve. *Think,* 19-23.

McGregor, D. M. (November 1957). The human side of enterprise. *Management Review,* 22-28, 88-92.

Martinko, J. J., and Moss, S. (1988). A review of The greatest management principle in the world. In Pierce, J. L., and Newstrom, J. W., eds. *The manager's bookshelf: A mosaic of contemporary views.* New York: Harper & Row, 109-16.

Notes

1. Atop the Fortune 500: A survey of the C.E.O.s. (28 April 1986), *Fortune,* 26-31.

2. W. C. Hamner and E. P. Hamner (1976), Behavior modification on the bottom line, *Organizational Dynamics,* 4, 3-21.

3. A. H. Maslow (1943), A theory of human motivation, *Psychological Bulletin,* 50, 370-96.

4. Maslow, 382.

5. C. P. Alderfer (1972), *Existence, relatedness, and growth: Human needs and organizational settings,* New York: Free Press.

6. H. A. Murray (1938), *Exploration in personality,* New York: Oxford University Press; J. W. Atkinson and D. C. McClelland (1948), The projective expression of needs. II. The effect of different intensities of the hunger drive on thematic apperception, *Journal of Experimental Psychology,* 38, 643-58; D. C. Mc-Clelland, J. W. Atkinson, R. A. Clark, and E. L. Lowell (1953), *The achievement motive,* New York: Appleton-Century-Crofts.

7. J. W. Atkinson and A. C. Raphelson (1956), Individual differences in motivation and behavior in particular situations, *Journal of Personality,* 24, 349-63; R. C. DeCharms (1957), Affiliation motivation and productivity in small groups, *Journal of Abnormal Psychology,* 55, 222-76; D. Birch and J. Veroff (1966), *Motivation: A study of action,* Monterey, CA: Brooks/Cole; R. M. Steers and D. N. Braunstrin (1976), A behaviorally based measure of manifest needs in work settings, *Journal of Vocational Behavior,* 9, 251-66.

8. D. C. McClelland (1975), *Power: The inner experience,* New York: Irvington; D. C. McClelland, W. N. Davis, R. Kalin, and E. Wanner (1972), *The drinking man: Alcohol and human motivation,* New York: Free Press.

9. F. Herzberg, B. Mausner, and B. Snyderman (1959), *The motivation to work,* New York: Wiley; F. Herzberg (1968), One more time: How do you motivate employees? *Harvard Business Review,* 46, 54-62.

10. Herzberg, et al.

11. V. H. Vroom (1964), *Work and motivation,* New York: Wiley; R. J. House and L. A. Wigdor (1967), Herzberg's dual-factor theory of job satisfaction and motivation: A review of the evidence and a criticism, *Personnel Psychology,* 20, 369-89.

12. House and Wigdor.

13. R. J. Bullock and E. E. Lawler III (1984), Gainsharing: A few questions and fewer answers, *Human Resource Management,* 23(1), 23-40; E. A. Locke, D. B. Feren, V. M. McCaleb, K. N. Shaw, and A. T. Denney (1980), The relative effectiveness of form methods of motivating employee performance, in K. D. Duncan, M. M. Gruneberg, and D. Wallis, eds., *Changes in working life,* New York: John Wiley and Sons, 363-88.

14. R. N. Kanungo (1987), An alternative to the intrinsic-extrinsic dichotomy of work rewards, *Journal of Management,* 13, 751-66; L. Dyer and D. F. Parker (1975), Classifying outcomes in work motivation research: An examination of the intrinsic-extrinsic dichotomy, *Journal of Applied Psychology,* 60, 455-58.

15. Hamner and Hamner.

16. G. C. Homans (1961), *Social behavior: Its elementary forms,* New York: Harcourt, Brace, and World.

17. J. S. Adams (1965), Inequity in social exchange, in L. Berkowitz, ed., *Advances in experimental social psychology,* vol. 2, New York: Academic Press; also see R. T. Mowday (1987), Equity theory predictions of behavior in organizations, in R. M. Steers and L. W. Porter, eds., *Motivation and work behavior,* New York: McGraw-Hill, 89-110.

18. E. A. Locke and G. P. Latham (1984), *Goal setting: A motivational technique that works!* Englewood Cliffs, NJ: Prentice-Hall.

19. E. A. Locke (1982), Relation of goal performance with a short work period and multiple goal levels, *Journal of Applied Psychology,* 67, 512-14; G. P. Latham and J. J. Baldes (1975), The practical significance of Locke's theory of goal setting, *Journal of Applied Psychology,* 60, 187-91; G. P. Latham and E. A. Locke (1979), Goal setting—a motivational technique that works, *Organizational Dynamics,* 68-80; H. Garland (1983), Influence of ability-assigned goals and normative information of personal goals and performance: A challenge to the goal attainability assumption, *Journal of Applied Psychology,* 68, 20-30; E. A. Locke, K. N. Shaw, L. M. Saari, and G. P. Latham (1981), Goal setting and task performance: 1969-1980, *Psychological Bulletin,* 90, 125-52; E. A. Locke, G. P. Latham, and M. Erez (1988), The determinants of goal commitment, *Academy of Management Review,* 13, 23-39.

20. Locke, 1982.

21. J. R. Hollenbeck, C. R. Williams, and H. J. Klein (1989), An empirical examination of the antecedents of commitment to difficult goals, *Journal of Applied Psychology,* 74 (1), 18-23.

22. This treatment of expectancy theory is based primarily on the work of Lyman Porter and Ed Lawler, although many others have contributed to various aspects of this theory, c.f., L. W. Porter and E. E. Lawler (1968), *Managerial attitudes and performance,* Homewood, IL: Irwin; V. H. Vroom (1960), *Some personality determinants of the effects of participation,* Englewood Cliffs, NJ: Prentice-Hall; Vroom, 1964; J. Galbraith and L. L. Cummings (1967), An empirical investigation of the motivational determinants of task performance: Interactive effects between instrumentality-valence and motivation-ability, *Organizational Behavior and Human Performance,* 2, 237-57.

Jack Dobbins' Problem

By David Kenerson, University of South Florida

Jack Dobbins left the vice-president's office feeling elated as well as concerned about the new responsibilities he was about to assume. Ralph Barnes, State College's vice-president and comptroller, had just told Jack of the Executive Committee's decision to appoint him superintendent of buildings. Jack was concerned because Mr. Barnes had gone into considerable detail about the many management and morale problems among the college's custodial workers and their supervisors.

The Situation

State College is located in a rural area just outside of St. Louis, Missouri. It is one of several universities run by the state and is less than ten years old. In this short time it has grown rapidly to 9500 students, the majority of which live off campus and commute to school each day.

The superintendent's major function is to plan, organize, direct, and control the activities of about eighty employees and supervisors involved in keeping all college buildings, except for the dormitories, in a clean and orderly condition. There are ten major buildings ranging in size from 24,000 square feet to 137,000 square feet. Total square footage under the jurisdiction of the superintendent amounts to 1,025,000. This space includes classrooms, faculty offices, administration and library buildings, student center, and the like.

Of the eighty employees in the department, sixteen are women, and sixty-four are men, including the four male supervisors who report to the superintendent. Starting wages are $11,000. Employees can only receive one raise per year, usually on July 1, at the beginning of the fiscal year. It is within the superintendent's authority to grant raises up to a maximum of 10 percent the first year, 7 percent the second year, and 5 percent the third and subsequent years. To qualify for the maximum, however, employees have to receive a performance rating of "outstanding." The work week is forty hours. Vacation leave of ten working days is allowed, while sick leave is accrued at the rate of one day per month to a maximum of thirty days. Group life insurance and medical and hospitalization insurance are available through payroll deduction at employee expense. Employees participate in the state retirement system under which both the state and the employee contribute. The total budget for the department amounts to about $1,015,000, with $900,000 for wages and salaries and $115,000 for supplies and materials.

Turnover among employees is unusually high. In July and August of the previous year, turnover amounted to 15 percent and 20 percent respectively. Typically, in this type of work in universities, turnover averages 75 percent per year. Most of the employees at State College hold second jobs outside of the college.

Departmental Work Organization

There is no organization chart for the department, but it appears to Jack Dobbins that it would look pretty much like the chart shown in Figure 13A. Work is assigned on the basis of special tasks. Although supervisors are assigned responsibility for different buildings, night crews are specialized into floor-mopping crews, followed by waxing and buffing crews. Supervisors decide when particular floors are to be mopped, waxed, and buffed and coordinate and schedule the different crews in proper sequence. The day crews work largely on restroom detail in all buildings, with special groups assigned for carpet cleaning, window washing, and straightening and cleaning up meeting rooms before and after meetings.

Jack Dobbins' Background

Jack Dobbins is a retired military officer with twenty years' service in various posts as a management analyst and operations and training officer. As a young man, he graduated from a midwestern engineering school. On resigning from the military, he enrolled in an M.B.A. program to earn a degree in management. Now at forty-five he is looking forward to a new career in a new environment in a field in which he feels

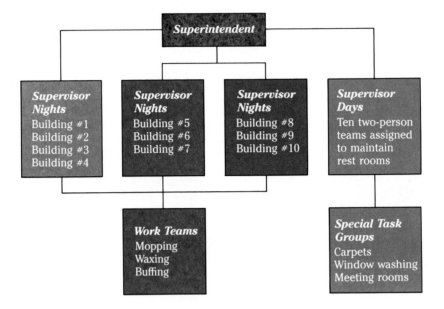

his experience, knowledge, and training could be most effectively used.

During the last hour and a half in his talk with Mr. Barnes, he has learned much about the current problems of the department. Harry Kraft, the superintendent he is replacing, had come to State College when the first students were admitted. He is fifty-five years old, of limited education, and with a varied background as a supervisor in construction firms. When the college was small with only a few buildings and few employees, he had been reasonably successful; however, four months ago, Harry fired one of the supervisors, with rather disastrous results. Rank-and-file employees were indignant and sent a petition all the way to the state capitol in an attempt to get Harry's

decision reversed. Some were threatening not to come to work. Morale was low, turnover was high, and top officials of the college, as well as the department itself, were being deluged with complaints about the lack of good housekeeping in all buildings. Toilets were not adequately serviced; classrooms and offices frequently went untouched for a week at a time.

Although Jack is concerned, he is not dismayed, because he feels strongly that his recent exposure to a wide variety of management courses will make it relatively easy to show substantial improvements in this department, despite the fact that no raises could be given to any employees before the next fiscal year, eleven months away.

Questions

1. Analyze the custodial employees' situation using two different motivational theories.
2. Assuming Jack Dobbins has studied the same theories that you have, which, if any, are going to be of help to him?
3. What should Jack Dobbins do?

14

Interpersonal Factors in Organizations

Student Learning Objectives

After reading this chapter, you should be able to:

1. Explain the sources of interpersonal power and the ways in which these sources work together.

2. Describe how people use and abuse power.

3. Describe the major steps in the communication process.

4. Enumerate ways to improve communication in organizations.

5. Identify conflict and explain why it occurs in organizations.

6. Discuss the personal styles of conflict management and the situations in which each is appropriate or inappropriate.

7. Explain how organizational politics affect interpersonal behavior.

*B*ob Johnson and Karin Sandberg-Brennan both attended the University of Cincinnati, where each received an M.B.A. in accounting in 1979. Today, both Bob and Karin are department managers at the Cincinnati Fan Company. Next week Karin will become the company's new director of accounting. Missing out on this promotion has been the last in a long string of disappointments for Bob, who has considered his job an increasing struggle since becoming a manager in 1984.

When Karin asks her subordinates to do something, they usually comply quickly. When Bob makes requests, he is never sure whether people will comply with them. Karin's subordinates and co-workers always seem to understand her instructions, memos, and other communications. Bob's attempts at communication frequently elicit a puzzled "What do you mean?" Karin and her workers function as a team; Bob struggles with almost constant conflict within his department.

Bob is failing as a manager because he cannot competently manage a variety of interpersonal factors. If an organization is to function effectively, its managers must direct subordinates' motivation and behavior toward meeting the organization's goals. Four interpersonal factors play a major role in this process: power, communication, conflict, and politics.

Interpersonal Power

Just as there are many sources of electrical energy, there are many sources of interpersonal power.

Electrical power lets people operate machines. **Interpersonal power** lets people influence other people. The greater a person's total supply of electricity, the greater his or her capacity to operate machines. The greater a manager's total supply of interpersonal power, the greater his or her ability to influence others. Just as there are many sources of electrical energy—water, coal, wind, and nuclear fission—interpersonal power has many sources. Just as it would be politically and ecologically undesirable for the United States to rely entirely on one source of electricity, it is not suitable for a manager to rely on just one source of interpersonal power.

Sources of Power

As you learned in Chapter 10, there are several major sources of social power (see Table 14.1).[1] A person's total power derives from a combination of these six sources, and a strength in one area can compensate for a weakness in another.

TABLE 14.1 *The Sources of Power*

Type of Power	Description
Legitimate	Based on perceived authority: the *right* to influence
Reward	Based on perceived ability to provide/withhold rewards
Coercive	Based on perceived ability to provide/withhold punishment
Expert	Based on willingness to share/withhold desired expertise
Resource	Based on willingness to share/withhold desired information/resources
Referent	Based on charismatic attractiveness of power holder

Legitimate Power. **Legitimate power** exists when one person believes that another person has the right to influence him or her. Legitimate power is usually thought of as authority: the authority of a manager over a subordinate, of a board of directors over a manager, or of a teacher over a student. A manager's formal authority is specified by his or her position in the organization's hierarchy and typically is limited to the right to influence only certain behaviors—such as work-related activities—for a given group of organization members—usually subordinates. A machine foreperson can tell machinists how many units to produce, for example, but he or she generally cannot tell the vice-president what to do (unless the vice-president sees the influence attempt as legitimate). Legitimate power can also be derived informally. The leader of an informal work group or of a social group may be recognized by other group members as having legitimate power over them: power to speak for them to their boss, to help them solve problems, and to suggest improvements.

Like all other sources of power, legitimate power is in the eyes of the beholder. The fact that a manager is assigned a position of authority does not guarantee that others will respect his or her authority. For authority to translate into power, the individuals to be influenced must accept the manager's right to influence them. Until this happens, the manager has authority but no power.

Reward Power. Managers have **reward power** if they can and will provide or withhold rewards from those whom they wish to influence. **Formal rewards,** such as increases in pay or a promotion, are stipulated by an organization to help its managers develop power. **Informal rewards** are provided from the leader's own resources. An elementary-school teacher may use personal funds to purchase school supplies or treats to influence student behavior. A manager can provide employees with special recognition, do them a favor, or send them to dinner at the manager's expense. Incorporating reward power, either formally or informally, is a common way to enhance a leader's legitimate power.

Coercive Power. Managers have **coercive power** if they can and will provide or withhold punishment from those whom they wish to influence. As with reward power, a manager holds coercive power over another person if that person believes the manager has the *ability* to punish, can *control* the punishment, and is *willing* to provide or withhold that punishment. Managers who threaten punishment but never inflict it soon lose whatever coercive power they had.

Like legitimate and reward power, coercive power can be formal or informal. An organization can provide managers with the right to administer various forms of punishment, such as suspending or firing employees or reducing their pay. Managers can administer other punishments, even if they have not been assigned the formal right to do so. A high-school drama instructor may publicly criticize a student actor. A manager can give a worker an undesirable work assignment.

Coercive power is like the punishment described in Chapter 13. That is, unpleasant consequences of behavior tend to reduce the recurrence of that behavior. Coercive power, like punishment, easily generates negative side effects, and managers must use it carefully. Coercive power can create dissatisfaction and resentment. It can also lead to unexpected and undesirable results if employees fight back. It also can reduce the effectiveness of a manager's other power sources if employees resist his or her use of punishment.

Expert Power. Mary Ellen Murnin, a chemistry instructor, has used her knowledge of personal computers to generate recordkeeping programs and to design computer demonstrations. Her co-workers, seeing how fast Mary Ellen can complete report cards at the end of the semester and how positively her students evaluate her classes, are eager to get copies of her programs. Further, by updating her knowledge with new computer languages and graphics programs, Mary Ellen is able to sustain her expert knowledge base and convince management to award her with requested teaching assignments and curriculum development grants. Mary Ellen has **expert power.**

For a manager to have expert power, the following conditions must exist: the employees to be influenced must believe that the manager possesses expert knowledge they do not have, employees must want that expert knowledge, and employees must believe that the manager is willing to share (or withhold) the expert knowledge at his or her discretion. Less-skilled organization members need the expert's help and, therefore, are willing to be influenced.

Resource Power. **Resource power** is the ability to influence others because they desire (nonexpert) resources a manager controls. These resources could be information, time, materials, or anything else of value to the person who wants it. For a manager to have resource power, others must believe that he or she controls the resource and is willing to share it. For example, Corporal Walter "Radar" O'Reilly in the movie and TV series "M*A*S*H" possessed an incredible amount of resource power. Everyone, including his commanding officers, believed that Radar could obtain virtually any resource if he chose to do so. For this reason, mild, unassuming Radar was capable of exerting tremendous influence over others.

Referent Power. The final source of power commonly found in organizations is **referent power,** the ability to influence another person because he or she wants to be associated or affiliated with the power holder. People are drawn to others for a variety of reasons, including physical or social attractiveness, fame, and prestige. Charisma often finds its base in referent power. Throughout the history of the United States, such politicians as John F. Kennedy have added substantially to their power base through personal charisma. Referent power is a potential source that almost anyone can use regardless of his or her legitimate power.

John F. Kennedy added substantially to his power base through great personal charisma.

The Coordination of Power Sources. As you have learned, managers develop a total power base by combining various sources of power. An individual's overall power position is not, however, simply the sum of the power derived from each source. In reality, some combinations of power sources are synergistic: they are *greater* than the sum of their parts. Referent power, for example, tends to magnify the impact of other sources (particularly legitimate, resource, and expert power) because they are especially valued when coming from a respected person. Reward power frequently increases the impact of referent power because people tend to like those who reward them. In other words, certain power profiles may be more potent and effective than others.

The reverse can also be true. The power produced by some source combinations can be *less* than the sum of the individual sources. For example, high coercive power can dilute the impact of referent power. A manager who constantly threatens employees to obtain compliance usually becomes disliked and, therefore, has little referent power.

An individual's power profile, then, reflects his or her total amount of power and its sources; thus, organization members have different power profiles. The most effective managers recognize that legitimate power is seldom sufficient and, therefore, carefully build an integrated power base.

Uses and Abuses of Power

In January 1985, James Miller became the executive vice-president of a 500-employee service corporation. He developed a very strong overall power base out of a combination of legitimate, reward, and coercive power. Several ways in which James influenced other members of the organization include the following:

1. He asked his assistant to prepare a summary report of an impending business deal. The assistant worked until midnight to prepare the report on time.
2. He instructed the company's five division heads to develop and present him with a Management by Objectives program. They did so.
3. He asked his secretary to pick up his laundry on her way home. The secretary complied.
4. He asked a low-level staff accountant to spend a couple of hours tutoring his college-age son. The accountant obeyed.
5. He told the company's expense account manager to reimburse him for expenses for which he had no receipts (and which he had not actually incurred). The manager did so.
6. He asked all executives who earned frequent flyer awards from company travel to give them to his secretary "for company use." They did so, and James then used several of the awards on his family's vacation.
7. He invited an attractive woman from the human resources department to accompany him on an overnight business trip. She went. During the trip, James made repeated sexual overtures.

James soon found himself looking for a new job. He was fired by the president of the company, who used all but the first two items from this list as reasons for the termination. James Miller had power in the organization, which he abused.

Power can be used to encourage organization members to do things they might not otherwise do. When that behavior has little, if any, relationship to legitimate organizational activities, the power is abused. Abuses of power raise ethical questions for which there are no easy answers. Although asking a subordinate to run a personal errand for a manager during the lunch hour is not an extreme case of abuse, it may not be an ethical use of the power that was developed to *serve the organization.*

It is not unethical for an organization to train its leaders to develop a power base. Power is needed to run an organization; however, each person who develops power is ethically bound to consider carefully the impact it will have on others.

To close this discussion, consider again the electrical power analogy. Many resources are required to generate both electrical and interpersonal power. Without the resources necessary to generate sufficient electricity, a machine will not function effectively. Generating more electrical power than needed to run the machine, however, is a waste of resources. The same is true for interpersonal power; managers must determine how much is needed to direct the behavior of others effectively. The development of more than this amount of power is a waste of resources. Just as too much electrical power can damage a motor, too much interpersonal power can damage working relationships. Egos and self-esteem are even more sensitive than are electrical motors.

Organizational Communication

Managers spend a great deal of time communicating with individuals and groups, both inside and outside of their organization. "Joe, here are the sales figures for your territory." "I'd like everyone in the group to take a look at this chart." "How about adding some of our unscented products to this month's order?" Some managers communicate well and become more effective. Others communicate poorly and become less effective. This section explores the role of communication in directing behavior in organizations.

The Communication Process

Communication is the process of transferring information from one person or group (the sender) to another (the receiver). *Effective* communication takes place when the information, or message, received matches the information the sender intended to transmit. Communication occurs, however, whenever a message is received—even if the received message is different from that which was intended; thus, two major communication-related problems are *communication failure* (no meaningful information changes hands) and *miscommunication* (the message received is different from the one intended). Signs of communication failure include such telltale remarks as, "Oh, I guess I didn't hear you say that," "No, I never got that report," and "He didn't have anything new to say." Examples of miscommunication include a professor who requests a ten-page term paper but receives a two-page paper and a manager who says and means Wednesday December 15, but whose subordinate hears and understands Wednesday December 22.

Managers communicate for many reasons. They often communicate to provide receivers with needed information. From a control perspective, communication clarifies duties, authority, and responsibilities for organization members. Managers also communicate to motivate employees to commit to organizational objectives. Communication allows managers or their employees to express their feelings. In fact, most communication serves more than one of these functions. It transmits information, motivates, expresses feelings, and informs.

The complexity of the communication process grows as the number of communication purposes increases. In turn, increased complexity makes distortion more likely. Despite the greater risk of distortion, however, complex communications are often necessary and can be quite effective. Bill Cornett, for example, is a manager concerned about his organization's ability to fill a major order. He decides to send a message to production workers that: (1) shows that there is a large upcoming order; (2) relates that large orders have been poorly handled in the past; (3) indicates who is responsible for filling the upcoming order; (4) motivates by promising that success at filling this order will contribute to the company's success and, thus, the size of the profit-

FIGURE 14.1 The Communication Process

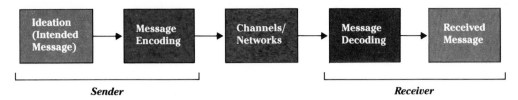

The communication process diagram shows: Ideation (Intended Message) → Message Encoding → Channels/Networks → Message Decoding → Received Message. The first two boxes are grouped as *Sender*; the last two boxes are grouped as *Receiver*.

sharing pool for production workers; and (5) conveys his feelings about the importance of the upcoming order. Bill's fairly complex communication serves several purposes: it provides information, clarifies duties, motivates, and expresses feelings.

Communication Components

The communication process has five components: ideation, message encoding, channels/networks, message decoding, and a received message (see Figure 14.1). Communication begins when a sender identifies the need to send a message, formulates the message, and places it in the channels needed to transmit it. Communication concludes when a receiver accepts the message and interprets its meaning.

Ideation, the first step of the communication process, occurs when a manager decides to communicate and develops the nature and content of the intended message based on his or her reasons for communicating. "I'm worried about that order," Bill Cornett thinks. "I'd better let my people know."

Encoding is the second step: converting an intended message into a transmittable form, such as speech, a written message, computer code, or any other form that can be sent to a receiver. A manager must be careful during the encoding stage, or the message sent will be different from the one intended. "I'd better note exactly who is responsible for filling the new order, or we'll have the same problems as last time," Bill thinks as he makes notes for his message.

Once a manager has encoded a message, he or she must send it. Bill decides to distribute typed copies to each worker personally, to post a copy on the bulletin board, and to send a copy to his supervisor. Messages are sent through communication *channels.* Any medium capable of transmitting a message is a communication channel, including mail systems, phone lines, and computers. Communication *networks* tie channels together to facilitate the flow of information. It is imperative that a manager choose channels and networks appropriate for the nature of the message and of sufficient quality to preserve its integrity. Writing a letter but forgetting to mail it halts the communication process.

Decoding, the fourth step, is the process by which a receiver interprets a message to derive meaning from it. As you read this book, you are decoding the messages that were encoded and transmitted to you in book format. As his subordinates read Bill's memo, they interpret his message. Managers must recognize that effective communication depends as much on the receiver as on the sender. A message is *received* when it has been decoded, even if the receiver's interpretation of its meaning differs from the sender's intent. Com-

Realistically, the individual manager can be more precise when communicating the overall unit goals, individuals' roles, and standards of performance expected. This provides a clear set of expectations against which performance can be measured. When conflict, misunderstanding, or poor performance occur, they can be judged and resolved by referring to the objectives which have been defined.

—Marx

Creative Communication: The Annual Report

Every shareholder of every publicly held corporation in the United States receives a copy of the company's annual report. One section of the annual report contains financial figures that must conform to specific standards set by the Securities and Exchange Commission (SEC) and the Financial Accounting Standards Board. These figures also must be examined by auditors who certify their accuracy. As a result, this section usually provides a fairly forthright picture of the company's finances.

Virtually every annual report, however, also contains other information, often in the form of a message from the chairperson, which is not subject to audit. According to *Business Week*, this message "doesn't always give a brutally frank version of the year's events . . . . Part of the challenge is learning how to translate this verbiage."[1] To this end, *Business Week* offers some illustrated translations of common messages from the chair (see below).

1. Reading between the lines of an annual report (23 March 1987), *Business Week*, 164.

Illustrations from "Reading Between the Lines of an Annual Report." Reprinted from the March 23, 1987 issue of *Business Week* by special permission. Copyright © 1987 by McGraw-Hill, Inc.

WHEN THEY SAY THIS:
The uncertain regulatory climate poses challenges for our business.
THEY MAY MEAN THIS:
The SEC has subpoenaed our records and our lawyers are scared to death.

We can prosper only by being better managed than our competitors.
If we can sell below cost long enough, we'll have the field to ourselves.

Your company is now posed for earnings growth.
We lost so much money earnings can't get worse.

We're seizing the growing opportunities for global out-sourcing.
We're moving production to the Far East, where wages are dirt-cheap.

We are vigorously seeking creative techniques to bring our costs in line.
We are going to slash salaries by 20% and cash in our pension plan.

Last year we substantially strengthened the ranks of our senior management.
After the latest series of indictments, heads rolled.

plicating this step of the communication process is the fact that the decoding process is influenced heavily by the perceptual process (see Chapter 12). Many people, for example, throw away mail that is sent bulk rate without bothering to open it, but they read all of their express mail.

As you can see, the communication process is not simple. As a manager, you must do more than plan what you want to say. You must also choose your words carefully and send them appropriately. Furthermore, you need to consider the receivers and design your message so they will notice it, choose it for decoding, and interpret it as you intended.

Communication Channels

Selecting a communication channel to transmit a timely, accurate, complete, and understandable message is very important. People are channels who use speech, sight, and body motions to communicate. Mechanical channels go beyond the capabilities of the human body and include newsletters, magazines, telephones, radio, television, and computers. At this moment, messages about the process of management are coming to you through a textbook, a mechanical channel that is more efficient than your instructor's sitting down with you and your classmates individually and imparting such information. Audio or video recording is also an alternative. In fact, for students with visual or learning disabilities, this book can be translated by Recording for the Blind, Inc. (20 Rozel Road, Princeton, NJ 08540).

Most managers have personal preferences about communication channels. Some believe that face-to-face communication is best whenever possible. Others rely on memos. More and more managers use computer channels as a first choice. There is no single best communication channel. Because of their differences in capacity, modifiability, duplication, speed, feedback, and appropriateness, some channels convey particular messages better than others.

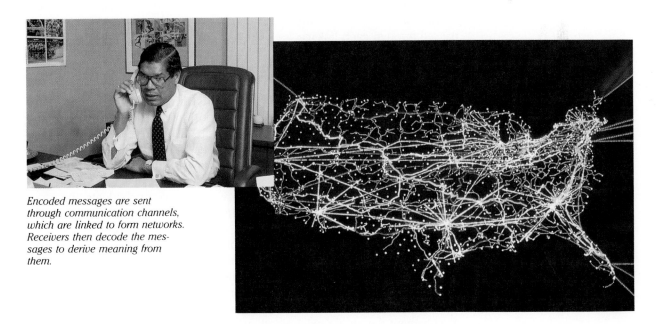

Encoded messages are sent through communication channels, which are linked to form networks. Receivers then decode the messages to derive meaning from them.

Channel *capacity* is the amount of information a channel can transmit without significant distortion. A television broadcast, for example, has greater channel capacity than a memo. Channel *modifiability* is the degree to which a transmission can be changed while in progress. A training session presented using a video recorder can greatly increase modifiability if trainees can replay a passage or freeze an important frame on the screen. Channel *duplication* involves the use of subchannels to repeat or elaborate on a message, as when a professor places key terms on a chalkboard while discussing them in detail. Channel *speed* is how fast a message can be sent. Overnight delivery is fast compared to first-class mail but slow compared to a faxed message. Channel *feedback* permits bilateral (two-way) communication. A telephone, for example, allows information to flow in both directions. Channel *appropriateness* asks, "Is this the right way to send this particular message?" If a manager wants to persuade a job candidate to accept a job offer, for example, should the manager's secretary call the candidate with the offer, or would a personal call from the manager be more effective? In addition to evaluating such objective characteristics as capacity, modifiability, and speed, a manager should think about whether the channel(s) under consideration are appropriate to the message.

Communication Networks

Each communication between two people or groups is called a *linkage*. A **communication network** is a series of linkages connecting individuals or groups for communication purposes. The number of linkages in a network is important because each linkage tends to introduce some distortion. If Melissa Graves Robin, president of a hierarchical organization, wants to send a message to first-level supervisor Otis Taylor, she might give the message to vice-president Bill Tobey, who gives it to division head Dorothy Duerr, who passes it down the chain of command until it reaches Otis. Direct communication from Melissa to Otis probably would be more accurate and more efficient, because it would eliminate the opportunity for the message to be lost or distorted as it passed through each linkage.

Managers often excel in their ability to build relations with other managers in interdependent departments. . . . In short, they are best when communicating laterally, weakest when communicating upward or downward.

—Marx

Formal Communication Networks. Because there is no single best network for all communication needs, most organizations use a variety of networks. In a network using **vertical communication,** information flows between individuals in superior-subordinate positions. When employee Delma Eckman reports on sales calls to district manager Pat Kelley, and when Pat tells Delma which calls to make in the next sales period, they are engaging in vertical communication. **Horizontal communication** transfers information between individuals or groups at the same hierarchical level. When Tom Logan, vice-president of marketing, shows other vice-presidents the story boards for a new advertising campaign, horizontal communication occurs. In **diagonal communication,** information flows across *both* vertical and horizontal components, as when a salesperson receives information from the vice-president of human resources or when the head of research and development solicits information from one of the organization's purchasing agents.

Managers can choose from among many types of networks when creating a communication system within their organization. If they adhere to classical management theory, for example, they may design very rigid communication networks in which employees are discouraged from talking with anyone except their immediate supervisor. Such a system enables supervisors to maintain control over subordinates and to remain highly informed about various activities in their departments. Managers in more open systems, such as those found in organically designed organizations, are likely to create flexible communication systems that encourage workers to seek and transmit information as dictated by the nature of the task on which they are working. Figure 14.2 illustrates five common communication networks.

Informal Communication Networks. Although the communication networks discussed so far are formal and created by organizations, informal networks also exist. Created by employees and often referred to as "the grapevine," informal networks emerge through natural and spontaneous human interaction. They "flow around water coolers, down hallways, through lunch rooms, and wherever people get together in groups."[2] Although informal networks can benefit an organization by distributing important information, they can also wreak havoc when the messages they carry thwart organizational objectives.

Managing Communication Effectively. In sum, effective communication requires careful planning and considerable skill. There are many opportunities for things to go wrong, and two or more sources of distortion can have compounding effects, as when a poorly encoded message sent over inadequate channels through an inappropriate network produces disastrous results. Table 14.2 contains suggestions to guide managers along each step of the communication process so that they can reduce the barriers to effective communication.

FIGURE 14.2   Communication Networks

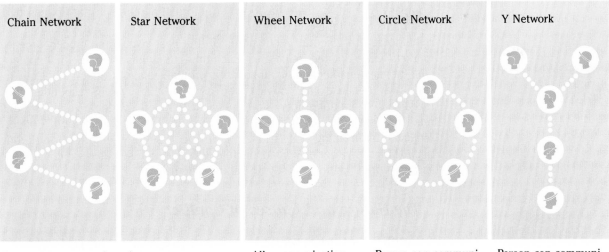

Chain Network	Star Network	Wheel Network	Circle Network	Y Network
Person can communicate directly only with persons one step higher or lower in chain.	Any person can communicate directly with any other person.	All communication must flow through person at hub of wheel.	Person can communicate only with persons adjacent in the circle.	Person can communicate only with persons one step higher or lower in chain; most communication flows through key person.

TABLE 14.2   A Guide for Systematic Communication

1. Establish the intended message and communication objective(s).
2. Establish the communication needs of the message.
3. Appraise the characteristics of the receiver(s).
4. Identify the available communication channels and networks.
5. Identify noise in the environment likely to interfere.
6. Evaluate the adequacy of each channel for the communication needs.
7. Evaluate the adequacy of each network for the communication needs.
8. Select channel(s) and network(s) for use.
9. Reduce noise in the environment if necessary/possible.
10. Encode the message to match the channels, networks, and receivers.
11. Carefully send the message.
12. Obtain feedback (was the message received as intended?).
13. Follow up if necessary with additional communication.
14. Learn from your communication experiences.

Note that Table 14.2 shows a final step in effective communication that takes place after the message has been received. The final step is *learning*. Every communication experience can teach you something. You may learn about new channels or discover additional strengths and weaknesses of various networks. You might learn more about your ability to encode messages or about the characteristics of your receivers. Take advantage of every opportunity for enhancing your communication effectiveness.

Interpersonal Conflict

Colleen Anderson is angry, frustrated, and determined to get back at Craig Gagstetter. Colleen and Craig are sales representatives for the Lepley Calculator Company. For years, there has been an informal agreement that Colleen had sole rights to sell the company's products at grocery stores, and Craig had the rights to sell to discount retail stores. In the past year, three grocery "mega-markets" have opened in the area. Each time, Craig has made the first contact with the megamarket and obtained large, profitable sales. Colleen told Craig to stay away because she "owned" the grocery stores. Craig responded that megamarkets are not grocery stores because they sell a wide range of discount retail products for cars, homes, and recreation in addition to food. Colleen retaliated by invading Craig's Kmart stores because they sell a few food products. Things have gotten so bad that the two sales representatives spend almost as much time fighting as they do selling calculators.

The Nature and Causes of Conflict

Conflict exists when two or more people have incompatible goals, and one or both believe that the behavior of the other prevents their own goal attainment. The presence of incompatible goals alone is not sufficient to produce conflict, however; conflict does not occur until the behavior of one person interferes with the efforts of the other.

In organizations, incompatible goals come about for a variety of reasons. Workers' needs, values, or personalities might clash, as sometimes happens when an intense, aggressive, highly energetic worker is paired with a slower, less aggressive, less intense co-worker. Incompatible goals—for example, between a production department that concentrates on quantity and a quality assurance department that focuses on quality—are often created through job assignments or the structure of an organization. Organizations with limited resources are more likely to experience conflict as their members and departments fight to obtain a share of those resources. A job design or organizational structure that makes individuals or departments interdependent also increases the likelihood of conflict, because the goals of one person or group cannot be reached without the other's cooperation. Neither Colleen nor Craig can sell calculators unless the company's shipping department consistently delivers products on time. The shipping department, in turn, can do little unless the production department provides the goods.

The Conflict Process

Conflict does not suddenly appear in full bloom. It evolves from a series of occurrences (see Figure 14.3).

Stages of Evolution. People may first become aware of the evolution of conflict when they *experience frustration.* This frustration can concern anything of importance: not receiving a promotion, receiving only a small pay raise, or having difficulty accomplishing a work objective. The magnitude of conflict is usually in proportion to the magnitude of the frustration. Colleen was frustrated because Craig's invasion of her territory prevented her from reaching her sales goals and earning bonuses. Frustration, regardless of the cause, can lead to dissatisfaction, anxiety, anger, depression, and aggression.

After experiencing frustration, people try to figure out why the conflict is occurring. Some ask one question: "Why is that person doing this to me?" Others are more analytical, asking such questions as:

1. Why do I feel this frustration?
2. What has that person done to contribute to my frustration?
3. What have I done to contribute to that person's frustration?
4. What would I like to obtain that I am currently being prevented from obtaining?
5. What do I think that person would like to obtain that he or she is currently being prevented from obtaining?
6. How do I expect that person to behave during the remainder of this conflict?
7. How do I plan to behave during the remainder of this conflict?

FIGURE 14.3   The Conflict Process

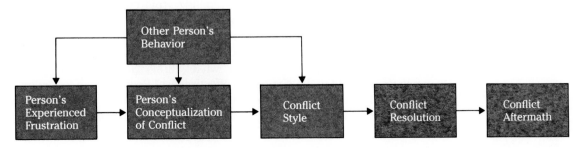

The more systematic managers can be, the better they will conceptualize the nature and meaning of the conflict.

After people have conceptualized a conflict, they can take action to deal with it. The actions they engage in, of course, influence the reactions and behavior of the others involved in the conflict. Conflict behavior can take many forms, depending on the levels of cooperation and assertiveness of those involved. As shown in Figure 14.4, various combinations of cooperativeness and assertiveness create five styles of conflict behavior: competing, collaborating, compromising, avoiding, and accommodating. Although most people have a dominant conflict style, they usually incorporate aspects of the other styles as well. Furthermore, their dominant style may differ from one conflict to another, depending on how they conceptualize the situation.

The *competing* conflict style is an aggressive, often combative, strategy, in which one party tries to overpower the other. If Colleen were to adopt a competing style, she would take whatever steps were necessary to meet her own goals and to prevent Craig from reaching his. The *collaborating* conflict style tries to satisfy all parties' interests, producing what University of Wisconsin management professor Alan Filley has referred to as a "win-win" solution (because both parties get most of what they want.)[3] Colleen and Craig could collaborate if they agreed to figure out why problems have arisen and to develop a mutually acceptable and beneficial solution. The *compromising* style typically leads to a "lose-lose" solution, because both parties have to give up something they value. If Colleen agreed to give Craig one megamarket in exchange for two Kmarts, both would lose something in the compromise. A person who uses an *avoiding* style is uncooperative, unassertive, and attempts to withdraw from conflict, as would be the case if Colleen did not even try to resolve the conflict. Finally, a person with an *accommodating* conflict style tries to satisfy the interests of the other party at his or her own expense, producing a "win-lose" solution (because the other party is given what he or she wants but the accommodator gets nothing in return except resolution of the conflict). If Colleen chose this style, she would say to Craig, "All right, you can sell to megamarkets."

The next segment of the conflict process shown in Figure 14.3 deals with the other person's behavior. After all, there would be no conflict without the presence and behavior of another person. It is Craig's behavior that first caused Colleen to sense frustration. Your perceptions of another person's style substantially influence your own choice of conflict style. You are likely to behave differently, for example, if you perceive the other person to be accommodating than you probably would behave if you perceived him or her to be competing. In conflict situations, it is important to remember that you and the other person simultaneously perceive and react to each other's behavior.

Finally, there is conflict aftermath. Think back to your last big conflict with someone. The fact that you can remember this conflict is proof that things are not the way they were before the conflict. This conflict process leaves an aftermath that costs both the competing parties and their organization. Feelings of satisfaction, motivation, trust, and cohesiveness, for example, are likely to be affected. If Colleen wins the conflict with Craig, and he is prohibited from selling to any of the megamarkets, what will her victory do to their working relationship and to the company's effectiveness? Regardless of the outcome of the conflict, its presence costs the organization time, energy, and money. Clearly, the conflict consumed Colleen's and Craig's time. It cost their company

FIGURE 14.4   *Conflict Behavior Styles*

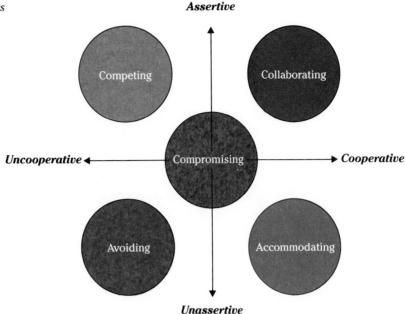

money due to sales lost while they fought. The company also lost some of the effectiveness and productivity of their manager, Dorian Ring, as he spent time trying to referee the dispute.

The aftermath of conflict can also be positive. Conflict resolution often leads to needed organizational change, stronger feelings of cohesion, and greater individual or group maturity. Dorian suggested that Colleen and Craig find a collaborative way to settle their dispute. Eventually they arrived at a win-win solution in which Colleen created and became the manager of a new mail-order division. Craig then acquired Colleen's grocery stores. Colleen finds her new job much more rewarding than her previous job, and Craig is pleased to have the expanded market. By working out the solution together, each gained respect and admiration for the other.

Managing Conflict Effectively.   People's instinctive choices in conflict situations are not necessarily good ones. For this reason and because there is no one best conflict style, managers must carefully conceptualize each conflict situation and react appropriately. A competing style might be called for when quick, decisive action is vital and the other person in the conflict has a history of attacking noncompetitive opponents. An accommodating style might be more fitting when people discover they were wrong, when they know they will lose no matter what, or when future relations with the other person are more important than the outcome of the conflict at hand. Table 14.3 provides further suggestions for situations in which each of the five conflict styles might be appropriate.

In sum, not all conflict must be avoided, but all organizational conflict must be managed. Good managers possess the skills to minimize conflict and to emphasize the benefits of the conflict that does emerge (see "A Closer Look: Conflict Management").

TABLE 14.3   *Appropriate Situations for Conflict Management Styles*

Conflict-Handling Styles	Appropriate Situations
Competing	1. When quick, decisive action is vital—e.g., emergencies 2. On important issues where unpopular actions need implementing—e.g., cost cutting, enforcing unpopular rules, discipline 3. On issues vital to company welfare when you know you are right 4. Against people who take advantage of noncompetitive behavior
Collaborating	1. To find an integrative solution when both sets of concerns are too important to be compromised 2. When your objective is to learn 3. To merge insights from people with different perspectives 4. To gain commitment by incorporating concerns into a consensus 5. To work through feelings that have interfered with a relationship
Compromising	1. When goals are important but not worth the effort or potential disruption of more assertive modes 2. When opponents with equal power are committed to mutually exclusive goals 3. To achieve temporary settlements to complex issues 4. To arrive at expedient solutions under time pressure 5. As a back up when collaboration or competition is unsuccessful
Avoiding	1. When an issue is trivial or more important issues are pressing 2. When you perceive no chance of satisfying your concerns 3. When potential disruption outweighs the benefits of resolution 4. To let people cool down and regain perspective 5. When gathering information supersedes immediate decision 6. When others can resolve the conflict more effectively 7. When issues seem tangential or symptomatic of other issues
Accommodating	1. When you find you are wrong—to allow a better position to be heard, to learn, and to show your reasonableness 2. When issues are more important to others than to you—to satisfy others and maintain cooperation 3. To build social credits for later issues 4. To minimize loss when you are outmatched and losing 5. When harmony and stability are especially important 6. To allow subordinates to develop by learning from mistakes

Source: Based on Table 1 of K. W. Thomas (1977), Toward multidimensional values in teaching: The example of conflict behaviors, *Academy of Management Review*, 2, 487.

Politics

Organizational politics, "the management of influence to obtain ends not sanctioned by the organization or to obtain sanctioned ends through non-sanctioned influence means," surface in every organization as individuals and groups promote their own best interests.[4] Coalitions form, labor and management bargain, and payments are made "on the side." In fact, James March, a noted organization scholar from Carnegie-Mellon University, has suggested that organizations are political coalitions in which decisions are made and goals are formed through the bargaining processes that unfold between individuals and groups.[5] Good managers must recognize the importance of organizational politics and either act to reduce their importance or skillfully play the political game themselves.

Conflict Management: Disagree with Your Boss? Let Your Peers Settle It

"I don't agree with you, but you're the boss." These words have been spoken millions of times to thousands of bosses. In recent years, however, a number of progressive companies have decided that simply being higher in the organizational hierarchy does not necessarily make a boss right. These companies have created a variety of "speak up" and "open door" policies, which typically allow a worker to skip over his or her boss and go directly to a higher-level manager to appeal an action the employee considers unfair or unwise.

For many organizations, such as IBM, speak up and open door programs have worked well. For many others, however, employees have viewed such grievance systems as a waste of time. Convinced that upper-level managers usually support lower-level management decisions, employees have not felt it worthwhile to complain.

Some progressive organizations, such as Federal Express, Digital Equipment, General Electric, and Borg-Warner, have therefore created peer review panels to resolve employ-ees' grievances. According to *The Wall Street Journal,* most peer review panels contain peers of both the aggrieved employee and his or her manager.[1] On a typical panel, however, peers outnumber managers three to two. How do the panels work? A couple of examples follow.

An employee at Control Data Corporation was fired. According to his boss, the employee refused to cooperate in a performance improvement program. According to the employee, however, the "boss's idea of feedback consisted of verbal abuse and threats."[2] The employee appealed to a peer review panel. After taking statements from both parties, the boss was overruled and the employee was reinstated with back pay.

Consider a case at Deseret Generation & Transmission Cooperative of Salt Lake City. When Leesa Story was passed over for a job in a power plant control room, she claimed she was treated unfairly when a man with less experience was given the job. She complained to her boss and then to her boss's boss. They refused to budge. She appealed to the peer board, which reversed the decision of management and awarded her the promotion.

Peer appeal boards are clearly risky business. They threaten to undermine the authority of management, but they also promise to open communication, to create a trusting atmosphere, and to keep managers on their toes. Such boards may also "help deter union organizing and, perhaps most importantly, stem the rising number of costly lawsuits claiming wrongful discharge and discrimination."[3]

Is there a risk that peer boards will give away too much to complaining employees? So far, it does not appear likely. Often peers are tougher on the complainant than even the boss would be. In fact, in the majority of cases to date, peer boards have sided with management.

1. More firms use peer review panel to resolve employees' grievances (3 December 1986), *The Wall Street Journal,* 25.
2. *Ibid.*
3. *Ibid.*

Politics and Interpersonal Behaviors

In early 1989, the Lepley Calculator Company merged with The Electronic Abacus. Both companies manufactured and marketed electronic calculators and had often competed in the same marketplace prior to the merger. After the merger, the companies formed a new management team with members from both companies and created a management council to make significant decisions for the new organization.

On February 15, 1989, the first meeting of the council took place. The primary focus of the meeting was on how best to serve the needs of the new organization. It was very difficult, however, for committee members to forget that they had once been a Lepley or an Abacus employee. Coalitions clearly existed and vested interests endured. Former members of each company seemed intent on demonstrating that their company had been the better of the two and, thus, should play the dominant role in the new organization. Such political issues could not be ignored, but they could not be allowed to supersede the interests of the new organization. Sandy Manly, president of the new company, deemed effective management of the political issues within the council to be essential or the company would suffer significantly.

Organizational politicians often obtain gratification by demonstrating their power. Kent Merrill, former general manager of The Electronic Abacus, had a political decision to make as a member of the management council. He could serve as a rallying person for council members from his former company and attempt to imbue that group with the strongest power base, or he could side with Patrick Penry, former president of Lepley, and attempt to acquire political power by siding with the new regime. His decision was based as much on personal interests as on a consideration of what would be best for the company.

It is widely believed that organizational decisions, such as whom to promote, where to locate a new facility, and how to administer pay, are influenced by political issues.[6] It is also commonly believed that such political considerations damage an organization and its members. Even so, most managers believe that they must be politically effective to succeed.

Living in the Political Environment

What can you do about organizational politics? First, you cannot ignore them. Recognize that individuals and groups are interested in the acquisition of power and probably will use this power to serve their own interests. Be aware of the fact that decision making is often based not only on the merits of an issue but also on the political consequences. Does the accounting department, for example, want to hire additional workers to help the organization function effectively or to build power for the accounting department? Be sensitive to the political concerns and interests of various individuals and groups as you evaluate the probable effects of alternative decisions. In short, learn about the political realities of your organization and anticipate their effects.

A second tactic used by some is to take advantage of organizational politics. Supporting a politically powerful organization member can yield payoffs. If pay raises and promotions are influenced by people's political stance, learning the "party line" and behaving accordingly probably will increase wages and enhance employees' positions. Combining forces with other individuals or groups to build a political power base that dominates less powerful interests can also be effective.

Third, if you decide to play the political game, be aware of the possible ramifications. You cannot gain political advantage without expending energy that could be used for other purposes, such as increased performance. Furthermore, reliance on political support can be costly if the view you espouse falls from power. If your favored status in an organization is heavily influenced by affiliation with a strong political leader, for example, what happens to you when that leader is replaced by an opponent? You undoubtedly will lose whatever political benefits you were enjoying. When you must stand on your capabilities rather than on your politics, you may also find that the energy you devoted to the political cause may have prevented you from being an effective, competitive organization member.

Rather than play the political game, you might wish to reduce the role of politics in your own life. Avoid using power solely as a show of force. Use it for organizational purposes when you need to, but do not flaunt it. Unfortunately, others may feel your behavior is politically motivated even if it is not. Take care to explain the reasons for your actions and be sensitive to the political concerns and awareness of others. Encourage open decision making and problem solving, because decisions made behind closed doors are often politically suspect.

A fourth alternative is to try to reduce the role of politics in an organization as a whole and to diffuse responsibility throughout the organization rather than center it in the hands of a favored few. This atmosphere makes the development of strong political coalitions less likely. Where political power does exist, try to channel it toward the accomplishment of organizational goals rather than toward special-interest objectives.

As a member of an organization, you must decide whether to use or to diffuse political power. You should realize, however, that failure to recognize and deal with the political realities of organizational life will decrease your effectiveness, be it as employee or manager.

Interpersonal Factors in Organizations in Review

Interpersonal factors affect a manager's ability to direct the behavior of organization members. These factors include interpersonal power, communication, interpersonal conflict, and politics.

Every member of an organization can accumulate legitimate, reward, coercive, expert, resource, and referent power. Some of these sources can be formally created by an organization, but others must be nurtured by individuals. Regardless of the source of power, a person has power only to the extent that others believe it to be true. To develop an appropriate power base, managers must carefully coordinate the sources of power. Some combinations of sources can produce very strong power; others are self-defeating.

Communication is an intricate but critical organizational process. The communication process includes the formulation of an intended message, the encoding of that message, the transmission of the message through channels and networks, and the decoding of the message by receivers. Distortion can occur at each step of the process. Managers must be very careful to match their communication choices to each situation for their message to be received and interpreted as intended.

Conflict is a situation in which two or more people have incompatible goals, and one or both believe the other will prevent their own goal attainment. A person going through the conflict process first experiences frustration, then tries to conceptualize or understand what is happening, reacts to his or her perceptions and to the behavior of others involved, and lives with the aftermath.

In reacting to conflict, people choose one or a combination of styles: competing (trying to win at all costs), collaborating (trying to see that both parties win), compromising (finding a solution in which both parties renounce something), avoiding (withdrawing from the conflict altogether), and accommodating (acceding to the other party's wishes so that the conflict will end). Most people have a dominant conflict management style that can—and usually should—be altered according to their opponent's behavior and the degree of interdependence between them. The most effective managers are aware of the conflict styles available to them, and they select those styles that are appropriate for a given conflict situation.

Finally, much behavior in organizations is influenced by political considerations, so an awareness of these issues is essential. Each person must decide how to respond to political pressures. Some available choices include learning to play the political game, avoiding politics as much as possible, and trying to diffuse the importance of politics in a specific organization.

Issues for Review and Discussion

1. Identify the major sources of organizational power and discuss how they can work with or against one another.
2. Describe the major steps of the communication process.
3. What steps can a manager take to guide organizational communication systematically?
4. Describe the stages in the evolution of conflict.
5. Identify the five major styles of conflict management.
6. How can you capitalize on politics in organizations?
7. How can you reduce the impact of organizational politics?

Key Terms

interpersonal power	referent power
legitimate power	communication
reward power	communication networks
formal rewards	vertical communication
informal rewards	horizontal communication
coercive power	diagonal communication
expert power	conflict
resource power	organizational politics

Suggested Readings

Blanchard, K., and Johnson, S. (1981). *The one minute manager.* LaJolla, CA: Blanchard-Johnson. For a review of this book, see Manz, C. C. (1988). In Pierce, J. L., and Newstrom, J. W., eds. *The manager's bookshelf: A mosaic of contemporary views.* New York: Harper & Row, 104-9.

Cavanagh, G. F., Moberg, D. J., and Velasquez, M. (1981). The ethics of organizational politics. *Academy of Management Review,* 6, 363-74.

Davis, K. (1969). Grapevine communication among lower and middle managers. *Personnel Journal,* 48, 269-72.

Filley, A. C. (1975). *Interpersonal conflict resolution.* Glenview, IL: Scott, Foresman.

French, J. R. P., Jr., and Raven, B. H. (1959). The bases of social power. In Cartwright, D., ed. *Studies in social power.* Ann Arbor, MI: University of Michigan Press.

Gandz, J., and Murray, V. (1980). The experience of workplace politics. *Academy of Management Journal,* 23, 237-51.

Murray, V., and Gandz, J. (December 1980). Politics at work. *Business Horizons,* 11-23.

Smith, H. (1987). *The power game.* New York: Random House.

Notes

1. J. R. P. French, Jr., and B. H. Raven (1959), The bases of social power, in D. Cartwright, ed., *Studies in social power,* Ann Arbor, MI: University of Michigan Press; D. Mechanic (1964), Sources of power of lower participants in complex organizations, in W. W. Cooper, H. J. Leavitt, and M. W. Shelly II, eds., *New perspectives in organizational research,* New York: John Wiley, 136-47; G. R. Salancik and J. Pfeffer (1983), Who gets power—and how they hold onto it: A strategic-contingency model of power, in R. W. Allen and L. W. Porter, eds., *Organizational influence processes,* Glenview, IL: Scott, Foresman, 52-71.

2. K. Davis (1969), Grapevine communication among lower and middle managers, *Personnel Journal,* 48, 269-72.

3. A. C. Filley (1975), *Interpersonal conflict resolution,* Glenview, IL: Scott, Foresman.

4. B. T. Mayes and R. W. Allen (1977), Toward a definition of organizational politics, *Academy of Management Review,* 2, 672-78.

5. J. G. March (1962), The business firm as a political coalition, *Journal of Politics,* 24, 662-78.

6. J. Gandz and V. Murray (1980), The experience of workplace politics, *Academy of Management Journal,* 23, 237-51.

The Open Door

By Mabry Miller and Thomas Pursel, Drake University

The U.S. Navy has an airborne weapons evaluation facility located on an Air Force base in New Mexico. The primary mission of the command is to test weapons used with various types of aircraft deployed throughout the fleet. As a secondary mission, it provides personnel administration services for Naval personnel assigned to inter-service commands in the vicinity and to many retired naval personnel located in central New Mexico. At the time of the incidents related here, the organizational structure for the facility was as shown in Figure 14A.

Background

The technical requirements of the primary mission were accomplished in the nuclear engineering, special applications, and surface applications departments. The other departments fulfilled a supporting role. The secondary missions were coordinated by the administrative support department (ASD). For example, the command might be called on to provide color guards, escorts, and pallbearers for military funerals or to provide units to participate in civic events, such as parades. The military personnel who

actually took part in these events were, of necessity, provided by the aircraft maintenance department. These events tended to occur on weekends, holidays, and other times that would normally be off-duty hours.

All departments formally reported through the executive officer. Navy regulations also provided that department heads had direct access to the commanding officer for matters related to the mission of their departments. In reality, however, the nuclear engineering, special applications, and surface applications

FIGURE 14A

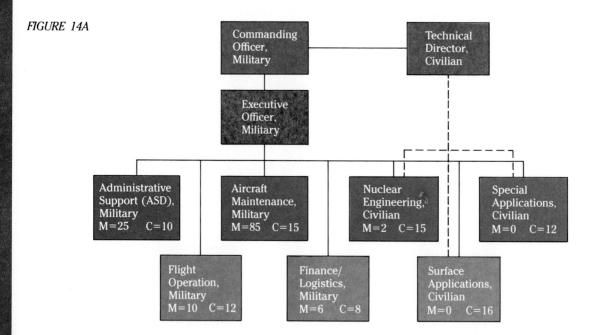

Note: The terms *Military* and *Civilian* within each block denote the status of the department head. *M* indicates the number of military personnel assigned to the department, and *C* indicates the number of civilian personnel.

department heads dealt almost exclusively with the technical director, who had complete—or nearly complete—autonomy, depending on the incumbent commanding officer's management style. The technical director and the three technical department heads were all senior civilian employees, as were most of their assigned engineers and analysts. All were long-term employees with an average of fifteen years' service at the facility. In contrast, military personnel were usually assigned for only two-year tours of duty.

As indicated in the organizational chart, the personnel mixture of the facility was approximately 50 percent military and 50 percent civilian. Most of the military personnel were assigned to the ASD and aircraft maintenance. With the exception of pilots, who were assigned to management positions, all of the personnel in the ASD held nonaviation ratings. In contrast, all personnel in the aircraft maintenance department were in positions that required aviation ratings.

The facility occupied space in two widely separated locations. The commanding officer, executive officer, technical director, and three departments—flight operations, finance/logistics, and aircraft maintenance—were located in the main hangar. All other departments were located in an area requiring a lower security clearance. The nuclear engineering, special applications, and surface applications departments needed to be accessible to visitors. The ASD also

needed to be accessible because it was responsible for servicing the needs of Navy personnel assigned to other commands in the area and the needs of retired naval personnel living in the area.

This separation prevented the incidental interactions normally associated with cohesive military or civilian units. A particular source of resentment was the assignment of personnel from the aircraft maintenance department to funerals, parades, and other ceremonial functions by the ASD. These personnel blamed the ASD for ruining their weekends and holidays.

Captain Rahl

Captain Rahl had been recently assigned as the new commanding officer. Having previously served a two-year tour at the base as a department head, he was aware of the latitude normally granted to both civilian and military department heads by previous commanding officers. Captain Rahl, however, insisted that he should be involved in every detail. In addition, he wanted to be thought of as being completely accessible to every member of the facility on any matter. To accomplish this, he instituted an "open door" policy, whereby he was accessible to anyone on the same day they requested to speak to him.

Shortly after Captain Rahl established his open door policy, Petty Officer Jones of the aircraft mainte-

nance department asked to speak to the captain. Captain Rahl then advised Commander Smith, who was head of Jones' department, that Jones had scheduled an interview; however, he did not invite Smith to be present, nor did he discuss the interview with Smith afterwards. After this, Jones often spoke privately with Captain Rahl without Smith being advised either by Jones or Rahl that the conversations were taking place.

When it was seen that Captain Rahl really honored his open door policy, the members of other departments, from the lowest-ranking sailor to the most senior petty officer and civilian employees, took advantage of the opportunity for personal discussions with the commanding officer.

Not long after his conversations with Petty Officer Jones, Captain Rahl called Commander Smith into his office and said, "I understand that favoritism is being shown in the assignment of personnel for special functions on weekends and holidays. Morale in your department is not what it should be because some of your people are being treated unfairly. Straighten this out or I'll have to make note of it on your fitness report [performance evaluation]." Smith sought in vain to learn the source of the Captain's information, to obtain specific details, and to refute the accusation. He was simply advised to "Shape up your ship."

As the Captain's open door policy gained momentum, no department head, civilian or military, was immune from "Rahl's Rockets." Even though formal grievance procedures were readily accessible, the Captain's open door became the accepted channel for the resolution of perceived problems within the command.

This had a dramatic effect on the department heads. Commander Green of the ASD, who felt her department had been particularly victimized, made this private assessment:

It would be bad enough if problems that I can easily handle were taken to the commanding officer merely to speed up routine actions, but it appears that some people are trying to earn credit with the 'old man' or to embarrass someone who is totally unaware that a problem exists. The results are devastating. Personnel in the departments affected have withdrawn from all but the most essential contacts with the rest of the facility. Inaction is deemed to be safer than an unpopular action which can be misinterpreted. As a consequence, productivity and morale are both suffering. Requests for early reassignment have been received from practically all military personnel in the ASD and not a single person has reenlisted upon completion of obligated service. This includes many who have many years of service.

The same results occurred with civilian personnel in the ASD and in the nuclear engineering, special applications, and surface applications departments. Many sought new positions in other activities or simply resigned. The technical director and two of the three technical department heads resigned during Captain Rahl's tour of duty.

Questions

1. What barriers to effective communication are present in the situation described in this case?
2. Discuss the motives that led Captain Rahl to establish his open door policy.
3. Has the open door policy helped or hindered the flow of effective communication in this organization? Why?
4. What alternative to the open door policy could Captain Rahl have used to get good information about department performance?
5. What would you recommend to Captain Rahl?

15 Leadership

Student Learning Objectives

After reading this chapter, you should be able to:

1. Understand the nature of leadership and the leadership process.

2. Explain and describe the trait perspective on leadership.

3. Explain the relationship between power and various forms of leadership.

4. Distinguish between Theory X and Theory Y leader attitudes.

5. Understand the behavioral perspective on leadership.

6. Discuss how situational theories of leadership can help managers.

7. Describe what is meant by charismatic leadership.

*S*uzie Pendergast is the manager of a district claims office for a large insurance company. Fourteen people work for her. The results of a recent attitude survey indicated that, as a group, these fourteen people have extremely high job satisfaction and motivation. Conflict is rare in Suzie's office. Furthermore, productivity ratings indicate that her group of employees is among the most productive of all claims groups in the entire company. After reviewing these facts, the company's vice-president of human resources visited the claims office in an attempt to discover the secret to her success as a manager. Suzie Pendergast's peers, superiors, and subordinates all gave the same answer: she is an outstanding leader.

The perfect answer to the question "What makes a leader effective?" has not been—and probably never will be—found. Nevertheless, because leadership is considered so critical to organizational effectiveness, managers and researchers have devoted enormous amounts of time, effort, and money pursuing this issue. Their massive joint efforts have identified several perspectives, and this chapter reviews the most useful of these.

The Nature of Leadership

There are many definitions of leadership. Most people agree that **leadership** is an interpersonal process involving the exercise of influence within a social system, such as a group, family, community, or work organization. In work organizations, effective leadership influences individuals and/or groups to achieve organizational goals.

The Leadership Process

As shown in Figure 15.1, the leadership process is a complex, dynamic, and interactive exchange in which leaders influence followers, followers influence leaders, and all are influenced by the context in which the exchange takes place. The by-products of any leader-follower exchange can influence future interactions. A *leader,* as defined by Webster's dictionary, is a person who takes charge of or guides a performance or activity. A *follower* is a person who performs under the guidance and instructions of a leader. The *context* is the situation—formal, informal, social, military, emergency, routine, and so on— surrounding a leader-follower relationship. The nature of the leadership process varies substantially with the context in which it occurs. For example, the context for the leader of a recreational softball team is very different from that of a military commander on a battlefield, and leadership tactics that work in the former context might fail miserably in the latter. The *by-products* of leadership are many and varied—for example, animosity produced by a punitive leader's actions and respect for an able leader's decisions; they can also influence future interactions.

Leaders

Leaders hold a unique position in their group by exercising influence and providing direction. As a symphony director, for example, Leonard Bernstein is a part of the symphony. His role, however, is distinctly different from that of the

FIGURE 15.1   The Leadership Process

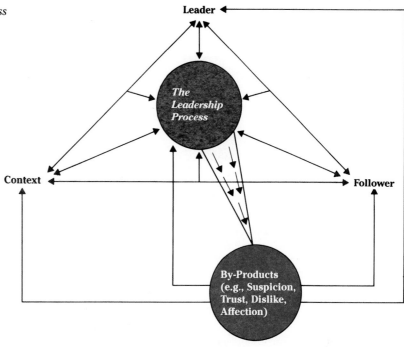

Leaders provide direction, as does Leonard Bernstein in his role as symphony director.

other symphony members. He is responsible for coordinating the sounds and tempo for the musicians. In this capacity, his identity in the group is unique.

Two kinds of leaders can usually be identified in organizations: formal and informal. A **formal,** or **designated, leader** is an individual appointed *by the organization* to serve in a formal capacity as its agent. Suzie Pendergast is the formal leader of the claims office, and Leonard Bernstein is the formal leader of the symphony. As you learned in Chapter 1, practically every manager is called on to act as a formal leader as part of his or her interpersonal role.

An **informal leader,** in contrast, frequently emerges as the group's natural leader. Athletic teams often have informal leaders who exert considerable influence on team members, even though they hold no official (formal) leadership positions. In fact, most organizational work groups contain at least one informal leader. Informal leaders can benefit or harm an organization, depending on whether their influence encourages group members to behave consistently with organizational goals.

The terms *leader* and *manager* are not synonymous. Informal leaders, for example, often have considerable leverage over their colleagues but are not designated as managers by the organization. Even formal leaders do not exercise all of the managerial functions of planning, organizing, directing, and controlling if they are not managers. Leaders who are also managers find that leadership falls under the directing function.

Power and Leadership Styles

Because leadership includes influencing others, power is an essential ingredient for effective leadership. So important is power to the exercise of effective leadership that many leaders (and writers about management) treat leadership as little more than the development and application of interpersonal power. Consider the ways in which the use of power is reflected in leadership styles.

FIGURE 15.2   Tannenbaum and Schmidt's Leadership Continuum

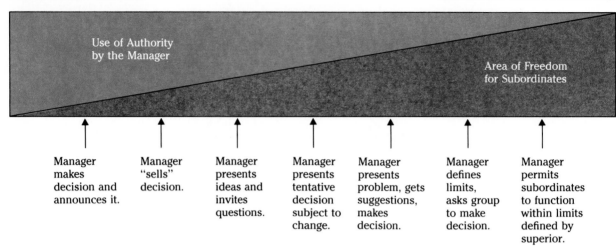

Boss-Centered Leadership   **Subordinate-Centered Leadership**

Use of Authority by the Manager

Area of Freedom for Subordinates

| Manager makes decision and announces it. | Manager "sells" decision. | Manager presents ideas and invites questions. | Manager presents tentative decision subject to change. | Manager presents problem, gets suggestions, makes decision. | Manager defines limits, asks group to make decision. | Manager permits subordinates to function within limits defined by superior. |

Source: Modified from R. Tannenbaum and W. H. Schmidt (May-June 1973), How to choose a leadership pattern, *Harvard Business Review*, 167.

The Tannenbaum and Schmidt Continuum.   While at the University of Michigan in the late 1950s, Robert Tannenbaum and Warren Schmidt developed a continuum depicting different degrees of power and influence exercised by a manager in a leadership position (see Figure 15.2).[1] At one extreme is the boss-centered leader who makes decisions and announces them. At the other extreme is the subordinate-centered leader who engages in participative leadership, with the leader and group acting as a single social unit. At the center of the continuum is a leader whose consultative decision-making style encourages both the leader and subordinates to assume joint responsibility for decision making.

Autocratic, Participative, and Free-Rein Power Styles.   Another way to categorize leaders and the way they use power is through the autocratic, participative, and free-rein styles described by management professors Keith Davis from Arizona State University and John W. Newstrom from the University of Minnesota-Duluth (see Figure 15.3).[2] Davis and Newstrom's autocratic leader corresponds to Tannenbaum and Schmidt's boss-centered leader, and their participative leader is consistent with Tannenbaum and Schmidt's subordinate-centered leader. A third extreme, the *free-rein (laissez-faire) leader,* avoids power and responsibility. Free-rein leaders tend to give assignments to work groups and offer support as needed but otherwise leave the groups alone. Under this "hands-off" form of leadership, subordinates assume operating authority, define their own work goals and procedures, and resolve performance-related problems as they occur.

Directive/Permissive Leadership Styles.   According to Jan P. Muczyk and Bernard C. Reimann of Cleveland State University, a contemporary approach to leadership and the exercise of power should distinguish between *making* decisions and *executing* them.[3] Their perspective builds on variations in decision making and execution and results in four types of leadership styles:

FIGURE 15.3   *Leader Style and Distribution of Power*

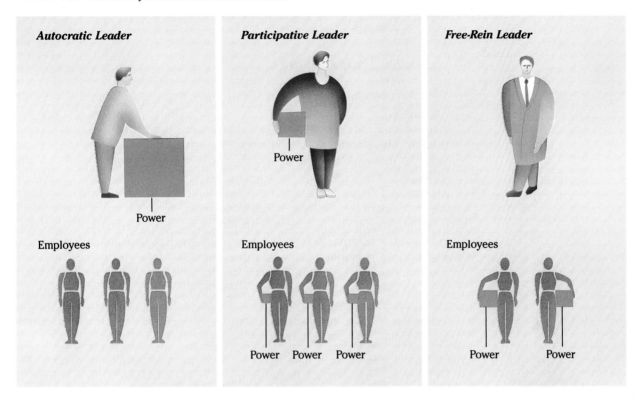

directive autocrat, permissive autocrat, directive democrat, and permissive democrat.

A *directive autocrat* retains power, makes unilateral decisions, and directs the activities of subordinates with close supervision. A *permissive autocrat* retains decision-making power but permits subordinates some discretion in executing those decisions, as would be the case if software manager Patty Stark were to tell programmer Mark Weber, "I have decided that this program should offer the option of keyboard, mouse, or joystick input. Please write the code to accomplish this." A *directive democrat* shares power through participative decision making but retains the power to direct employees in the execution of their roles. Surgeon Kimberly Workman, for example, allows her surgical team to help develop a plan for a surgical procedure, but Kimberly is in charge once the actual surgery has begun. Finally, a *permissive democrat* shares power with group members, soliciting involvement in both decision making and execution. Patty Stark would have been acting as a permissive democrat if she had asked Mark Weber to help choose the input devices to be supported by her computer program.

Trait Approaches to Leadership

One of the oldest approaches to the study of leadership is known as the **trait approach.** Those who follow a trait approach attempt to identify physical, psychological, attitudinal, and/or ability traits associated with effective leaders.

Proponents of this approach believe that certain people are "born leaders," and organizations should, therefore, select leaders who possess the appropriate physical and intellectual characteristics.

Leader Trait Research

In the late nineteenth century, researchers began a serious search for the specific traits that characterized "the great person." The **great person approach** to leadership states that some people—for example, Julius Caesar, Joan of Arc, Napoleon, Mahatma Gandhi—are born with a set of personal qualities that enables them to become effective leaders. During the 1930s and 1940s, trait theorists made numerous attempts to identify the traits that made certain leaders great, hoping that organizations could use this information to select the right people for key leadership positions.

Ralph Stogdill was a pioneer of the modern study of leadership.[4] In his early research, he studied physical characteristics (such as appearance, height, and weight), demographic characteristics (such as age, education, and socioeconomic background), personality characteristics (such as dominance, self-confidence, and aggressiveness), intellective factors (such as intelligence, decisiveness, judgment, and knowledge), task-related characteristics (such as achievement drive, initiative, and persistence), and social characteristics (such as sociability and cooperativeness). Stogdill observed that:

> *The average person who occupies a position of leadership exceeds the average member of his or her group in . . . (1) intelligence, (2) scholarship, (3) dependability in exercising responsibilities, (4) activity and social participation, and (5) socioeconomic status.[5]*

Although some traits were found to differentiate leaders from nonleaders, many of the effects attributed to certain leader traits were quite small and of limited practical value. Furthermore, even though certain traits may increase the likelihood that a leader will be effective, they do not guarantee effectiveness. It is the demands of the situation that in large part determine the qualities, characteristics, and skills most important for a leader to be effective. For these reasons, the notion that leaders are born, not made, has largely been put to rest.

Theory X and Theory Y

During the 1950s, Douglas McGregor presented a unique view on leadership that quickly became very popular among managers.[6] McGregor's work resembled that of earlier trait theorists in that he argued that effective leaders had certain identifiable characteristics. Unlike the earlier trait theorists, however, McGregor focused on the attitude and belief structures of leaders. He felt that most leaders adopted one of two basic attitude and belief structures about employees, which, in turn, influenced how they fulfilled their leadership role (see Table 15.1 on page 354).

As you learned in Chapter 4, a leader who subscribes to Theory X assumes that the average individual dislikes work and is incapable of exercising adequate self-direction and self-control; thus, a Theory X leader is likely to engage

Leadership: The Leader of Tomorrow—What Is She Like?

If you look at research on leadership from the first third of this century, you will find a profile of the person thought most likely to be an effective leader. The leader should stand six feet tall, weigh around 175 pounds, have well-conditioned (but not bulky) muscles, and be "ruggedly handsome" and well groomed. The research did not usually say so outright—it was simply *assumed*—the ideal leader was a man.

Even today, many people assume that men can lead and women cannot. "Mention women in management and the instant association in the minds of many men (and women) is: Women have babies . . . . [W]omen can't be counted on to make a full-time, open-ended commitment to their careers."[1] Such beliefs are strongly rooted in age-old stereotypes that resist change even in the face of contradictory evidence: the thousands of women who manage effectively every day.

Felice N. Schwartz is the president of Catalyst, an organization that helps organizations further the careers of women. As she says, "A significant number of working women are determined to reach the top of their field. Many of the most gifted and able leaders of the future will be women to whom career is primary, women who are ready to make the same trade-offs that male leaders traditionally have made. Companies that do not spot and groom these women are shortsighted."[2]

Schwartz notes that there has always been a shortage of individuals able to become effective leaders. She predicts that this shortage will worsen as the United States economy shifts further into service industries, where leadership is critical, and as many of the young people entering the workforce increase their interests in nonwork activities. "Within a few years, as the effects of an aging baby boom are felt, the [leadership] talent of women will become indispensable. Companies that start now to develop the leadership potential of women will have a competitive edge."[3]

The challenge of identifying and developing effective leaders is not an easy one, and finding female leaders is particularly challenging for the traditional male CEO. "The very qualities that bespeak motivation—determination, drive, aggressiveness, single-mindedness—still tend to provoke discomfort and uncertainty . . . ."[4] Employers who are smart enough to identify and develop women as managers will soon benefit by obtaining " . . . the difference between getting employees who simply put in their hours and those who perform with enthusiasm and effectiveness."[5] They will capture the best people available for leadership positions; generate important female role models for the next generation of female leaders; provide motivating evidence that anyone can advance in the organization; and create a healthier, more socially responsible environment.

1. Don't write women off as leaders (8 June 1987), *Fortune*, 185.
2. *Ibid.*
3. *Ibid.*
4. *Ibid.*
5. *Fortune*, 188.

in a highly controlling leadership style, treating each employee as a cog in the machinery of the organization. Such managers concentrate on the ability of people to *do*. Theory Y leaders, in contrast, believe in the ability of people to *think* and to exercise self-direction and self-control. They typically allow employees to exercise significant amounts of discretion in their jobs and to participate in departmental and organizational decision making. Suzie Pendergast, the district claims manager, is a Theory Y leader. She permits her employees to accept or reject claims, schedule work and vacation time, and handle departmental grievances. Suzie's philosophy is that her employees are creative, resourceful, and responsible; therefore, she does not have to make these intradepartmental decisions on their behalf.

TABLE 15.1   *Theory X and Theory Y Assumptions*

Theory X

1. The average human being has an inherent dislike of work and will avoid it if possible.
2. Because of their dislike of work, most people must be coerced, controlled, directed, or threatened with punishment to get them to put forth adequate effort toward the achievement of organizational objectives.
3. The average human being prefers to be directed, wishes to avoid responsibility, has relatively little ambition, and wants security above all.

Theory Y

1. The expenditure of physical and mental effort in work is as natural as play or rest.
2. External control and the threat of punishment are not the only means for bringing about effort toward organizational objectives. Workers will exercise self-direction and self-control in the service of objectives to which they are committed.
3. Commitment to objectives is a function of the rewards associated with their achievement.
4. The average human being learns, under proper conditions, not only to accept but to seek responsibility.
5. The capacity to exercise a relatively high degree of imagination, ingenuity, and creativity in the solution of organizational problems is widely, not narrowly, distributed in the population.
6. Under the conditions of modern industrial life, the intellectual potentialities of the average human being are only partially utilized.

Source: D. McGregor (1960), *The human side of enterprise,* New York: McGraw-Hill, 33-34, 47-48.

Behavioral Approaches to Leadership

During the late 1940s, those interested in understanding leadership began to wonder if effective leadership was a function of the way a leader behaved rather than the result of inborn traits. Two major research programs were launched to explore this possibility.

The Ohio State University Studies

During the late 1940s, a group of Ohio State University researchers, under the direction of Ralph Stogdill, began an extensive and systematic set of studies that attempted to identify leader behaviors associated with effective group performance. The data they collected led to the identification of two major sets of leader behaviors: consideration and initiating structure.

Consideration is the "relationship-oriented" behavior of a leader. It is instrumental in creating and maintaining good relationships with subordinates. Consideration behaviors include being supportive and friendly, representing subordinates' interests, communicating openly with subordinates, recognizing subordinates, respecting their ideas, and sharing concern for their feelings.

Suzie Pendergast, for example, often behaves considerately toward the members of her department. When the corporate office told her that three new counties were to be added to her geographic region and two new claims

Ralph Stogdill helped identify leader behaviors associated with effective group performance.

personnel were to be assigned to her office, she realized this would require at least some reassignment for everyone in her district. As soon as Suzie heard the news, she called a meeting of everyone in her office. She explained what was going to happen, acknowledged that the transition would be rough, and encouraged people to discuss their concerns.

Initiating structure involves "task-oriented" leader behaviors. It is instrumental in the efficient use of resources to attain organizational goals. Initiating structure behaviors include scheduling work, deciding what is to be done (and how and when to do it), providing direction to subordinates, planning, coordinating, problem solving, maintaining standards of performance, and encouraging the use of uniform procedures. When a new computer system was installed, Suzie Pendergast provided initiating structure for members of her department:

> *As you all know, I have been trained by our corporate management information systems department on the new computer system. I would like to take this opportunity to explain the new system. On April 21, a computer terminal will be installed on each desk. You will use the system to record the information that you would normally enter by hand on the old form 23A. To sign on to the computer, simply press the key labeled 'alert' and then enter your employee ID when asked to do so by the computer. You are to use the computer for all noninjury settlements. Continue to use the old method for injury settlements. . . .*

After the importance of consideration and initiating structure behaviors were first identified, many leaders believed that they had to behave one way or the other. If they initiated structure, they could not be considerate, and vice versa. It did not take long, however, to recognize that any combination of these two behaviors was possible.

Although the Ohio State studies were important because they identified two critical categories of behavior that distinguish one leader from another, the effects of consideration and initiating structure are not consistent from situation to situation.[7] In some of the organizations studied, for example, high levels of initiating structure increased performance. In other organizations, the amount of initiating structure seemed to make little difference. Although most subordinates reported greater satisfaction when leaders acted considerately, consideration behavior appeared to increase performance in some studies but had no clear effect in others.

Initially, these mixed findings were disappointing to researchers and managers alike. It had been hoped that a profile of the most effective leader behaviors could be identified so that leaders could be trained how to behave. Research made clear, however, that there was no one best style of leader behavior for all situations.

The University of Michigan Studies

At about the same time that the Ohio State studies were under way, researchers at the University of Michigan also began to investigate leader behaviors. As at Ohio State, the Michigan researchers attempted to identify behavioral elements that differentiated effective from ineffective leaders.[8]

The two types of leader behavior that stood out in these studies were job-centered and employee-centered. **Job-centered behaviors** were devoted to

Job-centered behaviors are devoted to planning, scheduling, and coordinating work activities.

supervisory functions, such as planning, scheduling, coordinating work activities, and providing the resources needed for task performance. **Employee-centered behaviors** included consideration and support for subordinates. These dimensions of behavior, of course, correspond closely to the dimensions of initiating structure and consideration identified at Ohio State. The similarity of the findings from two independent groups of researchers added to their credibility.

Subsequent research at Michigan identified two additional behaviors associated with effective leadership. First, effective leaders were found to adopt an active leadership role by setting goals and basic guidelines for subordinates while still allowing subordinates to decide how their job was to be done and how to pace themselves. For example, as you saw, Suzie Pendergast provided her employees with company guidelines on processing claims and let them handle all aspects of the process, as long as they met departmental goals and followed organizational guidelines. Second, effective leaders were found to exert influence upward to obtain resources and the support needed for their subordinates. As it turns out, this was something Suzie Pendergast also did quite well. When she discovered, for example, that her employees were uncomfortable about using a new computer system, she convinced her boss to allow each member of her department to spend a day at corporate headquarters learning how to use it.

The studies at Michigan were important because they reinforced the importance of leaders' behaviors. They also provided the basis for later theories that identified specific, effective matches of work situations and leader behaviors.

System 4 Leadership

Influenced heavily by the work of his University of Michigan colleagues, Rensis Likert identified the *System 4* approach to organizational design (see Chapter 11).[9] Figure 15.4 summarizes the leadership model Likert identified as a part of this approach. According to Likert, a System 4 leader should provide:

- *Supportive behavior.* This includes understanding employees, providing recognition, keeping subordinates informed, and showing appreciation. Suzie Pendergast, for example, was behaving in a supportive fashion when she took the time to give her followers advance notice of the impending changes and when she offered to help them cope with the new arrangements.

- *Group methods of supervision.* Likert suggested that effective leadership is group oriented, rather than based on one-on-one relationships. When Suzie called her meeting to inform subordinates of the new territorial and staff assignments, she was capitalizing on the effectiveness of the group method.

- *High performance goals.* For effective group performance, a leader should guide the group toward setting high (although realistic), specific performance goals.

- *Linking pin functions.* As discussed in Chapter 11, managers collect, dispense, and coordinate information and influence among organizational units to enhance communication, cohesiveness, and organizational decision making. Suzie fills this role in part by attending a weekly meeting of all managers at her district claims office, at which she shares information

FIGURE 15.4 Likert's
Leadership Process Model

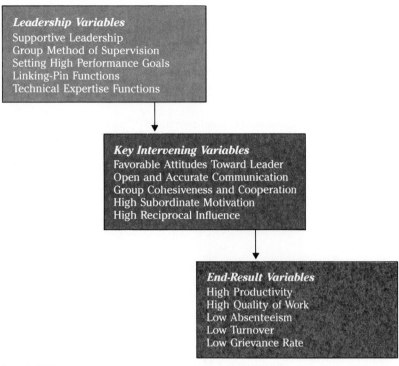

Leadership Variables
Supportive Leadership
Group Method of Supervision
Setting High Performance Goals
Linking-Pin Functions
Technical Expertise Functions

Key Intervening Variables
Favorable Attitudes Toward Leader
Open and Accurate Communication
Group Cohesiveness and Cooperation
High Subordinate Motivation
High Reciprocal Influence

End-Result Variables
High Productivity
High Quality of Work
Low Absenteeism
Low Turnover
Low Grievance Rate

From Garl Yukl, *Leadership in Organizations,* © 1981, p. 117. Reprinted by permission of Prentice-Hall, Inc., Englewood Cliffs, New Jersey.

on the claims department with other managers and negotiates the resources her department needs.

- *Technical expertise functions.* The leader serves as a source of expert knowledge for subordinates, thereby making their work more effective. Suzie's employees know that they can rely on her for the latest information from trade journals and monthly update sessions on company claims practices.

As illustrated in Figure 15.4, these five leadership behaviors should produce favorable attitudes toward leadership, open channels of communication, create group cohesiveness and cooperation, motivate employees, and ensure a high level of reciprocal influence between leaders and subordinates. These, in turn, should enhance organizational and group effectiveness (high productivity—both in quantity and quality—and low rates of absenteeism, turnover, and grievance).

The Managerial Grid®

Much of the credit for spreading knowledge about important leader behaviors to managers must go to Robert R. Blake and Jane S. Mouton, who developed a method of classifying styles of leadership compatible with many of the ideas from the Ohio State and Michigan studies.[10] In their classification scheme, *concern for production* involves an emphasis on output, cost effectiveness, and (in for-profit organizations) profits. *Concern for people* involves promoting friendships, helping subordinates with work, and paying attention to

FIGURE 15.5 Blake and Mouton's Managerial Grid®

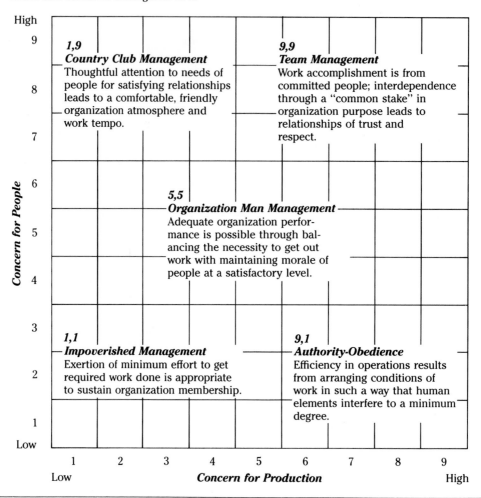

Concern for People — High 9, 8, 7, 6, 5, 4, 3, 2, 1, Low

1,9
Country Club Management
Thoughtful attention to needs of people for satisfying relationships leads to a comfortable, friendly organization atmosphere and work tempo.

9,9
Team Management
Work accomplishment is from committed people; interdependence through a "common stake" in organization purpose leads to relationships of trust and respect.

5,5
Organization Man Management
Adequate organization performance is possible through balancing the necessity to get out work with maintaining morale of people at a satisfactory level.

1,1
Impoverished Management
Exertion of minimum effort to get required work done is appropriate to sustain organization membership.

9,1
Authority-Obedience
Efficiency in operations results from arranging conditions of work in such a way that human elements interfere to a minimum degree.

Low 1 2 3 4 5 6 7 8 9 High
Concern for Production

issues of importance to employees. As their Managerial Grid® shows, any combination of these two leader behaviors is possible (see Figure 15.5). The combinations produce five styles of leadership: (1) *country club* (concern for people but little time and energy devoted to production), (2) *impoverished* (low concern for both people and production), (3) *organization person management* (moderate concern for both people and production), (4) *authority-obedience* (low concern for people but a strong production orientation), and (5) *team* (strong regard for employees and a strong production orientation).

Blake and Mouton contend that the team leader (9,9) style is universally the most effective. Furthermore, they claim that experienced managers prefer the team style of leadership in many types of situations.[11] The fact that the 9,9 style may be preferred, however, does not mean that it is necessarily effective. Evidence suggests that there is no universally effective style of leadership (9,9 or otherwise).[12]

Situational Approaches to Leadership

Geoff Priest was a drill instructor (DI) for the United States Marine Corps. Tough and extremely task oriented, he became one of the most effective DIs in the Corps. Geoff's leadership style was tough and straightforward. He wasted little time talking with recruits; he talked *at* them. Rather than discuss recruits' problems, he told them to keep their problems to themselves. He carefully and completely explained what was expected of his subordinates and then demanded compliance.

At age forty-five, Geoff Priest retired from the Marine Corps with a full pension. Anxious to continue working and to supplement his pension, he accepted a job as a supervisor in a small manufacturing plant. Convinced that he knew the most effective way to lead subordinates, Geoff treated his subordinates, who belonged to a union, in the same way he had treated Marine recruits. The results were disastrous. Satisfaction among workers plummeted, absenteeism increased, productivity dropped, and Geoff's subordinates filed many grievances against him. How could Geoff have been such an effective leader in the Marine Corps but so unsuccessful in his new leadership role? As Geoff came to learn, different situations demand different leadership qualities or behaviors. As early as 1948, Ralph Stogdill stated that "the qualities, characteristics, and skills required in a leader are determined to a large extent by the demands of the situation in which he or she is to function as a leader."[13]

Because the characteristics of a situation are so important, managers must identify them and then select the appropriate match of leader traits or behaviors. One such situation-contingent behavioral approach, the Vroom-Yetton normative theory of leadership, was discussed in Chapter 7 on decision-making tools because it focuses primarily on the conditions under which leaders should select particular types of decision-making strategies. Two other well-known situational approaches to leadership are Fiedler's contingency model and House and Evans' path-goal theory.

Fred E. Fiedler developed a popular contingency theory of leadership. His work helped show the importance of good leader-situation matches.

Fiedler's Contingency Model

One of the earliest and best-known situation-contingent leadership theories was set forth by Fred E. Fiedler from the University of Washington.[14] This theory is known as the **contingency theory of leadership.** Fiedler classified leaders according to an underlying trait, described situations that leaders face, and identified optimal matches between leaders and situations. According to Fiedler, organizations must do the same thing: assess the leader, assess the situation, and construct proper matches between the two.

The Leader Trait. Fiedler measured traits by asking leaders about their **least preferred co-worker (LPC).** Leaders described the person with whom they could work *least* well along a number of dimensions—pleasant/unpleasant, friendly/unfriendly, helpful/frustrating, and so on—and used the results to calculate an LPC score, that is, their underlying disposition toward others. You can use the descriptions presented in Figure 15.6 to assess your own LPC score.

FIGURE 15.6 Fiedler's LPC Scale

Think of the person with whom you can work least well. This may be someone you work with now or someone you knew in the past. It does not have to be the person you like least well but should be the person with whom you had the most difficulty in getting a job done. Describe this person as he or she appears to you.

	8	7	6	5	4	3	2	1	
Pleasant	8	7	6	5	4	3	2	1	Unpleasant
Friendly	8	7	6	5	4	3	2	1	Unfriendly
Rejecting	1	2	3	4	5	6	7	8	Accepting
Helpful	8	7	6	5	4	3	2	1	Frustrating
Unenthusiastic	1	2	3	4	5	6	7	8	Enthusiastic
Tense	1	2	3	4	5	6	7	8	Relaxed
Distant	1	2	3	4	5	6	7	8	Close
Cold	1	2	3	4	5	6	7	8	Warm
Cooperative	8	7	6	5	4	3	2	1	Uncooperative
Supportive	8	7	6	5	4	3	2	1	Hostile
Boring	1	2	3	4	5	6	7	8	Interesting
Quarrelsome	1	2	3	4	5	6	7	8	Harmonious
Self-assured	8	7	6	5	4	3	2	1	Hesitant
Efficient	8	7	6	5	4	3	2	1	Inefficient
Gloomy	1	2	3	4	5	6	7	8	Cheerful
Open	8	7	6	5	4	3	2	1	Guarded

Note: LPC score is the sum of the answers to these sixteen questions. High scores indicate a relationship orientation; low scores, a task orientation.

Source: F. E. Fiedler and M. M. Chemers (1974), *Leadership and effective management,* Glenview, IL: Scott, Foresman.

Fiedler states that leaders with high LPC scores are *relationship oriented* and tend to evaluate their least-preferred co-workers in fairly favorable terms. These individuals need to develop and maintain close interpersonal relationships. Task accomplishment is a secondary need to this type of leader and becomes important only after the need for relationships is reasonably well satisfied. In contrast, leaders with low LPC scores tend to evaluate the individuals with whom they would least like to work fairly negatively. They are *task oriented* and are likely to work on establishing good social and interpersonal relations only after tasks are accomplished.

The Situational Factor. Some situations are more favorable for leaders than are others. To Fiedler, situational favorableness is the degree to which a

Failed Leadership: The Bottom Line Is Not Enough

In 1982, 1983, and 1984, Dravo Corporation, an international engineering and construction firm, lost money. In an attempt to turn the company around, Dravo named Thomas F. Faught, Jr., president and chief executive officer. He cut costs. He reduced employment by almost 50 percent. In both 1985 and 1986, Dravo made money. The value of the company's stock increased over 50 percent. Faught clearly had started the company on a fiscal turnaround. These and other actions led business analysts to conclude that the company had been put back on a successful path.

In January 1987, however, Faught was fired by the Dravo board of directors. Why would the company rid itself of the very person who had engineered its comeback? Simply put, there is more to management than making money. Faught was fired, in

large part, because he was not a good enough *leader*.

Apparently, Faught remained distant from all but a few top managers. In his interactions he was often erratic, alienating and eventually driving away a number of key members of the organization. "Mr. Faught's lieutenants complained that he gave contradictory orders and ruled by fear."[1] He gave himself a raise while freezing or even cutting the salaries of subordinates. "One month he would be demanding from a subordinate completion of existing orders and the next fuming that the subordinate wasn't finding new business . . . ."[2]

The effects were more problematic. For instance, James P. Kelly, senior vice-president to Faught, was considered one of the company's most talented managers. He tried to reason with Faught but finally left

Dravo and soon lured away a number of other key Dravo employees. Kelly found that he "was able to pick up the best Dravo people because they were so disenchanted."[3] Dravo may have been doing well financially for the first time in years, but managers were so unhappy with the company's leadership that they chose to leave.

Leadership is part of only one of the four major functions of management—directing—but without effective leadership, managers will find it difficult to exercise their other functions. As Dravo's experiences showed, performance is not just a matter of profit.

1. Dravo seeks leadership to pursue turnaround strategy: Chief's downfall shows how performance isn't judged only by profit (24 February 1987), *The Wall Street Journal*, 6.
2. *Ibid.*
3. *Ibid.*

---

leader has control and influence and, therefore, feels that he or she can determine the outcomes of a group interaction.[15] Three factors work together to determine how favorable a situation is to a leader: (1) *leader-member relations* (the leader's degree of acceptance by the group and the members' level of loyalty to the leader), (2) *task structure* (the degree to which the task specifies a detailed, unambiguous goal and how to achieve it), and (3) *position power* (a leader's ability to influence subordinates through any of the sources of power discussed in Chapter 14). The situation is most favorable for a leader when the relationship between the leader and group members is good, when the task is highly structured, and when the leader's position power is strong.

Leader-Situation Matches. Some combinations of leaders and situations work well and others do not. In search of the best combinations, Fiedler examined a large number of leadership situations. He argued that most leaders have a relatively unchangeable, dominant leadership style—be it task or relationship oriented—so managers should design job situations to fit the leader rather than the other way around.[16]

Relationship-oriented (high LPC) leaders are much more effective under conditions of intermediate favorability than in either highly favorable or highly unfavorable situations. A high LPC leader's nondirective, permissive attitude

works better in this situation than does a more directive attitude that could lead to followers' anxiety, conflict, and lack of cooperation.

In highly favorable conditions in which the leader-follower relationship is good, task structure is high, and leader position power is strong, task-oriented leaders (low LPC) leaders are effective. They do not, for example, need to impose task-directed behavior when tasks are already highly structured. Low LPC leaders are also effective under highly unfavorable conditions in which such task-oriented behaviors as setting goals, detailing work methods, and guiding and controlling work behaviors move the group toward task accomplishment.

Leaders with midrange LPC scores can be more effective in a wider range of situations than can high or low LPC leaders.[17] Under conditions of low favorability, for example, a middle LPC leader can be task oriented to achieve performance but show consideration for employees and allow them to proceed on their own under conditions of high situational favorability.

Controversy over the Theory. Although Fiedler's theory can often identify appropriate leader-situation matches, it is not without critics. As some of those who study leadership in organizations see it, Fiedler's theory characterizes leaders through reference to attitudes or personality traits (LPC) but explains the effectiveness of leaders through reference to their behaviors; that is, leaders with a certain trait (high or low LPC) will behave in a particular fashion. In addition, the model has not been fully tested, and tests that have been conducted have often produced mixed or contradictory findings.[18] Perhaps of most concern is that it does not explain how attitudes determine effectiveness through behavior.

The Path-Goal Theory

Robert J. House of the Wharton School of Management and Martin Evans of the University of Toronto have developed a useful leadership theory. Like Fiedler's, it asserts that the type of leadership needed to enhance organizational effectiveness depends on the situation in which a leader is placed. Unlike Fiedler, however, House and Evans focus on the leader's observable behavior and believe that managers can either match the situation to the leader *or* modify the leader's behavior to fit the situation.

According to the path-goal theory, leader behavior should match the work environment.

The model of leadership advanced by House and Evans has been called the **path-goal theory of leadership** because it suggests that an effective leader provides subordinates with a *path* to a valued *goal*. According to House:

> *The motivational function of the leader consists of increasing personal payoffs to subordinates for work-goal attainment, and making the path to these payoffs easier to travel by clarifying it, reducing road blocks and pitfalls, and increasing the opportunities for personal satisfaction enroute.[19]*

Effective leaders, therefore, give specific instructions so that ambiguities about work are reduced and employees understand how to do their jobs effectively. They provide coaching, guidance, and training so that employees can perform the task expected of them. Effective leaders also remove barriers to task accomplishment by correcting shortages of materials, inoperative machinery, or interfering policies. In addition to these actions, effective leaders provide pay increases, recognition, promotions, and other rewards that give employees an incentive to work hard to achieve performance goals.

According to the path-goal theory, the challenge facing leaders is twofold. First, they must analyze situations and identify the most appropriate leadership style. For example, a leader who supervises experienced employees working on a highly structured assembly line does not need to spend much time telling the workers how to do their jobs—they already know how. The leader of a group of laborers excavating an archeological site, however, will need to spend a great deal of time telling them how to excavate and care for the relics they uncover. Second, leaders must develop the capacity to be flexible enough to use different leadership styles as appropriate. For example, a group vice-president who leads executives with strong needs for autonomy must use a different style of motivating and directing from a drill sergeant who teaches enlistees to clean their weapons. The degree to which leadership behavior matches situational factors will determine the level of subordinate motivation, satisfaction, and performance.[20]

Substitutes for and Neutralizers of Leadership

Relatively recently, several factors have been discovered that can substitute for or neutralize the effects of leadership behavior.[21] Sometimes an employee's characteristics make leadership less necessary, as when a master craftsperson or highly skilled worker performs up to his or her own high standards without the need for outside prompting. Sometimes it is a task's characteristics that take over, as when the work itself—solving an interesting problem, for instance, or working on a familiar job—is intrinsically satisfying. Sometimes the characteristics of an organization make leadership less necessary, as when work rules are so clear and specific that workers know exactly what they must do without help from a leader.

Substitutes for leadership behavior can clarify role expectations, motivate employees, or satisfy employees (making it unnecessary for a leader to attempt to do so). In some cases, these substitutes supplement the behavior of a leader. The presence of a highly professional workforce is a good example of this. Standardized accounting practices, for example, are established by that profession; a good accountant knows and follows these standards and does not need a leader to develop or administer them. In other words, some substitutes act as substitutes when they are necessary but do not interfere when not needed. Effective leaders can use them to good advantage. When an accounting manager need only say, "Follow standard procedures" to provide much of the structure needed by the organization's accountants, for example, it allows the manager to spend more time on other leader behavior.

Neutralizers of leadership are not always so helpful; they prevent leaders from acting as they wish. A computer-paced assembly line, for example, prevents a leader from using initiating structure behavior to pace the line. A union contract that specifies that workers be paid according to seniority prevents a leader from dispensing merit-based pay. Sometimes, of course, neutralizers can be beneficial. Union contracts, for example, clarify disciplinary proceedings and identify the responsibilities of both management and labor. Leaders must be aware of the presence of neutralizers and their effects so that they can work at either eliminating troublesome neutralizers or take advantage of any benefits that accompany them (such as the clarity of responsibilities provided by a union contract). If a leader's effectiveness is being

> *Neutralizers are unlikely to be viewed positively by a leader. . . . Substitutes for leadership, on the other hand, are often employed by an effective leader to his or her own advantage. . . . [For] example, a leader may elect to use a formula-based reward system as a substitute for personal salary judgments that would inevitably appear to subordinates as arbitrary.*
>
> —Kerr

neutralized by a poor communication system, for example, the leader might try to remove the neutralizer by developing (or convincing the organization to develop) a more effective system.

Charismatic and Transformational Leadership

Ronald Reagan, Jesse Jackson, and Evita Peron have something in common with Martin Luther King, Jr., Corazon Aquino, and Winston Churchill. The effectiveness of each of these leaders is (or was) due in part to **charisma,** a special personal magnetic charm or appeal that arouses loyalty and enthusiasm.

Sociologist Max Weber showed an interest in charismatic leadership during the early 1920s, calling charismatic leaders people who possess legitimate power that arises from "exceptional sanctity, heroism, or exemplary character."[22] Today there is renewed interest in people who can "single-handedly" effect changes even in very large organizations.

The charismatic leadership phenomenon involves a unique interplay between the attributes of a leader and followers' needs, values, beliefs, and perceptions.[23] At the extreme, leader-follower relationships are characterized by followers' unquestioning acceptance, trust in the leader's beliefs, affection, willing obedience, emulation of and identification with the leader, emotional involvement with the leader's mission, and feelings of self-power directed toward that mission.[24]

What are the characteristics of people who can exert such a strong influence over their followers? Charismatic leaders have a strong need for power and tend to rely heavily on referent power as their primary power base.[25] They are strongly self-confident and convinced of the rightness of their own beliefs and ideals. Charismatic leaders often paint exciting visions for followers, encouraging them to rely on and have hope for the future, as when Martin Luther King, Jr., told listeners of his "dream." Charismatic leaders also are likely to set high

While most effective leaders are able to clarify goals and paths to goals, charismatic leaders are uniquely able to create goals and articulate them in a way that galvanizes subordinates and those who are not subordinates—indeed, those who may not even be members of the organization. . . . [R]eplacement of a charismatic leader is one of the most difficult tasks confronting any organization.

—Kerr

Charismatic leaders are strongly self-confident and convinced of the rightness of their beliefs and ideals.

goals for their followers and to instill in them the belief that they can meet these high expectations.

Today much attention is focused on people who can bring about major organizational transformations, such as Lee Iacocca did when he saved Chrysler Corporation from bankruptcy.[26] **Transformational leadership,** in which a leader inspires enough strategic change in an organization to transform its identity, relies on leaders' charisma and "deeply held personal value systems that include such values as justice and integrity."[27] John Welch of General Electric, for example, has been the transformational leader guiding the metamorphosis of GE during the late 1980s. Welch divested the company of many historically key product lines that had lost their value and began the construction of a new corporate identity. Of at least equal importance were the changes in the GE culture nurtured by Welch.

Although there has been little empirical research on charismatic and transformational leadership, many people believe that major organizational events can be influenced by the leadership efforts of people with such magnetic personalities. Most attention until now has been focused on charismatic leadership at the top of organizations. It will be interesting to learn whether charismatic leadership is a significant factor at other levels in the organizational hierarchy.

Reprinted with special permission of King Features Syndicate, Inc.

Leadership in Review

Leadership is a primary vehicle for fulfilling the directing function of management. Organizations typically have both formal leaders chosen by the organization and informal leaders chosen by group members. Leadership and management, therefore, are not the same. Although effective leadership is a necessary part of effective management, the overall management role is much larger than leadership alone. Managers plan, organize, direct, and control. As leaders, they are engaged primarily in the directing function.

There are many diverse perspectives on leadership. Some managers treat it primarily as an exercise of power. Others maintain that a particular belief and attitude structure makes for effective leaders. Still others argue that it is possible to identify a collection of leader traits that produces a leader who should be universally effective in any leadership situation. Even today, many believe that a profile of behaviors can universally guarantee successful leadership. Unfortunately, such simple solutions fall short.

It is now clear that there is no one best way to be an effective leader in all circumstances. Rather, the nature of the situation dictates the type of leadership most likely to work well. Fiedler focuses on leader traits and argues that the favorableness of the leadership situation dictates the type of leadership approach needed. He recommends selecting leaders to match the situation or changing the situation to match the leader. The path-goal theory focuses on leadership behavior that can be adapted to the demands of a particular work environment and subordinate characteristics. Path-goal theorists believe that leaders can be matched with the situation as well as the situation changed to match leaders. Together, these theories make clear that leadership is effective when the characteristics and behavior of a leader match the demands of the situation.

Aspects of subordinates, tasks, and organizations can substitute for or neutralize many leadership behaviors. Leaders must remain aware of these factors, no matter which perspective on leadership they adopt. Such awareness allows managers to use substitutes for and neutralizers of leadership to their benefit rather than be stymied by their presence.

Finally, in recent years, there has been a renewed interest in charismatic leadership and its transformational effects on organizations. Charismatic leaders have certain attributes that persuade people to follow them and their directives.

Issues for Review and Discussion

1. Define leadership and distinguish between leadership and management.
2. Discuss the relationship between power and variations in types of leadership.
3. What has been learned from the universal leader trait perspective?
4. What were the central leader behaviors identified in the Ohio State University and University of Michigan studies, and how are they different from one another?
5. What are the leadership types identified by Blake and Mouton's Managerial Grid®, and how does this leadership model look from the perspective of situation theories of leadership?
6. Compare and contrast Fiedler's contingency theory of leadership with House and Evans' path-goal theory.
7. What are the distinguishing features of charismatic leadership?

Key Terms

leadership
formal (designated) leader
informal leader
trait approach
great person approach
consideration
initiating structure

job-centered behaviors
employee-centered behaviors
contingency theory of leadership
least preferred co-worker (LPC)
path-goal theory of leadership
charisma
transformational leadership

Suggested Readings

Bennis, W. (1987). *Why leaders can't lead.* San Francisco: Jossey-Bass.

Bennis, W., and Nanus, A. (1985). *Leaders: The strategies for taking charge.* New York: Harper & Row.

Collins, N. W., Gilbert, S. K., and Nycum, S. H. (1988). *Women leading: Making tough choices on the fast track.* Lexington, MA: Stephen Green.

Conger, J. A. (1988). *Charismatic leadership.* San Francisco: Jossey-Bass.

House, R. J. (1977). A 1976 theory of charismatic leadership. In Hunt, J. G., and Larson, L. L., eds. *Leadership: The cutting edge.* Carbondale: Southern Illinois University Press.

Kotter, J. P. (1988). *The leadership factor.* New York: Free Press.

Loden, M. (1985). *Feminine leadership: Or how to succeed in business without being one of the boys.* New York: Time Books. For a review of this book, see Rubenfeld, S. (1988). In Pierce, J. L., and Newstrom, J. W., eds. *The manager's bookshelf: A mosaic of contemporary views.* New York: Harper & Row, 97-103.

Manz, C. C., and Sims, H. P., Jr. (1988). *Superleadership: Leading others to lead themselves.* New York: Prentice-Hall. For a review of this book, see Manz and Sims (1988). In Pierce, J. L., and Newstrom, J. W., eds. *The manager's bookshelf: A mosaic of contemporary views.* New York: Harper & Row, 327-35.

Schriesheim, C. A., and Von Glinow, M. A. (1977). The path-goal theory of leadership: A theoretical and empirical analysis. *Academy of Management Journal, 20,* 398-405.

Yukl, G. A. (1981). *Leadership in organizations.* Englewood Cliffs, NJ: Prentice-Hall.

Notes

1. R. Tannenbaum and W. H. Schmidt (March-April 1958), How to choose a leadership pattern, *Harvard Business Review,* 95-101.

2. N. R. F. Maier (1965), *Psychology in industry,* Boston: Houghton Mifflin, 157; K. Davis and J. W. Newstrom (1989), *Human behavior at work: Organization behavior,* 8th ed., New York: McGraw-Hill.

3. J. P. Muczyk and B. C. Reimann (1987), The case for directive leadership, *The Academy of Management Executive,* 1, 301-11.

4. R. M. Stogdill (1948), Personal factors associated with leadership: A survey of the literature, *Journal of Applied Psychology,* 25, 35-71; R. M. Stogdill (1974), *Handbook of leadership: A survey of theory and research,* New York: Free Press.

5. Stogdill, 1948, 63.

6. D. McGregor (1957), The human side of enterprise, *Management Review,* 46, 22-28, 88-92; D. McGregor (1960), *The human side of enterprise,* New York: McGraw-Hill.

7. E. A. Fleishman (1953), The description of supervisory behavior, *Personnel Psychology*, 37, 1-6; E. A. Fleishman and E. F. Harris (1962), Patterns of leadership behavior related to employee grievances and turnover, *Personnel Psychology*, 15, 43-56; A. W. Halpin and B. J. Winer (1957), A factorial study of the leader behavior descriptions, in R. M. Stogdill and A. C. Coons, eds., *Leader behavior: Its description and measurement*, Columbus: Bureau of Business Research, Ohio State University; J. K. Hemphill and A. E. Coons (1975), Development of the leader behavior description questionnaire, in R. M. Stogdill and A. E. Coons; S. Kerr and C. Schriesheim (1974), Consideration, initiating structure, and organizational criteria—an update of Korman's 1966 review, *Personnel Psychology*, 27, 555-68.

8. D. Katz and R. L. Kahn (1952), Some recent findings in human relations research, in E. Swanson, T. Newcomb, and E. Hartley, eds., *Readings in social psychology*, New York: Holt, Rinehart and Winston; D. Katz, N. Macoby, and N. Morse (1950), *Productivity, supervision, and morale in an office situation*, Ann Arbor, MI: Institute for Social Research; F. C. Mann and J. Dent (1954), The supervisor: Member of two organizational families, *Harvard Business Review*, 32, 103-12.

9. G. A. Yukl (1981), *Leadership in organizations*, Englewood Cliffs, NJ: Prentice-Hall, 114-18; R. Likert (1961), *New patterns of management*, New York: McGraw-Hill.

10. R. R. Blake and J. S. Mouton (1964), *The managerial grid*, Houston: Gulf; R. R. Blake and J. S. Mouton (1981), *The versatile manager: A grid profile*, Homewood, IL: Dow Jones-Irwin; R. R. Blake and J. S. Mouton (1984), *The new Managerial Grid III*, Houston: Gulf.

11. R. R. Blake and J. S. Mouton (1981), Management by Grid® principles or situationalism: Which? *Group and Organization Studies*, 6, 439-55.

12. L. L. Larson, J. G. Hunt, and R. N. Osborn (1976), The great hi-hi leader behavior myth: A lesson from Occam's razor, *Academy of Management Journal*, 19, 628-41.

13. Stogdill, 1948, 63.

14. F. E. Fiedler and M. M. Chemers (1974), *Leadership and effective management*, Glenview, IL: Scott, Foresman.

15. F. E. Fiedler (1976), The leadership game: Matching the men to the situation, *Organizational Dynamics*, 4, 9.

16. F. E. Fiedler (September-October 1965), Engineering the job to fit the manager, *Harvard Business Review*, 115-22.

17. R. B. Dunham (1984), [Interview with Fred E. Fiedler], *Organizational behavior: People and processes in management*, Homewood, IL: Richard D. Irwin, 368; J. L. Kennedy, Jr. (1982), Middle LPC leaders and the contingency model of leadership effectiveness, *Organizational Behavior and Human Performance*, 30, 1-14.

18. See, for example, the supporting results of M. M. Chemers and G. J. Skrzypek (1972), Experimental test of the contingency model of leadership effectiveness, *Journal of Personality and Social Psychology*, 24, 172-77; and the contradictory results of R. P. Vecchio (1977), An empirical examination of the validity of Fiedler's model of leadership effectiveness, *Organizational Behavior and Human Performance*, 19, 180-206.

19. R. J. House (1971), A path goal theory of leader effectiveness, *Administrative Science Quarterly*, 16, 324.

20. R. J. House and T. R. Mitchell (Autumn 1974), Path-goal theory of leadership, *Journal of Contemporary Business,* 86; R. J. House and G. Dessler (1974), The path goal theory of leadership: Some post hoc and a priori tests, in J. Hunt and L. Larson, eds., *Contingency approaches to leadership,* Carbondale: Southern Illinois University Press; R. T. Keller (1989), A test of the path-goal theory of leadership with need for clarity as a moderator in research and development organizations, *Journal of Applied Psychology,* 74(2), 208-12.

21. S. Kerr (1977), Substitutes for leadership: Some implications for organizational design, *Organization and Administrative Sciences,* 8, 135-46; S. Kerr and J. M. Jermier (1978), Substitutes for leadership: Their meaning and measurement, *Organizational Behavior and Human Performance,* 22, 375-403; J. P. Howell and P. W. Dorfman (1981), Substitutes for leadership: Test of a construct, *Academy of Management Journal,* 24, 714-28.

22. S. N. Eisenstadt (1968), *Max Weber: On charisma and institution building,* Chicago: University of Chicago Press, 46.

23. J. A. Conger and R. N. Kanungo (1987), Toward a behavioral theory of charismatic leadership in organizational settings, *Academy of Management Review,* 12, 637-47.

24. R. J. House and M. L. Baetz (1979), Leadership: Some empirical generalizations and new research directions, in B. M. Staw, ed., *Research in organizational behavior,* 1, Greenwich, CT: JAI Press, 341-423; Conger and Kanungo.

25. R. J. House (1977), A 1976 theory of charismatic leadership, in J. G. Hunt and L. L. Larson, eds., *Leadership: The cutting edge,* Carbondale: Southern Illinois University Press.

26. B. M. Bass (1985), Leadership: Good, better, best, *Organizational Dynamics,* 13, 26-40; N. M. Tichy and D. O. Ulrich (Fall 1984), The leadership challenge—a call for the transformational leader, *Sloan Management Review,* 26, 59-68.

27. K. W. Kuhnert and P. Lewis (1987), Transactional and transformational leadership: A constructive/developmental analysis, *Academy of Management Review,* 12, 650.

28. See Part 1, "Manager Profile: Jack Welch" in this textbook; Inside the mind of Jack Welch (27 March 1989), *Fortune,* 38-50.

Mrs. Loomis

By Roger Smitter,
North Central College

The Student Counseling Center of Miller University had experienced considerable internal turmoil over the past three years, but when Dr. Beth Sims took over as the new director, she knew little of the history of the center. Having been in student counseling for nine years, she knew Miller's center had always been considered one of the best in the region. It was especially well known for the excellent mentoring its now-retired director, Bob Grimes, had given to many young counselors. Many of his protégés had moved on to become directors and deans at other institutions. She also knew that Grimes' replacement, John Youngs, had resigned rather surprisingly after only two years. The most senior counselor on the staff, Carl Bearman, had been appointed an interim director while the university conducted a national search.

The center had a staff of six counselors (three men and three women) in addition to Dr. Sims. She had met all of them during her interviews, as well as Mrs. Loomis, the secretary. Mrs. Loomis had proudly told her she had been with the center for eighteen years.

Sims came into the position with a suspicion that she was not the counseling staff's first choice. During her interviews, she had sensed some hostility from the staff. When she mentioned this to the dean after he had offered her the job, he said it was probably due to what had happened in that office. Sims felt it may have been due to the fact that she had a Ph.D., something the other counselors had not yet earned. Also, she had only two years of admin-

istrative experience at the big-ten university where she had earned her doctorate in counseling. At thirty five, she was older than all of the staff counselors and did have considerable counseling experience. The dean told her she was just the person the university had been searching for. With his encouragement and because she wanted to gain more administrative experience, she took the job.

Acquiring Information

During her first week, Sims began a review of the center files. Mrs. Loomis was proud to show her these files, and Sims quickly learned why. The records were clear, precise, and very complete. She learned that her predecessor had resigned about midway through the previous year. Two counselors had left after his first year as director, and another had resigned at the start of his second year. The records also indicated that the number of student appointments dropped considerably just before Youngs resigned.

Youngs had sent out many memos to the staff counselors informing them of changes in the office routines for making appointments and keeping records. Apparently, there had been few formal procedures when Grimes was director. Many of Youngs' memos were responses to complaints and justifications for his new procedures. Sims also noted that under Grimes, Mrs. Loomis had sat in on staff meetings to take notes. Under Youngs, however, a staff counselor took notes and Mrs. Loomis was not present.

The minutes written by staff became increasingly terse and even cryptic just before Youngs' departure.

After this review of the files, Sims set out to get to know the staff better. During her first staff meeting, she announced she would have Mrs. Loomis make appointments for all the staff. "I just want to get to know all of you on a one-to-one basis." She also announced her goal of restoring the center to a position of respect on campus and in the profession. She mentioned several possible ideas and new programs the staff could undertake. Sims did most of the talking at the staff meeting and came away from it frustrated. The staff had little overt reaction other than, "That's interesting," and, "We might try that."

Carl Bearman was Sims' first appointment later that week. He nervously waited outside her office, talking with Mrs. Loomis. In a whisper, she told him she was "disappointed in that young woman." She told him how she had baked a batch of cookies and brought them to Dr. Sims' apartment when she was moving in. She had invited her to dinner during the moving-in period. "She was nice and thanked me for the invitation, but she's never mentioned it again. And I've given her all the information about how we used to run the office, but I think she wants to do it her way."

Carl Bearman entered Sims' office at the appointed time, smiling warily to Mrs. Loomis. Within a few minutes, Mrs. Loomis could hear animated talking from the office. Then, there was some laughter. Bearman's session was scheduled to last thirty minutes but took over an hour. Mrs.

Loomis had to tell the next staff member to wait.

After emerging from the appointment, Bearman reported to Mrs. Loomis that he and Sims had a great time together. "She knows a lot about counseling. She encouraged me to go on for a Ph.D. In fact, she knows a lot of people in grad schools. And, she's got some terrific ideas about what needs to be done with this office." Then he added, "She seemed especially appreciative of what I told her about the office routine. She had guessed some of the problems we had with Youngs, but she said the detail I added was very helpful in understanding what's going on."

Similar results ensued from the next interview that day. When Mrs. Loomis left work, a third interview was still going on. The sessions were the main topic of conversation among the staff counselors for the next few days.

The next staff meeting went beyond its scheduled time. Mrs. Loomis could hear laughter and excited discussions coming from Sims' office. As she typed the minutes of the meeting, Mrs. Loomis saw that several new program ideas were raised at the meeting.

Over the next several weeks, Sims learned a great deal about what had happened in the center with Youngs and before that with Grimes. During one staff session, a counselor said that Youngs had imposed a lot of rules, which "I guess were needed since things had been pretty loose, but he always made you feel like a hired hand, not a professional." Sims learned that Youngs had imposed a strict 8 A.M. to 5 P.M. work schedule.

He changed the system for making appointments and expected staff to begin publishing in the field, in order to "get the name of this place known." He wanted all staff and students to refer to him by his title, "Doctor Youngs." Within his first year, a rebellion was brewing.

During an informal discussion with one of the experienced counselors, Sims learned that the staff had confirmation of serious trouble when Mrs. Loomis stopped defending Youngs. The counselor said, "I'd never heard her say an angry word about anyone until Youngs came here. She would tell us to be patient. 'He's young. He'll learn,' she would say. She thought that since he was the boss, he was right. Then she overheard him call her a fussbudget one day. He'd been trying to do the budget without her help. She always did most of it for Bob Grimes. That persuaded her." "What happened?" asked Sims. "She let everyone know in her own way that she was displeased with what he was doing. She could be the same old gabby Mrs. Loomis with us until Youngs stepped out of his office. Then, she would shut right up," said the counselor. "That was when she started talking about retiring several years early. I'm glad it didn't come to that."

Only once did Sims ever attempt to talk about Youngs with Mrs. Loomis directly. Sims had asked her for some files, which she promptly retrieved. When Sims asked why Youngs had established these files, Mrs. Loomis said only, "He had his ideas." When Sims pressed her a little with, "How so?" Mrs. Loomis would only say that she was glad Mr.

Youngs was gone. Then she added, "But I'm so sorry for all the grief it caused poor Carl when he took over. I just know Carl is a better counselor than Dr. Youngs ever will be. But heavens, that young man knew nothing about running an office. You should have seen him struggle with the budget. It's a good thing I've been around this office since the dawn of time."

After two months on the job, Sims asked Mrs. Loomis to schedule a lunch appointment with Bob Grimes. The former director still lived in the small university town but he did little on campus and never came to the center. At lunch, Grimes recalled with fondness his days of helping students deal with all kinds of problems. "Everything from homesickness to the serious stuff," he said. Sims complimented him on his reputation as a mentor. He recalled his retirement dinner when many former counselors came back to praise him for helping him get positions of responsibility. Then he paused and said in a hushed tone, "But don't let that fool you. It was Mrs. Loomis who really ran things in that office. Without her, I wouldn't have had time to work with students and those young counselors. I never really liked all that stupid paperwork. Counseling is about people, not paper!"

He went on to praise Mrs. Loomis for helping new counselors feel at home. "She always brought them a meal when they moved in. She had them over for dinner plenty of times, especially after her husband died. She never had any of her own kids but was just as proud of those young people as any parent."

Grimes also told her he had advised the university not to hire Youngs. "Sure, he had a fancy Ph.D. and all that, but it's important to come through the ranks like I did. I know if someone is a people person. So does my staff. Youngs wasn't that kind of fellow." Beth shared with him some of her perceptions of the university and the center but let Grimes do most of the talking.

The Confrontation

After this session, Sims tried especially to have a friendly but professional relationship with Mrs. Loomis. She made it a point to compliment her exactness and attention to detail. She gave her plenty of advance notice on major typing projects. Mrs. Loomis usually replied with, "Oh, I don't mind. Heavens, Mr. Grimes was always coming in at the last minute." Beth also encouraged her to take the standard ten minute coffee break with other secretaries in the building, but Mrs. Loomis told her, "It's important to be at my desk and get your phone messages, especially in the Counseling Center. We have so many students coming in, who would keep the appointments straight?"

Indeed, there were many students coming into the office. The Counseling Center's new reputation had quickly spread across campus. Sims was asked to speak in residence hall meetings; the counselors were also busy with appointments and campus programs. Sims seemed pleased with what had been accomplished by spring.

Sims' rapport with the staff carried over to the students who worked in the office as file clerks. She got to know them on a first-name basis. One in particular, Susie Dunn, had worked in the office for three years. She and Mrs. Loomis would often talk when she worked. One day, when Sims was putting on her coat to leave for a meeting, she overheard Susie say to Mrs. Loomis, "You know, for a couple of years, this was just a job, but now, I'm really interested in looking into a master's degree in counseling after I graduate."

"Well, that may be nice," said Mrs. Loomis, "but a nice young lady like you should have no trouble finding a handsome man and settling down." Just as Sims was leaving, she said to Susie, "See if Mrs. Loomis can find a time in my appointment book. Let's talk about those plans for graduate school." Susie readily agreed.

Sims returned late that afternoon to the office after a series of long and difficult budget meetings with the dean. She greeted Mrs. Loomis with a quick "Hello" and went directly into her office. Once seated, she was surprised to find Mrs. Loomis standing in the doorway with a handful of phone message slips. Mrs. Loomis said, "Now Dr. Sims, here are some important phone messages for you." As was her custom, she began to read to Sims what she had already written in detail on the sheets.

With a sigh, Sims said, "You know, Mrs. Loomis, I can read. Just give me the message slips."

Mrs. Loomis slumped, threw the messages on the desk, turned around, and left the office. Sims went out to the reception area by Mrs. Loomis' desk only to see the secretary putting on her coat with tears in her eyes as she walked out the door.

Questions

1. Characterize the leadership styles of Bob Grimes, John Youngs, and Beth Sims. Which style do you think most appropriate for the Counseling Center?

2. What factors made Mrs. Loomis a powerful person in the organization? What factors made her a weak person in the organization?

3. What messages was Sims sending to her staff and to Mrs. Loomis?

4. What should Sims do now?

5. Given what Mrs. Loomis said to Susie Dunn, does she belong at a university counseling center?

PART 5

Controlling

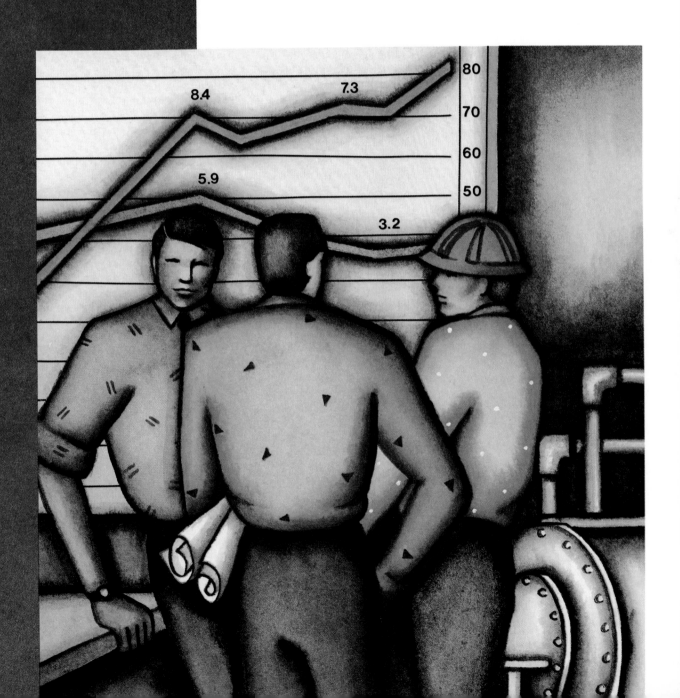

John Sculley

After receiving an M.B.A. from the Wharton School at the University of Pennsylvania, John Sculley went to work for PepsiCo. Sculley arrived at about the time Pepsi developed the goal of taking on Coke in a marketing battle, with the objective of surpassing its archrival in market share. Sculley was placed on the fast track, and, with his marketing skills, he responded successfully to each of the challenges presented to him. After a series of rapid promotions, he was moved to the presidency of PepsiCo's international foods operation. This promotion was a major challenge for him, since this division, with all of its problems and complexities, had been the dead end for many executives before him. Donald Kendall, then the CEO of PepsiCo, was grooming Sculley as his eventual replacement.

Innovation must be carefully managed.

The international foods operation was characterized by inefficient plants, unsanitary conditions, terrible products, poor distribution, and nonexistent advertising. Sculley successfully tackled the operation, and three and one half years later he was promoted to the presidency of PepsiCo, Frito-Lay, and the food group.

John Sculley claims that the more difficult and challenging the task, the greater the satisfaction he derives from task accomplishment. Sculley appears to be driven by intrinsic rewards—feelings of accomplishment and success he gives to himself while responding to challenging tasks. Like most individuals with a strong need for achievement, Sculley possesses a need to feel in control of things. At

PepsiCo, Sculley became bogged down in numerous contractual squabbles, began to feel a lack of challenge, failed to find intrinsic rewards in the myriad tasks he was working on, and experienced a growing sense of helplessness. He eventually left PepsiCo and journeyed to Apple Computer, fascinated with the computer whiz-kid entrepreneur, Steven Jobs. Sculley saw Apple as an organization in which he could make a difference. The team of Sculley and Jobs would be one in which Sculley would teach Jobs management and marketing skills, and Jobs would teach Sculley about his vision for a world wrapped up in the information age—a new social, cultural, economic, and technological revolution.

The early months at Apple were exhilarating. Creativity was emphasized by everyone; they were working on the cutting edge, learning about the ways that people process information; everyone was involved in the decision-making process; and there was an intense sense of commitment and direction that seemed to bind the organization together. A highly intrinsically motivated individual himself, Sculley was fascinated by the intrinsic motivation of the Apple employees who surrounded him. The commitment level was high, people were energized, and excitement filled the organization.

After one and one half years of Apple prosperity, major problems began to emerge. As he worked on these issues to no avail, Sculley began to doubt himself, and once again that feeling of helplessness began to set in. People around him began to criticize him for allowing Steven Jobs to become more and more involved in day-to-day decision making, the very job, they claimed, for which Sculley had been hired.

Sculley thought about leaving Apple, but then threw aside his feelings of helplessness and took a number of major steps in order to regain control. He replaced Apple's product structure with a functional structure. He removed Steven Jobs from his position as general manager of Macintosh and eventually fired him—the man who had brought him to Apple. He repositioned the Macintosh computer line for businesspeople, and he instituted massive layoffs. Running the risk of stifling creativity, he became directive and reduced the level and form of participation that had characterized Apple during its early stages.

Sculley strongly believes that it is important for a manager to have a clear vision for the organization and views on how to position it within its external environment. It is also critically important that the manager communicate that vision to his or her subordinates. A key to effective leadership is that the manager must clearly understand his or her strengths and weaknesses and attack problems with these strengths.

Sculley suggests that an innovative organization does not manage itself. If an organization is going to grow and continue to be innovative, the process of innovation must be carefully managed. Management has the responsibility to be proactive. According to Sculley, there are six general principles that can be used to manage creativity.[1]

First, *the safer you can make a situation, the higher you can raise the challenge.* An environment that is risk free, coupled with easy goals, breed arrogance and complacency; therefore, management needs to create an environment in which people are not afraid of making mistakes and must simultaneously make the task confronting them extremely difficult.

Second, *do not give people goals; tell them which way to go.* In order to get people to have creative ideas, management needs to avoid specifying where it wants to be tomorrow based on extrapolations from where it was yesterday. Instead, people need to envision what tomorrow will be like and then come back to today and design ways to get there.

Third, *encourage contrarian thinking.* There is a need for low levels of dissent within an organization; there should be a modest amount of tension between discipline and anarchy. Instilling a measured amount of anarchy into an organization encourages people to express varying opinions without worrying about the implications. Tension properly placed between points of view brings out the best in people. Dissention stimulates discussion and influences decision making for the better.

Fourth, *build a work environment to extend not just people's aspirations but also their sensibilities.* There are tools that foster creativity, and the major tool is an environment that is conducive to fun and to thinking in nonstandard ways. The work environment should be egalitarian, informal, relaxed, devoid of symbols of management, and open, while possessing a culture (norms, values, symbols) that reflects creativity. It is the relaxation at the level of consciousness that is the seed for creativity at the level of the subconscious mind.

Fifth, *build emotion into the system.* "Defensiveness is the bane of all passion-filled creative work."[2] Problems need to be thought about in positive instead of negative terms. Large and public reward systems that provide immediate reinforcement of major breakthroughs can contribute to the creation of emotion within the system. For example, reward problem finding as well as problem solving.

Sixth, *encourage accountability over responsibility.* Creative people need to feel free to let their creative instincts work. As a result, organizational responsibility should be attached to the desired outcome, namely the production of creative ideas. Accountability should be attached to the results of the work assigned to people.

According to Sculley, "while management demands consensus, control, certainty, and the status quo, creativity thrives on the opposite—instinct, uncertainty, freedom, and iconoclasm."[3] If Sculley's early successes in managing creativity at Apple continue, it would seem that he has developed an effective means to mesh the demands of management and the needs of innovative organization members.

1. Sculley's lessons from inside Apple (14 September 1987), *Fortune*, 108-19.

2. *Fortune*, 119.

3. *Fortune*, 118.

Sources: J. Sculley with J. A. Byrne (1987), *Odyssey: From Pepsi to Apple*, New York: Harper & Row; D. A. Greenberger (1988), A review of Odyssey: From Pepsi to Apple, in J. L. Pierce and J. W. Newstrom, eds., *The manager's bookshelf: A mosaic of contemporary views*, New York: Harper & Row, 313-19; Sculley's lessons from inside Apple (14 September 1987), *Fortune*, 108-19.

16 Organizational Effectiveness

Student Learning Objectives

After reading this chapter, you should be able to:

1. Explain why there is disagreement about the meaning of organizational effectiveness.

2. Identify various criteria that can be used to measure organizational effectiveness.

3. Discuss four major systematic approaches to assessing effectiveness and identify the major differences among these perspectives.

4. Explain the competing values perspective on organizational effectiveness and the way in which it incorporates the merits of each of the four major approaches.

5. Describe each of the four models of effectiveness included in the competing values perspective.

6. Consider how organizational life cycles can help managers decide which of the four competing values models is most appropriate for their organization.

*T*his book has identified management techniques that should contribute to the effectiveness of organizations. Most people would agree that the development and maintenance of an effective organization requires careful and systematic planning, organizing, directing, and controlling. Beyond this general agreement, however, the waters get murky. When comparing two organizations, for example, how does a person know which is more effective? In 1988, General Motors had $121 billion in sales compared to Ford Motor Company's $92.4 billion. Does this make GM more effective than Ford? In 1988, Ford had a $5.3 billion profit compared to GM's $4.9 billion profit. Does this make Ford more effective? In 1988, Ford's profits equaled 5.7 percent of sales compared to GM's 4 percent. Abbott Laboratories had "only" $4.9 billion in sales, but over 15 percent of this was profit. Does that make Abbott Laboratories a more effective organization than either GM or Ford?

The Nature and Importance of Organizational Effectiveness

Previous chapters in this book have addressed the planning, organizing, and directing functions of management. This part of the book examines the fourth function: controlling. As you learned in Chapter 1, the controlling function involves monitoring both the behavior of organization members and the effectiveness of the organization itself, determining whether plans are achieving organizational goals, and taking corrective actions as needed. To execute the controlling function, managers must understand the nature of organizational effectiveness, because organizational effectiveness is largely what they must control. This section on the controlling function, thus, begins with an examination of organizational effectiveness. Chapters 17 and 18 follow up by exploring methods for controlling effectiveness.

Webster's defines *effectiveness* as the production of or the power to produce a desired result. Management scholars and managers have a much harder time agreeing on a definition of **organizational effectiveness.** Many managers in the private sector, for example, consider organizational effectiveness to be reflected by the bottom line (profits). Defining organizational effectiveness strictly in terms of dollars and cents, however, fails to capture the complexity of organizational operations and the full meaning of effectiveness. After all, managers in the public sector sometimes overspend their current year's budget to justify a larger budget request for the next year. This chapter explores a wide range of definitions of organizational effectiveness and offers an integrated model that permits organizations to define effectiveness in ways that are relevant to them. As you will see, these definitions focus on the degree to which organizational goals are met.

Assessing Effectiveness

Managers have used a wide range of specific criteria to assess organizational effectiveness. They have also used four systematic approaches in defining organizational effectiveness. This section explores these traditional criteria and approaches. The next section presents an integrating perspective that can guide managers in selecting effectiveness criteria that are appropriate to their particular organizational situations.

Potential Criteria

Just as it is difficult to agree on a definition of organizational effectiveness, selecting criteria to use in assessing organizational effectiveness is not an easy task. Managers tend to use a single effectiveness criterion or a limited number of criteria, and many managers select a criterion because it "looks right." For example, many managers concentrate on profit because it seems to be an intuitively appropriate measure of organizational effectiveness. As you will see, however, excellent arguments can also be made for using such effectiveness criteria as employee job satisfaction and flexibility in adapting to changing environments. Table 16.1 presents many criteria that managers have used to assess organizational effectiveness.

TABLE 16.1 *Criteria and Measures of Organizational Effectiveness*

1. *Productivity.* Usually defined as the quantity or volume of the major product or service that the organization provides. It can be measured at three levels: individual, group, and total organization via archival records or ratings or both.

2. *Efficiency.* A ratio that reflects a comparison of some aspect of unit performance to the costs incurred for that performance.

3. *Profit.* The amount of revenue from sales left after all costs and obligations are met. Percentage return on investment or percentage return on total sales are sometimes used as alternative definitions.

4. *Quality.* The quality of the primary service or product provided by the organization that may take many operational forms, which are determined largely by the kind of product or service provided by the organization.

5. *Accidents.* The frequency of on-the-job accidents resulting in lost time.

6. *Growth.* Represented by an increase in such variables as total workforce, plant capacity, assets, sales, profits, market share, and number of innovations. It implies a comparison of an organization's present state with its own past state.

7. *Absenteeism.* The usual definition stipulates unexcused absences, but even within this constraint there are a number of alternative definitions.

8. *Turnover.* Some measure of the relative number of voluntary terminations, which is almost always assessed via archival records.

9. *Job satisfaction.* Has been conceptualized in many ways but the modal view might define it as the individual's satisfaction with the amount of various job outcomes that he or she is receiving.

10. *Morale.* The model definition seems to view morale as a group phenomenon involving extra effort, goal communality, commitment, and feelings of belonging. Groups have some degree of morale, whereas individuals have some motivation (and satisfaction).

11. *Flexibility/adaptation.* Refers to the ability of an organization to change its standard operating procedures in response to environmental changes.

12. *Planning and goal setting.* The degree to which an organization systematically plans its future steps and engages in explicit goal-setting behavior.

13. *Managerial interpersonal skills.* The level of skill with which managers deal with supervisors, subordinates, and peers in terms of giving support, facilitating constructive interaction, and generating enthusiasm for meeting goals and achieving excellent performance.

14. *Utilization of environment.* The extent to which the organization interacts successfully with its environment and acquires scarce and valued resources necessary to its effective operation.

15. *Stability.* The maintenance of structure, function, and resources through time and, more particularly, through periods of stress.

16. *Value of human resources.* A composite criterion that refers to the total value or total worth of the individual members, in an accounting or balance sheet sense, to the organization.

Source: Adapted from S. P. Robbins (1983), *Organization theory: The structure and design of organizations*, Englewood Cliffs, NJ: Prentice-Hall, 22-23.

Few organizations will find all of these criteria to be appropriate indicators of effectiveness. Most organizations, however, should be evaluated along many of these and other dimensions. Despite this, many managers often aim at only one or two in a *rifle approach* to assessing effectiveness (see Figure 16.1). The problem with this approach is that a manager who uses a single indicator might miss information that has an important bearing on organizational effectiveness. Focusing only on sales volume, for example, could permit a manager to classify an organization as effective even if it is losing money or experiencing other major problems.

One reason managers use such a narrow approach is that they frequently adopt criteria largely according to their personal interests and values. Compounding this is the fact that managers tend to choose criteria that make them look good. For example, economically oriented managers of organizations generating high sales might choose a profit criterion to gauge organizational effectiveness, whereas human relations-oriented managers in organizations with low turnover levels might focus on such criteria as job satisfaction, motivation, or cohesion.

Although an overly narrow approach to measuring effectiveness is ill-advised, so is the opposite approach. Some managers overreact by using a *shotgun approach* that aims at every criterion in sight (see Figure 16.2). Managers who adopt too many criteria may lose sight of important individual criteria. If, for example, morale is just one of thirty effectiveness criteria being used, it is easy to overlook its importance. As you will see later in this chapter, some criteria are significantly more important than others under certain circumstances.

One of the first challenges facing managers is to identify and use the proper mix of criteria to assess organizational effectiveness. Managers should take a

FIGURE 16.1   The Rifle Approach to Assessing Organizational Effectiveness

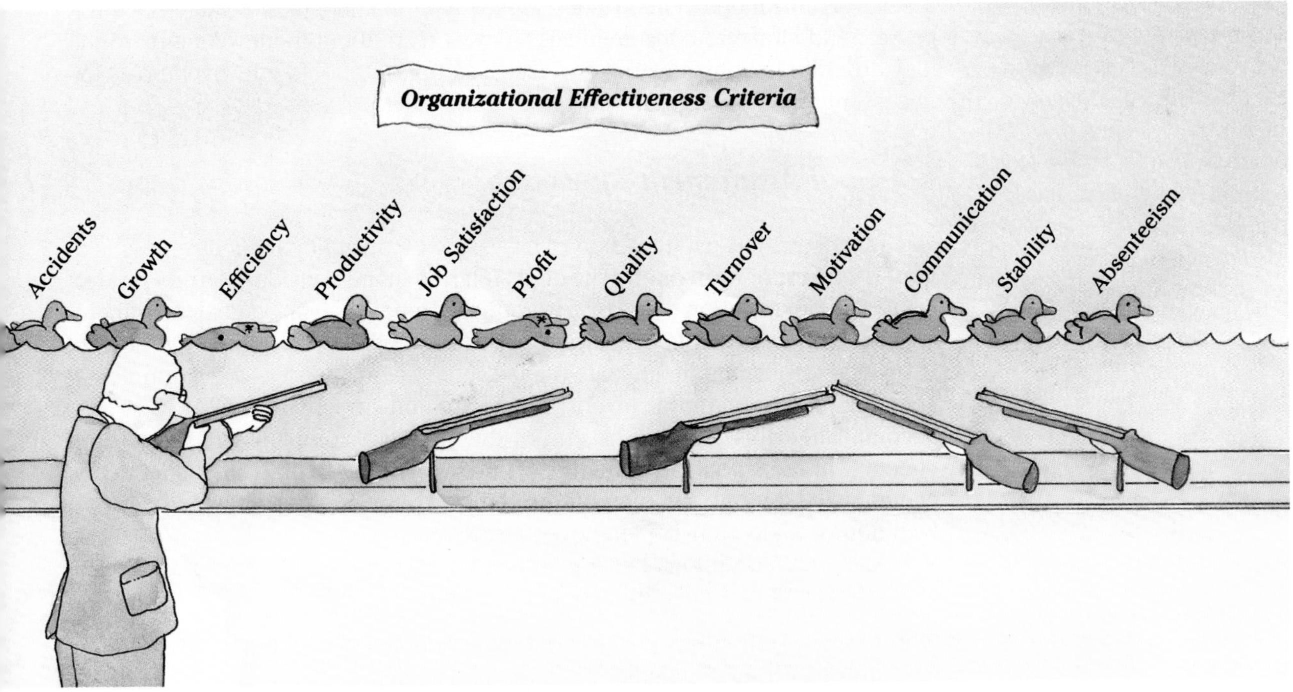

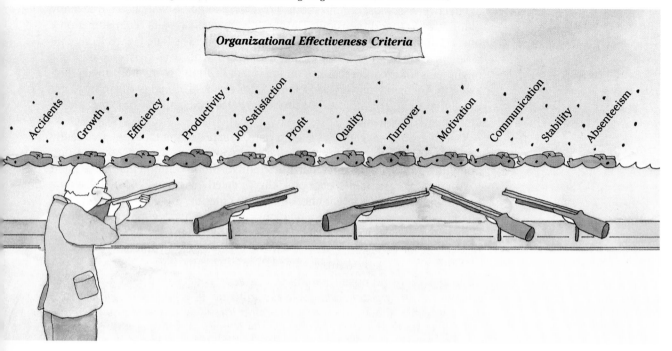

A MANAGER'S WORD

[O]fficial company definitions of effectiveness are almost always so general as to be meaningless. Mission statements or credos that define effectiveness as service to customers, contribution to society, highest-quality products, and so on are largely constructed for public-image purposes or to meet legal requirements.

Kim S. Cameron
Associate Professor of
Organizational Behavior and
Industrial Relations
University of Michigan

focused approach that does not rely on too few or too many criteria, selecting only those that are relevant to their particular organization based on its current stage of activity and development. An integrated perspective, such as the one presented later in this chapter, is designed to help managers do exactly this. Consider the four major systematic approaches that managers have used to assess organizational effectiveness: goal attainment, systems, internal processes, and strategic constituencies. As you read about them, remember that they describe how managers *have* assessed organizational effectiveness—not necessarily how they *should* do so.

A Goal Attainment Approach

The most widely used method of assessing organizational effectiveness is a **goal attainment approach.** The goals referred to are considered **ends goals:** what is an organization trying to accomplish? Managers using a goal attainment approach, thus, evaluate organizational effectiveness by assessing the degree to which one or more specified goals are met. Consider, for example, a company that sets a goal of clearing $5 million in profits in 1991. If it has accomplished this goal by the end of the year, the company will have been effective from a goal attainment perspective—even if that $5 million was accumulated through a combination of aggressive marketing, deceptive pricing techniques, and extensive employee layoffs.

Under what conditions has a goal attainment approach worked reasonably well? Managers often use this approach when:

- An organization has specific outcome-oriented goals (this holds true for any organization, whether it is a football team trying to win the Super Bowl or a branch of the military attempting to recruit enlistees).

- Specific goals are stated, defined, and understood by management.
- Management agrees that the stated goals are appropriate indicators of effectiveness.
- It is possible to measure the degree to which goals are being met.
- The number of goals is small enough to be manageable.

Many managers like a goal attainment approach. They can use it relatively easily, and it allows them to obtain regular feedback about progress toward goals. Managers can regularly see, for example, how close they are to reaching targeted sales quotas or profit margins. If used as the sole indicator of assessing effectiveness, however, a goal attainment approach may condone or mask inappropriate, abusive, and even unethical behaviors. The Boise Cascade Company, for instance, met or exceeded a 20 percent growth goal for twelve consecutive years but ended up in bankruptcy and a forced reorganization as a result of its risky and environmentally unsound methods of achieving that goal. Furthermore, managers may have trouble agreeing which goals are to be pursued and in what order.

If managers can deal with the limitations presented by a goal attainment approach, this perspective can provide a reasonable assessment of the major aspects of organizational effectiveness. Using this approach well, however, requires at least the following from organizations:

1. Ensuring that management receives input from all individuals who have a major influence on formulating official goals, even if they are not part of senior management
2. Including recognition of all goals attained (by observing the behavior of organization members), whether or not they were included in the official goals set forth by management
3. Recognizing the necessity of both short- and long-term goals
4. Insisting on tangible, verifiable, and measurable goals rather than relying on vague statements that merely mirror general expectations
5. Viewing goals as dynamic entities that change over time rather than as rigid or fixed statements of purpose[1]

A Systems Approach

In contrast to managers who use a goal attainment approach and focus on *what* is accomplished, managers who use a **systems approach** to assess organizational effectiveness care mostly about *how* things are accomplished. This approach is also goal oriented, but the goals referred to are **means goals:** how should an organization and its members behave? Managers using a systems approach, thus, evaluate organizational effectiveness by assessing the degree to which their organization acquires resources, processes these resources, and distributes the resulting goods or services in order to maintain environmental stability and balance.[2] Consider, for example, an organization with means goals that define a particular mix of products and the use of an aggressive marketing strategy. If the organization met these goals, it would be considered effective according to the systems approach, even if its profits were low.

A personal analogy might help differentiate the goal attainment and systems approaches. Suppose you were planning to drive your car from Chicago to

The effectiveness of a police department should be assessed in terms of its interaction with the public as well as in terms of its success in meeting ends goals.

Denver. The goal attainment approach for measuring effectiveness might focus on such ends goals as reaching Denver by noon on Thursday and keeping expenses under $150. The systems approach, on the other hand, might focus on such means goals as not exceeding the speed limit and driving between 350 and 400 miles each day. If you reach Denver Thursday night and spend over $150 to do so, your trip has been ineffective according to a goal attainment approach. If, on the other hand, you get to Denver by noon Thursday, having spent no more than $150, but had to drive for 24 hours at 75 miles per hour to make it because you were snowbound in Nebraska for a day, your trip has been ineffective from a systems approach.

Why do some people favor a systems approach over a goal attainment approach? According to some advocates, a systems approach is appropriate because:

- Goals are attained only when an organizational system operates effectively; therefore, managers should concentrate on assessing system effectiveness rather than on determining whether a profit was made or a particular sales goal was reached.
- An organization is a collection of interdependent segments, all of which must perform well to ensure the smooth operation of the overall organization. Just as your car's ignition, cooling, power-train, and other systems must work well to make it to Denver on time, an organization's communication, decision-making, and other systems must work well for it to be effective (see the discussion of systems theory in Chapter 4).
- A systems approach is based on the belief that an organization's survival and effectiveness depend on its ability to replenish the resources it consumes. Raw materials must be replenished, departing employees must be replaced, and outdated information (on customer needs, technological processes, and regulatory requirements) must be refreshed.

An Internal Processes Approach

An **internal processes approach** defines effectiveness as the degree to which organization members are integrated with organizational production and management systems to function smoothly with a minimum of internal strain. In an effective organization, according to this approach, communication flows freely, members trust management, and the organization is benevolent toward members.[3] An effective organization identifies and satisfies employees' needs, nurtures cohesion, reduces dysfunctional interpersonal conflict, and treats the integrity of internal systems (such as communication, work coordination, group functioning, and safety systems) as its most important concern. Managers can gauge effectiveness with the internal processes approach by assessing the degree to which these systems work appropriately for organization members. A communication system, for example, can be evaluated by the timeliness and accuracy of its information exchanges. An examination of accident records and inspection results can reveal safety system results. A survey program—such as the one used by Sears to assess employees' attitudes toward such factors as leadership, work design, physical working conditions, and communication—can reveal the extent to which employees are satisfied.

An internal processes approach and a systems approach are similar in that both are concerned with an organization's systems. An internal processes approach, however, has a much narrower scope, focusing on an organization's *members;* thus, managers using an internal processes approach must satisfy members' needs, both as the *means* to accomplishing goals and as an *end* in itself.

A Strategic Constituencies Approach

The newest of the four approaches, a **strategic constituencies approach,** assesses effectiveness by evaluating the degree to which the needs of an organization's constituents have been satisfied.[4] An organization's constituents are its stakeholders—that is, its suppliers, customers, unions, regulatory bodies, and any other group whose cooperation is required for the organization to survive. According to this approach, achieving effectiveness involves three steps: (1) identifying critical constituents; (2) identifying the important demands of each critical constituent; and (3) satisfying these demands.

Recall Progressive Video Images, the videotape shop introduced in Chapter 7. At PVI, owner Cindy Mertes' strategic constituencies include the bank that loaned her the capital to purchase supplies, the wholesale outlets that sell her tapes at reasonable prices, the employees who transform customers' tapes into the desired products, and—of course—the customers who want to use PVI for movie conversion and custom editing. PVI can be considered effective from a strategic constituencies approach if it can meet the needs of each of these groups.

A strategic constituencies approach overlaps somewhat with the other three approaches to organizational effectiveness. Managers trying to satisfy critical constituents, for example, may need to develop and pursue specific goals related to constituent satisfaction. In most cases, satisfying constitutents also requires managers to focus on internal processes and on integrating organization members with organizational systems. What distinguishes a strategic constituencies approach from the others is its concentration on one primary

TABLE 16.2   Four Systematic Approaches to Assessing Organizational Effectiveness

Approach	Characterized By	Sample Effectiveness Statement
Goal attainment	Focus on the degree to which ends goals are met	"The company was effective, having met its profit goal of $5 million."
Systems	Focus on how systems acquire, process, and export processed resources (i.e., means goals)	"The company was effective, having obtained necessary resources, produced a supply of products, successfully marketed these products, etc."
Internal processes	Focus on the integration of members with systems producing a smoothly functioning organization	"The company was effective, having good communication systems, satisfied employees, cohesive employee groups, and little internal conflict."
Strategic constituencies	Focus on the degree to which the needs of the organization's constituents have been met	"The company was effective, having identified and met the needs of critical constituents, including suppliers, employee unions, customers, and regulatory bodies."

ends goal (to satisfy constituent needs) rather than on other goals or on the means by which this ends goal is achieved.

Table 16.2 summarizes the main emphasis of the four systematic approaches presented in this section and gives examples of effectiveness statements for each.

An Integrated Approach to Controlling and Managing Organizational Effectiveness

The four approaches just presented are the most common ones used in recent years by U.S. organizations to define, measure, and control effectiveness. Unfortunately, managers do not always choose the approach most appropriate for their organization. For instance, an organization that is just getting started sometimes uses a goal attainment approach to specify what it expects its first-year results to be. Any of the other three approaches would be a better choice at a time when the organization should be concentrating on the future. The **competing values perspective** on organizational effectiveness attempts to address these problems by integrating ideas from the four systematic approaches.[5]

Development of the Competing Values Perspective

[A] company's stockholders may define effectiveness as return on assets or earnings per share, whereas its managers may define it as product quality or meeting production schedules.
—Cameron

The competing values approach takes its name from the belief that what a person values or considers effective depends on who that person is and what he or she represents. If her organization has yearly sales of $1 million, sales manager Theresa DePalo may consider it to be effective. On the other hand, human resources director Susie Carlisle may consider the same company ineffective if its unethical sales practices have caused three top salespeople to

FIGURE 16.3
Organizational Life Cycles

Maturity

Maturity Level

Birth

Entrepreneurial   Collectivity   Formalization   Elaboration of Structure

Stages of Development
(Life Cycles)

resign in disgust. Competing values create different and potentially conflicting goals among organization members and constituents. According to this perspective, therefore, there is no single goal against which effectiveness should be measured, and managers are not likely to agree on the importance of goals. The competing values perspective acknowledges a number of important effectiveness measures and specifies a viable way to deal with this fact consistent with an organization's stage of development and the values held by its key members.

The Importance of Organizational Life Cycles.   In choosing a model of organizational effectiveness, managers must take an organization's **life cycle** stage into account. The competing values perspective considers four stages, or cycles, to be important (see Figure 16.3):

1. *Entrepreneurial* ("birth") stage—the focus is on collecting resources needed for an organization's survival and the support of future activities
2. *Collectivity* stage—the concentration is on activities revolving around informal communication and structure, the development of cooperation among members, and the building of members' commitment to the organization
3. *Formalization* stage—the emphasis is on stability, efficiency of operations, and rules and procedures to guide operations
4. *Elaboration of structure* stage—the attention is refocused on the external environment and opportunities for additional growth

As you will discover in the next section, the competing values perspective offers four models of effectiveness. None of them is best for all organizations at all times, but each is well suited to particular stages of the organizational life cycle. Later in this chapter, you will see how managers can determine which model(s) to emphasize based, in part, on their organization's stage of development.

Critical Values and Effectiveness Criteria. The developers of the competing values perspective examined the many criteria others used to define effectiveness, and they identified three sets of competing values that appeared to influence which criteria managers choose to use in assessing effectiveness:

1. *Flexibility vs. control*—the degree to which an organization values flexibility over control. If innovation, adaptability, and change are important to an organization, flexibility is emphasized. If, on the other hand, order, consistency, and maintenance of the status quo are more important, the organization will accentuate control.

2. *People vs. organization*—the degree to which an organization values the well-being of organization members vis-à-vis the development and promotion of the organization. The competing values approach does not assert that these two must conflict with one another, merely that an organization should determine which it wishes to emphasize as it assesses effectiveness. When managers believe that the feelings and needs of organization members are of utmost importance, they express a value similar to that promoted by the internal processes approach to organizational effectiveness.

3. *Means vs. ends*—the relative importance of each type of goal to the organization. If ends are valued more highly, a perspective similar to that found in the goal attainment approach is favored. If means are preferred, managers maintain a perspective such as that presented in the systems approach.

As shown in Figure 16.4, the three sets of critical values can be placed into eight possible combinations. Each combination is associated with a particular type of effectiveness criterion. An organization that values *O*rganization over people, *E*nds over means, and *C*ontrol over flexibility, for example, would probably want to include criterion set 1 (OEC) in its assessment of effectiveness, because its emphasis on productivity and efficiency is consistent with that combination of values. As shown in the figure, a manager might measure this effectiveness criterion by assessing the amount of output generated by the organization or by looking at the ratio of output to input.

Because the developers of the competing values perspective believed that no one effectiveness criterion is adequate, they grouped the eight criteria shown in Figure 16.4 into compatible combinations. This results in four models that managers can use to assess effectiveness in organizations.

Four Models of Effectiveness

This section describes the four models of effectiveness proposed by the competing values perspective and shows how managers can assess effectiveness using each (see Table 16.3 on page 388). As you read, you will notice that some of these models have names similar to the four systematic approaches discussed earlier in the chapter. Do not let these (or other) similarities between

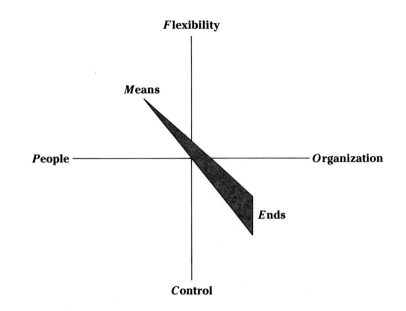

FIGURE 16.4 A Three-Dimensional Model of Organizational Effectiveness

The three-dimensional model shows the three value sets. The eight cells represent the ways the value sets can be combined. The criterion to the right of each cell is often used to measure effectiveness for that particular combination of values.

The Eight Cells	The Eight Criteria
OEC	1. *Productivity/efficiency*—volume of output, the ratio of output over input
OCM	2. *Planning and goal setting*—the amount of emphasis on the planning, objective setting, and evaluation process
OFE	3. *Resource acquisition*—the capacity to capture assets and develop external support
OFM	4. *Flexibility-readiness*—the ability to adapt to shifts in external conditions and demands
PCE	5. *Stability-control*—Smoothness of internal conditions, continuity, equilibrium.
PCM	6. *Information management-communication*—sufficiency of information flows, adequacy of internal orchestration
PFE	7. *Value of human resources training*—the enhancement and maintenance of overall staff capacity
PFM	8. *Cohesion-morale*—the level of communality and commitment among the staff members

Source: Based on R. E. Quinn and K. Cameron (1979), *Organizational life cycles and the criteria of effectiveness,* working paper: SUNY-Albany.

the four *models* and the four *approaches* confuse you. Recall that the four systematic approaches discussed earlier were *descriptions* of how some organizations have assessed effectiveness. The four models proposed by the competing values perspective are *prescriptions* of what organizations should do to evaluate effectiveness. Unfortunately, relatively few organizations have followed these prescriptions thoroughly.

TABLE 16.3   Models, Values, and Effectiveness Criteria

Model	Values	Effectiveness Criteria	
		Means	Ends
Human relations	People and flexibility	Maintaining cohesion and morale	Value and development of human resources
Open systems	Flexibility and organization	Maintaining flexibility and readiness	Growth, resource acquisition, and external support
Rational goals	Organization and control	Planning, objective setting, and evaluation	Productivity and efficiency
Internal processes	Control and people	Information management and coordination	Stability and equilibrium

From Stephen P. Robbins, *Organization Theory: Structure and Design of Organizations,* © 1983, p. 39. Reprinted by permission of Prentice-Hall, Inc., Englewood Cliffs, NJ.

The Human Relations Model.   The **human relations model** characterizes an organization that values the well-being of its members over the development and promotion of the organization itself. This model is further characterized by the beliefs that flexibility is necessary for innovation, adaptation, and change and that the need for flexibility is more important than the need for control and maintenance of the status quo.

Given this orientation, managers should assess the effectiveness of means goals by measuring the degree to which cohesion and morale are developed and maintained among organization members. Cohesion can be measured by evaluating the degree to which organization members like each other, work well together, communicate fully and effectively, and successfully coordinate work with each other. Morale can be measured by evaluating the degree to which members feel they are important to the organization; share goals; are committed to the organization and its interests; and, as a group, desire to contribute to the organization.

Managers adopting a human relations model assess the model's effectiveness of ends goals by measuring the value and development of an organization's human resources. Just as investors judge the worth of their stocks by whether they increase in value, another indication of the economic worth of an organization's workforce is whether it improves over time. An organization that is unable to retain valued employees and that replaces them with less-skilled, less-experienced, or less-accomplished workers would see a decline in the worth of its workforce and would be considered ineffective under a human relations model. On the other hand, an organization that recruits, retains, and improves its members increases the worth of its human resources and, thus, its effectiveness. The human relations model, by its nature, considers the worth of a workforce as indicative of an organization's chances of functioning effectively.

The Open-Systems Model.   An open system of management, as described in Chapter 2, characterizes an organization that is sensitive and responsive, capable of both receiving information from and projecting information to the external environment. Managers of an **open-systems model** organization,

Managers adopting a human relations approach value trained, experienced, skilled workers capable of producing at high levels, even though such a workforce tends to be more expensive for an organization.

thus, value the need for flexibility over the need for control, as do managers using the human relations model. The open-systems model, however, emphasizes organizational development and promotion over the well-being of organization members.

Given this orientation, managers should assess the effectiveness of means goals by measuring the degree to which their organization maintains flexibility and readiness for change. Flexibility can be measured by determining how easily the organization can alter its policies and practices in response to changes in its environment. In a flexible organization, managers can make changes in standard operating procedures relatively quickly. Managers in a less flexible organization must "move heaven and earth" to change the way work is performed. Readiness for change can be assessed by determining how easily the organization can perform alternative tasks if called on to do so and by measuring the degree to which workers are receptive to change (see Chapter 18).

Ends goals in an open-systems model focus on organizational growth, the acquisition of needed resources, and the procurement of external support for the organization. Managers, thus, can measure the production capacity of the workforce and the organization's assets, sales levels, market share, and (in for-profit organizations) profits. Managers can assess resource acquisition, for example, by evaluating the degree to which sufficient raw materials, inventories, and employees are obtained from the environment and by evaluating the cost of doing so. External support can be measured by the degree to which critical external constituents—suppliers, customers, regulatory agencies, and so on—are loyal to the organization, have confidence in it, and provide support when needed.

The Rational Goals Model. When management values an organization over its members and control over flexibility, its focus is considered to be on rational goals. Like the open-systems model, the **rational goals model** is concerned with organizational development and promotion. Unlike the open-systems model, however, the rational goals model values control, consistency, and maintenance of the status quo more than it values flexibility.

Organizational Effectiveness: Who's on First?

The competing values perspective stresses that there is no universal goal against which organizational effectiveness can be measured. The criteria appropriate for judging one organization's effectiveness should differ from those used to judge another, depending on each organization's values, life-cycle stage, and so on. Sometimes, however, people want to compare the effectiveness of one organization to that of another. Is a "blue chip" company still considered strong, for example? Which companies are poised for rapid growth and which are ripe for a takeover bid? *Business Week, Fortune,* and other publications generate lists each year to satisfy readers' demands to know what the "top" companies are.

To compile these and other comparison lists, standard criteria of effectiveness must be adopted. Five standard criteria are used here to examine the effectiveness of three well-known companies: Du Pont, Merck, and Amoco. In 1988, these companies were similar in market value, ranging from $20.8 billion to $25.4 billion. Their CEOs received similar compensation: $2.4 million, $1.4 million, and $1.3 million, respectively. Deciding which company is most effective is not an easy task. Which

company comes out on top depends on the effectiveness criterion that is used. As you examine the accompanying five charts, look at how the lead changes according to whether the criterion is sales revenues, profits (income after expenses), margin (profit as a percent of sales), sales growth (the increase in sales over those from the previous year), or profit growth (the increase in profit over that from the previous year). Note, for example, that Du Pont comes out on top on the basis of both sales and profits. Merck, however, excels on the basis of sales growth and margin, while Amoco appears best in terms of profit growth. This illustrates the importance of using more than one effectiveness criterion to understand an organization's overall effectiveness.

As you examine the charts, you will note that they (and many of the "top" lists published) are based mostly on ends criteria. Understanding *how* ends effectiveness is obtained, however, would require examination of means criteria. Although it is more difficult to compare means criteria than ends criteria across organizations, some means measures can be compared. In fact, when *Fortune* publishes the results of its annual survey of America's most admired

corporations every January, many of the criteria examined are means criteria. It is very likely that Merck's success on ends criteria is largely attributable to its strong means performance. Of the 305 companies included in *Fortune*'s survey, Merck ranked first overall and first in six of eight criteria, including: the ability to attract, develop, and keep talented people; innovativeness; quality of products and services; and use of corporate assets. It ranked no lower than third on any criterion.[1]

1. America's most admired corporations (30 January 1989), *Fortune,* 71ff.

This combination of values results in means goals that focus on organizational planning and the setting of objectives—in short, on setting and reaching rational goals. Managers assessing the effectiveness of an organization's planning techniques can measure the degree to which the organization follows the procedures suggested in Chapters 5 and 8 as they plot its course for the future. For example, does the organization establish objectives, premise (forecast and formulate assumptions), determine a course of action, and then formulate supporting plans for the plotted course of action? Managers also can evaluate

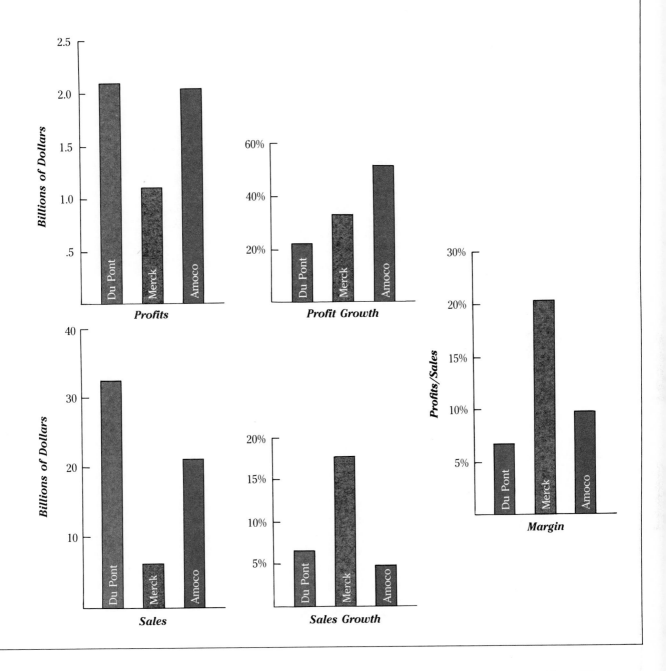

these goals to determine the degree to which they are specific, difficult, properly formulated, and reachable.

The important ends goals in the rational goals model usually involve productivity and operations efficiency. Generally, managers measure productivity by assessing the amount of goods or services generated in a specific period of time. This assessment can be conducted for individual organization members, for specified groups, and for the overall organization. Managers can measure efficiency by comparing productivity to production costs. The greater the productivity per dollar of cost, the greater the organization's efficiency.

Managers can measure efficiency by comparing productivity to production costs. The greater the productivity per dollar of cost, the greater the organization's efficiency.

The Internal Processes Model. Like the traditional internal processes approach and the human relations model, the **internal processes model** of organizational effectiveness values the well-being of organization members. Unlike either of them, however, the internal processes model shares the rational goals model's emphasis on the values of control, consistency, and the status quo over flexibility.

One set of means goals important in an internal processes model involves information management. Managers can assess the effectiveness of their information-collection and distribution processes by measuring the completeness and accuracy of the information received from and delivered to their external and internal environments. Managers can also take into account the efficiency with which the information is collected. The effectiveness of other information-management means goals should be assessed by determining the adequacy of the organization's analysis and interpretation, as well as by the adequacy of its communication of information, evaluations, and directives.

Another important set of means goals for this type of model involves coordination processes. For example, how much are organization members aware of their individual and group responsibilities? Do they understand how to interact with other individuals and groups to serve the organization?

Ends goals in the internal processes model relate to an organization's stability and equilibrium. Managers can assess these attributes by measuring the degree to which their organization maintains its structure, distribution of functions, and allocation and use of resources over time. Particularly important is the degree to which these factors remain unchanged in the face of stress or external threats.

Guidelines for Managers

As you can see, each of the four models advocated by developers of the competing values perspective provides a way for managers to assess organizational effectiveness. Confounding the situation, however, is that characteristics of all four effectiveness models can be found, to a degree, in most organizations. Furthermore, as you have learned, not all key members champion the same model, because they hold different values. The obvious question for managers is "Which model of effectiveness should I favor?" Sometimes, the answer is to provide different models of effectiveness for different parts of an organization. The criteria for assessing the effectiveness of a research and development department, for example, usually favor the values expressed by the open-systems and/or human relations models, whereas an audit or quality assurance department usually needs a rational goals model. Most of the time, however, managers should choose a model of effectiveness based on their organization's level of maturity.

An organization in the *entrepreneurial stage*, for example, often is best served by the open-systems model of effectiveness. After all, the organization's chances of survival depend on its flexibility (a means goal in the open-systems model) and whether the organization exists for reasons beyond the personal interests of a few individuals. The ends goals of growth, resource acquisition, and external support, which characterize the open-systems model, are also appropriate for this stage in an organization's life cycle. In its entrepreneurial stage, for example, Apple Computer should have gauged effectiveness by measuring how well it maintained flexibility and readiness for change and by measuring its growth rate, the adequacy of the resources it obtained, and the level of support it received from those outside the organization. Not only were these appropriate measures of effectiveness for Apple in its early years, but they were based on goals that had to be accomplished in order for the company to advance to the next stage in its life cycle.

The *collectivity stage* of an organizational life cycle is consistent with the characteristics of the human relations model of effectiveness. At this point in an organization's life cycle, that model's means goals of maintaining cohesion and morale match the organization's emphasis on informal communication and structure and the development of cooperation and commitment among its members. The human relations ends goals relating to the value and development of human resources also fit well, because the organization is trying to build a strong "family" of members during this stage. The onset of this life-cycle stage was particularly noticeable at Apple in the early 1980s, given the company's rapid growth and the high visibility of its revolutionary product line. During its collectivity stage, Apple was proud of its human relations orientation and devoted tremendous amounts of resources to developing employee morale and cohesion. Even its advertising revealed the company's emphasis on its members.

For organizations in the *formalization stage*, the combined use of the internal processes and rational goals models could be appropriate. An organization at this point in its life cycle usually becomes somewhat conservative relative to its earlier stages, and the combined use of these models offers the control the organization seeks as it concentrates on efficiency and stability. For instance, as Apple Computer entered this life cycle stage during the mid-1980s, its managers were faced with the company's first quarterly loss and employee layoffs. Particularly between 1985 and 1987, after John Sculley took control of the company, Apple shifted its means criteria to systematic and rational planning, formal objectives, careful information management, and comprehensive internal coordination. Ends effectiveness criteria became measures of productivity, efficiency, and stability. For most of this period, the combination of means and ends goals enabled the company to become profitable again.

Managers and Effectiveness: Do Managers Matter?

In 1988, Maria Castañeda of Texas A&M University and Nancy Johnson, vice-president of corporate research for American Family Insurance, conducted a study to find out whether the performance of individual managers influences the effectiveness of their work units. Approximately seventy-five American Family district claims managers (DCMs), who oversee the investigation and settlement of claims filed by or against the company's policy holders, participated in the investigation.

Performance was defined as the degree to which a manager fulfilled each of ten major managerial responsibilities identified through job analysis (see Chapter 22), three of which were planning, directing, and controlling. (The terminology in this "Closer Look" is consistent with that used elsewhere in this book, even though different terms were sometimes used in the study at American Family.) How well each DCM performed each of ten managerial behaviors was rated by his or her boss. Seven measures of effectiveness involved various business outcomes of the manager's unit, three of which were productivity, employee satisfaction, and financial effectiveness. Productivity was assessed by the number of claims handled by the technicians working for the DCM. Employee satisfaction was measured by surveying the technicians. Financial effectiveness was assessed by measuring annual loss payments and expenses.

The results of the study showed little relationship between the managers' performance and four effectiveness criteria of customer retention, customer satisfaction, customer attraction, and timeliness of claims service. All of the management behaviors examined, however, were related to at least one of the three effectiveness criteria of productivity, employee satisfaction, and financial effectiveness. Perhaps most importantly, managers who were better at planning, directing, and controlling had more positive, effective work units. The better managers planned, the more satisfied were their employees. Managers who directed better than their peers also had employees who were more satisfied and more productive and who contributed more to the company's financial effectiveness. Lastly, the better managers executed the controlling function, the more satisfied and more productive were their employees (who contributed more to financial effectiveness).

It would appear from this study that managers *do* matter. Better managers have more effective work units. These findings are helping American Family Insurance improve managerial selection and training programs to obtain a result desired by every organization: improved organizational effectiveness.

As an organization matures further, it may find that it has become too stable, too conservative. When it reaches the *elaboration of structure stage,* it must again become flexible and open to change in its search for new growth opportunities, additional resources, and new and continuing sources of external support. This point in the life cycle encourages a return to the open-systems model of effectiveness so that the organization can take advantage of any opportunities it finds. In practice, however, organizations at full maturity are unlikely to adopt the open-systems model as a sole perspective on organizational effectiveness, even if they did so during their entrepreneurial stages. Instead, they may adopt an open-systems model and—perhaps to a lesser extent—both the internal processes and rational goals models. As a result, the definition and measurement of organizational effectiveness can become quite complex.

Apple has not abandoned the rational goals and internal processes models that served it so well during the mid- to late 1980s, but John Sculley appears ready to incorporate some open-systems characteristics in his plans for the company's future. Developing new products, capitalizing on rising interest in such issues as network computing, and spending over $150 million per year on

TABLE 16.4 *Life Cycle Stages and Matching Effectiveness Models*

	Entrepreneurial Stage	Collectivity Stage	Formalization Stage	Elaboration of Structure Stage
Characterized By	Emphasis on collection of resources needed for survival and future activities	Emphasis on informal communication and informal structure	Emphasis on stability and efficiency	Emphasis on monitoring the external environment
	Use of resources to find creative, innovative business methods and/or products/services	Development of cooperation among members and the building of members' commitment to the organization	Development of rules and procedures to guide operations; use of a conservative approach	Searches for opportunities for renewal and further growth; attempts to become less conservative
Appropriate Effectiveness Model	Open-systems model	Human relations model	Internal processes model combined with rational goals model	Open-systems model and, to a lesser extent, internal processes model and rational goals model

research are some indications that Apple is taking the open-systems effectiveness criteria seriously.[6]

Another possible avenue for mature organizations is to create a unit or division targeted for growth and development and to use an open-systems model of effectiveness for that unit, but to continue to emphasize internal processes and/or rational goals models for the remainder of the organization. This, in effect, is what IBM did when it created an independent business unit to develop the IBM PC. In fact, IBM's success in this venture contributed heavily to Apple's problems in the early 1980s and is a testimony to this model's potential usefulness.

[G]ood managers can improve organizational effectiveness. Bad managers, on the other hand, can lead their organizations into decline.
—Cameron

As you can see, an organization's stage of development significantly influences the models of organizational effectiveness managers adopt—or, rather, it should. Too often, managers choose a model based strictly on personal values, sometimes selecting inappropriate models as a result. For years, Steven Jobs, one of the founders of Apple, successfully used the human relations model. When his preference for this model matched the company's needs, Apple was successful. As the company matured beyond the collectivity stage, however, Job's insistence on using this model and the company's newly conservative behavior contributed to its profitability problems.

In sum, managers should assess their organization's dominant life-cycle stage and choose effectiveness criteria from a model compatible with that stage. This means only that one (or perhaps two) models should be emphasized during certain life stages, not that all other effectiveness criteria are irrelevant. In fact, many internal problems encountered at Apple during its formalization stage were due largely to the company's failure to attend to the effectiveness criteria used during the two earlier life-cycle stages. To quote former employees, "It's just another big, boring company." "Why bother? You're a cog in a wheel."[7] Table 16.4 summarizes the characteristics of each of the four stages of development and indicates which model (or combination of models) of effectiveness is appropriate for each stage in an organization's life cycle.

Organizational Effectiveness in Review

There is no universally accepted definition of organizational effectiveness. This is unfortunate, because managers need to know what organizational effectiveness is in order to control it. This ambiguity is evident in the haphazard rifle and shotgun approaches managers often use to assess organizational effectiveness.

In recent years, however, managers have used four major systematic approaches that assess organizational effectiveness by considering both where an organization is going (ends goals) and how it intends to get there (means goals). A goal attainment approach, which evaluates effectiveness by assessing whether specified ends goals are met, has been the most widely used approach. A systems approach concentrates on means goals and, thus, examines the degree to which organizations successfully acquire and transform important resources. Less common is an internal processes approach, which measures whether organization members are well integrated and the organization is functioning smoothly. Finally, the strategic constituencies approach concentrates on the degree to which the needs of critical organizational constituents, such as suppliers and customers, are satisfied.

The competing values perspective on effectiveness, which observes that organizations define effectiveness differently depending on the values held by key organization members, integrates each of the four systematic approaches into four models. The human relations model values the well-being of organization members. The open-systems model emphasizes flexibility. The rational goals model stresses control and consistency. The internal processes model values both the well-being of organization members and control. Each model can be used individually or in combination with others.

Organizations usually select an effectiveness approach or a model based on their managers' values, but total reliance on personal values can lead to poor choices. The competing values perspective states that managers should evaluate their organization's life cycle to identify the model most appropriate for its stage of development: entrepreneurial (creation), collectivity, formalization, and elaboration of structure.

Issues for Review and Discussion

1. Compare and contrast the rifle and shotgun approaches to organizational effectiveness and identify the primary drawback of each.
2. Present an example of a goal attainment approach to organizational effectiveness for an organization at which you have worked.
3. Describe how a systems approach to effectiveness would differ from an internal processes approach for an organization such as McDonald's.
4. Describe a strategic constituencies approach to effectiveness for a college fraternity or sorority and identify at least two important factors that would be overlooked in using such an approach.
5. Develop a brief argument that could be presented to the board of directors of Ford Motor Company, making clear how a competing values perspective could benefit that organization.
6. List the main similarities and differences among the four models in the competing values perspective.

7. The competing values perspective argues that an organization's life-cycle stage should dictate the model of effectiveness it uses. Construct an argument against this.

Key Terms

organizational effectiveness
goal attainment approach
ends goals
systems approach
means goals
internal processes approach
strategic constituencies approach

competing values perspective
life cycle
human relations model
open-systems model
rational goals model
internal processes model

Suggested Readings

Cribben, J. J. (1982). *Leadership: Strategies for organizational effectiveness.* New York: AMACOM.

Goodman, P. S., Pennings, J. M. and Associates, eds. (1977). *New perspectives in organizational effectiveness.* San Francisco: Jossey-Bass.

O'Toole, J. (1987). *Vanguard management.* New York: Berkley.

Peters, R. (1987). *Thriving on chaos.* New York: Alfred A. Knopf; for a review of this book see Noe, A. W. (1988). In Pierce, J. L., and Newstrom, J. W., eds. *The manager's bookshelf: A mosaic of contemporary views.* New York: Harper & Row, 320-26.

Peters, T. J., and Waterman, R. H., Jr. (1982). *In search of excellence.* New York: Harper & Row.

Quinn, R. E., and Cameron, K. (1983). Organizational life cycles and shifting criteria of effectiveness: Some preliminary evidence. *Management Science,* 29(1), 33-51.

Notes

1. S. P. Robbins (1983), *Organization theory: The structure and design of organizations,* Englewood Cliffs, NJ: Prentice-Hall, 27.
2. E. Yuchtman and S. E. Seashore (1967), A systems resource approach to organizational effectiveness, *American Sociological Review,* 32, 891-903; E. Yuchtman and S. E. Seashore (1967), Factorial analysis of organizational performance, *Administrative Science Quarterly,* 12, 377-95.
3. B. Bass (1952), Ultimate criteria of organizational worth, *Personnel Psychology,* 5, 157-73; B. S. Georgopoules and A. A. Tannenbaum (1957), The study of organizational effectiveness, *American Sociological Review,* 22, 534-40; W. Bennis (1966), *Changing organizations,* New York: McGraw-Hill.
4. J. Pfeffer and G. Salancik (1978), *The external control of organizations,* New York: Harper & Row.
5. J. Rohrbaugh, G. McClelland, and R. Quinn (1980), Measuring the relative importance of utilitarian and egalitarian values: A study of individual differences about fair distribution, *Journal of Applied Psychology,* 65, 34-49; K. S. Cameron and D. A. Whetten (1981), Perceptions of organizational effectiveness over organizational life cycles, *Administrative Science Quarterly,* 26, 525-44; Robbins.
6. Apple's comeback (19 January 1987), *Business Week,* 86; Tremors from the computer quake (1 August 1988), *Fortune,* 42-60.
7. Apple is getting a few gray hairs (19 January 1987), *Business Week,* 88.

The Night Shift

By Cyril Ling, University of
Wisconsin-Whitewater

Jean MacDuff, the night nursing director of St. Amos Hospital, was disturbed by a memo from the hospital administrator, Paul Seay. Reports from the controller's office indicated that linen replacement costs, particularly for bed sheets, had doubled within the past three months due to shortages. A check by the day staff of laundry room procedures and nursing floor supplies had not accounted for the continued shortages. Paul's memo concluded, "In view of rising operating costs, I suggest that you institute immediate close checks on all your personnel."

The hospital had two main sections of eight floors each, including fifteen nursing units and an operating room, and one small wing consisting of three nursing units. Soiled linen was collected from two main laundry chutes in the basement of the main sections and from linen hamper trucks in the adjoining wing. The hospital laundry operated at peak capacity for eight hours, six days a week, starting at 9 A.M. Daily supply orders were filled and checked by the laundry manager before the laundry closed at 5 P.M. The night shift ran from 11 P.M. to 7 A.M. At 11 P.M., the night orderlies began distributing loaded hampers to each of the nursing units and the operating room. Floor personnel stored the linen in closets during the night as time permitted. The empty hampers were returned to the basement chutes by orderlies before they checked out at 6:30 A.M.

The night shift was a close-knit group, and its employment turnover was the lowest in the nursing department. Since the hospital was located in the far southwest corner of the city, many of the night employees, including several members of the professional nursing staff, carpooled from downtown areas. Many of the night-shift nurses' aides and orderlies were long-time employees; some were related to other employees or were second-generation St. Ames employees.

Jean MacDuff, being of ample proportions, was affectionately referred to as "Miz Mac" directly and "Big Mac" indirectly. With her approval, the night shift's 2:30 A.M. break had become a respected ritual; employee birthdays, anniversaries, and pay raises were always celebrated with food and fellowship between the units. Henry Sharon, the head orderly, often wrote a poem in honor of special occasions. Of undetermined age and handicapped with an artificial leg, Henry was the most agile and light-hearted worker on the night-time staff. He proudly carried his keys dangling from his belt, which indicated that he was in charge of laundry cart deliveries. He had been at the hospital for more than twenty years, and he tutored new orderlies with skill and understanding. Many student nurses also learned much from Henry in handling difficult patients and deaths.

Because of the size of the hospital and her many administrative duties, Jean considered Paul's directive to be an impossibility. On rounds that evening, she simply read the memo to each of the nursing unit supervisors and asked them to observe the handling of linen closely, to report any irregularities, and to make suggestions for changes. That night during the break, Jean asked Henry if he had noticed any outsiders hanging around while the linen hampers were being moved from the laundry. Henry reminded her that there were six exits in the hospital, which fire regulations stated must be kept open at all times, and that only one night watchman was on duty, usually at the emergency entrance. No suggestions or ideas were reported to Jean by any of the night personnel. Since there was no apparent shortage of clean linen during the 11-to-7 shift that evening, Jean and the night shift did nothing further about the linen problem.

Two weeks later, a second memo from Paul advised, "Due to continued shortages in linen sheets, effective immediately, all linen closets in nursing units will be kept tightly locked. Sheets will be dispensed only upon request by the nursing unit supervisors, and delivery and storage of the next day's linen must be personally supervised by the supervisor in each unit."

This regulation was met with much opposition and resentment from night staff, because it would require so much time and personnel. Orderlies unloading floor linen hampers were often called from the floor, and patient calls could not be handled promptly as a result of the regulation. With the extra work, the 2:30 A.M. break was frequently delayed until 3 or 4 A.M., and on some floors was omitted entirely. On two occasions, Paul was observed counting hampers and checking the basement laundry room at 6 A.M. Empty hampers often filled the service elevators when the day shift reported for duty; Henry Sharon explained to Jean that his orderlies no longer had time to get the empty hampers back to the basement, because the floors were too slow in unloading them. Nurses' aides reported frequent backaches from so much heavy unloading and complained that they could not guide the hampers, even when they were empty and blocking the hallways.

Absenteeism, which had never been a problem on the 11-to-7 shift, became more frequent, and several aides asked for transfers to the day shift. Jean questioned one very capable aide who resigned from the hospital. She said, "It's just no fun working here like it used to be. Everybody's got to be so careful and looking at each other. What do they think we would do with those missing sheets anyway, Miz Mac? We're all double bed sleepers! You can ask anybody!"

The following month, the hospital began using linens with its name printed in large blue letters in the middle. In spite of the addition of two new guards at employee exits and the checking of all personal parcels,

linen losses continued, although at a reduced rate.

About three weeks later, Jean resigned as night nursing director, complaining that she simply "couldn't take all this bickering and suspicion anymore."

Six months later, Paul still had not found a qualified replacement for Jean. Nursing care during night hours had been reduced sharply, and many staff doctors admitted acutely ill patients to the hospital only if private-duty night nurses were available.

Questions

1. Which of the four approaches to assessing organizational effectiveness was Paul using?
2. How might other approaches have helped him devise a better solution to the problem of the missing linen?
3. How would you have handled this problem?
4. Describe how you would go about identifying an appropriate organizational effectiveness model for use in the hospital.

17 Control Methods and Their Effects

Student Learning Objectives

After reading this chapter, you should be able to:

1. Define the managerial function of controlling and discuss the levels at which controlling activities take place.

2. Identify the targets of the control activity.

3. Distinguish among the four steps of the integrated control process and understand why an effective control system must include all four steps.

4. Explain why it is important to integrate strategic planning and controlling.

5. Understand the advantages and limitations of cybernetic and noncybernetic control systems.

6. Discuss the time perspectives that may be found in a control system.

7. Recognize the specific characteristics of good control systems and explain how each characteristic can improve the effectiveness of a control system.

8. Identify some of the most important positive and negative effects of control systems on organization members and explain the importance of this knowledge for managers.

*M*arianne Rowe is an assistant manager at Burger Barn #382 in Greensboro, North Carolina, one of 750 virtually identical fast-food restaurants in the Burger Barn chain. The parent organization has established a collection of very detailed ends and means goals for each restaurant in its chain, including the amounts of sales and profits each restaurant must generate per square foot, exactly how much each hamburger patty should weigh, and the word-for-word greeting employees should give customers. Robert Frank, the company's national franchise director, sends a report to each franchise at the beginning of every quarter that recaps the previous quarter's activity for that store and specifies corrective actions for the next quarter.

Yesterday Marianne received the report for store #382. It noted that her franchise met its sales goals for the preceding quarter, did not achieve its profits goals, treated customers according to procedure, and exceeded its food wastage allowance. As always, the report detailed the actions Marianne and her manager should take to improve performance. When Marianne met her friend Phyllis Klarner after work that night, she told her about the report. Phyllis asked Marianne how she felt about working for a company with so many rules and procedures to follow, and Marianne replied:

> *Actually, most of the time I like having the rules to depend on. They tell the people working for me how to do their jobs, and I can almost always anticipate what the other assistant managers will or won't do. Sometimes the rules do get on my nerves, though, especially if I feel the company uses them to treat me like a machine instead of a person. When I really get mad (and my boss isn't around), I get even by putting extra meat in the hamburgers and giving the staff complimentary meals.*

Robert Frank's quarterly reports are part of the control process used by the Burger Barn chain. It is a good system, but when Marianne feels overly controlled by the process, she vents her dissatisfaction and hurts the company's profitability by putting too much meat in the hamburgers and by giving free meals to employees. This illustrates the challenge of maintaining an organization's control systems while taking into account members' reactions to the control process.

The Control Process

In Chapter 16, you learned that the primary reason managers exercise control is to make their organization as effective as possible. **Controlling,** therefore, is defined as the process of monitoring and evaluating organizational effectiveness and initiating the actions needed to maintain or improve effectiveness. The control system in the Burger Barn chain, for example, collects information about the franchises through a variety of monitoring systems, including company observers who pose as customers. It then sends this information to Robert Frank, who compares it to the company's standards and forwards feedback and instructions for improvements to the stores in his quarterly reports.

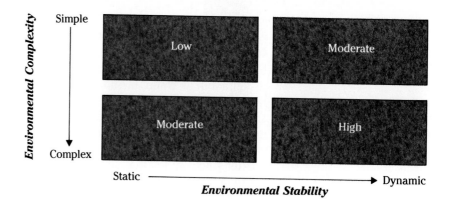

FIGURE 17.1 Need for Control

Environmental Complexity — Simple / Complex

| | Low | Moderate |
| | Moderate | High |

Static ────────────────→ Dynamic

Environmental Stability

The Need for Control

Like the managerial functions of planning, organizing, and directing, controlling is a complex activity that managers must perform at many organizational levels. Upper-level managers, for example, must monitor their organization's overall strategic plans, which can be implemented only if middle-level managers control the organization's divisional and departmental plans, which, in turn, rely on lower-level managers' control of groups and individual employees (see the discussion of goal hierarchy in Chapter 5). For instance, Robert Frank controls franchise effectiveness in the Burger Barn organization; Marianne's boss controls the effectiveness of Barn #382; Marianne controls the effectiveness of her shift.

Although there is a continual and universal need for control in organizations, the importance, amount, and type of control vary across organizational situations. Probably the most important influence on the nature of an organization's control systems is the amount of environmental change and complexity.

Organizations that operate with relatively stable external environments usually need to change very little, so managers eventually are able to control such organizations using a set of routine procedures. Consider, for example, the rules and procedures used to control the loan-making decisions, cash handling, dress codes, treatment of customers, and other means goals of a large bank and its branch offices. With greater levels of environmental change, however, controlling requires more continual attention from managers. Traditional routines and rigid control systems are simply not adequate for such conditions, as U.S. investment firms discovered in October 1987, when their computerized trading programs were unable to cope with dramatic and unanticipated changes in the stock market.

The amount of environmental complexity also affects the nature of control systems. Simple environments contain a limited number of highly similar components that are relatively easy to control through common sets of rules and procedures that address similar goals. The same bureaucratic control system, for example, can be used at most branch offices of a large bank. As complexity increases through organizational growth, product diversification, and so on, managers' needs for up-to-date information and coordination among organizational activities intensify. The complexity that calls for increased control, however, also requires open, organic systems that can respond quickly and effectively to complex environments. In such complicated situations, organizations often specify the development of flexible systems as a

FIGURE 17.2 The Traditional Control Model

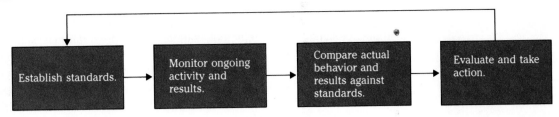

means goal: "To allow us to manage the complexities of our organization, we must remain flexible and open." Other control activities shift to ends goals, such as "We want to increase market share 10 percent in each of our divisions." Flexibility allows substantial choice as to how ends goals will be met: "Each division may decide how to achieve its 10 percent increase in market share." Figure 17.1 shows the level of control organizations need under different environmental conditions.

A Traditional Control Model

Traditional control models (see Figure 17.2) suggest that control is a four-step process in which managers:

- *Establish standards.* Standards are the ends and means goals established during the planning process; thus, planning provides the basis for the control process by providing the standards of performance against which managers compare organizational activities.
- *Monitor actual organizational behavior and results.* Managers determine what should be measured, by whom, when, and how so that they can determine what has actually taken place.
- *Compare actual behavior and results against standards.* Similar to the gap analysis performed during the strategic planning process (see Chapter 8), this comparison provides managers with the information they will evaluate in the final step.
- *Evaluate and take action.* Using their comparative information, managers form conclusions about the relationships found between expectations and reality and then make decisions to maintain the status quo, to change the standard, or to take corrective action.

The integrated control model presented later in this chapter expands the traditional model to deal with the complexities of today's organizational environments and to meet managers' needs to monitor both ends and means criteria of organizational effectiveness.

Organizational Targets

In essence, control affects every part of an organization: the resources it receives, the output it generates, its environmental relationships, and all managerial activities. Especially important are the targets of control in the essential functional areas of operations, marketing, finance, and human resources.

Product control is one system managers have devised to control productivity and quality.

To regulate productivity and quality, *operations controls* include systems that oversee design, product, service and use, materials, inventory, production, and employee behaviors.[1] Operations specialists for the Burger Barn chain, for example, designed quick, efficient, sanitary food preparation systems that produce tasty food.

Marketing controls often focus on systems that regulate sales, prices, costs, and market share.[2] The Burger Barn marketing department identified the prices each Barn would charge for food items and the sales volume expected per square foot of restaurant space.

Financial controls take place at many different levels within an organization. At an individual level, for example, Robert Frank's travel budget specifies how much he can spend on hotel rooms and meals when traveling to the franchises. The department Robert manages operates under an annual budget that governs how much money it can use to recruit and hire employees. The chain has an annual operating budget that specifies how much each Barn can spend for hamburger meat, condiments, paper supplies, labor, maintenance, and so forth, as well as a nonmonetary budget that defines the number of hours each company manager will donate to charity.

Two common targets of *human resource controls* are the regulation of managerial and nonmanagerial activities carried out on behalf of an organization and the improvement of its human resources so that its people can respond to and initiate new organizational ventures.[3] For instance, Melissa Zuravner-Lerner, human resource manager for Burger Barn, has implemented systems that specify, monitor, and control employee selection procedures, training and development programs, performance appraisals, and compensation methods.

An Integrated Control Model

Whether the need for control is high or low, whether the target is marketing or operations, the essential purpose of the controlling function is to monitor and enhance organizational effectiveness. As you learned in Chapter 16, both ends goals (*what* an organization is trying to accomplish) and means goals (*how* an organization and its members behave) contribute to the overall effectiveness of organizations. In the integrated model of the control process presented in Figure 17.3, managers assess the degree to which their organization has met both ends and means goals established during the planning process, examine the relationship between means behavior and ends results, and develop prescriptions for maintaining strengths and correcting weaknesses.

Step One: Assessment of Ends Goals

At Step One, managers measure actual organizational accomplishments and compare them to planned ends goals. The purpose of Step One of the control process is to identify what happened, not why it happened or what to do next. For managers concerned only with ends goals, this step would constitute the complete assessment of organizational effectiveness, which is one argument against the goal attainment approach (see Chapter 16). Consider, for example, Lil'America Builders, the remodeling company introduced in Chapter 7. Know-

FIGURE 17.3   *An Integrated Organizational Control Model*

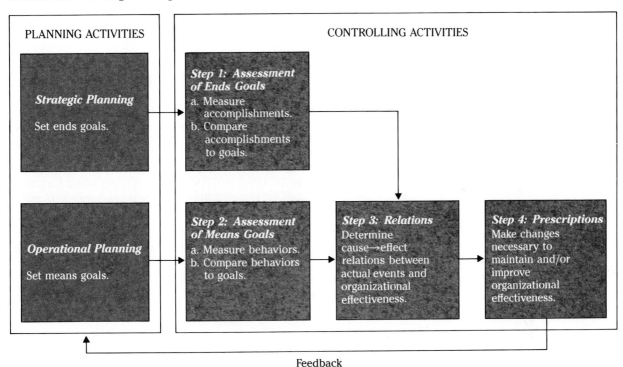

Feedback

ing that half of his jobs were completed on time does not tell owner Butch Ledworowski why the other half ran behind schedule.

Step Two: Assessment of Means Goals

At Step Two, managers measure actual behaviors and compare them to planned means goals. As in Step One, the purpose of Step Two of the control process is to identify what happened. By itself, it does not permit managers to conclude whether adherence to the plan accounted for the successes detailed in Step One, or whether deviations from the plan caused the weaknesses identified. For managers concerned only with means goals, this step would constitute the complete assessment of organizational effectiveness, which is one argument against the systems approach (see Chapter 16). Knowing, for example, that PERT (see Chapter 7) was not used for every project does not tell Butch what effect this had on completion timeliness.

Step Three: Examination of Ends and Means Goals Relationships

At Step Three of the control process, managers try to answer the question "What effect did behaviors aimed at means goals have on the attainment of ends goals?" Although it is possible for managers of some organizations to examine statistically the relationships between behaviors (the degree to which means goals are met) and results (the degree to which ends goals are met), most perform such examinations subjectively. Butch sees that PERT was used on nearly every job that was completed on time and on only a few of the delayed projects. He also finds that employees spent too much time correcting errors that could have been detected earlier. Butch concludes that project completion delays are caused by Lil'America's failure both to monitor progress using PERT as planned and to conduct daily inspections.

Step Four: Development of Prescriptions

In Step Four, managers use the cause-and-effect conclusions reached in Step Three to determine what actions their organization could take to maintain effectiveness already achieved and to improve effectiveness where needed. Often these actions can be categorized into three main groups:

1. If means criteria were planned and followed, and they helped achieve ends goals, they should be retained to maintain organizational effectiveness.
2. If means criteria were planned but not consistently followed, they should be retained and followed more consistently to improve organizational effectiveness.
3. Some means criteria should be added or changed. Sometimes the determination of cause-and-effect relationships shows that a means activity helped achieve an ends goal, even when the activity was not specifically intended to do so. In that case, this new means criterion should be added to the organization's plan. At other times, the relationship analysis shows that planned means criteria failed to produce ends results. In such cases, the criteria should either be changed or eliminated.

Accordingly, Butch should retain and encourage greater adherence to the means goals of using PERT to schedule and monitor each project's progress. He also should specify that inspections are to be conducted daily and include this means criterion in Lil'America's plan.

Variations in Control Systems

Whereas all good control systems should follow an integrated control model, such as that just described, not all control systems are identical. Control systems differ in terms of the degree to which they are self-managing, as opposed to externally managed, and by the point in the process at which control is exercised.

Cybernetic and Noncybernetic Systems

Control systems differ in the amount of outside attention required for them to operate effectively (see Figure 17.4). Systems using **cybernetic control** are based on self-regulating procedures that automatically detect and correct deviations from planned activities and effectiveness levels. Control systems that are operated completely independently from the work system itself involve **noncybernetic control.** They rely on external monitoring systems in much the same way that a manufacturing company might use a separate quality assurance department to monitor and enforce quality standards rather than allowing production crews to perform this activity.

FIGURE 17.4   The Cybernetic Continuum

Totally Noncybernetic   **Totally Cybernetic**

Cybernetic Control.   Everyone is quite familiar with—and, in fact, personally operates—a number of highly sophisticated cybernetic control systems. One of these determines the body's need for oxygen, assesses whether the supply is adequate, and causes action (breathing) to maintain an adequate supply. Few organizational control systems are totally cybernetic, but some come close. The control system for a coal-fired electrical generating station at Detroit Edison, for example, uses computers to monitor the flow of pulverized coal into the burning chamber. The computers speed up or reduce the flow as necessary to maintain adequate fuel supplies.

Although totally cybernetic systems are difficult to design for many organizational activities, they have a number of advantages. The cybernetic portions of the control system at the generating station are able to identify and document deviations much more rapidly than any human worker could. Furthermore, electronic and mechanical cybernetic systems can provide this analysis consistently and for long periods of time without getting tired and subsequently losing effectiveness. Finally, cybernetic control systems are often much more cost effective. Only a few employees are required to operate the entire electrical generating station, primarily because significant portions of the control process are conducted by computerized cybernetic control systems.

The mere automation or computerization of a *work* system does not necessarily mean that the *control* system is cybernetic. The drone submarine sent to explore and photograph the sunken Titanic was fully automated, but humans on the surface monitored the effectiveness of the sub's operations and its adherence to the planned mission. To be classified as a cybernetic system, a work system must have built-in automatic control capabilities, although the built-in control need not be machine-based. A group of workers that controls its own activities without assistance from people outside the group would constitute a cybernetic system.

Noncybernetic Control.   With so many advantages inherent in cybernetic control systems, why would an organization want to use noncybernetic controls? Sometimes it is not possible to develop a completely cybernetic system. Universities, for example, have not yet developed cybernetic systems for monitoring and correcting teaching effectiveness. Even the cybernetic control system at the Detroit Edison generating plant relies on noncybernetic controls in nonroutine situations, as when a human worker must inspect the coal conveyors, pulverizers, or feeders to determine what has caused an alarm to sound.

Sometimes it is possible, but not economically or socially feasible, to use a cybernetic system. Technology currently exists, for example, to enable Burger Barns to use a completely cybernetic system to control food preparation, delivery, and payment. Customers could approach the counter, gaze at the menu, and press the button next to their menu choice. Automated systems could prepare the food, signal the customer to pick it up at a designated delivery station, and require the customer to insert payment into a receptacle before releasing the meal. The cybernetic system could automatically monitor and control inventory and conduct appropriate financial audits of payments received. Possible? Yes. Economically feasible? No. The cost of products would probably have to rise dramatically to support the expense of such a system.

Time Perspectives

Organizations can introduce the control activity at three stages in the work process: prior to, during, or after the performance of a work activity.[4] Managers use **precontrols** (or *preaction controls*) to prevent deviation from a desired plan of action before work actually begins. For example, Butch Ledworowski inspects all construction materials before they are used to see that they meet industry standards.

Managers use **concurrent controls** to prevent deviation from the planned course of action while work is in progress. **Steering controls** are reactive concurrent controls; they occur after work has begun but before it is completed. At Lil'America, for instance, Butch visits each construction site and watches his carpenters, offering advice and instruction as they work. **Screening controls** (also referred to as *yes/no controls*) are preventive concurrent controls. As activity at a critical stage is completed, managers use screening controls to assess work performed to that point and to judge whether progress is adequate. If it is, a yes decision is made to proceed to the next stage. At Lil'America, for example, Butch always inspects carpentry work after walls have been framed. Unless he approves the work, electricians cannot begin wiring the structure.

Managers use **postaction controls** after the product or service is complete to examine the output. After each remodeling job, Butch assesses the work to determine whether it met specifications, was completed on time, and came in at or under budget. Postaction controls play an important role in future planning, but their primary function is to provide feedback by describing the degree to which previous activities have succeeded.

In practice, most managers use a hybrid control system that incorporates all three types of control systems so that managers can prepare for a job, guide its progress, and assess its results.

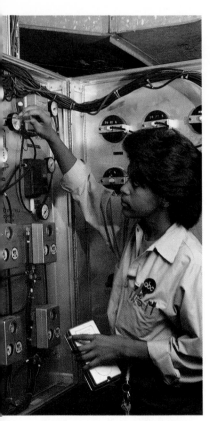

Steering controls are intended to keep work operations on track and to make adjustments if deviations occur.

Characteristics of Effective Control Systems

Successful control systems have certain common characteristics. First, a good control system systematically follows an integrated model, such as that described in this chapter (review Figure 17.4), and adequately addresses each organizational target. Next, to the extent possible, an effective control system takes a hybrid approach so that precontrol, concurrent, and postaction control systems can be used to monitor and correct activities at all points in an organization's operations. Other characteristics of a good control system include its treatment of information, its appropriateness, and its practicality.[5]

Evading Control: Games People Play

Carleton Arthur works for the bridge inspection office in a Western state. His boss, Peter Johnson, decided last year that all bridges in the state should be inspected at least every other year, and he assigned each inspector a monthly quota of bridges to inspect. To make sure all bridges were inspected as required by the quota, Peter required the inspectors to paint a control number on the side of each bridge after each inspection, log the entry in a control book, and turn in their control books for review at the end of each month.

Carleton and his co-workers soon found that they could not complete the number of assigned inspections in a month. Initially, they simply turned in their logs showing that they were failing to meet their quotas while they continued to make comprehensive bridge inspections. When Peter started to place inspectors on probation for substandard performance, however, some of the inspectors began to "pad" their logs by listing inspections they had not actually conducted. As part of his control system, though, Peter examined some of the bridges at random. Discovering that the painted control numbers were missing on some bridges that had been logged as inspected, he terminated an inspector

for falsifying records. Now inspectors inspect every other bridge, but they paint the inspection number on every bridge and log each entry.

Carleton and his co-workers are players in the "let's see who can beat the system" game. They and other employees who systematically try to circumvent control systems are sometimes able to fulfill the letter of the law but clearly not its spirit. The increased use of computerized monitoring systems may have eliminated some such players but has encouraged creativity from others. Some computers have been fooled when workers have left machines running while the workers are away from their desks. Students who are required to complete computerized exercises as a course requirement have evaded control by using a work processor to type a facsimile of the verification printout. Typists whose performance is monitored by the number of keystrokes entered on computers have placed staplers on the keyboard to produce keystrokes (and deleted the nonsensical characters afterwards).

Sometimes, employees try to "pull a fast one" because they are lazy. Usually, however, workers try to circumvent control systems they consider unfair, unreasonable, or of-

fensive. Bypassing the rules without getting caught is one way to strike back at a dehumanizing control system. Unfortunately, many organizations respond to these types of actions by further tightening controls, making them even more offensive and oppressive. The dehumanizing factor aside, it often would make good economic sense for organizations to look at the cause underlying the behavior they are trying to control. At one of the Burger Barns, for example, a manager reprimanded for exceeding the food wastage allowance instructed employees to allow unsold food to remain on the shelf for ten minutes rather than the specified eight minutes before throwing it out. Who knows how many customers never returned because they were unhappy with their lukewarm hamburger but did not want to complain?

In short, managers should consider whether a stringent control system will be accepted by workers. So-called foolproof systems may well end up being foolhardy if they fail to acknowledge that the object of control is a thinking individual with feelings.

The control process itself—and, certainly, all effective control systems—are based on information. Without good information, managers cannot assess whether ends and means goals are met. They cannot determine the relationship between them or provide feedback to planners. To be effective, information must be accurate, objective, timely, and distributed to organization members who need it.

Another characteristic of a good control system is its focus on issues of importance to an organization. Managers who develop control procedures for virtually all work activities and outcomes waste resources and, as will be discussed later in this chapter, risk creating a control system that produces negative feelings and reactions among employees (see "A Closer Look: Evading Control").

When evaluating whether a control system is right for a particular organization, managers should ask the following questions:

1. "Does the control system deal with important issues?" A good control system focuses on significant ends and means goals and deemphasizes minor issues. Butch Ledworowski, for example, does not concern himself with the brand of tool boxes used by his carpenters.
2. "Is the control system placed at critical junctures in the work process?" For example, should Butch inspect carpentry work after walls have been framed or would it suffice to wait until wallboard has been installed?
3. "Can managers do anything about these issues to improve their organization?" A disciplinary system, for example, should recognize the difference between voluntary absenteeism (a behavior that managers may be able to change) and absences caused by accidents and illnesses (events over which managers have little control).

A final characteristic of a good control system is its practicality. Something may have worked well for another organization or may look wonderful in print, but unless it is applicable to the organization in question, it will not work well there. Some practical characteristics to look for in a control system include feasibility, flexibility, the likelihood that organization members will accept it, and the ease with which the system can be integrated with planning activities.

Table 17.1 lists many of the characteristics discussed in this section. Managers can use such checklists to evaluate current or planned control systems.

TABLE 17.1 Checklist for Evaluating Control System Characteristics

	Inadequate	Unknown	Adequate
Follows Stage One of control process	_____	_____	_____
Follows Stage Two of control process	_____	_____	_____
Follows Stage Three of control process	_____	_____	_____
Follows Stage Four of control process	_____	_____	_____
Incorporates precontrols	_____	_____	_____
Incorporates steering controls	_____	_____	_____
Incorporates screening controls	_____	_____	_____
Incorporates postcontrols	_____	_____	_____
Information accuracy	_____	_____	_____
Timeliness of information	_____	_____	_____
Objectivity of information	_____	_____	_____
Appropriate distribution of control information	_____	_____	_____
Appropriate focus	_____	_____	_____
Feasibility (economically and organizationally)	_____	_____	_____
Flexibility	_____	_____	_____
Acceptance	_____	_____	_____
Is well integrated with planning	_____	_____	_____

The Impact of Control on Organization Members

To this point, you have been learning about the importance of the controlling function to an organization. Consider now what the controlling function does for or to an organization's members. If designed well, control systems can have many positive effects both for organizations and for the people who work in them (see Table 17.2).[6] Unfortunately, sometimes a number of dysfunctional effects also occur (see "A Closer Look: Controlling Employee Behavior").

Positive Effects

Organizational control systems can provide many positive effects for organization members through the influence they exert on motivation, performance, and satisfaction. This influence is created by providing adequate structure, appropriate feedback, and effective goal-setting programs.

As you learned in Chapter 15, when workers want clarification of what they are expected to do, a leader can improve both their performance and satisfaction by providing initiating structure. The guidance provided by both precontrol and concurrent control systems can likewise be received favorably. In her conversation with her friend Phyllis, for example, Marianne Rowe remarked that she liked how the rules enabled her to predict the behavior of other assistant managers at the Burger Barn. Another potential and related benefit for employees with a low tolerance for ambiguity (see Chapter 12) is that the structure of a good control system tends to reduce the uncertainty of a work situation. Recall that Marianne also liked the fact that her subordinates could depend on the rules to tell them how to do their jobs.

A good control system also provides feedback to organization members. It has long been known that most employees react quite favorably to the timely provision of accurate feedback about their effectiveness.[7] Feedback provides the guidance workers need to correct ineffective behaviors. Perhaps more importantly, feedback can be very rewarding. People who have a need to succeed are gratified when feedback tells them that they are, in fact, succeed-

TABLE 17.2   The Impact of Control on Organization Members

Potential Positive Effects of Control	Potential Dysfunctional Effects of Control
• Clarifies expectations	• Consumes resources
• Reduces ambiguity	• Creates feelings of frustration and helplessness
• Provides feedback	• Creates "red tape"
• Facilitates goal setting	• Creates inappropriate goals
• Enhances satisfaction	• Fosters inappropriate behavior
• Enhances performance	• Decreases satisfaction
	• Increases absenteeism
	• Increases turnover
	• Creates stress

Controlling Employee Behavior: Here's Looking at You, Kid

In the United States, when over 1.5 million employees talk, more than 14,000 employers listen—at the keyhole, that is.[1] The amount of eavesdropping on employees' phone calls is exceeded only by the amount of surreptitious monitoring of their computer workstations. An estimated 40 percent of the 15 million Americans using workstations are being monitored by the computer itself.[2] At a number of airlines, for example, computer monitoring programs tell managers how much time each reservation agent spends with a caller, the intervals between calls, and how long each agent is away from the phone for bathroom breaks and the like. The same optical scanners that tell grocery store cash registers how much items cost are used to control clerks and inventories by checking how many items are handled per minute. Computers at *The New York Times* keep track of clerks who accept advertising over the phone. In addition to electronic surveillance, there is the traditional company spy, like the ordinary passenger who really is an airline employee on board to observe flight-crew behavior.[3]

These examples are just a few of the ways in which managers are trying to control workers' behavior. Allan Clyde, president of Clyde Digital Systems, brags that his company's software monitoring program "permits total surveillance of all users, all of the time."[4] Some computerized control programs deliver (sometimes subliminal) messages to boost productivity, such as "You're not working as fast as the person next to you."[5] The companies that use these programs, as well as the firms that develop them, claim that they greatly facilitate the effectiveness of organizational control. R. Douglas MacIntyre, senior vice-president of Management Science America, says that his company's programs " . . . are letting management make better, quicker decisions based on facts, not emotions."[6] Some employees like programs that reward them financially for typing the most keystrokes, booking the most reservations, and so forth. Many employees feel that monitoring helps identify and eliminate ineffective co-workers. One flight attendant, for example, is not bothered by reports that her behavior is monitored by spies, "because I know I do my job. . . . Maybe if they checked a little more they'd spot the ones who don't."[7]

Other workers and their representatives are less pleased. One national worker advocacy group, 9 to 5, believes that surveillance systems invade workers' privacy, cause stress, and show a lack of trust for and concern about employees. Employees complain that the feeling of being watched makes them "a nervous wreck. . . . The stress is incredible. . . . It's a very oppressive way to work."[8] Because it appears these systems are here to stay, however, perhaps the best approach is to come to an agreement on their use. Managers who want both to use monitoring devices and to maintain good working relations with subordinates should consider following these guidelines:

1. Tell employees when their work will be monitored and why.
2. Create reasonable work standards that account for different types of tasks and for short-term variations in employee performance.
3. Monitor and measure employees' performance only as often as is necessary to make effective calculations.
4. Allow employees to have complete access to their own records.[9]

1. I. M. Shepard and R. L. Duston (1987), *Workplace privacy*, Washington, DC: Bureau of National Affairs, 59.
2. The boss that never blinks (28 July 1986), *Time*, 46.
3. Ghost riders in the sky (April 1988), *Frequent Flyer*, 80 ff.
4. *Time*, 47.
5. *Ibid.*
6. *Time*, 46.
7. *Frequent Flyer*, 86.
8. *Time*, 47.
9. Shepard and Duston, 66.

ing. Feedback can improve job performance if workers use it to adjust their goals appropriately. Both concurrent and postaction controls provide employees with feedback about the appropriateness of their behavior and the degree to which their work is producing successful results. When Marianne watches a counter worker and comments on how well he or she is doing or suggests a change, she is providing feedback that can be both satisfying and helpful.

You have already seen that goal setting can be an important contributor to effective management. A good control system is very useful for identifying appropriate goals. Consider the control system used by the sales company at which Maurice Prater works. It specifies an expected sales approach (means goal) that helps him work toward a specific, difficult sales goal (ends goal). Precontrols help him understand how to achieve the desired sales level by providing such means goals as specific sales calls to make and promotional specials to offer. Concurrent controls and postcontrols provide feedback that helps Maurice monitor his progress. The combined effects of goal setting and feedback about goal progress are particularly powerful.

Dysfunctional Effects

Unfortunately, control systems can also produce dysfunctional side effects. Excessive controls are quite simply a waste of money and energy. Peter Johnson, for example, needs a larger travel budget because he must personally inspect bridges under his new control system (review "A Closer Look: Evading Control"). His inspectors spend the time they could have used to inspect bridges in logging entries, painting numbers, and griping about the unfairness of the situation. Not only do excessive controls waste money because they fail to enhance effectiveness, but they can also create additional problems. For example, Carleton and his co-workers have changed from good corporate citizens who kept accurate records and conducted comprehensive inspections into harried workers who falsify log entries. Worse, unsuspecting motorists travel over what might be unsafe bridges.

The vast amount of paperwork and documentation called for by an excessive control system can also cause the dysfunctional effects of frustration and helplessness. The "red tape" created by many universities' control systems, for example, wastes students' time. Standing in lines for hours, they wait to pay dorm fees, purchase meal tickets, rent parking spaces, pay tuition, and register for classes. Their frustration and dissatisfaction are mirrored by many organization members who question the competence, the reasonableness, and perhaps even the intelligence of supervisors who insist on maintaining excessive control.

Another dysfunctional result of poor control systems can be seen in their effect on goal-setting programs. Whereas a good control system can help design and monitor valuable goal-setting programs, a poor control system can accomplish quite the opposite. A control system focused on unreasonable ends and means goals can motivate workers to establish inappropriate individual goals. For instance, the ends goal Peter Johnson established of having all bridges inspected within two years was unreachable, and his monthly inspection quotas (means goals) were unobtainable. Peter's insistence on maintaining these inappropriate goals was evident in his reactions when the inspectors failed to meet them. Consequently, Carleton and his co-workers focused on preserving their jobs as a primary goal, rather than on conducting quality inspections.

In addition to encouraging the formation of inappropriate goals, organizational control systems often emphasize and reward behaviors that, although not necessarily inappropriate, may hinder more productive behavior. Managers who concentrate on workers' attendance, for example, may not promote such desirable behaviors as creativity, cooperation, and team building.[8] Although there is nothing wrong with encouraging attendance, a control system that fosters attendance (by punishing tardiness) because it is easier to measure than creativity tends to encourage rigid, uncreative behavior (on the part of employees who are almost always at work). An advertising agency that controls attendance but not creativity, for example, would soon be in serious trouble.

Even when control systems help identify appropriate goals and encourage appropriate behavior, rigid adherence to narrow goals can create problems. A large number of specific, concrete goals, for example, can inhibit creativity. The vast amount of time organization members must spend tending to concrete goals leaves them little time or energy to create. It is not only creativity that suffers, however. Every minute used taking attendance in a classroom is one less minute available for teaching. Every hour a police officer spends completing paperwork is one less hour available for public service. Managers should use only the goals they need, no more.

The Need for Personal Control

A MANAGER'S WORD
[T]he issue of control is probably much larger than most managers envision.
David B. Greenberger
Associate Professor of Management and Human Resources
The Ohio State University

Management can and probably should keep control over [an organization's] members, but management must also allow them to feel a sense of accomplishment and success at work. This can be achieved by allowing members to participate in decision making, but it also can be achieved by removing obstacles to successful task completion.

—Greenberger

Organizations clearly have a need to control their members and operations, but individuals also have a need for personal control, a need to believe that they have the "ability to effect a change, in a desired direction, on the environment."[9] Sometimes organizations make people feel they have too little control. Colleges and universities, for example, tell students which classes they are allowed to take and when, what grades they have to maintain, how to behave outside the classroom, and so on. Work organizations tell members when to come to work, how many hours to work, what to wear, when to take breaks, how to perform their jobs, and many other things. The challenge facing managers is to strike a balance between the amount of control their organization needs to assert and the amount of personal control needed by its members. A 1989 study suggests that, when this balance is reached, both the satisfaction and performance of organization members can be enhanced.[10]

Finding the optimum balance between organizational and personal control is not an easy task, however, because most employees desire more personal control than their organization allows them. People will strive to gain greater control "in spite of (and frequently because of) the barriers and constraints the organization places on the attainment of personal control."[11] Repeated failures to gain personal control may cause workers to develop what has been called **learned helplessness.**[12] People who learn that they are helpless to influence their work environment are likely to be the source of low productivity, low quality, high absenteeism, dissatisfaction, and turnover. They tend to react with depression, anxiety, stress, frustration, hostility, anger, and alienation. Furthermore, once helplessness has been learned, people often continue to behave helplessly, even if the environment changes to permit them greater control. Managers, thus, must prevent subordinates from developing learned helplessness because reversing it is very difficult. They should do so by allowing workers to control the aspects of their work lives that they can adequately control and by using only the necessary amount of organizational control. Butch instructs his highly skilled carpenters to frame a wall, for example, but he does not attempt to control how this is done (his best carpenters know how to do it).

In Search of Balance

At this point, it might seem that managers should just accede to workers' persistent demands for greater control. Research has shown, however, that indiscriminately giving an employee large amounts of control can actually cause performance to suffer if such control exceeds the individual's capacity to use it.[13] In other words, if Marianne Rowe's boss gives her a lot of control, and she exercises it but still fails, Marianne probably will not be highly motivated, because her use of control leads to failure, not to success.

Management must be less concerned with losing control than with providing opportunities for individuals to derive their own control.
—Greenberger

If an organizational control system that is too excessive does not work, and if giving workers all of the personal control they desire is not effective, what should managers do to achieve the proper balance? First, because people need to possess personal control, managers should give them the amount of control they are able to handle. Second, managers should take steps to make certain that workers given control believe they can use it effectively. Managers should also help them translate their effort into successful performance. (The techniques and managerial skills discussed in the directing section of this book—Chapters 12-15—can help managers in these endeavors.) Third, managers must recognize that organizational control systems influence the personal control perceptions of organization members. These, in turn, change workers' behavior and attitudes.

By interviewing and/or surveying employees, managers can learn more about those employees' needs for control. Through organizational scans (see Chapter 8), managers can determine the amount and location of control already existing within the organization, as well as the areas needing control. The objective then becomes one of achieving the best possible match between organization members and their work environment.

Control Methods and Their Effects in Review

The primary purposes of the controlling function are to monitor the extent to which an organization's plans are being followed and their effectiveness and to identify when and where it is necessary to take corrective action. To accomplish these ambitious tasks, managers construct control systems that touch most aspects of an organization's functional areas, its relationships with the external and internal environments, and its relationships across different hierarchical levels.

The control process consists of four steps. In Steps One and Two, managers determine the extent to which ends and means goals have been met. In Step Three, managers examine the relationships between means and ends goals. In Step Four, managers develop prescriptions to correct problems, to maintain strengths, and to provide feedback to an organization's planners.

Whereas all control systems have the same general purposes, they differ in their specifics. Some are self-managing cybernetic systems; noncybernetic systems require regular external supervision to be effective. Other variations in control systems include the point at which control activities are applied: before work has begun (precontrols), while work is in progress (concurrent controls), and after work is completed (postaction controls). A hybrid control system engages a variety of control activities at many points in time.

Although there are variations in control systems, all good systems have characteristics that enable them to work well in a given organization. Managers evaluating a control system, thus, might wish to gauge its adequacy in providing accurate, timely, objective information to appropriate people in the organization. They also should examine whether the system focuses on the most critical aspects of their organization's condition in a feasible, flexible manner that will be accepted by organization members. Because of the importance of the information it provides, a good control system should also be integrated with planning activities.

Any control system can produce both positive and dysfunctional effects on organization members. If it is well designed, a control system helps provide needed structure and feedback and can facilitate the development and execution of effective goal-setting programs. The result of this can be a satisfied, motivated, productive workforce. Inappropriate control systems, however, can produce dysfunctional effects, including frustration, dissatisfaction, and poor performance. Being aware of a control system's potential effects on organization members can help managers capitalize on its positive aspects, reduce the impact of dysfunctional effects, and promote workers' acceptance of the system.

The effort to maintain control is not restricted to managers. All organization members have a need for personal control, a need that sometimes conflicts with their organization's need to maintain control. To achieve effectiveness, managers must balance the control needs of both the organization and its members.

Issues for Review and Discussion

1. Define controlling and explain its importance.
2. Identify the levels and targets of the control activity.
3. Identify and discuss each step of the control process.
4. Distinguish between cybernetic and noncybernetic control systems and list the advantages and drawbacks of each.
5. Identify, compare, and contrast the various time perspectives found in control systems.
6. Name the common characteristics of effective control systems.
7. Identify and discuss three positive and three dysfunctional effects often associated with control systems.
8. How does the desire for personal control affect managers, and how can they balance it with organizational control systems?

Key Terms

controlling
cybernetic control
noncybernetic control
precontrols
concurrent controls

steering controls
screening controls
postaction controls
learned helplessness

Suggested Readings

Green, S. G., and Welsh, M. A. (1988). Cybernetics and dependence: Reframing the control concept. *Academy of Management Review,* 13(2), 287-301.

Greenberger, D. B., and Strasser, S. (1986). Development and application of a model of personal control in organizations. *Academy of Management Review,* 11, 164-77.

Martinko, M. J., and Gardner, W. L. (1982). Learned helplessness: An alternate explanation for performance deficits. *Academy of Management Journal,* 7, 195-204.

Merchant, K. A. (1982). The control function of management. *Sloan Management Review,* 23(4), 43-55.

Notes

1. D. H. Holt (1987), *Management: Principles and practices,* Englewood Cliffs, NJ: Prentice-Hall, 546-81.

2. W. H. Cunningham, I. C. M. Cunningham, and C. M. Swift (1987), *Marketing: A managerial approach,* Cincinnati: South-Western, 785-89.

3. H. C. Carlson (1979), Personnel control systems, in D. Yoder and H. G. Heneman, Jr., eds., *ASPA Handbook of Personnel and Industrial Relations,* Washington, DC: The Bureau of National Affairs, Inc., 31-56.

4. W. H. Newman (1975), *Constructive control,* Englewood Cliffs, NJ: Prentice-Hall, 6.

5. Newman; W. H. Newman (1984), Managerial control, in J. E. Rosenzweig and F. E. Kast, eds., *Modules in management series,* Chicago: Science Research Associates, 1-42; W. H. Newman, J. R. Logan, and W. H. Hegarty (1985), *Strategy, policy, and central management,* 9th ed., Cincinnati: South-Western; W. H. Sihler (1971), Toward better management control systems, *California Management Review,* 14, 33-39; E. P. Strong and R. D. Smith (1968), *Management control models,* New York: Holt, Rinehart and Winston.

6. M. S. Taylor, C. D. Fisher, and D. R. Ilgen (1984), Individuals' reactions to performance feedback in organizations: A control theory perspective, in K. M. Rowland and G. R. Ferris, eds., *Research in personnel and human resources management,* Greenwich, CT: JAI Press, 81-124.

7. E. A. Locke and G. P. Lathan (1984), *Goal setting: A motivational technique that works,* Englewood Cliffs, NJ: Prentice-Hall.

8. Interview with Steven Kerr appearing in R. B. Dunham (1984), *Organizational behavior: People and processes in management,* Homewood, IL: Irwin, 147; S. Kerr (1975), On the folly of rewarding A, while hoping for B, *Academy of Management Journal,* 18, 769-83.

9. D. B. Greenberger and S. Strasser (1986), Development and application of a model of personal control in organizations, *Academy of Management Review,* 11, 164.

10. D. B. Greenberger, S. Strasser, L. L. Cummings, and R. B. Dunham (1989), The impact of personal control on performance and satisfaction, *Organizational Behavior and Human Decision Processes,* 43, 29-51.

11. Greenberger and Strasser, 174.

12. J. B. Overmier and M. E. P. Seligman (1967), Effects of inescapable shock upon subsequent escape and avoidance learning, *Journal of Comparative and Physiological Psychology,* 63, 28-33; M. J. Martinko and W. L. Gardner (1982), Learned helplessness: An alternate explanation for performance deficits, *Academy of Management Journal,* 7, 195-204.

13. M. H. Bazerman (1982), Impact of personal control on performance: Is added control always beneficial? *Journal of Applied Psychology,* 67, 472-79.

The Two Edges of Control

Adapted from R. S. Schuler and D. R. Dalton (1985), Case problems in management, *3rd ed., St. Paul, MN: West, 184–86.*

"Tom, do you have a minute?" asked David Morrison.

"Sure, come in," responded Tom Davidson, plant manager of Mayberry Manufacturing. "What do you have on your mind?"

"I'll tell you, Tom. At times it is just frustrating as can be around here. Sometimes you can't get a straight answer from anyone. There are times when absolutely no one can seem to help you," answered David with some irritation.

"What specifically is bothering you, Dave?"

One Story

"It's just one thing after another. For instance, two days ago one of my employees asked me for a six-week leave of absence for surgery and a recuperation period. Frankly, I was not familiar with the leave policy around here. I must have asked a half a dozen people, including the shift supervisors, what the policy is. They told me there is no specific policy and that I will have to use my best judgment on the matter. I am to examine the circumstances of the request and decide accordingly. I thought I had better check with you before I acted in one way or another on the request for the six-week leave," explained David. "Ordinarily, I wouldn't bother you with something like this. I just can't seem to find a policy anywhere."

"Well, I appreciate the fact that you checked with me. The advice you've received, however, is essentially correct. We don't have a specific policy for leaves of absence. In the past, they have been handled on a case-to-case basis. I will say this, though. I don't think that this request has come at a very opportune time. As you know, we have a large order due for delivery and we'll need every employee we can get. In fact, I'll be very surprised if we get through this without paying a lot of overtime. Obviously, I hate to see us give any employees that much time off when we'll have to replace them with employees on overtime at time-and-a-half pay," said Tom.

"You haven't heard the half of it," continued David. "Yesterday, another employee requested a six-week leave of absence as well. It seems that this employee's daughter works for a major airline and can get tickets to Europe for very reasonable rates. I don't know exactly what is happening there, but apparently the airline is in the middle of some kind of promotion for their overseas flights and employees are entitled to an extraordinary discount. To hear my employee tell it, this is the dream of a lifetime—the opportunity to visit Europe for very little money. There's no telling when, if ever, the employee will have this opportunity again."

"Given our circumstances," said Tom, "I can hardly see how that leave of absence could be justified."

"Well, I really have a problem," replied David. "Both of these are excellent employees. At first, I thought that I could justify the leave of absence on medical grounds for the surgery but would have trouble with the vacation; however, I looked into the matter more carefully and it turns out that the surgery is elective—this is not a life-threatening situation. The surgery could be put off for a time. Interestingly, the vacation really can't be put off. Well, of course, it *can* be put off, but only at great expense. We can be sure of one thing. The vacation is at least as important to the one employee as the surgery is to the other. I really wish we had a policy on this. It would make things a lot easier for me," David finished with some irritation.

"I see your point, Dave, but let me share a problem I recently had that involves policy."

Another Story

"We were talking about overtime a few minutes ago. Our corporate headquarters recently sent a memorandum to all department heads concerning the use of overtime. The memo essentially stated that, in the future, no overtime could be authorized without the personal permission of the plant manager. In this case, of course, such permission would have to come from me. Let me remind you that I did not send the memo to the department managers. That memo was sent by corporate headquarters. I was, as you would expect, notified of the memo," Tom explained.

He continued, "Now, in the past, any department manager could authorize overtime for his or her department if the need should arise. Evidently the corporate offices are concerned about the amount of overtime that has been authorized and are seeking to control it by having all overtime okayed by me before its use. The company is trying to reduce costs, and the reduction of overtime is a high-priority item.

"This worked fairly well for a while. Of course, the department heads did not especially like the new policy. The policy did, however, reduce overtime somewhat. The department heads were a little more careful. For the most part, I approved any overtime that was requested. I think that the department heads just thought it over a bit more carefully before they called me.

"This all came to an unfortunate conclusion last Friday. As it happened, I was out of town that day. At the same time, two unforeseen circumstances caused a problem in the shipping department. First, there was an unusually high incidence of employee absenteeism, so shipping was very shorthanded. Second, there was a delay in sending the finished goods from production to the shipping department. In other words, they were short of people, and the goods they were to send out were coming in late. It became absolutely obvious to Ms. Bates, head of the shipping department, that there was no way that all of the orders were going to be dispatched by Friday's deadline. The following Monday was a holiday. So, if these orders didn't go out on Friday, they would not be processed until Tuesday. The sum of this is that the orders would go out four days late."

"What happened?" asked David.

"Nothing, and that's the problem," replied Tom with some exasperation. "Ms. Bates tried to reach me, but I was, of course, out of town. She knew that in the past, orders that were not processed by the deadline have been returned by customers and subsequent orders canceled. The memo clearly stated that my personal permission was required to authorize overtime. She badly needed that overtime so the orders could be processed Friday and not wait until Tuesday. If she had authorized the overtime, she would have exceeded her authority. If she didn't, we ran the risk of product returns and cancellation of future orders."

"What did she do?" asked David.

"Oh, she took the safe course. She did not use the overtime," answered the plant manager disgustedly. "It would seem, Dave, based on your recent experiences and mine, that policy is a two-edged sword."

Questions

1. What type of control is exemplified by the corporate policy on approval of overtime? Is this the kind of control being sought by David Morrison?

2. Since a policy on granting leaves of absence would restrict David's freedom to act, why does he seek such a policy?

3. Why does Tom Davidson refer to policy as a "two-edged sword"?

4. What should David do about the leave requests? What should he do to prevent a reoccurrence of the overtime authorization problem? to prevent a reoccurrence of the problem with leave requests?

18

Organizational Change and Development

Student Learning Objectives

After reading this chapter, you should be able to:

1. Identify the five primary reasons that change does and should occur in organizations.

2. Understand the difference between proactive and reactive change.

3. Describe the major types of change that occur in organizations.

4. Describe the range of reactions people have to organizational change and the reasons underlying their reactions.

5. Identify and describe the seven major techniques for developing support for organizational change.

6. Understand the special role of organizational development (OD) and how it can enhance organizational effectiveness and benefit organization members.

7. Describe the major stages of a systematic approach for planning and managing organizational change.

C hapters 16 and 17 of this section on the controlling function of management have shown that managers must control their organization's effectiveness by comparing what it has accomplished (means and ends goals) to what it was supposed to accomplish (the standard), by determining the cause-and-effect relationship between the two, and by making necessary changes to maintain and/or improve effectiveness. As you are about to find out, however, managers must do more than have a good "change" idea—they must have the skills to make that good idea work well.

This chapter is designed to give you those skills by exploring some of the causes of organizational change, the types of changes managers are likely to face, and the potential reactions of organization members to change. This chapter also explores the ways managers can develop support for organizational change; some organizational development techniques for developing structured, systematic changes; and a step-by-step model for planning and managing the change process. As you will see, managing change is not easy, but it is necessary if an organization is to succeed.

Why Change Occurs: Forces to Change

)))) A MANAGER'S WORD

Long ago, Peter Drucker said, "The purpose of an organization lies outside itself." Organizations that do not adapt to changing environments wither and die.

Donald L. Hawk
Executive Vice-President and Manager, Administration Department
Texas Commerce Bancshares

Organizational change does not occur spontaneously. It takes place when the forces encouraging change become more powerful than those resisting change. Sometimes an organization faces **internal forces to change** that emanate from within the organization itself, such as a new strategic plan that calls for product diversification. At other times, **external forces to change** rush at an organization from outside its boundaries. A new technological development from outside an organization can provide a powerful external force to change, such as the way in which the creation of compact audio disks (CDs) revolutionized the music industry.

As Figure 18.1 on page 422 shows, one useful way to categorize forces to change is by their nature. *Technological* forces to change can arise from internal sources, as when Federal Express' Memphis development center created the company's "supertracker," a portable device that allows agents to enter shipping information at a customer's site and transmit it to the company's central computer. This system dramatically changed the company's previous tracking and control procedures. Technological forces to change can also arise from external sources. For instance, the discovery of bovine growth hormone (BGH) will allow U.S. dairy farmers to decrease herd size without reducing milk production.

Employee needs and values are another important change force, because organizations must attract, retain, and motivate workers. Change may be needed if organization members change their minds about what is of value to them—preferring vacation time over insurance benefits, for example. *Social* forces also can bring about change, as when Tree Top, Inc., stopped buying apples from Alar-using growers in 1989 because of customers' growing disenchantment with products that contain the chemical. Social forces extended their impact later in 1989 when Uniroyal, the maker of Alar, withdrew the chemical from the U.S. market (but not from foreign markets, where there had been less social pressure). *Business and economic* forces exert tremendous

FIGURE 18.1 *Major Forces to Change*

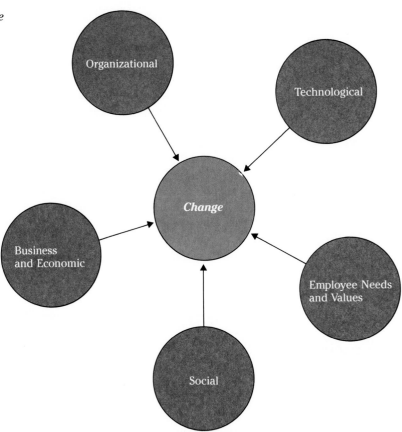

change forces, including inflation rates, gross national product, money supplies, interest rates, and industry competition. Often, the *organization* itself is the primary force behind a change, as when key decision makers implement an MBO program or install a new communications system. Some of the unique characteristics of organizationally driven change are discussed in the organizational development section later in this chapter.

Typically, the total force driving change is a combination of two or more individual forces. For example, organizations introduced robotics because technological advances made it possible to do so *and* because of economic constraints, employees' desire for more challenging work, and societal demands for better-quality products.

Types of Change

Changes occur either in reaction to a driving force or forces or on a proactive, planned basis initiated by an organization. Either type can involve technological, structural/procedural (administrative), and human components.[1] Changes can also be distinguished based on the degree to which they are innovative or simply different from what was done previously in the organization.

Reactive vs. Proactive Change

Reactive change occurs when the forces driving change provide so much pressure that an organization *must* change. The failure of existing equipment or systems, for example, is a powerful impetus for change, as NASA discovered following the failure of the space shuttle *Challenger*'s O-rings. Redesign of those and other critical shuttle parts were reactive changes. Organizations seldom welcome unplanned, reactive change, because it usually results in poorly coordinated, inefficient management that plays havoc with virtually any strategic plan.

Proactive change occurs when an organization's managers conclude that a change would be desirable (as opposed to necessary). Generally, proactive change is more orderly and more efficient because it is planned (although, as noted in previous chapters, not all planning is done well). The section on organizational development later in this chapter deals primarily with proactive, planned change.

Change and Innovation

"All innovation is change, but not all change is innovation."[2] Although many people equate these two concepts, it is important to differentiate them. Change involves any modification of an organization's established ways of operating. An organization that replaces its word processors and laser printers with manual typewriters is making a change, but hardly an innovative one. **Innovation** occurs when an organization is first or an early user of an idea within its set of similar organizations.[3] The first airline to provide scheduled service in orbital altitudes will be innovative, and the first hospital to use a newly discovered treatment for AIDS will be innovative. Because innovation provides more excitement, challenge, and uncertainty than does most change, managing innovation requires special care.

Technological Change

Some of the most visible and dramatic changes made in organizations during the past decade introduced new technologies. Organizations increasingly use robotics in manufacturing processes. Computers are leading to paperless offices. For better or for worse, technological change is occurring at a rate unprecedented in history (see Figure 18.2 on page 425).

Structural/Procedural Change

While changes in technology focus on the tools used to accomplish work objectives, structural changes concentrate on an organization and the methods it uses to coordinate work (as described in Chapter 11). For example, movement from a functional form of organization (such as one based on finance, operations, or marketing) to a divisional form (such as one centered on product lines, customer groups, or territories) is a structural change. Structural organizational changes have been very popular in recent years as organizations struggle to find effective coordinating work designs (see "A Closer Look: Restructuring").

Technological Change: Kellogg's Profits Snap, Crackle, and Pop

Tony the Tiger may not strike you as the high-tech type, but innovation got Tony where he is today. Frosted Flakes' developer, the Kellogg Company, was founded on an experimental new idea, and Americans have been chomping on the results for almost 100 years.

In the 1890s, W. T. Kellogg was the manager of a sanitarium in Battle Creek, Michigan. Kellogg, a vegetarian, sought to provide a healthy diet for his patients and eventually came up with a hearty, but unpalatable, whole wheat meal. Although able to convince many members of his captive audience to eat the unappetizing concoction, Kellogg was in little danger of taking the world by storm. He, therefore, set out to find a way to retain the nutritional value of the meal, while making it more attractive. It turned out that using a set of rollers to flatten day-old wheat dough produced little flakes as opposed to the previous damp, mushy concoction.

The result has shaped the cereal market for nearly a century, but the Kellogg Company has not remained king of the breakfast table by sticking to one tried-and-true product. The continued development of new methods for manufacturing and handling no-sugar, no-preservative cereals has made it possible to market "health foods" to the masses. The Nutri-Grain line of whole-grain cereals, for example, created a new market niche. Super-secret, advanced techniques resulted in Crispix, a product that no competitor seems able to duplicate. With it, Kellogg introduced the first cereal piece in history to combine two different grains. Similar technological breakthroughs produced Raisin Squares, a crispy cereal with a chewy fruit center.

The Kellogg Company is not afraid to change its production methods for existing product lines. Its 1988 capital budget was close to $600 million. It was among the first to use statistical sampling to check product quality. Kellogg involves production workers in the generation of ideas for improving quality and decreasing costs. It has been willing to introduce new equipment, but only after carefully evaluating its effectiveness. So committed is Kellogg to this idea, in fact, that it uses an experimental plant in Canada to test experimental equipment and production methods before replacing existing equipment. The company also has a new "Building 100" in Memphis that, according to *Fortune*, is the most efficient cereal factory in the world.[1]

The results seem well worth the planning and execution complexities that accompany change. In 1988, Kellogg ranked second in profits among the 48 food companies ranked by *For-* *tune*.[2] Sales increased almost 15 percent over those in 1987, and profits soared over 21 percent. Margin (profits as a percent of sales) were 11 percent, compared to the top 500-company composite of 4.8 percent. Return on invested capital was 26 percent. Tony the Tiger is not the type to let success go to his head, though. According to Kellogg Chairperson William E. LaMothe, "[w]e look at ourselves as a small company dealing with giants. . . . We spend a lot of time talking about small things that top management in more diversified companies probably don't get involved with."[3]

To avoid missing an opportunity, the company reevaluates its strategic plan every year, even when it appears to be succeeding. New products and innovative manufacturing and marketing methods just keep coming. About the only thing that has not changed at Kellogg is Tony's famous slogan, and it could just as easily be applied to the company's operations as to the taste of its cereals: They're G-R-R-REAT!

1. How King Kellogg beat the blahs (29 August 1988), *Fortune*, 54ff.
2. The *Fortune* 500 (24 April 1989), 383.
3. The health craze has Kellogg feeling G-R-R-REAT (30 March 1987), *Business Week*, 53.

People-Oriented Change

No matter how marvelous the technology or how well suited the structure, success cannot be achieved without the appropriate contributions of individual organization members. For this reason, many organizational changes are people oriented, such as improving the skills, attitudes, motivation, and behaviors of organization members (see the discussions of people-oriented issues in

FIGURE 18.2   Rate of Technological Change

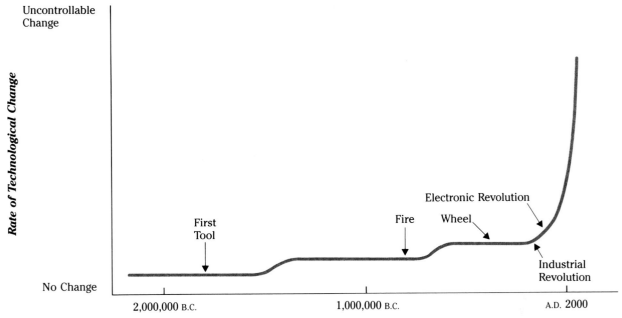

Source: R. B. Dunham (1984), *Organizational behavior,* Homewood, IL: Irwin, 465.

Chapters 12–15). These factors are so important that they constitute a major part of the work conducted by organizational development specialists.

Technostructural and Sociotechnical Change

It is often fairly easy to distinguish between technological, structural, and people-oriented changes in theory. In reality, however, organizational change is rarely so neatly categorized, representing instead a combination of these approaches. Accordingly, hybrid approaches that "affect the work content and method and . . . the sets of relationships among workers" have been developed to reflect certain combinations of the three specific types of change.[4] **Technostructural changes,** thus, involve concurrent changes in organizational technology and structure. **Sociotechnical changes** involve changes in people and the technology.

As you may have guessed, even these distinctions are seldom made so clearly in practice. In fact, most changes using either of these hybrid titles involve changes in all technological, structural/procedural, and people-oriented change areas. Rather than fighting over the appropriate label to assign a given change, it is more important to address effectively all three areas of potential change.[5]

Reactions to Change

Organization members' reactions to change can range from quite positive and supportive to quite negative and very resistant. In fact,

Restructuring: Changes Contribute to Eczel Excellence

"Bust-ups? Oh, no! The whole company gets blown to smithereens, as if by dynamite. What crazy, wasteful destruction!"[1] Although a common attitude, bust-ups (separating a corporation into its component parts, often selling off the pieces) and the restructuring that usually follows do not have to portend doom and gloom. Many bust-ups benefit more than hurt the economy and the individual businesses involved.

Eczel is a fast-growing organization that distributes office supplies to a wide range of large corporations. Until 1985, Eczel was a subsidiary of Crown Zellerbach Corporation, then a huge forest-products company. In 1985, however, Sir James Goldsmith gained control of Crown Zellerbach and got rid of everything but Eczel, which he felt had great potential. Goldsmith installed Al Dunlap as the new operating head of Eczel, and Dunlap immediately initiated major structural changes. He reduced Eczel's twenty-two distribution centers, each with its own vice-president, to four centers and four VPs. He also created a highly centralized buying center to replace Eczel's inefficient decentralized buying operation. These and other structural changes, accompanied by a new "this company is important" approach to management, have turned Eczel's deep losses into profits. Why couldn't giant Crown Zellerbach do the same? Dunlap explains, "We operate it like it's the only company in the world."[2]

Eczel's excellence following restructuring is not an isolated case. Goldsmith also took over and broke apart Diamond International, whose egg carton manufacturing business has flourished as an independent entity. Its new bosses attribute much of their success to " . . . being liberated from the three layers of bureaucracy between them and a decision. . . . [T]hey can make instant product improvements instead of waiting months for the go-ahead."[3] Consider a former TRW subsidiary that, as part of the TRW conglomerate, scrapped 24 percent of the aircraft turbine parts it manufactured because they failed to meet specifications. After the subsidiary was sold to Precision Castparts and given a new boss, the scrap rate was cut in half, orders skyrocketed, and the company became profitable. Why? The business was managed systematically, focusing on quality and providing a new structure to support this focus.

Bust-ups and restructurings offer opportunities for organizations to make changes that can yield improvements. They do not, however, guarantee improved effectiveness. It is up to the managers to provide the systematic strategic planning and implementation of change that produce the results. Given this, it is not surprising that most popular current topics in executive education programs focus on strategic planning and the management of organizational change.

1. Restructuring really works (2 March 1987), *Fortune*, 41. Other facts for this "Closer Look" were derived from pages 38ff of this article.
2. *Fortune*, 43.
3. *Fortune*, 42.

. . . [P]eople experience change in all manner of ways. For some, a particular change will bring satisfaction, joy, advantage, a sense of job well done; for others, that same change may bring disadvantage, pain, sadness, even humiliation. Still others may barely perceive the change at all, experiencing it indifferently at most.[6]

The Range of Reactions

Because not even good change ideas will work well unless they receive favorable reactions from organization members, managers must understand the types of reactions that might result from the planned change. Figure 18.3 shows the continuum of possible change reactions.

Usually, the most extreme reaction an organization member shows to a change is to *leave the organization*. Sometimes workers quit because they

FIGURE 18.3   *Continuum of Change Reactions*

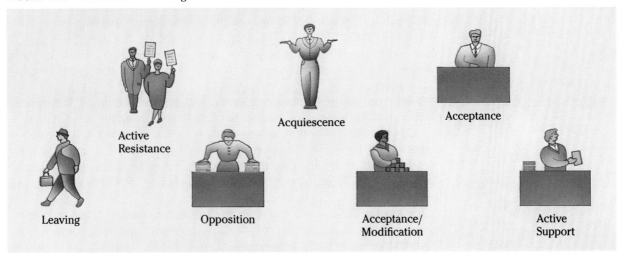

believe the change is so obnoxious that staying would be intolerable. Sometimes they depart even if the change is a good one because they find it personally difficult to cope with the change. Many of the employees who left Apple Computer after John Sculley took over in 1985 appear to have done so because they preferred the open, informal Apple of old to the expected constraints of the new Apple. Although leaving an organization may be the most extreme reaction to change, things probably proceed more smoothly if the most adamant opponents of a change leave rather than stay to fight.

The next reaction along the continuum is *active resistance.* Workers who actively resist a change may try either to prevent it from occurring or to modify its nature. At its extreme, active resistance sends the message "No, I will not do this." Active resistance often goes beyond personal defiance and includes attempts to encourage others to resist the change. A strike by a trade union is a good example of group-oriented active resistance.

Somewhat less extreme than active resistance is behavior that can be labeled *opposition.*[7] Usually a passive behavior, opposition might consist of simple "foot-dragging" or any other stalling tactic either to delay implementation or to bring about a scaled-down version of a proposed change. For example, an air traffic controller who gives the Congressional Oversight Committee an anonymous tip that a planned change in control may reduce safety margins falls into the opposition category. (A public whistleblowing, as described in Chapter 3, would be considered an active resistance maneuver.)

Sometimes those opposed to a change feel powerless to prevent or alter it and, thus, allow the change to occur without interference. This *acquiescence* to an unwanted change may arise from an impending sense of its inevitability. "People put up with the inevitable as best they can, shrugging their shoulders, gritting their teeth, steeling themselves to face a tragic event."[8]

Still farther to the right on the continuum shown in Figure 18.3 is *acceptance/modification.* For example, suppose manager Marie Archer has been told that her employer intends to move the company's headquarters out of state. Marie supports the idea of moving operations because local taxes and other restrictive ordinances are hurting the company's ability to compete. On the other hand, she is worried that the change may alienate many of its major

The acceptance of a change is characterized by passive support. Employees who accept, for example, new technology in their work environment are likely to participate in the change but are not likely to actively promote it.

customers and adversely affect its supply and delivery systems. On a personal level, she would rather not move so far from friends and relatives. Acceptance/ modification responses to change usually can be characterized as "bargaining over details (albeit, perhaps, important ones), rather than over principles."[9] Marie, for instance, could accept the need for a relocation but might try to persuade her employer that there are sound reasons for finding a different site in the same state.

A more positive response is a clear-cut *acceptance* of change. This type of reaction is likely when people are either indifferent toward the change (that is, they do not dislike it) or they agree with it. Acceptance reactions to change are characterized by passive support. If asked whether they like a change, for example, workers might agree that they do, but they are unlikely to volunteer such information. If asked to participate in the change, they will cooperate, but they probably will not initiate participation.

The most positive reaction is an *active support* of change. Active supporters try to increase a change's chances for success, often by initiating conversations in which they explain why they like the change and think others should too. For example, when American Family Insurance decided to implement work teams for service employees at its office in Eden Prairie, Minnesota, a group of workers promoted the idea with banners and a party celebrating the change. Active support also includes "pitching in" and making the change work.

It is important to recognize that the range of reactions to change shown in Figure 18.3 lies along a continuum. Consider the label *acceptance,* for example. A workforce that approves of a change is more likely to support it actively than is one that merely does not dislike it. Both situations, however, can produce passive acceptance. There is also a big difference between active supporters who make favorable comments about a change and those who work overtime to make the change succeed. In reality, an individual's reaction to change can fall at any point along the continuum.

The Underlying Causes

Although some people occasionally resist change just to be difficult, most people usually have a reason for their reaction (see Figure 18.4). Knowing what causes people to react as they do should help managers anticipate when support or resistance is likely and should encourage them to manage actively the development of support for change.[10]

Gain or Loss of Value. People who review a proposed change and conclude that it would cause them to lose something they value have a vested interest in resisting the change. Workers, therefore, resist changes they believe would cause them to lose status, would restrict their promotional opportunities, would reduce their control over their work, or would threaten anything else they value. The greater the expected loss, the more likely they are to resist. Conversely, the more people expect to gain from a change, the more they will support it. Many proposed changes win the support of those affected by offering something of value, such as a job redesign effort that promises to make their jobs more interesting or leads to greater pay and recognition.

Understanding. Because most people have some fear of the unknown, they are less likely to support a change if they do not understand it. Many

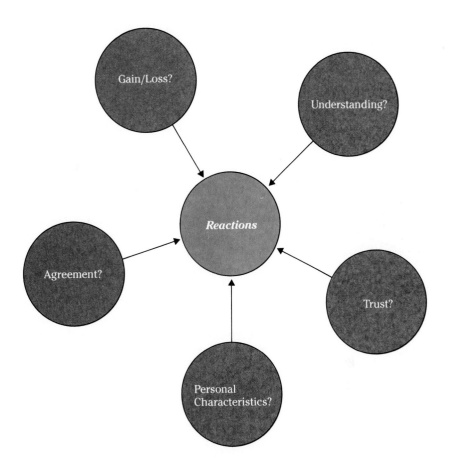

FIGURE 18.4 *The Causes of Reactions to Change*

organization members who are confused about the implications of a particular change assume the worst and react accordingly. For example, workers may resist switching to a flextime schedule if they believe that supervisors will arbitrarily assign them new (and perhaps undesirable) hours. If a manager assumes a change will be well received if it is understood, he or she can usually make workers' support for it more likely by increasing their understanding. Telling the workers they will be allowed to choose their hours, for example, may encourage them to support the flextime schedule. Understanding a change does not guarantee support for it, however. In fact, sometimes the more completely people understand an idea, the more reasons they discover to dislike it. In such a situation, managers may have to redesign (improve) the change or try to focus employees' attention on the reason(s) for the change and its importance to their organization.

Trust in the Change Initiators.   Organizations vary substantially in the degree to which members trust management. If a change is proposed when trust is low, a natural first reaction is to ask, "What is really going to happen and how is it going to hurt me?" When the initiators of change are not trusted, any change can be received negatively. When trust is high, employees are more likely to support a proposed change.

Agreement with the Change.   Organizations planning change often fail to assess who is likely to agree with the introduction of a change and who might disagree. It is logical to expect that those who think the change is a good idea will be more likely to support it than those who feel the change is a bad idea.

Personal Characteristics. A number of personality characteristics (see Chapter 12) affect support for and resistance to a change. Workers who have a low tolerance for ambiguity may resist a change because it pushes uncertainty beyond their personal comfort level. On the other hand, organization members with a high tolerance for ambiguity may welcome such uncertainty as something that will make their lives more interesting. Highly dogmatic individuals are likely to support a change if it is consistent with their view of how things should be but resist strenuously if the change challenges their personal points of view. Strong authoritarian personalities tend to support change if they believe that the initiators have the right to order the change.

In addition to the influence of these and other personality attributes, workers' attitudes toward change itself can play an important role in shaping their reactions to the change process. The eighteen items listed in Table 18.1 assess the cognitive, affective, and behavioral tendency components of a person's attitude toward change and, thus, help managers anticipate the worker's probable reactions to change.[11] Cognitive items concentrate on whether a person believes change tends to produce positive or negative effects. Affective items measure the degree to which a person enjoys change. Behavioral intent questions deal with the degree to which a person tends to support or resist change.

TABLE 18.1 *Measuring Attitudes Toward Change*

	Strongly Disagree	Disagree	Neither Agree nor Disagree	Agree	Strongly Agree
Cognitive Items					
1. Changes usually benefit the organization.	1	2	3	4	5
2. Most of my co-workers benefit from change.	1	2	3	4	5
3. Change often helps me perform better.	1	2	3	4	5
4. Other people think that I support change.	1	2	3	4	5
5. Change usually helps improve unsatisfactory situations at work.	1	2	3	4	5
6. I usually benefit from change.	1	2	3	4	5
Affective Items					
7. I look forward to changes at work.	1	2	3	4	5
8. I don't like change.	5	4	3	2	1
9. Change frustrates me.	5	4	3	2	1
10. Change tends to stimulate me.	1	2	3	4	5
11. Most changes are irritating.	5	4	3	2	1
12. I find most changes to be pleasing.	1	2	3	4	5
Behavioral Intent Items					
13. I usually resist new ideas.	5	4	3	2	1
14. I am inclined to try new ideas.	1	2	3	4	5
15. I usually support new ideas.	1	2	3	4	5
16. I often suggest new approaches to things.	1	2	3	4	5
17. I intend to do whatever possible to support change.	1	2	3	4	5
18. I usually hesitate to try new ideas.	5	4	3	2	1

Source: R. B. Dunham, J. A. Grube, D. G. Gardner, and J. L. Pierce (1989), *The development of an attitude toward change instrument.* Paper presented at the 49th Annual Meeting of the Academy of Management, Washington, DC.

Developing Support for Change

This section explores several techniques managers can use to reduce resistance to and/or develop support for an impending change: education and communication, participation and involvement, facilitative support, emotional support, incentives, manipulation and co-optation, and coercion. Table 18.2 summarizes these approaches and their respective advantages and potential drawbacks.

Education and Communication

Education and communication provide information about an impending change: *what* it is, *when* it is to be introduced, *how* it will be introduced, and *why* it is considered necessary. Education and communication can also reveal the logic behind the change, as well as the intended objectives. This technique addresses the underlying causes of resistance to a change, first by reducing misunderstanding about the change and the worst-case assumptions often made in the presence of misunderstanding. Next, education and communication can clarify the ways in which the change can benefit organization members. Finally, this technique can increase employees' trust of management if workers view the education/communication as an honest, straightforward attempt to describe the impending change. Otherwise, the method may appear to be an attempt at manipulation.

TABLE 18.2   Advantages and Drawbacks of Change Techniques

Technique	Advantages	Potential Drawbacks
Education and communication	After being convinced, members often assist with implementation.	It costs time and money.
Participation and involvement	Participants' input can be useful, and they are likely to be supportive.	It has heavy time costs; it can lead to poor change suggestions and disillusionment if ideas are not followed.
Facilitative support	It enhances the successful implementation of change.	It costs time and money for support materials and training programs.
Emotional support	It is relatively inexpensive; it is a good way to help with personal adjustment problems.	It is often done nonsystematically, resulting in time and cash outlays that may not remedy the problem.
Incentives	It can "head off" major resistance before it arises.	It can be expensive and can encourage resistance in hopes of gaining "compensation."
Manipulation and co-optation	It works fairly rapidly without substantial cost.	It is unethical and can destroy trust if workers find out they have been intentionally misled.
Coercion	It is usually the fastest method; it suppresses resistance regardless of cause.	It decreases satisfaction, increases resentment, and makes other techniques less effective.

Participation and Involvement

The second technique, participation and involvement, elicits information from members that might help improve the quality or effectiveness of a change. This method also increases the likelihood that employees will accept the change and become committed to its success. Active participation substantially increases the understanding of a change. Managers can deal with workers' personal concerns about potential losses at the design stage, and, because members help design the change, they are more likely to agree on its advisability. Trust can also be substantially enhanced, as management conveys the message "We trust you and value you enough to ask you to help with this important task."

Facilitative Support

Facilitative support consists of the assistance an organization provides its members to help make a change effective.

Most change efforts fail unless they are adequately supported. Facilitative support, the third technique available to managers, is the assistance an organization provides its members to help make a change effective. For example, if an organization intends to introduce new technology to conduct tune-ups of electronic ignition systems, managers should identify the tools and equipment that will be needed to implement the change and provide them to the mechanics. A mechanic who lacks some of the skills required to use the new tools should be offered a training program. Appropriate amounts of facilitative support can make the difference between a moderate and major success for a change program. It not only directly facilitates effectiveness, it also does so indirectly by reducing employees' fears about new techniques and procedures. It also shows that the organization is competent enough to plan ahead and cares enough about employees to provide support needed in the face of change.

Emotional Support

When faced with major changes, employees can require support that goes well beyond the technical aspects of facilitative support. In these cases, managers can use emotional support as a fourth technique to reduce resistance and bolster workers' support for an impending change. Emotional support addresses organization members' personal concerns, often through such formal methods as employee assistance programs that provide a counselor with whom individuals can discuss their fears and concerns. In the majority of cases, however, emotional support comes primarily from a member's immediate supervisor and co-workers. Emotional support can remove potential stumbling blocks to change by emphasizing, once again, that "this organization cares about its members."

Incentives

As you will recall, a major reason people choose to support or resist a change involves their judgment of whether they will personally gain or lose because of the change.[12] Managers can emphasize the potential for personal gain by providing incentives when the change is implemented. This can be done in two ways. First, managers can identify people who are likely to lose something of value when a change is implemented and compensate them for their loss with an additional pay increment, some time off, an extra vacation day, or a particularly desirable work assignment. When an organization provides a compensatory incentive, it is saying, "I know this change will hurt you, and I want to do something to make up for it." This type of incentive also carries the risk that members might decide that the way to obtain special rewards is to resist. If it becomes known that "the squeaky wheel gets the grease," organizations may suddenly discover a large number of squeaky wheels.

A second way managers can provide incentives is to design a change in such a way that the change itself benefits organization members. Job redesign, for example, can provide a substantial incentive for employees who value more interesting, challenging work. Incentives inherent in a change tend to be more powerful and benefit the organization far longer than do one-time compensatory changes.

Manipulation and Co-optation

Manipulation involves the systematic control or distortion of information provided to organization members about a change. Information is provided that makes a change appear to be one that members should like and support. Information that might discourage support is withheld or distorted. Some managers believe that it is perfectly acceptable to provide only part of the information related to a change as long as it is accurate. This approach is risky, however. There is no easier way to damage trust and ensure resistance—for both the immediate change and for future changes—than to have employees discover that they have been intentionally deceived.

Co-optation is a special type of manipulation, which, on the surface, appears very similar to participation and involvement. Managers using co-optation ask employees to participate—or even to lead others—in adapting to a change. Although this creates the impression of participation and involvement, the chosen employee is really a figurehead; his or her ideas are neither wanted nor are given serious consideration. The biggest risk managers face when using co-optation is that the people deceived will discover the truth. Reactions to such discoveries can be quick, strong, and actively resistant. The damage can last for a long time. Another risk in creating a figurehead is that others in the organization may believe the role and allow themselves to be influenced by the figurehead—hardly what the change initiator had in mind.

Coercion

Often the most forceful, most powerful, and quickest technique for developing support (at least, on a short-term basis) is coercion. The principle underlying the use of coercion is very simple: "Do this or else." For coercion to work, organization members must believe that resistance to a change would result in punishment, either through the loss of something of value or at a significant cost to them. Managers using coercion can threaten the loss of jobs, promotion, pay, recognition, or anything else that organization members value.

Coercion can be quite effective, and managers sometimes use it when support is needed because a change must be implemented quickly to avoid

TABLE 18.3   Techniques for Developing Support/Reducing Resistance
and Examples of Appropriate Uses

Technique	Common Uses
Education and communication	When knowledge would help alleviate fears due to inaccurate or sketchy information
Participation and involvement	When change initiators need information from others to design change and when the probability of resistance is high
Facilitative support	When people lack the necessary skills or tools to be effective following change
Emotional support	When people have personal concerns and anxiety about a change that supportive reassurance could help alleviate
Incentives	When key people will resist the change unless they benefit from it
Manipulation and co-optation	When change is absolutely necessary and all other techniques would be ineffective or too costly
Coercion	When change must occur quickly and the initiators have significantly more power than the resistors

great loss. There are some problems, however. First, people who are coerced to behave in a particular manner often seek alternative ways to regain control; thus, workers who are forced to support a change they dislike may react by increasing absenteeism, lowering performance, or possibly even engaging in organizational sabotage (see Chapter 17). Coercion usually results in reduced satisfaction and increased resentment. An organization's ability to use many of the other techniques for managing change is reduced, as most employees lose respect for the coercive change manager.

Many of the techniques for developing support discussed in this section are used extensively during the organizational development efforts discussed in the next section. Their use should be considered when implementing any organizational change. In most situations, managers will want to choose an appropriate combination of techniques to manage change most effectively. Table 18.3 provides examples of situations in which each technique may be appropriate.[13]

The Special Role of Organizational Development (OD)

The techniques for managing change discussed in this chapter have been developed and refined, to a large extent, by individuals referred to as *organizational development (OD) specialists.* OD specialists tend to apply these techniques in a particular manner and for a particular purpose. In general, they attack substantial, often organizationwide issues for the purpose of achieving a planned, systematic improvement of organizations.

What Is OD?

Michael Beer, a well-known OD specialist from Harvard University, defines **organizational development** as "a process for diagnosing organizational problems by looking for incongruencies between environment, structures, processes, and people."[14] Although this may sound like a very broad and loose description of what has developed into a distinct discipline over the past thirty years or so, it can be argued that OD's openness provides the breadth and flexibility necessary for the effective enhancement of organizations.

OD specialists use a variety of theories from psychology and organizational behavior. The OD process consists of a series of planned actions designed to improve the effectiveness of an organization and/or its members' well-being. OD practitioners refer to such actions as *interventions*. An OD specialist analyzes an organization's problems and needs and then plans an intervention. Interventions could involve anything from individual or group counseling sessions to organizationwide structural changes.

An OD specialist can be likened to a doctor. A good physician talks with a patient to identify apparent health weaknesses and strengths. He or she then conducts a more formal assessment, using the tools of the medical trade to determine the condition of each major component of the patient's body. If a problem is found, more extensive diagnostic techniques are used to find the source(s) of the apparent problem. Based on this information, the doctor makes a diagnosis and identifies alternative treatment plans. He or she discusses these alternatives with the patient and, based on the patient's preferences and the physician's expert opinions, a course of treatment is undertaken. If treatment goes beyond the expertise of the examining physician, he or she seeks assistance from other experts. The doctor reassesses the patient's progress periodically and adjusts the treatment if necessary. If all goes as planned, the patient improves.

An organizational doctor (OD specialist, or "Dr. O") follows a virtually identical procedure. Dr. O talks with organization members to identify apparent organizational weaknesses and strengths. He or she then conducts a more formal assessment, using such tools as surveys and interviews, to determine the condition of each organizational component. For problem areas, Dr. O extends the diagnosis to locate the source(s) of the organizational problem (for example, is it based on technological, structural, or interpersonal problems?). Based on this information, Dr. O identifies potential interventions that might remedy the problem(s) and discusses them with key organization members. Based on the organization's preferences and Dr. O's opinions, appropriate interventions are undertaken. When necessary, Dr. O might consult engineers, accountants, psychologists, or others who possess the knowledge and expertise needed to design and implement the needed organizational changes effectively. Throughout the intervention period, Dr. O assesses the organization's progress, fine-tunes the interventions as necessary, and guides the improvement of organizational effectiveness. As is the case with medical doctors, Dr. O sometimes succeeds and sometimes fails, but the treatment of every organization, whether it leads to success or failure, enhances the doctor's ability to treat future patients.

Common OD Activities

Because OD involves such a flexible, adaptive process, it is very difficult to create a list of tools that are always used. Medical doctors do not use every available tool each time they examine a patient. The same is true for Dr. O, although there are specific activities that reflect some of the most basic values and assumptions inherent in the OD process (see Table 18.4).[15] These values

TABLE 18.4 *Frequently Used OD Techniques*

Technique	Examples
Organizational diagnoses	Interviews, surveys, group meetings
Team building	Improvement of existing groups; creation of teams for problem solving
Survey feedback	Provision of survey results to members; interpretation of results by members
Education	Classroom training for "sensitivity" skills and interpersonal skills
Intergroup activities	Communication development; conflict reduction
Third-party peace making	Negotiation, mediation by "outsider" for interperson and intergroup conflict
Technostructural/sociotechnical activities	Joint examination of technology, structure, and people systems
Process consultation	Observation of groups in action with immediate feedback on processes observed
Life/career planning	Future oriented—development of personal goals and acquisition of skills to help individuals fit into the organization and the organization match individual needs
Coaching	Nonevaluative feedback to individuals describing how others see them
Planning and goal setting	Training of individuals to improve personal-planning and goal-setting effectiveness; emphasis on individual's place in the overall organization

and assumptions include, for example, the belief that organization members seek satisfaction of high-level needs, personal development, and growth. It is also believed that people wish to contribute to organizational effectiveness and are capable of doing so. OD values tend to stress that group relationships have a major impact on the satisfaction and productivity of individual members and that groups are the key to organizational success. Finally, OD specialists tend to assume that the design, structure, policies, and practices of organizations influence the attitudes and behaviors of their members and that management must recognize this and be prepared to change these factors to benefit both the organization and its members.

How Effective Is OD?

It is hard to know how well organizational development actually works. Most OD activities must remain open to change while underway in order to adapt to organizational and individual complexities. Such flexibility can make it difficult to judge an intervention's success. Many OD specialists do not collect evidence that could be used to assess their effectiveness. Perhaps they are too busy with the intervention itself to conduct an independent "research" study at the same time, or perhaps they are so convinced they will be successful that they do not see the need for doing so. The literature contains many case studies reporting apparently successful OD interventions.[16] Reports of success, however, tend to be based on subjective rather than objective evaluation. Although there is nothing wrong with subjective evaluation of OD interventions, the use of such reports to guide future work is limited by the lack of substantiating evidence. The few "objective" attempts to evaluate OD effectiveness have uncovered mixed results.[17]

Many OD interventions have been conducted well and have produced moderate-to-substantial positive effects. Others have been conducted less well and have often damaged an organization and its members. Some OD practitioners expect too much from their interventions and promise too much. They should have a more realistic set of expectations; less puffery in the promotion of OD activities; and improved, more systematic documentation of the effects of their interventions. Finally, the OD interventions that prove most effective tend to follow a systematic approach, such as that presented in the next section on planning and managing the change process, and are begun without prejudice about the nature of needed organizational change. The best OD practitioners appear to be those who practice the trade systematically and follow the principles that give OD so much promise.

Planning and Managing the Change Process

The key to the effective management of change is the use of a *systematic* and orderly change process. Such a process is shown in Figure 18.5. Managers can use this four-stage process as they plan and manage change.

Stage 1: Change Identification

The first stage of the change process requires managers to recognize a need for change and to identify the nature of the change. Normally the need for change is indicated by the forces to change discussed at the beginning of this chapter. Employee complaints, dropping sales, and technological developments are a few of the signals that might alert managers that a change is needed.

Once the need for change has been identified, managers should clarify the nature of the change. Sometimes the signals that indicate the need for change suggest the general nature of the change, while at other times they also reveal the specific types of change needed. An increase in turnover in one office, for example, might indicate that a turnover-management change is needed. On the other hand, exit-interview complaints of poor supervision may more precisely identify the nature of the needed change. Sometimes a needed change is identified quite specifically, as might be the case when a machine breaks down and cannot be repaired.

During this first stage, it is important that managers specify, at least in a general sense, the proposed change's objectives and the criteria they will use to determine whether these objectives are met. At times the change can be very specifically and completely identified at Stage 1. At other times—for instance, when significant employee input is needed to design the change—final planning of the change carries over to the second stage.

FIGURE 18.5 The Systematic
Management of Change

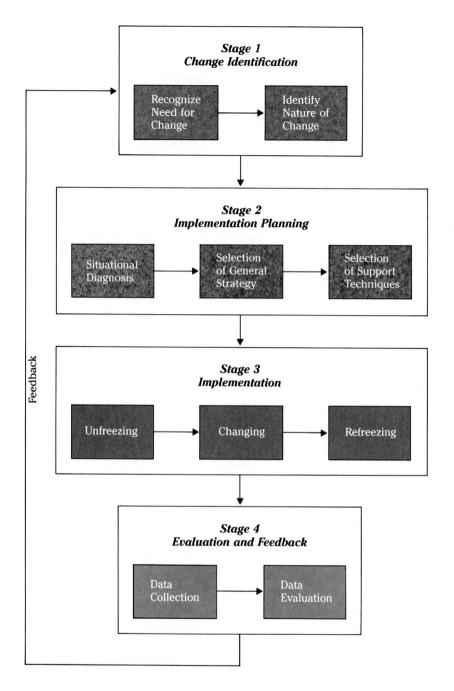

Stage 2: Implementation Planning

In this stage, managers diagnose the situation in which the change is likely
to occur, select a general strategy for managing the change, and choose
specific techniques to develop support for and reduce resistance to the
change. To perform a situational diagnosis, managers must collect a broad
range of information. It is necessary, for example, to identify where the change
will be implemented and which organization members will potentially be
affected by it. Managers must also discover who possesses the information
needed to design the change effectively and pinpoint the key individuals who

must support the change for it to work well. Equally important is the identification of those who are likely to support or resist the change and the determination of why they are expected to do so. Finally, managers should assess the expected risk(s) and benefit(s) of making the change.

After conducting a situational diagnosis, managers must select a general change strategy. They must decide, for example, how quickly the change must be implemented and how completely the plan should be designed before it is revealed to organization members.

The final step of the implementation planning stage involves selecting techniques to develop support and reduce resistance. The information obtained from the situational diagnosis, along with the choice of a general change strategy, should aid in the selection of these techniques. In choosing from among the available alternatives, managers should try to construct an effective combination of techniques. Combining participation and involvement with facilitative support, for example, might encourage general support for an impending change that might otherwise be worrisome to employees.

Stage 3: Implementation

A thoughtfully planned change implemented too late has no value. Consequently, every attempt must be made to institutionalize a change as quickly as possible.

—Hawk

Once a change has been identified and implementation planning completed, it is time to implement the change. Psychologist Kurt Lewin has developed a widely accepted and very useful model that identifies three necessary steps for effective change implementation: unfreezing, changing, and refreezing.[18] *Unfreezing* systematically upsets the equilibrium between the forces driving change and those discouraging it so that others will also feel the need for change. Managers should create a felt need for change if it does not currently exist—for example, by providing organization members with information that helps them understand the need for change.[19] *Changing* introduces the change, such as putting a new machine in place or adopting new work procedures. *Refreezing* requires managers to restabilize the situation and to encourage the long-term acceptance and success of the change.

Stage 4: Evaluation and Feedback

A learning organization is capable of creating matches between the design and implementation of its actions and the actualization of its intended behaviors.

—Argyris

The fourth stage of a systematically managed change process is extremely important for an organization's long-term success, although managers often overlook it. At this final stage, managers should collect data and evaluate them so they can compare what was accomplished by the change to what was desired. If discrepancies are found, managers should plan to modify the change or the processes by which the results of the change are managed. Based on this evaluation, the managers should provide feedback to those involved in planning and/or implementing the change, and, if necessary, the change process should begin again from Stage 1.

Organizational Change and Development in Review

Change must occur for organizations to succeed. Now, more than ever, a key factor that distinguishes effective managers from those who are less effective is an ability to manage change well. Most changes occur because of forces exerted by technological factors; employee needs and values; and social, business, economic, and organizational factors.

Many types of organizational change are possible. Some changes are reactive (the forces to change are so strong that an organization must change). Other changes are proactive (an organization concludes that change would be desirable). Innovation is a special type of change that occurs when an organization is the first or an early user of an idea. Some changes involve the introduction of new technologies; others focus primarily on organizational structure and procedures; still others are people-oriented. Many of the most effective changes—often referred to as technostructural or sociotechnical changes—involve combinations of these last three types of change.

Many reactions to change are possible, ranging from active resistance to active support. The reason for this is that people react based on whether they expect to personally gain or lose something of value because of the change. Their reactions are also based on how well they understand the change, on whether they trust the change initiators, and on whether they agree to the advisability of the change. Finally, reactions to change are influenced by organization members' personal characteristics. Knowing why people react as they do can help managers select appropriate techniques to reduce resistance and to develop support for an impending change. These techniques include education and communication, participation and involvement, facilitative support, emotional support, incentives, manipulation and co-optation, and coercion.

Organizational development (OD) is a process by which specialists systematically apply their knowledge about change management to enhance organizational effectiveness and the quality of the work experience for organization members. The actions specialists take to remedy an organization's problem areas are called interventions. It is often difficult to evaluate the success of an OD intervention objectively because OD specialists usually do not complete comprehensive documentation of their cases.

It is essential that OD specialists and managers follow a systematic procedure for planning and managing the change process. Four stages are included in this process: recognizing the need for change and identifying the nature of the change, planning its implementation, implementing it, and evaluating the results and providing feedback.

In many ways, this chapter is the most important one in this text. If you have ideas that are worth implementing, you must implement them well or they will fail to realize their potential. Good ideas only work well when they are managed effectively. Regardless of your ultimate field of interest, you should recognize that one of the major factors that distinguishes excellent managers from merely adequate ones is the degree to which they are able to design and effectively manage organizational change.

Issues for Review and Discussion

1. Describe how the five forces to change combine to create the need for organizational change.
2. Why is it important to differentiate proactive (planned) change from reactive change?

3. Explain why you would expect a variety of reactions from students if your college proposed to change its grading system so that all courses would be graded pass/fail only.

4. Briefly describe which of the techniques for developing support for change might be useful for an organization planning to change from traditional assembly-line production to a heavily automated operation.

5. Outline the procedures an OD specialist follows when working with an organization.

6. What problems arise in trying to determine the effectiveness of OD, and why do these problems exist?

7. In your own words, summarize the systematic procedure presented in this chapter for the planning for and management of organizational change. Briefly note why each stage and each step is necessary.

Key Terms

internal forces to change
external forces to change
reactive change
proactive change

innovation
technostructural changes
sociotechnical changes
organizational development (OD)

Suggested Readings

Beer, M., and Walton, A. E. (1987). Organization change and development. *Annual Review of Psychology,* 38, 339-40.

Buller, P. (Winter 1988). For successful strategic change: Blend OD practices with strategic management. *Organizational Dynamics,* 42-55.

Connor, P. E. (1988). Strategies for managing technological change. *Harvard International Review,* 10(2), 10-13, 42.

Connor, P. E., and Lake, L. K. (1988). *Managing organizational change.* New York: Praeger.

Joiner, C. W. (1987). *Leadership for change.* Cambridge, MA: Ballinger.

Kanter, R. M. (1985). *The change masters.* New York: Touchstone Books.

Kilmann, R. H., Covin, T. J., and Associates (1988). *Corporate transformation.* San Francisco: Jossey-Bass.

Naisbitt, J., and Aburdene, R. (1985). *Re-inventing the corporation.* New York: Warner. For a review of this book, see Boal, K. (1988). In Pierce, J. L., and Newstrom, J. W., eds. *The manager's bookshelf: A mosaic of contemporary views.* New York: Harper & Row, 275-281.

Sashkin, M., and Burke, W. W. (1987). Organization development in the 1980's. *Journal of Management,* 13, 393-417.

Notes

1. H. J. Leavitt (1964), Applied organization change in industry: Structural, technical, and human approaches, in W. W. Cooper, H. J. Leavitt, and M. W. Shelly II, eds., *New perspectives in organization research,* New York: John Wiley & Sons, 55-71.

2. Based on a similar quote by J. L. Price (1972), *Handbook of organizational measurement,* Lexington, MA: D.C. Heath, 118.

3. This definition is consistent with that provided by S. W. Becker and T. L. Whisler (1967), The innovative organization: A selective view of current theory and research, *Journal of Business,* 40, 462-69.

4. F. Friedlander and L. D. Brown (1974), Organization development, *Annual Review of Psychology,* 25, 320.

5. Leavitt.

6. C. A. Carnall (1986), Toward a theory for the evaluation of organizational change, *Human Relations,* 39, 745-66.

7. Carnall.

8. B. Moore (1978), *Injustice: The social bases of obedience and revolt,* New York: Macmillan, 490.

9. Carnall, 756.

10. Many of the issues covered in this section are based on those discussed by J. P. Kotter and L. A. Schlesinger of Harvard University in (March/April 1979), Choosing strategies for change, *Harvard Business Review,* 106-13; and in J. P. Kotter, L. A. Schlesinger, and V. Sathe (1979), *Organization: Text, cases, and readings on the management of organizational design and change,* Homewood, IL: Irwin. In addition, both Kotter and Schlesinger graciously submitted to interviews with one of the authors of this text to discuss some of their ideas. It should be noted that these authors organized these issues somewhat differently and focused primarily on reasons for resistance. Treatment of these issues in this textbook has been expanded to include reasons for support as well as for resistance.

11. R. B. Dunham, J. A. Grube, D. G. Gardner, and J. L. Pierce (1989), The development of an attitude toward change instrument. Paper presented at the 49th Annual Meeting of the Academy of Management, Washington, DC.

12. L. W. Mealiea (1978), Learned behavior: The key to understanding and preventing employee resistance to change, *Group & Organization Studies,* 3, 211-23.

13. Some of these are based on Kotter and Schlesinger, 11.

14. M. Beer (1980), *Organization change and development: A systems view,* Santa Monica, CA: Goodyear, 7; M. Beer and A. E. Walton (1987), Organization change and development, *Annual Review of Psychology,* 38, 339-40.

15. W. L. French and C. H. Bell, Jr. (1978), *Organizational development: Behavioral science interventions for organization improvement,* 2nd ed., Englewood Cliffs, NJ: Prentice-Hall.

16. Z. E. Barnes (February 1987), Visions, values, and strategies: Changing attitudes and culture, *The Academy of Management Executive,* 33-42; R. N. Beck (February 1987), The theory practice gap: Myth or reality? *The Academy of Management Executive,* 31-32; J. J. Renier (February 1987), Turnaround of information systems at Honeywell, *The Academy of Management Executive,* 47-50.

17. B. A. Macy, C. C. M. Hurts, H. Izumi, L. Norton, and R. R. Smith (1986), An assessment of U.S. work improvement and productivity efforts: 1970-1985, 46th Annual Academy of Management Convention, Chicago, IL; J. Nicholas (1982), The comparative impact of organization development interventions on hard criteria measures, *Academy of Management Review,* 9, 531-43; W. M. Vicars and D. D. Hartke (1984), Evaluating OD evaluations: A status report, *Group Organizational Studies,* 9, 177-88.

18. K. Lewin (1947), Frontiers in group dynamics, *Human Relations,* 1, 5-41; K. Lewin (1951), *Field theory in social science,* New York: Harper & Row.

19. W. G. Bennis, D. E. Berlew, E. H. Schein, and F. I. Steele (1973), *Interpersonal dynamics: Essays and readings on human interaction,* Homewood, IL: Dorsey Press; D. A. Nadler (1981), Managing organizational change: An integrative perspective, *The Journal of Applied Behavioral Science,* 17, 191-211.

The Wyatt-Boyer Insurance Company

Loren W. Kuzuhara and
Randall B. Dunham,
University of Wisconsin

Wyatt-Boyer Insurance is a multiline insurance firm located in a major city of a midwestern state. The primary functions of the company's service division are to accept policy applications from agents, rate (price) the policies, and issue the policies.

Figure 18A illustrates the initial workflow layout (job design) for the services division at Wyatt-Boyer Insur-ance. Policy applications received (new work) are first routed to a gen-eral sorting room, where policies are separated by type (A, B, or C). The sorted policies are then sent to the appropriate policy-type sorting rooms (room A, B, or C) where they are pre-pared for distribution to policy-type supervisors. These supervisors assign the work to entry clerks, who enter policy information into a computer and send the work to underwriters. The underwriters authorize the pol-icies and send them to rating clerks, who are responsible for rating (pric-ing) the policies. The rated policies are then printed out and sent to a policy-type sorting room, where the work is processed and assigned to distribution clerks. Three copies of each policy are made by distribution clerks and then sent on to the mail-room. The mailroom sends one copy of the policy to Wyatt-Boyer files, one copy to the policy holder, and one copy to the appropriate insurance agent.

Recently, management at Wyatt-Boyer administered a survey to cler-ical workers in the service division in order to assess core job charac-teristics and worker responses. The

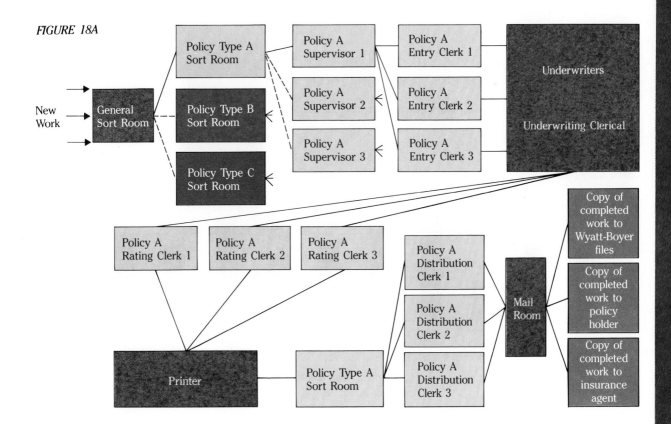

FIGURE 18A

results of this survey are displayed in Figure 18B. The dotted line running across each bar graph represents the national norm (average value) for a large, representative sample of clerical workers in the United States. The top graph shows clerical workers' perceptions of core job characteristics. The bottom graph represents workers' satisfaction with various aspects of their jobs, along with attendance levels and an index of productivity. Finally, it should be noted that the clerical workers at Wyatt-Boyer Insurance were generally very competent individuals who had a strong desire to engage in challenging work (they had high growth-need strength).

Questions

1. Are the clerical jobs at Wyatt-Boyer in need of redesign? Explain why you feel redesign is or is not needed.

2. Describe the process you would follow to redesign the jobs at Wyatt-Boyer. Pay particular attention to the systematic management of the change process.

3. Discuss the expected resistance to change if the clerical jobs at Wyatt-Boyer were to be redesigned. From whom would you expect resistance and for what reason(s)?

4. Describe how you would change the design of the clerical jobs at Wyatt-Boyer if you were required to do so based on the information presented in this case. Explain why you would choose this particular redesign.

5. Describe the changes you would expect in perceived job characteristics, job satisfaction, attendance, and performance given your redesign of the jobs. Explain why you would expect these effects.

6. Briefly discuss the types of actions that might encourage supervisors to actively support the redesign of the clerical jobs.

FIGURE 18B

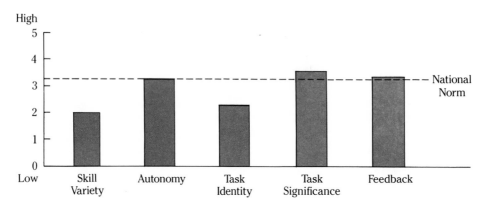

Core Job Characteristics

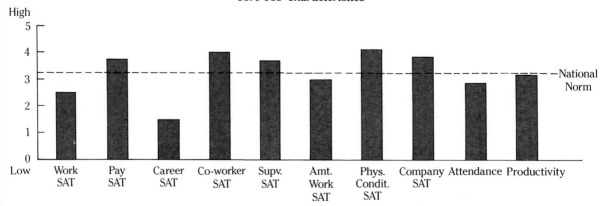

Worker Responses

PART 6

Special Topics

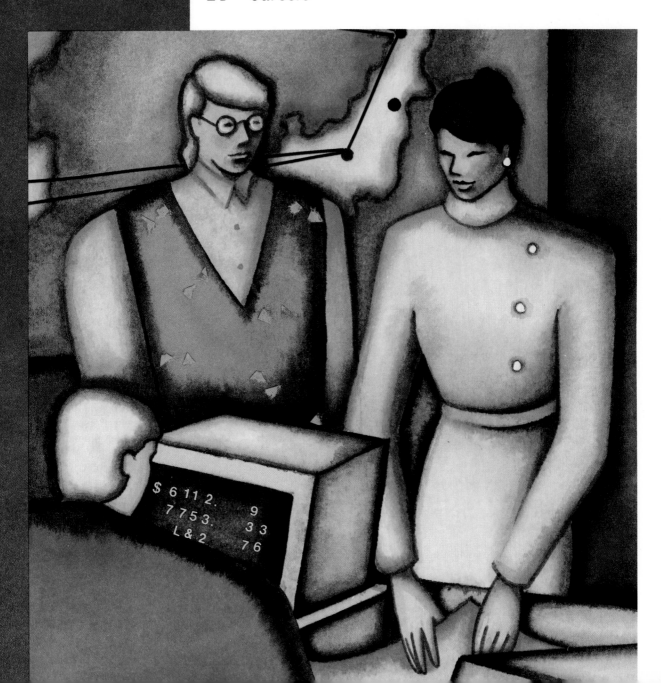

Mary Kay Ash

Her organization is characterized by a humanistic management philosophy. A free and entrepreneurial spirit is encouraged and rewarded, and emphasis is placed on self-esteem, self-confidence, and an endless stream of self-competition. She motivates her employees with public praise and an elaborate reward system. Rewards of increasing value are given for increasing performance, and as employees climb upward, pins, diamonds, fur coats, and pink cadillacs await them. If a person slips downward while trying to achieve, the rewards slide down as well. The system is designed so that people can compete with themselves, not with others or with a bureaucratically defined performance standard. People set goals, compete with themselves, and are rewarded for their effort and performance.

> *She motivates her employees with public praise and an elaborate reward system.*

The founder and chairperson of this organization is its corporate symbol, its heroine. The company is Mary Kay Cosmetics, and the woman at the helm is Mary Kay Ash. A woman with an entrepreneurial spirit—a sense of drive, the need to succeed, and a strong sense of self-confidence—born out of a need to overcome myriad obstacles confronted during childhood, Ash developed a "you can do it" conviction. This conviction is the cornerstone of her cosmetics empire.

As a young child, Ash nursed her tubercular father, cleaned house, cooked, and attended school while her mother worked long days managing a restaurant. "When I was growing up, we had very little and I had to work hard. That experience made me want to excel and to work hard. We had plenty of love and my mother always encouraged me by saying, 'You can do it, Mary Kay! . . . You can do it.'" Sacrifice and hardship carried her past high-school graduation, when a lack of money prompted her to go to work instead of to college. Starting out as a salesperson with Stanley Home Products, it was not long before she was recognized as one of Stanley's top performers.

While achieving forms of personal success at work, Ash continued to face a series of hardships. Divorce, rheumatoid arthritis, an emotional breakdown, and facial paralysis scarred her life and yet made her strong in a unique way. She has woven this strength of character into her management style and organizational culture. Ash developed a strong sense of competitiveness and a desire for recognition. In 1963 she founded Mary Kay Cosmetics, Inc. As founder and chairperson, she heads an organization with over $300 million in revenue, selling a facial care system to over 180,000 beauty consultants.

Self-competition, rewards for achievement (once a year at the annual Mary Kay seminar, diamonds, mink coats, and "Mary Kay Pink" cadillacs are presented), and peer recognition are an integral part of her management system. Her objective is to create a work environment that encourages and brings out the best in people. She awards people with the diamond bumblebee, which symbolizes the personal ability to overcome great odds—aerodynamically the bumblebee cannot fly, yet it does. Ash attempts to bring out this spirit in the people with whom she works. Her management style emphasizes the creation of a humanistic work environment in which self-strength is a core component.

William MacPhee writes that entrepreneurs are characterized by vision, resourcefulness, and self-confidence. They are risk takers—managers of odds, constraints, and obstacles. They are the types of people who make things happen. As a manager, Ash values goal setting and self- and time management. She manages her own day with a set of goals and an agenda that tackles the most challenging task first. Her problem-solving style consists of breaking problems down into manageable pieces, so that they can be dealt with one issue (piece) at a time until the entire problem has been resolved.

Entrepreneurial spirit is valued in the Mary Kay organization. People are encouraged to establish their own goals and try to exceed them. Achievement is nurtured, while control that stems from the bureaucracy is minimized. Ash's operating philosophy encourages striking a balance between the need to nurture the entrepreneurial spirit and certain elements of managerial necessity.

"By eliminating stress . . . you can increase and inspire productivity."

It has been said that Ash's management style is built around seven basic principles, the Mary Kay "Golden Rules of Management":

1. *Recognize the value of people:* "People are your company's number one asset. When you treat them as you would like to be treated yourself, everyone benefits."

2. *Praise your people to success:* "Recognition is the most powerful of all motivators. Even criticism can build confidence when it's 'sandwiched' between layers of praise."

3. *Tear down the ivory tower:* "Keep all doors open. Be accessible to everyone. Remember that every good manager is a good listener."

4. *Be a risk taker:* "Don't be afraid. Encourage your people to take risks, too, and allow room for error."

5. *Create a stress-free workplace:* "By eliminating stress factors, fear of the boss, [and] unreasonable deadlines, [etc.] . . . you can increase and inspire productivity."

6. *Develop and promote people from within:* "Upward mobility for employees in your company builds loyalty. People give you their best when they know they'll be rewarded."

7. *Keep business in the proper place:* "At Mary Kay Cosmetics, the order of priorities is faith, family and career. The real key to success is creating an environment where people are encouraged to balance the many aspects of their life."

MacPhee concludes his look at Ash and her company by noting that "Mary Kay Cosmetics has a people philosophy." The organizational culture is one that "encourages self-esteem and self-confidence" through its slogan "You can do it." Management encourages "free spirited [and] visionary thinking."

Source: W. MacPhee (1987), *Rare breed: The entrepreneurs, an American culture,* Chapter 2, Chicago, IL: Probus, 21-36.

19 International Management

Student Learning Objectives

After reading this chapter, you should be able to:

1. Explain why companies go abroad.

2. List the major factors that must be considered when managing in an international environment.

3. Understand the managerial problems and opportunities of joint ventures.

4. Describe how and why wholly owned subsidiaries need highly trained international managers.

5. Identify the staffing considerations faced by international human resource managers.

6. Describe the basic tasks of international marketing managers.

7. Understand why the tasks of international finance managers are complex.

By Heidi Vernon-Wortzel, Northeastern University-Boston

B ritish business raider Jimmy Goldsmith, owner of France's second-largest publishing company, sent Goodyear Tire & Rubber Company executives and Wall Street scrambling with his $5 billion bid to take over Goodyear.[1] The Bertelsmann Group of Germany now owns Doubleday Publishers.[2] France let Sweden's L. M. Ericsson purchase Compagnie Generale Construction Telephoniques—and 16 percent of the French telecommunications market—while Britain's electronics group GEP PLC merged with Dutch electronics giant Philips.[3] By 1980, the volume of world trade exceeded one trillion U.S. dollars; it was $800 billion in 1975.[4] Foreign direct investments by U.S. firms grew from approximately $215 billion in 1980 to approximately $260 billion in 1986.[5]

Fifty years ago, few managers predicted the current high degree of interrelationship among trading countries. Few have foreseen the rise of the small Asian countries to their powerful position in world business and the simultaneous decline of U.S. power. Currently no company, however small, can ignore foreign competition. **International management** is the process of carrying out the managerial functions of planning, organizing, directing, and controlling in an organization that operates in more than one country.

The International Environment

In going international, an organization's environment becomes more complicated. Its task environment grows larger and more complex as a result of increased numbers and/or varieties of customers, suppliers, competitors, regulatory agencies, and allies. Its general environment contains a greater variety of sociocultural, political/legal, economic, and technological factors. These four general environmental factors represent the four major forces on an organization's international operations (see Figure 19.1).

International managers work within complex sociocultural systems. They plan, organize, direct, and control organizational activities in accordance with the cultural norms that operate both in their home country and in the host environment.

FIGURE 19.1 The International Environment

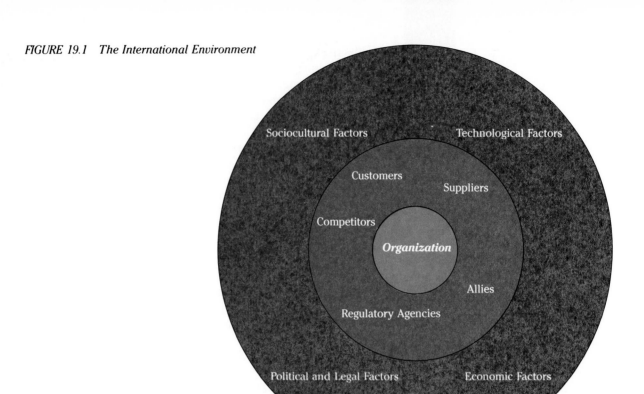

Sociocultural Factors

Managers of an international operation perform tasks from either domestic headquarters or a foreign subsidiary. Regardless of location, managers must be sensitive to social and cultural differences. Doing business in New York is not like doing business in Saudi Arabia or even in Canada; rules of behavior and differences among institutions can vary substantially. Most people take their own culture for granted, rarely thinking about why they behave in a particular way. It is only when they deal with different cultural expectations that they think about what culture is and how it changes their behavior as they conduct business internationally.

Culture can be defined as a complex whole that includes the knowledge, beliefs, art, morals, law, customs, and any other capabilities and habits acquired by people as members of society.[6] Rules of behavior are passed from generation to generation through the *enculturation process* (socialization). Language and the many forms of nonverbal communication transmit the elements of culture so subtly that individuals are not usually aware that they act in response to cultural norms. Cultural elements relevant to organizations include the simple act of meeting a foreign counterpart, the amount of personal space that people from different cultures like to maintain, the concept of being "on time," and the range of subjects that can be covered in "small talk." It is not necessary, or even possible, for a manager to learn every element of a foreign culture, but it is critical that he or she learn enough about a host-country culture to avoid major gaffes.

Legal and Political Factors

Firms operating simultaneously in several countries must deal with a variety of legal and political systems, which can be positioned along a continuum ranging from democratic to totalitarian. Democratic systems rely on a representative form of government. People and organizations operating in such systems play active roles through the electoral process, influencing national priorities, policies, and laws and electing individuals and groups to serve as their representatives. Within totalitarian systems, countries are frequently governed through dictatorships and/or single-party rule. Organizations are permitted to play a very minimal role in governmental policy and regulation.

Organizations are obligated to abide by the legal/political system of the country in which they operate, as well as by the legal/political system of their home country. A number of legal/political factors can have a major impact on an organization's international operations, including governmental stability, terrorism, and laws and regulations governing foreign investment and international trade.

Economic Factors

A sufficient, accessible knowledge base within a host country enables an organization to deliver its products efficiently and effectively.

World economies fall somewhere along a continuum between free-market and centralized-planned economies. *Free-market economies* operate under the laws of the marketplace and the dynamics of supply and demand. The United States and Canada have free-market economies. In *centralized-planned economies,* the central government makes basic economic decisions for the entire nation. Resource allocation, pricing and distribution, wages, and production quotas are defined in accordance with a master societal economic plan. The challenges and responsibilities of management are quite different under these two economic systems. To be successful, international organizations must adapt their management practices to the realities of this part of the external environment.

Many other economic factors also influence the nature of operations across various countries. Managers should consider a country's infrastructure, focusing on such factors as its education, communication, and transportation systems; its level of economic development; the exchange rates and the government's trade, monetary, and fiscal policies; and the country's resource and product markets.

Technological Factors

Technology is another component of an organization's foreign and general environment that significantly influences its operations. Technological dimensions consist of the availability of equipment, machinery, and components that will be used to transform the organization's inputs into outputs. For example, is there an accessible knowledge base within the host country sufficient to enable the organization to deliver its product efficiently and effectively?

International Management Functions

Because going international complicates an organization's general and task environments, the management process also becomes more complex. Environmental scans needed to aid in the decision-making and planning process are more complicated; new kinds of organizational structures may be needed; directing strategies have to cope with a variety of cultural differences; and organizational control systems need to be larger, more elaborate, and capable of integrating a greater variety of information.

Planning

International planning requires managers to set objectives and to design strategies and policies for an organization that faces constraints unique to its host country or countries. Foreign laws and regulations may subject the organization to forces beyond its control. International managers, therefore, approach the planning function knowing they have to provide a framework to help their organization reach its objectives in many different environments. International managers may be able to state objectives in broad terms without much more difficulty than their domestic counterparts, but when specific objectives require directions and guidelines for employee action, managers have to consider the constraints and opportunities in each country in which their organization is located.

The international planning function often takes place in a context characterized by multiple and varied languages, political systems, currencies, governmental regulations, business climates, and values, as well as by diverse and distant sources of information.[7] Thus, successful planning efforts greatly depend on accurate, timely, objective information. Given the increased environmental segmentation that accompanies international activities, managers need to invest in an information-management system that is sensitive to environmental issues.

International managers must make international strategic planning an integral part of their overall long-range strategic planning process. Without intense planning and detailed observation of operations, an international organization is at great risk.

Organizing

In the international context, managers approach the organizing function from the same perspective as do those in the domestic context. For example, the characteristics of the environment, the technology, the people, and the size of the system all influence organizing decisions. It is as important for an organization with international operations to create an environment-structure match as it is for an organization operating only in a single U.S. state.

For small organizations just beginning to enter the international arena through importing or exporting, structural arrangements are likely to be simple. As the scale of international operations increases and becomes more complex, however, managers may have to create specialized departments. Further growth in international operations may cause managers to develop an interna-

FIGURE 19.2 *The Evolution of an International Organization Structure*

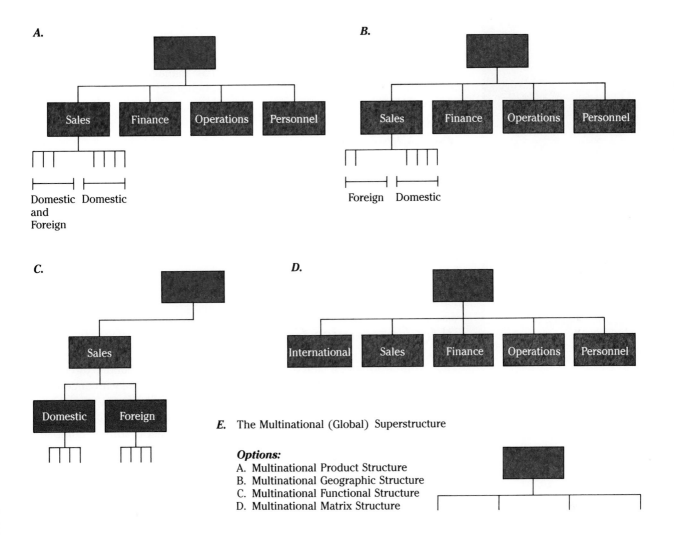

E. The Multinational (Global) Superstructure

Options:
A. Multinational Product Structure
B. Multinational Geographic Structure
C. Multinational Functional Structure
D. Multinational Matrix Structure

tional division within their organization. Finally, an organization can develop a truly multinational organizational structure. The evolution of international organizational structures is illustrated in Figure 19.2.

Directing

Once an organization has been designed and its plans developed, these plans must be carried out. To guide and motivate employees to help the organization meet its objectives, managers must provide leadership to people from other countries. They must communicate with and motivate foreign employees in ways that may be very different from the methods used in the organization's home country. International managers must know what incentives are appropriate, what constitutes supportive behavior, and how to give feedback in such a way that foreign managers are encouraged to meet the

At the Gold Star Company near Osan, South Korea, production line workers meet weekly with supervisors for quality control circle discussions.

organization's goals. Imagine how an American manager might motivate an employee in a culture in which monetary rewards are not considered important. International managers must understand what foreign employees value.

Managers cannot assume that U.S. models of motivation, leadership, political and communication processes, and group management are equally effective across cultural boundaries. International managers, therefore, must carefully develop directing strategies that are anchored in the culture in which their organization operates.

Controlling

The international controlling function is influenced by many of the same opportunities and constraints as is the planning function. Multiple environmental factors dictate the types of control systems that are effective in different locations and cultures. Management's information needs are usually great. In addition, specific controlling activities may be more or less acceptable in different countries. Unions in France, for example, place greater limits on an organization than is possible in Mexico.

Why Companies Go International

Managers who invest abroad, purchase from foreign manufacturers, or simply export goods to another country enter a situation fraught with uncertainties and risks. Why, then, do they even contemplate doing business internationally? The answer is that there is no domestic environment in the United States or in any other country that has not felt the impact of foreign competition, and there is no organization so small that there are not opportunities to be found abroad.

Opportunities for very large and diversified organizations abound. Walking through the Guangzhou (Canton, China) Foreign Trade Center, for example, tourists might see the Jolly Green Giant staring at them from a huge poster and suggesting, in Chinese characters, that they buy Niblet corn. Western expatriates working in China are making the bulk of such purchases, but increasing numbers of Chinese are developing a taste for western food. A tiny market for western foods today can be a huge market tomorrow.

Some international opportunities can also be exploited even by very small firms. Managers contemplating expansion to other countries might look at the example of Otto Clark, whose little company, Clark Copy International Corporation, won a contract with the Chinese despite fierce competition from American, German, and Japanese conglomerates. In 1981, Clark won a twenty-year, $5.5 million contract to deliver desktop copiers and parts to China because he was able to win the trust of the Chinese and respond quickly to their needs.[8]

Foreign Companies in the United States

Increasingly, foreign companies are capturing U.S. domestic markets, companies, and real estate. Nissan Foods makes dry ingredients for noodle soup in a factory a few miles from Campbell. Benetton of Italy dresses American teenagers, their younger siblings, and even their parents. British Petroleum now has the controlling interest in America's largest single oil field in Alaska. American managers must learn to develop a global perspective to combat this home-turf competition from foreign-owned companies, which are often better organized, better financed, "hungrier," and better managed.

U.S. Firms Competing Abroad

One of the most common reasons that organizations decide to go international has to do with *market* opportunities. Saturated domestic markets and perceived opportunities to expand sales by entering foreign markets prompt many organizations to become involved in international activity. Some organizations go international in order to acquire *resources* they need to produce goods or to gain access to products that are not available domestically. Many organizations have gone international for *production* reasons. Lower labor costs in other countries, for example, can reduce a firm's production costs. Finally, in many instances, fear that its major *competitors* might enjoy lower costs and/or higher sales gains may prompt an organization to follow their lead into foreign markets.

International business is certainly not new to American organizations. American entrepreneur Isaac Singer manufactured his sewing machine in Scotland only twenty years after he invented it in Boston. In the late nineteenth and early twentieth centuries, many other American firms began to move abroad with their operations and grew rapidly in size and strength. Even so, just twenty-five years ago, about one quarter of the companies on *Fortune*'s 500 list had no overseas manufacturing subsidiaries.[9] Currently the majority of *Fortune* 500 firms have a substantial overseas presence.

Many American managers and entrepreneurs of firms much smaller than the *Fortune* 500 have also realized the opportunities offered by foreign investment and have taken advantage of them. Consider, for example, Scott Karppinen of Hibbing, Minnesota. At peak production, his company makes 1.6 billion chopsticks a year, or 7 million pairs per day. The factory's entire output is exported to the Far East.

In sum, a growing number of American organizations are heeding the advice of the Business Roundtable, which exhorts American companies to get involved abroad: "The major responsibility falls on each company to stress the development of strategies and methods in a framework of global and long-term performance . . . to foster effective and timely development of competitive products."[10] Actually, because U.S. organizations no longer can depend on domestic markets, they have little choice but to go abroad. The questions now concern the mechanisms used and how effectively their managers carry out the management tasks.

Linkages Abroad

Organizations can make many arrangements as they go abroad. At one end of the spectrum, managers simply pack up a product and ship it to an importer in another country. The importer assumes all responsibility for marketing, thereby relieving the company of these decisions. Other organizations prefer to

Organizations can enter international business by exporting goods to buyers in other countries or by importing goods from sellers in other countries.

manufacture abroad and use their own resources to market their products. International managers may enter into licensing agreements with foreign counterparts or become involved in complex product trades with a foreign government. The largest corporations may use a complex web of international arrangements. To a great extent, the kind of arrangements into which international managers enter are determined by their organization's product lines and by the size of its overseas operations.

Exporting and Importing

Organizations can enter international business by exporting or importing goods and/or services. International trade through **exporting** (selling goods to buyers in another country) or **importing** (buying goods from sellers in another country) is perhaps the simplest level of international operation. At this level, managers need to make few changes in the organizing or directing function. Planning, of course, is influenced by the importing/exporting strategy, and some control systems may have to be adjusted to accommodate such operations.

Joint Ventures

A **joint venture** is formed when two or more parent firms collaborate to produce and/or market a product. The new venture may be located in the country of one of the parents or anywhere else. Organizations make joint ventures for many reasons. In some cases, they want access to a market and are forced by the host government to take on a local partner. In China, for example, the government links foreign investors to local organizations in an attempt to gain access to foreign technology and to enjoy income from foreign sales by exporting the joint-venture output. Accordingly, Orlando Helicopter Airway Company of Florida teamed with Guangdong No. 3 Machine Tools Factory to make Guangdong Province's first helicopters, and a Wisconsin organization's Scottish subsidiary agreed to manufacture trucks with the Inner Mongolia Second Machinery Company.[11]

Another reason that organizations enter joint venture arrangements is to gain technological cooperation and achieve scale economies. Telecommunications is one industry in which joint ventures give partners scale economies and a way of handling high entry costs. Joint ventures in the steel industry provided South Korean and Brazilian companies access to technology from their American partners that they would not have had otherwise.[12]

Another benefit of a joint venture is the possibility of avoiding tariff barriers. For example, the Chinese Jiangsu Provincial International Economic and Technical Cooperation Corporation is in a joint venture with Kingsboro Holding Company in Barbados.[13] Because the United States has a policy that offers Caribbean countries preferential access to U.S. markets, textile goods from Barbados are not subject to the same quotas that goods from China encounter.

Still another benefit is access to a country's market that would not otherwise be available and, thus, the economic and political advantages that partnership can bring. Investment risks can even be reduced if managers use a partner's existing infrastructure of local marketing and distribution resources. For instance, China's state planning system has traditionally handled all of the marketing and distribution of joint-venture output. Foreign partners contribute technology, foreign currency, and training.

Joint ventures can also present many problems for managers. Many joint ventures fail or are terminated when one partner's contribution of technology does not prove to be as good as expected, or when partners cannot get along. Problems also arise when partners fail to deliver on their part of the agreement, or when owners who have promised to contribute resources or information cannot get their own personnel to deliver what has been promised.[14] Many of these problems can be managed if organizations plan ahead and are firmly committed to making the venture work. Joint ventures are complex organisms that require trust on the part of all participants, careful selection of managers, and nurturing by parent firms.

Licensing Agreements

In a **licensing agreement,** a licensor gives a licensee the right to use a patent, trademark, copyright, technology, or other asset in return for a royalty or fee. A licensing agreement usually lasts for five to ten years, after which time the technology belongs to the licensee. One of the benefits of a licensing agreement is that it circumvents import barriers that may limit the quantity or add excessively to the price of the product. Small manufacturers find licensing agreements advantageous because they do not have to commit precious resources to building a plant overseas.[15] On the other hand, the risks involved in licensing agreements may be unacceptable, as was the case when United States companies licensed their patents to Korean pharmaceutical companies. Local Korean laws grant patents that cover production techniques but not the products themselves. When a popular U.S. product is licensed to a Korean firm, it is usually imitated within two to four years because a competitor can legally produce the same product with a slightly different process. The licensor has little legal recourse.[16]

Franchises

Franchising, a form of investment that is relatively new in international business, is a variation on a licensing agreement. A franchisor licenses an entire business system, as well as industrial property, to an independent person (a franchisee).[17] In **franchise** arrangements, the franchisor retains the right to inspect the franchisee's operations and to prohibit activities that may harm the product or service. For instance, McDonald's keeps a close eye on its overseas operations. When customers in Thailand stores wanted Filet-O-Fish sandwiches, the president of international operations tasted cod substitutes until he found one that was satisfactory. Franchisees sometimes come up with some new menu ideas, as was the case with the Egg McMuffin. Such ideas can benefit all of the franchisees. This combination of tight control over operating systems and encouragement of new ideas has resulted in thousands of international outlets.[18]

Franchising is a relatively new form of international management. A franchisor licenses an entire business system to an independent franchisee in another country.

Wholly Owned Subsidiaries

A **subsidiary** is an entity that is legally separate from the parent company and organized under the laws of the country in which it is located. In a **wholly owned subsidiary,** the parent company owns 100 percent of the voting stock, but its liability is generally limited to the assets of that subsidiary. Many companies, both U.S. and foreign owned, prefer to have total control over subsidiaries so that foreign governments do not have access to their technology or control over their strategy.

Companies with a variety of overseas linkages, of which a significant number are wholly owned subsidiaries, are often referred to as **multinational corporations (MNCs)** or multinational enterprises (MNEs). MNCs are large and have a substantial proportion of their workforce outside the home country. There is no magic number of linkages that define an MNC, but it is generally agreed that if a company has more than six foreign operations, it can be considered a multinational. MNCs usually hire local personnel to be managers, to work in factories, and to run operations. Although many strategic decisions for the organization are made in the home country, the number of host-country personnel is substantial.

In the past decade, the pattern of international competition has changed somewhat. In some key industries, the environment is now dominated by a small number of worldwide competitors. Multinational corporations that respond to world markets through a unified strategy are referred to as **global enterprises.** Michael Porter from Harvard Business School defines a global industry as one in which "a firm's competitive position in one country is significantly influenced by its position in other countries."[19] Television, copier, semiconductor, automobile, and pharmaceutical manufacturers are a few of the industries that exhibit a global pattern.

Wholly owned subsidiaries, whether of a multidomestic or global firm, must conform to the labor laws, wage laws, and hiring practices of their host countries. They also have to pay taxes and, in general, act very much like local companies. Such organizations have involved and difficult management tasks.

Countertrade

Countertrade involves simultaneous importing and exporting, or the exchange of goods for goods. An economist at the U.S. Department of Commerce estimated that by the year 2000 countertrade would account for one third of all world trade. Other estimates reach as high as one half.[20]

Barter, the exchange of goods for goods, is the simplest form of what has turned into an elaborate, complex set of linkages. Countertrade might occur when one country does not have easy access to foreign currency yet needs to engage in international trade. Developing countries that face foreign exchange difficulties when they try to sell their goods in developed-country markets, or that find that developed-country markets are protected, also may turn to countertrade. These arrangements can be extremely complex and very often include investment, technology transfer, and compensation trade. Briefly, countertrade can occur in situations in which foreign suppliers are required to market developing-country goods abroad (*counterpurchase*) or are required to receive goods as payment (*buy-back*). For instance, French companies have helped construct a steelworks in Nigeria in return for oil, and Caterpillar Inc. has taken iron ore from a Central American country in return for machinery.[21]

Critical International Organizational Functions

Although international managers must consider a wide range of forces in carrying out all organizational functions, three that are particularly influenced by the world arena are human resource, marketing, and finance management.

International Human Resource Management

Of all the functional areas, human resources is the most affected by the cultures of the host countries in which an organization operates. In many ways, the organization's success rests on how effectively it selects and manages its personnel. Although managers must deal with many human resource components—compensation, benefits, labor relations, and management technique—this section deals specifically with the critical issue of international staffing.

One of the most fundamental decisions an international organization must make is whether to staff foreign facilities with managers from the home country, the host country, or both. Staffing with home-country personnel, called **ethnocentric staffing,** offers headquarters tight control. Japanese organizations, for example, often use Japanese managers wherever subsidiaries are located. One rationale for this is that Japanese is a very difficult language that few outsiders speak, and communication with headquarters would be impeded by having a local manager at the top of the subsidiary. Another reason for ethnocentric staffing in Japanese subsidiaries is that Japanese managers need to have overseas experience for upward career moves within their parent organization. Very recently, Japanese organizations have been increasing their use of highly enculturated local managers, but only because of host-country insistence.

Host-country staffing, or **geocentric staffing,** is increasingly common. Host countries, particularly developing countries, prefer that managers be locals, and there are compelling reasons for organizations to adopt this policy. Host-country managers are not as expensive to maintain as home-country executives; there is no long-term training or extra payments for housing, schooling, and moving. Salaries for local managers are based on host-country scales, which may be considerably lower than in the home country. Local managers speak the language and are more aware of the political and economic situation in their own country.

Polycentric staffing puts the best managers in jobs regardless of their nationality. This concept often makes very good sense; a global organization should pursue a global human resource management policy. If a Japanese manager of a U.S. subsidiary in Japan has the finance skills that are needed in Taiwan, it should make sense to send him or her there. If the skills of an Italian marketing manager of a French organization are needed in Hong Kong, why not arrange a transfer? Merely because a manager possesses excellent functional skills, however, does not necessarily ensure that he or she will be effective. An organization that wants to build an international management force must embark on a broad (and expensive) training program. Salaries have to be adjusted for living conditions, taxation, and currency fluctuations. Organizations must commit to upward mobility so that regular transfers of these managers are rewarded. Finally, host-country governments have to be persuaded to accept the fact that an organization will not hire host-country personnel unless they fit the needs of the company as a whole.

International Marketing Management

International marketing managers carry out activities that may be as basic as exporting to one customer or as complex as selling a number of products in many countries. They make decisions about product, promotion, price, and distribution. When the marketing mix has international dimensions, managers may have to tailor it to the varied needs of foreign customers.

Product. Good marketing managers know it is dangerous to assume that simply because a product sells well in the home country it will sell well abroad. Marketing managers must use data collected by researchers to assess the product's suitability for the chosen market. Although some products are considered standard across cultures—a bottle of Coke in Denver should be basically the same as a bottle of Coke in Beijing—international marketing managers should ask three fundamental questions before introducing a product abroad: (1) Should the organization sell the same product abroad that it sells in the home market? (2) Should the organization change or adapt the

Marketing managers must analyze research data to assess the suitability of a product in a foreign market. Even when a product is standardized and does not change when introduced abroad, foreign consumers may have expectations that will affect sales.

product it sells at home to meet the specific needs of people in different cultures? (3) Should the organization develop a completely new product?

Usually, marketing managers in multinational corporations adapt products when they go abroad. Sometimes they make simple changes, such as putting less salt in a canned soup or rewiring an electrical appliance. Other times, no matter what they do, their products do not sell in a foreign environment. Microwavable packaged dinners, for example, may not find a ready market in cultures that prepare food by stirring over high heat (as in the Orient) or in cultures that value cooking "from scratch." Market research, done effectively, helps uncover adaptation needs and product requirements.

Promotion. The promotion component of the marketing mix requires managers to determine the blend of advertising, personal selling, and sales promotion in national markets; to determine the extent of worldwide standardization; to develop the most effective message(s); to select effective media; and to establish the controls necessary to achieve worldwide marketing objectives.[22] Sometimes managers do not achieve a successful mix, as when General Motors' Belgian marketing slogan "Body by Fisher" was interpreted by Flemish customers as "Corpse by Fisher."[23] Other campaigns go more successfully, as long as managers heed the information discovered through market research. The candid advertisements for women's sanitary products that are now quite acceptable in the United States would be insulting and illegal in the Middle East.

Managers must also remember that media vary widely across cultures. While most people in developing countries listen to radios, they may not be able to read. Even if they can read, they may not have access to magazines or newspapers. In West Africa, for instance, buses are traveling billboards and are a very effective means of getting messages to the public—a fact that is not likely to be obvious to a foreign organization.

Pricing. Although perhaps the most baffling component, pricing is a critical part of the marketing mix. International managers must consider the prices permitted by the market, by competition, and by government regulation. They must deal with tariffs that differ from country to country, which change the price of their product. For example, a $15,000 car made in the United States and exported to South Korea may cost over $40,000 after Korea imposes duties, taxes, and fees.

Sometimes managers have control over the price of a good in a foreign market; at other times that price is largely dictated by the host government. Some governments do not allow companies to discount or to raise prices. Until recently, the Japanese tobacco monopoly added charges to American cigarettes to make them prohibitively expensive to all but the most determined consumers. Although the Japanese agreed to pricing changes, they used a multilevel intermediary structure that continued a slow, inefficient distribution of American cigarettes.

Pricing decisions involve an extremely complex combination of factors, including multiple competitors, multiple costs, and widely varying government regulations. International managers must take all of these factors into account when determining policy, yet remain flexible enough to allow for price movements.

Physical Distribution. Every product, regardless of where it is marketed, must go through a physical distribution system. This system includes the physical handling of goods; the passage of ownership; and the buying and selling negotiations among producers, intermediaries, and consumers. International managers must understand the channels available in each market. The key elements include: "(1) the availability of middlemen, (2) the ability and effectiveness of the alternatives in performing the functions, (3) the cost of their services, and (4) the extent of control that the company can exert over the middlemen's activities."[24]

Some American organizations have had frustrating experiences, such as those often encountered with the complex Japanese system, but others have managed to forge arrangements that are quite satisfactory. Levi Strauss has set up its own independent system. Goods the company imports into Japan are sent to its own distribution center; salespeople contact retailers directly and arrange for products to be delivered by trucks. Department stores in Japan, unlike their U.S. and European counterparts, often carry designer items in an exclusive relationship. If a designer makes an arrangement with one store, none of the others carries the same line.[25]

International Finance Management

Several major issues distinguish the tasks of international finance managers from those of finance managers who work solely in the domestic environment. Chief among these are coping with the risks involved in managing foreign exchange rates in foreign markets and import/export financing.

When currency values fluctuate, companies' competitive positions change at home and abroad. A finance manager's task is to reduce or eliminate foreign exchange risk.

Foreign Exchange Risk Management. Consider what happens when companies are involved in the exchange of foreign currencies. Goods exported from the home country are priced in home currency. For example, a John Deere tractor is priced in dollars. If the tractor is sold in France, its price is converted to francs. The standard rate at which one currency is converted to another, called *the exchange rate,* is listed daily in *The Wall Street Journal* and in other major newspapers.

Say that a John Deere tractor costs $50,000 when priced in the United States. In 1982, 1 U.S. dollar could be exchanged for about 10 francs, so the tractor cost its French owner 500,000 francs. In 1989, the exchange rate of 6 francs to a dollar meant that a French customer had to pay only 300,000 francs for a similarly valued tractor. For international finance managers, anticipating and responding to changes in exchange rates is one of the most exciting and challenging parts of their job. When currency values fluctuate, as they have done dramatically since the early 1980s, companies find that their competitive positions change both at home and abroad. One task of finance managers is to use techniques that reduce or eliminate foreign exchange risk. The measure of the foreign exchange risk is called *exposure.*

Most organizations manage economic exposure by diversifying their operations into different countries and by financing internationally. It makes sense, therefore, for an organization to be prepared to shift sources of production or financing into countries where currency is undervalued. With the low dollar, organizations doing business abroad might reasonably be expected to consider shifting some of their production to the United States if other variables, such as cost and prices, warrant it. France's Airbus Industrie, the Netherlands Fokker, and the United States Lockheed Corporation have discussed making commercial aircraft in the United States to cut the high costs of manufacturing in Europe. West Germany's Siemens has already shifted production and currently exports hundreds of millions of dollars of U.S.-made goods.[26]

Import and Export Financing. Importers and exporters have a wide range of financial services available to them; it is important for international finance managers to understand what these services are and how they work. Commercial banks with international facilities handle the collection of payments for goods. When a transaction is completed, the seller is paid for the goods through the bank.

Except in rare instances in which a buyer pays for the goods before they are delivered, the terms of an export transaction often are negotiated between the buyer and seller using an instrument called a **letter of credit (LC).** Say that U.S. buyer Nancy Flannery agrees to buy goods from Taiwanese shirt manufacturer Ito Kuzu. Under the terms of their sales contract, Ito is to be paid through a letter of credit. Nancy arranges with her own bank to open a letter of credit, which is usually irrevocable if the terms of the letter are met. The LC establishes an account in favor of Ito. For example, if Nancy agrees in the sales contract to pay Ito $4000 for the shirts, she sets up an LC for that amount by having her bank fill out a standard letter of credit form that guarantees payment for the goods. Nancy's bank sends this letter to Ito's bank, where it is held until the terms of the contract are met.

It is possible for Ito to borrow against the LC to finance the purchase of materials and the payment of workers. In essence, the LC becomes the collateral against which his loan is made. Nancy is usually not required to pay for the goods until she has received the shipping documents from Ito. Ito, on the other hand, must prepare shipment of the goods within the stipulated delivery schedule. Once shipment is completed, he presents all the documentation to his bank for payment under the terms of the letter of credit. In due course, his bank will send the documentation to Nancy's bank, where the money has been deposited, and the bill will be settled. Nancy will use the shipping documents to take possession of the shipment in the United States.

In addition to the LC, other necessary documentation includes commercial invoices, bills of lading, and insurance certificates. The commercial invoices must be signed by the exporter and must describe the goods exactly as they are described in the LC. A bill of lading serves as a document of title to the goods at the place of destination, and it shows that shipment has taken place as stipulated in the LC. An insurance certificate, which is usually called for in an LC, must be issued by an insurance company or its agents, and the sum for which the cargo is insured must be the same as in the LC.[27]

The tasks involved in international finance management are concerned with making profits for an organization, just as they are for a purely domestic organization. International operations complicate the task and add such dimensions as developing an adequate financial information system and juggling multiple currencies. Perhaps the most important task for international finance managers is to reduce the risks of exposure.

International Management in Review

In the international arena, managers must effectively carry out the planning, organizing, directing, and controlling functions in one or more foreign countries. Whether located in a domestic or foreign environment, international managers must deal with forces that influence business operations in foreign countries. These forces are created by sociocultural, legal/political, economic, and technological factors.

No U.S. company can ignore the opportunities and risks involved in international business. Managers have become increasingly aware of the impact of foreign competition at home; many American companies are now partially or wholly owned by foreign investors. In addition, many American managers now realize that there are major opportunities in foreign markets and that it may be more cost effective to use foreign human and production resources than to maintain strictly domestic operations.

Organizations can enter international trade simply through exporting or importing goods and services. Managers can also form joint ventures in which they trade technological and marketing expertise with foreign companies. They may also participate in licensing agreements, in which they give a foreign operation the rights to use a process or product for a limited period of time. A foreign franchisee operates a business that is directed and controlled by the parent franchisor.

Large companies frequently have foreign subsidiaries, many of which are wholly owned. A wholly owned subsidiary may be completely staffed and operated under host-country policies, but 100 percent of its stock is owned by the domestic parent company. Multinational companies and global enterprises encompass many wholly owned subsidiaries.

Both small and large companies may participate in international countertrade. Countertrade involves importing and exporting goods in exchange for one another; it can involve pure barter or complex systems of product and monetary exchange.

Three areas that have special complexities for international managers are human resource, marketing, and finance management. International staffing can be conducted by placing home-country managers in foreign locations (ethnocentric staffing), by using host-country managers in host-country operations (geocentric staffing), by placing managers from various countries in operations where their functional expertise is deemed most useful (polycentric staffing), or by combining these approaches. International marketing management involves making decisions concerning products, pricing, promotion, and physical distribution based on forces operating in foreign environments. International finance management is heavily influenced by fluctuating currencies and monetary conversions.

Issues for Review and Discussion

1. Why would a manager become involved in international business?
2. Explain why the issue of culture is important to international managers.
3. How might an organization use a joint venture for its linkage? What are some of the benefits and drawbacks?

4. What is a licensing agreement, and what use does it make of managerial expertise?
5. What is countertrade, and why do organizations use it?
6. List three major staffing policies available to international human resource managers.
7. Explain how a letter of credit works.

Key Terms

international management
culture
exporting
importing
joint venture
licensing agreement
franchise
subsidiary

wholly owned subsidiary
multinational corporations (MNCs)
global enterprises
countertrade
ethnocentric staffing
geocentric staffing
polycentric staffing
letter of credit (LC)

Suggested Readings

Cole, R. E. (1980). Learning from the Japanese: Prospects and pitfalls. *Management Review*, 69(9), 22-28.

Hayashi, K. (1978). Corporate planning practice in Japanese multinationals. *Academy of Management Journal*, 21, 221-26.

Marsland, S., and Beer, H. (Winter 1980). The evolution of Japanese management: Lessons for U.S. managers. *Organizational Dynamics*, 49-67.

Schein, E. H. (Fall 1981). SMR Forum: Does Japanese management style have a message for American managers? *Sloan Management Review*, 55-68.

Schonberger, R. J. (1982). The transfer of Japanese manufacturing management approaches to U.S. industry. *Academy of Management Review*, 7, 479-87.

Thurow, L. (1987). *The management challenge: Japanese views.* Cambridge, MA: M.I.T. Press.

Walton, M. (1986). *The Deming management method.* New York: Dodd, Mead.

Wheelwright, S. C. (July/August 1981). Japan—where operations really are strategic. *Harvard Business Review*, 67-74.

Zussman, Y. M. (Winter 1983). Learning from the Japanese: Management in a resource-scarce world. *Organizational Dynamics*, 68-80.

Notes

1. The two worlds of Jimmy Goldsmith (1 December 1986), *Business Week*, 42.
2. Europe goes on a shopping spree in the States (27 October 1986), *Business Week*, 54.
3. Hands across Europe: Deals that could redraw the map (18 May 1987), *Business Week*, 64-65.
4. N. J. Adler (1986), *International dimensions of organizational behavior*, Boston: Kent; International Monetary Fund and ACLI International, Inc., *The Wall Street Journal* (28 May 1981), 50.
5. B. Toyne and P. G. P. Walters (1989), *Global marketing management: A strategic perspective*, Boston: Allyn and Bacon, 31.

6. E. B. Tylor (1978), Primitive culture, in V. Terpstra, ed., *The cultural environment of international business,* Cincinnati, OH: South-Western.

7. G. Hofstede (Summer 1980), Motivation, leadership, and organization: Do American theories apply abroad? *Organizational Dynamics,* 9, 46-49.

8. Small firm outmaneuvers big-time rivals in winning copier sales from the Chinese (26 April 1982), *The Wall Street Journal.*

9. R. Vernon (1971), *Sovereignty at bay,* New York: Basic Books, 11.

10. *American excellence in a world economy: A summary of the report* (15 June 1987), Washington, DC: The Business Roundtable, 7.

11. U.S., China form joint venture to manufacture helicopters (10 December 1988), *Journal of Commerce,* 58; Joint ventures held key to succeeding in China (24 November 1987), *Journal of Commerce,* 5A.

12. West coast steel users in a bind (1 May 1987), *Journal of Commerce.*

13. Orienting the Latin connection (February 1988), *South,* 21.

14. K. R. Harrigan (July 1987), Why joint ventures fail, *Euro-Asia Business Review,* 6(3), 20-26.

15. F. R. Root (1982), *Foreign markets entry strategies,* New York: AMACOM, 97-100.

16. Patents battle (February 1986), *South,* 48.

17. Root, 122-23.

18. McDonald's combines a dead man's advice with lively strategy (18 December 1987), *The Wall Street Journal,* 1.

19. M. E. Porter (Winter 1986), Changing patterns of international competition, *California Management Review,* 28(2), 11.

20. Are companies ready for countertrade? (Summer 1986), *International Marketing Review,* 28.

21. Managing countertrade (October 1987), *Euro-Asia Business Review,* 6(4), 45.

22. P. R. Caetora and J. M. Hess (1979), *International marketing,* 4th ed., Homewood, IL: Irwin, 417.

23. D. A. Ricks (1983), *Big business blunders,* Homewood, IL: Dow Jones-Irwin, 82.

24. Caetora and Hess, 477-78.

25. Keys to success in the Japanese market (1980), *JETRO,* 9-10.

26. U.S. exporters that aren't American (29 February 1988), *Business Week,* 7.

27. G. Tianwah (1984), *Guide to letters of credit,* Singapore: Rank Books, 10-69.

Bridgestone

S. B. Prasad, Central Michigan University

Bridgestone is named after its founder, Ishibashi, whose name means "stone bridge." Shojiro Ishibashi founded Bridgestone in 1951 in Kurume, Japan, to produce tires using domestic capital and technology. In the years since, two principles have consistently guided the conduct of Bridgestone's business in both tires and chemical and industrial products. The first is an unswerving commitment to "enhancing the quality of life," a commitment served by the second principle: "serving society with products of superior quality." Bridgestone attributes its growth in large part to its emphasis on quality. The company exercises strict control over every aspect of tire production, from the manufacture of cords to the finishing process.

In 1978, Bridgestone reached a landmark: total production topped 500 million tires, a first for Japanese tire makers. Today Bridgestone operates twelve factories in Japan. It is also the only Japanese tire maker to manufacture tires abroad and has four overseas plants. Bridgestone leads the Japanese rubber industry in sales and has climbed to sixth place among rubber-product manufacturers around the world.

In 1979, the Japanese economy faced rising costs of raw materials because of sharply higher crude oil prices and the lower value of the yen on foreign exchange markets. Even so, strong personal consumption and public-sector investment combined to boost the gross national product. In this climate, Bridgestone intensified its sales efforts in order to uplift overall corporate performance. The company also pursued ongoing programs to develop innovative new products, raise productivity, and contain costs.

The results were excellent. Total consolidated sales rose to 579.7 billion yen (in U.S. currency, $2,645.1 million), up 16 percent over 1978. Before-tax income amounted to 69.9 billion yen (U.S. $318.9 million), 68 percent over 1978, and net earnings reached 29.1 billion yen (U.S. $132.8 million), a 72 percent advance. These unprecedented returns far exceeded the targets for the year.

Tire sales grew especially because of higher demand both in Japan and overseas. Steel-belted radial tires for automobiles sold well because of the economic recovery and brisk automobile production. The company stepped up marketing activities and introduced new products, such as the Super Filler radial tire (RD-207 STEEL), to achieve solid gains both in the original-equipment and replacement-tire markets. Sales of truck tires also advanced. Exports were up significantly as the company focused on sales of steel radials and large tires for mining and construction vehicles, particularly to North America, the Middle East, and Europe. The drop in the value of the yen had a positive effect on exports.

The company invested 40.2 billion yen (U.S. $167.7 million) in plant and equipment in 1979. Priority went to increasing capacity for producing steel-belted radial tires. Recreational and welfare facilities were also expanded, and a data-management system for domestic sales was enlarged.

The company actively cultivated overseas markets. It marketed the Super Filler radial in West Germany and Australia. Eastern Airlines and Frontier Airlines in the United States adopted Bridgestone aircraft tires. Exports accounted for more than 23 percent of total sales, with the Overseas Division reporting its highest sales on record. Vigorous overseas demand and the decline of the yen by nearly 10 percent were contributing factors. Among overseas factories, Thai Bridgestone Co., Ltd., hailed the tenth anniversary of its founding by expanding its production facilities.

On January 5, 1980, Chairman Kanchiro Ishibashi met with foreign dignitaries who were visiting the Bridgestone Museum of Art adjacent to the headquarters of Bridgestone Corporation. As the guests were led to the reception area, President Shigemichi Shibamoto also joined them, and as they strolled, Shibamoto mentioned to Chairman Ishibashi that he would ask Mr. K. Hattori, the executive vice-president of Bridgestone, to report on whether Bridgestone should consider the issue of direct investment in the United States. "My feeling," he said, "is that we can't wait too long." Chairman Ishibashi nodded in agreement.

Mr. Hattori called for a preliminary meeting of the senior managing directors to consider the possibility of more active and direct participation in the United States passenger-car and truck-tire markets. American business journalists had long speculated that, with mounting concern over car and truck imports from Japan, Japanese car manufacturers, such as Toyota, Honda, and Nissan, had to consider direct investment in the United States.

At the meeting, among various other important matters, Mr. Hattori suggested to K. Ishikure, senior managing director (international operations), that he develop a preliminary strategic analysis of manufacturing in the United States. He was to look at the competitive, regulatory, and production environments and at the labor situation. Mr. Hattori had seen the December 1, 1980, issue of *Business Week*, which reported that Michelin, the giant French tire company, had developed critical problems in its United States operations. Mr. Ishikure responded that he would immediately ask one of the planning assistants, a recent M.B.A. graduate from Purdue University, to prepare such a report.

Questions

1. What are the motives for Bridgestone's investments in manufacturing abroad? in industrial countries such as the United States? in developing countries such as Thailand?

2. By the late 1980s, the value of the yen had risen dramatically against the dollar. How would such decisions as Bridgestone's investment in U.S. manufacturing facilities be influenced by such changes in the currency rates?

3. What kind of difference between the U.S. and Japanese business environments do you think would be considered in Mr. Ishikure's report?

4. Do you think it is a good idea for the United States to allow foreign corporations to build and own factories in the United States?

20 Management Information Systems (MIS)

Student Learning Objectives

After reading this chapter, you should be able to:

1. Explain what a management information system (MIS) is and discuss its purpose.

2. Describe the three stages of Herbert Simon's decision-making model and explain how managers can use an MIS at each stage.

3. Understand the difference between routine and nonroutine decisions and how an MIS is applicable for each.

4. Define artificial intelligence and its potential effect on management information systems.

5. Describe knowledge/expert systems and their benefits.

6. Relate the ways in which managers at each hierarchical level can use an MIS.

7. Distinguish between the types of organizational information systems.

By Thomas Duff, University of Minnesota-Duluth

*N*ear the end of the eighteenth century, Benjamin Franklin said that the only two certainties in life are "death and taxes." During the 1990s, almost all Americans would add "change" to Franklin's list. As the twentieth century gives way to the twenty-first, the certainty and rapidity of change will probably have a greater impact on managers and management practices than on society in general. According to futurist Marvin Cetron:

> This will put a premium on management's ability to make speedy decisions. At the same time, the stakes riding on those decisions will climb because more activities will become increasingly capital intensive. Running tomorrow's companies won't be a task for the timid.[1]

Ironically, one of the factors perpetrating the rapidity of change in general—technology—will be the instrument that contributes most to managers' ability to make speedy decisions based on timely, accurate information. The technological tool becoming most common today is the computer.

Where computers are present, most of the information about an organization's activities is provided by computer-based information systems. For example, grocery stores rely on computers to furnish information about inventory levels, stock ordering, advertising expenses and results, unit and dollar sales volume, employee work schedules, payroll, and other planning and controlling functions. As computers become more intricately involved in the processing, storing, and distributing of information, managers must develop more formal management information systems to organize and manage these data.

The decreasing cost and overall improvements in computer technology have made it a part of most organizations.

What Is a Management Information System?

There may be as many different definitions or descriptions of an MIS as there are textbooks written on the topic. Stated most simply, a **management information system (MIS)** provides managers with information that enables them to make better decisions and to improve their job performance.

The MIS concept has appealed to managers for a long time. Managers have always sought as much information as possible to help them make decisions while carrying out planning, organizing, directing, and controlling activities at various levels in their organization. Before the advent of such office machines as typewriters, electronic calculators, and copiers, managers used a variety of manual tools and methods to create and distribute information. Although office machines changed the type of information provided to managers and the way it was provided, the pervasiveness of computer and telecommunications technologies in modern organizations has changed information systems even more dramatically. The next sections explore the *information* and *system* components of an MIS.

Information

As it is used in this chapter, the term **information** can be defined as meaningful data. **Data** are representations of basic facts pertaining to people, things, ideas, and events. The facts are represented by symbols, such as numerals or letters of the alphabet. Data can be groups of symbols combined in various ways. The words you are reading now consist of data—alphabetic symbols combined to represent facts.

Organizations collect and process large amounts of data as they make and receive payments.

For data to yield information, they must be processed and presented in a way that users find meaningful. The foundation of any information system is data processing. It is hoped, for example, that the combinations of data you are reading have been processed and are being presented in a way that makes them meaningful to you. As you read the words, you are taking in data, processing them, and trying to derive meaning from them. The mental data-processing techniques you use are much more complicated than those used by even the most sophisticated computers now available. The goal of your processing activities and that of a computer are the same, however; both attempt to make data meaningful or to create new information from them.

Like alphabetic characters, numerals are data until they are processed or combined so they become meaningful. When a person buys something with a charge card at a department store, several data items represented by numerals are collected. The credit card or account number, an identification number for the purchased article, the article's price, the amount of tax, and the total amount of the charge are recorded. Individually, each of these is a meaningless data item. It is only when they are combined in a particular manner and recorded together that they become information about a business transaction.[2]

Even small organizations collect and process large amounts of data as they complete their production and marketing activities, keep track of customer and employee activities, make and receive payments, and carry out other activities. All data related to a certain transaction or individual are combined to create a record; closely related records are combined to form a file. The data in all the records and files are considered to be the base of an organization's data, sometimes called its *database.*

In computer jargon, a **database** is an organization's computer data files, which are structured and stored so they can be easily processed and used by those who need information about the organization. Most routine business data-processing activities are done by computers, which can do them much faster and with greater accuracy than humans can. The power and processing speed of computers have been primarily responsible for the increasing amount of information available to managers in organizations and to society in general. As the amount of information has increased, organizations have found it necessary and beneficial to study different ways of systematically organizing and distributing it. This has resulted in an increased interest in the development of information systems within organizations.

Systems

As you will recall from Chapter 4, a **system** can be defined as a set of interrelated elements that functions as a unit for a specific purpose. These elements are often called *components;* each one affects and is affected by the others. The basic components of an organizational system are people, machines, buildings, and so on. There are usually several subsystems within a system, and managers use a process known as *systems analysis* to study all of the subsystems and components—as well as the nature of their interrelationships—to identify the smallest subsystems needed to accomplish a given task.

A variety of organizational subsystems are interdependent and must be linked through an organization's information network. The college or university you attend is an example of such a system. One of its major purposes is to improve society in general. To achieve this, it probably has established subsystems to facilitate the creation of knowledge through research and the dissemination of that knowledge through teaching. These research and education subsystems also contain a variety of system components—professors, support staff, classrooms, computers, libraries, and printed material—that must be integrated to transform the university's input (students) into output (graduates).

Purpose

The ultimate purpose of an MIS is to improve organizational decision making and behavior. Managers develop and operate an MIS to improve both their performance and that of other organization members by providing the information needed to make decisions. An MIS should provide the type of information upper-level managers need to develop long-range plans and objectives for an organization. It should also provide information to help managers organize, direct, and control their organization's resources so they are used most efficiently and effectively to achieve those objectives.

The most important criterion for judging the success of an MIS is its ability to support the improved performance of the people in the organization in which it operates.[3] It is generally agreed that one of the keys to improving managers' performance is to get the right information to the right person at the right time. One might sum up the purpose of an MIS in precisely that way.

Providing Information to Managers

Managers at all levels are involved to varying degrees in planning, organizing, directing, and controlling activities in an organization. Because the purpose of an MIS is to help managers improve their performance, it should provide the information they need to carry out their managerial activities. That is easier said than done, however. Managers in different areas of an organization may require special information to aid them in making decisions unique to their particular position. For example, a first-line supervisor at a furniture company needs detailed information, such as raw materials requirements, personnel availability, and shipping dates, to direct and control the production of sofas. The president of the company, on the other hand, may be interested in furniture sales trends in general, the availability and price of timber, and the predictions for general economic activity nationwide when making long-range plans for the organization. An information system, therefore, must be designed to fulfill many different managerial needs for information.

What factors determine the kinds of information managers need to make decisions, and how can an MIS be used to provide the appropriate information? The next sections address these issues by relating the MIS concept to the decision-making process and to various managerial activities.

The Decision-Making Process

As you will recall from Chapter 6, the first step in the decision-making process is to recognize the need for a decision. Three types of situations usually trigger the decision-making process: the belief that a problem exists, the emergence of a crisis, or the availability of an opportunity. According to Herbert Simon, once a manager recognizes the need to make a decision, the process continues through three stages: intelligence, design, and choice. An organization's MIS should collect and process data to provide information that will help managers during all three stages so they can solve problems, resolve crises, or take advantage of opportunities.

Intelligence. In Simon's description, the term *intelligence* is used as it is in the military sense. During the intelligence stage, decision makers collect, classify, process, and arrange information from their organization's internal and external environments for use during the next two stages of the process. Managers typically receive most of their information from periodic reports that are routinely produced and distributed by their organization's data-processing, or information-services, unit. The content of the reports, as well as their number and frequency, should be based on an analysis of managers' needs. These reports provide much of the information managers seek during the intelligence stage, such as quantities or dollar value of goods or services produced and sold and the cost of raw materials, human resources, and other things used to produce and sell them.

Periodic reports are usually designed to meet the perceived needs of several managers. In addition, an MIS should provide an opportunity for each manager to access, collect, combine, and manipulate easily as much information as he or she believes is needed to provide the most accurate picture of a problem or opportunity and the internal and external environment in which an upcoming decision will be made.

Most of the information managers seek during the intelligence stage can be gathered and presented by a computer-based system. Managers who are not able to use terminals or microcomputer technology to access the computer-based system directly depend on others to get the information they desire. Managers who are familiar with and able to use the technology of their organization's computer-based system have the advantage of being able to search through its information in whatever way they think will generate the most meaningful results and will best describe the conditions under which they must make decisions.

Design. During the design stage, managers outline alternative sets of action they could take to address the problem or opportunity, given the conditions identified during the intelligence stage. They assess each possible alternative to determine its pros and cons on the basis of established criteria. The data and information collected during the first stage are now used in various ways in an attempt to forecast the outcomes of each alternative.

To assist managers at this stage, an MIS should provide planning and forecasting models that are easy to use and understand. Management-science and information-system professionals have developed programmed models and analytic tools to forecast, predict, and assess outcomes (review the quantitative tools section in Chapter 7). To use these models and tools successfully, managers must know enough about them to be able to select the appropriate one for each situation. They also must have accurate data and information for the variables involved. Managers may enter the data and run the models personally, or they may direct others to provide them with the results.

LOTUS is a popular and powerful design-stage tool. It can be used on microcomputers and is relatively easy to learn and to use.

In addition to allowing managers to search, combine, and manipulate data to meet their unique needs, current database systems let managers develop their own models based on their understanding of current and future conditions. LOTUS 1-2-3 and other electronic spreadsheets are popular design-stage tools because they are powerful planning devices, they can be used on microcomputers, and they are relatively easy to learn and to use. The term *decision-support system (DSS)* is frequently used to describe many of the models and analytic tools managers use in the design and choice stages.[4] This is because they do not replace human decision makers; they aid or support managers at this stage.

Choice. Choosing a set of actions to take is the final stage in Simon's model. No matter how much quantitative and statistical analysis managers perform, decisions often come down to qualitative judgments. This occurs for many reasons. For example, the trade-offs among alternatives are not always easy to measure in monetary terms. Uncertainty surrounds future events, and managers must often subjectively assess the probabilities of future events. Nevertheless, a DSS can provide some simulation tools and other software packages to help managers at this stage by answering "what-if" questions. For example, a model might project what would happen to total revenue, costs, and profits in an organization if there were an increase or a decrease in the inflation rate or in federal income taxes.

As it does during the design stage, an MIS provides managers with support at the choice stage. MIS and computer professionals are currently researching and developing additional support tools, such as artificial intelligence and expert systems, to aid managers in the choice stage. Again, it is important to note that human beings make the final choices; machines and software packages only provide support.

Routine and Nonroutine Decisions

Herbert Simon and others who investigated the decision-making process made another important contribution to MIS development by identifying the differences between routine and nonroutine decisions, respectively referred to in Chapter 6 as *programmed* (structured) and *nonprogrammed* (nonstructured) decisions. As you would expect, decisions do not usually fall clearly into one category. Instead, they can be placed on a continuum ranging from routine to nonroutine, and the role of an MIS changes as the nature of each decision shifts.[5]

Routine Decisions. Routine decisions are decisions made repeatedly because the occasion for the decision occurs frequently. Examples of routine decisions include deciding when to send an overdue notice to a customer, when to reorder an inventory item, what premium to charge an insured party, and when to buy or sell a stock.

Computers can be programmed to make routine decisions. That is, managers can write instructions for making such decisions into a computer system; the computer can compare the conditions for each subsequent case to arrive at a decision. For example, automatic teller machines can "decide" whether to let someone withdraw money by comparing the amount of cash requested with the amount of funds available in the account. In such cases, a computer program substitutes for a human decision maker.

A computer can be programmed to make routine decisions.

Nonroutine Decisions. Nonroutine decisions usually involve the use of intuition, expert judgment, common sense, and trial-and-error. These decisions are unique (novel), as the occasion for making the decision in its present form occurs only once. They are made over and affect longer periods of time than routine decisions. The important factors about the conditions and outcomes related to a problem or an opportunity involved are vague and usually more qualitative than quantitative. The conditions under which nonroutine decisions are made are encountered infrequently, perhaps only once. A procedure used to make such decisions, therefore, may have limited—if any—future applications. Consequently, developing a formal computerized procedure usually will not meet the cost-benefit test applied by most organizations. Thus, the computerized management-science and operations-research models that are appropriate for routine decisions are not very useful in nonroutine situations. Two areas of computer-based support being explored to remedy this problem involve artificial intelligence and knowledge, or expert, systems.

Artificial intelligence (AI) can be defined simply as the ability to program computers for use with tasks requiring the human characteristics of intelligence, imagination, and intuition. AI systems have a knowledge base similar to that of a human being. They also are able to communicate in a natural human language rather than in a machine language, so a user can ask questions with the same English syntax he or she would use with another person. The system tries to understand the question and then presents a response. If the system becomes confused, it asks for more information from the user to clarify the question. Although such products as INTELLECT, CLOUT, and GURU do not enable a computer to substitute for a human being, many MIS professionals believe they are the forerunners of natural languages and artificial intelligence that will continue to become more "human."

Knowledge, or **expert, systems** may be thought of as computer programs that store representations of human knowledge about a specific subject and process it in various ways to draw conclusions. Of all the research and development efforts in AI, this work has produced the greatest return. Knowledge systems currently exist for specific areas of medicine, geology, chemistry, computer configuration, and diesel engine repair. There is an expert system that helps airlines weigh such factors as date and time of departure, prices charged by competing airlines for service on the same route, and number of passengers using the flight in the past. The system suggests how many seats to offer in each price range in order to maximize revenues. Such a system helps managers structure nonroutine situations.

Although the work done to develop AI and expert systems to their present state is admirable, the systems are not widely used for a number of reasons. Many managers believe that they can apply these systems to only a very limited class of decisions. Others assert that the systems are time consuming and expensive to develop and maintain and that they are not well suited to managerial decision making. Even the harshest critics of AI and expert systems, however, point out that research in these areas is useful because of the help it may give managers in the future.

Managers who are higher up in an organization's hierarchy are generally involved in making more nonroutine or unstructured decisions than are those in the lower levels. Usually, the more unstructured the decision, the less managers are able to find relevant or directly related information from an MIS to support their decisions. Periodic reports and other routine information generated by data-processing systems provide only a small portion of the information managers need to make nonroutine decisions.

Decisions at Different Organizational Levels

As you know, research and investigation have indicated that there is a difference in the types of decisions made by managers at different levels in an organization. Robert Anthony's work in the area is representative. He classifies managerial activity and decision making into three categories—strategic planning, management control, and operational control—and relates each to a hierarchical level in an organization. In addition, he believes the decisions made by those at various levels are sufficiently different to require different types of information.[6]

Senior Managers (Strategic Planning).   The strategic planning process usually involves a small number of people in the highest levels of an organization. The complexity of the situations with which these managers deal and the nonroutine, creative way in which they handle them make it difficult to specify the type of information they need. As a consequence, designing an effective MIS is difficult.

Because strategic planning deals with broad policies and goals, senior managers have a crucial need for information that addresses their organization's relationship to its environment. Strategic planners usually need summarized, aggregated information, much of it obtained from external sources. The scope and variety of the information are large, but the requirements for accuracy are not particularly stringent. The decisions made at this level are nonroutine and nonrepetitive.[7]

To meet the needs of senior managers, an MIS must gather, process, and provide information about conditions outside an organization. Further, the MIS must be structured so that senior managers are comfortable using the system to obtain data or information to meet their unique needs while making nonroutine decisions. Because senior managers are relatively highly paid and make decisions that have a major impact on their organization, MIS professionals must work with them to ensure that they are using the system efficiently and effectively.

Middle Managers (Management Control).   Decision makers in this category generally require summarized information that compares present and past performance. Although they need mostly internal information, they also require some external information. The decisions made at this level are somewhere between routine and nonroutine and are often referred to as *semistructured*. Only part of the decision-making process is structured. Much of the information needed at this level is obtained through interpersonal interaction.[8]

To serve the needs of middle managers, an MIS should provide several types of periodic internal reports, exception reports, and perhaps some forecast and historical information. In addition, it should be structured so that middle managers, like senior managers, can easily use the system to obtain information they might need for their unique organizing, directing, and controlling activities. For example, middle managers may need information to help them develop personnel policies, build and monitor budgets, and determine an appropriate marketing mix.

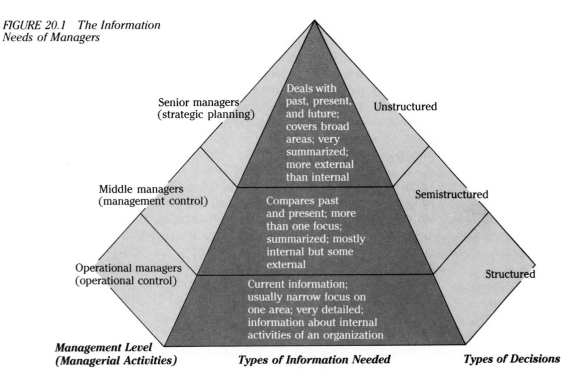

FIGURE 20.1   The Information
Needs of Managers

Senior managers
(strategic planning)

Deals with past, present, and future; covers broad areas; very summarized; more external than internal

Unstructured

Middle managers
(management control)

Compares past and present; more than one focus; summarized; mostly internal but some external

Semistructured

Operational managers
(operational control)

Current information; usually narrow focus on one area; very detailed; information about internal activities of an organization

Structured

**Management Level
(Managerial Activities)**   **Types of Information Needed**   **Types of Decisions**

Operating Managers (Operational Control).   According to Anthony, operational control is "the process of assuring that specific tasks are carried out effectively and efficiently."[9] Operational control is primarily concerned with tasks rather than with people and deals with very short-term activities.

In this area, managers need well-defined, detailed, accurate information that is usually narrow in scope. They use this information frequently, so it is often available and reported routinely through their organization's data-processing system. Many of the decisions at this level are routine and lend themselves to structured approaches.[10]

To meet the needs of operating managers, an MIS provides a variety of information designed to help them direct and control the resources and activities for which they are responsible. Most of the information needed at this level is provided by regular internal reports, detailed transaction reports, procedures manuals, and the like. Operating managers need this type of information to plan and implement production, to exercise inventory control, and to manage credit and other types of activities at lower levels of their organization.

Figure 20.1 shows the information needs of managers by level and general type of decision. It summarizes the major points made in this section related to getting the right information to the right person.

The Types of Organizational Information Systems

As described in this chapter, an MIS is the broadest, most comprehensive information system in an organization; thus, an MIS includes both computer-based information and information collected or provided to managers in other ways. The emphasis in this chapter—and in most current information-system discussions—is on how managers get and use computer-based information. In fact, most discussions about an organization's MIS are related only to the formal, structured MIS. Although this is typical, remember that managers receive information from both the formal MIS and the informal networks within and outside the organization. Managers use both informal and computer-based information while making decisions.

Informal Information

Decision makers at all levels are influenced by the information they pick up consciously or by happenstance through informal conversation. It is difficult to pin down how big a factor such information plays in managerial decision making. It has little, if any, influence on the routine decisions made at the operational level; however, it may be given some consideration in various management control situations and has its greatest influence in nonroutine decisions made at the strategic-planning level.

Some believe informal information is the most important factor in decision making. Henry Mintzberg, a supporter of this belief, has studied the content of managers' information and what they do with it. He says:

Large mainframe and supercomputers, such as the CRAY-2, process data and create information for large organizations.

> The evidence here is that a great deal of the manager's inputs are soft and speculative—impressions and feelings about other people, hearsay, gossip, and so on. Furthermore, the very analytical inputs—reports, documents, and hard data in general—seem to be of relatively little importance to many managers.[11]

J. F. Rockart agrees that a great deal of information must be dynamically gathered as new situations arise for top executives and that much of it is not computer based but is communicated informally. There is, however, some information that should be supplied regularly to chief executives through a computer-based information system.[12]

Computer-Based Information

In organizations, quantitative data related to the production and sale of goods or services are recorded, processed, stored, and distributed by a computer. Large mainframe and supercomputers process data and create information for such large organizations as the U.S. Department of Defense, the Social Security Administration, General Motors, and Exxon. Microcomputers are now being used to do the same thing—but on a smaller scale—for farms, bakeries, churches, PTAs, and the like. Computers provide a fast, accurate way of handling and processing the data in organizations.

Just as a computer-based information system is one subsystem of an overall MIS, subsystems make up a computer-based system. There can be a number of different subsystems, and different terms may be used for them, depending on how one chooses to analyze an organization. Three common subsystems of an organization's computer-based information system are a transaction-processing system, an information-reporting system, and a decision-support system.

Transaction-Processing System. In business and accounting vocabulary, a *transaction* is an economic event that affects the resources or financial position of a business. Buying something, paying an invoice, selling goods or services, and reducing or adding to inventory are examples of transactions. A **transaction-processing system (TPS)** records, processes, and manages data related to an organization's everyday activities. Management information produced by a TPS usually takes the form of a listing of transactions or business events that have occurred recently or are scheduled to occur. Because it is usually very detailed—current information focusing on one area of an organization's internal activities—the information output from a TPS is most frequently used by managers for making structured decisions at the operating level. A TPS also is important because it contains the database on which the information provided in information-reporting and decision-support systems is based.[13] This information then becomes a database that is available to managers when they move into the intelligence stage of Simon's decision-making model.

Information-Reporting System. Middle and senior managers need more general types of information than are provided by a TPS. An **information-reporting system** retrieves, sorts, pools, and manipulates an organization's transaction data in other helpful ways. The information is summarized, aggregated, and otherwise transformed in such a way that it is quite different from the original transaction data. In fact, additional data or information may be added to the transaction data to create meaningful reports. One of the major advantages of a computer-based information system is that, once it is programmed to prepare an organization's most frequently used reports, it can do so efficiently and repeatedly without additional work. The system is programmed and designed to begin preparing these reports in various ways. It is often this system that organizes the information used during the intelligence stage and delivers it to managers.

An information-reporting system prepares three types of reports of special interest to middle managers. *Periodic reports* (daily, weekly, monthly, and so on) are prepared and distributed after their specific period of time has elapsed. *Exception reports* are distributed when something unexpected (an "exception") occurs. For example, a manager may be reminded that sales are more than 15 percent below target or that labor costs are more than 20 percent above budget. *Demand reports* are distributed to managers who ask for specific information because they wish to analyze a particular issue in more depth. These and other prespecified reports compare summarized information related to past and present activities within an organization. Some of these reports, or specific information from several of them, may be combined to create even more summarized reports. The information they provide is used mostly by middle managers to monitor business activities, to spot problems and opportunities, and to analyze specific issues. The summarized reports are then used by senior managers as part of a decision-support system.[14]

Decision-Support System. A **decision-support system (DSS)** consists of the data, information, and reports of an organization's transaction-processing and information-reporting systems. In addition, it includes a variety of computer software that enables managers to access and use information in the other two systems to produce desired output that is not routinely available. The structure of a DSS is usually flexible because it is intended to be used by managers in whatever way they feel is most helpful in a given situation. The results of analysis, modeling, and forecasting programs offered by a DSS help managers during the design and choice stages of the decision-making process.

As is evident, a DSS is probably of great value to senior managers who make many nonroutine, one-time-only decisions in their role as strategic planners; however, a DSS is also helpful to middle-level operating managers in certain situations. For example, a DSS can help an inventory control manager decide when to order new inventory, how much to order, and when to take delivery. All parts of a DSS must be designed and developed so managers can learn about and use them easily. Otherwise, managers will not use the system to support their decision making.

As you can see, the conventional targets of all three computer-based MIS subsystems have been a manager's planning and controlling activities (Anthony's strategic planning, management control, and operational control activities). While it is generally agreed that an MIS can also aid managers in their organizing and directing activities, less formal work has been done to develop standard applications and tools that managers can use to obtain information from a computer-based system for these purposes.

Managers who invest just a small amount of time in learning to operate a computer-based information system reap the reward of time saved in the long run.

What Managers Need to Know to Use an MIS Effectively

As is true for most management- and decision-support resources in an organization, an MIS is an essential tool for managers to use in order to improve their performance. They will be more inclined to do so if their MIS is user friendly—although people developing the computer-based parts of such systems have complained that the system must be "user seductive" to get some managers involved. Even a user-friendly MIS cannot be effective, however, unless managers are familiar with the process of management and the roles that managers play. They must also be able to understand and apply some of the traditional principles of management, and they must possess some basic technical and decision-making skills.

There are no generally established criteria for what a manager must know about computer-based systems to use them effectively. Knowing about bits and bytes, storage size and processing speed, computer architecture and compatibility, and other technical aspects of the system may be helpful; however, there is no empirical evidence that this is true. At this time, it is still advantageous for managers to be able to use a computer keyboard, although systems that allow managers to touch the screen or use their voices may soon change that. Managers also need to know enough about their system to easily access data, programs, and communication devices. These technical skills are not difficult to master for anyone willing to invest the time to learn them, and they will pay large dividends in time saved in the long run.

Management Information Systems in Review

The quantity, quality, and timeliness of information are of paramount importance to managers. Modern technology provides ever-increasing amounts of information, but it must be managed appropriately to be of maximum use. A management information system (MIS) offers managers information they can use and manipulate to improve the performance of all organization members.

One of the most valuable aspects of an MIS is the support it can offer managers as they make decisions. An MIS can collect the necessary data (during the intelligence stage), provide forecasting models and analytic tools that manipulate the data (during the design stage), and answer "what-if" questions (during the choice stage). Although managers often make the final decisions on a subjective basis, good managers also take advantage of the objective information an MIS can offer.

Sometimes computers are able to substitute for human decision makers. For routine decisions in which issues can be structured and programmed, computers can analyze a current situation according to previous instructions and make decisions. Nonroutine decisions are much more difficult, because they occur infrequently and under unusual circumstances. The creativity needed to make nonroutine decisions is not widely available from computer-based systems, although artificial intelligence and expert systems currently being developed and tested may be able to provide this assistance to managers in the future.

A good MIS must be able to help managers at all levels of an organization. Senior managers must construct strategic plans, and need far-reaching, often abstract information. Middle- and lower-level managers usually need narrower and more concrete information, much of which comes from computer-based sources. Computer-based information is generally obtained from three subsystems: a transaction-processing system (TPS), an information-reporting system, and a decision-support system (DSS). A TPS provides very detailed information about an organization's everyday activities. An information-reporting system provides summarized periodic reports that manipulate the TPS data in ways that middle managers find useful. A DSS enables senior managers to add, alter, or restructure the statistical information obtained by the other two systems in any way that will help them make complex, often creative decisions.

The ultimate goals of both an MIS and the managers who use it are congruent; both are concerned with getting the right information to the right decision makers so that the best possible decisions can be made. Managers who are personally able to use a computer-based system instead of relying on technical staff can access and manipulate information quickly for their unique needs. This does not mandate a high level of computer literacy; the only requirement is to learn the technical skills necessary to use organizational information systems effectively.

Issues for Review and Discussion

1. Explain what a management information system is and discuss its purpose.
2. What role can an MIS play in each stage of the decision-making process?
3. Comment on the observation "MIS should not be a decision-making system, but rather a decision-support system."
4. Identify three organizational information subsystems and explain the purpose of each.
5. How is an MIS beneficial for managers at each level in an organization's hierarchy?
6. Compare and contrast artificial intelligence and expert systems.

Key Terms

management information system (MIS)
information
data
database
system

artificial intelligence (AI)
knowledge (expert) systems
transaction-processing system (TPS)
information-reporting system
decision-support system (DSS)

Suggested Readings

Huseman, R. C., and Miles, E. W. (1988). Organizational communication in the information age: Implications of computer-based systems. *Journal of Management*, 14 (2), 181–204.

Keen, P. (January 1985). A walk through decision support. *Computerworld*.

McGarrah, R. E. (September-October 1984). Ironies of our computer age. *Business Horizons*.

Magee, J. F. (Winter 1985). What information technology has in store for managers. *Sloan Management Review*.

Millar, V. E. (January 1984). Decision-oriented information. *Datamation*.

Porter, M. E., and Millar, V. E. (July-August 1985). How information gives you competitive advantage. *Harvard Business Review*.

Power, D. J. (September 1983). Impact of information management on the organization. *MIS Quarterly*.

Shoor, R. (June 1986). The new breed of executive information user. *Infosystems*.

Wrapp, H. E. (July-August 1984). Good managers don't make policy decisions. *Harvard Business Review*.

Notes

1. M. Cetron (1985), *The future of American business*, New York: McGraw-Hill, xiv–xv.
2. D. R. Adams, G. E. Wagner, and T. J. Boyer (1983), *Computer information systems: An introduction*, Cincinnati: South-Western, 48–50.
3. R. H. Sprague, Jr. (December 1960), A framework for the development of decision support systems, *MIS Quarterly*, 4, 4.
4. Adams, et al., 36–42.
5. B. J. Finch and J. F. Cox (1988), Process-oriented production planning and control: Factors that influence system design, *Academy of Management Journal*, 31 (1), 123–53.
6. R. N. Anthony (1965), *Planning and control systems: A framework for analysis*, Boston: Harvard University Graduate School of Business Administration.
7. A. G. Gorry and S. Morton (1987), A framework for management information systems, in H. J. Watson, A. B. Carroll, and R. J. Mann, eds., *Information systems for management*, Plano, TX: Business Publications.
8. Gorry and Morton, 70.
9. Anthony, 69.
10. Anthony, 70–71.
11. H. Mintzberg (July-August 1976), Planning on the left side and managing on the right, *Harvard Business Review*, 54.
12. J. F. Rockart (March-April 1979), Chief executives define their own data needs, *Harvard Business Review*.
13. T. H. Athey and R. W. Zmud (1986), *Introduction to computers and information systems*, Glenview, IL: Scott, Foresman, 265–67.
14. Athey and Zmud, 267–68.

On Target, Inc.

Richard A. Scudder, University of Denver

On Target, Inc., is a Michigan-based direct marketing company for real estate firms. It has been in existence since the 1950s and has enjoyed reasonable success. On Target made a well-thought-out, well-designed entry into computer-based information systems in 1972. During its early years it was extremely progressive, always successful at implementing the latest technology.

By the late 1970s, On Target was recognized as one of the leaders in the use of computer-based information systems. It was written up in *Business Week,* a major coup in the industry. The leader of the MIS group, as well as many of his executive staff, were often asked to make presentations at conferences explaining how their system worked.

As a result of the success of On Target's information systems, other organizations continually attempted to recruit both its information-systems management and its technical staff. Over a period of years leading up to the mid-1980s, the top talent at On Target was stolen away by other corporations.

Initially, the management at On Target was quite content with its information-systems staff. The staff did a good job of maintaining the systems developed in the late 1970s and early 1980s that created On Target's reputation. They were able to meet the needs of their clients and received few complaints. They were not overly ambitious, nor were they able to make the kind of innovative changes that earlier employees had.

By 1988, however, the world of information systems was quickly leaving On Target behind. The staff was still primarily working to maintain systems that were by now becoming quite ancient. They were losing clients quickly because they were not adapting to massive changes in the financial industry. Other marketing companies, as well as most of the large brokerage shops, had created massive systems focused to give a strategic advantage to their organizations. On Target, on the other hand, had not begun to take advantage of newer, more sophisticated techniques.

On Target's board, recognizing the fact that it did not have much time left to turn the company around, decided on a bold move. In a 1988 general shake-up of top management, a new president, Jim Swanson, was recruited from a top real estate marketing shop in New York. This firm had much the same reputation that On Target possessed during the late 1970s.

Initially, Swanson had trouble convincing management of the need to invest in new, strategic information systems. Many of the firm's executive team felt they were getting along fine, no matter what the board said. Among the most adamant of the old-line managers was the director of information systems, Brad Swanke.

Swanke was a manager who had come up through the ranks. He began as a programmer, progressed to manager, and then to operations manager. When the originator of On Target's MIS system left in the early 1980s, Brad was promoted to assistant director. Later, as director, Brad was insistent that the system in place was more than adequate to meet the current challenges.

Recognizing the need to move swiftly, Swanson completed an evaluation of On Target's information systems—both the system and the people running it. The Information Systems Report highlighted the complete lack of forward momentum. Soon afterwards, Brad Swanke quietly retired.

The Information Systems Report led to a series of in-depth discussions with the key information-systems managers currently at On Target. Swanson found that the managers were not familiar with the new database management technologies or end-user computing. He concluded that if he was going to pull On Target out of its slump, it would require new leadership at all levels of the organization. He began an immediate search for a team of capable, leading-edge information managers. He was able to come up with an MIS executive named James Wilson within about two months.

Wilson immediately went on a national search to hire twelve first-rate MIS specialists. Having successfully recruited these people, he began to spread them among the different information-systems activities within the MIS function. He also began to recruit his immediate staff. He was able to bring in Patricia Mann as a systems development manager and Ed Farley to head up production. Both individuals were young, capable managers who were well versed in both the current technology and MIS management techniques.

Wilson quickly became entangled in a variety of complex corporate issues involving end-user computing, information-systems planning, and steering committees. At the end of a year, much to Wilson's surprise, three of his twelve newly hired MIS specialists left On Target. The grapevine indicated that all the new MIS specialists were dissatisfied with their positions and were looking for other employment.

Alarmed and concerned, Wilson called a meeting of his top advisers. Both Mann and Farley indicated that they were as concerned and confused as Wilson. The new hires had been given high-profile, challenging positions; none had complained openly about the organization. Wilson asked Mann and Farley to call a meeting of the remaining nine specialists.

Unfortunately, the meeting provided little help. The specialists talked in vague terms about job stress and time pressure. It was apparent to the executive team that they were not completely happy but were unwilling to make specific complaints. In desperation, Wilson made luncheon appointments with the three specialists who had left the organization.

Wilson met with the first of the departed employees early the next week. James Lockhart explained his reasons for leaving candidly.

Lockhart: I was brought in as a specialist to help the organization develop a more flexible project management system. We were supposed to create a system that would allow managers to adjust project management techniques to the specifics of the project they were assigned. I thought when I interviewed for the position that I was going to get support to try out my ideas. Both you and Ms. Mann were very encouraging when I discussed the ideas with you originally. Unfortunately, Mr. Baker, my direct supervisor, was not nearly as supportive. Every time I brought a set of ideas to him, he told me to go back to the drawing board. When I wanted to recommend new methods for estimating the time it would take to complete a programming job, he laughed and said that he had been counting lines of code produced per week for years, that it had worked well, and that he didn't think there was any need to change.

Wilson: I don't suppose that sat too well with you.

Lockhart: Not after all the other frustration that I'd been through. I'd tried to get a chance to talk to you or Mann but was told to keep my nose clean and not go over people's heads. Besides that, I wasn't getting any support from my peers in the office. Most of them considered me an interloper and had little to do with me. All-in-all, I decided that it was best to cut my losses and quit. It worked out fairly well for me, actually. I got a $10,000 raise at the place I'm at now.

Wilson: I don't suppose there's any chance of hiring you back, is there?

Lockhart: None.

A couple of days later Wilson met with Joan Becket, another former employee. Like Lockhart, she was very candid in her remarks.

Becket: I was hired to assist in operations. I was sure we would be bringing in new machines and systems soon after I came to work at On Target. We did bring in some new systems after about six months, but it was taking forever to get through the process of putting together specifications for new machines. Most of us knew what systems would do the job we wanted to accomplish, but getting management to support us was like pulling teeth. As you know, it's important in this field to keep up with the changes in technology. When I came to On Target, I was at the leading edge in knowledge about what IBM machines would do. After being buried in that backward, unprogressive shop for fourteen months, I felt I was about to become irretrievably outdated. I had to get out. My career is important to me, and I had to move forward. I couldn't move forward at On Target. You've got to understand, Mr. Wilson. We felt that you and the top management of the MIS department were progressive and understood what needed to be done. Unfortunately, your subordinates don't share that understanding. It's not that they oppose what you plan, it's just that nothing ever happens.

When Wilson met later that week with his team, he reported that the interviews had been very useful. All of them were surprised at first by the comments from Lockhart and Becket, but on reflection, what they said made sense. Young MIS specialists were in great demand from other organizations, and most of them felt that their careers came first. If they couldn't work in a progressive organization, they were likely to move elsewhere.

The executive team was faced with a dilemma. The middle level of management was passively blocking much of what they wanted to do. Swanson was becoming impatient with the pace of forward progress in the organization. He had asked Wilson to make a report with recommendations next week.

Questions

1. What should that report say, and what recommendations should be made? What specific actions can be taken to get middle management to support the strategic thrust of the organization?

2. What actions could On Target have taken to prevent the loss of its MIS specialists during the early part of the 1980s? What could have been done to better integrate the new specialists into the organization when they began rebuilding the organization?

3. Should Swanson recommend the replacement of the middle managers?

4. Why did Wilson neglect this problem until it reached the point at which valuable people were leaving?

21 Operations Management

Student Learning Objectives

After reading this chapter, you should be able to:

1. Describe the transformation process.

2. Show how the design and use of the operations function are central to the attainment of an organization's goals and objectives.

3. Define the interrelationships between operations and other functions in an organization, such as marketing, research and development, finance, and human resource management.

4. Distinguish among the types of production processes.

5. Describe the decisions involved in designing and using an operating system.

6. Discuss the concept of world-class operations.

7. Understand important concepts (such as just-in-time) that are shaping current operating decisions.

By Peter Billington, Northeastern University

E very organization has an operations function that produces a product or delivers a service. **Operations management** is the process of designing, planning, organizing, directing, and controlling this operations function, and the person in charge is the operating manager. The central task of an operating manager is to transform resources into products or services that are useful to customers. The design and use of an operating system must complement an organization's overall objectives, whether this means faster delivery, higher quality, or any other attribute that gives the organization a competitive advantage. This chapter examines the transformation process that is the heart of the operations function, as well as the important operations concepts used by foreign competitors, such as just-in-time and total quality control.

The Transformation Process

An operating system consists of four components: random events, resources, a transformation process that converts the resources into products or services, and a feedback loop (see Figure 21.1). *Random events* are external and internal environmental occurrences that may be out of management's control. *Resources* consist of labor, material, technology, information, and management. The *transformation process* changes these resources into products and services for customers. Some examples of the transformation process include an assembly line, information gathering and transmitting, college lectures and assignments, hamburgers being made at a fast-food restaurant, and patient care and diagnosis at a hospital.

A *feedback loop* is needed to monitor output, which managers measure and compare to a standard. Feedback tells managers if a product or service has not met the standard and resource adjustments are necessary. If, for example, a product does not meet quality-assurance specifications, managers must obtain better raw materials, increase inspection of the raw materials, purchase new machinery, train workers, or make any other changes that will bring the product up to standard. Table 21.1 provides examples of operating system components for four organizations.

FIGURE 21.1   Schematic Diagram of an Operating System

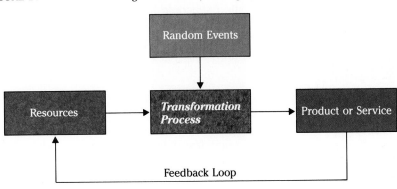

TABLE 21.1 Component Elements of the Operations Function in Several Organizations

| Organization | Inputs | Transformation Processes | Outputs | | Feedback Loops |
			Products	Services	
Fast-food restaurant	Food Labor Grill Building	Cooking Mixing Assembling	Burgers Fries Drinks	Seating areas Drive-up window Speed of delivery	Customer returns Inspections
Hospital	Medicines Physicians/nurses Diagnostic equipment	Surgery Therapy Treatment	Bandages Pacemakers Prostheses	Patient wellness	Customer surveys Patient returns
Automobile manufacturer	Steel Rubber Glass Labor Machines/tools Conveyors	Metal stamping Welding Molding Assembling Painting	Automobiles Service parts Service manuals	Service training Warranty Financing	Warranty charges Inventory levels Quality-control inspections Customer surveys

University	Textbooks
	Faculty
	Students
	Classrooms
	Computers
		Lectures
		Exams
		Assignments
		Writing
			Diplomas
			Books
			Research papers
				Educating
				  students
					Alumni donations
					Job offers to students
					Teacher/course
					  evaluations

Management Decisions

Management of the transformation process entails a wide range of decisions. Managers must make decisions about product design, production processes, equipment, workers' skill and pay levels, the location of the operation, its capacity, and the internal layout of the facility. After design decisions have been made, the system must be used. Utilization decisions fall into three types: planning, managing (organizing and directing), and controlling. Managers must plan how the system will be used, organize and direct its use to produce goods and services, and then control the system using feedback loops.

All of these decisions must be coordinated through an organizational structure that allows an operating system to produce products or services in a way that meets organizational goals. It is important for managers to ensure that all of these activities are coordinated. For example, if the paint buyer of a boat manufacturer does not coordinate the purchase of blue paint with the production schedule for blue boats, there are bound to be serious repercussions: production might come to a halt when the blue paint runs out; fewer blue boats than needed might be produced; or more blue paint might be produced in a hurry, often at a higher cost.

Operations Function Objectives

An organization's product or service must have some features—whether low price, fast delivery, or something else—that set it apart from its competitors. These features can be translated into the objectives of the operations function in four dimensions: (1) the *cost* per unit to produce a product or service (low

TABLE 21.2   Product/Process Objectives

Objectives of the Production Process	Sedan	Race Car
Cost	Low	High
Quality/features	Standard	Customized
Flexibility	Slow (model changes once a year)	Fast (can be redesigned and rebuilt quickly)
Dependability	High volume of same product, fast delivery from dealer's lot	Lowest volume, every car different, longer lead time to custom build

vs. high), (2) the ability to produce a product or service with a certain *quality* or features (high customization vs. a commodity product), (3) the *flexibility* to change the product design and volume (quickly vs. slowly), and (4) the *dependability* to deliver a large volume of the same product (high vs. low reliability).

To succeed in all four of these dimensions at the same time generally is considered impossible. Most operating systems can succeed in two dimensions, which define the systems' distinctive competence. For example, consider the difference between a producer of four-door sedans and a producer of custom-made race cars. The operating system that delivers the sedans can do so at a relatively low cost and with high dependability. The cars are affordable to a large segment of the population and are readily available. The cost of the custom-made race cars, by contrast, is very high, but the manufacturer can produce cars that meet drivers' high-quality specifications and that can be redesigned and rebuilt almost on a whim. Table 21.2 compares the production process dimensions for these two automotive products.

Operations for Strategic Advantage

To succeed, organizations must try to "get an edge" on their competition. An organization gains a **competitive (strategic) advantage** when the characteristics of its product or service induce customers to choose it over the competition. Competitive advantages are not just marketing gimmicks; they provide tangible benefits to customers. For example, a fast-food restaurant's advantage is its convenience, both in its location and in its ability to deliver a low-cost meal quickly. An operating system must be designed and used to provide competitive advantage. A fast-food restaurant's kitchen and serving facilities must deliver low-cost food quickly, or the restaurant will have no competitive advantage.

Managers must link their organization's overall strategy to operations to ensure that the organization's operating system can produce products or services that allow the organization to attain its goals. For example, when conducting an organizational scan during Step Four of the strategic planning process (see Chapter 8), managers should consider what the organization's operating system does well. What type of materials can it work with (metal, plastic, and so on)? How flexible is its equipment? Can it produce custom products or only standard designs? If the overall strategy determines that customer service is important, should the operating system include many small facilities near customers, or can fast delivery from a central location be equally effective? An operating system's design and utilization considerations, such as inventory procedures and production schedules, are important to an organization's overall competitive ability. Managers must analyze the abilities of their organization's existing operating system to see if it can carry out the organization's strategy.

Contemporary Strategy Factors

In the modern global marketplace, organizations must be able to compete with foreign firms in domestic markets and in other countries. Rapid transfers of information and products among countries break down advantages that may have been inherent in domestically based companies. For instance, foreign banks now compete in the U.S. market with U.S.-based banks, and many large U.S.-based banks have branches in other parts of the world.

Because of the globalization of competition, a new set of factors shapes the operating environment. Previously, capacity, location, and other factors were considered critical to successful competition. Although still important, those factors are now not as important as shorter new product lead time, faster inventory turnover (less inventory), shorter delivery lead time, higher quality, increased flexibility, better customer service, decreased waste, and higher return on assets. Companies that are successful in meeting all or some of these objectives have a competitive advantage. Note that these factors are all operationally based. It is no longer adequate to have only the best advertising campaign or the lowest cost to compete successfully. Consumers are now demanding higher quality, better service, and faster delivery.

Service providers must have operating systems and must make decisions regarding product design, capacity, and location.

Contemporary operating managers can no longer meet customers' demands by focusing exclusively on their operating system. Operating managers also should concentrate on the activities conducted in other functional areas. For example, they should have more contact with marketing managers, first to understand what marketing advantages would be useful and then to translate those advantages into improved operating systems. Would shorter delivery times be a competitive advantage and a good marketing tool? If so, how can the operating system be designed and used to accomplish faster delivery?

Operating managers must be prepared to make changes continuously, because product and technological innovations in operating processes are occurring rapidly. It is no longer important to be a good "housekeeper" of a production system, as that process is likely to change. Competition is forcing managers to reduce inventory, increase quality, and speed up delivery lead times.

Service Industries and Manufacturing

Historically, operations management has focused on the manufacturing part of business. Most concepts and techniques in operations management were first developed for manufacturing. This was a natural extension of the fact that, at one time, manufacturing was the largest sector of the U.S. economy. At this time, however, the service sector of the economy is larger. Not only do banks and insurance companies provide services as their primary products, but many manufacturing companies provide much of the service necessary to sell their products.

Service companies have "production" departments with delivery objectives similar to those of manufacturers. A parts supplier must deliver parts when the customer needs them. A hospital has a limited number of patient beds and certain objectives regarding the average length of stay.

Service providers must have operating systems and must make the same types of decisions regarding product design, capacity, location, and so forth that manufacturers make. Even so, service industries have lagged behind their manufacturing counterparts in implementing many operations-management concepts. Hospitals, for example, have been slow to implement inventory control procedures, perhaps because their desire not to run out of medical supplies is at odds with the high costs of maintaining large inventories.

In the 1970s, many jobs in manufacturing industries were lost to foreign competition. The causes of this phenomenon are complex and varied; the simple view is that the quality of foreign-made products improved while the quality of U.S.-made products did not. Service industries should learn from manufacturing industries that foreign competition will probably arise, and that it may represent lower costs and higher quality. The service industries must learn how to design and produce their services for continuing improvement.

Interaction of Operations with Other Functions

The operations function must interact effectively with all other functions in an organization. Competitive advantages an organization wants to achieve are best found through the coordinated efforts of all functional areas. For example, the ability to deliver a product or service more quickly than the competition can provide a tremendous marketing advantage. Marketing managers must, therefore, ask operating managers about potentially fruitful operational improve-

Marketing managers interact with operating managers to create strategies to gain competitive advantage through product delivery, design, and redesign.

ments. In the other direction, if marketing managers plan to promote a product to increase sales, operating managers must be told so they can determine the proper production and inventory levels. Failure to do this could result in customer demand for an unavailable product. Marketing managers must also interact with operating managers about such factors as product delivery, product design, and product redesign.

Research and development functions are active in the design of new products, the redesign of products, and the design of substitutions for raw materials and parts. Product redesign may have a direct impact on the production process in that different types of material require different types of equipment. New products must be considered in light of the strengths and capabilities of the existing production process.

The finance function also interacts significantly with the operations function. The major assets of manufacturing organizations are usually inventory, plant, and equipment. The finance managers in most firms must know the planned levels of inventory to determine inventory financing. Finance managers can assist operating managers in determining the expected benefits of new equipment and the location of new facilities.

The accounting department is responsible for operating a system that collects and analyzes the costs of producing products or services. Operating managers need accurate information about production costs in order to make the proper decisions regarding new product cost estimates, equipment purchasing, and scheduling for improved productivity.

Types of Processes

Recall the example of four-door sedans made on an assembly line and race cars custom-made in a small shop. The production processes used to create these two automobile types have very different functions, produce very different products, and require different sets of management actions. Figure 21.2 shows how different products relate to various process structures. Generally, a facility falls on the diagonal from the upper left to the lower right. This ensures a good match of product and process: the process produces the desired product with high efficiency. It is not unusual to find an organization that is not on the diagonal; this is not necessarily an incorrect position, as long as the organization can exploit its product/process combination to competitive advantage.

In a **job shop,** work centers are arranged around particular types of equipment or functions. Examples of job shops include photocopy centers, universities, and hospitals. Each job, or customer, flows through the process from function to function according to requirements that may be different for each customer. Although an engineering student takes one set of courses and a business student takes another, they may share some similar functions, such as taking English and math courses. A job shop allows a high degree of customization and is very flexible.

In a **repetitive process,** functions are arranged in a sequence according to product specifications. An auto assembly line is a classic example. This

FIGURE 21.2   *The Product/Process Matrix*

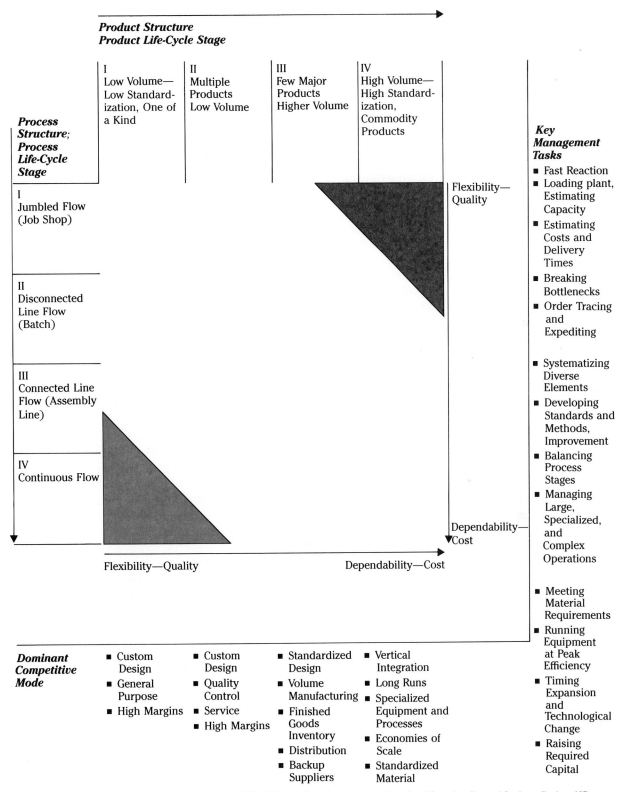

Source: W. Hayes and S. Wheelwright (January-February 1979), Link manufacturing process and product life cycles, *Harvard Business Review,* 137.

process results in a high volume of similar products at relatively low costs, owing to the specialized equipment that is placed where it is needed.

A **batch,** or **disconnected-line, process** falls midway between a job shop and a repetitive line. Products or services can be produced in a line manner but are usually processed in large batches because of a particular feature of the product or process. For example, soup can be made in large batches because it must cook for a certain amount of time. After cooking, the soup flows out to the canning operation. The next batch, possibly of a different soup, can then be made in the same kettle (after cleaning, of course). This operation shares some of the characteristics of a job shop in that there is some flexibility in the types of products. The operation also has some characteristics of an assembly line in that all types of soup must go through the same process (mix, cook, and can).

A **continuous process** operating system is a higher-flow version of a repetitive line; the product flows continuously through the process. Examples are sugar refining and oil refining. A continuous process operating system creates very high volume with very little variability in final product. The result is low cost and high dependability of volume output.

Generally an operation does not rely strictly on one type of process. A fast-food restaurant, for example, may have a batch process (the grill on which hamburgers are cooked), a repetitive process (the assembling of the burgers), and then a job shop (counter workers who custom-assemble the final product). Each of the four operating processes has different competitive abilities. A job shop can produce custom products and services with a large amount of flexibility, while a continuous process is capable of delivering large volume at low cost.

Job shop, repetitive, batch, and continuous processes require different management tasks, some of which are shown in Figure 21.2. Because it may involve many different jobs moving in many different routes, a job shop requires managerial skills in scheduling production, tracing orders, estimating capacity, and determining costs and delivery times. For instance, the manager of a hospital emergency room is concerned with the scheduling of patients, doctors, and nurses. Because each patient has a different illness or injury with varying degrees of severity and because patients arrive randomly, the emergency room must have a scheduling system that moves the most critically ill or injured patients through the facility most efficiently and effectively.

A repetitive operation (such as an assembly line), owing to its high volume of standard product, requires management skills in determining the timing of expansion and technological change; in managing large, specialized, and complex organizations; in running equipment at peak efficiency; and in raising the capital to pay for expensive equipment and facilities. For example, since an auto assembly plant is usually dedicated to one or two basic models, managers spend little time making decisions about which models to produce in one day or week. On the other hand, managers must deal with the complex task of ensuring that the thousands of parts necessary for each car are available at the right time. Changes in the process, such as the addition of a new painting facility, involve major decisions that may take years to move from planning to implementation. Changes in technology are major ones that must be made at the appropriate time, or competitors may gain an advantage.

Designing and Using an Operating System

Operating managers must first design an operating system and then use it to generate products and services. All parts of an operating system should be designed and used in harmony with each other. If a purchasing agent buys low-quality parts, it may result in an unreliable product. If the purchasing agent, design engineers, and warranty department staff discuss the product before the parts are purchased, however, their coordinated efforts should ensure a reliable product.

A typical product or service goes through the following sequence of activities: (1) product and process design, (2) planning and control system design, (3) production or delivery, (4) distribution, and (5) after-sales service and support. Managers must integrate these five activities in dealing with vendors and customers. For example, when product designers are working on a design, they must approach materials vendors to find out the types of available materials. Automobile designers, for instance, approach radio vendors to identify the latest technology so they can design the proper wiring into the cars.

Design Decisions

Design decisions are long-term and usually are made by upper or upper-middle managers. Decisions about the location and size of a facility are not easily changed once it is built.

Product and service design, although not usually carried out within the operations function, has a major impact on how a product will be produced or on how a service will be delivered. For example, in luxury cars, air conditioning is standard and is factory installed. In less-expensive cars, by contrast, holes and supports must be placed properly to permit dealer installation of an air conditioning unit, at a buyer's request.

Process design involving the type of process and types of equipment must be coordinated with product design. The design of a product (standardized vs. customized) results in different production processes. The "have-it-your-way" hamburger chain has a process that allows customization without excessive costs, while the other major hamburger chain has a process that produces an identical product every time.

Capacity is the maximum amount of product or service that can be delivered in a stated time frame—for example, 400 sweaters per shift on an assembly line, or 50 customers per hour at a car wash. For large operations, such as those involving auto assembly, this is a difficult decision; extra assembly plants waste money if they are not used, but insufficient capacity when demand is high results in lost sales. An operation's capacity must be matched with the expected or anticipated demand.

Organizations can locate near customers, near sources of raw material, or near sources of labor. **Location decision** is a function of the nature of the product or service, the type of inputs, and other factors. For instance, a supermarket must be located near its customers. The location decision is often combined with the capacity decision, because it is possible to balance production between one large, central plant and many small, scattered plants.

The **layout** of a facility is a function either of the product or of the process used in production. A product layout arranges the processing equipment or functions in sequence as they are needed in production. An assembly line is an example: a car is assembled in a certain sequence, which is a function of its design, and the processing equipment must be arranged in that order.

Finally, jobs must be designed around the type of processing equipment being used, and the wage scale must be tailored to the skill level required to accomplish the jobs. For example, managers do not hire high-cost gourmet chefs to cook at a fast-food restaurant, nor do gourmet restaurants hire fast-food cooks. The skill levels, pay scales, and final products are different.

Utilization Decisions

Utilization decisions are short term and may be constrained by a system's design. Before managers determine the plan for each product, department, and machine, they create an **aggregate plan** for the entire operating system. Managers use an aggregate plan for using the operating system at this aggregate level for each month of the year. For instance, based on the forecast for total car production, General Motors can plan auto production for each of its assembly plants for each month of the coming year, balancing the cost of inventory, back orders, and changing production rates. This allows the corporation to plan monthly hiring, raw material and parts purchases, and inventory levels.

The determination of which employees will work when and at which machines or departments, along with decisions about the work that will flow through the operating system, is known as **scheduling.** Decisions must frequently be made on a day-to-day, sometimes hour-to-hour, basis.

Inventory is a measure of physical goods that are produced but not yet sold. Inventories can include raw materials and purchased parts, work-in-process (WIP), and finished goods. Because storing inventory can be very costly, production scheduling decisions must be made to increase or decrease inventory. For example, inventory could be kept in raw-material form and finished products made only when customers demand them; at the other extreme, products could be produced and kept in finished-good form for rapid delivery.

Quality assurance relates to the fact that it is important to produce a product or service that meets customers' expectations. Inspection during production can ensure that the product or service will meet specifications; proper design ensures that it will fill customers' needs.

More emphasis is now being placed on the role of **purchasing** in determining the quality of products or services. At one time, purchasing agents were merely required to find the lowest-cost suppliers of raw materials, parts, and services. Managers now recognize that using the lowest-cost supplier may not result in the lowest cost if many defective supplies must be discarded or returned or if low quality causes customer dissatisfaction. The role of purchasing is to work with vendors to obtain the best product at the lowest cost.

Finally, **distribution systems** include warehouses and delivery systems, such as track and rail operations. Decisions must be made regarding the location of warehouses and inventory and the best way to transport that inventory to customers.

Inventory is a measure of physical goods that are not yet sold. Since storage costs can be high, many decisions must be made about the scheduling of production to regulate inventory.

World-Class Operations

Because of the competitive disadvantage of many U.S.-based companies, a significant revolution in operations management has been underway since 1980. During the 1970s and 1980s, Japanese manufacturers produced high-quality products at low prices and took over significant market shares in many industries. The American response to this has been to study several Japanese methods that have contributed to Japan's superior market position. Contrary to popular opinion, the Japanese advantage has not been gained solely through cheap labor rates and government subsidies. It has usually been achieved through superior production systems that result in high quality at low cost.

The production of a product or service that can compete successfully anywhere in the world is known as **world-class operations.** Because the most common application of this principle has been in the manufacturing sector, it has been called *world-class manufacturing (WCM)* in the popular press. The concepts used in WCM are applicable to service industries as well, so this description is not entirely accurate; *world-class operations* would be more appropriate.

Operating-system changes necessary to achieve world-class operations call for very different approaches to operations management. World-class operations focus on three key areas: inventory planning and scheduling, quality, and automation and process technology. These areas are addressed through just-in-time, total quality control, and computer-integrated operations.

Just-in-Time (JIT)

The concept of **just-in-time (JIT)** involves a particular philosophy of managing inventory and scheduling production. In the "requirements era" in the United States, beginning in the 1970s and continuing in the present, computerized systems have been used to determine the best production schedules and inventory locations. During that time, Japanese managers were developing the key JIT philosophy: inventory is a fundamental liability that must be reduced. Inventory hides problems and costs that are not readily noticed.

This view forces managers to think of ways to reduce inventory rather than to determine the best place to store it. For example, suppose that a fast-food restaurant cook places 100 cheeseburgers in inventory at the front counter to meet lunchtime demand. The first customer to receive a burger notices that there is no cheese on it. An inspection reveals that there is no cheese on any of the burgers; the cook made an error. The restaurant has to discard most of the 100 burgers because the demand for hamburgers without cheese is low.

Consider what would have happened if the cook had made 10 small batches of 10 cheeseburgers each, rather than a single batch of 100 burgers to meet the lunchtime demand. Obviously, the inventory level would have been much smaller. This means that, although the first defective cheeseburger would have been discovered at about the same time as before, the restaurant would have had to discard only 10 hamburgers. On receiving feedback that cheese had been omitted, the cook could have made an immediate correction by adding cheese to the next batch of 10, thus rectifying the cheeseless cheeseburger situation.

The premise behind total quality control is that quality is everyone's responsibility.

Notice that this example of inventory reduction through smaller batch size also results in improved quality, reduced wastage (and, consequently, lower costs), and smaller space requirements for holding the inventory. Also consider that the cook would have been more productive, because he or she would not have had to remake 100 cheeseburgers. The inventory of 100 cheeseless cheeseburgers might also have inconvenienced customers, a cost (perhaps of future lost sales) that is hidden and very difficult to detect.

For a JIT system to work well, the quality of incoming parts and supplies must be high. Because production occurs in small batches with little inventory to cover any variation in production rate, there can be no defective parts, or the production process will not meet demands. In a JIT system, if defective parts come into the process, they are discovered quickly.

The overall effect of JIT is to improve the total operating process, not just to reduce inventory. Quality improvement and scrap reduction are typical in a JIT environment, with increased productivity. It is very difficult to argue with the success of this technique in the face of successful Japanese-dominated industries that produce automobiles, cameras, and electronic home consumer products, all characterized by high quality and relatively low price.

Total Quality Control (TQC)

The premise behind **total quality control (TQC)** is that quality is everyone's responsibility, not just the responsibility of a quality assurance department. In essence, all organization members must work together to determine how quality can be improved. The quality of a product or service has a direct bearing on how customers perceive the product.

Like JIT, TQC requires a philosophy of continual improvement through the discovery and correction of problems, with a resulting increase in quality. This is counter to the conventional quality control practice that has endured for many years in the United States. In this system, products are inspected at several points along the process and defective ones are removed. This attitude ignores the time wasted in producing defective products, with resulting productivity decreases and large amounts of scrap. The TQC approach is different: find the problems and fix the process so that only defect-free products are produced.

Computer-Integrated Operations

Recent advances in electronic technology have resulted in a significant improvement in managers' ability to control manufacturing and service processes by computer—**computer-integrated operations.** For example, an automated bank teller can accept deposits, dispense cash, and show account balances. This process also links account balances and can be used to show the bank's financial controllers its immediate cash position. Various bank functions are integrated by computer.

In manufacturing, product design can be assisted by engineering design software, which provides computerized procedures for producing parts. Computer-controlled equipment that is scheduled with computer-driven systems can then produce products with little human intervention. This technology allows a high degree of flexibility—in both volume and product variety—in the production of high-quality parts and products. With computer-integrated operations, there is no need for inventory, because units can be produced on demand.

The three areas of world-class operations—JIT, TQC, and computer-integrated operations—are linked, although the third concept does not need to be put into effect to gain the advantages of the first two. Significant implementation of JIT and TQC has begun in the United States, whereas computer-integrated operations are still in infancy, owing to new technology. These three topics, which are revolutionizing the management of manufacturing, can also be applied to service functions.

Operations Management in Review

Operations management is concerned with the production of goods and the delivery of services. Inputs of material, information, labor, and capital are used in the transformation process to produce goods and services. Managers must make many decisions when designing an operating system, in planning and managing its use, and in controlling it.

The design and use of a production system are crucial to successful competition in a rapidly changing global economy. Continual improvement is required to maintain a competitive edge. Both service and manufacturing operations can benefit from using the latest concepts of operations management.

An operating system must be integrated with other important functions, such as marketing, finance, accounting, and human resource development. Management of the process is highly dependent on the type of product or service and the type of delivery system. There are different types of production systems; each competes differently and requires different management skills.

Global competition has forced organizations to determine how to compete with world-class operations. The best Japanese techniques of just-in-time and total quality control are now being applied in U.S. companies with excellent results. Computer integration requires new management tasks and results in more competitive advantages for organizations that can produce products and deliver services more quickly, of higher quality, with more customization, and at lower prices.

Operations managers are concerned with systems that not only must be operated on a day-to-day basis but also encompass increasing complexity and change. Product and process innovation is changing, and managers must be able to change as well.

Issues for Review and Discussion

1. In your own words, define operations management.
2. What is the role of operations in an organization?
3. Watch a television commercial and list the attributes that are presented to induce you to buy the product or service. Which of those attributes are direct results of the design and utilization of the operations function?
4. Think of the different types of restaurants in which you have eaten. Which ones could be considered job shops? batch processes? assembly lines? Do the objec-

tives of those restaurants match the process objectives? Place the restaurants on the product/process matrix in Figure 21.2.

5. Many people who cook at home shop for food about once a week, buying enough for a week's worth of consumption. Other people eat in a cafeteria, thus avoiding the purchase of food ahead of time. Discuss these two approaches in terms of JIT, TQC, and inventory management.

6. Discuss the operating objectives of the college in which you are enrolled in relation to a competing college. Use the operations objectives of cost, quality, flexibility, and dependability. Which of these does your college use as a competitive advantage? What form of production process does your college use? Does this fit its objectives?

7. How can computer-integrated operations increase an organization's ability to compete?

Key Terms

operations management
competitive (strategic) advantage
job shop
repetitive process
batch (disconnected-line) process
continuous process
capacity
location decision
layout
aggregate plan

scheduling
inventory
quality assurance
purchasing
distribution systems
world-class operations
just-in-time (JIT)
total quality control (TQC)
computer-integrated operations

Suggested Readings

Chase, R. B., and Aquilano, N. J. (1985). *Production and operations management: A life cycle approach*, 4th ed. Homewood, IL: Irwin.

Ferdows, K., and Skinner, W. (Fall 1987). The sweeping revolution in manufacturing. *Journal of Business Strategy*, 64-69.

Garvin, D. A. (1987). *Managing quality*. New York: The Free Press.

Gunn, T. S. (1987). *Manufacturing for competitive advantage*. Cambridge, MA: Ballinger.

Hayes, W., and Wheelwright, S. (January-February 1979). Link manufacturing process and product life cycles. *Harvard Business Review*, 133-40.

Hayes, W., and Wheelwright, S. (March-April 1979). The dynamics of process-product life cycles. *Harvard Business Review*.

Schonberger, R. J. (1982). *Japanese manufacturing techniques—nine hidden lessons in simplicity*. New York: The Free Press.

Stevenson, W. J. (1986). *Production/operations management*, 2nd ed. Homewood, IL: Irwin.

Vonderembse, M. A., and White, G. P. (1988). *Operations management, concepts, methods, and strategies*. St. Paul, MN: West.

HSB Manufacturing, Inc.

Paul M. Bobrowski, University of Oregon

Neil Christy is just starting his third week at HSB Manufacturing in the newly formed position of manufacturing manager. He arrived at work at 7:30 A.M. in anticipation of the weekly meeting with Charlie Maxwell, the shop owner, and Ted Lepcio, the head of sales and customer service. Also attending this meeting would be Neil's subordinate, Virgil Trucks, the production control manager. This meeting was important because it would be the first at which Neil was expected to make a contribution. Neil was concerned about shop congestion and the bottlenecks that were most acute in the punch press department. Walking through the shop, Neil noticed that there seemed to be a large amount of work in process around the machines. Pans and baskets of semifinished parts were stacked around each machine, three to five in each stack, with each representing a separate customer order.

HSB Manufacturing, Inc. is a typical midsized job shop with annual sales between $12 and $15 million. The 150 nonunionized workers are paid from $8.50 to $13.50 per hour, with an incentive based on the job standard. During peak business periods, their wages are augmented by extensive overtime. In the past ten years, there had been three unsuccessful attempts to unionize. The last attempt, three years earlier, had failed by only 12 votes.

The plant is arranged by function or department. HSB has eight departments: single spindle lathes, multiple spindle turret lathes, cold heading, milling machines, drills, punch presses, finishing, and heat treating

and plating. The machinery is a mix of old equipment and modern machines using computer technology. All equipment, regardless of its age or technology, is flexible. Each machine must be able to perform a generic function on a wide variety of parts, components, and modules. The flexibility of the machinery requires a complement of highly skilled machinists who often have to design the process and set up machines to meet the specifications of a custom order.

HSB depends on customer orders for 90 percent of its business. Since it is a make-to-order operation, HSB has no ability to inventory items during the leaner economic times. All of HSB's customers are large manufacturing, construction, or mining companies dependent on the business cycle. As a result, customers choose a job shop to manufacture a component or part based primarily on quality and delivery reliability; price is usually a less-important criterion.

HSB receives orders by bidding on a job as specified by the customer. Based on customer-provided blueprints and specifications, HSB quotes a price for the required quantity. Since HSB has a well-established reputation for quality, the bidding process is usually a mere formality rather than competitive.

Setting delivery dates, however, is not a straightforward process. It primarily involves the customer, HSB sales personnel, and Charlie Maxwell. The tightness of the delivery schedule is influenced by the overall business cycle; during the boom periods, the lead time from order to delivery could be in excess of nine months.

By 8:00 A.M., the first shift had been working one hour. In the punch press department, Milt Bolling, the department foreman who had been with the company for twenty years, was discussing some technical problems with one of the machine operators. At the conclusion of that conversation, Neil approached Milt to discuss the bottleneck problem.

Milt: The problem with the department is that marketing is constantly interfering with the schedule and expediting different orders. This causes two problems; first it gives us multiple set-ups. You might not know yet, but Mr. Maxwell really has stressed that we should minimize the number of set-ups. So we usually take all the jobs with a particular set-up and run them back to back. This is great since it usually keeps the workers' morale up by increasing their incentive pay. The second problem is that, using the sales departments' revised schedule, we can't choose the next job to minimize the down time. Set-ups are just eating up our capacity, and nobody wants to authorize very much overtime. And another thing, the sales department people that come down to revise the schedule are not consistent; they are constantly juggling the orders so we end up having everything as some sort of priority or rush job. What can I do but sort of muddle through? If anybody tells you different, just ask Virgil [Trucks].

Neil assured Milt that he was investigating the problem and told him that the punch press department is not the only department experiencing this; it was merely more acute here and, therefore, that department was the center of attention.

On his way to the weekly meeting with Ted and Charlie, Neil swung by the loading dock. There he noticed almost no available space and that completed orders were stacked all the way into the raw material holding area. At random, Neil pulled a few orders to see what was waiting to be shipped. The first order was to Craig Mining. The order said the job was not to be delivered before August 23, which was nine weeks from now. The next order was for C-Gap Mfg. and carried a series of due dates; the original was for June 24, but pen-and-ink changes had taken the due date out to October 4. The other orders Neil looked at told similar stories; the current due dates were either earlier or later than the original due date, or the completed orders were not to be delivered before dates that were substantially in the future.

When Neil arrived at the meeting, Ted Lepcio, the sales and customer service manager, was ready to begin. He held a stack of message sheets that he handed to Charlie and Neil. He started his presentation.

Ted: Each of you have in your hands the recorded dissatisfaction with our delivery record. According to our calculations, 45 percent of our orders are delivered over two weeks late. Twenty percent are over two months late. This is having a detrimental effect on getting future orders. Our good customers are beginning to tell us that having a quality product at a reasonable price is not enough when our delivery reliability is so atrocious. As these customers get into the just-in-time concepts, I expect the howls will get louder, and we will begin to experience a loss in business.

Charlie looked at Virgil, who was responsible for loading the shop floor with the right mix of orders, as well as for tracking the jobs as they progressed on the shop floor.

Virgil: Well, I don't get the same kinds of figures, because my weekly hot sheet, which projects jobs that are scheduled to be late according to the original due date, never exceeds 20 percent. Part of my problem lately is manpower in my department. I don't have enough expeditors to adequately cover the shop floor with this many open jobs. An extra two expeditors would surely clear up the problem. And for the good news, we have been able to maintain over an 85 percent utilization rate in the two lathe departments and the header department.

Virgil knew that this would be good news to Charlie, who was constantly harping on keeping the utilization as high as possible in these three departments because of the tremendous capital investment in machinery. Charlie, however, shook his head slowly.

Charlie: We seem to be busier than ever, and yet, the customers are screaming for their orders. How come our internal numbers on late orders are inconsistent between sales and production control? Maybe Neil can shed some light on this dilemma now that he has been with us for two weeks.

With that, Neil went to the front of the room, and as he walked he remembered what Milt had told him, what he had seen on the loading dock, and what had been said here in the meeting. Being the new manager meant he had to explain what was going wrong without blaming, while making it plain to everyone that business as usual would not solve the problems.

Questions

1. Identify and explain the main source of the operational problem Neil has observed.
2. Once Neil lays out the problem, what should Charlie Maxwell do?
3. How can the system be redesigned to solve the scheduling problem?
4. Why do Ted Lepcio, the sales and customer service manager, and Virgil Trucks, the production control manager, have different figures on late deliveries?
5. How can this problem be solved?

22 Human Resource Management

Student Learning Objectives

After reading this chapter, you should be able to:

1. Discuss how the human resource function supports the overall strategy of an organization.

2. Explain how factors in the external environment influence the human resource function.

3. Explain why job analysis is required for the successful design and execution of most human resource activities.

4. Describe the process for obtaining and keeping staff members.

5. Clarify why training and development programs are needed even when an excellent staffing program exists.

6. Understand the purposes, techniques, and problems associated with appraising performance.

7. Delineate the forms of cash and noncash compensation and the ways in which they are used to motivate and reward employees.

8. Explain why unions exist and how they interact with the management of organizations.

*O*rganizations are systems of interacting people. To realize their goals, organizations must depend on those people. An organization's success and survival largely depend on how well its human resources are managed. How does an organization identify the types of people it needs and then convince them to join it? What does it take to train them, to evaluate their performance, and to encourage them to stay with the organization and contribute to its mission? All of these tasks fall within the realm of **human resource management.**

In most organizations, the management of human resources is a joint venture. It involves all of the managers in an organization, plus a human resource department (often called a personnel or industrial relations department). In most cases, individual managers do the everyday hiring, training, evaluating, and promoting. The human resource department usually identifies standards and provides resources to managers, including performance appraisal forms, training, information about how to select employees, and so on.

For many years, some managers considered personnel departments to be an organization's weak link. They felt that such departments had little to offer and created more problems than they solved. Part of the reason for this reputation was the fact that few personnel managers were professionally trained in the personnel function. Over the last couple of decades, however, human resource departments have earned a much better image. Managers now recognize the importance of the function and demand high-quality human resource employees and programs.

The Role of the External Environment

The external environment affects all parts of an organization, and human resource management is no exception. Human resource managers must cope with at least four important components of the external environment: economic forces, labor markets, laws and regulations, and labor unions. The top

In most organizations, the management of human resources is a joint venture.

FIGURE 22.1 The Human
Resource Management Model

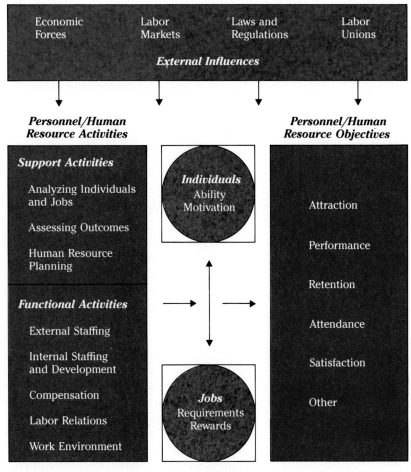

Source: Based on H. G. Heneman III, D. P. Schwab, J. A. Fossum, and L. D. Dyer (1989), *Personnel/
human resource management,* 4th ed., Homewood, IL: Irwin, 8.

part of Figure 22.1 identifies these four major external influences.* The left side
of the figure shows two kinds of human resource activities: support and
functional. Support activities include analyzing individuals and jobs, assessing
outcomes (such as performance), and planning human resource activities.
Functional activities include staffing and overseeing compensation plans, labor relations, and aspects of the working environment. The middle panel of the
figure shows the need for these activities to match workers' abilities with job
requirements and to enhance motivation through rewards. If these are matched
appropriately, workers can achieve the objectives shown on the right side of
the figure.

Economic Factors

Business organizations operate in a marketplace. They must respond sen-
sitively to economic changes. The level and health of economic activity in the

*This figure and much of the general approach to human resource management presented in this
book are based on H. G. Heneman III, D. P. Schwab, J. A. Fossum, and L. D. Dyer (1989),
Personnel/human resource management, 4th ed., Homewood, IL: Irwin.

external environment, for example, strongly influence an organization's volume of business. This volume, in turn, affects the types and number of employees the organization requires. If new car sales slump, for example, steel orders decline and the need for employees at steel mills drops substantially.

Economic factors strongly influence an organization's demands on its human resource department. For instance, in response to tight financial conditions during the 1980s, human resource departments were called on to identify and implement work design, training, and motivational programs to enhance productivity and increase the value of work output per employee. Human resource departments also dealt with recent financial difficulties by designing and implementing early-retirement programs to help reduce payroll costs.

Labor Factors

The **labor market** defines the number and types of people present in the workforce. The labor market typically is discussed in terms of the number of employed and unemployed individuals in various labor groups, such as those described as skilled, unskilled, professional, and technical. It is also typically described in terms of the characteristics of the people in these groups, such as their age, gender, and level of education.

The labor market influences virtually every aspect of human resource management. Jobs, recruiting programs, training programs, and even work schedules must draw on the talent available and address the personal needs and work interests of the people in the labor market. In some cases, for example, companies must offer alternative work schedules, such as job sharing or flextime, or must design jobs in particular ways to attract and retain certain segments of the labor market. To do their job effectively, human resource managers must not only recognize changes in the labor market but anticipate them as well. Job design, the nature of compensation, training programs, and retirement programs all depend on the profile of workers hired by the organization.

Legal Factors

Recent successful lawsuits brought by former employees against employers show that managers do not have complete discretion in hiring, managing, and letting workers go.[1] Human resource managers must juggle a number of legal considerations, including:

- *Hours/wages.* The U.S. Fair Labor Standards Act, The Walsh-Healy Act, and other federal and state laws govern the number of hours that some employees can be asked to work and specify the minimum wages they must be paid. Laws also decree that time-and-a-half pay must be given to certain employees who work more than a certain number of hours (usually forty) per week.
- *Worker safety.* Of the laws that apply to worker safety, the most notable is the Occupational Safety and Health Act (OSHA). This and other laws dictate that employers have a duty to provide workers with safe working conditions.

- *Financial protection.* The Federal Unemployment Tax Act, state workers' compensation laws, the Employee Retirement Income Security Act (ERISA), and the Social Security Act are some of the laws designed to protect employees financially in case of involuntary unemployment, disability, or retirement.
- *Discrimination.* Federal and state laws, regulations, and executive orders protect certain subgroups in the labor force. In a nation dedicated to the principles of equal opportunity and nondiscrimination, human resource managers must become familiar with the laws and regulations that enact these principles, such as the Civil Rights Act of 1964, Age Discrimination in Employment legislation, and the Equal Pay Act of 1963.

Many other laws and regulations place additional constraints on employers, and human resource practices must conform to them all. Labor law issues are particularly important and are discussed later in this chapter.

Job Analysis

Newspaper publisher, photographer, delivery truck driver, real-estate broker, lawyer, assembly line worker—all of these are jobs. A **job** is a collection of tasks that can be performed by one person. **Job analysis** is the process of identifying and defining those tasks and their associated responsibilities and requirements. Virtually every human resource activity is influenced by the results of job analysis. For this reason, job analysis is considered to be the *core* of human resource operations.

One of the most important uses of job analysis lies in the preparation of job descriptions. At a minimum, a **job description** should list the duties and responsibilities that managers expect the holder of that job to accomplish, the procedures the job holder should follow in carrying them out, and the qualifications—education, skills, and experience—a person needs to accomplish these duties and responsibilities. Human resource managers use the information gathered in a job analysis to develop job descriptions, such as that shown in Figure 22.2 on page 508.

Hundreds of job analysis techniques are in use.[2] They differ substantially in their methods of collecting job information, in their focus of analysis, and in their expression of results. The range of jobs covered by job analysis techniques also varies. Some techniques are designed for small subsets of jobs. Others are intended for very broad use. Job analysis techniques also vary substantially in quality. Without high-quality job analysis information, a human resource program cannot meet an organization's needs. Some good techniques that human resource managers use to conduct job analyses include:

- *Direct observation*—watching workers continuously during a specified period to identify every relevant activity
- *Work sampling*—a variation of the direct observation approach, in which a human resource manager periodically observes workers
- *Critical incidents*—another variation of the direct observation method, which examines only those job behaviors that most influence successful or unsuccessful performance

FIGURE 22.2 *Sample Job Description: Legal Clerk*

Title: Legal Clerk III   Grade: C   4/15/90
                             Hours: 7:30 A.M.–4:00 P.M. (some flexibility)
Minimum: $12,580/year   Division: Legal

The Duties of This Position Involve the Following:

1. Answer telephone, screen calls as required, take messages or refer for proper handling.
2. Make photocopies and overhead transparencies as requested.
3. Utilize typewriter, word processor, and personal computer for typing needs of the Legal Division staff (reports, letters, memos, charts, etc.).
4. File and maintain records as assigned, including maintenance of sublicense agreements file and list.
5. Assist in preparation of materials for printing, production, and mailing.
6. Distribute completed work, photocopies, and research files as needed.
7. Maintain inventory of office supplies and replenish as needed.
8. Provide assistance and support to Legal Division secretaries.
9. Perform other duties as assigned.

Qualifications:

High-school diploma plus one year of office experience. Two-year secretarial certificate may be considered in lieu of experience. Sixty wpm typing speed, excellent oral and written communication skills, excellent organization skills, proofing/editing efficiency, and ability to work under pressure required. Word processing, personal computer, telephone, and dictaphone experience required. Additional relevant experience may be considered in lieu of educational requirements as stated.

- *Interviewing*—discussions between a job incumbent and/or supervisor and a human resource manager to identify important aspects of a job that may not be obvious through direct observation
- *Structured questionnaires*—standardized forms, such as the Position Analysis Questionnaire (PAQ) and the Professional and Managerial Position Questionnaire (PMPQ), which elicit answers about a job, the activities it involves, and other relevant data[3]

Staffing

Job analysis tells what *a* person must be able to do to carry out a job, but **staffing** is the process of finding *the* person to do so. Human resource managers must find people who meet the specified requirements, must narrow the field to the candidates who best appear to have those abilities, and must develop them into effective organization members. Staffing also describes the processes that human resource managers go through to separate members from organizations through layoffs, firings, and retirement.

External Recruiting

When searching for viable job candidates, managers can look either outside or inside their organization. Human resource managers perform **external**

TABLE 22.1 *How to Find Job Candidates*

Type of Job	*How to Look*
Blue-collar	Direct applications, advertising
Clerical	Advertising, direct applications, employee referrals
Sales	Advertising, private employment agencies, employee referrals
Professional/technical	Advertising, private employment agencies, educational institutions
Managerial	Advertising, private employment agencies, executive search firms

Source: *Recruiting policies and practices* (1979), Washington, DC: Bureau of National Affairs.

recruiting when they find a qualified pool of candidates outside their organization. External recruiting consists of five steps:

1. *Planning.* Human resource managers see how many and what types of people the organization is likely to need, how many people in the external labor market are likely to meet the requirements, and how many of those are likely to accept a job if it is offered.

2. *Strategy development.* Once managers know the types and number of candidates to contact, they must develop a strategy that specifies where, how, and when to look. *Where* to look for candidates depends on the nature of the job in question. A potential legal clerk can probably be found locally, for example, but the search for a new chief legal counsel may extend to the entire state. *How* to look for candidates also depends on the type of job (see Table 22.1). *When* to look for candidates depends on how long it is likely to take to complete the search. The search can involve advertising, checking résumés, issuing invitations for and conducting interviews, screening candidates, and so forth.

3. *Searching.* Once they have planned the strategy, human resource managers begin the search process. They seek and get applications and exchange information with job applicants.

4. *Screening.* After receiving applications, human resource managers screen them to identify the candidates who meet the job's basic qualifications. A legal clerk, for example, must have personal computer and word-processing experience, so the candidate with a B.A. who has worked as a receptionist in a law office but cannot type is screened out. After the screening process has reduced the pool of applicants to the qualified candidates, managers use a selection process (described later in this section) to choose the individual to hire for the job.

5. *Program evaluation.* Like any other strategic plan, a recruiting program must be monitored, evaluated, and controlled. Human resource managers must determine whether recruiting activities have occurred as planned and assess the results. How many candidates were contacted and at what cost? How effective was the search from equal employment and affirmative action perspectives? Such evaluations let managers identify the strengths and weaknesses of their organization's external recruiting program and allow them to make changes for the future.

Internal Recruiting

Human resource managers use **internal recruiting** to find employees already inside the organization who are qualified for new job openings. Internal recruiting involves the same five steps used for external recruiting: planning, strategy development, searching, screening, and program evaluation. In fact, most organizations integrate internal and external recruiting, at least to a degree, such as when a company places a classified ad in a local newspaper and posts the job opening on an employee bulletin board. An organization's hiring policies, often specified in employee handbooks and union contracts, usually dictate the degree to which current employees will be given priority over candidates from outside the organization for new openings.

Selection

The purpose of recruiting is to identify a pool of qualified candidates for a job opening. Managers use a **selection** process to evaluate each candidate, to predict the probable levels of job performance by each, and to choose a candidate for the job. Any technique or procedure for choosing candidates is referred to as a **selection device.** A wide range of selection devices is available to give human resource managers information on which to base their decisions. These selection devices include:

- *Application blanks.* These are forms that ask for personal information, as well as information about previous training and work experiences, that might give an indication of a candidate's probable job performance. Many states have laws limiting the types of questions that can be asked on the application to avoid discrimination on the basis of age, race, religion, marital status, and so forth.[4]

- *References and recommendations.* Human resource managers often seek information from someone other than the candidate—usually a previous or current employer—about the candidate's past performance record. Sometimes references and recommendations are honest, helpful, and reliable. They can be unreliable and lack validity, though, if the source allows personal opinions and feelings (positive or negative) to override an objective evaluation of the candidate.

- *Interviews.* Organizations usually hold question-and-answer sessions between the candidate and the prospective employer. Although interviews probably are the most commonly used selection device, they often fail to identify the most qualified candidate because of time constraints, managers' personal biases, and poor interviewing techniques. For an interview to produce valid information, interviewers must be properly trained to use a structured approach that asks the same relevant, job-related questions of each candidate, questions that are written out in advance and scored on a standardized rating scale.

- *Tests.* Human resource managers can use a wide range of instruments to examine candidates' abilities, skills, behaviors, and attitudes. The best tests assess, in a standardized manner, those factors that job analysis has identified as necessary for a candidate to perform well on the job. For instance, the three top candidates for the legal clerk job could be given typing and dictation tests.

- *Assessment centers.* This selection device sets up an environment in which managers conduct a simulation of the job in question, usually over a two- or three-day period. Typically, observers independently rate each candidate on a standardized scale on a number of dimensions that job analysis has identified as important parts of the job. The three top legal clerk candidates, for example, could receive in-baskets containing identical samples of mail, phone messages, and reports and be given one hour to respond to its contents. At the end of the time period, observers would assess how effectively each candidate handled the material.

Career Development

Job candidates want to know what their promotion possibilities are if their performance is satisfactory. Organizations want to know who will be available to fill job openings all along career paths. By considering potentially available jobs as they evaluate candidates, human resource managers can develop career plans that benefit the organization's overall and long-term staffing strategy.

The most effective career development plans identify career paths (see Figure 22.3 on page 512), along with estimates of the likelihood that an employee will advance to higher-level jobs (see Chapter 24 for a detailed discussion of careers and career development). They also estimate the amount of time it typically takes employees to reach each step along the path. By meeting with supervisors or career counselors, employees can see how they fit into a generic career path.

Separation Issues

Sometimes human resource managers must ask employees to leave an organization, such as when the organization needs fewer or different types of employees or when employees are not meeting their job requirements. Asking employees to leave an organization is (perhaps euphemistically) called *separating* them. Separation methods include:

- *Layoffs*—stopping someone's employment either temporarily or permanently through no fault of the employee
- *Dismissals*—ending someone's employment "for cause," such as habitual tardiness, poor performance, or undesirable behavior at work
- *Retirement*—allowing (usually) older employees to leave an organization in good standing. Federal law prohibits mandatory retirement before age seventy, except for some executives and policymakers and for certain types of jobs, such as airline pilot.

Training and Development

Organizations identify and hire people who meet their requirements as closely as possible, but the match is seldom perfect. Usually, employees hired through even the best staffing programs need to be taught how to apply their abilities and skills to the requirements of the specific job. This instruction,

FIGURE 22.3   Career Paths
in an Insurance Company

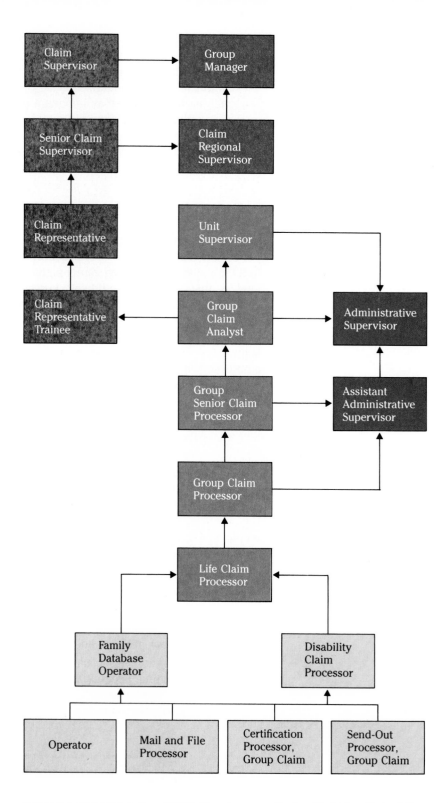

Source: M. London and S. A. Stumpf (1982), *Managing careers,* Reading, MA: Addison-Wesley, 140.

Employees hired through even the best staffing programs need training and development.

which prepares an employee for a job, is known as **training.** In contrast, **development** usually refers to preparation that extends beyond the present job, such as the instruction the employee will need if the design of the current job changes or if the employee changes jobs through transfer or promotion.

Determining Training and Development Needs

First, managers must identify particular *areas* in which performance problems have been experienced or may develop. If there are extreme quality control problems on a particular assembly line, the organization may have to train workers in that area. If the organization can expect to run short of qualified first-level managers, its human resource manager should begin to prepare some nonmanagerial employees to make the transition into management. Good human resource plans, in other words, anticipate needs rather than react to emerging problems.

After learning where problems are likely to occur, human resource managers focus on the specific *types* of training needed. Here, too, job analyses often are useful. Managers can compare job requirements with employees' abilities and, thus, pinpoint the types of training required. A manager analyzing a robotic technician's job, for example, might determine that the ability to work a computer keyboard is essential. If the employees who are or who will become robotics technicians do not know how to use a keyboard, they should receive training *before* they are placed in the new job.

In planning employees' development, human resource managers also can create formal career paths that draw on a progression of closely related skills for each succeeding job (review Figure 22.3). The presence of career paths helps managers plan how to use each employee over a series of years. It also helps employees aspire to appropriate future jobs and to prepare for them. For instance, a legal clerk can take advantage of his or her organization's continu-

TABLE 22.2   Examples of Training and Development Methods

On-the-Job	Off-the-Job
Coaching ■ Tutoring ■ Role modeling	Information presentation ■ Written/visual materials ■ Lectures
Special assignments ■ Projects ■ Task forces	Information processing ■ Conference groups ■ Discussion groups
Job rotation ■ Departmental transfers ■ Functional transfers	Simulations ■ Role playing ■ Vestibule training

ing education policy to gain paralegal training (to progress along a non-managerial path) or managerial courses (to prepare to manage the legal division's clerical staff).

Training and Development Methods

Managers conduct training and development in several ways (see Table 22.2), usually while employees are on the job. *On-the-job training* consists mostly of coaching, special assignments, and job rotation. *Coaching* occurs as a supervisor guides a subordinate through the day-to-day activities of a job. The supervisor observes the subordinate at work and provides suggestions for maintaining or improving performance. Employees sometimes get *special assignments,* such as membership in a task force or responsibility for a particular project, so that they can learn or refine skills for their current job or for a future one. A teacher who wants to become an administrator, for example, may accept membership in a task force to devise a community outreach program. *Job rotation* systematically moves a subordinate through a series of relatively brief job assignments to broaden his or her abilities, skills, and knowledge about the organization. For instance, a person hired as a group claims analyst in an insurance company might spend some time processing group life claims, then disability claims, then health claims, so that he or she will better understand the workings of the organization.

Organizations are increasingly turning to *off-the-job training,* including information presentation, information processing, and simulation.[5] In *information presentation,* employees are given information via written material, films, videotapes, lectures, or a computer. For example, students can use computer-assisted review and tutorial modules to assess their mastery of text material. This method has proved to be popular and effective for job training.[6]

To manipulate information—to generate ideas and discussions, for example—rather than merely to learn facts is the goal of *information-processing techniques.* In discussion groups, employees meet with management development trainers, who are likely to supplement the information presented in training manuals and lectures by guiding trainees in experiential exercises; discussing case studies; and helping them complete questionnaires to learn more about themselves, such as what kind of leaders they are. Information-processing techniques are useful for presenting complex material, and they often increase trainees' motivation.

Simulation techniques give trainees a chance to encounter important aspects of a job in a safe environment, where they are free to perform inexpertly or to make mistakes. Airline pilots, for example, can practice landing planes under various weather conditions without risk to life or limb. Physicians can diagnose and treat computer-simulated patients rather than practicing on people. Learners can solve real cases, play roles to be faced on the job, and practice coping with business scenarios that depict real issues.

Performance Appraisal

Performance appraisal is the process of evaluating how effectively employees are fulfilling their job responsibilities and contributing to the accomplishment of organizational goals. It is a task that most managers find very difficult. To appraise performance effectively, a manager must be aware of the specific expectations for a job, monitor employees' behavior and results, compare the observed behavior and results with the expectations, and measure the match between them. In most cases, a manager must also provide feedback to employees, a process that can elicit strong feelings.

Although they may be difficult to conduct, performance appraisals are extremely important to an organization.[7] They tell organizations whether their selection devices are effective. They show where training, development, and motivational programs are needed and later gauge whether these have been effective. In fact, many organizational policies and practices are evaluated, in large part, through their impact on performance. Performance appraisals are the basis on which managers make decisions about compensation, promotion, and dismissal. In short, without good measures of employees' performance, managers find it very difficult to identify and encourage organizational effectiveness.

Appraisal Techniques

Managers have two ways of comparing actual with anticipated performance. They can try to assess an employee's output through *objective methods* based on verifiable physical objects or events. One objective measure of performance used by Producers Color Service's lab in Detroit, for example, is the amount of scrap produced while processing movie film. Sales performance can be measured by how much of a product or service is sold, either in units or in dollars. Objective methods can be useful because numbers are readily understandable and easy to explain.

For most jobs, though, objective measures are neither possible nor completely adequate. For instance, in some jobs, performance—and measurable output—are the combined effort of many workers. How, for example, is a manager to determine who made the steel at a steel mill? In other cases, an objective count says nothing about the quality of performance. An artist's performance is not judged on the number of paintings completed in a year. For these reasons, managers often use *subjective methods* to judge performance instead of, or in addition to, objective measures.

In one subjective approach, the *comparative method,* supervisors compare the perceived performance of each employee with the perceived performance

For some jobs, objective measures say nothing about quality of performance.

FIGURE 22.4 Traditional Rating Scale

Behavior	Unsatisfactory	Questionable	Satisfactory	Outstanding
A. Quantity of work	1	2	3	(4)
B. Quality of work	1	2	(3)	4
C. Work initiative	1	(2)	3	4
D. Efficiency	1	2	(3)	4
E. Overall	1	2	(3)	4

Employee rated: Jean Smith
Rater: Susanne Rowe

of co-workers. In another subjective method, the *absolute standards approach,* managers compare the performance of each employee with a certain standard instead of with the performance of other employees. Figure 22.4 shows a traditional rating scale completed by managers using an absolute standards approach.

Behaviorally anchored rating scales (BARS) have been developed to improve the accuracy and usefulness of absolute standards rating scales.[8] The BARS approach also uses a scale for each relevant dimension of performance, but this scale has behavioral anchors at various points along it. For each performance dimension that is to be evaluated, specific and observable behaviors that reflect various degrees of performance effectiveness are described. A rater chooses the description of the behavior most characteristic of an employee's actual performance (see Figure 22.5).

Managing Appraisal Problems

Performance appraisals that rely on subjective methods are influenced by many of the perceptual problems discussed in Chapter 12. For example, some supervisors base their ratings heavily on first impressions of an employee's performance; others base them primarily on very recent job performance. Some supervisors distort performance ratings because of prejudices against or stereotypes of people of certain race, gender, religion, age, or other characteristics.

How can managers do a better job of appraising performance? Improvements require an integrated set of actions. First, raters should be taught to recognize and avoid perceptual pitfalls. Rating instruments also must be improved and raters trained to use them properly. Then, dimensions of performance and the scales for rating them must be described clearly so that raters understand what they mean. The rating process should involve standardized procedures, and the raters must be motivated to follow them.

Compensation and Benefits

Money can motivate workers to meet goals. Although people join organizations for a variety of reasons, including their desire for interesting challenges, enjoyable interactions with other people, and simply a need to get away from

FIGURE 22.5   *Behaviorally Anchored Rating Scale*

Supervising Sales Personnel

Gives sales personnel a clear idea of their job duties and responsibilities, exercises tact and consideration in working with subordinates, handles work scheduling efficiently and equitably, supplements formal training with his or her own "coaching," keeps informed of what the salespeople are doing on the job, and follows company policy in agreements with subordinates.

Effective	9	Could be expected to conduct full day's sales clinic with two new salespeople and thereby develop them into top salespeople in the department.
	8	Could be expected to give his or her sales personnel confidence and strong sense of responsibility by delegating many important jobs to them.
	7	Could be expected *never* to fail to conduct training meetings with his or her people weekly at a scheduled hour and to convey to them exactly what is expected.
	6	Could be expected to exhibit courtesy and respect toward his or her sales personnel.
	5	Could be expected to remind sales personnel to wait on customers instead of conversing with each other.
	4	Could be expected to be rather critical of store standards in front of his or her own people, thereby risking their developing poor attitudes.
	3	Could be expected to tell an individual to come in anyway even though he or she called in to say he or she was ill.
	2	Could be expected to go back on a promise to an individual whom he or she had told could transfer back into previous department if he or she did not like the new one.
Ineffective	1	Could be expected to make promises to an individual about his or her salary being based on department sales even when he or she knew such a practice was against company policy.

Source: Adapted from J. P. Campbell, M. D. Dunnette, R. D. Arvey, and L. V. Hellervik (1973), The development and evaluation of behaviorally based rating scales, *Journal of Applied Psychology*, 57, 15-22.

home, being paid for their efforts is certainly a major attraction. Organizations pay their members in two ways, through cash compensation and through benefits.

Cash Compensation

Organizations compensate people in cash to attract them, to keep them, to motivate and reward their performance, and to give them feelings of satisfaction. To accomplish these objectives requires the management of pay levels, pay structure, and individual pay.

TABLE 22.3   Sample Pay Structure

Pay Grade	Annual Pay Range		
	Minimum	Midpoint	Maximum
A	10,200	12,000	13,800
B	11,220	13,200	15,180
C	12,580	14,800	17,020
D	14,280	16,800	19,320
E	16,065	18,900	21,735
•			
•			
•			

Pay Level.   **Pay level** is the relationship between an organization's rate of cash compensation and the general level for comparable jobs in the labor market. Appropriate pay level varies with many different factors, such as the supply and demand for workers and the financial health of an organization. Managers may have to offer relatively high pay levels to recruit employees in a tight labor market. In contrast, when labor is plentiful, unemployment is high, and jobs are highly structured and controlled, organizations may be able to offer lower pay levels.

Much of the information managers can use to keep abreast of prevailing pay rates comes from **wage surveys** that contain summarized information on prevailing pay practices collected from organizations within a given labor market. Information about pay levels is also available from such sources as the U.S. Bureau of Labor Statistics, the American Compensation Association, and the American Management Association. In addition, many industry groups collect data relevant to their own industries, as do some organizations and professional associations.

Pay Structure.   Whereas pay level involves the comparison of the amount of cash compensation offered by one organization with that of another, **pay structure** describes the relative values and pay ranges for jobs in one organization. Pay structures specify the minimum, midpoint, and maximum pay levels for each organizational job or group of jobs (also called *pay grades*). Table 22.3 contains part of the pay structure from a hospital's legal department (the legal clerk III job shown in Figure 22.2 is a C pay grade).

Managers develop and price pay structures by combining the results of wage surveys and their organization's human resource goals with the information provided by job evaluation. **Job evaluation** is the process of determining the overall value of a specific job relative to the value of other jobs in the pay structure. Generally, managers evaluate a job based on the results provided by job analysis and the resulting job description. They compare the content of a specific job with standards (sometimes called *compensable factors*) that indicate the value of the job based on its importance to the organization.

Of all the procedures used to conduct job evaluations, the point method is the one most widely used. The **point method** identifies a group of compensable factors, which typically parallel the factors in job analyses, and assigns

TABLE 22.4 The Point Method of Job Evaluation

Job	Compensable Factor				
	Skill	Effort	Responsibility	Job Conditions	Total Points
File clerk	50	45	60	50	205
Receptionist	70	60	70	45	245
Medical secretary	85	75	85	60	305
Lab technician	100	80	95	55	330

points to each job according to the level of responsibility for each factor. A rater then adds the points and arrives at a total for each job. Table 22.4 provides an example of the point method of job evaluation. Note how each job is rated in each of four areas to arrive at an overall point value for it. The total number of points indicates the relative overall value (responsibility level) of the evaluated job.

Once jobs have been evaluated, human resource managers usually group jobs containing approximately the same number of points into grades. The legal clerk III job, for example, was grouped with such jobs as secretary II and placed in job grade C. Human resource managers then check the pay surveys for each grade and set midpoints for pay ranges for each job grade based on the organization's decision to lead, trail, or match market pay levels. Finally, they assign minimum and maximum levels of pay within each range. It was through this process that a pay range of $12,580 to $17,020 was determined for the legal clerk III job shown in Figure 22.2. Managers usually adjust pay structures annually to take into account changes in market compensation and in the job's requirements.

Individual Pay. Once pay ranges are established for jobs, how does a manager determine what to pay an individual? Decisions about **individual pay** usually are based on a combination of an employee's *qualifications* (prior work experience), *seniority* (the length of time he or she has worked), and *merit* (actual performance on the job). As you learned in Chapter 13 and other chapters in this book, pay based on performance can motivate workers to perform effectively.

For jobs in which it is possible to measure performance objectively, **incentive** systems are sometimes used. With a piece rate plan, for example, employees are paid a certain amount for each unit of work they produce. Some organizations have production bonuses that pay "extra" when a worker produces more than a standard amount in a given time period. For instance, commission plans for salespeople provide compensation based on the amount of product or service they sell.

Benefits

Many employees get benefits (noncash compensation) as well as cash compensation from their organizations. Benefits can include almost anything from medical insurance to retirement plans and vacations to college tuition for

Day-care benefits are becoming increasingly popular.

workers' children. The U.S. Chamber of Commerce Research Association annually estimates the cost of benefits to American organizations. Twenty years ago, organizations spent an amount equal to about 30 percent of cash compensation on benefits for employees. Currently the figure is closer to 40 percent.

What do organizations hope to receive in exchange for the billions of dollars they spend on benefits? Some organizations have a simple paternalistic motivation: they want to protect and provide for their employees. For example, they offer health care and life insurance policies. Most organizations, however, view benefit costs as a business investment. They expect benefits to help them attract qualified job candidates and persuade them to accept and keep positions.

Types of Benefits. Organizations offer an extremely wide range of benefits. Some common benefits that many employees have come to think of as standard include:

- *Time not worked*—pay for "time off," such as coffee breaks, holidays, and vacations
- *Insurance*—primarily coverage for disability, medical care, and death
- *Retirement*—private plans, such as savings, thrift, and stock options, offered in addition to the percentage of cash compensation that most organizations must contribute to Social Security
- *Income maintenance*—insurance and other policies that continue an employee's income in case of unemployment or disability

Other forms of benefits are not yet so firmly established. Fitness and wellness programs, such as memberships in health clubs or on-site exercise facilities, have become extremely popular. Some employees want day-care benefits for their children. An increasing number of organizations are setting up "employee assistance programs" to provide counseling and treatment, such as self-improvement seminars, stress-management programs, and financial and tax planning.

Flexible Benefits. During the past ten years, more and more organizations have begun to offer flexible benefit plans that allow employees to choose a combination of benefits that meets their personal needs. These plans are often called **cafeteria plans,** because employees choose benefits much as they would choose a meal in a cafeteria line. Every benefit is priced, and employees are told how much money their organization will give them to spend. Employees can spend their allotment however they please, choosing day care over dental coverage, life insurance protection for dependents over increased health policies, and so on.

Labor-Management Relations

Labor unions developed to protect employees from undesirable management practices. Traditionally, unions have concentrated on improving health and safety conditions at work, controlling the hours employees could be asked to work, protecting job security, and improving pay.

Union Formation

Research indicates that employees vote to join a union when they are dissatisfied with their own ability to meet their economic and noneconomic goals at work.[9] For example, they may feel that their working conditions are unsafe or that their pay levels are exploitive. The National Labor Relations Board (NLRB) has established rules that union organizers must follow when trying to start a union for a group of employees. Organizers begin by encouraging employees to sign *authorization cards* stating that they wish to be represented by a union. When a sufficient number of cards has been signed (usually 30 percent of the employee group), the NLRB identifies a *bargaining unit* (the employees to be covered if the union prevails) and conducts a *representation election.* If a majority of employees voted to establish a union, the NLRB certifies it to act as the employees' representative. If not, at least one year must pass before another representation election can be held.

Collective Bargaining

Winning a representation election gives a union the right to require an organization to negotiate a *union contract,* which is an agreement between labor and management that covers wages, working hours, and the terms and conditions of work. The negotiation process between management and labor in which both parties try to agree on the terms of the contract is called *collective bargaining.* Table 22.5 on page 522 contains a wide range of collective bargaining items and shows the broad impact that a union can have on the human resource function.

If the two sides cannot reach an agreement, an *impasse* is said to exist. If requested, the Federal Mediation and Conciliation Service will provide an impartial third party, known as a **mediator,** to work with the bargainers to identify a mutually acceptable agreement. If the parties do not request a mediator, or if the mediator cannot get them to agree, one or both parties may take more forceful actions to encourage the other side to agree to their terms.

A primary tool of a union is a **strike.** If a contract has expired, employees can legally refuse to return to work until an agreement is reached, an arrangement known as an *economic strike.* Sometimes a union calls an *unfair labor practice strike* to try to force an employer to conform to agreed-upon terms. A *wildcat strike,* although unauthorized and illegal, is sometimes conducted by union members in violation of an existing contract.

Organizations also can take actions. Under certain circumstances, for example, they can conduct a **lockout** by closing down operations and refusing to offer work to union members until an agreement is reached. Sometimes an organization hires nonunion members, called **scabs,** to work in place of striking union members. These actions, although legal, usually generate bitter reactions from union members.

Grievance Activities

A union contract specifies the agreed-upon conditions of employment. If a union member feels that part of a contract has been violated, he or she may file a **grievance,** which describes the alleged violation. An employee designated

TABLE 22.5 *Items Mandatory for Bargaining*

Wages	Stock-purchase plan	Partial plant closing
Hours	Workloads	Hunting on employer forest preserve
Discharge	Change of employee status to	where previously granted
Arbitration	independent contractors	Plant closedown and relocation
Holidays—paid	Motor carrier—union agreement	Change in operations resulting in
Vacations—paid	providing that carriers use own	reclassifying workers from
Duration of agreement	equipment before leasing	incentive to straight time, or cut
Grievance procedure	outside equipment	workforce, or installation of
Layoff plan	Overtime pay	cost-saving machine
Reinstatement of economic strikers	Agency shop	Plant closing
Change of payment from hourly	Sick leave	Job-posting procedures
base to salary base	Employers' insistence on clause	Plant reopening
Union security and checkoff	giving arbitrator right to enforce	Employee physical examination
Work rules	award	Union security
Merit-wage increase	Management-rights clause	Bargaining over "bar list"
Work schedule	Cancellation of seniority on	Truck rentals—minimum rental to
Lunch periods	relocation of plant	be paid by carriers to
Rest periods	Discounts on company products	employee-owned vehicles
Pension plan	Shift differentials	Musician price lists
Retirement age	Contract clause providing for	Arrangement for negotiation
Bonus payments	supervisors' keeping seniority in	Change in insurance carrier and
Price of meals provided by	unit	benefits
company	Procedures for income tax	Profit-sharing plan
Group insurance—health,	withholding	Company houses
accident, life	Severance pay	Subcontracting
Promotions	Nondiscriminatory hiring hall	Discriminatory racial policies
Seniority	Plant rules	Production ceiling imposed by
Layoffs	Safety	union
Transfers	Prohibition against supervisor	Most-favored-nation clause
Work assignments and transfers	doing unit work	Vended food products
No-strike clause	Superseniority for union stewards	
Piece rates	Checkoff	

Source: R. Richardson (1979), Positive collective bargaining, *ASPA handbook of personnel and industrial relations*, D. Yoder and H. G. Heneman, Jr., eds, Washington, DC: Bureau of National Affairs, 7-120–7-121.

to represent the union members, known as a **steward,** attempts to resolve the grievance by meeting with the complaining employee's supervisor. If this does not lead to satisfaction, higher-level representatives of the union and the organization typically meet to develop a solution. Finally, if the employee does not feel that the issue has been resolved, the grievance can be submitted to an outside third party, called an **arbitrator.** This step, called **binding arbitration,** is the last available remedy. Both parties are obligated to accept the arbitrator's findings.

Public-Sector Considerations

In the public sector, conditions are somewhat different. In most states, for example, it is illegal for public employees to strike, a fact that clearly can limit union power. Instead of allowing strikes, many states require binding arbitration or fact finding, which is when a neutral party, after studying the dispute, issues a public recommendation of a reasonable settlement with the intent of facilitating—not pressuring—a settlement. States that do not require binding arbitration must rely on voluntary arbitration. One disadvantage to these methods is that they are slow. Employees sometimes must work for long periods of time without a contract, and mountains of paperwork build until the delayed contract is finally signed. The obvious advantage of and prevailing rationale for these methods is that agreements can be reached without work stoppages, and, as the argument goes, public-sector employees—such as police, fire-fighters, and teachers—are so important to the social welfare that they must not strike.

Human Resource Management in Review

The purpose of the human resource function is to match the abilities and motivation of individuals with the requirements and rewards of jobs. If done well, the human resource objectives of attraction, performance, retention, attendance, and satisfaction will be met. To meet these objectives, human resource managers must, among other things, pay attention to the economic, labor market, legal, and union factors in the external environment.

The task at the core of human resource management activities is job analysis, which uses direct observation and structured questionnaires to gather information and to document the responsibilities and associated requirements of jobs within organizations. All other human resource activities—staffing, training and development, performance appraisals, motivation and reward programs, and labor-management relations—are built on the foundation that job analysis provides.

Staffing is the human resource activity that locates, selects, and prepares career paths for organization members (including separating them from the organization when necessary). Human resource managers are also responsible for training and developing the people hired and then appraising their performance on the job, usually through a combination of objective and subjective methods. Organization members expect to receive something for their efforts, and it is part of the human resource function to determine what that compensation ought to be. Usually it takes the form of cash and benefits, with managers and human resource managers working together to determine specific pay levels.

If workers belong to a union, managers do not have total discretion over the working conditions and amount of pay they can offer. Contracts specify these and other terms of employment. If the two sides cannot agree on a contract, an outside party may be brought in to help them reach agreement. In extreme cases of disagreement, union members who work for private-sector (and, in some states, public-sector) organizations may go on strike. The organization may retaliate by hiring nonunion workers or by locking employees out of the workplace. In the public sector, laws usually govern the settlement of management-labor disputes and prevent strikes by public employees.

Issues for Review and Discussion

1. What are the major goals of the human resource function?
2. Identify the major factors of the external environment and explain how they influence the effectiveness of the human resource function.
3. What are the primary reasons for conducting job analyses?

4. Describe the most important goals and functions of the following activities: external recruiting, internal recruiting, selection, career development, separation.

5. How can an organization identify its training and development needs?

6. Discuss why the performance appraisal and feedback process is troublesome to many managers.

7. Briefly describe how a labor union is formed and how its existence changes the nature of the human resource function.

Key Terms

human resource management
labor market
job
job analysis
job description
staffing
external recruiting
internal recruiting
selection
selection device
training
development
performance appraisal
pay level
wage surveys

pay structure
job evaluation
point method
individual pay
incentive
cafeteria plans
mediator
strike
lockout
scabs
grievance
steward
arbitrator
binding arbitration

Suggested Readings

Brett, J. M. (1980). Why workers want unions. *Organizational Dynamics,* 8(4), 47-59.

Cascio, W. F. (1987). *Costing human resources: The financial impact of behavior in organizations.* Boston: PSW-Kent.

Kravetz, D. J. (1988). *The human resources revolution: Implementing progressive management practices for bottom-line success.* San Francisco: Jossey-Bass.

Latham, G. P. (1988). Human resource training and development. *Annual Review of Psychology,* 39, 545-82.

Shepard, I. M., and Duston, R. L. (1987). *Workplace privacy: Employee testing, surveillance, wrongful discharge, and other areas of vulnerability.* Washington, DC: BNA.

Zimmerman, J. H. (April 1986). Human resource management at MCI. *Management Review,* 49-51.

Notes

1. Fired employees turn the reason for dismissal into a legal weapon (2 October 1986), *The Wall Street Journal,* 31; It's getting harder to pass out pink slips (28 March 1988), *Business Week,* 68; I. M. Shepard and R. L. Duston (1987), *Workplace privacy: Employee testing, surveillance, wrongful discharge, and other areas of vulnerability,* Washington, DC: BNA.

2. Information on job analysis techniques can be found in the following sources: U.S. Department of Labor, Manpower Administration (1972), *Handbook for analyzing jobs,* Washington, DC: U.S. Government Printing Office; S. E. Bemis, A. H. Belenky, and D. A. Soder (1983), *Job analysis,* Washington, DC: Bureau of National Affairs; E. L. Levine (1983), *Everything you always wanted to know about job analysis,* Tampa, FL: Mariner.

3. E. J. McCormick, P. R. Jeanneret, and R. C. Mecham (1972), A study of job characteristics and job dimensions as based on the position analysis questionnaire (PAQ), *Journal of Applied Psychology,* 56, 347-68; W. W. Tornow and P. R. Pinto (1976), The development of a managerial job taxonomy: A system for describing, classifying, and evaluating executive positions, *Journal of Applied Psychology,* 61, 410-18; J. L. Mitchell and E. J. McCormick (1979), *Development of the PMPQ: A structured job analysis questionnaire for the study of professional and managerial positions,* West Lafayette, IN: Department of Psychological Sciences, Purdue University.

4. C. M. Koen, Jr. (1984), Applications forms: Keep them easy and legal, *Personnel Journal,* 63(5), 26-29.

5. H. G. Heneman III, D. P. Schwab, J. A. Fossum, and L. D. Dyer (1989), *Personnel/human resource management,* 4th ed., Homewood, IL: Irwin, 432-37.

6. K. W. Wexley (1984), Personnel training, *Annual Review of Psychology,* 35, 519-51.

7. Bureau of National Affairs (1983), Performance appraisal programs, *Personnel Policies Forum,* 135.

8. P. C. Smith and L. M. Kendall (1963), Retranslation of expectations: An approach to the construction of unambiguous anchors for rating scales, *Journal of Applied Psychology,* 47, 249-55; J. P. Campbell, M. D. Dunnette, R. D. Arvey, and L. V. Hellervik (1973), The development and evaluation of behaviorally based rating scales, *Journal of Applied Psychology,* 57, 15-22.

9. W. C. Hamner and F. J. Smith (1978), Work attitudes as predictors of unionization activity, *Journal of Applied Psychology,* 63, 415-521; J. M. Brett (1980), Why workers want unions, *Organizational Dynamics,* 8(4), 47-59.

The River City Library

By William Ross, University of Wisconsin at La Crosse

John Switzer, the head of the River City Citizens' Library Board (CLB), had a problem. His board was charged with evaluating the performance of the library director, who was responsible for the daily affairs of the library. The board had just finished the director's performance evaluation for the previous year, and the entire process left John dissatisfied, although he could not put his finger on the problem.

John called the River City personnel office to see if they would develop a new performance evaluation form for the position of library director. The personnel director explained that her employees were unable to accept new projects at that time and recommended that he hire a consultant. After several phone calls, John obtained the necessary authorization from the proper city officials and arranged a meeting with Fred Sawyer, a private consultant.

Meeting with the Consultant

At the meeting, John explained that the CLB was supposed to supervise the library director, and that he had misgivings about using the existing performance appraisal system.

Fred: So, you'd like my firm to design a new performance appraisal system the board can use to evaluate the library director?

John: Right. I called you because nobody on the board knows how to tackle this situation, and the people at the city personnel office have their hands full with other things.

Fred: How often do you get a chance to observe the library director at work?

John: That's the problem. No one on the board has any formal education in library matters; we all have other jobs. What we know about the library, we've learned from serving on the board. Unless we're also on special committees, we only see the library director at monthly meetings, so we really don't see him at work. He just reports to us.

Fred: Do you have a copy of a job description that I could have?

John: Yes, a job analysis was conducted about a year ago by the city personnel department. Here's the job description they created. [See Figure 22A on page 528.]

Fred: What type of performance appraisal have you been using?

John: It's one we borrowed from another library. [See Figure 22B.] We set up a three-member CLB personnel committee. Each member did ratings individually and then discussed them jointly. Then, they made a final rating based on the average of the three.

Fred: What happened to the average ratings made last year?

John: We sent one copy to the library director. A second copy went into his personnel file at city hall. The third copy went to me. I could go before the city and use the ratings to argue for a raise or bonus for the library director if the ratings were high or no raise at all if he received low ratings. Let me emphasize that, while there are problems with the library, we feel that the director is doing an effective job, so there is no hidden agenda. This is not an attempt to replace the library director by changing the rules. We just aren't sure that the present system is adequate. If it is, that's fine. If you know of something better, then we'd like to hear about it.

Fred: OK, I'll see what I can do. I'll need to talk to the other board members and to the library director. I may also ask you for other information later. Otherwise, I'll get back to you in about three weeks.

Organizational Problems

Fred reviewed the job description John gave him and interviewed several city officials, including the library director. Fred discovered a growing list of organizational problems. The relationship between the library and other city agencies was deteriorating. Library staff members refused to cooperate with other departments' requests, and sometimes even disregarded their own director's orders. Complaints were mounting and there was talk of the library employees' unionizing. One person in another city agency even said that "things at the library are out of control."

The library had recently undergone a number of changes. Chief among these was that the library had been a private, nonprofit organization until the city assumed responsibility for it two years before. New facilities were built, the collection was enlarged, and a museum was added. More staff members were hired, doubling the number of library employees in a short time. An extremely well-liked head librarian retired after many years of service, and the city then established higher qualifications for a more professional library director. For the first time, the library was required to use citywide personnel procedures and to follow city personnel rules.

The mayor appointed local residents to a nine-member CLB to set policy, to approve major projects, and to provide general supervision to the library director. John met with the mayor every six months to brief him on library projects and to explain anticipated future library needs. The CLB also supplied the mayor's office with an annual report, which included the library director's performance appraisal. While the library director reported to the CLB, the position was made equal in status with other city department heads (for example, the police chief and the director of public works) and the director represented the library at bi-weekly executive council meetings called by the mayor.

The city provided about 80 percent of the library's annual operating budget of $1.2 million. A private trust fund had been established for capital improvements. Under the terms of the trust, the trustees, who were separate from the library board, were required to spend all of the interest from the trust, about $300,000 annually, but were prohibited from spending any of the principal. Among city officials, only the library director had any regular contact with these trustees.

Recent Developments

River City CLB members were not experts in organizational change. Most were owners of small businesses, a few were attorneys, two were homemakers, and one was an elementary-school principal. They assumed that after an initial period of transition after the changes, relations with the library staff would improve; however, the situation continued to deteriorate. One female employee filed a complaint with the state Equal Employment Opportunity Commission, charging the library with sex discrimination by hiring a male library director rather than promoting the female head librarian. The library director reported increased bickering between the new staff members and older library employees, and, on a recent visit to the library, Fred overheard one staff member refer to the director as "the city's man."

The relationship between the library and other city agencies also worsened. For example, one agency head argued that the library budget should be cut because it received funding from the private trust. Fred reviewed the facts that he had uncovered during his inquiry. He realized that the problems facing the CLB went far beyond an inadequate performance appraisal system. He wondered whether he should try to address these other problems, and if so, how he should begin.

Questions

1. Is the job description for the library director's position adequate? Explain.

2. Are the performance appraisal form and procedures adequate? Why or why not?

3. The consultant believed that a poor relationship existed between the library staff and the city. What caused this? What can be done?

4. If you were the consultant, what recommendations would you make to the Citizens' Library Board?

A. RESPONSIBILITIES

Listed below is a brief description of the library director's duties for each of several dimensions. In each instance it is suggestive, not inclusive, of the director's duties in that area.

Dimension I. Managing the Library Staff

1. Develops and implements equitable personnel policies
2. Motivates the staff to achieve high goals and evaluates their performance as appropriate
3. Contributes to employee job satisfaction, low absenteeism, and a low grievance rate and handles grievances that do occur in a proper and timely fashion
4. Contributes to staff selection, training, and development
5. Sees that staff organization and use are efficient
6. Ensures that physical facilities are maintained by proper personnel

Dimension II. Planning, Implementing, and Maintaining Projects

1. Establishes priorities
2. Works with the Library Board to establish long- and short-range plans
3. Presents well-developed ideas clearly and concisely to the Board
4. Provides the Board with sufficient information for planning and monitoring projects
5. Is willing to make the difficult decisions that are necessary to fully implement Library Board policies
6. Establishes guidelines and actively sees that projects stay within those guidelines

Dimension III. Coordinating Work with Other Agencies

1. Sees that library policies and procedures are consistent with those of the city
2. Coordinates plans with appropriate city agencies
3. Gives presentations to and/or attends relevant governmental committee meetings
4. Coordinates City Library work with that of the county and of the regional library system as necessary
5. Actively works to maintain harmony between the library and other city agencies
6. Sees that physical facilities are maintained and repaired by the appropriate city agencies

Dimension IV. Budgeting

1. Adequately researches budget proposals
2. Sees that budget proposals are explained clearly to the Library Board
3. Sees that budget covers necessary expenses
4. Ensures that adequate funds are requested for unanticipated contingencies
5. Proposes budget to the city in a clear, concise, and effective manner
6. Maintains the library's share of the overall city budget
7. Effectively communicates special library needs before the Washington Board (the private fund trustees)

Dimension V. Professional Activities

1. Actively participates in state library system activities
2. Is active in the regional library system
3. Is involved in professional organizations
4. Does not allow professional activities to unduly interfere with the administration of the library
5. Keeps abreast of current laws and procedures affecting library administration
6. Maintains high ethical standards

Dimension VI. Customer Service

1. Communicates services to the public
2. Solicits public input to better identify and meet customer needs in developing the library collection
3. Is visible to the community
4. Seeks to increase circulation rate in all areas of library service
5. Promotes the Friends of the Library organization

B. QUALIFICATIONS

Essential Knowledge and Abilities

1. Advanced administrative ability
2. Knowledge of local, state, and library law
3. Ability to communicate effectively with people from diverse backgrounds
4. Ability to speak effectively in public
5. Extensive knowledge of modern library organization, procedures, policy, aims, and service
6. Considerable knowledge of current and world literature and a diverse liberal arts background
7. Ability to plan, motivate, direct, and coordinate the work of others

Training and Experience

1. Masters of Library Science from an accredited library school
2. Five years' progressively responsible public library experience
3. Eligibility for Grade I state library certificate
4. Administrative or supervisory experiences

Library Director _____   Date _____

Board President _____

Directions: Circle the response that *best* reflects the consensus of the Board with regard to each of the following
items.

Library Director	Always true	True most of the time	True about half of the time	Seldom true	Never true	Not enough information to rate	Board Comments (Required for a rating of 1 or 2)
1. Presents proposals to the Board in a clear and concise manner	5	4	3	2	1	0	
2. Provides Board with sufficient information that members can make intelligent decisions	5	4	3	2	1	0	
3. Effectively plans projects	5	4	3	2	1	0	
4. Anticipates crises and takes appropriate preventive action	5	4	3	2	1	0	
5. Delegates work to subordinates	5	4	3	2	1	0	
6. Meets deadlines	5	4	3	2	1	0	
7. Effectively identifies budgetary needs and keeps expenses within the budget	5	4	3	2	1	0	
8. Maintains harmonious working relationships with other government agencies	5	4	3	2	1	0	
9. Effectively manages library staff	5	4	3	2	1	0	
10. Performs all duties conscientiously	5	4	3	2	1	0	

Overall Performance Rating   (Outstanding) 5   4   3   2   1   0 (Unsatisfactory)

Acknowledgment of Receipt and Discussion   _____
                                                                        Library Director

529

23 Entrepreneurship and Intrapreneurship

Student Learning Objectives

After reading this chapter, you should be able to:

1. Define and discuss entrepreneurship and intrapreneurship.

2. Describe typical personal characteristics and experiences of entrepreneurs and intrapreneurs.

3. Describe the types of behaviors common among entrepreneurs and intrapreneurs.

4. Describe the key phases of the intrapreneurial process.

5. Discuss the methods of facilitating and supporting intrapreneurship.

6. Describe and discuss the three major strategies available to entrepreneurs and intrapreneurs.

_I_n the 1960s, actress Barbara Walden landed a minor role in the Paul Newman movie _What a Way to Go._ Anxious to see herself on the big screen, Barbara rushed to a movie theater when the film was released. What she saw was an attractive black woman who looked purple on screen because the makeup she used was formulated to enhance the appearance of white women. When her search for cosmetics better suited to black women failed to identify existing products, she decided to create her own. Beginning with a hair-styling lotion and expanding to a full line of personal care products, Barbara Walden Cosmetics now captures over $5 million in annual sales through national department store chains.[1]

Chuck House, an engineer at corporate giant Hewlett-Packard, worked on a project intended to develop a new cathode ray display for use by air traffic controllers. When the display failed to meet specifications, Hewlett-Packard management wanted to cut their losses and drop the project altogether. Chuck persevered, however, arguing that the display held promise for other markets. Working mostly on his own, he identified potential market applications and customers. The result was success in three separate markets. Chuck had turned one failure into three successes.[2]

Both Barbara Walden and Chuck House are innovators. Each identified a need, developed products to satisfy the need, and made their products succeed in the marketplace through personal effort and perseverance. Barbara, who accomplished this on her own, is known as an _entrepreneur._ Chuck, who innovated within an existing organization, is known as an _intrapreneur._ This chapter explores the nature and importance of entrepreneurial and intrapreneurial activities and examines the factors that contribute to their success.

Entrepreneurship

Loren, Sharon, and Arlene Krok, the founders of EPI Products, embody the entrepreneurial spirit. They have identified the needs of the marketplace and developed innovative products to satisfy those needs.

Entrepreneurship is the development of a product or service idea and the creation of an organization to further its growth.[3] One attribute often used when discussing entrepreneurship is _innovative._ In fact, Peter Drucker, who wrote the stimulating book _Innovation and Entrepreneurship,_ argues that the creation of an organization should not be considered entrepreneurial unless the new organization is also innovative.[4] Others, such as William Gartner of Georgetown University, acknowledge that many of the most interesting entrepreneurial ventures are indeed innovative, but they do not believe that innovation is required for entrepreneurship to take place. What entrepreneurship does require, of course, is a person whose ideas and energy make it happen. The first part of this chapter is concerned with what entrepreneurs are like and what they do.*

The Entrepreneurial "Type"

Jeff Lemieux was fourteen years old when he received a $30 box of baseball cards, which he built into a $10,000 collection and thriving business one year

---

* More research has been conducted on the characteristics of entrepreneurs than on those of intrapreneurs. It appears, however, that the vast majority of the characteristics of entrepreneurs also apply to intrapreneurs. Many of the examples in this section are of intrapreneurs.

TABLE 23.1 *Personal Characteristics of Successful Entrepreneurs*

High need for achievement	High self-confidence
Low fear of failure	Optimism
Low need for power	Determination
Strong internal locus of control	High energy level
High tolerance for ambiguity	Strong individualism

later. Orville Redenbacher was sixty-four when he first marketed his gourmet popcorn. Barbara Walden is a black female. Dr. An Wang, founder of Wang Laboratories, is an oriental male. Obviously, there is no easy way to spot an entrepreneur at first glance. Nonetheless, many successful entrepreneurs share somewhat similar characteristics. Although it is sometimes difficult to separate personality from the behaviors that result, the next two sections briefly explore some of the things that entrepreneurs often have in common.[5]

Personal Characteristics. One way to describe entrepreneurs is on the basis of their personal characteristics (see Table 23.1). Entrepreneurs, for example, tend to have a high need for achievement (review Chapter 13) and perhaps gravitate toward entrepreneurial situations because they offer a chance to compete against a standard of excellence. Success (and, therefore, satisfaction of the need) depends on the effectiveness of the individual entrepreneur. For instance, it took Frances Lear two and one half years to get *Lears,* her magazine for women over the age of forty, onto national newsstands. With a current circulation exceeding that of *Harper's Bazaar,* Frances describes her success as "a sock in the ego."[6] Perhaps a strong need for achievement encourages certain individuals to select entrepreneurial situations they think provide a greater opportunity for personal achievement than would most opportunities elsewhere. Once a person with entrepreneurial leanings is in the situation, the challenge to succeed becomes a powerful motivator.

A high need for achievement is particularly powerful when coupled with a low fear of failure. Put quite simply, many entrepreneurs love to achieve but are not afraid to fail. They recognize that success requires some risks and are not devastated by periodic failure. Some people, in fact, make their initial forays into entrepreneurship only after a failure. Consider, for example, Louis Centofanti, former Carter administration official, who developed a revolutionary way to clean up PCBs after being fired by the Reagan administration in 1981.[7] By the late 1980s, Louis had turned his invention into USPCI, the fifth largest hazardous waste company in the United States.

Many people assume that the search for power is important to entrepreneurs. Often, however, the most successful entrepreneurs actually have a low need for personal power. It appears that power is important only to the extent that it facilitates successful goal attainment, rather than being an end in itself. For example, Bill Gates, cofounder of Microsoft, hired professional managers to help run the growing computer software company (sales for 1988 were $590.8 million) because he "learned at a young age that you've got to give up power to get power."[8]

Successful entrepreneurs also tend to have a strong internal locus of control (review Chapter 12). In other words, they believe that their accomplishments

TABLE 23.2 *Personal Experiences Before Becoming Entrepreneurs*

Difficulty working for someone else
Challenging educational experiences
An early experience running an organization

result primarily from their own capabilities and efforts. Failures are attributed to a lack of ability or adequate effort or both. Particularly when combined with a high need for achievement, an internal locus of control can produce powerful effects. People possessing this combination of characteristics value achievement but believe it cannot be obtained without personal effort. One example can be found in Kenneth Olsen, founder of Digital Equipment Corporation. After more than thirty years at the helm of the giant company, Ken still "draws strength from nuts and bolts. He can spend hours sweating the homely, low-tech details of DEC's computers—making sure, for example, that the plugs and connectors on the backs of DEC machines are neatly laid out."[9]

Tolerance for ambiguity is another quality characterizing many successful entrepreneurs. They are able to cope with the tremendous amount of uncertainty typically present in entrepreneurial situations. In fact, although those with low tolerance for ambiguity might be threatened and frustrated by this amount of uncertainty, many entrepreneurs actually find it stimulating and challenging. For example, Scott McNealy, the thirty-three-year-old cofounder of Sun Microsystems, relishes situations that depend on courage and intuition. Scott attributes one of Sun's most recent successes—a new microprocessor licensed to AT&T, Xerox, and Unisys—to an abrupt strategy change based on "90% assumption and 10% fact."[10]

Other characteristics sometimes attributed to entrepreneurs include self-confidence, optimism, determination, a high energy level, and a strong sense of individualism.

Personal Experience. Certain experiences apparently are common among potential entrepreneurs (see Table 23.2). Some argue that these life experiences may contribute to the development of an interest in entrepreneuring and to the nurturing of the abilities to do so effectively.[11]

One common early experience is that entrepreneurs-to-be encounter *difficulty working for someone else.* People with the personality profiles just discussed would naturally want to avoid situations in which someone else controlled their ability to succeed and/or treated failure as something to shun at all costs.

Many entrepreneurs mention *challenging educational experiences* as instrumental in their journey toward entrepreneurship, even though some insist that their real education did not begin until after graduation. To an extent, these educational experiences simply provide students with early opportunities to be an entrepreneur by allowing them to solve difficult or challenging class problems. In 1947, for example, MIT student Ken Olsen worked with other students as part of the research team that developed the Institute's first computer.

Other life experiences that have turned up as entrepreneurial antecedents include running an organization early in life (usually before the age of thirty), being the first-born child, and having a supportive spouse.

Scott McNealy, cofounder of Sun Microsystems, relishes situations that call for courage and intuition. Hardworking McNealy has led his company through the troubled computer market.

TABLE 23.3   *Typical Entrepreneurial Behaviors*

Goal-oriented behavior	Moderate risk taking
Commitment to goals	Acceptance of responsibility
Perseverance	Innovative behavior
Problem-solving behavior	

Entrepreneurial Behaviors

Not only do entrepreneurs have different personal characteristics and experiences, but they also engage in different behaviors than do nonentrepreneurs. Some typical entrepreneurial behaviors appear in Table 23.3. Many of the behaviors shown in this table might be expected, given the characteristics of entrepreneurs discussed earlier. It is not surprising, for example, that entrepreneurs set specific goals for themselves and their organizations, become committed to these goals, and persevere until succeeding or recognizing that success cannot be obtained. If failure does result, an entrepreneur is typically willing to accept responsibility for it. For example, Jerry Chazen, cofounder of Liz Claiborne Inc., blames himself for the failure of the company's high-hemlined dresses in 1987, saying, "I should have known better. . . . It was the biggest boo-boo that I know of in my 35 years in the business."[12]

Entrepreneurs spend much of their time engaged in problem-solving behaviors. This is consistent with a high self-confidence that lies in the belief that solutions can be found if sought hard enough. Maybe it is an entrepreneur's high tolerance for ambiguity that allows him or her to wallow in uncertainty while searching for solutions. Solutions that emerge are often innovative, due, perhaps, to the entrepreneur's willingness to try new ideas in the face of failure, coupled with the desire to demonstrate strong individualism.

Intrapreneurship

As you will recall from the example of Hewlett-Packard engineer Chuck House, not every person who identifies a need, develops products to satisfy the need, and makes the products succeed in the marketplace through personal effort and perseverance is an entrepreneur. **Intrapreneurship** takes place when individuals who identify the need for often innovative change in an organization create the environment in which the change can succeed and champion the implementation of the change.[13] Rather than creating a new organization in which to develop an idea, as entrepreneurs do, intrapreneurs create a new climate within their existing organization to further the idea's growth.

Given that intrapreneurs typically have most of the characteristics and behaviors of entrepreneurs, why would a person choose to develop his or her ideas within someone else's organization rather than starting a new one? According to Gifford Pinchot, it may be very difficult under certain circumstances "to develop the new business independently of the corporation. This is true whenever the new venture (or intraprise) requires access to proprietary technology, the firm's marketing system (e.g., company name, distribution channels), production facilities, financial resources, or managerial ca-

TABLE 23.4 *Intrapreneurial Phases*

Phase 1:	The Solo Phase
Phase 2:	The Network Phase
Phase 3:	The Bootlegging Phase
Phase 4:	The Formal Team Phase

pabilities."[14] Given a potential strong need for achievement, the choice to become an intrapreneur rather than to start from scratch might depend on one's perceptions of whether the organization can help improve his or her chances of success.

The Intrapreneurial Process

The intrapreneurial process involves both creative and analytical activities. Together, these activities create the new ideas and develop what has been called the "intraprise" necessary for their successful implementation. Table 23.4 presents the four phases of intrapreneuring. Managers should encourage workers through all four phases to promote the emergence and success of entrepreneurial activity. In practice, this often means stimulating a willingness for risk taking and change in the organization.

Phase 1: The Solo Phase. In this stage of the process, intrapreneurs typically work alone. First, they must identify the intrapreneurial idea. Next, they begin to develop the idea and submit it to three feasibility tests:

1. Will the idea provide a clearly identifiable benefit for customers or clients?
2. Is the idea compatible with the organization's resources and overall strategy?
3. Are the idea and its potential implementation compatible with the intrapreneur's personal character and skills?

If the idea passes these tests, the next phase begins.

In the solo phase, an intrapreneur typically works alone to determine if an idea will clearly benefit customers and if it is compatible with the organization's resources and overall strategy.

Phase 2: The Network Phase. In this stage, intrapreneurs share the idea with other members of the organization. Seeking feedback on the idea's merits, intrapreneurs elicit suggestions on how to capitalize on existing strengths and ask members to identify the idea's potential weaknesses.

Phase 3: The Bootlegging Phase. In this stage of the process, intrapreneurs start to build an informal team that will pursue the idea. Typically, this group maintains independence by remaining informal and, often, by operating outside of the (physical and psychological) walls of the organization. The purpose of this phase is to refine the idea before its formal presentation to the rest of the organization.

Phase 4: The Formal Team Phase. At this phase, the intraprise becomes a visible organizational entity, usually subjected to the organization's "normal" policies and practices for the first time. Prior to this phase, the idea was primarily a concept. It now begins to harden into reality.

Formal sponsors ensure that intrapreneurs are provided with needed funds, that their work is accepted politically, and that they are free to think and create.

Developing a Supportive Environment

How can organizations enjoy the benefits of entrepreneurship when a major characteristic of entrepreneurs is that they do not want to work for someone else? The answer lies in convincing workers to become intrapreneurs; however, intrapreneurs-to-be are often frustrated by the restrictions of freedom typically imposed in larger organizations. Existing organizational structures frequently are designed for stability rather than for change. Organizations seeking to capitalize on the potential benefits of intrapreneurial activity, then, should seek ways to overcome these barriers.

Pinchot identifies a number of actions that managers should take to create an environment that supports intrapreneurial activity:

1. *Sponsorship.* Formal sponsors can be anyone, from the intrapreneur's immediate supervisor to the president of the company, who is identified and empowered by an organization. Formal sponsors ensure that needed funds are provided, that the work is accepted politically, and that the intrapreneur is free to think and create. In short, the sponsor frees the intrapreneur from the hassles of the organization.

2. *Self-selection.* Managers should recognize that it is virtually impossible to command someone to become an intrapreneur. Instead, they should focus on identifying likely candidates—those who might choose to be and succeed at being intrapreneurs—and allow the intrapreneurial activity to occur.

3. *No hand-offs.* Managers should allow intrapreneurs and their teams to stay with projects as long as possible. When managers say, "Thank you for the idea; now we will hand it off to someone else to develop," organization members probably will feel inhibited and less likely to generate future ideas. Moreover, hand-offs tend to reduce the commitment to the effective development of the ideas that are generated.

4. *The doer decides.* Managers should allow intrapreneurs and their groups to make as many decisions as possible rather than concentrating decision making at higher levels. The purpose of this is to facilitate the rapid development of the ideas as well as commitment to them.

5. *Corporate slack.* Managers should allow individuals the time and freedom to explore new ideas. Tight controls inhibit creativity by removing the opportunity for it to occur.

6. *Ending the home-run philosophy.* Big ideas should not be discouraged, but the organization that supports only big ideas is unlikely to get many small ones. Small ideas sustain an organization.

7. *Tolerance of risk, failure, and mistakes.* Good intrapreneurs are people who like to take risks, who can live with failures, and who accept mistakes as learning opportunities. Managers who permit this facilitate intrapreneurship.

8. *Patient money.* Managers must recognize that ideas take time to mature. Withdrawing financial support too quickly when results do not appear is short-sighted, prevents potential successes from developing, and discourages others from attempting innovation.

9. *Freedom from "turfiness."* Intrapreneurs are known for stepping on toes. When developing ideas, they frequently cross organizational boundaries. Managers must take care to see that the organization's culture discourages workers from digging in and protecting their own turf, which erects barriers to innovation.

10. *Cross-functional teams.* Intrapreneurs should be encouraged to develop self-contained teams whose members possess all of the functional expertise needed by the venture. Managers should support these teams to reduce the need for hand-offs and to encourage the development of ideas.

11. *Multiple options.* Intrapreneurs must be given flexibility in developing, producing, and marketing their products and services. If the organization's traditional methods do not match the needs of the new idea, other options should be permissible.

12. *An effective reward system.* Managers should design systems that encourage, recognize, and reward intrapreneurial behavior without becoming dysfunctional for the organization. Promoting an effective intrapreneur to a managerial position, for example, is usually a mistake, because it significantly reduces future intrapreneurial output from that person. It would be better to provide direct financial rewards, to reward the intrapreneur by supporting his or her future endeavors, or both.

13. *Use an intracapital system.* Intracapital is money that intrapreneurs may spend on a discretionary basis. In this way, they have the financial support they need to develop ideas without encountering bureaucratic barriers to spending decisions. Pinchot recommends that a portion of the funds generated by an intrapreneurial idea be funnelled back into the intrapreneur's intracapital account for further discretionary intrapreneurial spending. This rewards a successful intrapreneur by providing the support needed to pursue his or her valued ideas.[15]

The guidelines just presented are not designed to guarantee intrapreneurial success. The purpose is to offer opportunities for such success by providing a barrier-free, supportive environment.

Entrepreneurial and Intrapreneurial Strategies

Emphasizing that stereotypes of successful entrepreneurial efforts are too narrow, Peter Drucker has described several alternative strategies for identifying and developing entrepreneurial and intrapreneurial ideas (see Table 23.5).[16] Each strategy has been used both by entrepreneurs and by intrapreneurs. For simplicity the term *entrepreneurship* is used exclusively in the following section, although the strategies are equally applicable to intrapreneurship.

Leadership in a New Market or Industry

Leadership in a new market or industry, the approach most people associate with the idea of entrepreneurship, involves creating and then dominating a new product or service area. The plastics industry, for example, was created using this entrepreneurial approach.[17] In the 1920s, Du Pont (then a leading producer of explosives) hired chemist Wallace H. Carothers to develop synthetic fibers using polymer chemistry. After years of failure, the first truly synthetic fiber was created and given the name *nylon.* The rest is history, thanks to Du Pont's massive manufacturing and marketing efforts.

Leadership in a new market or industry has been successful in areas other than big business. Consider the case of the two surgeons who, early in the twentieth century, decided to establish a medical center in remote Rochester, Minnesota.[18] Their goals included: to create a center based on the then-unheard-of practice of staffing medical teams with outstanding specialists, to dominate the field in the treatment of complex medical problems, and to attract patients who would pay extremely high fees for such superior medical care. They were the first to pioneer this approach to medical treatment and they did so in a big way. The two entrepreneurial physicians were named Mayo, and the clinic they founded is the renowned Mayo Clinic.

The aim of Du Pont and of the Mayos was the same: to create a new industry and to dominate it. They succeeded. So, too, did Hofmann-LaRoche, the pharmaceutical company that pioneered and dominated the vitamin market. So did Dr. An Wang, who created—and for many years dominated—the word processing industry. So did the founders of Apple Computer. So have many others who have followed this strategy. The key to success with this strategy, Drucker says, is to aim high; set one goal and focus all effort on it. Succeed, and like the Mayos and Du Pont, you have made history. Miss your target by even a little bit, though, and you are in big trouble because the approach requires a large investment and sustained effort. Furthermore, although the potential payoff may be quite large, the chances of achieving it are small. There is great risk, and most entrepreneurs prefer moderate risks; thus, this may be the flashiest of approaches but it is not the most popular.

Creative Imitation

Creative imitation, the second entrepreneurial/intrapreneurial strategy, is based on improving someone else's innovation. Although somewhat a contra-

TABLE 23.5 *Entrepreneurial and Intrapreneurial Strategies*

Leadership in a new market or industry
Creative imitation
Entrepreneurial judo

diction in terms, this approach is used by entrepreneurs who understand the meaning and uses of the innovation better than its creator.

Creative imitation is a market-driven, rather than a product-driven, strategy. It is appropriate for a rapidly growing market in which a creative imitator can satisfy existing market demand better than a pioneer can. A successful creative imitator capitalizes on a pioneer's success by perfecting and positioning the product or service more appropriately. This approach does not even require the entrepreneur to take customers away from the pioneer; instead, he or she can simply focus on customers new to the market. This approach has been particularly successful in high-tech areas in which, according to Drucker, innovators "are least likely to be market-focused, and most likely to be technology- and product-focused. The innovators therefore tend to misunderstand their own success and to fail to exploit and supply the demand they have created."[19]

Creative imitation requires alertness, flexibility, an ability to "read" the market, and plenty of hard work. Consider, for example, the over-the-counter painkiller market.[20] For years, aspirin dominated this market in spite of such side effects as nausea and bleeding. An alternative to aspirin, acetaminophen, was available, but only by prescription. When acetaminophen was approved for over-the-counter sales, it was promoted as "the painkiller of choice for those with reactions to aspirin." The marketer of the drug quickly captured that relatively small market. Johnson & Johnson creatively imitated by positioning the drug as a safe, universal painkiller. In less than two years, Johnson & Johnson dominated the market with its version of the drug, Tylenol.

Other examples of creative imitation include IBM's success with personal computers following Apple's innovations. IBM has used this strategy in other areas as well, including the photocopying market. Another example of a repeatedly good creative imitator in the home products market is Procter & Gamble. Although creative imitation has much less inherent risk than does the leadership strategy, entrepreneurs following this approach have to take care not to be *too* creative. This approach succeeds by filling an existing need in an existing market better than existing products and services, so creative imitators must keep their focus on the market rather than on the product or service.

Entrepreneurial Judo

Entrepreneurial judo, the final strategy, capitalizes on the weaknesses of an organization holding a leadership position. As with judo, the martial art, entrepreneurial judo:

> *first aims at securing a beachhead, one which the established leaders either do not defend at all or defend only half-heartedly. . . . Once that beachhead has been secured, that is, once the newcomers have an adequate market and adequate revenue, they then move in on the rest of the territory.[21]*

TABLE 23.6   *Five Bad Habits to Attack with Entrepreneurial Judo*

The "not-invented-here" syndrome
Creaming the market
The misunderstanding of quality
The use of premium pricing
Maximization attempts

Like a martial artist, an entrepreneurial judo expert attacks weak points. According to Drucker, organizational weaknesses are the result of five bad habits (see Table 23.6). The next sections examine these bad habits and the opportunities they present to entrepreneurs who follow this strategy.

Five Bad Habits.   When an organization falls into one or more of the bad habits shown in Table 23.6, it exhibits a weakness that allows an entrepreneurial judo artist to attack. Furthermore, an organization with these habits tends to repeat them, making future judo attacks even easier for ambitious entrepreneurs.

- *Bad habit #1: the "not-invented-here" syndrome.* This bad habit occurs when managers reject a new idea simply because it was invented by someone else. In 1947, for example, U.S.-based Bell Laboratories invented the transistor. Leading American radio and television manufacturers delayed using the new technology, however, partially because Bell had invented it and they had not. Conversion to transistors was planned for a couple of decades later. Akio Morita, president of SONY, had no such qualms about the transistor. Paying a paltry $25,000, Morita obtained a license to use the transistor in consumer electronics products. Through the quick and effective use of entrepreneurial judo, Morita captured the portable radio market for years to come.

- *Bad habit #2: creaming the market.* Managers who fall prey to this bad habit attempt to skim the high-profit portion of the market, as Xerox did by concentrating on its customers who purchased the greatest number of the most expensive copy machines. Small users received relatively little attention, which left many feeling dissatisfied. Identifying this weakness as an opportunity, other American manufacturers and a number of Japanese competitors stepped in and courted and won the small user market. The exploration of this weakness was the competitors' stepping stone to bigger markets, and Xerox paid the price for its bad habit.

- *Bad habit #3: misunderstanding quality.* "Contrary to what most manufacturers believe, a product is not 'quality' because it is hard to make and costs a lot of money. . . . Customers pay only for what is of use to them and gives them value. Nothing else is 'quality.'"[22] The manufacturers of vacuum tube radios advertised the "quality" of their radios in the 1950s, citing the expertise, time, and materials required to build them. To consumers, however, reliable, inexpensive transistor radios presented far greater quality.

- *Bad habit #4: premium pricing.* Premium pricing involves charging the highest prices the market will accept. This may seem like a wonderful practice to an organization that has no competitors, but an excessive price

When Xerox creamed the high-volume copier market, the competition stepped in and won over small users.

Reprinted with special permission of King Features Syndicate, Inc.

is an attractive target to an entrepreneur looking for a weak point to attack. When IBM priced its first personal computers relatively high, potential clone makers saw the opportunity to enter the market by providing low prices, even if they could not compete with IBM on other bases. A market leader who uses premium pricing may do quite well on a short-term basis but is vulnerable in the long term.

- *Bad habit #5: maximization attempts.* The fifth common bad habit Drucker identifies involves trying to make a product or service "all things to all people." He again cites Xerox as an organization that exhibited this weakness. Concentrating on developing copy machines that could do almost anything, the company created machines that many customers simply could not use. When the competition offered small, simple, but functional machines for users with small, simple copying needs, they again hit Xerox where it hurt.

Entrepreneurial Judo Opportunities. The five bad habits just described combine to create three principal opportunities for entrepreneurial judo artists who wish to attack established leaders' weak points. First, challengers can try to *beat them to the punch*—that is, to look for unexpected success or failure to which leaders are not reacting properly and to deliver a new product or service before the leader has a chance to do so. Second, entrepreneurs can *undercut price*—that is, they can look for a rapidly growing market in which leaders are creaming the market and/or using premium pricing, target the part of the market slighted by the leader, and price the entrepreneurial product lower. Third, challengers must *seize the moment*—that is, they must look for a volatile market in which the nature of the products or services is changing quickly, identify an area where leaders have not kept up with new demands, and satisfy these demands before the leaders react.

The entrepreneurial judo strategy may not be as flashy as the leadership in a new market or industry approach, or as creative as the creative imitation approach, but it can be effective and reliable (less risky). It seldom produces the magnitude of results that the other approaches do, but it has a much higher success rate and generally requires fewer resources to pursue.

Entrepreneurship and Intrapreneurship in Review

Entrepreneurship involves the development of a product or service idea and the creation of an organization to further its growth. Intrapreneurship involves identifying the need for change in an organization, creating the environment in which the change can succeed, and championing the implementation of the change.

Many entrepreneurs and intrapreneurs are characterized by particular personal characteristics, such as a high need for achievement combined with a low fear of failure and a strong internal locus of control. They also have certain common life experiences, such as difficulty in working for someone else, challenging educational experiences, and early practice at running an organization.

Intrapreneurship involves entrepreneurial activities within an existing organization. Intrapreneurs should proceed through a four-step process to achieve maximum creative and analytical success. In Phase 1, the solo phase, intrapreneurs identify an idea and begin to develop it. In Phase 2, the network phase, they share the idea with other organization members to gain feedback. In Phase 3, the bootlegging phase, they refine the idea. In Phase 4, the formal team phase, they present the final concept to the entire organization.

Intrapreneurs are becoming more and more important to organizations, but organizational policies and practices can often discourage and stifle their initial attempts. Managers must create an environment conducive to intrapreneuring by offering sponsorship, tolerance, rewards, and other organizational support.

Three entrepreneurial and intrapreneurial strategies can help challengers establish a place for themselves in the market. The first, leadership in a new market or industry, focuses on creating and then dominating a new product or service area. The second, creative imitation, concentrates on the creative improvement of someone else's innovation to better serve the market. The final strategy, judo, capitalizes on an organization's weaknesses to obtain a small entry point from which further inroads can be attempted.

Issues for Review and Discussion

1. Discuss why you feel entrepreneurs and intrapreneurs are or are not the key to the future of American organizations.
2. Discuss steps that a college could take to encourage the development of entrepreneurs and intrapreneurs.
3. Describe the systematic steps that a large corporation, such as General Motors, could take to encourage intrapreneurial behavior. Would you recommend that GM do this?
4. If you were an entrepreneur looking for opportunities, which of the strategies described in this chapter would be most attractive to you? Explain why.
5. Discuss how a market leader could defend itself against entrepreneurs attempting to challenge it using the creative imitation strategy.
6. Discuss how a market leader could defend itself against entrepreneurs attempting to challenge it using the entrepreneurial judo strategy.

Key Terms

entrepreneurship   creative imitation
intrapreneurship   entrepreneurial judo
leadership in a new market or industry

Suggested Readings

Drucker, P. F. (Winter 1985). Entrepreneurial strategies. *California Management Review*, 27, 2, 9-25.

Drucker, P. F. (1985). *Innovation and entrepreneurship.* New York: Harper & Row.

Kent, C. A., Sexton, D. L., and Vesper, K. H., eds. (1982). *Encyclopedia of entrepreneurship.* Englewood Cliffs, NJ: Prentice-Hall.

Mancusco, J. R. (October 1974). What it takes to be an entrepreneur. *Journal of Small Business Management,* 16-22.

Pinchot, G. III (1985). *Intrapreneuring.* New York: Harper & Row.

Rifkin, G., and Harrar, G. (1988). *The ultimate entrepreneur: The story of Ken Olsen and DEC.* Chicago: Contemporary Books.

Notes

1. What do women want? A company they can call their own (22 December 1986), *Business Week,* 60-62.

2. G. Pinchot III (1985), *Intrapreneuring,* New York: Harper & Row.

3. Similar definitions are contained in W. B. Gartner (1985), A conceptual framework for describing the phenomenon of new venture creation, *Academy of Management Review,* 10, 696-706; K. H. Vesper (1980), *New venture strategies,* Englewood Cliffs, NJ: Prentice-Hall.

4. P. F. Drucker (1985a), *Innovation and entrepreneurship,* New York: Harper & Row.

5. This section is based on ideas and findings from J. Timmons (1985), *New venture creation,* Homewood, IL: Irwin; Pinchot; C. A. Kent, D. L. Sexton, and K. H. Vesper, eds. (1982), *Encyclopedia of entrepreneurship,* Englewood Cliffs, NJ: Prentice-Hall; M. J. C. Martin (1984), *Managing technological innovation & entrepreneurship,* Reston, VA: Reston Publishing.

6. The year's 25 most fascinating business people (2 January 1989), *Fortune,* 42.

7. L. F. Centofanti (October 1986), So I said to myself, why not? *Venture,* 128.

8. The billion-dollar whiz kid (13 April 1987), *Business Week,* 69.

9. America's most successful entrepreneur (27 October 1986), *Fortune,* 26.

10. America's fastest-growing companies (23 May 1988), *Fortune,* 32.

11. J. R. Mancusco (October 1974), What it takes to be an entrepreneur, *Journal of Small Business Management,* 16-22; J. A. Welsh and J. F. White (Summer 1978), Recognizing and dealing with the entrepreneur, *S.A.M. Advanced Management Journal,* 22-24.

12. *Fortune,* 1988, 36.

13. Gifford Pinchot III has written a fascinating book on this subject appropriately entitled *Intrapreneuring.* Much of this chapter is based on an excellent review of that work prepared by Filip Caeldries and Arnold C. Cooper (1988) contained in J. L. Pierce and J. W. Newstrom, eds., *The manager's bookshelf: A mosaic of contemporary views,* New York: Harper & Row, 135-41. The concept is also discussed at length by Peter Drucker (although he uses somewhat different terminology).

14. Caeldries and Cooper, 137.

15. Caeldries and Cooper, 138-41.

16. Also see P. F. Drucker (1985b), Entrepreneurial strategies, *California Management Review,* 27 (2), 9-25.

17. Drucker, 1985b, 10.

18. Drucker, 1985b, 11-12.

19. Drucker, 1985b, 18-19.

20. Drucker, 1985b, 17.

21. Drucker, 1985b, 23.

22. Drucker, 1985b, 21.

I Had No Authority

By S. Neaman (1976), I had no authority, in For the good of the company: Work and interplay in a major American corporation, *New York: Grosset & Dunlap, 43–44, 52–54.*

I had no authority . . . but here was an opportunity. Here was a store that had lost so much money. I wanted to know what it took to make a good store. So I said to John, a store manager, "Look, we are going to bring into this store a group of people, a team, and you'll be the quarterback. You and they will go and visit all the competition in town and write up what you find. You'll check our merchandise and write it up. Every evening you'll hold classes with a blackboard and will have a consultation with everyone. In addition, I'm gonna bring in the regional manager, merchandisers, buyers, and other store managers. I want to know the sum total of our know-how by taking a sampling of a group of people dedicated to finding out what they can do thinking together." For weeks they studied the store. They had a tough time agreeing with each other, but they did. The spirit was sky-high; excitement was beyond description. Why? For the first time they were given a chance to express themselves as individuals and as a group, each one giving the best that he or she knew. Not a nickel was spent. Every change was made from what was in the store. Floors were changed, aisles widened, walls painted. It was a new store, a pleasure to the eye.

What put that store across? They knew they had to visit all the competition and then look at our store with a cold eye. They applied what they learned. Until then, they had to look at the eyeballs of the boss and guess what he wanted. All I did was ask them to use their senses and their heads, and I got a good store. Over the next two years, it reduced its losses and then started making money. After all the hustle-bustle, the whole company became aware of it. The chairman and his entourage came running to see what was happening. Now everybody jumped on the bandwagon. Everybody wanted a district, every vice-president, the executive vice-president, even the chairman.

Show the people a way. That's what I did. I even had a place to send everyone. Indianapolis. "Go to Indianapolis in Indiana," I told them. "Go there, look at the store and learn. It was put together by people like you, using spit and polish and only their own normal talents." A little while later, in the home office, I changed the pattern. To a variety chain vice-president who was in charge of buying, I said, "All right, Joe, you don't have to go to the Midwest. Do me an Indianapolis right here in New York. You have seen what can be done. So go do an Indianapolis in Flushing. But I don't want you to copy it. We'll keep Indianapolis as a sort of school." I told him to give me his version of a good variety store in Flushing.

Well, several weeks later he invited me to the store and I found one of the most beautiful retail stores I have ever seen. I immediately invited a few others to see it. You never would have believed that his horrible store would be the attraction of the neighborhood and the jewel of the company. Sales began rising right away and the store became our best in New York. But what it did was to challenge the other home-offices to go out and "Do an Indianapolis."

As the parent company began to brag more and more, I expanded the variations. I used the idea of the Indianapolis store as a visual aid. This meant devising a system of selecting one unit for improvement, getting the people to bring it into shape, then bringing others to see what they did so they could learn from it. This became a substitute for writing memos or giving instructions on the phone. Instead, I said, "Come look and see. This is the new company—nothing else is—this is it!" I instructed every district (ten to fifteen stores) that it must have its own model store. Every district manager would have to reflect all his or her knowledge in one store and from that "Indianapolis" improve all the stores in the district. It would be the model for everyone who would look at it. The idea caught on like wildfire. They did it evenings, Sundays, holidays. The Sundays became big shindigs with beer and food provided by the store's restaurant manager. They had the year of their life getting the chain in shape, all forty-seven districts.

Questions

1. What does Mr. Neaman's account tell us about developing an entrepreneurial spirit in a corporation?

2. What is needed to get people to look at their business with a "cold eye" instead of looking to the bosses to find out what they want?

3. What does the account tell us about the spread of innovation?

4. Once the Indianapolis store was proven successful, why didn't the company just copy it elsewhere instead of repeating the change process over and over?

5. What do you think of using the idea of selecting one store in a region for change and then using it as a "visual aid" instead of "writing memos or giving instructions on the phone"?

24 *Careers*

Student Learning Objectives

After reading this chapter, you should be able to:

1. Define career.
2. Identify the stages of Miller and Form's life-span model.
3. Identify the stages of Super's life-span model.
4. Explain the five career anchors identified by Schein.
5. Discuss Dalton and Thompson's career stages model.
6. Apply the career models to your own career development.
7. Discuss the methods of increasing organizational effectiveness through the application of career theory.

By Ann Cope, (Novations consulting firm) in consultation with Gene Dalton, Brigham Young University

For most people, their career is a primary factor in determining the overall quality of life.[1] For managers, career development and progression means attending to subordinates' careers as well as to their own. Giving organization members opportunities to grow, advance, and develop is extremely important. Workers need to know what their organization values and rewards for two reasons: to understand promotion decisions and to assist and counsel others toward successful and satisfying careers. A solid comprehension of career dynamics contributes to overall organizational effectiveness. Organizational needs are met as people's talents are best used, as planning for the future is carried out, and as managers anticipate organizational needs for new generations of leaders and managers.

Once the importance of learning about and studying career development is realized, a question remains to be answered: what is a career? Two simple definitions are that a **career** can be either a series of movements in an organization or a certain line of work or profession, such as a career as an accountant. Another way to define *career* is in terms of stages that take into account the role that organizations play in an individual's career.[2] As individuals perform needed functions in organizations, they are valued and rewarded. If people do not understand that career progression is linked to organizational needs, they will often fail to advance or to feel rewarded and satisfied. These and other definitions have been incorporated into various models that explain the ways in which individual careers progress and develop: life-span models, individual differences models, and organizationally based models of career development.

Life-Span Models

Life-span models of careers are built around the biological life cycle and, thus, are very similar to one another. The models provide such a broad framework that they accommodate a great diversity of empirical findings and points of view. In fact, although they were constructed at a time when most employees were young men who remained in the workforce until retirement, the models are often applicable to modern employees, both men and women.

Miller and Form's Life Stages Model

Delbert Miller and William Form were among the first to formulate a developmental model for careers.[3] They viewed a career as a series of social adjustments imposed on workers by a culture. Depending on the culture in which one lives, certain standard activities and vocations are desirable and acceptable; to function in the culture, an individual must adjust to these standards. These social adjustments fall into a pattern of five periods:

1. The *preparatory work period,* characterized by the socialization of a child, at home and at school, into the work patterns of society
2. The *initial work period,* when a young worker is initiated into the work world through part-time employment
3. The *trial work period,* which begins with the first full-time job and continues to a permanent work position

In the initial work period, a young worker is initiated into the labor force through part-time employment.

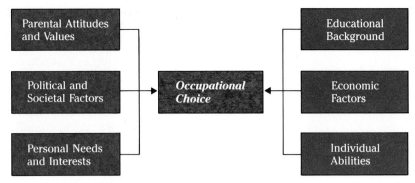

FIGURE 24.1 The Factors Involved in Determining Occupational Choice

Source: D. C. Feldman (1988), *Managing careers in organizations*, Glenview, IL: Scott, Foresman, 29.

4. The *stable work period,* the period of job permanence

5. The *retirement period*

In their explanation of what happens within and between these periods, Miller and Form emphasize the importance of social class in predicting which occupational level an employee will attain. They cite research evidence of a relationship between occupational level attained and the following five factors: (1) father's occupation, (2) worker's intelligence, (3) father's income and education, (4) accessible financial aid and influential contacts, and (5) social and economic conditions in the society.

Because four of these five factors demonstrate a relationship between an individual's environment and occupational level, the accident of birth into a certain social class may be more of a determinant of an individual's attainments than anything the individual does (see Figure 24.1). In this view, a person's developmental pattern is determined largely before the developmental process even begins. Although this approach may be seen as rather fatalistic, its implications for career counseling are enormous. The Miller and Form model should be used informationally to create a context in which to discuss the many possible directions that a person's career development can take.

Super's Model

Donald Super, an authority in vocational counseling, uses self-concepts to examine career development. He sees a career as a synthesis of a person's self-concept and the external realities of the work environment.[4] The synthesis develops as a person becomes aware of his or her self-concept, faces opportunities and requirements in particular occupations, and implements his or her self-concept by working. This evolution takes place through five stages of a life-span model that Super based on the work of Charlotte Buehler.[5] The five stages include:

1. The *growth stage,* extending from conception to approximately age fourteen, during which one's self-concept begins to form through identification with key figures in the family and at school

2. The *exploratory stage,* ordinarily including the period from ages fifteen to twenty-five, during which the self-concept is emerging and being tested

against reality. This stage often includes the transition from school to employment.

3. The *establishment stage,* spanning the years from twenty-five to about forty-five, during which a person finds an appropriate field and puts forth an effort to make a permanent place in it. During this stage, the tested self-concept is modified and implemented.

4. The *maintenance stage,* stretching from age forty-five to retirement. The main concern for an individual during this stage is to hold on to a place already made in the world of work.

5. A *decline stage,* in which an individual concludes his or her work life by leaving the organization and must adjust to a new self-concept

Like Miller and Form, Super postulates that such environmental influences as family, disabilities, and economic factors have a part in occupational choice. This is apparent if people follow in their parents' footsteps, if not by entering the same occupation, at least by choosing a similar work environment and socioeconomic level.

Individual Differences Model

Through extensive research, Edgar Schein has formulated an "individual differences" model that describes various needs, or "anchors," that individuals meet through their careers.[6] Schein's model was developed from a ten-to-twelve-year longitudinal study of forty-four male M.B.A. graduates from the Sloan School of Management at MIT. The forty-four interviews revealed a number of common ideas about what people are fundamentally looking for in their careers. These common themes can be defined as the underlying **career anchors**—technical/functional competence, managerial competence, security and stability, creativity/entrepreneurship, and autonomy and independence—that pull people back if they stray too far from what they really want (see Table 24.1).

Career Anchors

People with a **technical/functional competence anchor** are motivated by the challenge of the technical work in financial analysis, engineering, marketing, strategic planning, or any other area related to technology or business. Their anchor is the technical field or functional area, not the managerial process itself. In fact, people with this set of needs would often rather leave a company than be promoted out of their technical/functional area. Such people are often functional managers, technical managers, senior or junior staff members, and external consultants.

People with a **managerial competence anchor** are motivated to be competent in the complex set of activities that make up the concept of "management." Particularly important are the areas of *interpersonal competence* (the ability to influence, supervise, lead, manipulate, and control people toward the achievement of organizational goals), *analytical competence* (the identifica-

TABLE 24.1 *Schein's Career Anchors Model*

Career Anchor	Characteristics	Typical Career Paths
1. Technical/functional competence	1. Excited by work itself 2. Willing to forgo promotions 3. Dislikes general management and corporate politics	1. Research-oriented positions 2. Functional department management jobs 3. Specialized consulting and project management
2. Managerial competence	1. Likes to analyze and solve knotty business problems 2. Likes to influence and harness people to work together 3. Enjoys the exercise of power	1. Vice-presidencies 2. Plant management and sales management 3. Large, prestigious firms
3. Security and stability	1. Motivated by job security and long-term careers with one firm 2. Dislikes travel and relocation 3. Tends to be conformist and compliant to the organization	1. Government jobs 2. Small, family-owned businesses 3. Large government-regulated industries
4. Creativity/ entrepreneurship	1. Enjoys launching own business 2. Restless; moves from project to project 3. Prefers small, up-and-coming firms to well-established ones	1. Entrepreneurial ventures 2. Stock options, arbitrage, mergers, and acquisitions 3. General management consulting
5. Autonomy and independence	1. Desires freedom from organizational constraints 2. Wants to be on own and set own pace 3. Avoids large businesses and governmental agencies	1. Academia 2. Writing and publishing 3. Small business proprietorships

Source: Adapted from E. H. Schein (1978), *Career dynamics,* Reading, MA: Addison-Wesley, 124-60.

tion and solution of conceptual problems under conditions of uncertainty and incomplete information), and *emotional stability* (the capacity to be stimulated by emotional and interpersonal crises rather than exhausted or debilitated by them—the capacity to exercise authority without fear or guilt). People with a managerial competence anchor usually become line or general managers, depending on their rank.

Individuals with a **security anchor** are motivated to stabilize their careers by linking them to particular organizations or locations and probably will remain there for the greater part of their careers. They are not concerned with achieving brilliant success but, rather, with maintaining a degree of comfort. These individuals rely on organizations to recognize their needs and competencies; they trust organizations to do the best possible for them. This hope, however, is not always fulfilled, and such people are often willing to accept less pay or to sacrifice some autonomy to stabilize their total life situation.

People with a **creativity/entrepreneurship anchor** are motivated to create something new that can clearly be identified with themselves. They also exhibit a need for autonomy and independence but do not have to leave the business world to achieve their autonomy and creative goals (review the discussion of intrapreneurship in Chapter 23).

Individuals having an **autonomy and independence anchor** find organizational life to be restrictive, irrational, and/or intrusive into their private lives. Some leave the world of business altogether, seeking careers that provide more autonomy. Others remain in the business world by operating on their own as consultants.

Implications of the Individual Differences Model

Not surprisingly, Schein found that the managerial competence group was the most successful purely in terms of income. This is because climbing the managerial ladder is congruent with society's definition of success—organization executives are well paid and generally well respected. The creativity/entrepreneurship anchor group had the greatest net worth. Schein postulates that it perhaps is more important for those with a creativity anchor, often entrepreneurs, to build total assets than to consume what they have amassed. At the lowest end of the income scale was the autonomy and independence group, who had left large organizations. This group included a freelance writer, a professor, and other people in vocations that allowed them plenty of freedom from institutions.

Several implications are inherent to this model. First, organizations need to help employees recognize and work with their anchors toward more effective careers. Along with this, organizations would do well to create multiple paths and reward systems to permit the effective use of employees' managerial, technical, and other professional talents. Business organizations can learn to identify individual career anchor orientations and, subsequently, steer individuals in the directions that will allow the greatest satisfaction and productivity.

An Organizationally Based Model

From years of study about professional employees, Gene W. Dalton and Paul H. Thompson developed a model based on organizational career stages.[7] Their model applies best to people they call "knowledge workers"—that is, people in professions such as engineering, accounting, business management, and science. The principles also apply to people in other professions; however, those who work their way up in organizations by engaging in more highly valued activities typically move through the stages as well.

Traditional organizational models did not explain what Dalton and Thompson found in studying the careers of college graduates. For example, the pyramid model typified by most organizational charts suggests that authority, status, and pay increases come as a person moves higher up the chart. The implication is that a person should try to move up as quickly as possible. Also, the pyramid model was often taken to imply that willingness to perform is the sole criterion for advancement, recognition, and reward.

Another model that has been used frequently to think about careers is the obsolescence model. This view holds that quickly changing technology results in a rapid outdating of the skills of older professionals. New college graduates are hired to replace obsolete workers. The obsolescence model could not explain, however, why some older professionals were classified as high performers and rewarded as such, while others were seen as having outdated skills.

In their study of 550 professionally trained employees, Dalton and Thompson found that the professionals who were rated as high performers throughout their careers played successively different roles in their organizations. They engaged in new activities and developed new skills. Their organizations valued these new roles and gave them high performance ratings (see Figure 24.2).

FIGURE 24.2 Age and
Performance: Managers'
Evaluation of Engineers

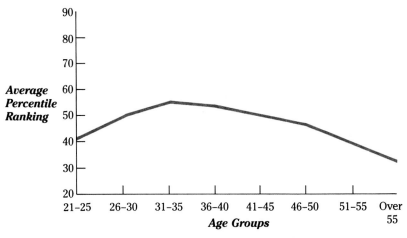

Source: G. W. Dalton and P. H. Thompson (1986), *Novations: Strategies for career management,*
Glenview, IL: Scott, Foresman, 4.

Employees fulfill new roles throughout four stages of their careers: the apprentice stage, the independent contributor stage, the mentoring stage, and the sponsor stage. Each stage differs in the activities people must perform, in the relationships they encounter, and in the psychological issues they face (see Tables 24.2 and 24.3).

Stage I: The Apprentice

People in Stage I, the **apprentice stage,** typically lack experience and credibility and are closely supervised. Apprentices perform routine duties and detailed tasks; however, to be successful, they must also exhibit initiative and innovation. The incongruity of these two approaches can be difficult.

Activities. This stage involves three types of learning. First, apprentices must learn to perform at least some of the organization's tasks competently. This can involve learning to run a computer, to draw up an account, or to perform any other necessary task. Second, Stage I employees must learn which elements of the work are critical and which require the greatest attention.

TABLE 24.2 *Central Activities, Relationships, and Psychological Issues in Four Career Stages*

	Stage I	*Stage II*	*Stage III*	*Stage IV*
Central Activity	Helping, learning, following directions	Independent contributor	Training, interfacing	Shaping the direction of the organization
Primary Relationship	Apprentice	Colleagues	Mentor	Sponsor
Major Psychological Issues	Dependence	Independence	Assuming responsibility for others	Exercising power

Source: G. W. Dalton, P. H. Thompson, and R. L. Price (Summer 1977), The four stages of professional careers—a new look at performance by professionals, *Organizational Dynamics,* 23.

TABLE 24.3   *Characteristics of Career Stages*

Stage I	Stage II
Works under the supervision and direction of a more senior professional in the field	Goes into depth in one problem or technical area
Work is never entirely his or her own but assignments are given that are a portion of a larger project or activity being overseen by a senior professional	Assumes responsibility for a definable portion of the project, process, or clients
Lacks experience and status in the organization	Works independently and produces significant results
Expected to willingly accept supervision and direction	Develops credibility and a reputation
Expected to do most of the detailed and routine work on a project	Relies less on supervisor or mentor for answers: develops more of his or her own resources to solve problems
Expected to exercise "directed" creativity and initiative	Increases in confidence and ability
Learns to perform well under pressure and accomplish a task within the time budgeted	

Stage III	Stage IV
Involved enough in his or her own work to make significant technical contributions but begins working in more than one area	Provides direction for the organization by: a. "Mapping" the organization's environment to highlight opportunities and dangers b. Focusing activities in areas of "distinctive competence" c. Managing the process by which decisions are made
Greater breadth of technical skills and application of those skills	Exercises formal and informal power to: a. Initiate action and influence decisions b. Obtain resources and approvals
Stimulates others through ideas and information	Represents the organization: a. To individuals and groups at different levels inside the organization b. To individuals and institutions outside the organization
Involved in developing people in one or more of the following ways: a. Acts as an idea leader for a small group b. Serves as a mentor to younger professionals c. Assumes a formal supervisory position	
Deals with the outside to benefit others in organizations—i.e., working out relationships with client organizations, developing new business	Sponsors promising individuals to test and prepare them for key roles in the organization

Source: G. W. Dalton and P. H. Thompson (1986), *Novations: Strategies for career management,* Glenview, IL: Scott, Foresman, 8, 9.

Apprentices can focus attention on these activities, concentrating on learning the intricacies involved in the tasks. Finally, people in this stage must learn how to get things done using both formal and informal channels of communication. It is critical that apprentices perform all of their duties thoroughly and well, even if the tasks appear small and menial, for two reasons: because they must learn the skills involved and because they are being closely observed for indications of competence and potential.

Relationships.   The primary relationship that apprentices experience in Stage I is that of subordinate. Stage I employees are typically low on the totem pole and must take direction and instruction from their superiors. Ideally, each apprentice works with a mentor, learning from observation and trial-and-error the approaches, organizational savvy, and judgment that cannot be learned from textbooks. Apprentices perform detailed, often boring work in exchange for things that they can learn only from a mentor. A mentor supports, instructs, provides opportunities for apprentices to try new tasks, and makes sure they do not make important errors. As apprentices learn, they are given more responsibilities—but if they fail, they remain longer under supervision.

Apprentices generally work on assignments that are part of a larger project or activity directed by a senior manager.

Psychological Issues. Apprentices are expected to "willingly accept supervision and direction" and to "exercise directed creativity and initiative."[8] This can be difficult for new employees, who had anticipated finishing their education so they could be free of professors' demands and could find some independence. Instead of freedom, new employees are confronted with a high degree of supervision, direction, and routine work.

When a person leaves college or graduate school, he is automatically demoted from the senior level to freshman again. He's been the experienced student who's mastered the system, then all of a sudden he's forced back to the bottom of the heap. Many of our new MBAs have a rough time swallowing it. As students, they analyzed and discussed cases from the point of view of the president. Now they see themselves as the peons, doing all the detail work. Those that resist making this shift get off to a very poor start.[9]

If apprentices learn to perform and stick with the seemingly endless routine work, they will be valued and rewarded by their organization. On the other hand, if they lose interest or do sloppy work, they may earn a poor reputation and have difficulty in subsequent career stages.

Stage II: The Independent Contributor

By developing a reputation as a technically competent professional who can work independently to produce significant results, an apprentice passes from Stage I to Stage II, the **independent contributor stage.** There is little, if any, supervision in Stage II, and people work with others only in coordinating projects.

Activities. Independent contributors have their own projects or areas of responsibility, although they often must coordinate their projects with others. Stage II employees are given general instructions and can complete their work in whatever way they think is best, as one young physicist discovered.

Since my early days at the laboratory, I'd always worked with Chuck Robinson on research projects. It took three years before I had confidence to submit a proposal on my own. But even with my own project, I never made a decision or wrote a final draft without consulting Robinson. When he took a six-month assignment in Kwajalein, I was paralyzed. I couldn't think for four months. Eventually, I figured out that I could get opinions from other people in the department and make a decision using their input. It was a major discovery for me to realize that I didn't need a boss to approve my decisions.[10]

Independent contributors have a high level of professional skills and are very good in a certain area. The dilemma for those in Stage II is how much to specialize. A generalist is useful, but to be valued by an organization, a person needs to develop and demonstrate solid competence in a critical task area. If this does not happen, it becomes a major block to a person's career.

There are two approaches to selecting areas of specialization. The first is to focus on content, as does a CPA who concentrates on tax problems for banks, a scientist who focuses on testing, or a banker who concentrates on loans to utilities. The second approach is to focus on a set of specialized skills—for example, applying computer technology or dealing with clients—that independent contributors can use to solve a variety of problems. There is often a risk of becoming pigeon-holed in a phased-out specialty, but a good specialty is usually a solid base for a career.

Relationships.   The main relationships in this stage are with peers. Independent contributors can receive a great deal of support and information from their colleagues. **Networking** is a process by which a person gains knowledge and support from many sources, including mentors, peers, peers' associates, and other individuals from within and outside the organization. Independent contributors rely less on supervisors and mentors for direction, a change that is difficult for both subordinates and supervisors. Subordinates lose the direction and dependency that come with a Stage I relationship, and supervisors must learn to release their students/helpers.

Psychological Issues.   Employees entering Stage II must make the transition from dependence to independence. They learn to develop ideas about what is required and personal standards of performance. Help and guidance are less available from superiors but are more available from peers and professional standards than during Stage I. Still, Stage II employees must learn to find confidence in their own judgment.

It is important that employees spend some time in this stage; problems arise when a person moves out of Stage II too quickly. Before moving into management, independent contributors need time to understand the technical aspects of the work they will supervise. Otherwise, they risk undermining others' confidence.

Dalton and Thompson found that many professional workers stay in Stage II throughout their careers. In this stage, the employees are able to make substantial contributions and experience a high degree of personal satisfaction through the technical work they perform; however, high ratings tend to diminish with time for those in Stage II. As such workers get older, they are expected to begin filling new roles in their organization.

Stage III: The Mentor

In Stage III, the **mentoring stage,** a person begins to influence, direct, and develop other people. Additionally, mentors broaden their interests and capabilities; they are a natural source of ideas for people in Stages I and II.

Activities.   A mentor performs three roles, which are not mutually exclusive. The first is that of an informal mentor. Mentors are asked to do more work because of their demonstrated competency (which was most probably developed in Stage II). To shoulder this load, they need help from Stage II employees, who do the detail work.

The second role enacted in Stage III is that of an "idea person." Stage III people may act as consultants for small groups, with others coming to them for suggestions. From their experience, they can glean information that will be helpful for others.

The third and most common role is that of manager. Stage III managers are distant from the work and, thus, manage at a more abstract level. They deal more with concepts and less with technical activities. Nonetheless, they assume responsibility for the technical work others do.

Relationships. In Stage III, people learn to take care of others by mentoring and to assume responsibility for subordinates' work. Employees who advance to Stage III need to demonstrate interpersonal skills in setting objectives, delegating, supervising, and coordinating. They must satisfy many people, as they have responsibilities upward as well as downward. Always looking upward means losing loyalty from below. On the other hand, Stage III individuals need to have influence with superiors to be able to obtain resources and provide ways for subordinates to perform their duties.

Psychological Issues. Stage III employees need to develop a sense of confidence in their own ability to produce results and to help others do the same. Mentors must also avoid feeling threatened by subordinates' successes, or they will not provide the guidelines and freedom that Stage I and II employees need to progress. Somehow a balance must be found between directing others and providing them with freedom. Because mentors rarely perform the tasks involved in a project, they must learn to derive satisfaction from seeing subordinates move away, become independent, or take on new mentors.

A mentor needs to be willing and able to take responsibility for someone else's output. Occasionally, a person begins to fill Stage III roles but then feels frustrated and unhappy. At times, the supervisory responsibility seems confining; in this case, it is possible to find a role that allows broad influence without supervisory duties. On the other hand, a person who feels restricted by this role can move back into Stage II. In some organizations, this move is acceptable; in others it is viewed as a demotion and a lowering of status.

To achieve a sense of long-term satisfaction, mentors meet challenges by broadening their thinking, by increasing their knowledge through forays into new areas, and by applying present skills to new problems. They also derive satisfaction from social involvement and recognition from peers and by helping junior professionals further their careers.

People in the sponsor stage influence the direction of an organization or a major portion of it.

Stage III can be the climax of a career. The psychological and physical rewards may be substantial, and professionals enjoy a fairly high degree of status within organizations. Others may feel stagnant and hard-pressed to keep up with younger competitors. Some move on to Stage IV, where their roles again shift to meet another set of organizational needs.

Stage IV: The Sponsor

People in the **sponsor stage** influence their organization's direction or a major portion of it. They exercise this influence in several ways: through negotiating and interfacing with key parts of the environment; through developing new ideas, products, markets, or services that lead the organization into new areas of activity; or through directing organizational resources toward specific goals. Because these functions are so critical to the growth and survival of an organization, those who perform them are highly valued, and only those whose skill and judgment have been proven in the past are trusted to play Stage IV roles.

Activities. In Stage IV, a person performs at least one of three roles. As in Stage III, one role is that of manager. It is important, however, to remember that managers in Stage IV are not close enough to the details of daily work to perform technical roles. Instead, they formulate policy and initiate and approve broad programs.

The second role Dalton and Thompson identified within Stage IV is that of "internal entrepreneur" or "intrapreneur." This is a person with new ideas and a strong sense of direction for the organization's future (see Chapter 23).

The third role of people in Stage IV is described as "idea innovator." The biggest opportunities and the most significant breakthroughs most often originate with these people. Idea innovators may puzzle for years over a problem or an idea before a solution finally presents itself. They may work quite closely with a manager or someone else to "sell" their ideas. Often Stage IV people have established a reputation outside their organization, which enhances credibility within the organization and may allow Stage IV people to play key roles in recruiting and business development.

Relationships. The first major relationship has to do with selecting and grooming key people from Stage II or III who show promise of performing Stage IV activities in the future. Stage IV individuals focus on opening up opportunities, assessing work, and providing feedback for subordinates, rather than on such mentoring activities as giving instruction. Sponsors watch potential organization leaders, looking for strengths and weaknesses; they counsel candidates and guide them to areas where they can be most effective.

The second primary relationship is directed outside a sponsor's organization. This relationship is critical because it brings current information about events and trends into the organization. Such a relationship can be seen in professional associations and legal and banking communities.

Psychological Issues. Because sponsors are invariably pulled away from organizational operations, they must learn not to second-guess subordinates on operating decisions. Instead, they must learn to influence those under them through ideas, personnel selection, reviews, resource allocation, changes in organizational design, and so on. Stage IV individuals may find it difficult to allow the distancing from day-to-day activities to take place, but they must do so if people in each of the other stages are to function effectively.

Sponsors have broad perspectives and far-reaching time horizons. They think about their organization as a whole and act in that framework, planning beyond the time frame in which they are personally affected for scenarios that take place in the next five to ten years and beyond. Stage IV people must become accustomed to using power to fight for their programs. In addition, they need to form alliances and take strong positions without feeling permanent enmity toward those who differ.

Implications of the Organizationally Based Model

People in all four stages make important contributions to their organization. Obviously, a number of people in each stage are necessary for organizational effectiveness. To maintain high performance ratings throughout their careers, however, people should seek to move at least to Stage III. Depending on an organization's climate, organization members may move back and forth between stages, although for many this implies demotion. The stages model also implies that, unlike the pyramid or hierarchy model, Stages III and IV are not always limited to formal management positions. Engineers and accountants, for example, can continue to work in their chosen fields without forgoing the organizational rewards that typically come with advancement into management:

> I assumed when I came here that being a good scientist was all that was necessary. Later, I found that science was more than just research. You have to conceive, sell, and direct a program. I began to do all those things and found myself in management mainly because I didn't want to work for the other guys they were considering. . . . I have stayed close to my field, written papers, and still consider myself to be a scientist.[11]

Careers in Review

There are several reasons for studying career development and progression. First, it is useful for individuals to understand the reasons behind their successes and failures. Second, people in organizations need to understand the ways in which they can assist and counsel others toward successful and satisfying careers. Third, a solid comprehension of career dynamics contributes to overall organizational effectiveness. Career development also contributes to the process of anticipating organizational needs for new generations of leaders and managers.

One definition of *career* is a series of movements in a company; *career* can also mean a certain line of work or profession, such as a career as an accountant. Dalton and Thompson's definition of *career* as a set of stages considers the role organizations play in individuals' careers.

There are several models that examine career progression and development: the life-span models, the individual differences model, and the organizationally based model of career development. Life-span career models are built around the biological life cycle. Miller and Form's life-span model views a career as a series of social adjustments that culture imposes on workers; it emphasizes the importance of social class in predicting and determining the occupational level a person attains. Super's life-span model views a career as the refinement of a person's self-concept through five stages.

Schein formulated an individual differences model that describes the various needs (called anchors) individuals fill through a career: technical/functional competence, managerial competence, security, creativity/entrepreneurship, and autonomy and independence. People with a technical/functional competence anchor are motivated by the work itself. Those with a managerial competence anchor are motivated by managerial activities. To satisfy the security need, workers remain with a certain company or in a particular geographic area. To satisfy the creativity/entrepreneurship need, workers create something independently of established organizations. To satisfy the autonomy and independence need, workers leave organizations they find to be restrictive, irrational, and/or intrusive into their private lives.

Dalton and Thompson developed a model based on career stages, each different in the tasks people are expected to perform, the types of relationships they develop, and the psychological adjustments they make. Stage I, the apprentice stage, is typified by individuals' entering organizations and learning their duties. Stage II, the independent contributor stage, is filled by people who are experts in a certain area and who are no longer closely supervised. People in Stage III, the mentoring stage, help subordinates develop and learn. In Stage IV, the sponsor stage, people determine policy and direction for their organization.

Careers are very important, both for individuals and for organizations. It is critical that managers see the value of fostering the development of organization members. Career progression and development of human resources help an organization merge individual goals with organizational needs to achieve effectiveness.

Issues for Review and Discussion

1. Define career.
2. What are some implications of measuring career success from an individual's perspective rather than from an organization's perspective?
3. Compare and contrast the life-span career models identified by Miller and Form and Super. How do these compare with Dalton and Thompson's career stages?
4. Describe Schein's individual differences model and discuss how career anchors are useful in describing career development.
5. Based on your reading of Dalton and Thompson's career stages model, what organizational programs or policies might improve the career development of individuals at various stages in their careers?
6. What are the similarities and differences among the life-span, individual differences, and organizationally based models of careers?
7. How can bosses aid subordinates' career development?

Key Terms

career

life-span models

career anchors

technical/functional competence anchor

managerial competence anchor

security anchor

creativity/entrepreneurship anchor

autonomy and independence anchor

apprentice stage

independent contributor stage

networking

mentoring stage

sponsor stage

mentor

Suggested Readings

Dalton, G. W., and Thompson, P. H. (1986). *Novations: Strategies for career management.* Glenview, IL: Scott, Foresman.

Feldman, D. C. (1988). *Managing careers in organizations,* Glenview, IL: Scott, Foresman.

Kram, K. (1985). *Mentoring at work: Developmental relationships in organization life.* Glenview, IL: Scott, Foresman.

Levinson, D. (1978). *The seasons of a man's life.* New York: Alfred A. Knopf.

Notes

1. D. T. Hall (1976), *Careers in organizations,* Pacific Palisades, CA: Goodyear.
2. G. W. Dalton, P. H. Thompson, and R. L. Price (Summer 1977), The four stages of professional careers—a new look at performance by professionals, *Organizational Dynamics,* 23.
3. D. C. Miller and W. H. Form (1951), *Industrial sociology,* New York: Harper.
4. D. E. Super (1957), *The psychology of careers,* New York: Harper & Row.
5. C. Buehler (1933), *Der menschliche lebenschauf als psychologisches problem,* Leipzig: Hirzel.
6. E. H. Schein (May-June 1975), How career anchors hold executives to their career paths, *Personnel,* 11-24.
7. G. W. Dalton and P. H. Thompson (1986), *Novations: Strategies for career management,* Glenview, IL: Scott, Foresman.
8. P. H. Thompson and G. W. Dalton (November-December 1976), Are R&D organizations obsolete? *Harvard Business Review,* 108.
9. Dalton and Thompson, 22.
10. Dalton, Thompson, and Price, 28.
11. Dalton, Thompson, and Price, 31.

The Token Woman

Linda P. Fletcher, Westchester
College, and Susan Phillips,
University of Iowa

The Mainstream Life Insurance Company, to forestall possible affirmative action pressure because of the lack of women in the insurance industry's managerial ranks, decided to actively recruit a woman to fill a recent opening in the research division of the company's trust department. The position, that of research analyst, was one of several middle-management jobs at Mainstream that traditionally have been stepping stones for promotion into the executive ranks.

The required credentials for this particular opening were an M.B.A. (or a comparable graduate degree) with a major emphasis in finance, at least two years of academic or business experience, and proven research capability in the investment field. An exhaustive search and meticulous screening resulted in the hiring of Claire Meredith. Claire was an attractive, twenty-seven-year-old woman whose M.S. degree in finance was awarded "With Distinction" and whose master's thesis was published by a prestigious university press. She had been employed as a broker in a highly respected Wall Street investment banking firm, and had written numerous publications based on theoretical and applied research projects. Mainstream was able to hire her only after John Forbes, her potential immediate supervisor, assured her of equal opportunity in all organizational levels. An additional inducement was a starting salary $2000 higher than other offers she had recently received.

At the end of her third month on the job, Claire privately acknowledged a pervasive feeling of frustration with her new position. She began reviewing the activities of the past three months in an attempt to determine the basis of her negative reaction.

During the first day on the job, each of Claire's colleagues had expressed delight at having her "on board." One colleague observed that "it's high time the company hired a woman for our section—we've needed some beautification of the office for a long time now." Another chimed in with the remark, "We'd better tell our wives that Claire is married so they won't think we're researching monkey business!" When Claire suggested that they all have lunch together, Roy James, a division programmer, told her that "each of the guys brings a brown bag for lunch, and we eat and talk shop in one or the other's office." Accordingly, Claire decided to join her colleagues and announced that she was joining the brown-bag league. She was surprised, therefore, when at noon the following day, Roy James opened his office door and urged, "Come on, you guys, let's research our brown bags. Frank, you and Jim get the coffee while David and I get the ice cream, and don't forget Don wants double cream in his coffee." Since Claire's name was not mentioned specifically, she decided, after some hesitation, to eat alone in her office. Claire did not feel she should join the secretaries and clerks for lunch, although she knew she would be welcome. This routine, with minor variations, subsequently became the established pattern.

Breaks for coffee in the company cafeteria were no exception to the seemingly established separation principle. Only once during the three-month interval had Claire been invited to join her colleagues for coffee. At that coffee break, Claire felt particularly uncomfortable. Although she thought she had an excellent working relationship with her associates, she had little in common with them outside of the work environment. In addition, it was quite obvious that the men in the division seemed to get together both after work and on weekends. Although her colleagues were very friendly in the office, they never included her in their plans.

Having reviewed the informal social structure of her employment, Claire recognized similar frustrations with respect to various functional aspects of her position. She recalled John Forbes, the head of the research division, explaining the operational features of the section: "We meet once a week in committee to determine the status of current projects, discuss proposals for the future, and make individual assignments on new research projects to be initiated. Any ideas you have, write them up in memo form for distribution to everyone prior to the next meeting, and we'll go over your suggestion at the earliest possible meeting to determine the feasibility of your idea."

Because she was the most recent addition to the staff, Claire deliberately maintained a low profile during the first few weekly committee meetings of the research division. The other committee members appeared to endorse her strategy by seeking her opinions only infrequently and by failing to draw her into their policy deliberations. During the fourth weekly gathering, John Forbes, who acted as chairman, noted that his secretary was unable to be present as usual to record the minutes of the meeting. Frank Howard suggested sending a replacement from the secretarial pool, but John shook his head and casually replied that "a replacement is unnecessary since the logical substitute is Ms. Meredith. Besides, brushing up on her shorthand will give her something to do during the meeting." Claire hastened to reply. "Since I do not know shorthand, I must decline the honor of this additional responsibility."

Shortly after the meeting, Claire decided to abandon her sideline role in the committee. She decided that the next time the group gathered formally, she would present a research proposal that she had been developing in the area of commission reduction through the use of regional exchanges.

Claire's specific assignments included the responsibility for several ongoing projects that required only infrequent attention. The major portion of her time was spent on a "cost allocation" project. Cost allocation was a computer system that, when completed, would provide complete investment information for each of Mainstream's trust customers. All trust funds were pooled for investment purposes. The pooling was necessary, since some of the trust ac-

counts were so small that each alone would generate little investment income, and income would virtually be wiped out by commission expenses.

The current method of determining income for each trust account was to apply the average new investment rate to the pro rata portion of each account's share of the total investment funds. Consequently, several of Mainstream's larger trust accounts had complained that their investment income was "supporting" the smaller accounts. Threatened with the loss of these large trust accounts, the financial vice-president of Mainstream, Bill Newbit, instructed John Forbes to develop an allocation system in which each account could be properly charged with expenses while simultaneously enjoying the income of the pooled fund investment mechanism.

John had developed the specifications for the cost allocation system and had turned over the system design and programming to a research analyst who had resigned several months before Claire joined the division. Claire later found out through the grapevine that he quit because he felt he was getting nowhere with cost allocation. When Claire was hired, she was told she would have full responsibility for the completion of the system, including supervision of the programming by Roy James, development of comprehensive test data, and ultimately getting the system on line. Since investment income for each account was currently calculated by hand under the supervision of Frank Howard, Claire anticipated the usual problems of employee resistance to a new computer system. Therefore, she had begun system-orientation classes for the personnel involved. Claire had determined that the existing personnel, with training, would be adequate

to effectively use and run the new system. No personnel displacement would be necessary.

Claire was in the final stages of testing the system with Roy James and decided it was time to show some results to John Forbes. When she took the first test run in to John, he expressed complete surprise. He admitted, "I can't believe that the cost allocation project got off the ground. This system had been knocking around for three years—we never had any usable output and I really never expected to get any. Frankly, we had just about decided to write off the $800,000 development costs as 'sunk.' I guess we'll have to start thinking about moving on this thing—manpower, planning, and so on."

When Claire left John's office, she was disappointed at his reaction. As she reviewed his comments, she really began to wonder just what she was supposed to be doing at Mainstream, and how she could go about doing it.

Questions

1. Are the problems that Claire Meredith is having typical for a young woman in management?

2. Where would you place Claire in a life-span career model and why?

3. Can you identify Claire's current career anchor?

4. What could John Forbes do to improve Claire's situation?

5. How well do you think Claire has handled herself?

6. What suggestions would you have for Claire?

GLOSSARY

Acceptance view of authority View in which authority flows upward from subordinates to superiors based on the nature of the relationship between people and their perception of this relationship. (Ch. 10)

Accounting management System of management that plans, organizes, directs, and controls the successful execution of financial transactions between an organization and other parties. (Ch. 2)

Acquired needs Needs learned through experience. (Ch. 13)

Action statements Statements that reflect the means by which an organization moves forward to attain its goals. (Ch. 5)

Administrative plans Managers use administrative plans to allocate organizational resources and to coordinate their organization's internal subdivisions. These plans are associated with the organizational responsibility of middle management. (Ch. 5)

Affective component Part of an attitude that includes how people feel about a person, task, or the like and that arises from their reactions to the cognitive component of the attitude. (Ch. 12)

Aggregate plan Plan for entire operating system done before the actual plan for each product, department, and machine is determined. (Ch. 21)

Analyzer organization True blend of the defender and prospector styles; attempts to balance the risk and aggression of a prospector with the conservative, protective nature of a defender. (Ch. 8)

Apprentice stage Stage in Dalton and Thompson's career model in which individuals enter organizations and perform detailed and routine tasks under close supervision. (Ch. 24)

Arbitrator Third party outside of an organization to whom a grievance can be submitted if an employee does not feel an issue has been resolved. (Ch. 22)

Artificial intelligence Computers' tasks requiring the human characteristics of intelligence, imagination, and intuition. (Ch. 20)

Assessment of means goals Review of actual processes and procedures used toward planned outcomes. (Ch. 19)

Attitude Beliefs, feelings, and intentions about behavior that people have toward a person, event, task, or organization. (Ch. 12)

Authoritarian Person who feels that power and status should be clearly defined and that there should be an organizational hierarchy of authority. (Ch. 12)

Authority Legitimate right of a person to exercise influence. (Ch. 10)

Authority relationships Relationships between people and between people and their work: line, staff, and functional authority. (Ch. 10)

Autonomy and independence anchor Need to be able to work without direction or restraints, often manifested in a departure from traditional jobs. (Ch. 24)

Batch (disconnected-line) process Operating process that falls midway between a job shop and a repetitive line. Products or services can be produced in a line manner but are usually processed in large batches because of a particular feature of the product or process. (Ch. 21)

Behavioral approach Job design approach that rejects the idea of treating people like automated machines that continuously perform simple and repetitive activities. (Ch. 9)

Behavioral model Organizational design model that focuses less on the rational and mechanical aspects of organizational design and more on the social and psychological sides of an organization. (Ch. 11)

Behavioral school Behavioral management theorists viewed organizations from social and psychological perspectives. (Ch. 4)

Behavioral science movement Movement that stressed the need to conduct systematic and controlled studies of workers and their attitudes and behaviors. (Ch. 4)

Behavioral tendency component The part of an attitude that identifies how

people intend to behave toward a person, task, or the like. (Ch. 12)

Binding arbitration Process in which both parties are obligated to conform to the findings of an arbitrator. (Ch. 22)

Boundary roles Positions that link an organization to its external environment. (Ch. 2)

Boundary-spanning process One means through which organizations conduct transactions with their external environment. (Ch. 2)

Bounded rationality Situation wherein managers try to behave rationally within the limits of their information-processing capabilities and within the context of their attitudes and emotions. (Ch. 6)

Brainstorming A qualitative tool; a technique designed to stimulate people to develop alternatives during the planning and decision-making process. Brainstorming encourages the sharing of ideas in a setting free of the interruptions and risks of immediate evaluation and discussion. (Ch. 7)

Break-even analysis Identification of the point at which sales revenues equal the total cost of producing a product or service. (Ch. 7)

Budgets Single-use plans, expressed in numerical terms, sometimes called *numerized programs,* that deal with the allocation and use of organizational activities for a specified accounting period. (Ch. 5)

Bureaucratic model Organizational design that bases its legitimacy on inherent rationality and relies on a set of rules that specifies employee rights and duties and on standard operating procedures to control work-related activities. (Ch. 11)

Business unit strategy Functioning of an individual business within a corporation; specifies how an organization will interact with its task environment. (Ch. 8)

Cafeteria plans Benefit plans that allow individual employees the flexibility of picking and choosing plans that meet their personal needs. Employees choose benefits much as they would choose a meal in a cafeteria line. (Ch. 22)

Capacity Maximum amount of product or service that can be delivered in a stated time frame. (Ch. 21)

Career Individually perceived sequence of attitudes and behaviors associated with work-related experiences and activities over the span of a person's life (Hall). (Ch. 24)

Career anchors Schein's description of the needs that individuals fill through their careers. (Ch. 24)

Cash cows SBUs within a portfolio matrix with a large share of a low-growth market. (Ch. 8)

Causal modeling Quantitative model that attempts to forecast future events in statistical terms. Causal models document the causes of past events. (Ch. 7)

Cautious shifts Tendency of groups to make decisions that are more cautious than an average individual's decision. (Ch. 6)

Centralization Extent to which formal authority is concentrated within the hierarchy of an organization determines its degree of centralization. (Ch. 10)

Certainty Situation wherein a decision maker is aware of all available alternatives and the factors (outcomes) associated with each. (Ch. 6)

Charisma Leadership trait involving a personal magnetic charm or appeal that arouses loyalty and enthusiasm. (Ch. 15)

Choice making Narrow set of activities associated with choosing one option from a set of already identified alternatives. (Ch. 6)

Classical approach Task approach wherein labor is divided into jobs made up of a small number of simple, repetitive, standardized tasks. (Ch. 9)

Classical authority theory Authority is the institutional right of organizations to act, to decide, and to exercise influence. (Ch. 10)

Classical organization theory Concentrates on the management of an entire organization. Deals with the structure of an organization and with designing processes that improve its operations. (Ch. 4)

Classical school Includes the scientific-management movement and classical organization theory. It emphasized the economic rationality of decisions made by organizations and their members and the role of economic incentives as primary motivators. (Ch. 4)

Closed system Organization that operates as though it were in a world by itself. It blocks out ideas, information, and external environmental forces. (Ch. 2)

Coercive power Power a person has because people believe that he or she can punish them by inflicting pain or by withholding or taking away something that they value. (Ch. 14)

Cognitive component Part of an attitude that includes what people think they know about a person, task, or the like and is generally descriptive. (Ch. 12)

Communicating Process of transmitting information. (Ch. 2)

Communication Process of transferring information from one person or group (sender) to another (receiver). Five components are: ideation, message encoding, channels/networks, message decoding, and received message. (Ch. 14)

Communication networks Interconnected linkages. Together these linkages connect individuals or groups for communication purposes. (Ch. 14)

Competing values perspective Approach to assessing organizational effectiveness that attempts to integrate ideas from the four systematic approaches when none of them is an ideal solution. (Ch. 16)

Competitive advantages An organization's unique position compared to other organizations in its task environment. (Chs. 8, 21)

Compulsory staff consultation Action that forces line personnel and staff personnel to discuss issues before taking action. (Ch. 10)

Computer-integrated operations Operations based on the ability to control manufacturing and service processes by computer. (Ch. 21)

Conceptual skills Skills that allow people to see, to diagnose, and to understand concepts at an abstract level. (Ch. 1)

Concurrent controls Control device used by managers to make certain that deviation from a planned course of action does not occur while work is in progress. Two common forms of concurrent control are steering controls and screening controls. (Ch. 17)

Concurring authority Authority whereby a designated staff member can formally approve or disapprove an action to be taken. (Ch. 10)

Conflict Situation that exists when two or more people have incompatible goals and one or both believe that the behavior of the other will prevent his or her own goal attainment. (Ch. 14)

Consideration Relationship-oriented behavior of a leader. (Ch. 15)

Content theories Theories based on the premise that all people have needs, both innate and acquired. (Ch. 13)

Contingency approach Managers organize work and design jobs to fit the characteristics of workers who will perform the jobs, the organization's technology, and other design characteristics of the organization. (Ch. 9)

Contingency plans Plans created to deal with events that might occur if certain assumptions turn out to be wrong. (Ch. 5)

Contingency theory of leadership Leadership theory (Fiedler) that classifies leaders according to an underlying trait, describes situations that leaders face, and identifies optimal matches between leaders and situations. (Ch. 15)

Continuous process Operating system that is a higher-flow version of a repetitive line. (Ch. 21)

Continuous schedules of reinforcement Schedules of reinforcing or punishing every time a behavior is shown. (Ch. 13)

Controlling Monitoring and evaluating organizational effectiveness and initiating the actions needed to maintain or improve effectiveness. (Chs. 1, 17)

Conventional career pattern Pattern in which individuals move from an initial job to a trial job to stable employment. (Ch. 25)

Coordinating process Linking two or more organizational units so that they work harmoniously together. (Ch. 12)

Corporate strategy Strategy that defines the domain of an organization and lets its members know which priorities have been set. (Ch. 8)

Cost leadership strategy Generic strategy wherein managers find a market niche by selling their organization's products or services more cheaply than its competitors'. (Ch. 8)

Countertrade Simultaneous importing and exporting. (Ch. 19)

Craft approach Task approach wherein a single skilled worker designs and builds one product at a time from beginning to end. (Ch. 9)

Creative imitation "Drucker" strategy based on improving someone else's innovation. (Ch. 23)

Creativity/entrepreneurship anchor Need to create, to develop, or to invent something in one's career. (Ch. 24)

Culture Complex whole that includes knowledge, belief, art, morals, law, customs, and any other capabilities and habits acquired by people as members of society. (Ch. 19)

Custom solutions Solutions developed specifically for a current situation. (Ch. 6)

Cybernetic control Control system based on self-regulating procedures that automatically detect and correct deviations from planned activities and effectiveness levels. (Ch. 17)

Data Representations of facts (represented by symbols, such as numerals or letters of the alphabet) pertaining to people, things, ideas, and events. (Ch. 20)

Database An organization's set of computer data files that are structured and stored so they can be easily processed and used by those who need information about the organization. (Ch. 20)

Decentralization Extent to which, by design, authority is spread throughout an organization and, thus, characterizes the organization's structure. (Ch. 10)

Decisional (strategy-making) roles Managerial roles in which a manager functions as entrepreneur, disturbance handler, resource allocator, or negotiator. (Ch. 1)

Decision making Process of identifying a set of feasible alternatives and, from these, choosing a course of action. (Chs. 2, 6)

Decision-support system (DSS) Data, information, and reports of the TPS and information-reporting system. (Ch. 20)

Decision tree Tool that helps a manager decide the extent to which subordinates should be involved in making decisions for particular situations. (Ch. 7)

Defender organizations Organizations in which managers develop strategies that they hope will create and maintain a stable niche in the market for their organization's products or services. (Ch. 8)

Delegation Process managers use to transfer formal authority from one position to another within an organization and to put the authority system they have designed into place. (Ch. 10)

Delphi technique Qualitative tool that is a group process designed to bring information and the judgments of people together to facilitate planning and decision making. (Ch. 7)

Departmentalization Process of grouping jobs into organizational units and those units into larger units. (Ch. 9)

Development Preparation that extends beyond a job, such as the instruction an employee will need if the design of the current job changes or if the employee changes jobs through transfer or promotion. (Ch. 22)

Diagonal communication Communication that occurs as information flows across both vertical and horizontal components. (Ch. 14)

Differentiation strategy Generic strategy to help an organization establish itself as different from the competition. (Ch. 8)

Directing The process through which employees are led and motivated to make effective and efficient contributions to the realization of organizational goals. (Ch. 1)

Distribution systems Systems by which an organization's inventory is transported to its customers. (Ch. 21)

Distributive justice George Homans held that distributive justice is a question of fairness; does a person believe that fair exchange has occurred between himself or herself and the organization? (Ch. 13)

Divestiture strategy Within portfolio matrix, managers get rid of an SBU that is financially unsuccessful and unlikely to respond to the retrenchment/turnaround strategy. (Ch. 8)

Divisional superstructure Organizational superstructure designed according to nonfunctional factors, such as territories, products, customer base, process, or projects. (Ch. 11)

Dogmatism Theory in which a person has a rigid belief system and sees the world from a narrow perspective. (Ch. 12)

Dogs SBUs within portfolio matrix with a small portion of a low-growth market. (Ch. 8)

Domain/directional planning Development of a course of action that moves an organization toward one identified domain and, therefore, away from other domains. (Ch. 5)

Economic order quantity (EOQ) Mathematical model for identifying the amount of inventory to order when managers know their inventory use, product cost, cost of procuring inventory, and annual inventory carrying costs. (Ch. 7)

Employee-centered behaviors Leader behaviors that include consideration and support for subordinates. (Ch. 15)

Ends decisions Decisions that are oriented specifically toward achieving a goal. (Ch. 6)

Ends goals Specified goals in goal attainment approach to assessing organizations' effectiveness. (Ch. 16)

Entrepreneurial judo Strategy that capitalizes on the weaknesses of an organization that holds a leadership position. (Ch. 23)

Entrepreneurship Involves the development of a product or service idea and the creation of an organization to further its growth. (Ch. 23)

Environmental change Change that reflects the degree to which an organization's task environment is stable or shifting. (Ch.2)

Environmental segmentation Similarities and differences among components of the task environment and the demands that they place on an organization. (Ch. 2)

Equity theory As proposed by Adams, suggests that people compare their own distributive justice ratio to the ratio they perceive for other people (an individual, a group, one's self in another situation, or one's idealized self). (Ch. 13)

ERG Theory Hierarchy of needs developed by Alderfer (existence, relatedness, and growth). (Ch. 13)

Establishment stage Period in Super's life-span model in which an appropriate field is found and effort is put forth to make a permanent place in it. (Ch. 25)

Ethics Set of standards and code of conduct that define what is right, wrong, and just in human actions. (Ch. 3)

Ethnocentric staffing International staffing wherein the staffing of subsidiaries is based on putting home-country personnel in place. (Ch. 19)

Existing solutions Alternatives that have been used (or at least considered) by other decision makers in similar situations. (Ch. 6)

Expectancy perception Part of expectancy theory, which holds that it is likely that a given alternative will lead to a particular performance level. (Ch. 13)

Expectancy theory Theory that holds that individuals make their decisions by thinking through the implications of each alternative and choosing the one that is most attractive. (Ch. 13)

Expert power Power that exists when an individual is perceived as having greater knowledge or ability than those around him or her. (Ch. 14)

Exporting Selling goods to buyers in another country. (Ch. 19)

External environment Conditions, circumstances, and influences that surround and affect the functioning of an organization. (Ch. 2)

External recruiting Human resource managers' attempting to find a qualified pool of candidates from outside of an organization. (Ch. 22)

Extrinsic motivators Motivators within organizational behavior modification program that are based on rewards provided by someone other than the person being motivated. (Ch. 13)

Financial management Staff function that applies the management process to an organization's financial assets. (Ch. 2)

Focus strategy Generic strategy in which organizations focus on a specific segment of a total market and concentrate their resources on competing within that segment. (Ch. 8)

Force Part of expectancy theory that refers to the overall attractiveness of an alternative, which drives a person to choose that alternative. (Ch. 13)

Formal (designated) leader Individual appointed by an organization to serve in a formal capacity as an agent of the organization. (Ch. 15)

Formal groups Groups consciously created within organizations to serve organizational objectives. (Ch. 12)

Formal organization Organization that exists as a result of the official structures and systems designed by managers through the organizing activity. Usually contains a structured communication and command system that helps people pool their time, energy, and talents to reach common objectives. (Ch. 9)

Formal rewards Rewards, such as increases in pay or receipt of a promotion, that are stipulated by an organization to help its managers develop power. (Ch. 14)

Franchise Licensing of an entire business system as well as industrial property by an independent person. (Ch. 19)

Functional authority Right to direct or control specific activities that are under the span of control of other managers. (Ch. 10)

Functional departments Departments in which activities are grouped according to the nature of the work performed. (Ch. 9)

Functional managers Managers classified according to their area of specialized activity (also known as organizational function served). (Ch. 1)

Functional strategy Comprehensive plan for each major functional area (such as marketing, finance, and production) within a business unit. Functional strategy should support and conform to the strategy of the business unit. (Ch. 8)

Functional superstructure Superstructure in which upper-level managers are organized around the basic organizational functions similar to the departmentalization-by-function approach adopted at lower levels. (Ch. 11)

Gap analysis Step in strategic planning process that identifies the expected gaps between where managers want their organization to go and where it will go if they maintain the current strategy. (Ch. 8)

General environment Overall environment within which an organization operates, including its social and cultural context, the economic system surrounding the organization, the legal and political atmosphere, the technology from which knowledge and tools for reaching goals are derived, and the international climate. (Ch. 2)

Generic strategies Three strategies—cost leadership, differentiation, and focus—that are pursued by managers. (Ch. 8)

Global enterprises Multinational corporations that respond to world markets through a unified strategy. (Ch. 19)

Goal attainment approach Method by which managers evaluate organizational effectiveness by assessing the degree to which one or more specified goals are met. (Ch. 16)

Goal hierarchy Illustration of the complexities posed by many interrelated systems of goals and major plans. (Ch. 5)

Goal planning Setting specific goals and creating action statements. (Ch. 5)

Goals End states (targets) that managers hope to attain. They emerge from forces in both internal and external environments of an organization. (Ch. 5)

Goal theory Theory that specifies that particular kinds of goals motivate organization members most effectively. (Ch. 13)

Great person approach Leadership approach that states that some people are born with the necessary attributes to be great leaders. (Ch. 15)

Grievance Complaint filed if a union member feels that part of a contract has been violated. (Ch. 22)

Group Two or more people who interact, who perceive themselves to be a group, and who have a common purpose or common goal. (Ch. 12)

Group norms Stipulations of the limits of expected and acceptable behavior for group members. (Ch. 12)

Groupthink A group drive to reach consensus at almost any cost. (Chs. 6, 12)

Growth strategy Strategy within portfolio matrix that is required for stars and for questions marks that an organization hopes to transform into stars. (Ch. 8)

Heterogeneous task environment Highly segmented or differentiated task environment. (Ch. 2)

Hierarchy Set of managerial levels of authority and responsibility within an organization. (Ch. 1)

Homogeneous task environment Task environment characterized by very little segmentation. (Ch. 2)

Horizontal communication Flow of information between individuals or groups who occupy positions at the same hierarchical level. (Ch. 14)

Horizontal coordination Coordination within a single hierarchical level. (Ch. 9)

Horizontal specialization Job design that creates many low-skill-level, repetitive jobs. (Ch. 9)

Human (interpersonal) skills An individual's ability to work with and understand others, to lead, to motivate, to manage conflict, and to build group effort. (Ch. 1)

Human relations model Model of assessing organizational effectiveness characterizing an organization that values the well-being of its members over the development and promotion of the organization itself. (Ch. 16)

Human resource management Managerial function that tries to match an organization's needs to the skills and abilities of its employees. (Chs. 2, 22)

Hybrid approach Simultaneous use of two or more departmentalization strategies. (Ch. 9)

Hybrid planning Planning that moves from domain planning to goal planning. Planners begin with more general domain planning and establish their commitment to move in a particular direction. (Ch. 5)

Hybrid superstructure Superstructure that combines the characteristics of two or more structural approaches. (Ch. 11)

Hygiene needs Needs, classified by Herzberg, that are not directly related to work itself. Instead they relate to the context of a job and consist of such factors as pay, working conditions, coworkers, supervision, and security. (Ch. 13)

Importing Buying goods from sellers in another country. (Ch. 19)

Independent contributor stage Stage in Dalton and Thompson's career model in which individuals develop in areas of expertise and work independently. (Ch. 24)

Individual pay Amount a manager decides to pay an individual within an established pay range. (Ch. 22)

Influence Ability to produce results and to bring about a change in the environment. (Ch. 10)

Informal groups Groups that arise spontaneously and whose activity may or may not be helpful in reaching organizational objectives. (Ch. 12)

Informal leader A leader created because group members choose him or her as their natural leader. (Ch. 15)

Informal organization Two or more people who interact for a purpose or in a manner beyond that specified by managers. Often, informal organizations evolve in a natural, unplanned manner. (Ch. 9)

Informal rewards Rewards provided from a leader's own resources. (Ch. 14)

Information Meaningful data. (Ch. 20)

Informational (environmental) scan A step in the strategic planning process by which an organization collects information from the external environment about factors that can influence the organization. (Ch. 8)

Informational roles Roles in which managers collect and disperse knowledge, thus becoming an important nerve center for an organization. (Ch. 1)

Information-reporting system System that retrieves, sorts, pools, and manipulates transaction data in other ways to produce summary or management reports. (Ch. 20)

Initiating structure Structure that involves "task-oriented" leader behaviors and is instrumental in the efficient use of resources to attain organizational goals. (Ch. 15)

Innate needs Inborn needs, such as the needs for food and water. (Ch. 13)

Innovation Phenomenon that occurs when an organization is the first or early user of an idea among its set of similar organizations. (Ch. 18)

Institutional zone Zone of responsibility in which managers are primarily responsible for two aspects of an organization's external environment. (Ch. 1)

Instrumentality perception Perceived likelihood that a given performance level will lead to one or more outcomes. (Ch. 13)

Intermittent schedules of reinforcement Schedules that provide a consequence following some (but not all) responses. (Ch. 13)

Internal environment Wide range of factors within an organization's formal boundaries. (Ch. 2)

Internal forces to change Forces emanating from within an organization that encourage change. (Ch. 18)

Internal processes approach Approach that defines organizational effectiveness as the degree to which members are integrated with organizational production and management systems to function smoothly with a minimum of internal strain. (Ch. 16)

Internal processes model Model of assessing organizational effectiveness that values the well-being of organization members. (Ch. 16)

Internal recruiting Human resource program of finding employees already inside an organization who are qualified for job openings. (Ch. 22)

International management Process of carrying out the managerial functions of planning, organizing, directing, and controlling a business that operates in more than one country. (Ch. 19)

Interpersonal power Power that enables individual organization members to exert influence over others and over their organization. (Chs. 10, 14)

Interpersonal roles Roles managers must fill because of their position in an organization. (Ch. 1)

Intrapreneurship Process that takes place when individuals who identify the need for (often innovative) change in an organization create an environment in which the change can succeed and champion the implementation of the change. (Ch. 23)

Intrinsic motivators Motivators within an organizational behavior modification program that arise from within an individual. (Ch. 13)

Inventory A measure of physical goods that are produced and not yet sold. (Ch. 21)

Job Collection of tasks that can be performed by one person. (Ch. 22)

Job analysis Process of documenting job tasks and their associated responsibilities and requirements. (Ch. 22)

Job-centered behaviors Leader behaviors devoted to supervisory functions, such as planning, scheduling, coordinating work activities, and providing the resources needed for task performance. (Ch. 15)

Job Characteristics Model (JCM) Model that specifies the critical job components that lead to positive results for both an organization and its workers. (Ch. 9)

Job description List of the duties and responsibilities that managers expect the holder of a job to accomplish, the procedures that the job holder should follow in carrying them out, and the qualifications that a person needs to accomplish these duties and responsibilities. (Ch. 22)

Job design Method of dividing work into tasks and then assembling these tasks into jobs. (Ch. 2)

Job enlargement Job design strategy that adds breadth to a job by increasing the number and variety of activities performed by an employee. (Ch. 9)

Job enrichment Job design strategy that adds depth to a job by adding "managerial" activities (planning, organizing, directing, and controlling) to an employee's responsibilities. (Ch. 9)

Job evaluation Process of determining the relative value of jobs, based on the job requirements identified in a job analysis. (Ch. 22)

Job involvement An employee's psychological involvement with a job. (Ch. 12)

Job satisfaction Affective component of people's attitudes toward their work. (Ch. 12)

Job shop Type of operation in which work centers are arranged around particular types of equipment or functions. (Ch. 21)

Just-in-time (JIT) Inventory control method based on the principle that inventory is a fundamental liability that must be reduced. (Ch. 21)

Labor market The number and types of people in the workforce. (Ch. 22)

Layout Arrangement that locates a facility's processing equipment or functions in sequence as they are needed in production. (Ch. 21)

Leadership Interpersonal process involving the exercise of influence within a social system, such as a group, family, community, or work organization. (Ch. 15)

Leadership in a new market or industry Process that involves creating and then dominating a new product or service area. (Ch. 23)

Least preferred co-worker (LPC) Person with whom leaders least wanted to work along a number of dimensions, such as pleasant/unpleasant, friendly/unfriendly. (Ch. 15)

Legitimate power Power that exists when one person believes that another person has the right to influence him or her. (Ch. 14)

Letter of credit (LC) Financial instrument used between a buyer and a seller in an export transaction. (Ch. 19)

Licensing agreement Agreement in which a licensor gives a licensee the right to use a patent, trademark, copyright, technology, or other asset in return for a royalty or fee. (Ch. 19)

Life cycle Stages of an organization's development: (1) entrepreneurial, (2) collectivity, (3) formalization, (4) elaboration of structure. (Ch. 16)

Life-span models Descriptive frameworks of careers built around the biological life cycle. (Ch. 24)

Linear programming (LP) Quantitative model by which managers not only can control inventory but can also identify the appropriate quantity of product to manufacture. (Ch. 7)

Line authority Command authority that gives a manager the organizational right to make decisions and to commit the organization to action. (Ch. 10)

Line managers Managers with a direct responsibility for producing the service or product line of an organization. (Ch. 1)

Linking pin roles Roles resulting from managers' participation in and connecting function with multiple groups. (Ch. 11)

Lockout Process in which management closes down operations and refuses to offer work to union members until an agreement is reached. (Ch. 22)

Long-range plans Plans that generally encompass a period of more than five years. (Ch. 5)

McKinsey 7-S framework Seven interdependent factors in organizations that must be managed harmoniously, because a change in one necessitates adjustments in the other six. (Ch. 4)

Management Process of planning, organizing, directing, and controlling organizational resources in the pursuit of organizational goals. (Ch. 1)

Management by Objectives (MBO) Process through which an organization's goals, plans, and control systems are defined through collaboration between managers and their subordinates. (Ch. 5)

Management information system (MIS) System that provides managers with information that enables them to make better decisions and improve their job performance. (Ch. 20)

Managerial competence anchor Need to be competent in the set of activities that comprise management. (Ch. 24)

Managerial (tactical) decisions Decisions that specify how an organization intends to integrate its institutional level with its technical core and how it will coordinate work systems within the technical core. (Ch. 6)

Managerial zone Zone of responsibility in which managers create and manage systems to coordinate and integrate various parts of the technical core. (Ch. 1)

Managers Organization members who are assigned the primary responsibility of carrying out the management process. (Ch. 1)

Marketing management Applies the management process to satisfying the needs and wants of an organization's customers through its goods and services. (Ch. 2)

Matrix boss Person who manages one of an organization's overlapping systems. (Ch. 11)

Matrix superstructure Superstructure that uses two or more integrated, coexisting structures simultaneously. (Ch. 11)

Means decisions Decisions that concern procedures or actions undertaken to achieve particular goals—in other words, how a goal is to be reached. (Ch. 6)

Means goals Specified goals that are directly tied to a systems approach. (Ch. 16)

Mechanistic system System characterized by clear definition and relative stability of tasks and responsibility. (Ch. 2)

Mediator Impartial third party who works with bargainers to identify a mutually acceptable agreement. (Ch. 22)

Mentor An experienced member of an organization who coaches, guides, and counsels newer members. (Ch. 24)

Mentoring stage Stage in Dalton and Thompson's career model in which individuals coach, teach, and guide people in Stage 1. (Ch. 24)

Motivation Stimulus that energizes, directs, and sustains human behavior. (Ch. 13)

Motivator needs Needs classified by Herzberg as achievement, recognition, responsibility, and advancement (like Alderfer's growth needs). (Ch. 13)

Multinational corporations (MNCs) Companies that have a variety of overseas linkages, of which a significant number are wholly owned subsidiaries. (Ch. 19)

Need for achievement Desire to accomplish difficult and challenging objectives. (Ch. 13)

Need for affiliation Desire for warm and friendly relationships with others. (Ch. 13)

Need for power Desire to control others and to influence their behavior. (Ch. 13)

Negative reinforcement Method of making a desired response more likely when a behavior causes something undesired to be taken away. (Ch. 13)

Networking Process by which individuals in organizations gain social support from many directions. (Ch. 24)

Nominal group technique (NGT) Qualitative tool that is a group decision-making process designed to generate a large number of creative potential solutions to a problem, to evaluate these solutions, and to rank them from best to worst. (Ch. 7)

Noncybernetic control Control system operated completely independently from the work system itself. (Ch. 17)

Nonprogrammed decisions Decisions generally made in unique or novel situations, when no prior routine or practice exists to guide the decision-making process. (Ch. 6)

Nonreinforcement Method of making desired responses less likely. Subordinate is permitted to engage in an undesired behavior but no consequence at all, positive or negative, follows that response. (Ch. 13)

Objective rationality Situation wherein managers know all possible alternatives and their probable consequences and rationally select the "one best" alternative. (Ch. 6)

Official goals An organization's general aims as expressed in public statements, in its annual report, and in its organizational charter. (Ch. 5)

Open system Organizational system that interacts with and depends on other systems. (Ch. 2)

Open-systems model Model of assessing organizational effectiveness that values the need for flexibility over the need for control, as do managers using the human relations model. (Ch. 16)

Operating decisions Decisions that deal with the day-to-day operations of an organization. (Ch. 6)

Operating plans Plans that cover the day-to-day operations of an organization. (Ch. 5)

Operational goals Goals that reflect managers' specific intentions; the concrete goals that organization members are to pursue. (Ch. 5)

Operational strategies Actions that are to be taken in order to accomplish strategic objectives. (Ch. 8)

Operations management Application of planning, organizing, directing, and controlling activities to that part of an organization in charge of making its product. (Chs. 2, 21)

Optimize Find the best possible decision. (Ch. 6)

Organic organization Organization that is fluid and dynamic and capable of evolution, redesign, and adaptation to both internal and external environments. (Ch. 11)

Organic system System characterized by a flexible structure that can change, loosely defined tasks to be performed by employees, consultative-type organizational communication, and authority that flows more from knowledge centers. (Ch. 2)

Organization System of consciously coordinated activities of two or more persons. (Ch. 1)

Organizational behavior modification (OBM) Systematic application of operant learning principles to manage behavior within organizations. (Ch. 13)

Organizational chart Schematic drawing of the positions within an organization. (Ch. 1)

Organizational climate Climate composed of such factors as structure, processes, and culture. (Ch. 2)

Organizational commitment Active association between individuals and organizations such that committed employees are willing to give something of themselves in order to contribute to the organization's well-being. (Ch. 12)

Organizational context Circumstances and conditions within which an organization operates. (Ch. 11)

Organizational culture Pattern of basic assumptions invented, discovered, or developed by a group as it learns to cope with its problems of external adaptation and internal integration. (Ch. 2)

Organizational design An organization's structure and the systems that help the organization operate. (Chs. 2, 11)

Organizational development (OD) Process of diagnosing organizational problems by looking for incongruencies between environment, structures, processes, and people. (Ch. 18)

Organizational effectiveness Degree to which organizational goals are being met. (Ch. 16)

Organizational mission Statement that specifies an organization's reason for being. (Ch. 8)

Organizational politics The management of influence to obtain ends not sanctioned by an organization or to obtain sanctioned ends through nonsanctioned influence means. (Ch. 14)

Organizational scan Step in strategic planning process that identifies an organization's present strengths and weaknesses by examining its internal resources. (Ch. 8)

Organizational structure Structure that identifies and distinguishes the individual parts of an organization and ties these pieces together to define an integrated whole. (Ch. 11)

Organizing Process by which managers design, structure, and arrange the components of an organization's internal environment to facilitate attainment of organizational goals. (Chs. 1, 9)

Path-goal theory of leadership Leadership theory (House and Evans) that suggests that an effective leader provides subordinates with a path to a valued goal. (Ch. 15)

Pay level Relationship between an organization's rate of cash compensation and the general level for comparable jobs in the labor market. (Ch. 22)

Pay structure Relative values and pay ranges for each job in an organization. (Ch. 22)

Perception Process by which a person gains information from the environment, organizes it, and derives its meaning. (Ch. 12)

Performance appraisal Evaluation of how effectively employees are fulfilling their job responsibilities and contributing to the accomplishment of organizational goals. (Ch. 22)

Personality Combination of the psychological characteristics and traits that make up each person's unique style of behavior. (Ch. 12)

Planning Process by which managers establish goals and define the methods by which these goals are to be attained. (Ch. 1)

Planning specialists Professional planners who work singly or in groups to develop organizational plans and to help managers plan. (Ch. 5)

Point method Most widely used job evaluation tool that identifies a group of compensable factors—which typically parallel factors in job analyses—and that assigns points to each job according to level of responsibility for each factor. (Ch. 22)

Policies Broad-based statements of understanding or general statements of intent; provide limits within which decisions are to be made. (Ch. 5)

Polycentric staffing International staffing with executives from any country if they are the best people available. (Ch. 19)

Portfolio matrix Phase of business portfolio approach that categorizes an SBU according to its relative market growth and market share. (Ch. 8)

Positive reinforcement Method of making a desired response more likely; occurs whenever a positively valued consequence follows a response to a stimulus. (Ch. 13)

Postaction controls Controls exercised after an entire set of work activities has been completed to produce a product or service. (Ch. 17)

Precontrols Control activities that occur before inputs enter the system or prior to the beginning of an activity. (Ch. 17)

Premising Forecasting what is likely to happen inside and outside of an organization. (Ch. 5)

Proactive change Type of change that occurs when an organization's managers conclude that a change would be desirable (as opposed to necessary). (Ch. 18)

Problem solving Finding and implementing a course of action to correct an unsatisfactory situation. (Ch. 6)

Procedures Standing plans that guide action rather than thinking; procedures establish customary ways for handling certain activities. (Ch. 5)

Process perspective View that focuses on the actions taken by managers. (Ch. 1)

Process theories Theories that focus on the reasons people choose to behave in certain ways and the reasons they react as they do to organizational events. (Ch. 13)

Product/service departmentalization Job design strategy whereby activities related to the development and delivery of a single product (or closely related group of products) are grouped together. (Ch. 9)

Programmed decisions Decisions that deal with frequently occurring situations, such as requests for vacations by employees. (Ch. 6)

Programs Single-use plans consisting of a complex set of policies, rules, procedures, and other elements necessary to carry out a course of action. (Ch. 5)

Project departments Department created to address specific, often unique, organizational goals. (Ch. 9)

Projects Projects have the same characteristics as programs but are generally narrower in scope, less complex, and frequently created to support or complement programs. (Ch. 5)

Prospector organizations Innovative organizations in which managers move rapidly from one domain to another in search of new opportunities. (Ch. 8)

Punishment Method of making desired responses less likely because the undesired behavior is followed by a distinctly undesirable consequence. (Ch. 13)

Purchasing Working with vendors to supply the best product at the lowest cost. (Ch. 21)

Qualitative tools Tools designed for collecting and processing ideas, opinions, and judgments; thought-processing procedures. (Ch. 7)

Quality assurance Method of assuring that products or services meet customer expectations. (Ch. 21)

Quantitative tools Tools that provide a way to examine, to measure, and to express information in numbers. (Ch. 7)

Question marks SBUs within portfolio matrix that possess a relatively small share of a rapidly growing market. (Ch. 8)

Queuing models Models that help managers identify the best number of waiting lines. (Ch. 7)

Rational goals model Model of assessing organizational effectiveness that is concerned with organizational development and promotion; values control, consistency, and maintenance of the status quo. (Ch. 16)

Reactive change Type of change that occurs when the forces driving change provide so much pressure that an organization must change. (Ch. 18)

Reactor organizations Organizations that react to environmental events before they analyze the meaning and possible consequences of such events. (Ch. 8)

Referent power Ability of managers to influence a person because he or she wants to be associated or affiliated with the power holder. (Ch. 14)

Regression analysis Process in which a mathematical model (equation) describes the relationship of one or more causal variables to a dependent variable. (Ch. 7)

Reinforcement theories Theories wherein a person repeats behaviors that result in desirable consequences and avoids behaviors that produce undesirable consequences. (Ch. 13)

Repetitive process Operating process in which functions are arranged in a sequence in accordance to the specifications of a product. (Ch. 21)

Resource deployment Internal distribution of an organization's resources, including how much money it will spend in pursuit of its goals. (Ch. 8)

Resource power Power a person has because others believe that he or she has and is willing to share resources that they need. (Ch. 14)

Retrenchment/turnaround strategy Within portfolio matrix managers can try to stimulate markets by finding new uses for existing products, by attempting to change the image of a product, or by modifying a product in a search for a market niche. (Ch. 8)

Reward power Power a person has because people believe that he or she can bestow rewards or outcomes—such as money or recognition—that others desire. (Ch. 14)

Risky shift Tendency of groups to make decisions that are more prone toward risk than an average individual's decisions. (Ch. 6)

Role ambiguity Uncertainty about the requirements of a role. (Ch. 12)

Role conflict Conflict that occurs when people occupy several roles whose expectations contradict one another or when demands of their roles conflict with their personal preferences. (Ch. 12)

Routine decisions Decisions in which the factors involved and the outcomes can be clearly defined, and the timelines involved are usually short; such decisions are based on clear logic, are repetitive, and are made at low levels in an organization. (Ch. 21)

Rules Standing plans that guide employee actions. (Ch. 5)

Satisfice To find the first satisfactory solution. (Ch. 6)

Scabs Nonunion members hired by an organization to work in place of striking union members. (Ch. 22)

Scheduling Determining which employee will work when and at which machine or in which department and determining the work itself. (Ch. 21)

Scientific management Management that conducts a business or affairs by standards established by facts or truths gained through systematic observation, experiment, or reasoning. (Ch. 4)

Scope An organization's present and planned interactions with its environment; also identifies the organization's domain, such as the markets in which it expects to compete, and the nature and character of these interactions, such as methods of competition. (Ch. 8)

Screening controls Forms of concurrent control by which managers often try to identify critical "go, no-go" stages of organizational activity. (Ch. 17)

Security anchor Need for stability in one's career, either by remaining with the same company or by staying in a particular geographic area. (Ch. 24)

Selection Process of evaluating candidates, making predictions of the probable levels of job performance by each, and choosing a candidate for the job. (Ch. 22)

Self-managing work group approach Job design strategy whereby groups of workers collaborate in performing and managing their work. (Ch. 9)

Short-range plans Plans that cover activities that unfold relatively quickly, in most organizations, from the next several hours to the next several months. (Ch. 5)

Single-use plans Plans developed for unique situations or problems that are usually replaced after one use. (Ch. 5)

Situational view of authority View that ultimate authority resides in the will and consent of the people who perform a particular task. (Ch. 10)

Social audit Detailed examination and evaluation of an organization's social performance. (Ch. 3)

Social facilitation Process whereby decision making is enhanced by the presence of others. (Ch. 6)

Social impairment Impairment of decision making by the presence of others. (Ch. 6)

Social responsibility An organization's obligation to engage in activities that protect and contribute to the welfare of society. (Ch. 3)

Sociological perspective Perspective that defines management as the group of organization members that occupies the social position responsible for making sure that an organization achieves its mission. (Ch. 1)

Sociotechnical changes Changes involving changes in people and the technology. (Ch. 18)

Sociotechnical systems theory Theory that balances the technical and social-psychological sides of an organization. (Chs. 4, 11)

Span of control Number of subordinates and activities that a manager oversees. (Ch. 9)

Sponsor stage Stage in Dalton and Thompson's career model in which individuals determine the direction and future of organizations. (Ch. 24)

Stable growth strategy Strategy within portfolio matrix appropriate for most cash cows and some dogs. (Ch. 8)

Staff authority Authority in the form of counsel, advice, and recommendation. (Ch. 10)

Staffing Finding the person to do a job well. (Ch. 22)

Staff managers Managers who support line managers but who are not directly involved in the production of goods or services. (Ch. 1)

Standard operating procedure (SOP) Procedure invoked under a standing plan when an issue is faced repeatedly. (Ch. 5)

Standing plans Plans designed to be used to cover the many issues that managers face repeatedly. (Ch. 5)

Stars SBUs within portfolio matrix with a relatively large portion of a high-growth market—for example, compact disk SBU of SONY. (Ch. 8)

Steering controls Forms of concurrent control that occur after work has begun but before the activity is completed. (Ch. 17)

Steward Employee designated to represent union members. (Ch. 22)

Strategic business unit (SBU) Segment of an organization with a mission, an external market, and a strategy (or potential strategy) for dealing with that market. (Ch. 8)

Strategic constituencies approach Newest approach to assessing an organization's effectiveness by evaluating the degree to which the needs of the organization's constituents (stakeholders) have been satisfied. (Ch. 16)

Strategic decisions Decisions that reflect management's strategies for positioning an organization in its external environment. (Ch. 6)

Strategic management That part of the management process concerned with achieving an overall integration of an organization's internal divisions, while simultaneously integrating the organization with its external environment. (Ch. 8)

Strategic objectives Statements of definable and measurable accomplishments that, when realized, fulfill an organization's mission statement. (Ch. 8)

Strategic planning Top managers' active, conscious attempts to design a scheme to position an organization within its external environment. (Chs. 8, 21)

Strategic plans Plans that define an organization's long-term vision and the organization's intent to make its vision a reality. (Chs. 5, 8)

Strategy The art and science of combining the many resources available to achieve the best match between an organization and its environment. (Ch. 8)

Subsidiary Company that is legally separate from the parent company and is organized under the laws of the country in which it is located. (Ch. 19)

Superstructure Division of activities at the top of the organizational hierarchy; provides the primary structural form of the organization. (Ch. 11)

Synectic technique Qualitative tool designed to develop creative ideas: problem statement and background information stage, goal-wishing stage, excursion stage, forced-fit stage, itemized response stage. (Ch. 7)

Synergy Combination of scope, resource deployment, and competitive advantages that produces positive results. (Ch. 8)

System Set of related parts that work together in an organized way to achieve a stated purpose. (Chs. 4, 20)

System 4 organization Organizational design that emphasizes openness. (Ch. 11)

Systems approach Approach to assessing organizational effectiveness in which managers care mostly about how things are accomplished. (Ch. 16)

Systems theory Theory that views organizations as complex networks of interrelated parts that exist interdependently with the external environment. (Ch. 4)

Tactical plans Plans that focus on subsets of an organization's overall programs, activities, and systems. (Ch. 5)

Task environment Means through which the general environment exercises its most immediate influences on an organization's management. (Ch. 2)

Technical core Zone in which managers have direct responsibility for producing and delivering an organization's goods and/or services. (Ch. 1)

Technical/functional competence anchor Need to be expert in a technical field or functional area. (Ch. 24)

Technical skills Managerial skills that enable a manager to understand and use the tools, procedures, and techniques needed to perform a given task. (Ch. 1)

Technology Processes that transform organizational resources into a product or service. (Ch. 2)

Technostructural changes Changes involving concurrent changes in the technology and structure of an organization. (Ch. 18)

Territorial/geographical departmentalization Job design strategy often used when organizations have widely dispersed operations or offices. (Ch. 9)

Theory X Leadership theory that assumes an average individual dislikes work and is incapable of exercising adequate self-direction and self-control. (Ch. 4)

Theory Y Leadership theory that assumes people have a creative capacity and both the ability and desire to exercise self-direction and self-control. (Ch. 4)

Theory Z Less a major theory of management than a set of organizational and management style characteristics that emphasizes terms of employment, decision making, evaluation and promotion, control, career paths, and concern for employees. (Ch. 4)

Time series analysis Quantitative model that examines past data for trends and forecasts events; assumes the past will predict the future without considering why past events occurred. (Ch. 7)

Top leader Person who heads the multiple command system of a matrix organization. (Ch. 11)

Total quality control (TQC) Belief that any errors should be caught and corrected at the source—that is, where the work is performed and within the production process. (Ch. 21)

Training Improving employees' levels of ability. (Ch. 22)

Trait approach Leadership approach that attempts to identify physiological, psychological, attitudinal, and ability traits associated with effective leaders. (Ch. 15)

Transaction processing systems (TPS) Systems wherein an organization records, processes, and manages the data related to these everyday business activities. (Ch. 20)

Transformational leadership Process that relies on leaders' charisma and deeply held personal value systems, which include such values as justice and integrity. (Ch. 15)

Two-boss manager Person who is at the point of intersection of two or more of an organization's multiple structures and, thus, is directly responsible for more than one matrix boss. (Ch. 11)

Type A personality Personality of a person who works intensely, impatiently, and well with pressure. (Ch. 12)

Type B personality In contrast to Type A, personality of someone who has a less-pressured style and tends to be more easy-going and relaxed. (Ch. 12)

Unit/functional-level plans Plans focused on the day-to-day operations of lower-level organizational units. (Ch. 5)

Valence Values attached to an outcome. (Ch. 13)

Vertical communication Communication that can flow downward, upward, or in both directions. (Ch. 14)

Vertical coordination Linkage of organizational units that are separated by hierarchical level. (Ch. 9)

Vertical specialization Job design that removes planning and controlling activities from production employees. (Ch. 9)

Whistleblowing A member's disclosing that someone within an organization has engaged in an illegal, immoral, unethical, or illegitimate act. (Ch. 3)

Wholly owned subsidiary Subsidiary in which the parent company owns 100 percent of the voting stock, but its liability is generally limited to the assets of that subsidiary. (Ch. 19)

Work unit design Method of grouping jobs into structures usually consisting of a relatively small number of employees. (Ch. 2)

World-class operations Producing a product or service that can compete successfully anywhere in the world. (Ch. 21)

NAME INDEX

ORGANIZATION INDEX

Herman Miller, 38
Hertz, 174
Hewlett-Packard Corporation, 87, 110, 192, 196, 197, 531, 534
Hilton, 174
Hitachi, 27
Hofmann-LaRoche, 538
Honda Automobiles, 86, 468
Honeywell, 251, 280
Hudson Bay Company, 28
Humana Hospital, 170, 172

Inner Mongolia Second Machinery Company, 456
Institute for Social Research, University of Michigan, 257
Intel, 227
International Business Machines (IBM), 24, 30, 54, 87, 125, 182, 185, 186, 192, 239, 251, 272, 395, 484, 539, 541
Iowa State University, 191

Jiangsu Provincial International Economic and Technical Cooperation Corp., 456
John Deere, 462
Johnson & Johnson, 539

Kellogg Company, 424
Ketchum, Lyman D., 205
Kingsboro Holding Company, 456
Kmart, 336

Lake Superior Paper Industries, 35
Lawn Doctor, 47
Lawrence Institute of Technology, 167
Lehigh University, 96
Levi Strauss and Company, 249, 250
Lewis Galoob Toys, Inc., 253
Liz Claiborne, Inc., 534
L. M. Ericsson, 449

McCabe/Gordon, 109
McDonald's, 180-81, 457
McGill University, 16
McGraw-Hill, 124
McKinsey and Company, 85, 87
Management Science America, 412
Mary Kay Cosmetics, 446-47
Massachusetts Institute of Technology (MIT), 261, 533, 548
Matsushita, 192
Mayo Clinic, 538
MCI, 182
Memphis State University, 220, 295
Mercedes-Benz, 170

Merck, 390
Metropolitan Edison, 50
Michelin Tire Company, 468
Microsoft, 532
Midvale, Simonds, and Bethlehem Steel, 76
Miller Brewing Company, 17, 108
Minnesota Innovation Research Program, 162
Minnesota Mining and Manufacturing Corporation (3M), 138, 162, 181
Mitsubishi, 86
Morton Thiokol, 136

National Aeronautics and Space Administration (NASA), 136, 423
National Labor Relations Board (NLRB), 521
New United Motor Manufacturing, Inc., (NUMMI), 86
New York Telephone Company, 161
9 to 5, 412
Nissan Automobiles, 468
Nissan Foods, 454
Nitro Green, Inc., 47, 48
Nivad Flornoy et Cie, 27
North Central College, 370
Northeastern University, 448, 486
Northwestern Mutual Life Insurance Company, 10
Northwestern University, 79, 224
Novations, 545

Occupational Safety and Health Administration (OSHA), 236
Ocean Pacific Sunwear, 253
Ohio State University, 354-55, 357, 414
Oregon State University, 250, 251
Orkin Lawn Care, 47
Orlando Helicopter Airway Company, 456
Osborne Computers, 102
Oscar Mayer, 40

Pan American Airlines (Pan Am), 60
PDQ Food Stores, 174
Pennsylvania Ashland Petroleum, 59
Pennsylvania State University, 179
PepsiCo, 374
Philip Morris, 105, 108
Philips Electronics, 449
Pick Kwik Food Stores, 174
Princeton University, 96, 196
Procter & Gamble, 40, 87, 124, 181, 205, 208, 239, 539
Producers Color Service, 515
Purdue University, 468
Purolator, 263

Radisson Corporation, 106
Rand Corporation, 160
Random House, 130
Recording for the Blind, Inc., 331
Reed Company, 300
Rinocon-Vitova, 48
R. J. Reynolds, 105
Robert Mondavi Vineyards, 60
Rodale Press, 200
Rubbermaid, 103
Rutgers University, 196, 272

San Francisco Bay Area Rapid Transit (BART), 106
Santa Clara University, 164
Scandinavian Airlines, 311
Scott, Foresman and Company, 214
Sears, Roebuck and Company, 6, 125, 173, 174, 180, 187, 261, 263, 282
Securities and Exchange Commission (SEC), 63, 330
Selection Sciences, Inc., 328
7Up, 108
Shell Oil Company, 167
Shenendoah Life Insurance Company, 205
Shimada, Haruo, 205
Shuwa Corporation, 27
Siemens, 463
Sloan School of Management, MIT, 548
Social Security Administration, 478
Sony Corporation, 174, 183, 540
Standard Oil, 261
Stanford University, 230
Stanley Home Products, 446
Sterling Vineyards, 28
Sun Microsystems, 533

Tandy Corporation, 185
Tavistock Institute, 256
Tenneco, 6
Tennessee Armature and Electric Company, 6
Tennessee Eastman Company, 6
Texas A&M University, 394
Texas Commerce Bancshares, 421
Texas Instruments, 27
Thai Bridgestone Co., Ltd., 467
Touchstone Pictures, 185, 256
Toyota Motor Corporation, 86, 468
Trans World Airlines, 231
Tree Top, Inc., 421
TRW, 426

Uniroyal, 421
Unisys, 533
United Airlines, 99, 115, 174
United Auto Workers (UAW), 86

Environmental scan, 176-77
Environments
    homogeneous task, 30
    internal, 33-39
    international, 449-51
    and organizations, 29-33
    segmentation, 30
    stability, 30
Equal Pay Act, 507
Equity theory, 312-13
ERG theory, 302-3
Esteem, 301
Ethics
    and *Challenger,* 61
    defined, 61
    and Janus-headed model, 66
    and justice theory, 66-67
    managerial, 62-63
    nature of, 61-67
    and OBM, 310-11
    and social responsibility, 49-71
    sources of, 62
    and unethical behavior, 64-65
    and utilitarian theories, 65-66
Ethnocentric staffing, 459-60
Exception principle, 214
Exception reports, 479
Existing solutions, 127
Expectancy perception, 315
Expectancy theory, 314-17
Expert power, 326
Expert systems, 475
Exporting, and importing, 456, 463
External environment, 24-28, 504-7
    and decentralization, 238
    and design, 260
External forces to change, 421-22
External recruiting, 508-9
Extrinsic motivators, 310

Facilitation, group, 289-92
Facilitative support, 432
Factors
    compensation, 518
    economic, 505-6
    interpersonal, 323-46
    labor, 506
    legal, 506-7
    situational, 360-61
Failure
    and isolation, 136
    and leadership, 361
Federal Unemployment Tax Act, 507
Feedback, channel, 331
Feedback loop, and transformation, 487-89
Fiedler's contingency model, 359-62
Fiedler's LPC scale, 359-60, 361, 362
Figurehead, 17
Financial management, 41-42, 462-63
Financial protection, 507

Financing, and importing and exporting, 463
Flexibility, need for, 129
Flexible benefits, 520
Focus strategy, 186
Followers, 348
Forecasting, and predicting, 151-57
Foreign companies, in United States, 454-55
Foreign exchange risk management, 462-63
Formal group, 286
Formal leader, 36-37, 349
Formal organization, 199, 200
Formal team phase, 535
Franchises, 457
Free-rein power style, 350
Frequency-of-use plans, 105-7
Functional authority, 229
Functional departmentalization, 207-8
Functional managers, 13
Functional strategy, 173
Functional superstructures, 248
Functions
    and dysfunctions, 109-10
    and international management, 452-54

Gap analysis, 177
General environment, 24-27
Generic strategies, 184-86
Geocentric staffing, 460
Geographical departmentalization, 208-9
Global enterprises, 458
Goal attainment approach, 380-81
Goals
    and design, 261-62
    ends, 380-81, 404-5, 406
    establishing, 100-102
    formulation, 111, 176
    hierarchy of, 110-11
    means, 381-82, 405-6
    and motivation, 313-14
    multiple, 110-11
    and path-goal theory of leadership, 362-63
    and planning, 100-102, 108-12
    rational, 389-92
    statements, 214
Great Depression, 51
Great person approach, 352
Grievance, 521-22
Groups
    and decision making, 132-36
    defined, 286
    and departmentalization, 205-11
    development and facilitation, 289-92
    formal, 286
    formation and cohesion, 286-87
    nature of, 274-97
    norms, 287

phenomena, 134-35
properties, 134
self-managing work approach, 204-5
Groupthink, 135, 288-89
Growth strategy, 184
GURU, 475

Hawthorne studies, 80-82
Helplessness, learned, 414
Herzberg's motivation/hygiene theory, 304-8
Hierarchical plans, 105
Hierarchy
    of goals, 110-11
    of needs, Maslow's. *See* Maslow's hierarchy of needs
Hold strategy, 184
Homogeneous task environment, 30
Horizontal communication, 332
Horizontal coordination, 214-16
Horizontal specialization, 202
Human relations model, of effectiveness, 388
Human relations movement, 82
Human resource management, 42, 459-60, 503-29
Human skills, 15
Humor, 197, 330
Hybrid approach, 211
Hybrid planning, 101-2
Hybrid superstructures, 249-50
Hygiene needs, 305

Ideation, 329
Imagination, creative, 538-39
Impersonal mode, of integration, 35-36
Implementation
    and change, 438, 439
    and strategic planning, 175-79
    of strategy, 178-79
Importing, and exporting, 456, 463
Incentives, and change, 432
Incentive systems, 519
Income maintenance, 520
Independent contributor stage, 553-54
Individual differences model, 548-50
Individual pay, 519
Individuals
    and decision making, 130-32
    nature of, 274-97
Influence, 223-26
Informal information, 478
Informal leader, 349
Informal organization, 199, 200
Information
    computer-based, 478-80
    defined, 470-71
    informal, 478
    systems. *See* Management information systems (MIS)

Management by walking around (MBWA), 197
Management information systems (MIS), 469-85
  defined, 470-72
  and managers, 472-79
  types of, 477-80
Managerial competence anchor, 548-49
Managerial decisions, 125
Managerial grid®, 357-58
Managerial linking role, 215
Managerial zone, 12
Managers
  and competence, 548-49
  defined, 5
  and effectiveness guidelines, 392-95
  and ethics. See Ethics
  functional, 13
  life of, 10
  line, 12
  and MIS. See Management information systems (MIS)
  and motivation, 314
  non-, 37
  and roles, 16-18
  senior, middle, operating, 476-77
  staff, 13
  two-boss, 254
  types of, 9-13
  See also Management
Manipulation, and co-optation, 433
Manufacturing
  and service industries, 490-91
  world-class. See World-class manufacturing (WCM)
Marketing
  international, 460-62
  management, 40-41
Maslow's hierarchy of needs, 82-83, 301
Matrix
  portfolio. See Portfolio matrix
  product/process. See Product/process matrix
  superstructure, 250-55
Maximize, defined, 128
Means decisions, 125
Means goals, 381-82, 405-6
Mechanistic management system, 30-31
Mediator, 521
Medium-range plans, 107-8
Mentoring stage, 554-56
Merit, 519
Middle managers, 476
Miller and Form's life stages model, 546-47
MIS. See Management information systems (MIS)
Mission statement, 170
Modifiability, channel, 331
Monitor, 18

Motivation
  and employees, 307
  and goals, 313-14
  theory, Herzberg's, 304-8
  and managers, 314
  and organization members, 298-322
Motivator
  intrinsic and extrinsic, 310
  needs, 305
Motives, defined, 275-76
Multinational corporation (MNC), 458
Myers-Briggs Type Indicator (MBTI), 281-82

National Labor Relations Board (NLRB), 521
Needs, 301-3
  and controlling, 402-3
  hierarchy of. See Maslow's hierarchy of needs
  innate and acquired, 300
Negative reinforcement, 308
Network, 554
  communication, 332-34
  organizations, 253
  phase, 535
Neutralizers, of leadership, 363-64
Nominal group technique (NGT), 162-64
Noncybernetic systems, 406-8
Nonmanagers, 37
Nonprogrammed decisions, 125, 474
Nonreinforcement, 309
Nonroutine decisions, 474-76
Nonstructured decisions, 474
Norms, group, 287
Not-for-profit organizations, 186-88

Objective rationality, 131
Objectives, strategic, 171
Occupational Safety and Health Act (OSHA), 506
OD. See Organizational development (OD)
Official goals, 108-9
Ohio State University studies, 354-55, 357
Open management system, 31-33
Open-systems model, of effectiveness, 388-89
Operating managers, 477
Operating plans, 105
Operating system, design and use, 495-96
Operational control, 477
Operational goals, 109
Operational strategies, 171
Operations management, 40, 486-502
Optimize, defined, 128
Organic management system, 30-31
Organic models, 258-59

Organizational behavior modification (OBM), 309-11
Organizational chart, 7
Organizational commitment, 282-83
Organizational design, 245-69
  approaches, 255-60
  influences, 260-64
Organizational development (OD), 434-37
Organizationally based model, 550-57
Organizational mission, 170
Organizational scan, 177
Organizational scope plans, 108
Organizational structure, 246-47
Organizational superstructure, 247-55
Organizations
  and analysis, 177
  analyzer, 181
  change, 420-44
  and classical theory, 76-78
  and climate, 38-39
  and communication, 328-34
  and culture, 37
  and decentralization, 238
  defender, 180-81, 182
  defined, 6
  design, 245-69
  development, 420-44
  and effectiveness, 376-99
  environment, 23-48
  and ethics. See Ethics
  formal and informal, 199, 200
  functions and management, 39-42
  interpersonal factors in, 323-46
  and levels of management, 476-77
  and life cycles, 385-86, 395
  and management, 5-7
  members, 274-322
  and model, 550-57
  and motivation, 298-322
  nature of, 6-7
  network, 253
  not-for-profit, 186-88
  and politics, 338-41
  and processes, 35-36
  prospector, 181
  reactor, 181-82
  small, 186-88
  and stakeholders, 52-53
  and structure, 34-35, 246-47
  and superstructure, 247-55
Organizing, 195-269
  and coordinating work, 198-221
  function, 9
  jobs, 201-5
  nature of, 199-201
Orientation, group, 289-90

Participation, 236, 432
Participative power style, 350

Sociotechnical change, 425
Sociotechnical systems theory, 84, 256
Solo phase, 535
SOP. *See* Standing operating procedure (SOP)
Span of control, 211-13
Span of management, 211-13
Span of supervision, 211-13
Specialization, vertical and horizontal, 201-2
Spokesperson, 18
Sponsor stage, 556-57
Stability
    emotional, 549
    environmental, 30
Stable growth strategy, 184
Staff, 508-11
    authority, 227-29
    compulsory consultation, 228
    ethnocentric, 459-60
    geocentric, 460
    and line, 12-13
    managers, 13
    polycentric, 460
Stakeholders, organizational, 52-53
Standardization, 213-14
Standing operating procedure (SOP), 106
Standing plans, 105-6
Stars, 183
Steering controls, 408
Steward, 522
Stewardship, principle of, 51
Strategic advantage, 489-92
Strategic business unit (SBU), 183
Strategic constituencies approach, 383-84
Strategic decisions, 125
Strategic management
    defined, 170
    and environmental fit, 169-93
    perspectives on, 179-86
    styles, 173-74
Strategic objectives, 171
Strategic planning, 476
    advantages and disadvantages, 174-75
    defined, 170-73
    and implementation process, 175-79
Strategic plans, 105
Strategy
    business unit (BUS), 173
    components, 172
    and constituencies, 383-84
    corporate, 173
    designing, 177-78
    entrepreneurial and intrapreneurial, 538-41
    functional, 173
    generic, 184-86
    implementation of, 178-79
    operational, 171
Strike, 521

Structure
    and change, 423, 424
    initiating, 355
    organizational, 34-35, 246-47
Structured decisions, 474
Subsidiary, wholly owned, 458-59
Substitutes, and leadership, 363-64
Super's model, 547-48
Superstructure, organizational, 247-55
Supervision, span of, 211-13
Support
    and change, 431-34
    facilitative and emotional, 432
Supportive environment, 536-37
Synectics, 160, 161
Synergy, 172
System 4 organizations, Likert's, 257-58, 356-57
Systems
    analysis, 471-72
    approach, 381-82
    controlling, 406-10
    cybernetic and noncybernetic, 406-8
    defined, 84, 471-72
    distribution. *See* Distribution systems
    incentive. *See* Incentive systems
    information-reporting. *See* Information-reporting systems
    knowledge or expert, 475
    management. *See* Management
    operating. *See* Operating system
    perspective, 84-85
    sociotechnical, 256
    theory, 84-85

Tactical decisions, 125
Tactical plans, 108
Tannenbaum and Schmidt continuum, 350
Task environment, 24, 27-28, 29
Task force, 215
Teams, work, 204-5
Technical core, 11
Technical skills, 15
Technological domain, 26
Technology, 35
    and change, 423, 424
    and design, 261
    and international management, 451
Technostructural change, 425
Territorial departmentalization, 208-9
Theory X, 83, 352-54
Theory Y, 83, 352-54
Theory Z, 87-88
Time, perspectives and allocation differences, 14, 408
Time-frame plans, 107-8
Time series analysis, 154-55
Tools
    planning and decision making, 145-68

qualitative, 157-64
quantitative, 146-57
Top leader, 253
Total quality control (TQC), 498
Traditional control model, 403
Training and development, 511-15
Trait approaches, and leadership, 351-54
Transaction-processing system (TPS), 478-79
Transformation
    leadership, 364-65
    process, 487-89
Translation, 285
Trend analysis, 154
Trusteeship management, 51
Turnaround strategy, 184, 185
Two-boss manager, 254
Type A personality, 279, 280-81
Type B personality, 279, 280-81

Uncertainty, and interdependence, 28
Understanding, 428-29
Unfair labor practice strike, 521
Union, formation, 521
United States Fair Labor Standards Act, 506
Unit/functional-level plans, 108
Universalism, of management, 8
University of Michigan studies, 355-56, 357
Utilitarian theory, and ethics, 65-66

Valence perceptions, 315
Value
    competing, 384-86
    gain and loss, 428
Vertical communication, 332
Vertical coordination, 213-14
Vertical specialization, 201-2
Vroom-Yetton model, 157-59, 163

Wages/hours, 506
Walsh-Healy Act, 506
Whistleblowing, 64
Wholly owned subsidiaries, 458-59
Wildcat strike, 521
Work
    involvement, 282
    organizing and coordinating, 198-221
    safety, 506
    teams, 204-5
    unit, and organizational structure, 34-35
Work-in-process (WIP), 496
World-class manufacturing (WCM), 497-99
World-class operations, 497-99

Zones of responsibility, 11-12

LITERARY CREDITS

page 47 Case: "Environcare" by James Clinton. Reprinted by permission of the author.

pages 55, 58, 59 From "Perceptions of Socially Responsible Activities and Attitudes" by Robert Ford and Frank McLaughlin, *Academy of Management Journal,* September, 1984. Copyright © 1984 by the Academy of Management. Reprinted by permission.

page 71 Case: "Frank Pearson and the Allied Research Corporation" by David B. Thompson and Michael J. DiNoto. Reprinted by permission of Michael J. DiNoto.

page 88 From William Ouchi, *Theory Z,* © 1981, Addison-Wesley Publishing Co., Inc., Reading, Massachusetts. Reprinted with permission of the publisher.

page 93 Case: "A Job Interview with Sterling Manufacturing" by Philip C. Fisher. Reprinted by permission of the author.

page 112 Reprinted by permission from *Organizational Goal Structures* by Max D. Richards. Copyright © 1978 by West Publishing Company. All rights reserved.

page 120 Case: "Product Development Planning at Display Electronics" by Philip C. Fisher. Reprinted by permission of the author.

page 124 From *Managerial Decision Making* by George P. Huber. Copyright © 1980 Scott, Foresman and Company.

page 142 Case: "AgBanCorporation" by Lowell D. Bourne. Reprinted by permission of the author.

page 157 Adapted and reprinted from *Leadership and Decision-Making* by Victor H. Vroom and Philip W. Yetton, by permission of the University of Pittsburgh Press. Copyright © 1973 by University of Pittsburgh Press.

page 167 Case: "Harvey Industries" by Donald F. Condit. Reprinted by permission of the author.

page 191 Case: "Xerox Corporation" by J. David Hunger, Thomas Conquest, and William Miller. Reprinted by permission of J. David Hunger.

page 220 Case: "Oscar Metz Tool Company" by James C. Hodgetts. Reprinted by permission of the author.

page 243 Case: "Bank Second Marriages: Conflict in Family Integration" by Dean Dudley. Reprinted by permission of the author.

page 268 Case: "Arnco Products Company" by Kenneth L. Jensen, The University of Tampa. Reprinted by permission of the author.

page 295 Case: "The Patterson Operation" by Thomas R. Miller. Reprinted by permission of the author.

page 321 Case: "Jack Dobbins' Problem" by David Kenerson. Reprinted by permission of the author.

page 338 Adapted from "Toward Multi-Dimensional Values in Teaching: The Example of Conflict Behaviors" by Kenneth W. Thomas, *Academy of Management Review,* July 1977. Copyright © 1977 by the Academy of Management. Reprinted by permission.

page 344 Case: "The Open Door" by Mabry Miller and Thomas Pursel. Reprinted by permission of Mabry Miller.

page 350 Reprinted by permission of *Harvard Business Review.* An exhibit from "How to Choose a Leadership Pattern" by Robert Tannenbaum and Warren H. Schmidt, May/June 1973. Copyright © 1973 by the President and Fellows of Harvard College; all rights reserved.

page 354 From *The Human Side of Enterprise* by Douglas McGregor. Copyright © 1960 by McGraw-Hill Book Company, Inc. Reprinted by permission.

page 360 Fiedler's LPC Scale from *A Theory of Leadership Effectiveness* by Fred E. Fiedler, 1967. Reprinted by permission of the author.

page 370 Case: "Mrs. Loomis" by Roger Smitter. Reprinted by permission of the author.

page 378 Adapted from John P. Campbell, "On the Nature of Organizational Effectiveness" in P. S. Goodman, J. M. Pennings and Associates, ed. *New Perspectives on Organizational Effectiveness* (San Francisco: Jossey-Bass, 1977). Reprinted by permission.

page 387 From "Organizational Life Cycles and Shifting Criteria of Effectiveness: Some Preliminary Evidence" by Robert E. Quinn and Kim S. Cameron, *Management Science,* January 1983. Reprinted by permission of Robert E. Quinn.

page 398 Case: "The Night Shift" by Cyril C. Ling. Reprinted by permission of the author.

page 418 Case: "The Two Edges of Control" adapted by permission from *Case Problems in Management,* Third Edition by Schuler and Dalton. Copyright © 1986 by West Publishing Company. All rights reserved.

page 425 From *Organizational Behavior: People and Processes in Management* by Randall B. Dunham. Copyright © 1984 by Richard D. Irwin, Inc. Reprinted by permission of Richard D. Irwin, Inc.

page 467 "Bridgestone Case" by S. B. Prasad. Reprinted by permission of the author.

PHOTO CREDITS